A Guid
CIVIL WA

SECOND EDITION

Patriotic Tokens and Store Cards
1861–1865
and related issues

History • Values • Rarities

Q. David Bowers

Foreword by
Susan Trask

Valuations editor
Steve Hayden

Reminiscence by
Dr. George Fuld

Whitman
Publishing, LLC
PUBLISHING SINCE 1934
www.whitman.com

A Guide Book of
CIVIL WAR TOKENS
SECOND EDITION

www.whitman.com

© 2015 Whitman Publishing, LLC
3101 Clairmont Road, Suite G, Atlanta, GA 30329

THE OFFICIAL RED BOOK is a trademark of Whitman Publishing, LLC.

Correspondence concerning this book may be directed to the publisher, attn: Civil War Tokens, at the address above.

ISBN: 0794842941
Printed in China

Disclaimer: Expert opinion should be sought in any significant numismatic purchase. This book is presented as a guide only. No warranty or representation of any kind is made concerning the completeness of the information presented. The author, a professional numismatist, regularly buys, sells, and sometimes holds certain of the items discussed in this book.

Caveat: The value estimates given are subject to variation and differences of opinion. Before making decisions to buy or sell, consult the latest information. Past performance of the rare coin market or any coin or series within that market is not necessarily an indication of future performance, as the future is unknown. Such factors as changing demand, popularity, grading interpretations, strength of the overall coin market, and economic conditions will continue to be influences.

Other books in The Official Red Book® series include: *A Guide Book of Franklin and Kennedy Half Dollars; A Guide Book of Double Eagle Gold Coins; A Guide Book of United States Type Coins; A Guide Book of Modern United States Proof Coin Sets; A Guide Book of Shield and Liberty Head Nickels; A Guide Book of Flying Eagle and Indian Head Cents; A Guide Book of Washington and State Quarters; A Guide Book of Buffalo and Jefferson Nickels; A Guide Book of Lincoln Cents; A Guide Book of United States Commemorative Coins; A Guide Book of United States Tokens and Medals; A Guide Book of Gold Dollars; A Guide Book of Peace Dollars;* and *A Guide Book of the Official Red Book of United States Coins.*

For a complete catalog of numismatic reference books, supplies, and storage products, visit Whitman Publishing online at www.whitman.com.

CONTENTS

FOREWORD

When Dave Bowers first suggested I write the foreword for the second edition of his *Guide Book of Civil War Tokens* I was stumped on where to begin. When the answer came to me it was so simple! Start at the beginning—with the first book on Civil War tokens I purchased, more than 20 years ago. It was used, slightly dog-eared, with much of the lettering worn off the cover. I paid $4 for the little black book, titled *A Guide to Civil War Store Card Tokens,* by George and Melvin Fuld. Issued in 1962 by Whitman Publishing Company, this little 96-page pocket book was my introduction to a hobby that would soon become a passion.

Until the day I purchased that book I had no idea Civil War tokens even existed. I was merely accompanying my coin-dealer husband, Frank, on his weekly rounds and stepped inside Riverside Coin and Stamp with him in an attempt to avoid the sweltering 100-degree summer heat in Southern California. A casual conversation about large cents with the proprietor led me to comment on how fascinating it was to think that very coin could have been in someone's pocket during the War Between the States. I was politely informed that what I was looking for was a Civil War token, as that large cent—along with most coinage—was hoarded during the war. An enthusiast of everything Civil War–related, I immediately asked to see one of these tokens, but none were available. In fact, he seldom ran across one and hadn't seen one in years—but he did have a little black book on them, if I was interested. I left that coin shop, book in hand, like a kid who had been offered her choice of anything she desired in a toy store! I had no idea what any of it meant but I was on a mission to find out more about this elusive emergency money.

It wasn't too long after that when my husband came home from the Long Beach Coin, Currency, Stamp & Sports Collectible Show saying he had heard on the loudspeaker an announcement that there was a meeting of the Civil War Token Society. He had attended and bought me a membership. Shortly thereafter I received a nice letter from Dale Cade, secretary of the Society, welcoming me to the group and encouraging me to order all of the books available through the club. This, he said, would help point me in the direction I would want to go with my collecting. Two more books authored by the Fulds arrived, one on patriotic tokens and a huge book on store cards. It seems my little black book had grown up!

I began attending those meetings in Long Beach. Front-row center with no less than Dale Cade (affectionately known as *the glue that held the CWTS together*) by my side, I would sit wide-eyed and all ears as the speaker wove a story about one token or another. It was Dale who introduced me to Steve Tanenbaum, Rich Rossa, Sterling Rachootin, Paul Cunningham, and eventually Q. David Bowers. It was also Dale who urged me to serve on the board of governors for the CWTS and eventually take over the treasurer's post, a position I held for 16 years. I think Dale saw in me a genuine interest in this hobby, and he was quick to tap into that enthusiasm. If he were here today I don't think he would be the least bit surprised at my having taken on the job as editor of our *Journal,* nor of my contributions to the soon-to-be-published third edition of the Fulds's store-card book, edited by John Ostendorf.

My numismatic library has experienced sizeable growth since that first Fuld book. While not all the additions to my library are pointed at Civil War tokens, those that are hold the most allure for me. When my copy of Dave's first edition of the *Guide Book of Civil War Tokens* arrived during the summer of 2013 I felt like that woman walking out of the coin shop 20 years ago all over again. Except this book told the history, shared

iv

fascinating stories, had suggestions on how to collect, and offered advice on ways to research. It incorporated patriotic tokens and store cards and had a pricing guide. And best of all, the color! Those tokens just jumped off the pages at me! It came as no surprise to me that shortly after receiving my copy, the *Guide Book* sold out at the American Numismatic Association's World's Fair of Money convention.

So with the second edition of this book comes more of Q. David Bowers's unique talent for turning a numismatic topic into something inherently readable and pleasurable. I couldn't wait to share that first edition with my fellow Civil War–token enthusiasts, and I eagerly await the opportunity for a repeat performance. Whether you are new to the hobby, a seasoned collector, or someone just looking for a comprehensive reference on Civil War tokens, this book deserves a prominent place on your library shelf. My new edition will find its place next to its very used, quite dog-eared, with some of the lettering worn off the front, older version.

Susan Trask
Sisters, Oregon

REMINISCENCE

As of 1943, like many youngsters I started to collect Lincoln cents. By 1946 I was deeply involved in collecting all United States coinage, and had completed my Lincoln cent set as well as a set of Indian Head cents and was pursuing earlier years of this denomination. In 1947 I talked my father, Melvin Fuld, into taking me to the American Numismatic Association convention held that year in Buffalo. For a precocious kid of 15, this was such an eye-opening experience. I met two collectors who made a complete change in my collecting interest. They were William Guild of West Newton, Massachusetts (later Florida), and Bill Jacka of Bedford, Ohio. They both told me of a new collecting interest—Civil War tokens. They suggested that this was a wide-open field with hundreds of different tokens available at 10¢ to 25¢ each.

At the show I met David Bullowa, who sold me dozens of different Civil War tokens at 25¢ each. At that time, my father had no interest in coin collecting. Over the next year or so he joined me in enjoying these tokens. In 1949, Bullowa acquired the 4,000-plus collection of Civil War tokens formed by Joseph Barnet and advertised in *The Numismatist*. He wanted $2,500 for the collection, a "huge" sum for me at the time. I proposed that Bullowa buy my collection of U.S. cents complete from 1794 to date (except the 1856 Flying Eagle) as partial payment in the amount of $900. My father agreed to make up the difference in cash. We packed up our collection and drove from Baltimore to Philadelphia to make the trade.

At that time the only reference available was the Hetrich and Guttag book published in 1924; Barnet had published an updated commentary on H&G varieties in *The Numismatist* and *The Numismatic Review* in 1943 and 1944. I aggressively continued to buy Civil War tokens, including small collections, and offered duplicates for sale. In 1951 my father and I bought the D.C. Wismer Collection of Civil War tokens, consisting of 11,000 pieces, from the New Netherlands Coin Company, at 6¢ each. We sold more than 5,000 of these, packed in a wooden crate, to Tatham Stamp & Coin Co. in Springfield, Massachusetts. These were all duplicates, mainly the "Dix" patriotic tokens. The other major collection we acquired was Henry Guttag's collection of about 5,000 pieces in 1958. It had first passed to Max Schwartz of New York City, who retained a hundred or so pieces, then to John Zug of Bowie, Maryland, who advertised it, but no buyer came forth. From there it went to New Netherlands, then to us. We traded with the few serious Civil War token collectors such as William Fayerweather, Clif Temple, Jim Curto, Ray Haggenjos, Charles Foster, Lionel Rudduck, Wayne Rich, Martin Jacobowitz, and Otto Kersteiner.

Starting about 1951 my father and I created articles on special series of Civil War tokens. About the same time I proposed a comprehensive compilation. I chose to do the patriotic series first, as there are only about 550 different patriotic token dies. Each die combination was assigned a number, as had been done by Hetrich and Guttag. I assigned rarity ratings of 1 to 10, which are still used today. The rarity of each combination was determined by checking inventories of all collections I knew of plus my experience of the many duplicates that I had seen. The photographs of each die were taken at two times actual size by Kenneth Bressett, after which I pasted and numbered them on 22 plates. This work was published serially in 1959 in *The Numismatic Scrapbook Magazine*, edited by Lee Hewitt, and in 1960 as one of the "little black books" that Hewitt printed for Whitman, then located in Racine. Two more editions were sold by Whitman Publishing Company, with a total run of more than 15,000 copies at $1 each.

Concurrently with the patriotic work, I was busy with a book covering the 8,500 or so store card varieties. In 1962 Whitman published *A Guide to Civil War Store Card*

Tokens as another of its "little black books." State by state, each city in which merchants issued Civil War tokens was assigned a number from 1 to 1000, following the style of *Atwood's Catalogue of United States and Canadian Transportation Tokens* published by the American Vecturist Association. The issues of the 900 or so store card advertisers were listed by merchant followed by a number representing the die varieties known of each advertiser. There were only occasional illustrations.

Starting about 1962 my father and I began working on a detailed catalog of store card varieties with photographs of the obverse die or dies used by each advertiser. As many dies were used repeatedly for token reverses, a new list of stock reverse dies with identification numbers starting with 1000 was prepared. One must remember that in 1962 there were no computers or word processors and of course no Internet. Starting about 1970, Doug Watson (who worked for Krause Publications) photographed all tokens at size and made paste-ups by hand of the descriptive text and photos of each token. The preparation of this massive text took about two years of time by Watson and me. The book was in large format (8-1/2 x 11 size), totaling 350 pages. I assigned copyright to the Civil War Token Society and it was printed by Krause in 1972. As I recall 1,000 copies were printed and sold out promptly. A slightly revised second edition was printed in a reduced format of 6 x 9 inches by Al Hoch of Quarterman Publications.

Along the way, in 1967, there was enough collector interest for the formation of the Civil War Token Society with Melvin Fuld as its first president. From a small group of about 100 the society grew to more than 1,000 members. Its journal was and is state of the art in publishing research, news, and other information.

By about 1970 my collection had grown to include about 6,500 different tokens. As new acquisitions were few and far between, I decided to sell it, mostly in groups by states. Now, over 40 years later, with updates on the patriotic and store card books and with interest increased by the Internet and other means, we have information that I never dreamed of in the 1940s, 1950, and 1960s. It has been a pleasure to have been a part of this growth.

When we started to publish articles on Civil War tokens in 1950, four important advances we enjoy today were not available: computers, word processors, digital photography, and the genius of Dave Bowers. As you read and enjoy this book you cannot help but wonder how Bowers has assembled so much useful information not in print in any other single source elsewhere.

Although much has been published on Civil War tokens, it has taken the gifted research and writing of Bowers to produce a book that will appeal to the novice collector and at the same time will provide much useful and often new information to the most experienced collector.

The author's first several chapters are very thorough, defining Civil War tokens and their setting in American history, replete with fascinating information on tokens prior to the conflict, then details of how they first appeared, became a necessity with the public, and then spawned a new generation of eager collectors. It may come as a surprise to learn that in 1863, the most prolific year of token issues, many numismatists formed extensive cabinets of pieces found in circulation while at the same time commissioning special strikings from the token-issuing diesinkers and shops. By the time the first serious catalog of such tokens was presented by Pliny E. Chase to the American Philosophical Society that September, there were a half dozen or so dealers in New York City engaging in a lively trade to supply Civil War tokens to collectors. In reading this book I had an "I am there" experience—in the midst of all of the excitement.

Dave Bowers goes on to give good suggestions as to how to collect Civil War patriotic tokens and store cards, discussing grading, elements that determine value, and aspects of rarity. A Rarity-9 token (2 to 4 known) can be worth only a few hundred dollars in many instances, but if issued in a "rare town" can run into the thousands.

The author gives excellent information on how dies were made and tokens struck, discussing different aspects and peculiarities. A "primitive" die, amateurishly made, can be more interesting and valuable to a collector than an expertly cut die with perfect details and letter alignments. Such rustic tokens are the numismatic equivalent of folk art.

This book will give a beginning collector enough information to develop into an expert. No book on Civil War tokens has ever been as thorough.

Patriotic tokens are the focus of chapter 6, with nearly every known die illustrated and described, together with information as to the market value of collectible varieties. Chapter 7 delineates all known issuers of Civil War store cards and gives information about them, together with illustrations of nearly all known reverse dies. The appendices are each a rich source for additional information.

Dave's narrative is not only informative, but it brings to life the lore, romance, and appeal of this fascinating branch of American numismatics. I expect that it will be a standard reference for years to come.

Dr. George Fuld

THE CIVIL WAR

19 67

TOKEN SOCIETY

Founded in 1967, the Civil War Token Society is a non-profit organization dedicated exclusively to educational purposes, with the objective of promoting and stimulating the study of Civil War tokens.

The Society issues a quarterly publication, *The Civil War Token Journal*.

For more information or to join the Society, visit our Web site at www.CWTSociety.com

INTRODUCTION

In 1958 I discovered the world of Civil War tokens through Dr. George J. Fuld, who at the time lived in Wakefield, Massachusetts and was a scientist working with the Massachusetts Institute of Technology. He invited me to come to his home where he offered me many thousands of these tokens in Uncirculated grade. The price was less than a dollar each. Soon, I put these into groups and offered them for sale through Empire Coin Company, which I co-owned with Jim Ruddy.

At the time the only reference book on such tokens was *Civil War Tokens and Tradesmen's Cards*, by Dr. George Hetrich, of Birdsboro, Pennsylvania, published in New York City by Julius Guttag in 1924. Guttag was also an enthusiastic collector of the series. The volume was long out of print. By that time I had built an extensive library of old numismatic magazines, auction catalogs, and books. In the pages of *The Numismatist* in particular there were scattered articles on the subject. In the August 1892 issue F. Green wondered why Civil War tokens were rarely seen even in large collections, and noted that their absence had always been a source of wonder. "Surely they are not without artistic beauty; their numbers are sufficient to form quite a collection in themselves, and besides they are cheap. Thus, three of the insurmountable barriers are removed," he observed. This evaluation is not much different today as you read these words, except that examples are more expensive. Still, rarity for rarity, Civil War tokens trade at fractions of the prices for such other specialties as colonial coppers, Hard Times tokens, and, of course, federal coins.

As a young dealer (having started in a small way as a high school student in 1954) I had many collecting interests, but only a modest budget. Most of my funds went to maintaining and buying and selling inventory for my business. I was a steady advertiser in *The Numismatist* and the *Numismatic Scrapbook Magazine* and issued my first illustrated printed catalog in 1955.

From the 1960s onward I built a modest collection of Civil War tokens selected to include issuers and dies I found to be interesting. Late in that decade a numismatist in Rochester, New York, Steve Tanenbaum introduced himself. He was just getting into Civil War tokens and had bought a few in the Wealth of the South series. Later, with partner Richard Rossa, he formed Rossa & Tanenbaum, pre-eminent dealers in tokens of all kinds. Steve loved research, and starting in the 1970s he and I exchanged information on various dies and their history. In the 1990s I bought a large section of his personal collection when he decided to raise money in order to broaden his collecting interests. He narrowed his tokens to one each of the circulation strike varieties and sold me nearly all of his numismatic strikes—issues in copper-nickel, white metal, nickel alloy, and silver, including many unique examples. In that era I also bought most of Cindy Grellman's collection which was brokered through Rossa & Tanenbaum and acquired several other specialized groups.

I created files on each and every die and, separately, each issuer of patriotic and store card tokens. Along the way I probably discovered at least a couple hundred varieties not listed in reference books, which by that time included *Patriotic Civil War Tokens* and *U.S. Civil War Store Cards*, each by George J. Fuld with the assistance of his father Melvin. I also corresponded with members of the Civil War Token Society who were interested in research, including those listed in the acknowledgements section of this book. Then came a quiet time for me from about 2005 to 2010, when I continued to buy tokens for my collection but did little additional study. That changed when I made the acquaintance of some newer researchers and jumped into the project of helping

John Ostendorf, editor of the third edition of *U.S. Civil War Store Cards*, offering much technical information, photographs, descriptions of new dies, and writing the preface.

As I write these words I treasure memories of those who are no longer with us, including Steve Tanenbaum who died in 2011 in a tragic incident when a deranged criminal ran him down on a Brooklyn street. The cast of players has changed, and the writers in *The Civil War Token Journal* are mostly different from those of decades ago (again, see the acknowledgements page). Happily, research methodology is more sophisticated and exact than ever before, and the Internet has opened wide the gates to new information.

To me, Civil War tokens are as exciting as they were when I bought my first ones as a young teenager. They form a special and wonderful niche in American numismatics. When Whitman Publishing, LLC, suggested that I write this book I jumped at the chance. In the pages that follow I share my enthusiasm and knowledge, with an appreciative nod to the many who have helped me.

Style, Terminology, and Arrangement Notes

Abbreviations: In modern (but not quoted) text, standard state abbreviations such as N.Y., Pa., etc., are used when needed; in original material such forms as Pa., Penna., Penn., etc., are retained. Relative to Fuld listings, postal abbreviations are employed. *JCWTS* refers to the *Journal of the Civil War Token Society* (which for a time was also known as the *Copperhead Courier* and today is known as the *Civil War Token Journal*).

Endnotes, including in quoted material, are those of the present author (QDB) unless specifically noted otherwise.

Fuld citations: Citations to the listings by George and Melvin Fuld are to *Patriotic Civil War Tokens* (5th edition) and *U.S. Civil War Store Cards* (forthcoming 3rd edition). In the numerous instances in which a single die has two different Fuld numbers, the patriotic die is listed first and the store card designation is given second. As an example of a die which has two Fuld numbers, a certain John C. Breckinridge die is listed as Fuld 508 and also as Fuld 1420. In the present text it is cited as Fuld 0508, 1420.

Occupations: Most Civil War store cards list the occupation, line or trade, or service offered by the issuer. In instances in which this was not done contemporary directories and advertisements often furnish useful information. The term *saloon* in the early 1860s did not necessarily refer to a tavern, as it usually does today, but to a nicely-furnished or appointed reception or public area. Tokens marked *saloon* can refer to a restaurant, ice cream saloon, coffeehouse (very often; accommodations for women and temperance advocates), billiard parlors, oyster house, and even hairdressing parlors.

Quoted material: Some quoted material has been lightly edited, but in all instances the original meaning has been preserved. Common misspellings found in catalogs (such as Stephen A. Douglass instead of the correct Stephen A. Douglas; John C. Breckenridge instead of the correct Breckinridge, Joseph Barnett instead of the correct Barnet, Benjamin F. True instead of the correct Benjamin C. True, etc.) have been corrected.

Image sizes: Although Civil War tokens range in size from 18 mm to 25 mm, all are enlarged to 30 mm herein for ease of viewing.

OVERVIEW AND KEY TO USING THIS BOOK

Civil War Tokens Defined

STRICTLY DEFINED

In the strictest interpretation a Civil War token is a struck metal token issued between April 1861 and April 1865 and intended for use as money, usually for the value of one cent, but other denominations were made as well. Most were made in copper, some were made in brass, and rare exceptions were struck in copper-nickel and white metal.

Added to these, still within the strict definition, are pieces made from Civil War era dies known as *numismatic strikes*. These comprise a diverse array of pieces in metals such as copper-nickel, German silver or nickel alloy, pewter or white metal, silver, and a few others. Also included are mulings or illogical combinations of dies—an obverse die mated with a reverse that might be illogical or inconsistent. Numismatic strikes constitute the vast majority of the over 10,000 die combinations and metals known to collectors today.

As numismatic strikes range from very rare to unique and are often expensive, in contrast a basic collection of tokens made to be used in circulation as monetary substitutes can be interesting and affordable, although there are many varieties that are elusive. The Civil War Token Society suggests that to be "official" a token must be of a diameter from about 18 to 25 mm. Nearly all of the copper tokens issued as monetary substitutes are in the range of 18 to 19 mm. (All are shown at 30 mm herein for ease of viewing.)

Civil War tokens are divided into two classes: patriotic tokens and store cards.

Patriotic Civil War Tokens

Patriotic Civil War tokens bear inscriptions relating to the war, events, and sentiments such as ARMY & NAVY, OUR LITTLE MONITOR, and others, often with the denomination stated as NOT ONE CENT to evade counterfeiting laws. Patriotic tokens are a catch-all category and many motifs not related to the war, such as historical figures, election candidates, Masonic and IOOF emblems, and others are included.

Curiously, tokens that advertise a product or service, such as clothing or medicine, are classified as patriotic if no specific name of an issuer is given. These have been nicknamed *half cards*. They probably should be classified under the next class, store cards, but tradition continues.

The fifth edition of *Patriotic Civil War Tokens* by George and Melvin Fuld is the standard reference and offers Fuld numbers. Obverse and reverse dies are given separate designations. Fuld 20/303a describes a token with obverse die 20 combined with reverse die 303. The lower-case "a" signifies the metal of striking, in this case copper (more will be said about metals).

Civil War Store Cards

Civil War store cards form a series of tokens issued by about 1,500 different merchants and other entities specifically mentioned on the dies. The standard reference, also by the Fulds, is *U.S. Civil War Store Cards.* The plan for these is somewhat different from that of patriotic tokens. The side with the name of the issuer is designated as the obverse and the other side the reverse. The reverse often has a portrait such as an Indian Head and the date and on a patriotic token would be called the obverse. Further, if the same die, say an Indian Head, was used on a patriotic token it was given a number ranging from 1 up into the 500s. If that die was used on a store card it was given a four-digit number with the listings beginning with 1000 and running to over 1400. As might be expected, this dual system requires some understanding. Fortunately, with books on hand most collectors can switch from one specialty to the other with little difficulty.

Fuld listings for store cards begin with the postal code for the state, then a number assigned for a particular town, then a letter from A onward for each merchant in that town (in alphabetical order), then a number for the variety, such as 1, 2, and onward, then a letter for the metal. In occasional instances in which such listings are out of order they are corrected in the present text.

An example is provided by IN-135-A-1d issued by an Indiana merchant in the town of Brooklyn (town number 135 in that state). The firm of Cox & Landers is listed as "A" in that community; the token is variety 1, and is struck in copper-nickel ("d"). By consulting the Fuld book you can learn of other merchants in a given town or city and of the different varieties of each merchant's tokens. This particular token uses reverse die 1046, an Indian Head made by the shop of John Stanton in Cincinnati.

"Adopted" Civil War Tokens

Long collected as adoptees of the series are certain tokens of 18 to 25 mm diameter and struck from 1858 to 1860, with evidence that certain of these were used interchangeably with other tokens during the war. Examples of such pieces are the pre-Civil War work of Chicago coiners Shubael D. Childs and, separately, Frederick N. Dubois. Those of Dubois lettered BUSINESS / CARD on the reverse are the size of contemporary federal cents and, in fact, have an agricultural wreath not unlike that on the Flying Eagle cent. These were first published in a numismatic reference in January 1860, verifying they were in circulation by 1859.

Loosely Defined

In modern times some medalets (small medals usually of 28 mm or slightly larger diameter) have been added to the series at the request of the late Stephen L. Tanenbaum and others. These will be included in the forthcoming third edition of *U.S. Civil War Store Cards.* These have various advertisements of coin dealers and others and were never intended as monetary substitutes. Certain medalets made for the numismatic trade by James A. Bolen of Springfield, MA, are also in this category. Joseph Merriam of Boston (also an issuer of Civil War store cards substituting for a cent) produced many such medalets, Alfred S. Robinson distributed over a dozen different from dies made by George H. Lovett, and the list goes on. Strange mulings were the rule, not the exception, and were not listed earlier. Only a few of these are treated in the present Whitman book, which concentrates on tokens traditionally collected as part of the series and featured in the second and first editions.

Hard rubber checks, sometimes round, other times elliptical or rectangular, are other modern additions to the third edition of *U.S. Civil War Store Cards.* What to include and what to exclude in *your* collection is up to you. There are no set rules. Rubber checks are not treated here.

Especially important numismatically from the Civil War era are encased postage stamps patented by John Gault on August 12, 1862, which are detailed in appendix V. These consist of a brass frame with a clear mica panel behind which is a standard postage stamp of a denomination from 1¢ to 90¢ issued during the period of coin shortages after the Treasury Department on July 17 authorized ordinary stamps to be *legal tender.* Over 30 different merchants advertised on the backs of encased postage stamps. Issued contemporaneously with Civil War tokens, they are an interesting related specialty today.

Sutlers' tokens are more closely related to Civil War store cards than are any of the pieces listed above under the "Assortment" heading. These are often made of brass, sometimes of copper, and were produced by the shops of Lanphear, Stanton, Childs, and others who also made patriotic tokens and store cards. Often, one side of a sutler's token is from a die as also used on store cards. These form a separate discipline well worth investigating. The standard reference is by David Schenkman, *Civil War Sutler Tokens and Cardboard Scrip,* 1983. See also the appendix of this volume.

Metals Used for Civil War Tokens

This listing of metals follows the Fuld guide. The abbreviations in lower-case letters follow each standard description. Examples: Patriotic token 124/417f is in silver (this being a metal used only for numismatic strikes). Civil War store card NY-630-A-1a is for a token struck in copper and issued by New York City merchant C. Bahr.

a = copper or bronze

b = brass

d = copper-nickel

e = white metal or pewter

f = silver

g = lead

i = tin or tin plated store cards (often the metal of the token beneath the plating is not known, but is usually copper or brass)

j = various nickel alloys including German silver (includes tokens earlier classified as "c")

k = gold plated (gilt)

m = tin patriotic tokens

n = iron

r = aluminum

z = zinc

Nearly all Civil War tokens made for circulation were made in copper (a) or, less often, brass (b). Many numismatic strikes were made in copper-nickel (d), often by filing down federal cents for use as planchets or striking over them. Nickel alloy (j) was also used for many numismatic strikes as was white metal, also known as pewter (e). Tin plating, described as (mpl) for patriotic tokens and (ipl) for store cards, was often used on numismatic strikes plus a few circulation issues. Tokens in silver (f) are the *crème de la crème* of numismatic strikes.

Some tokens, especially numismatic strikes, are over previously-struck tokens or coins. Such are designated by a lower-case "o" that follows the metal. A token with a "do" suffix is struck in copper-nickel (d) over (o) another coin, in this case likely an Indian Head or Flying Eagle cent. An example is provided by 1/391do, a certain patriotic token struck over an 1863 Indian Head cent.

Rarity Scale for Civil War Tokens

The following rarity scale devised by George and Melvin Fuld is used in standard references to estimate the number of tokens thought to exist today. Over a period of time the ratings can change, especially if additional examples are found.

Rarity-1: Greater than 5,000 (very common)

R-2: 2,001 to 5,000

R-3: 501 to 2,000

R-4: 201 to 500

R-5: 76 to 200

R-6: 21 to 75

R-7: 11 to 20

R-8: 5 to 10

R-9: 2 to 4

R-10: Unique (only 1)

The above scale is for *absolute rarity*. In many instances a token, particularly a circulation strike, can be, say, R-5 overall, but in Mint State can be R-7, R-8, or even unknown. There is no standard published source for *condition rarity*, although sale descriptions by knowledgeable dealers can be of help. Rarity can change if hitherto unknown tokens are brought on the market.

Getting Acquainted With Tokens

A first reading of Civil War token definitions and procedures might suggest that the field is complicated. However, with even slight experience in reviewing token listings or, better yet, viewing them on the Internet or at a coin show, everything will soon make sense.

A great deal of pleasure awaits you!

BEFORE THE CIVIL WAR

The North and the South

By 1860 there had been enmity between the North and the South for many years on the issue of slavery. In 1852 Harriet Beecher Stowe's novel, *Uncle Tom's Cabin, or Life Among the Lowly*, showcased the peril of a family of slaves attempting to flee to the North. In the first year 300,000 copies were sold, and before the end of the decade it was the best-selling American novel of all time. Many people who had been on the sidelines of the slavery issue took up the cause of abolition. The Supreme Court's Dred Scott decision in 1857 mandated that slaves who had escaped from their captivity must be returned to their "owners." This was viewed as a poor decision at the time and today it is a blot on the historical record of America's highest court. Africans working on plantations were bought and sold like common merchandise, families were broken up, and slave auctions were held within walking distance of the United States Capitol building.

By early 1860 the presidential election of November 6 was in the offing, and hopefuls in the North and South were well underway in their planning by spring. Meetings and finally the nominating conventions were held. On May 18 Abraham Lincoln was chosen by the Republican Party, besting hopefuls Salmon P. Chase and William H. Seward. The Democratic Party met in Charleston to pick a nominee, but confusion and dissention reigned and many delegates bolted. The result was that the Southern Democratic Party split off and chose John C. Breckinridge by default, and the Northern Democratic Party proposed Stephen A. Douglas. The recently formed Constitutional Union Party, which hoped to hold the North and South together, fielded John Bell of Tennessee.

Coin Collectors Active

While politicians dealt with factionalism and other issues, the economy in America was robust in 1860. Railroads were dynamic and dominated much activity on stock exchanges. The 1850s had been years of growth, punctuated by the Panic of 1857 which had an adverse effect on the financial community, less so on the average citizen. By 1859 most sectors of the economy had recovered. Among leisure-time pursuits the collecting of coins, tokens, and medals attracted many thousands of devotees. This was spurred by the announcement in 1857 that the old large copper cent, familiar since childhood days, would be discontinued, to be replaced by a small-diameter 72-grain copper-nickel alloy coin depicting an eagle in flight. A wave of nostalgia swept across the country as collectors young and old scrambled to find as many different dates of the old "pennies" as possible. Examples dating back to 1793 could be found in circulation, but those of early years were often worn nearly smooth, and those of 1793 and, in particular, 1799 were rare.

There were no reference books to tell what coins had been produced since the Mint opened in Philadelphia in 1792, joined by branch mints in New Orleans; Charlotte, North Carolina; and Dahlonega, Georgia, in 1838, followed by San Francisco in 1854. There were no guides to values and no system of grading.

As popular interest grew, collectors such as Jeremiah Colburn in Boston and Augustus B. Sage in New York City contributed information about coins to newspapers, spurring further interest. In January 1858 the Philadelphia Numismatic Society was formed, the first such group in the United States. It was quickly followed by the American Numismatic Society in March. In the meantime, *Historical Magazine*, launched in 1857, carried many items about coins, tokens, and medals each month.

Tokens of various kinds began to be collected by many *numismatologists*, as some were called in the days before *numismatist* became firmly established.

In 1858 Charles I. Bushnell, a New York City attorney and collector of tokens, medals, and early American coins, published *An Arrangement of Tradesmen's Cards, Political Tokens, also Election Medals, Medalets, &c. Current in the United States of America for the Last Sixty Years, Described from the Originals, Chiefly in the Collection of the Author.* A review in the December issue of *Historical Magazine* told this:

> The value of a record of this kind is greater than at first sight appears. It is not only the story of popular movements in politics, of a literal currency of ideas, of aid to the historian, and a means of itself preserving that history for the future in the cabinets of collectors; but it is also an important stimulus to the arts of design in the pursuits of the designer, medalist, die sinker and others.

A large (29 mm) cent of 1836. In the late 1850s there was a nationwide hunt to retrieve and preserve the old copper cents of childhood.

The new small-diameter (19 mm) Flying Eagle cent was first released on May 25, 1857. Four of them placed side by side spanned three inches, a handy measure.

The Beck's Public Baths, Richmond, token was among several hundred listed in Charles I. Bushnell's pioneering 1858 study, *An Arrangement of Tradesmen's Cards, Political Tokens, also Election Medals, Medalets, &c.*

> In this light, the notices of tradesmen's tokens by Mr. Bushnell may serve a liberal end by encouraging this species of production. It is a profitable means of advertisement to the merchant who has an opportunity to exhibit his taste and invention; and our merchants are by no means insensible to elegance of design which every year enters more and more into the pursuits of trade, in the decoration of packages, labels, etc. . . .
>
> In a similar field the token of copper, brass, or bronze might be made highly attractive for its artistical value and profitable in the same ratio to the direct objects of the merchant.

How exciting! Month by month, more people discovered the pleasure of forming a display of numismatic treasures.

At the Philadelphia Numismatic Society Mark W. Collet, J. Ledyard Hodge, and A.B. Taylor constituted a committee to study such pieces, whose findings were published by January 1860 under the title of *Catalogue of American Store Cards &c., With Space for Marking the Condition, Price, Rarity, &c., of Each Piece, Designed for the Use and Convenience of Collectors.* Four hundred and twenty-three items were listed.

In 1860 W. Elliot Woodward, who conducted an apothecary shop in Roxbury, Massachusetts, near Boston, issued his first auction catalog of coins, tokens, and medals. Woodward's star would rise rapidly, and in the next decade he would be recognized as one of the greatest of the early numismatic scholars. Tokens were among his favorite issues, and many issued in the late 1850s and early 1860s were individually described in his catalogs, even if they had values of, say, less than 10 cents each! Thus was created a printed record that is valuable to study today. This would change, and by the 1870s there were hardly any listings for such inexpensive tokens.

Washington tokens and medals were the hottest ticket in the marketplace in the late 1850s, due in no small part to Mint Director James Ross Snowden seeking such pieces to include in the Mint Cabinet and offering to strike to order and trade rare Proofs, restrikes, patterns, and other coins for them.

Demand increased, and several die cutters and private minters created tokens and small medals for collectors. In New York City, George H. Lovett turned out dozens of varieties with topics ranging from the completion of the Atlantic Cable in the summer of 1858 to the burning of New York City's elegant glass-enclosed Crystal Palace in the following October, to the chess exploits of Paul Morphy.

In Philadelphia, Robert Lovett Jr. created a series of tokens depicting events of the Revolutionary War and the accomplishments of George Washington. In Waterbury, Connecticut the Scovill Manufacturing Company turned out special strikings of tokens otherwise used by businesses ranging from daguerreotype parlors to patent medicines to hotels. Such store cards and medalets of the 1850s are in great demand today and are classified and priced in the *Standard Catalog of U.S. Store Cards 1700–1900* by Russell Rulau.

Token or medalet showing the destruction of the Crystal Palace by fire, from dies made by George H. Lovett in autumn 1858 and struck for dealer Augustus B. Sage. Tokens depicting current and past events in American history became very popular with collectors.

In Chicago in late 1858 or in 1859, Frederick N. Dubois produced the first series of store cards imitating the new small-diameter cent. The obverse lettering described various businesses and their locations and the standard or stock reverse depicted a wreath inspired by the Flying Eagle cent, but with BUSINESS / CARD at the center instead of ONE / CENT. In time such small-diameter pieces were also "adopted" by collectors of Civil War tokens. Today they are very popular and enthusiastically sought.

In his study of Dubois, Don Erlenkotter found a contemporary newspaper account and a reminiscence by the coiner. The *Chicago Press and Tribune* published this on August 11, 1859:

Struck by Frederick N. Dubois in 1859, this business card token is the same diameter as the current federal cent and imitates the wreath on the reverse of the Flying Eagle cent. The business of G.E. Gerts & Co. of Chicago is advertised. "Adopted" into the Civil War token series, this variety is designated as IL-150-Z-1a in *U.S. Civil War Store Cards,* by George and Melvin Fuld, the standard reference.

A Coin Nuisance

We wish that the business firms, some six or eight in number, who have chosen the more enterprising than sensible mode of advertising, by filling all collections of our smaller currency with spurious imitations of the new penny piece, might be visited by the fruits of their own devices. May they never take in twelve pennies whereof six at least are not their own "business cards."

At a recent collection in one of our Sabbath Schools, out of thirty-two pennies eight were the "business cards" of five different Chicago firms. We were shown yesterday a collection of thirty dollars in pennies taken in at a brewery for yeast, and of these four to five in each of several successive handfuls taken at random were these spurious little copper nuisances. We like advertising but this strikes us as overdoing it. It is an impudent and silly thing, this forcing "business cards" into your neighbor's pockets to jingle with honest pennies.

In Dubois's own words, including a comment on newspaper coverage:

The U.S. government had first coined the new cent which was very small, and I conceived the idea of making an advertising card of it. I had acquired some skill at making steel dies, so I made a die with the wreath of the new cent on it, and in place of the words "One Cent" on the coin, I put the words "Business Card" so there was no chance of counterfeiting the coin. On the other side of the coin I put the name and business of whoever wanted to buy them. I made a small machine that fitted on one of my presses and which was partly automatic. Then I purchased cheap scrap sheet copper, rolled it to the right thickness on my silver rollers, cut the little round pieces out with my press dies and put them through the stamping press and they were done. . . .

I did all this work myself so the cost of it was very small and more than half of what I sold them for was profit. I sold them to people who wanted to advertise for nine dollars a thousand, and they passed them off in their business for pennies, making a profit of ten percent. I don't recall how many of these pennies I made, but made them for the Chicago businessmen and county merchants until it ran into hundreds of thousands and they were in general circulation all around.

[The tokens] attracted the attention of Chicago newspapers where they were described as a nuisance, so I stopped making them. The public never knew where they came from, but I made quite a little money from the project to help my weak business.[1]

John Stanton's Tokens Become Popular

In 1860 in his Cincinnati shop at 139 West Fifth Street, John Stanton and his staff turned out a wide variety of tokens, baggage checks, stamps, and small metallic products from dies engraved by various artisans. One of the engravers working with him was Benjamin C. True.

Contemplating the lineup of four presidential candidates and being aware of the great interest in the campaign being played out in newspapers and magazines as well as the continuing contention between the North and South, Stanton commissioned True to create a series of 22 mm tokens depicting each of the four contenders. Dies were prepared showing Lincoln, Breckinridge, Bell, and Douglas in profile on the obverse, with a surrounding inscription giving the name and state of each. At the top was a tiny circle, indicating a spot to drill if the recipient wanted to make a hole to accommodate a cord or ribbon. The reverse illustrated the White House, called the "President's House." The official name for the structure at the time was the Executive Mansion.

Stanton solicited agents to buy these for five cents each wholesale, to be retailed at fifteen cents each. The following advertisement was placed in a Richmond newspaper

Tokens of the four presidential candidates of 1860—Lincoln, Breckinridge, Bell, and Douglas—with the standard President's House reverse, from dies by Benjamin C. True, struck in the shop of John Stanton. These were widely sold during the campaign. Later the dies were combined with irrelevant obverses and reverses to create tokens that became very popular with numismatists.

on August 14, 1860, to run five times. Similar notices were run elsewhere in the South, such as in the Charleston, South Carolina, *Mercury* on August 17 and 20:[2]

> Wanted—Agents to sell CAMPAIGN MEDALS. The likenesses of the candidates for President are correct. The price of the Medals is $5 per hundred. Agents are now selling from 100 to 200 per day. A specimen of either medal will be sent (by mail) upon receipt of the retail price, 15 cents.[3] Address John Stanton, Stamp and Brand Cutter, 139 Fifth Street, Cincinnati, O., August 14—5t.

In 1860 Stanton had other business with the South. A lively trade was conducted in 22 mm brass tokens depicting on the obverse various agricultural products and the inscription, THE WEALTH OF THE SOUTH. The reverse showed a palmetto tree with NO SUBMISSION TO THE NORTH. These had obvious appeal to Southerners who at the time were increasingly resenting the stance of many Northerners against slavery. Without slaves the products of Southern fields could not be harvested, or at least not as inexpensively. All of the tokens were in brass and many had a hole drilled at the top for suspension.

Many of the presidential and Wealth of the South tokens were lightly plated with tin—so light that on the many Wealth of the South tokens that were worn or otherwise handled by their recipients the plat-

The popular Wealth of the South / No Submission to the North token, this one holed and no doubt worn by a Southern sympathizer. These were struck in 1860 into 1861 with five different Wealth of the South obverse dies combined with various reverses. Later, both die types were combined with many irrelevant dies to create tokens for the numismatic trade.

ing quickly disappeared. The presidential tokens were kept as souvenirs, and few were suspended on cords or ribbons. These became wildly popular with collectors, and to accommodate them, in 1861 Stanton combined Wealth of the South and presidential candidate dies with many others, including advertisements by merchants. Some were whimsical, such as mating a die with the portrait of Lincoln on one side and "No Submission to the North" on the other! These continued to be produced into 1862. These are a very popular specialty within the Civil War token series today.

The November Presidential Election

After intense campaigning, often bitter and disruptive, the election took place on November 6. The results:

> *Republican Party:* Abraham Lincoln and Hannibal Hamlin. 1,865,908 popular votes, 180 electoral votes

> *Southern Democratic Party:* John C. Breckinridge and Joseph Lane. 848,019 popular votes, 72 electoral votes

Constitutional Union Party: John Bell and Edward Everett. 590,901 popular votes, 39 electoral votes

Democratic Party: Stephen A. Douglas and Herschel V. Johnson. 1,380,201 popular votes, 12 electoral votes

Lincoln's landslide victory portended difficult times for the South. While incumbent President James Buchanan, in office since 1857, endeavored to please both the North and the South (and succeeded in pleasing neither), Lincoln was an outspoken abolitionist. Slavery had no place in America he stated. On December 20, South Carolina seceded from the Union, followed in short order by other states. In early 1861 the Confederate States of America was formed with its capital in Montgomery, Alabama (moved later that year to Richmond, Virginia).

CHARLESTON
MERCURY
EXTRA:

Passed unanimously at 1.15 o'clock, P. M., December 20th, 1860.

AN ORDINANCE

To dissolve the Union between the State of South Carolina and other States united with her under the compact entitled " The Constitution of the United States of America."

We, the People of the State of South Carolina, in Convention assembled, do declare and ordain, and it is hereby declared and ordained,

That the Ordinance adopted by us in Convention, on the twenty-third day of May, in the year of our Lord one thousand seven hundred and eighty-eight, whereby the Constitution of the United States of America was ratified, and also, all Acts and parts of Acts of the General Assembly of this State, ratifying amendments of the said Constitution, are hereby repealed; and that the union now subsisting between South Carolina and other States, under the name of "The United States of America," is hereby dissolved.

THE
UNION
IS
DISSOLVED!

Broadside published in Charleston, South Carolina, proclaiming that at 1:15 p.m., December 20, 1860, the state seceded from the United States of America. (American Antiquarian Society)

MONEY OF THE CIVIL WAR

In Early 1861

A new nation had been born. At the outset many citizens on both sides hoped for a peaceful coexistence. Most who lived in the Confederate States of America (CSA) wanted to go about their business of using slave labor and wanted their country to be viewed by the United States (Union) as an adjacent independent nation over which the American Congress would no longer have jurisdiction. In March 1861 the Confederacy ordered its first bonds from the American Bank Note Company and its first paper money from the National Bank Note Company, both in New York City. Numismatic tradition has it that Philadelphia engraver Robert Lovett Jr. was commissioned to make patterns for a proposed coinage of one-cent pieces, although no CSA correspondence or other documentation has ever been found.

In contrast, Northerners, probably the majority, were not interested in such a scenario. By then the Confederates were viewed with contempt as secessionists or rebels who needed to be brought back into the Union, and soon.

By January 1861 economic uncertainty was increasing. On the 15th of the month the *London Post* printed this:

> The monetary intelligence from America is of the most important kind. National bankruptcy is not an agreeable prospect, but it is the only one presented by the existing state of American finance. What a strange tale does not the history of the United States for the past twelve months unfold? What a striking moral does it not point? Never before was the world dazzled by a career of more reckless extravagance. Never before did a flourishing and prosperous state make such gigantic strides affecting its own ruin.

At the time Great Britain was officially neutral, but many in government and business positions sided with the newly formed Confederacy, as the South was a prime source for cotton for the mills of Manchester and other textile-industry cities. Later, the South denominated many of its coupon bonds in British pounds and had great success selling them to investors there.

12

The presidential election past, John Stanton continued to issue "No Submission to the North" tokens to Southerners of this persuasion. This was not unpatriotic in early 1861 given that both sides were trading with each other in business. The Civil War was still in the future. Similar to what he did for the election tokens, Stanton solicited agents to sell the Wealth of the South pieces. This advertisement was run twice in Charleston, South Carolina, beginning on January 16, 1861.

> Wanted—AGENTS TO SELL SECCESSION MEDALS. The Medals are a beautiful pocket-piece or ornament for a watch chain. Sell readily and pay an agent from five to eight hundred per cent. A single specimen sent for 25 cents. Address JOHN STANTON, Covington, Kentucky.[1]

Covington, across the Ohio River from Cincinnati, was probably a better address to use at the time, for in nearby fields slaves were at work and Kentucky was considered to be a Southern state, although it remained independent (until later in the year when it sided with the Union). Picking up an exchange item from the *New Orleans Picayune*, the *Dallas Weekly Herald*, March 13, 1861, printed this:

> SOUTHERN COIN. We were shown this morning a very pretty and well executed medal made here, either in commemoration of the succession of the Southern States or suggested as a model for the coin of the future Southern Confederacy—we could not learn which.
>
> The medal is the size of a five-dollar gold piece. On one side is a palmetto tree, with cotton bales, sugar hogsheads, and a cannon at its base, beyond which appear the rays of the rising sun, and forming a semicircle immediately outside of the rays, fifteen stars. The motto "No submission to the North"—1860. On the reverse, rice, tobacco, and cotton plants form a tasteful group around the graceful sugar cane and mix their varied leaves. Around are engraved the words: "the wealth of the South—rice, tobacco, sugar, cotton." The finish of this pretty medal is as good and well executed as that of any gold piece issued by the mint. *N.O. Picayune.*[2]

Stanton's January 16, 1861, advertisement for what we know today as Wealth of the South tokens. He gave his address as Covington, Kentucky, across the Ohio River from Cincinnati.

Following the formation of the Confederate States of America in 1861 Southern militia began arming and training for the protection of their new nation. A commission was formed to explore future relations with that *other* country, the United States of America, while much commerce continued in the meantime. At the time the federal government was at an impasse. President James Buchanan in the last months of his presidency remained helpless. Cash reserves in the Treasury were low—the result of confusion caused by the secession, lack of revenue, and poor planning. Some Interest-Bearing Notes were issued by the government to raise money, but not in large enough quantities to materially affect the situation. The new Confederacy also had a low cash balance.

Meanwhile, many congressmen, government appointees, and other officials left Washington and headed to the South to their homes and families. This caused wide resentment and many charges of disloyalty and traitorism were printed in the Northern papers.

Civil War store cards were issued by the shop of John Stanton, from dies by Benjamin C. True, for *Steamer Lancaster No. 4*, launched in January 1861. Captain Lewis Morris was at the helm as she plied the Ohio River. These tokens measure 22 mm. Two varieties of these cards have perfect obverse dies lacking a crack after STEAMER. These were made in combination with THE WEALTH OF THE SOUTH die 1423 and Lincoln reverse die 1418. It is likely that tokens from the uncracked die were used aboard the steamer in early 1861. The route was on the Ohio River to the South, and this was a tribute to the South. Then when the war started in April, a Lincoln die was used instead. This same Lincoln die was used on other Civil War tokens. This die cracked and was replaced with Lincoln die 1419, by which time the obverse die had cracked from the rim past STEAMER. Illustrated are varieties OH-165-FXa-12a (early used with perfect obverse die) and OH-165-FXa-2a.

In New York City engraver George H. Lovett set about creating his Gallery of American Traitors series of 28 mm copper tokens in 1861. No. 1 was the only one ever issued. On the reverse 10 rascals who had gone to the Confederacy were listed, including erstwhile presidential candidates John Bell and John C. Breckinridge (surname misspelled) and Secretary of the Treasury Howell Cobb. J.B. Floyd, secretary of war under Buchanan (until December 29, 1860), had placed large amounts of debt with investors; these securities became worthless. Jefferson Davis became the president of the Confederate States of America.

Abraham Lincoln was inaugurated as president of the United States on March 4, 1861. William Henry Seward, long-time party stalwart who in early 1860 was among the Republican contenders for the candidacy, but lost to Lincoln, was appointed as secretary of state. Reviewing the situation, Seward stated that in recent events he saw not the establishment of an independent Confederate nation leading a willing people, but, instead, a temporary, unjustified, and unconstitutional challenge to the federal government. There was a question as to the sanctity of federal military posts, customs houses, and other government buildings in the South. Open trade with the North, as earlier envisioned, including the printing of paper money and bonds in New York City, diminished and by early April was no longer viewed as viable.

Fort Sumter

Then Fort Sumter. *Harper's New Monthly Magazine* told the story:

> Increased activity had been noticed in the navy-yards and forts in the North. Vessels were equipped and manned as rapidly as possible. About the 8th [of April] a fleet, having on board nearly 2,000 men and a large quantity of stores, was dispatched southward. It soon transpired that its object was to reinforce Fort Pickens, and if possible to throw provisions into Fort Sumter, the supplies of which were known to be nearly exhausted.
>
> On the 8th General [Pierre G.T.] Beauregard, the commander of the Confederate forces at Charleston, was formally notified that an attempt would be made to provision Fort Sumter. After communicating with his government, he was directed to reduce the fort.
>
> On the 11th Major [Robert W.] Anderson was summoned to evacuate the fort. He refused to comply, and on the morning of the following day fire was opened upon Fort Sumter from Fort Moultrie and the Confederate batteries. This was returned by Major Anderson with as much vigor as possible with the small force under his command. The bombardment continued with scarcely an intermission for 34 hours. The wood-work within the fort was set on fire by hot shot, the quarters were entirely consumed, the main gate burned, the gorge wall seriously injured, the magazine enveloped in flames, and the door closed from the heat, so that only four barrels of powder and a few cartridges were available.
>
> The garrison, which numbered only about 100 men, including laborers, were exhausted by fatigue and hunger, the only remaining provisions consisting of salt pork. Opposed to them were 7,000 men and powerful batteries. Further resistance being impossible, and the vessels not being able to afford any assistance to the fort, Major Anderson accepted the terms which had been offered before the commencement of hostilities, marching out with flying colors, saluting his flag with fifty guns. The men on both sides were so completely protected by the works that no loss of life occurred during the bombardment; but in saluting the flag a gun burst, by which several of the defenders of the fort were injured, one being killed.
>
> The evacuation of Fort Sumter took place on the afternoon of Sunday, the 14th of April, Major Anderson and his men embarking on a steamer for New York, where he was welcomed with distinguished honor. The Secretary of War subsequently addressed a note to him, expressing perfect satisfaction with the manner in which he had defended the post under his command.[3]

Uncertainty ended. Congress declared war. President Lincoln and his cabinet conferred, and his advisors suggested that no more than three months would be needed for Army troops to whip the rebels and restore peace. The North was a bastion of industrial strength, it was stated, while the Confederacy was a land of agriculture, sustained by the crops of rice, tobacco, sugar, and cotton, as delineated on the Wealth of the South token. It was not until July 13, however, that Congress formally authorized Lincoln to suspend commerce between the North and the South (and it was not until August 16 that the ban was fully implemented).

Lincoln called for 75,000 volunteers to enlist for 90 days. Parades and parties were held in New York City and elsewhere as men boarded trains and headed south. The capture of the Confederate capital of Richmond would quickly end matters.

The bombardment of federal Fort Sumter by Confederate States of America forces on April 12–13, 1861, initiated the Civil War. (John Gilmary, *History of the United States*, 1872)

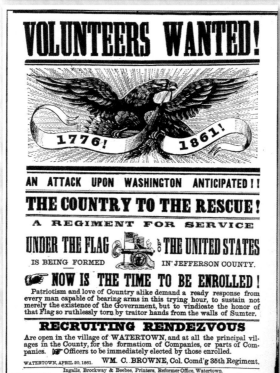

A Union recruiting poster published in Watertown, New York, on April 20, 1861.

Bull Run

In July the newspapers announced that the first significant battle between the North and South would take place near Manassas, Virginia, not far from Washington. Many sightseers hastened to be on hand to see the rebels vanquished. Great entertainment was in the offing! The date was July 21.

Brigadier General Irvin McDowell led his Union soldiers, nearly all of whom had received light training at best, to Bull Run, near Manassas, to take on the Confederate Army under Brigadier General P.G.T. Beauregard. McDowell's surprise attack against the flank of Beauregard's troops seemed to decide the matter, at least for a short time. The war was over. Or, was it? Confederate reinforcements came by rail from the Shenandoah Valley with Thomas J. Jackson of the Virginia Military Institute in command. Jackson stood fast (and earned the nickname "Stonewall") in a fierce counterattack. The Union forces became disorganized, then panicked and made a scattered retreat toward Washington, without any command or direction. Consternation prevailed. Onlookers could not believe what happened. Already 90 days had passed, and the first victory went to the South!

Regarding the flight of the Union soldiers, monetary scholar and banker Hugh McCulloch recalled:

> Members of Congress and other civilians who had gone out to witness a Union victory had returned stricken with terror. If the Confederates had known the real condition of Washington and the character of its defenses, they might have captured the city and placed their banners upon its public buildings.[4]

BATTLE OF BULL RUN.

The Battle of Bull Run. (Kurz & Allison print, Library of Congress)

Money in Circulation in Early 1861

The monetary situation in commerce remained normal as the year 1861 began, although the balances in the Confederate and Union treasuries were low. In the South federal mints were operating in New Orleans; Charlotte, North Carolina; and Dahlonega, Georgia. New Orleans produced silver and gold coins, while at the other two the output was limited to small-denomination gold. Each had been in continuous operation since 1838.

At the Philadelphia Mint denominations being struck included the copper-nickel Indian Head cent (a new design introduced in 1859 to replace the short-lived Flying Eagle cent), silver three-cent piece or trime, silver half dime, dime, quarter, half dollar, and dollar, and gold $1, $2.50, $3, $5, $10, and $20. In California the San Francisco Mint produced silver denominations from the dime upward and gold coins.

Most larger transactions in the channels of commerce were handled by bills issued by state-chartered banks, of which about 2,000 were in operation. Popular denominations included $1, $2, $3, $5, $10, and $20. Less often seen were $50 and $100 notes, and only a few banks issued bills of $500 and $1000 values.

In early 1861 the Confederacy paid out $50, $100, $500, and $1000 notes made in March by the National Bank Note Company in New York, imprinted with the Montgomery address of the capital. The $50 to $1000 "Montgomery notes," as they were called, traded at par with gold and silver coins but were made only in small numbers and were rarely encountered. Throughout 1861 federal coins and notes of regional state-chartered banks served business well in the South.

The mints at New Orleans, Charlotte, and Dahlonega were seized by Southern states' forces before war was declared. Using bullion on hand the New Orleans Mint struck thousands of half dollars and gold double eagles. The Dahlonega Mint produced a small run of gold dollars, and the Charlotte Mint presses were quiet. Afterward, the Charlotte and Dahlonega facilities passed into history. Years later in 1879 the New Orleans Mint was reopened for coinage and remained active through 1909.

Patriotic Civil War token 260/447b. The inscriptions suggest it may have been made very early in 1861 prior to Fort Sumter. Possibly engraved and struck by Joseph C. Merriam of Boston.

Money After Fort Sumter

Later in 1861, continuing through 1864, the Confederacy, with its capital now in Richmond, issued over 100 different designs and values of bills. No circulating coinage was produced in Dixie, but federal coins remained in commerce, eventually trading at a sharp premium when Confederate paper became depreciated.

In the North the outlook for the economy remained uncertain, as it had been for nearly a year. The Treasury needed further infusions of money. Congress met in extra session on July 4. Secretary of the Treasury Salmon P. Chase (a Lincoln appointee who had been a Republican presidential hopeful a year earlier) estimated that the government would require more than $318,519,581.87 (apparently, estimates were more than casual!) for the current fiscal year ending on June 30, 1862, to quell the rebellion and for other purposes.[5]

Lincoln requested the authority to borrow $400,000,000. The Act of July 17, 1861, was the result. However, just $250,000,000 was authorized. For starters, part of the "loan" was to be in the form of Demand Notes to be issued in denominations of not less than $10. The Act of August 5 added the $5 denomination, and modified certain provisions, and provided for convertibility of the Demand Notes into 20-year 6% bonds in denominations of $500 and more. These notes were authorized for up to a total of $50 million (until the Act of February 12, 1862, added an additional $10 million). These were redeemable at par in gold and silver coins, which gave them immediate acceptability. With the war in progress, conditions in Washington were anything but stable, as recalled by Senator John Sherman:

> We had to appeal to the patriotism of bankers to accept the Demand Notes of the United States as money, with no prospect of being able to pay them. Our regular army was practically disbanded by the disloyalty of many of its leading officers. Washington was then practically in a state of siege, forcing me, in May 1861, to go there at the heels of the 7th regiment of New York militia, avoiding the regular channels of travel.
>
> The city of Baltimore was decked under the flag of rebellion. Through the State of Maryland loyal citizens passed in disguise, except by a single route opened and defended by military power. The great State of Kentucky, important as well from its central position as from the known prowess and courage of its people, hung suspended in doubt between loyalty and secession. In the State of Missouri, St. Louis was the only place of unquestioned loyalty, and even there we regarded it a fortunate prize that we were able to take the public arms from a government arsenal. The whole State of Virginia, with the single exception of Fortress Monroe, was in the possession of the revolutionary force.[6]

The monetary situation remained more or less stable in coming months. In late December the condition changed abruptly. That the War of the Rebellion or the War of 1861, as many called it, would not be over anytime soon was a fact. Uncertainty increased, and as a safety measure many citizens in the North thought to obtain gold coins and hide them away for safekeeping. By the end of December banks stopped paying them out at par.

In the meantime in 1861 cent-size copper tokens, as conceived by Frederick N. Dubois in 1858 or 1859, were issued by other coiners. In Chicago, the shop of Shubael D. Childs made a specialty of these. Such pieces circulated effectively at the value of a cent and were the first true Civil War store cards used as a substitute for money.

Forts Henry and Donelson

Although there had been engagements between the South and the North since the Battle of Bull Run in July 1861, neither side could claim victories that might lead to the end of the war. The situation turned for the better for the Union in February 1862. General Ulysses S. Grant landed two divisions of his troops on the bank of the Tennessee River north of Fort Henry, Tennessee. On the 6th the Army was set to attack the fort while from the river Navy gunboats fired cannon at the fortification, which was also having problems with flood-tide water. The naval bombardment was definitive, and

EARLY STORE CARDS

Civil War store card made in 1861 by Childs for George Whitney (whose name did not appear), an issuer of drafts, a representative of the Royal Bank of Ireland. In this year Civil War tokens began to enter commerce in quantity, but the flood of such pieces was yet to come.

Civil War store card MI-60Aa struck by Childs in 1861 and issued by William Brooks giving both of his addresses—Elkhart (Indiana) and Battle Creek (Michigan), unique with two different states on the same die. Accordingly, numismatists specializing in either state find this token to be desirable.[7]

A well-worn example of Civil War store card IL-150-BB-5a issued by John Frederick Siehler and his family, who operated the German Guest and Boarding House on Larabee (Larrabee) Street, Chicago. The die work, especially the 1861 Indian Head on the reverse, is somewhat primitive, suggesting an amateur or an engraver with little experience. Such rusticity in a die is always a numismatic plus.

Civil War store card IL-150-BB-3a issued by Siehler has the same obverse die as IL-150-BB-5a. It isn't dated but is of the same 1861 era. Shown on the reverse is Gambrinus, the fictional king of Flanders, famous as the "patron saint" of beer. He is said to have learned the brewing craft from Isis, the goddess of ancient Egypt. In various depictions in the literature he is usually shown raising one hand aloft with either a stein or a foaming glass of beer. On this token the inscription on the barrel head is in German as LAGER / BIER. A differently styled image of Gambrinus is found on WI-510-E.

Civil War store card PA-750-H-1a good for one fare on the Chestnut & Walnut Passenger R.R. Co., a token also collectible by specialists in transportation tokens. The dies were made by Robert Lovett Jr. This municipal railroad was planned in 1858 and met with some local opposition. In 1861 the address was 228 Dock Street, which was soon changed to the office of the Germantown Passenger Railroad Co.

IL-150-BB-2a issued by Siehler and with Gambrinus, this with the description on the barrel head in English as LAGER / BEER. The obverse die is slightly different in its arrangement of letters.

the fort's commander, Brigadier General Lloyd Tilghman, surrendered before the Army arrived. For the next several days Union ships destroyed many Confederate vessels and bridges. Grant's army went overland 12 miles to win the Battle of Fort Donelson. Despite the victory, there was no end in sight, and both sides continued to expect a prolonged conflict.

Legal Tender Notes

The treasuries of both countries (and by now the CSA was considered by the world, if not by the Union, to be independent) were depleted. To raise funds Congress, under the Legal Tender Act of February 25, 1862, authorized the issuance of $150,000,000 in Legal Tender Notes, less the amount of Demand Notes still in circulation. Unlike the Demand Notes, the new bills were not redeemable in gold or silver coin, but were simply the government's promise to pay in the future. A $100 Legal Tender Note could be exchanged for two $50 notes or some other combination, but not at par for coins of significant intrinsic value.

On March 8 two "ironclad" vessels challenged each other off the coast of Virginia. The USS *Monitor*, especially constructed with iron and steel plating, faced off against the CSS *Virginia*, a wooden ship that had been converted by removing the upper deck

A $20 Legal Tender Note issued under the Act of February 25, 1862. Such bills could not be exchanged at par for gold or silver coins, causing the public to distrust them. At the time the outcome of the Civil War was increasingly uncertain.

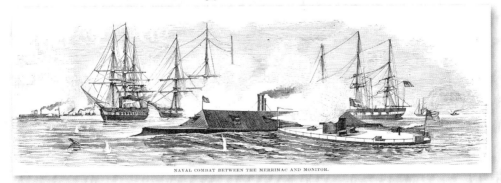

On March 8, 1862, the ironclads CSS *Virginia* (left) and USS *Monitor* engaged in not-so-mortal combat off the Virginia coast, an encounter that forever changed the course of naval history.

and other facilities of the USS *Merrimack* and replacing it with sloping sides of iron and adding cannon ports. Neither side was victorious, and each ship went back to its side, but a new chapter in naval history had been opened. In time, "Our Little Monitor" Civil War tokens were made in several varieties and became very popular.

At the time silver coins were still aplenty in commerce. Gold coins were available from banks and exchange brokers, but only at a premium. On March 22, 1862, it took $101.12 in bills from a sound bank, including 12 cents in change, to buy $100 worth of gold (by December 4 it took $124). In the meantime, federal silver and gold coins had been absent from commerce in the South since the summer of 1861. This was reflected by a May 1862 account of the Army's purchase of goods from Virginia citizens: "Silver Money. Some of the Virginians are delighted with the silver money which they get from our army in exchange for the things they sell, not having seen any for a year."[8] When Union troops went into that Confederate state they purchased agricultural goods as they went along.

Late Spring Into Summer 1862

When Legal Tender Notes were placed into circulation, public distrust of money increased. The war was ongoing, still with no resolution in sight. Silver coins from three-cent pieces to dollars were sought after by citizens who wanted to hold "hard money," and by early summer all were gone. Federal coins in circulation consisted only of Flying Eagle and Indian Head cents and the occasional stray old copper cent. Legal Tender Notes were a common sight at banks, stores, and elsewhere in trade, but most business was still conducted through notes issued by state-chartered banks. Inflation was rampant, and with the depreciation of paper money in terms of gold and silver, prices of goods rose steadily.

In the meantime the hobby of coin collecting continued to be active. William Harvey Strobridge, who would become prominent as an auction cataloger, held his first sale in May 1862 from the 26th to the 28th, featuring the William Lilliendahl Collection with memorable rarities. W. Elliot Woodward continued to attract clients, and Edward D. Cogan also had his hat in the auction ring. New York City dealer and cataloger Augustus Sage was no longer heard from and would serve a stint in the Army, as would many other numismatists, among whom were token issuer and collector Joseph N.T. Levick and Philadelphia dealer E.B. Mason Jr. Mark Collet, M.D., who helped the Philadelphia Numismatic Society compile its study of tokens, signed up and, sadly, lost his life. Had he lived, a bibliography of literature on tokens might be different from what we know today.

From June 25 to July 1, 1862, battles were fought for seven days in Virginia with Confederate troops under Robert E. Lee facing off against Union forces led by George B. McClellan. Results were mixed, but McClellan was out-generaled by Lee, who was the victor overall, further indicating that the war had a long way to go.

A Coinless America!

In the second week of July even one-cent pieces disappeared into the hands of hoarders. For the first time before or since, the United States was coinless!

In the absence of coins to pay for newspapers, haircuts, beer, lunches, and other goods a wide variety of monetary substitutes reached circulation in flood proportion. Making matters worse, a further $150,000,000 in Legal Tender Notes was authorized by Congress. The Act of July 17, 1862, sought to remedy the situation, at least in part, and made *postage and other stamps* legal tender in amounts up to $5 for certain debts (the government still had to pay interest on federal bonds in gold coins). This caused a great deal of excitement as the public took the view that stamps could buy anything. Various merchants and others had small paper envelopes printed to their order, with their name and a number such as 25 or 50 printed to indicate the face value of the stamps within. The act also prohibited the use of tokens as money, but nobody paid attention.[9]

Typical private scrip note issued in the summer of 1862 by Tucker & Stiles of Brookline, New Hampshire, who conducted a large general store above which was a large public meeting hall. The partners also operated a hotel, ran a farm, sold lumber, and manufactured wooden items, including kegs for the East Boston Sugar Refinery. All of the firm's assets were sold at public auction in August 1864.

THE CURRENCY QUESTION—MAKING CHANGE.
STOREKEEPER—"*I've no pennies—would you mind taking a ticket for the Broadway 'Free and Easy' instead?*"

Leslie's cartoon reflecting that in a coinless America all sorts of things were offered in the place of federal money, including Broadway show tickets.

"POSTAGE, OR OTHER STAMPS."

"The Secretary of the Treasury be and he is hereby directed to furnish to the Assistant Treasurers and such designated depositaries of the United States as may be by him selected, in such sums as he may deem expedient, *the postage or other stamps of the United States, etc.*"—U. S. Law, July 17, 1862.

Cartoon in *Frank Leslie's Illustrated Weekly* deriding the Act of July 17, 1861, authorizing common postage stamps to be used as money.

Soon, the Treasury Department authorized the printing of Postage Currency scrip notes in values of 5¢, 10¢, 25¢, and 50¢, using the same designs as on postage stamps. These were first distributed to Army paymasters in August and to the general public in September. By early 1863 about $100,000 of these notes reached circulation *per day*, but the demand remained unsatisfied.[10] The first of these notes had perforated edges just like stamps. These were followed in 1863 by the somewhat similar Fractional Currency notes.

On August 12, 1862, John Gault, who had recently come to New York City from Boston, patented the encased postage stamp. These consisted of a brass frame with advertising on the back and, on the face, a pane of clear mica behind which was a postage stamp and were made by the Scovill Manufacturing Company in Waterbury, Connecticut.[11] Denominations included 1¢, 3¢, 5¢, 10¢, 12¢, 24¢, and 90¢. These were circulated by the hundreds of thousands until well into 1863. More than 30 merchants advertised on them, dominated by patent medicine king J.C. Ayer, who advertised Ayer's Cathartic Pills and Ayer's Sarsaparilla. Drake's Plantation Bitters, an alcohol-laced cure-all put up in log-cabin shaped bottles, was another user as was Lord & Taylor, the New York City fashion house.

A Postage Currency note for 25 cents, with perforated edges. The ABNCo monogram of the American Bank Note Co. is at the lower right.

Encased postage stamp of Simon Steinfeld who had the agency to sell French Cognac Bitters, a patent medicine laced with alcohol.

Civil War store card of Steinfeld, NY-630-BU-1a. Dies by Emil Sigel with reverse signed E. SIGEL below the shield.

Merchants, towns, railroads, banks, and others circulated millions of small paper scrip notes, typically of values of 3¢, 5¢, 10¢, 25¢, and 50¢. These were printed locally or regionally, signed by the issuers, and were deemed for merchandise or exchange in appropriate quantities for Legal Tender Notes. Within a given community citizens, banks, and merchants generally agreed to accept such bills, and they were widely used by others than their issuers. The *Portsmouth* (New Hampshire) *Journal* printed this on September 13, 1862:

> PRIVATE FRACTIONAL BILLS. When silver change disappeared in July, four of our substantial firms procured the engraving of 25c bills, all of which were signed by such firms as issued them, and were redeemable by either firm in bank bills, whenever four might be presented. For a few days they were frequently returned for redemption. But after a week or two the matter was well understood to be only for a public accommodation, and without risk.
>
> They were then everywhere received like silver, in this and neighboring towns, and up to the time that Congress prohibited the issue, about five thousand, of these bills were issued and are now still in circulation—those who issued them not having a dollar's worth of them on hand. A premium has in some instances been paid for them. One of those who issued them had last week twelve bills presented at his counter. On handing out a three dollar bank bill, the lady replied, "Oh, I can get that for them anywhere—I thought you paid a premium!"[12]

Such scrip notes were made in even larger quantities in 1863 continuing into 1864. Although the government looked askance at anything but its own paper, the public could have cared less, as the federal monetary system was in disarray. Speculators, bankers, and exchange brokers sought to buy hoarded coins from the public, paying for them a premium in terms of paper and reselling them to others. Across the Northern border in Canada, Montreal became a trading center for American silver coins, and one writer stated that no less than $80,000 changed hands there every day in business conducted by 30 or more brokers.[13]

Civil War store card NH-120-A-1a, the only store card of New Hampshire. These were issued by Albert W. Gale, "restorator" (restaurateur) who operated the Depot House at 7 Railroad Square in Concord. Joseph Merriam, Boston diesinker and coiner, made the tokens. Only 500 were struck according to "A.W. Gale's Store Card," by Grovenor C. Nudd, *Journal of the Civil War Token Society*, Summer 1976. When the depot was torn down in the mid-20th century a hoard of about 200 Mint State tokens was found, accounting for most known to collectors today.

Scrip note for three cents issued and signed by A.W. Gale, March 20, 1863, and printed by McFarland & Jenks, a local shop.

In view of the continuing monetary confusion, many transactions were denominated in gold and silver, and when paid for in Legal Tender Notes an additional value was required to make up the difference. In the auction room sales of coins were called out in dollars and cents, with bills rendered in gold. Even the Philadelphia Mint would not accept Legal Tender Notes at par for gold and silver coins (which continued to be minted) or for Proof coins!

Meanwhile on the West Coast

The monetary situation was different in the far West, for in California paper money had been made illegal in commerce by an act of the state legislature in 1850. Neither bills from state-chartered banks nor Legal Tender Notes circulated there. The economy on the West Coast was entirely based on gold and silver coins. These continued to circulate at par, in contrast to the East and Midwest. When federal Legal Tender Notes were introduced in 1862, many were shipped to California as pay for federal employees.

Army and Navy troops were paid in paper money and could use the notes to buy items at their posts. Similarly, employees in federal offices such as at the Internal Revenue Department in San Francisco were paid in Legal Tender paper. Such notes, if spent in the outside world, were accepted only at deep discounts. However, postage stamps and revenue stamps (such as those applied to patent medicines, matches, etc.) could be bought at par in Legal Tender Notes, this, of course, simply being an exchange of paper for paper. However, the typical government employee had only a limited need for postage stamps and even less use for revenue stamps. He or she wanted money to buy food, shelter, and the other necessities and pleasures of life. It was found that a federal worker with a $20 Legal Tender Note had about as much spending power as a worker in the private sector who had $12 to $15 in gold and silver coins. This resulted in many grievances.

The uncomfortable situation continued. On November 8, 1863, "The S.S. *Moses Taylor* arrived [in San Francisco] with $1,000,000 in Legal Tender Notes and $50,000 in revenue stamps."[14] On August 25, 1864, the employees in the office of the Assessor of Internal Revenue in San Francisco went on strike seeking payment of their wages in gold coins or, alternatively, higher wages if they continued to be paid in Legal Tender Notes.[15]

Not adding any clarity to the situation was a ruling by the Supreme Court of California to the effect that Legal Tender Notes were, indeed, lawful money, *but* it was not required that "every kind of lawful money could be tendered in the payment of every obligation."[16] California passed a "specific contract" law under which debts could be collected in the form of payment specified by the makers of a given contract, who virtually always preferred gold coins, thus officially repudiating the use of Legal Tender Notes at par.[17]

More Copper Tokens

A reference book by Alfred H. Satterlee, *Arrangement of Medals and Tokens, struck in honor of the Presidents of the United States, and of the Presidential Candidates, from the administration of John Adams to that of Abraham Lincoln, Inclusive. Described chiefly from originals in the possession of the compiler and of Robert Hewitt, Jr., Esq.*, was published in 1862. Satterlee excluded George Washington, believing that his tokens and medals had already been well covered in numismatics, including in a book by James Ross Snowden published in 1861. Although this was too early to include tokens issued during the Civil War, the various 1860 presidential campaign tokens from dies by Benjamin C. True and sold by John Stanton were enumerated. Interest in collecting all kinds of tokens continued to increase. Curiously, current Liberty Seated silver and Liberty Head gold coins were only of passing interest to collectors, except for those who bought Proof sets each year. No one cared if coins had an "S" or other mintmark.

In 1862 more cent-sized copper tokens were made by various diesinkers. In Cincinnati the shop of Stanton took the lead with a series featuring advertisements on the obverse and an Indian Head on the reverse, the latter being a close copy of the federal cent except for stars around the border instead of UNITED STATES OF AMERICA. Three Indian Head dies were made with this date, each having a standard head at the center from a special punch and with the stars added one by one around the border. The Fuld numbers for these dies are 1007, 1008, and 1009. Distribution was by Cincinnati merchants. In the following year, 1863, Stanton created many more Indian Head token dies for merchants in over a dozen different states.

Stanton Indian Head obverse die 1007 used on OH-165-B-1a1, a store card of John Galvagni, a Cincinnati dealer in fancy goods and toys.

Die notes: Although this and other Stanton Indian Head dies are superficially similar, close examination will reveal features to differentiate, in this instance: Small date numerals. Most stars have two points toward the edge. Star 7 opposite tip of first feather. Star 13 slightly higher than tip of feather 8.

Stanton die 1008 used on OH-165-A-1a issued by Garret T. Dorland, a dealer in watches and jewelry in Cincinnati. If used on a patriotic token (one without mentioning a merchant) in the Fuld system this becomes die 57A and is the *obverse*. Giving the same die two designations is confusing at first, as noted in the text, but in using the two Fuld books, *Patriotic Civil War Tokens* and *U.S. Civil War Store Cards*, it becomes understandable.

Die notes: Large date. Most stars have one point toward the edge. Stars 6 and 7 double punched. Star 13 opposite tip of feather 8. 2 in date closer to the dentils than to the hair.

Stanton die 57A is the designation for 1008 when used for a patriotic token as 57A/444j as shown here. This is struck in German silver, a white alloy made of nickel and other ingredients and never used for circulating tokens but popular for numismatic strikes. The reverse die 444 shows a collage of fruit (when used on a store card, die 444 is known as 1279). The rim cud or break at the border below the 6 of the date indicates that this is a later use of the 57A die.

Stanton die 1009 used on OH-165-EJ-3a for Peebles, a Cincinnati grocer. If used on a patriotic token (one without mentioning a merchant) in the Fuld system this becomes die 57.

Die notes: Large date. Most stars have one point toward the edge. Star 7 left of tip of first feather. Star 13 between tips of feathers 7 and 8. 2 in date about centered between hair and dentils.

Beyond the Stanton Indian Heads there are relatively few other 1862-dated patriotic tokens or store cards. It is thought that in Chicago the shop of S.D. Childs continued the use of its several 1861-dated dies as the supply was adequate. In 1863 Childs would make dies with that date. Below are some miscellaneous tokens with the 1862 date.

Patriotic die 57 (a.k.a. store card die 1009) used with 57/467a. Die 467 was also used with store cards OH-DY-12a and OH-FN-1a. For the first time the third edition of *U.S. Civil War Store Cards* will assign this as die 1472. This represents a late state of the die with a rim cud below the 8 of the date.

NY-630-CA-1fo1 struck over an 1832 silver dime, a numismatic striking. Relatively few silver Civil War store cards are known today, and such are the *crème de la crème* of a specialized collection. The imprint is of liquor dealer J.H. Warner, 104 Barclay St., New York. Although copper strikings were made in quantity for circulation, most varieties are overstrikes made for collectors. One on a British sixpence sold for $1,900 in 1981 and into the 21st century was valued at several times that figure.

MI-370-D-2a with reverse die 1307 showing a Good Samaritan cast-iron kitchen stove.

TN-600-C-4a, a drayage check for moving goods such as from docks on the Mississippi River. Issued by B.E. Hammar & Co. of Memphis.

Patriotic token 71/456b in brass, combining obverse die 71 (same as store card die 1019) dated 1862 with reverse die 456 (known as 1401 when used with a store card) dated 1862, probably made as a numismatic specimen. From the shop of John T. Stanton.

On September 22, 1862, Lincoln issued his Preliminary Emancipation Proclamation stating that as of January 1, 1863, all slaves in rebellious states would be free. This had no effect on the Confederate States and did not take place in certain border states such as Missouri, Tennessee, West Virginia, and Maryland until later. In November 1862, Lincoln relieved McClellan of his command and appointed General Ambrose Everett Burnside in charge of the Army of the Potomac. In the next two years both men would become popular subject portraits for Civil War tokens.

Although no metal tokens as monetary substitutes were issued in the South, thought was given to the idea on several occasions.

The Confederate Senate actually passed a bill (S. 70) to provide for a copper token coinage for the Confederacy on September 25, 1862, but the House failed to take action on the bill after it was reported out of committee three weeks later. During consideration of the measure in the House *The Columbia Carolinian*, October 8, suggested that copper tokens might be of use:

> A light copper token, current for twenty-five cents, may be of the same weight as one for ten or five cents, the values of each being designated by some prominent emblem, with the aid of a little arithmetic, on either side of the piece. The intention of issuing tokens during war or a general interruption of ordinary trade is to affix a nominal value to some convenient object ultimately to be redeemed. Temporary copper "tokens" to take the place of silver coins will prove more convenient to the people of the Confederate States than the innumerable promise to pay small sums on bad paper.

New money in the South consisted of countless scrip notes, issues by state-chartered banks, and Confederate government bills. Federal silver and gold coins were hoarded and were worth multiples of the face value of CSA notes. Circulation of Yankee greenbacks in the South proved problematical and embarrassing to Confederate officials, leading to the Confederate Congress prohibiting dealing in "paper currency of the enemy" with certain exceptions, on February 6, 1864.

Tokens in 1863 and 1864

In 1863 the flood gates opened wide, and tens of millions of copper and, to a lesser extent brass, patriotic tokens and store cards were produced. In Chicago the shop of Shubael D. Childs, a pioneer in the field of cent-sized issues, produced many varieties for customers in several states. In Cincinnati the shop of John Stanton became the largest producer of store cards and served hundreds of customers in many states, primarily in the Midwest but also New York and New Jersey. Indian Heads were the main specialty, and he dominated production of this motif. Murdoch & Spencer (James Murdock Jr. and William W. Spencer) succeeded his interests in 1864 and kept using many of the older dies.

The shop of William K. Lanphear of Cincinnati turned out many tokens, including some from dies from the talented Frederick W. Lutz. Lanphear issued samples combining his own advertisement with dozens of different reverse motifs, giving customers a choice. Stock dies featured everything from eagles to clock faces and sets of teeth.

Most Chicago and Cincinnati makers emphasized store cards, with patriotic tokens in the minority.

In 1863 several diesinkers and token makers in New York City jumped into action. William Bridgens created over a dozen stock reverse dies and struck many store cards and some patriotics. Most of his customers were within a few hundred miles of his shop. Bridgens also advertised that he was a dealer in rare coins, although little is known about his involvement in that activity.

Bridgens's Civil War token dies are very distinctive, with the reverse dies including several interesting pictorial issues. Certain of his dies include some of the following features: The dentils of the die borders are composed of small triangles, a sawtooth arrangement called "dancetting" by the late Jack R. Detwiler. Die 1266 (a.k.a. patriotic

Patriotic token 281/468b in brass from dies by the Stanton shop. No doubt the reverse was intended to be used with a merchant's store card and perhaps was, but such is not located now. If discovered this would result in the die being given a store card number as well.

OH-165-FX-11a in copper, a store card advertising Stanton's business. The identity of the bearded man on the reverse die 1160 is unknown. It has been suggested that it might be Stanton himself. However, the die is used on tokens of other merchants as well. The obverse die has all letters in the same size font except for CARDS.

OH-165-DY-9a store card of James Murdock, who worked with John Stanton. Certain stock dies were used by both men for their advertising cards. The bison reverse die 1283 is an unusual motif for the era.

OH-165-GC-10a in copper issued by Vanaken ("Van.") Wunder of Cincinnati. Reverse die 1288 with a bull facing right was used on several other tokens as well.

IN-460-K-02a in copper with an inscription for J.F. Lenour of Minneapolis. This was an error die, as J.F. Senour was intended. Reverse 1311. Dies by the shop of W.K. Lanphear.

OH-165-BP-01d in copper-nickel, a numismatic strike by Lanphear. J. Hayes & Bro. Cincinnati. Reverse die 1169.

390A) is an exception. Ornaments included a spearhead found on the dies of no other diesinker. New York was sometimes abbreviated with a hyphen, as N-Y.

An auction held in the rooms of Bangs, Merwin & Co., New York City, January 29–30, 1863, that bore no consignor's or owner's name on the cover of the auction catalog, was attributed to William H. Bridgens by historian Emmanuel J. Attinelli, who also commented: "This collection belonged to the well-known diesinker, whose medals are numerous and fine."[18] This would seem to indicate that Attinelli may have known Bridgens. Alternatively, the catalog contents may have been attributed to Bridgens by virtue of the latter's advertisement on the back cover, which noted this (in part) and confirms his continuing activity in numismatics:

WM. H. BRIDGENS

Die sinker & Medalist

Dealer in

COINS, MEDALS & TOKENS

189 William Street, New-York.

N.B. Coins, bought, sold, or exchanged.

Certain of Bridgens's dies with pictorial motifs are illustrated below and on the page following.

Patriotic die 37 (also known as store card die 1387). Bridgens combined this die with many others. Depicted is his version of the French Liberty Head, the style used on certain French coins as early as the 1790s, but best known to numismatists on Robert Lovett Jr.'s 1860 store card and 1861 Civil War cent and an 1859 Marshall House token of Alexandria, Virginia. She is wearing a Phrygian cap, the ancient symbol of liberty (given to slaves or prisoners who were set free). The surrounding inscription, FOR PUBLIC ACCOMODATION includes a misspelling of the last word, which should be ACCOMMODATION.

The Washington Token die 120 (1137). Front row center among Civil War tokens bearing the portrait of the Father of Our Country is this Bridgens die, featuring an adaptation of the Jean Antoine Houdon 1785 portrait. Illustrated is the die used as the obverse of patriotic token 120/434d, a numismatic strike in copper-nickel made from a filed-down federal cent (note the file marks on the rim).

Bridgens die 138 (1152). Depicted is the head of a famous Civil War figure. There is no date on the die, but it was noted in print in 1863. In that year McClellan was a favorite national figure for those who opposed Abraham Lincoln, and in 1864 McClellan ran against Lincoln in the presidential election. Perhaps this die and the inscription on die 256 indicate that Bridgens was anti-Lincoln and against the war.

Bridgens Horrors of War die 256. This die is one of the "rarer" Bridgens issues and, like many of the others, was not extensively muled in combinations made for sale to numismatists, nor is it known combined with any store card dies. The dramatic and sad subject would not likely do any good for a commercial enterprise. At the center is the head of a distressed woman representing a Civil War soldier's widow. Two crossed cornucopias below her portrait represent what might have been, or will be, if there is peace instead of conflict.

Tradesmens Currency die 202 (1232) by Bridgens. At the center is a shield inscribed GOOD FOR ONE CENT, a rare wording as this is in contravention to law. The inscription indicates that this die was made as a currency substitute in the coin shortage of 1863. At the time *currency* referred to coins as well as paper money.

Bridgens political die 255. This features at the center a standing figure with cane, walking to the left, a representation of Diedrich Knickerbocker, the fictional early New Yorker created by Washington Irving in his light-hearted *History of New York*, 1809. The inscription, KNICKERBOCKER CURRENCY, completes the connection. The die is signed BRIDGENS below the standing figure, the only Civil War token die to bear his name. This die is not known in combination with any store card die. Interestingly, this die is also known mated with die 58A signed by another engraver, Louis Roloff, combination 58A/255, known in copper, unique, in the collection of the American Numismatic Society.

Bridgens die 434 (1215). An eagle is depicted on top of a world globe inscribed COPPER, with UNITED STATES above. Unusual for Bridgens, this die shows an error or mind-change as to the left of the first S (STATES) there is a trace of an earlier letter, possible an E, and a trace of another letter is at the lower right of the first T in the same word. The light striking on the higher parts of the eagle is due to the dies being spaced slightly too wide apart in the coining press. The eagle was from a hub punch and was used on dies 433 (a.k.a. 1214), 1215 (a.k.a. 1215), and store card NY-845-A (Skidmore's Head Quarters, Seneca Falls, NY).

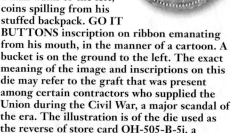

One of the numismatic favorites among Bridgens dies is 254 (1243). Around the border is the inscription MONEY MAKES THE MARE GO and the date 1863. At center a man walks to the left, coins spilling from his stuffed backpack. GO IT BUTTONS inscription on ribbon emanating from his mouth, in the manner of a cartoon. A bucket is on the ground to the left. The exact meaning of the image and inscriptions on this die may refer to the graft that was present among certain contractors who supplied the Union during the Civil War, a major scandal of the era. The illustration is of the die used as the reverse of store card OH-505-B-5j, a numismatic striking in nickel alloy.

Die 390 (1265). This popular Bridgens die is inscribed I-O-U 1 PURE COPPER CENT. A small portrait of Washington is seen to each side, both facing toward the center. Die 390 saw only limited use and is known only in combination with 434, the UNITED STATES COPPER die. Thus, copper metal is mentioned on both sides of the token.

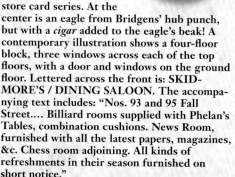

NY-845-A-1a. This motif is one of the most famous in the Civil War store card series. At the center is an eagle from Bridgens' hub punch, but with a *cigar* added to the eagle's beak! A contemporary illustration shows a four-floor block, three windows across each of the top floors, with a door and windows on the ground floor. Lettered across the front is: SKIDMORE'S / DINING SALOON. The accompanying text includes: "Nos. 93 and 95 Fall Street.... Billiard rooms supplied with Phelan's Tables, combination cushions. News Room, furnished with all the latest papers, magazines, &c. Chess room adjoining. All kinds of refreshments in their season furnished on short notice."

In New York City, Emil Sigel took the lead and turned out a large quantity of patriotic and advertising tokens, probably more than any other coiner in that metropolis or, possibly, even more than all of his competitors combined. For a long time he was located at 177 William Street. Curiously, his signature, which was usually a form of his initials ES, was often crudely added to even well-made dies.

The striking of tokens from his dies ranged from excellent to, more often, casual or indifferent to downright sloppy. It may be that some in the latter category were restrikes made outside of his shop, and studies of die states may eventually shed light on the matter. It is certain that many of his dies were used for a long time, often being relapped. Some dies were signed ES or E. SIGEL, others with his full name. It is easy to envision that from 1863 onward, including after the war ended, collectors visited Sigel's shop, or had Sigel make runs or sets of special strikings. Often, these special-order tokens were poorly struck, with light definition of details, weak rims, etc.

Louis Roloff conducted an engraving business at 1 New Chambers, New York City, during the Civil War. Roloff turned out the Gustav Lindenmueller and the J.L. Bode "birdstuffer" tokens, each about the size of a quarter, and served other clients as well, mostly with tokens of 19 mm diameter. He sometimes signed his dies as ROLOFF.

NY-630-U-1b store card for Carl Diem of the Constanzer Brauerei, New York City, from dies by Emil Sigel. Reverse die 1417 is signed EMIL SIGEL.

NY-630-AH-1a, a 24.2 mm store card by Roloff. With the prominent motif of a buck's head on the obverse and its overly large diameter, the J. Bode "Birdstuffer" token is one of the more curious issues among New York City merchants of 1863. L. ROLOFF is at the top of the obverse below the antler tips. This token was a playground for numismatic strikes, and various rarities were created from the dies. An example overstruck on an 1861 Liberty Seated quarter, pedigreed to John W. Haseltine's 65th Sale, March 1, 1883, lot 161, was offered in the Bowers and Ruddy sale of the Garrett Collection IV, lot 2045, and brought $4,400.

The curious 197/378a token combining a signed Sigel obverse die with a signed Roloff reverse die. In "Twice-Signed Patriotic CWTs," *JCWTS*, Fall 1984, Dr. Larkin Wilson noted that there are just four patriotic die combinations in which the obverse and reverse dies are signed by *different* engravers, these being: 58/439A (Roloff/Sigel), 58A/ 255 (Roloff/ Bridgens), 93/362 (H [probably Hörter] / JGW), and 197/378 (ES [Sigel] / L. Roloff).

In Philadelphia the shop of William H. Key, well-known in the field of tokens and small medals, created many Civil War motifs as well. In the same city Robert Lovett Jr. and Peter H. Jacobus were also in the business.

Joseph H. Merriam of Boston served many New England clients and created dies that were especially deeply and boldly engraved. His reverse die with a dog's head and GOOD FOR A SCENT became a classic in its own time. Innovative in the Civil War series were his modular dies that had a small cylindrical recess permitting a small round "slug" to be inserted to change the denomination, such as 10, 25, or 50 cents, of which more will be said.

The Milwaukee firm of Mossin & Marr, formed by Peter L. Mossin and John Marr, produced many dies for customers in Wisconsin and for scattered others. John Marr seems to have been the principal engraver, and certain of his dies are boldly signed MARR. Most tokens are deeply engraved and well struck. In face of legal threats the partnership suspended making these pieces in mid-1863 and advertised to redeem them. By 1864 the firm commenced making them anew, including strikings from a memorable 1863-dated die with an Amazonian warrior (sometimes called Minerva in 19th-century listings). The firm also made many restrikes and unusual die combinations for collectors.

PA-750-E-4a for M.F. Beirn and the Magnolia Hotel, Philadelphia. Dies by Robert Lovett Jr. Reverse die 1182. The Baltimore *Sun*, October 31, 1863, carried this: "Passing Tokens as Money: M. Beirn, keeper of a public house in Philadelphia, has been arrested on a charge of passing 'tokens' as money. The allegation is that he gives instead of cents for change small copper coins having upon them the name of M. Beirn and the location of his establishment. It was testified to that several of the tokens had been passed by Mr. Beirn and his bartender, and that upon the former being spoken to about it, he replied that he had a right to pass them, and they were good and would pass anywhere. The prosecution was brought under the Act of Congress, of 17th of July, 1862." [The disposition of the case was not stated.]

Joseph H. Merriam store card MA-115-E-1a with his famous GOOD FOR A SCENT reverse die 1384.

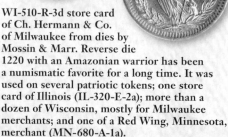

WI-510-R-3d store card of Ch. Hermann & Co. of Milwaukee from dies by Mossin & Marr. Reverse die 1220 with an Amazonian warrior has been a numismatic favorite for a long time. It was used on several patriotic tokens; one store card of Illinois (IL-320-E-2a); more than a dozen of Wisconsin, mostly for Milwaukee merchants; and one of a Red Wing, Minnesota, merchant (MN-680-A-1a).

WI-185-A-1a issued by C.W. Smith of East Troy, Wisconsin. Dies by Mossin & Marr. Reverse die 1174 dated 1864 with a boldly engraved eagle.

No sketch of Civil War token issuers would be complete without mentioning several "primitive" die cutters who turned out tokens with crudely aligned lettering and casually arranged motifs. Henry D. Higgins of Mishawaka, Indiana, is the best-known example, mainly due to a lot of attention paid to him by Wayne Stafford and David Gladfelter in the pages of the modern *Journal of the Civil War Token Society*, now named the *Civil War Token Journal*. Higgins, who made barometers and other devices, apparently decided to cut his own token dies to advertise his business and those of others. His naïve style with irregularly spaced and misaligned letters gave rise to the "Indiana primitive" series, a specialty in its own right. Certain of Higgins's dies are combined with those of Childs of Chicago, and it seems that Childs struck many of the tokens.

Alexander Gleason of Hillsdale, Michigan was another issuer of "primitives." Just as folk art is popular with collectors of art and antiques, tokens with rustic workmanship are more popular with collectors than are those from dies cut with precision. The Gleasons lived in Hillsdale in the 1860s into the 1870s after which they moved to Jackson, Michigan, and later to Darien, New York, where Alexander died and was buried. This was recorded in the family: "They did stencil work, and I can remember seeing father with a sharp instrument punching out designs."[19]

A.W. Escherich of Chicago, who was early in the game with tokens dated 1861, is also in the "primitive" category. His output seems to have been small, although sufficient enough that he made three different dies with his own advertisement.

Store card IN-630-A-5b advertising H.D. Higgins, who cut the dies. His rustic tokens are called "Indiana primitives." The reverse is designated as die 1328.

Patriotic Civil War token 155/431a, an "Indiana primitive" by H.D. Higgins.

Store card MI-450-G-8b issued by and for Alexander Gleason, reverse die 1187. The rustic die work gives "primitives" such as this extra numismatic appeal.

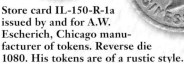

Store card IL-150-R-1a issued by and for A.W. Escherich, Chicago manufacturer of tokens. Reverse die 1080. His tokens are of a rustic style.

Store card IL-150-R-3a issued by and for A.W. Escherich with a different obverse die and with reverse die 1188.

William Johnston of Cincinnati turned out tokens that were satisfactorily lettered but which in some instances used rusted and cracked dies. Ditto for M. Lindermann of the same city. Both used reverse die 1247.

The Scovill Manufacturing Company of Waterbury, Connecticut, a leading maker of Civil War tokens, also made earlier Hard Times and other issues. The Waterbury Button Company was also important in this era.

W.C. Prime in *Coins, Medals, and Seals, Ancient and Modern*, 1861, commented on the two firms, his text being relevant for production of store cards commencing with the opening of the Erie Canal in 1825 and continuing to circa 1857. Nearly all were about the diameter of a large copper cent:

Store card OH-165-CF-5a by William Johnston. Reverse die 1388 is severely cracked.

Store card OH-165-DE-2a by M. Lindermann advertising his trade. Reverse die 1247 is deeply rusted.

> From this period the issue of such cards became more frequent, until now the catalogues show more than 500 extant, and large numbers have appeared which are not catalogued and are unknown to collectors.
>
> The die-cutters of New York and Waterbury, in Connecticut, are now constantly occupied in cutting these cards for tradesmen in all parts of the country. Hundreds of thousands are struck in every successive year by the Scovill Manufacturing Company and the Waterbury Button Company. They appear in copper, brass, and white metal and are largely circulated by their respective proprietors. But they disappear almost as rapidly as they appear, especially since the issue of the nickel cent [in 1857] which keeps them out of general circulation.[20]

During the war Scovill made encased postage stamps and in 1860 and 1864 ferrotype political campaign souvenirs. Relatively little is known about the firm's activities with Civil War tokens (but see notice of John Gault at 1 Park Place below). Many dies have been tentatively ascribed to Scovill—particularly the store cards with a brassy appearance (New York state issuers such as Robinson & Ballou, Wing, etc.) and similar patriotics (the 1863 "Flag" tokens and others), but not much of a factual nature has ever been confirmed. In the present text Scovill attributions are followed by a question mark.

In the Fall 1968 number of *JCWTS*, continued in the next two issues, Melvin Fuld presented an article, "Scovill Manufacturing Co." This gave a general history of the firm as supplied by E.H. Davis, company historian, with acknowledgment that records were incomplete, that in the late 19th century a fire had destroyed early documents, and some information was conjectural. Davis did find some early correspondence pertaining to the Army & Navy, Dix, and Boutwell tokens of 1863, suggesting that these may have been made by Scovill. The A. Ludewig token of Pittsburgh (PA-765-J) with reverse of a standing man and the legend COPPERS 20 Pr Ct PREMIUM, was mentioned as well.

However, among the tokens held in the Scovill archives were some known to have been made by others, including a card of E.E. Hasse (Yonkers, New York) signed by Roloff. Other store cards of 1863 included those of Brimelow (with Washington die) and Doscher (with Washington die), which are tempting to attribute to Scovill because of their general appearance. As there were non-Scovill tokens mixed among the firm's holdings, and no contemporary (1860s) accounting survives, the attribution of Scovill dies is conjectural as noted. On the other hand, a separate collection held by the firm contained many encased postage stamp varieties made for the inventor and distributor, John Gault.

Most of Scovill's Civil War tokens were made in brass or have a brassy appearance. The Waterbury Button Co. of the same city is thought to have made tokens of similar hue, but once again facts are elusive and no positive attributions have been made in the form of signed dies or original records.

In Rhode Island at least two "rustic" diecutters held forth. One laboriously hand-engraved letters and numerals with the result that in a word such as "Providence" both e's were differently shaped. Another engraver was illiterate, it seems, and placed the letters N and S backward.

A listing of other diesinkers and shops includes George J. Glaubrecht (New York City), Charles Hörter (New York City), Francis X. Koehler (Baltimore), Louis Leichtweis (New York City), H. Miller & Co. (Louisville, Kentucky, maker of many saloon tokens), Frederick B. Smith (New York City), and the roster could be extended. There are many Civil War tokens for which their makers are not known. The opportunities for research are extensive.

Store card of A. Ludewig, PA-765-J, 22 mm, may have been made by Scovill. With the obverse lettering, beaded border, and certain other characteristics it is surely seen as related to another Trade and Commerce token of like inscription and diameter, Fuld 259-445b, illustrated later in connection with John Gault.

NY-890-B-19b, one of many varieties of brass tokens issued by Oliver Boutwell, flour miller in Troy, New York. There is a good possibility the dies were made by the Scovill Manufacturing Company.

RI-700-G-4a store card for the City Fruit Store in Providence. The letters are all hand engraved, a style seen on some other Rhode Island and related tokens but rare elsewhere. On the reverse the stars are from a punch and have holes at the center, a style known as mullets (or molets).

RI-700-F-1a token, large 23.4 mm, for the Empire Saloon. The letters N and S are backward. Reverse 1294 with a beer mug.

Then there is the mysterious James A. Hughes of Cincinnati, who was associated with the Lanphear shop and issued store cards with METALIC / CARDS lettered within a wreath, the exact same style used by Lanphear. Hughes was a numismatist and had special pieces struck in silver. He seems to have had engraving ability as well, but whether he was ever involved in cutting dies for Civil War tokens is problematical.

George J. Glaubrecht prepared the dies for IL-890-B-2b issued by J.L. Loveday & Co. of Waukegan, Illinois. Reverse die 1142 is signed G.G. N.Y. at the bottom border. Loveday issued another token, IL-890-A, from dies ascribed to the Scovill Manufacturing Co., not shown here.

NY-630-A-1b from dies by Charles D. Hörter, signed H under the lyre, 21.5 mm, brass. The Atlantic Garden was an immense beer hall that was one of New York City's prime attractions in the Bowery in the late 19th century.

Interior of the Atlantic Garden as shown in a contemporary engraving. Articles of the time hailed it as a place to enjoy an afternoon or evening of beer and music or, alternatively thought by those who took a dim view of ardent spirits, a den for low life.

KY-510-D-2b issued by saloonkeeper George Brucklacher of Louisville, Kentucky. Dies by the H. Miller Co. of Louisville.

OH-165-BX-1f store card of J.A. Hughes, a Cincinnati numismatist who, it seems, also distributed tokens. The reverse is die 1131 by F.W. Lutz. This is one of several dozen store card varieties the Lanphear shop struck for him in silver, creating rarities.

John Gault in the Token Business

In 1863 when Civil War store cards and patriotic tokens flooded the channels of commerce federal cents were occasionally seen, but silver and gold coins continued to be absent (as they would be until the 1870s). In that year Postage Currency transitioned to become the Fractional Currency series (which lasted until 1876), and scrip notes, encased postage stamps (in relatively small numbers), and tokens facilitated the buying of small items and services as well as making change. Merchants found that copper tokens were more durable than paper scrip and were more effective as an advertising medium.

John Gault, the well-known patentee and issuer of encased postage stamps, was at 1 Park Place, New York City, and placed advertisements in 1863 to sell copper tokens in papers in the East and Midwest. Several examples follow.

Gault on March 22 placed this notice in the *New York Herald Tribune:*

> SUBSTITUTES FOR PENNIES.—COPPER, BRASS OR Nickel Tokens for business firms in any quantity and various designs. Also Encased Postage Stamps, with card stamped on back. Orders for the above promptly filled by JOHN GAULT, No. 1 Park Place, N.Y.

The above was repeated in the March 24 issue. On March 26 and 28 this notice appeared in the same paper:

> TOKENS OF BRASS OR COPPER, MANUFACTURED in any quantity, by JOHN GAULT, No. 1 Park Place, New York.

There was no mention of encased postage stamps in this new advertisement, perhaps signaling the end of the era of these encasements, which had been patented on August 12, 1862, and were familiar in circulation afterward. Significant to the present narrative the Scovill Manufacturing Company of Waterbury, Connecticut, nearly certainly made the encasements for Scovill, suggesting the likelihood that the same firm made the tokens he advertised. This is further strengthened by the fact that in 1864 Gault sold presidential campaign items made by Scovill, indicating that his connection was continuous.

The *New York Public Ledger*, March 9, 1863, reported that cents were "so scarce as to command a premium of 20 percent." This and related sentiments seem to have inspired Gault, for on May 30 this notice first appeared in the *New York Herald:*

> TRADE AND COMMERCE "TOKENS"—A new thing, having intrinsic value, manufactured and sold only by JOHN GAULT, Park Place, third door from Broadway, N.Y., first floor.

These tokens were 22 mm in diameter, larger than the usual 19 mm for the typical Civil War issues. Likely thousands were sold as these tokens are readily available in the marketplace today.[21]

Manufacturers typically charged $9 for 1,000 tokens at the outset, but by 1864 there were offers at $7.50 for the same quantity with Gault being the most prolific advertiser.

Trade and Commerce token, Fuld 259/445b, 22 mm, as offered by John Gault in the spring of 1863.

Events of 1864

The Act of April 3, 1864, introduced bronze as the alloy to replace copper-nickel in the manufacture of federal one-cent pieces. Mint officials had observed the success in circulation of copper/bronze tokens, had produced some patterns in bronze, and had concluded that this was a better alloy—cheaper and easier to coin. The act also prohibited the distribution of privately manufactured tokens. This time around, unlike with the Act of July 17, 1862, many people took notice, and warnings were published in the newspapers. By that time some 1864-dated dies had been made. After the legislation the solution for token makers was simple: keep using old dies and make new dies dated 1863! In one instance the new firm of Fisler & Chance, operators of a soda fountain and drug store in Urbana, Ohio, that announced its opening on July 4, 1866, set about issuing "Civil War" store cards made by Murdock & Spencer using earlier-dated dies. In the same city Charles McCarthy, who operated the Washington House, established after the war, did the same thing.

In July 1864 distrust of Legal Tender Notes and worries about the fiscal soundness of the Union drove the price of older silver and gold coins to a record high. It took $285 in such bills to buy $100 face value in coins. Coins were required for many transactions, and buyers of certain goods had no choice but to pay a high premium to banks, bullion dealers, and exchange brokers. The Philadelphia Mint would only accept such coins in payment for current Proof coins in various metals, and coin auctions, such as those conducted by W. Elliot Woodward, Harvey Strobridge, and Edward D. Cogan, had to be paid for in such coins or else in Legal Tender Notes at a stiff premium. The prices realized at auction sales were recorded in terms of dollars in gold and silver.

The total quantity of patriotic tokens and store cards issued is not known, but probably was on the long side of 50 million. When they were paid out by merchants a nominal profit was shown. In time, when federal cents reappeared in quantity beginning in 1864, many store cards were redeemed by their issuers. Patriotic tokens, which did not bear the name of an issuer, continued in circulation as no one knew where to turn them in.

Into the Year 1865

Absent any meaningful restrictions, issuers of paper scrip continued to turn out large quantities of such notes and routinely dated them 1864. By early 1865 the monetary crisis for pocket change was completely over, bronze Indian Head cents were common in circulation as were older copper-nickel cents that had emerged from hiding, and a new denomination, the two-cent piece, was made in quantity.

Civil War tokens of various kinds remained important in commerce throughout the 1870s after which time they gradually disappeared.

In the meantime in the late 1860s such shops as Lanphear, Sigel, Murdock & Spencer, and Mossin & Marr continued making Civil War tokens for collectors using earlier-dated dies.

Civil War Tokens and the History of Collecting Them

Collector Interest During the Civil War

By the time the Civil War started, tokens were already a prime focus of numismatic activity in America. The earlier-mentioned studies by Charles I. Bushnell (1858) and the Philadelphia Numismatic Society (1860) had attracted wide interest as had the tokens and medalets produced by Robert Lovett Jr., George H. Lovett, Joseph Merriam, and others. In 1861, as the conflict progressed, collector interest expanded. In that year no one knew if the war would be over soon or would last a long time. New tokens circulated in Chicago and elsewhere, but not enough varieties (yet) to create a Civil War tokens specialty.

By 1862 enthusiasm was in high gear. There was a scramble for mulings made by the shop of John Stanton from the dies used to strike the 22 mm Wealth of the South and presidential candidates' tokens of 1860, now mated with new store card dies for several Memphis and two Cincinnati businesses. Tokens combining two portraits of candidates, portraits with irrelevant store card dies, and others were made in copper, brass, tin-plated copper and brass, and white metal, to the delight of eager collectors. A few were struck in silver as well.

By 1863 numismatists were visiting the token shops of John Stanton and William K. Lanphear in Cincinnati, William Bridgens and Emil Sigel in New York, S.D. Childs in Chicago, and others to purchase new releases as well as buy mulings and off-metal strikes. Copper-nickel Flying Eagle and Indian Head cents, if filed down at the rims, made good planchets for such tokens, but sometimes a ghost image of the undertype cent design could still be seen. All of this was great fun. Confirmation of the desirability of these interesting pieces came quickly with listings of them in auction catalogs of W. Elliot Woodward, Edward D. Cogan, and others.

Collectors Will Be Collectors

A view of the collecting excitement in New York City in the spring of 1863 is revealed by this article in the *New York Evening Post*, Saturday, May 9:

The Penny Nuisance

The day after the battle of Roanoke Island it is related that not a rebel soldier lying on the field of battle, dead, was left with a button to his coat. Our soldiers are—or were—ravenous curiosity hunters, and every man who could secured a relic of that action and of the rebellion in the shape of a rebel button. There are collectors at home, too, and these are having a good time with the tokens and counterfeit pennies which are just now having a temporary "run."

Boys and idle curious men are busy making a collection of these coins; and this grows quickly into a business, so you may find petty merchants of this kind in the neighborhood of the post office, and doubtless elsewhere, who will not sell you a "Monitor" or a "Dix" or "copperhead" except at a premium.

Meantime, the general public good-naturedly accepts these almost worthless tokens as so many genuine cents, and the readiness with which they pass current has multiplied them, until there is reason to believe that not less than 200 different kinds have been manufactured in New York alone; and correspondents complain to us that engravers and die sinkers are so busy with this work that they have not time for legitimate work. Now it ought to be understood that while tokens, varying in name and promises to pay of responsible men, are not purporting to be cents, and many pass at the pleasure of those who take them. The rapidly increasing coinage of "Not One Cent," "Army and Navy," "Monitor," and other tokens of that kind, which bear no signature or name, are a clear fraud upon the public. They are not worth a quarter of what they pass for, and they are put forth by speculators, who are making a large profit by this totally irresponsible coinage. These tokens pass for a penny; they cost the ingenious makers at most 30 cents per 100; the profit on the venture of say 100,000 is therefore very considerable.

Of course no one is responsible for their redemption, and presently, when people discover the fact that pennies are not scarce, there will be a small panic. Everybody will refuse to take the sham pennies, and the loss will fall most heavily upon a class of people who ought not to suffer, namely the keepers of what are properly known as "cent shops," the little depots of toys, candles, needles, and thread, where women and children make so many purchases.

We advise these shopkeepers to refuse peremptorily at least all coins which do not bear some responsible name. In this way they can, with little inconvenience, drive out of circulation the irresponsible utterances and put a stop to a cheat from which otherwise they will eventually suffer most heavily. It would be well if the omnibuses and street rail companies would also refuse these tokens.

On May 12 the *New York Evening Post* had more to say on the subject:

Warning to Collectors and the Public

It ought to be known to the public and to the authorities that the manufacture of copper tokens to use instead of pennies is getting to be a considerable business, with promise of constant increase, and that while a very bold swindle is thus perpetrated against the public, the collectors of these coins and tokens have before them an endless task if they mean to complete their examples.

In this morning's papers not less than four advertisements point out where the dishonest dealer may purchase these substitutes for pennies there to be obtained, of any pattern design, at the rate of about 120 for a dollar; and we have reason to believe that a great many shopkeepers are regular customers of these die sinkers and coiners and put off daily a certain quantity of these coppers on unsuspecting customers, making a profit thereby of not less than 20%.

It is a profitable business, you see, but it is a shame to tempt small shop men to dishonest ways, and we hope the proper law officers will endeavor to put a stop to what is likely to demoralize and taint with dishonesty the whole minor retail trade. As for the collectors of these worthless tokens or spurious coins, they may well give up their task—it promises to be endless, for not only does every week see a new design, but the owner of a certain number of dies changes these about, and is thus able to strike off, from a dozen different matrices, a number of different coins frightful to the most patient and enthusiastic collector to think of. We suppose, for instance, that a manufacturer of coins has a dozen dies; he can from these strike off no less than 720 tokens, each differing from all the others in some way.

Moreover, we hear that the manufacturing of these things *only* for collectors is profitable and will go on for a long time to come. One maker told an inquirer that he was working now for "the trade," but when the rush was over he intended to turn out more careful copies for the benefit of collectors, so that those who now make up collections of half-debased poorly printed tokens are likely by and by to find themselves surpassed, with ease, by the more fortunate tokens who have a manufacturer of such relics at their command.

It is time to put a stop to the penny nuisance; and we hope that the ferry, stage, and city railroad companies will at once refuse them. That would almost of itself force out of circulation these cheats upon the public.

Far from being "warned," collectors increased their desire to add to their holdings. As noted above, the token makers in New York City had their hands full with mating dies in illogical combinations and producing scarcities and rarities for the numismatic trade. Priced scarcely above a cent each, this was a win-win situation for the coiners as well as for the expansion of interest in numismatics.

In the meantime on May 11 in the *New York Herald* this notice appeared, with the "Union Forever" title being the same as on some tokens, although there may have been no connection. The brokers dealt in coins and tokens:

NOTICE—UNION FOREVER—PROPRIETORS of hotels, restaurants, and stores are requested to call and see MATSON & ROBINSON, brokers, 163 Fulton Street, opposite St. Paul's Church. Nickels and Tokens supplied at the lowest market prices.

The May 12 issue of the same paper ran three advertisements adjacent to each other, reflecting the active market at the time:

COPPER TOKENS OF ALL KINDS furnished in any quantity. Merchants can be furnished with their business card on one side, at the same rates, $8.50 to $9 per 1,000, by the quantity, at D. MACKIE, 257 Broadway, upstairs.

COPPER TOKENS FOR SALE. J.G. Wilson, Medalist and Copper Token Manufacturer, 43 Centre Street, New York, in the rear. The trade supplied at the lowest prices.

COPPER TOKENS—THE ONLY TOKENS manufactured having any real value are those made by JOHN GAULT, No. 1 Park Place, two doors from Broadway, New York.

On May 17 the *New York Herald* printed this news item:

COPPERHEAD CURRENCY. We have before us fifty or sixty specimens of brass and copper cent tokens that are now circulating so extensively in this city and its environs. And this number is but a small proportion of the varieties that have come out within the last few months.

They are principally of a size approximating that of the nickel cent, though some few of them approach nearer to the size of the old copper cent. One set of the coins is stamped as Knickerbocker currency, another as tradesmen's currency; but the whole genus is popularly known as copperhead currency. The city is flooded with it, and, as at first, as no one thought of refusing it in change, of course the issuers of it were realizing immense profits.

Among those dealing in tokens in New York City was A. Ogden, who did business at 1 Park Place (the same street address used by John Gault, seller of encased postage stamps), in rooms 15 and 16. It is not known if he had any connection with Gault. Ogden advertised only briefly.

In the *New York Herald*, June 13, 1863, he ran an unusual notice offering to *buy* tokens from the public and to sell them to collectors:

WANTED—ANY QUANTITY OF COPPER TOKENS, at 30 cents per hundred; collections furnished; country orders filled. A. Ogden, No. 1 Park Place, New York, Room 15, first door from Broadway.

In *Harper's Weekly*, various issues that summer, Ogden ran small notices illustrated with an engraving of a token with ARMY / & / NAVY within a wreath:

COPPER TOKENS OR MEDALS, blanks, dies, business cards, and collections furnished cheap and in great variety. Also National Union League badges, Army Corps badges, National Union League pins, &c., at lowest jobbing prices. A. OGDEN, No. 1 Park Place, New York. Room No. 16.

Other postings were aplenty in 1863 in New York City, including these:

COPPER TOKENS. For sale in any quantity. Country orders promptly filled by express. Cut this out. JAMES MALONEY. 70 William Street, New-York.[1]

COPPER TOKENS MANUFACTURED BY NEAL & ENSCOE, 172 Centre Street. Agent at 950 Broadway in the store. Country orders attended to.[2]

A Collection Formed in 1863

The following account by an unknown writer, printed in an issue of the *New York Mercury* in 1863, gives another view of the tokens in the year in which they most actively circulated:[3]

Copper Tokens

One of the out-croppings of this Rebellion is just beginning to circulate among us, in the shape of "tradesmen's tokens" as they are called in England, or "store cards" as we name them. The material and stamping of these copper tokens cost quite a cent each. It is not therefore with a view to defraud the government that they are issued, but solely as a matter of convenience, and possibly with an eye to the advantages they offer as an advertising medium. Not one in five hundred of these tokens will ever be redeemed; not that they would not be, if offered, but they will go into the hands of collectors, into foreign museums, into the pockets of Western or Eastern men visiting the city, and who carry them away without knowing it, and when found, they are laid aside as curiosities, or given to the children to play with. When the loss does not exceed a few pennies, no one cares to take the trouble to repair it. These tokens will by-and-by obtain numismatic and historical value, and then the holders of their descendants will be envied.

Since the commencement of the present war, and indeed since 1857, many were issued of which no record has as yet been made. In the West, particularly in Illinois, there have been quantities struck, and even from Memphis we have seen one specimen quite creditable to Secessia. It is to be hoped for the benefit of history, and especially for that branch of history comprised in numismatics, that somebody is making collections of tokens, if any exist, in the States at present in rebellion.

They will form a most interesting as well as important feature in the future history of the war, and as being more ephemeral than almost any other species of illustration of history, should be carefully sought after, and securely hoarded, until the time for their practical use may have come. Here in the North we have no doubt many have already commenced collecting, and perhaps some, stimulated by the present writing, may commence the pursuit so interesting, and even infatuating, to the new beginner. . . .

We have collected no less than five different varieties of the Not One Cent pattern, in all of which the obverse is different, and in which there were three different types of the reverse. The legend on one of them is different, and in which there were three different types of the reverse. The legend on one of them is "Erinnerung an 1863," or "In memory of 1863," being in fact a souvenir, a memento, of the troubles and trials through which we are now passing, and of which the little coin is itself a sign and an accompaniment.

Still another very neat-looking token has a facsimile on the reverse side of the later issue of the nickel cents, with a head of Gen. McClellan in profile, facing right, on the obverse side; and this is known as the McClellan model.

Should the present scarcity continue for any lengthened period, it is probable that industrious collectors of the various tokens issued during the present year will have hundreds of different specimens to add to their collections.

A New Yorker Forms a Collection in a Few Hours

An article the next year in the San Francisco *Alta California*, July 18, 1864, described tokens collected in the space of a few hours in New York City in 1863. The journalist, who had a wry sense of humor, found the situation to be a bit confusing:

THE SPECIE CURRENCY OF NEW YORK.—We have been shown a collection of twenty-four specimens of copper coins, issued by private parties in New York in 1863 for circulation as small change, each being of the nominal value of one cent and readily passing for that amount.

The collection was made in a few hours by [news dealer and engraver] Mr. [Bernard B.] Steinbrink, of No. 35 Second Street, in this city, and the variety might have increased, with a little effort, almost indefinitely, so great is the number of these tokens in circulation in New York, where this is the only species of coin not held at over one hundred per cent premium. Most of these little jokers are of common copper, like the old American [large] cent, and about the size of the new "nickel" [Indian heads], although intrinsically worth less than half the value of the latter coin, and perhaps one-fourth that of the former.

Many of these "coppers" or "tokens" have the eagle or Indian head on one side, in partial imitation of the legitimate issue, and all are highly scented; in fact you could smell a man just about as many rods [1 rod = 5.5 yards] as he has cents of this description about him. The legends on some of these coppers are patriotic; on some they smack strongly of Copperheadism, and some are decidedly noncommittal, or merely of the advertising, or *carte de visite* style. Here they are, as we take them up in course:

"The Flag of Our Union." Reverse: "If anybody attempts to tear it down, shoot him on the spot—Dix. • "For Public Accommodation." Reverse: "Horrors of War; Blessings of Peace." • "Constitution Forever." Reverse: "Erinnerung, An. 1863." • "Union '61." • "Wilson's Medal." • "Gustavus Lindenmueller, New York" (with portrait resembling that of our old friend, Ovidius Naso). • "For Our Country, a Common Cause." Reverse: "Now and Forever." • Four coppers: "Army and Navy" (with the same legend, but different designs.) • Fine Ale Drawn from Wood, 95 Bowery." • "Not One Cent, U.S.A." (different designs). • "New York." • "Importers of Wines and Liquors." Reverse with address of advertiser. • "Gen. Geo. B. McClellan." Reverse: "United States Copper." (Would not the addition of "head" improve the last legend?—Reporter, *Alta California*) • "Broas Brothers Pie Bakery." Reverse: "United We Stand." (The Brothers, the Pies, or the Country?— Reporter, *Alta California*) • "Knickerbocker Currency Money Makes the Mare Go." Reverse: "Go it Buttons." • "Wright." (He is probably always so— Reporter, *Alta California*) • "Not One Cent" (different designs).

"When This Cruel War is Over." What a fruitful field for the researches of the numismatologist will be found in these unauthorized mint drops. A full text of all the issues of this kind would, like the roll of placards which adorned the walls of Paris on the successive days of the first French Revolution, afford an almost continuous history of the times and greatly facilitate the labors of the historian. It is worthy of note that these coppers have at last become so numerous as to seriously interfere with the circulation of the government "fractional currency," and a specific law prohibiting their issue was passed by the last Congress.[4]

The Pliny E. Chase Listing

The first known numismatic study of the series was the "Catalogue of Tokens Circulating During the Rebellion of 1861," by Pliny E. Chase, *Proceedings of the American Philosophical Society*, September 18, 1863, comprising 19 pages and describing 303 varieties. By that time interest was widespread, as noted above, but collectors had been busy acquiring them, not engaging in research. The listing began:

Mr. Chase presented for the Cabinet a collection of tokens, illustrating the trade currency illicitly circulating during the war, together with a catalogue.

An early print showing the home of the American Philosophical Society in Philadelphia. At a meeting held there on September 18, 1863, Pliny Elder Chase presented a paper listing the Civil War tokens he had found, this being the earliest known catalog of such pieces.

Collectors and others who may wish to assist in completing the collection of token currency in the Cabinet of the American Philosophical Society may send specimens, duplicates, or descriptions of such varieties as are not mentioned in this catalogue, to the curator, Mr. Fr. Peale, or to the librarian of the Society.[5]

The star (*) denotes such varieties as are described from other collections, but are wanting in the Society's collection.

B, brass; C, copper; L, lead. Where no letter is given, the token is of copper.

The sizes are given in sixteenths of an inch. Thus, size 12 denotes that the diameter is 12/16th of an inch. The average weight of the tokens examined by Mr. William E. Dubois, Assistant Assayer, United States Mint, is 51 grains.

Chase divided his study into seven different classes, excerpts from which are given below. How to properly sort Civil War tokens into distinct classes is a puzzle that to this day has never been solved to everyone's satisfaction. The tokens seem to have been gathered in the East. Therefore some of the Cincinnati and Chicago issues were not listed, nor are any with Indian Heads. This was a trial list, so to speak, the tip of the iceberg in relation to the tokens actually in the channels of commerce by that time.

It is significant to note that no copper-nickel, white metal, silver, or other numismatic strikings in existence by that time are listed, nor are intentional mulings of unrelated dies, but as they were not used in commerce, likely Chase's tokens were picked out of circulation. By this time many collectors had made-to-order rarities in their cabinets.

CLASS I.—*Business Cards.*

*1. "J.L. Agens & Co., No. 1 Commerce St., Newark, N.J. Newspapers." *Rev.* Eagle on globe. "Union forever." Size 13.

*2. Same. *Rev.* Two stars. "Good for 1 Cent." Size 13.

3. "Atlantic Garden, 50 Bowery, New York, 1863." *Rev.* Harp and wreath. "Grand Concert Every Night. Admission Free." Size 14.

4. "C. Bahr, cor. Cliff and Frankfort Sts., New York." *Rev.* Wreath. "Not One Cent. L. Roloff." Size 12+.

CLASS II.—*Portraits.*

187. Head of Washington, 6+7 stars. "1863." *Rev.* Shield, banners, liberty cap and pole, wreath and thirteen stars. Size 12.

188. Head of Washington, 6+6 stars. "1863." *Rev.* "New York." Wreath and stars. Size 12+.

*189. Head of Washington, two crossed flags and thirteen stars. "1863." *Rev.* "Exchange." Wreath. B. Size 12+.

190. Same, in copper. Size 12+. . . .

CLASS III.—*Equestrian Statues, Fancy Heads, and Human Figures.*
a. Equestrian Statues.

205. "1863. First in War, First in Peace." The date extends too far to the left to be symmetrical. *Rev.* Wreath, shield, and flags. "Union forever." Size 12+.

206. Same. Date more symmetrical. Figure of man somewhat larger. Size 12+.

b. Head with liberty cap.

207. "For Public Accommodation. 1863." *Rev.* "Horrors of War, Blessings of Peace. 1863." Female head. Two crossed cornucopias. Size 12+.

208. Same. *Rev.* Eagle on globe. "United States Copper." Size 12+.

209. Same. *Rev.* Man with cane. "Knickerbocker Currency." Size 12+. . . .

c. Head with feather crown.

233. No inscription on *obv.* *Rev.* Wreath. "Not one cent." 1863. Var. *a.* Size 12.

234. "Millions for contractors, 1863." *Rev.* "Not one cent for the widows." Var. n. Wreath and star. Size 12+.

235. "Union and Liberty. 1863." Two stars. *Rev.* "One Country." Wreath. Size 12+. . . .

d. Fancy Heads.

258. Head and thirteen stars. "L. Leichtweis. 1863." *Rev.* Wreath. "Millions for defence, Not one cent for tribute." Size 12.

259. Head, two arrow-points. "Liberty and no Slavery. 1863." *Rev.* Wreath, shield, flags, thirteen stars, liberty cap and pole. Size 12.

e. Human Figures.

260. Man with cane. "Knickerbocker Currency." *Rev.* As in No. 169. Size 12+.

261. 262. Same. *Rev.* "Good for 1 cent." Two stars. B. & C. Size 13.

*263. Same. *Rev.* Eagle. "Union forever." Size 12+. 264. Same. *Rev.* Man with bundle. "Go it buttons. Money makes the mare go. 1863." Size 12+. . . .

CLASS IV.—*Animals.*

*267. Eagle. "United States copper." *Rev.* "Good for 1 cent." Two stars. Size 12+.

*268. Same. *Rev.* "I-O-U 1 Cent. Pure copper." Size 12+.

269. Eagle on globe. "Union forever." *Rev* Female head; two horns of plenty. "Horrors of War, Blessings of Peace. 1863." Size 12+. . . .

274. Bees and hive. "Industry, C. D. H., 1863." *Rev.* Wreath. "Not one cent." Var. *r.* Size 12+.

CLASS V.—*Flags.*

275. Wreath, U.S. flag, and thirteen stars. *Rev.* Rays. "No North, No East, No South, No West. One Country." Size 12.

276. U.S. flag, thirteen stars, and liberty cap. "The Flag of our Union. 1863." *Rev.* "If any body attempts to tear it down, shoot him on the spot. Dix."[6] Five stars, two rings within the border. B. Size 12+.

*277. Same, with only one central ring, and one star. "1863," omitted on *obv.* B. Size 12+. . . .

CLASS VI.—*Miscellaneous Devices.*

282. Monitor. Thirteen stars. "C. D. H. 1863." *Rev.* Wreath. "Our Navy." Size 12. . . .

283. Monitor. "Our Little Monitor." Lower line of water nearly straight. *Rev.* Wreath.

285. Ship and six stars. "Trade & Commerce." *Rev.* "Coppers 20 per ct. Premium." Size 14.

286. U.S. Capitol and eight stars. "United States. 1863." *Rev.* Wreath. "Army & Navy." Var. *a.* Size 12.

287. Thistle. "United we stand, divided we fall." Two stars. *Rev.* "Drugs, Dry Goods, Groceries, Hardware & Notions." Four stars and six crosses. Size 12+. . . .

289. Cannon on wheels, with pile of shot, and thirteen stars. "1863." *Rev.* Wreath. "Army & Navy." Var. *b.* Size 12.

290. Cannon of a different design; thirteen stars. "Peace Maker." *Rev.* Flag, with liberty cap. "Stand by the flag. 1863." Size 12+.

291. Shield on star. "Pro Bono Publico. E. S. 1863." *Rev.* Wreath. "New York." Size 12+.

CLASS VII.—*Mottos.*

292–295. "Army and Navy." Var. *a, b, c, J.* Wreath. *Rev.* "The Federal Union, it must and shall be preserved." Thirteen stars. Size 12 J.

296. "Constitution forever." *Rev.* Wreath. "Not one cent." Var. *a.* Two stars on each face. Size 12+. . . .

301. "Liberty. 1863." Wreath. *Rev.* Wreath. "Union." Size 12.

302. "Remembrance of 1863." *Rev.* Wreath. "Not one cent." Var. *q.* Size 12+.

303. Same. *Rev.* Wreath. "One Country." Size 12.

The epilogue to the preceding is sad. On May 25, 1865, Chase submitted a revised list for publication, listing over 2,000 varieties. Research by Fred L. Reed through modern correspondence with the society revealed that the manuscript, never published, was later lost and that the collection of tokens, augmented by other donations, disappeared through looting.[7]

Collectors in Cincinnati

In Cincinnati at least two local numismatists—Thomas Cleneay and James A. Hughes—visited the shop of William K. Lanphear regularly and had special items struck to their order. In the *American Journal of Numismatics,* January 1869, Cleneay reminisced about Lanphear:

Letter from Cleneay

In answer to your inquiry about my store-cards of the Copperhead variety, and whether I would exchange silver or nickel duplicates for other rare pieces, as you are "running on those metals": The fact is that I have paid very little attention to store-cards, either the old or new. In 1862–3, I dropped in at the office of W.K. Lanphear almost every day, and would find trays full of the copperheads just from the press.

It occurred to me that they would be sought for and collected as mementos of the *War* if not as cards, and at the same time illustrate what our people had to resort to, when they were in the midst of a mighty rebellion (I might say that the most *infernal* rebellion that ever disgraced a civilized nation since the world was made), with their circulating medium depreciated so much that all even of the *base* metal coin of the realm was withdrawn from circulation, and these copperheads were substituted for the retired government coin.

In taking the above view of things, I concluded to call every day and get as many new pieces or names as were made. I also had some nickel cents prepared, filed and polished, and left with them at the shop; and an arrangement was entered into, when a new design was made to take an impression for me on one of my nickel planchets. This put me in possession of over one hundred most beautiful pieces. I believe I have every design gotten up by Lanphear. His designs are more artistic and finer, I think, than those of Stanton, or any other of our die sinkers.

I cannot tell you anything about either my old or new pieces, as they are not arranged, neither have I them catalogued. At some future time I will let you know what I can do for you in the way of exchange in cards. I do not believe there could be half a dozen nickel copperheads found in all the collections in this city, leaving out mine. I have also twenty-three silver cards made by Hughes. They are beautiful specimens. I believe there are several silver cards made by Hughes in different cabinets. I think Downing has one. Zanoni had one (his own card). Was it sold with his collection in New York? I don't remember. There was a Hughes card sold in some sale in New York in 1864. I bought Hughes' entire collection of American silver in 1865, and that is the way I came in possession of his silver and a few nickel copperheads which he made for his own collection.

Robert Downing, mentioned above, issued Civil War store cards lettered R. DOWNING / PUBLISHER / OF [horizontal comma to each side, tail oriented toward border] / SHEET SONGS / & DEALER IN / OLD / COINS / CINCINNATI. These were made by Stanton. Reverses included dies 1046, 1047, 1069, 1192, 1279, 1283, and 1370 to create numismatic strikes as each was made in small numbers and is a major rarity today.[8] It is curious that he didn't use even more of the reverses.

Store card of Robert Downing, Cincinnati coin dealer, OH-165-AK-4b, reverse 1192. Very few from this issuer are known today.

In 1867 Downing was a buyer in W. Elliot Woodward's sale of the Joseph J. Mickley Collection. On February 13, 1868, he was elected to corresponding membership in the American Numismatic and Archaeological Society following his sponsorship by J.N.T. Levick. In the December 1868 issue of the *American Journal of Numismatics*, Levick called Downing's collection of store cards one of the best in the country. By 1877 Downing's membership in the American Numismatic and Archaeological Society had lapsed. Upon making inquiry the society learned that Downing "was regarded as an unscrupulous man, void of any business reputation." Apparently, he had disappeared for a time, but as of 1877 he had been committed to a workhouse.[9] By that time, many articles had appeared in Cincinnati papers about disorderly conduct within the family, particularly a daughter who had many run-ins with the police.

After 1877, he took on a new life. Rather than being in a workhouse, as per conventional wisdom, in September 1867 he appeared in Syracuse, New York, after which he was known as Joseph Eugene Perkins!

Joseph Zanone, a Cincinnati ice-cream saloon operator, whose name in certain accounts is spelled Zanoni, was also active in numismatic circles and issued tokens. The word *saloon* meant *salon* in this era and not necessarily an establishment that served liquor. There were billiard saloons, oyster saloons, and even hairdressing saloons.

The Great Western Sanitary Fair opened in Cincinnati in Greenwood Hall on December 21, 1863, and closed on January 9, 1864.[10] Donations valued at $235,406.62 were received during this period and, after a two-week exhibition period, sold through

Exceedingly rare silver striking, OH-165-GX-1f, reverse 1131, probably arranged by James A. Hughes, to whom this F.W. Lutz reverse die (the only one of this general style) was a favorite.

Rare muling in silver, probably also arranged by Hughes, OH-165-GX-5f combining Zanone's die with one of S.A. Ingram of Chicago.

various venues.[11] On Friday, March 15, 1864, local auctioneer S.G. Hubbard commenced selling 825 numbered lots described in a 39-page catalog. Included were many coins, tokens, and medals donated by William K. Lanphear, John Stanton, R. Coulton Davis (Philadelphia), Alfred S. Robinson (Hartford, Connecticut), and others. The committee arranging and conducting the sale included T.C. Day (chairman), Geo. McLaughlin, Samuel B. Warren, Joseph Zanone, Thomas Cleneay, and Noah B. Wells.

On April 24–16, 1867, Zanone's collection, cataloged by Edward D. Cogan, was sold at the sale room of Bangs, Merwin & Co. "Zanoni" was the spelling used. The title page began with this text:

> A Catalogue of a valuable collection of COINS AND MEDALS Comprising American Gold, Silver and Copper, Washington and Colonial Pieces, Amongst which will be found some exceedingly rare and valuable Specimens in a fine state of preservation, The more valuable specimens of the collection is [sic] from Mr. Joseph Zanoni of Cincinnati, also a large & valuable Collection of Grecian & Roman Coins from the Cabinet of Mr. Henry Bogert of New York.

The described items were very miscellaneous and did not include any rare Civil War tokens.

A close friend of Zanone, and later business partner in a chess and whist club, was Samuel Bacciocco, who operated an ice-cream saloon and confectionery (misspelled on his token) at 176 Fifth Street. He is not known to have been a numismatist. Both Zanone and Bacciocco issued Civil War store cards from the shop of William K. Lanphear, including one that muled their obverse dies. Zanone's cards used card dies 1131, 1172, and 1274; also mulings with obverse of IL-150-AG (S.A. Ingram, Chicago, Illinois), IL-795-A (J.C. Yager, Springfield, Ohio), obverse of OH-165-H (Bacciocco). Bacciocco's cards OH-165-H used dies 1131, 1172, and 1274 plus the muling with the Zanone obverse. James A. Hughes was involved in the production of certain of these, such as silver strikings and mulings. All were made in small quantities and are rarities today.

OH-165-H-1a by Samuel Bacciocco, reverse 1131 by F.W. Lutz, a design sometimes called the "Phoenician Head."

Brass token issued by the Zanoni & Bacciocco Chess and Whist Club in the later 1860s. Here we have the Zanoni spelling. Dies by James W. Murdock Jr., who signed the bottom of the reverse.

Joseph N.T. Levick

W. Elliot Woodward in his catalog of the Joseph N.T. Levick Collection Sale, May 26–29, 1884, told of Levick's having special Civil War tokens struck to order (excerpts from a very large commentary and listing):

> The currency of the Rebellion, which for a time was almost the only circulating medium for retail transactions, was a necessity incident to the times. These trifling

pieces, few persons at the time thought it worth their while to collect and preserve. But a few collectors foresaw that their use was but temporary, and that the formation of a collection having any degree of completeness must be attended to at the time.

"The Smoker" medalet, 27.4 mm, was published circa 1860 by well-known numismatist Joseph N.T. Levick, who sold tobacco and related accessories at 904 Broadway, New York City. This antedates the Civil War token series.

Amongst these persons Mr. Levick was especially prominent, and, commencing early, he made it a business to obtain from every section of the country—in many cases from the die sinkers themselves—the finest specimens that could be procured, in all their variety of metals, etc. And in this way he gathered the cabinet which is now offered for sale. No accurate account has been taken of the number of pieces which it comprises, but it is presumed to contain not less than four or five thousand, and possibly more. I know of no other collection either so fine or so extensive. This cabinet, which it would be actually impossible to duplicate, together with the collection of the paper currency of the Rebellion catalogued in connection with it, ought to be preserved in a National Museum. If all other records were lost, the business and political history of the country during our great war could be written from the records here preserved.

In the preparation of a sale catalogue, it is, of course, impossible to give each one of these little coins a separate description: hence I remark generally that the impressions are the finest that it was possible to procure at the time. They are in all the metals that were issued. Those in silver are catalogued by themselves; the other metals are copper, nickel, brass, and tin, with occasionally one in lead or oroide. The size is generally that of the ordinary nickel or bronze cent. A few are of larger size, which, when catalogued, will be distinguished simply as "large." Their condition is generally absolutely perfect, bright and Uncirculated; the exceptions are so few that they are not particularly referred to.

Most of the nickel cards in Mr. Levick's collection are Proofs struck to order and cost in quantity 15 cents each at the time. All were struck expressly for collectors; none of them for circulation.

The following [silver tokens], as will be noticed, are generally of smaller size than the preceding; many, though not all, are of the period of the late war. Some of them are unique, and none are common. The degree of rarity I am unable to give; I only know that Mr. Levick availed himself of every opportunity to procure unique impressions in silver of the various issues of the period, and many of these are of that class, all silver.

A few lots in the sale:

Lot 1505. A selection all in brass; many of the tokens of this period for New York and the Eastern states were struck in a variety of metals. In the West, on the contrary, as a rule, copper only was used; hence all the brass tokens are scarce, and those in other metals are even rarer. Those in tin, and especially in nickel, were struck only for collections. 20 pieces.

Lot 2358. Mr. Levick's entire collection of Rhode Island copperheads in c. b. n. and t., all struck to order and bright and Uncirculated. The collection is believed to comprise a specimen of each variety that originated in that state. It contains business cards and numerous combinations. I notice Head of Burnside, Arms of the State, Bust of Lincoln, Sporting Scenes, and a vast number of varieties.[12] This set to a collector, being so varied and perfect, is most desirable. 124 pieces.

Is this man Lincoln as Woodward suggested? Or is he just a typical bearded man of the era? This has been debated by numismatists for years. Store card in nickel alloy of the Arcade House of Providence, Rhode Island. RI-700-A-1j. Reverse die 1147.

Lot 2359, Mr. Levick's entire collection of the Copperheads of New Jersey and of Pennsylvania, with the exception of the city of Pittsburgh and its vicinity. Like nearly all the pieces in this department of Mr. Levick's collection, these were struck to order in the various metals, and are nearly all in perfect to Proof condition. I do not know how nearly complete the collection is, but it is the most extensive of any that I have seen. Collectors are of course aware that but comparatively few of these tokens were issued in Penn. 76 pieces.

Lot 2446. Set of the cards of Stoner & Shroyer, Adamsville, Ohio; various revs., bust of Washington, Franklin, Lincoln, Grant, and others; c. b. n. and t., splendid Proofs on thick planchets; only a few sets struck to order. [Size] 12. 32 pieces.[13]

The *American Journal of Numismatics*

In June 1866 the American Numismatic and Archaeological Society launched the *American Journal of Numismatics.* On the first page of the first issue this was posted:

"COPPERHEADS"

In the present issue we commence a list of the "Copperheads," "Store Cards," or "Tokens" of the rebellion. This list will be, it is hoped, perfect and complete in every respect, as it is made from probably the largest collection in the country, and by a gentleman thoroughly qualified for the task. Such a catalogue cannot fail to be of the greatest value and importance to collectors and should, we think, alone make the *American Journal of Numismatics* a "welcome guest" among them. Any collector having, or knowing of, any piece not enumerated in this list, will confer a favor by informing us immediately of the fact, when the addition shall be made.

On page 13 the study began:

"COPPERHEADS"

A Descriptive Catalogue of the Copper and Base Metallic Currency issued in the several States of the United States, commencing in 1862 and ending in 1864. . . .

MAINE

1. Ob. "R.S. Torrey Inventor of the Maine State Bee Hive 5th St. Bangor, Me." Rev. Liberty head facing left, "Union" in small letters above, 13 stars, "1863." C.

2. Ob. "R.S. Torrey Inventor of the Maine State Bee Hive Bangor, Me. 1864." A circle of small dots and two stars.
Rev. Eagle on Shield inscribed "Union," Four Flags and an open wreath. C.

MASSACHUSETTS

Store card of R.S. Torrey of Bangor, Maine, with reverse die 1005 by S.D. Childs, called a "Liberty Head" in the quoted text.

1. Ob. "Dunn & Co.'s Oyster House. 1864" within a wreath, two small stars.
Rev. Bunker Hill Monument within a wreath. C.
2. Ob. "Jos. H. Merriam Medalist. Die Sinker and Letter Cutter Established 1850 No. 18 Brattle Square, Boston."
Rev. Dog's Head with collar inscribed "Merriam. Good for a Scent 1863" two small stars. C.

Civil War Tokens Minted in 1869

The *Journal* study was continued in later months, and in the autumn an especially comprehensive listing of Rhode Island tokens was given, including mintage figures for numismatic mulings and off-metals.

In 1869 in Cincinnati, William W. Spencer, successor to the businesses of John Stanton and Murdock & Spencer, used dies of earlier dates as well as new ones to strike tokens for the numismatic trade. Stanton die 1047 in particular, dated 1864, was employed to make many varieties. Die 1018 of 1863, now rusted, was another favorite. Likely the making of these extended into the early 1870s.

Edward Groh, Pioneer Civil War Token Collector

Edward Groh, born in New York City of German parents on June 2, 1837, was bitten by the collecting bug (literally) at an early age—with insects being his first interest, then when he was a teenager, old coins. Not long afterward he discovered tokens, including the Hard Times issue of T.D. Seaman. He later recalled that he was in Belleville, New Jersey, and spotted an old sign of T.D. Seaman, which made him put two and two together to identify him as the issuer of a Hard Times token lettered T. DUSEAMAN. Collectors at a later time suggested that the die had been made erroneously with a U instead of a period. No one knew who "Duseaman" was until Groh figured it out.

On March 8, 1858, Groh was one of five who signed a letter inviting interested collectors to meet at the home of Augustus B. Sage at 121 Essex Street, New York City, to establish what became the American Numismatic Society. Perhaps as a reward for his efforts and numismatic prominence, on April 6 Groh became resident member number one of the society. As did many collectors, Groh traded in coins and occasionally offered some at auction, including in a sale held at Bangs, Merwin & Co. on February 28–29, 1860, advertised as the "largest collection of American tokens ever offered for sale in this country." The offering of 835 pieces brought $418.70, plus 43 addenda pieces for $14.26.

In one caper Groh was too clever for his own good. He took an 1836 Gobrecht dollar and made castings from it, then had Abraham Posner, a jeweler in The Bowery, silver plate them. Posner was arrested for counterfeiting, but was released when he explained that the coins were worth three times face value and thus were not intended to be put into circulation. In the early 1860s when New York engravers and minters began issuing Civil War tokens Groh was fascinated. These became the love of his life. He had special strikings in odd combinations and metals struck to his order.

In the *American Journal of Numismatics*, May 1867, Groh's collection was described:

> 4,580 specimens of the two classes of Copperheads, viz: the tokens and the store cards, 140 of which are in silver, and all in the finest condition. Mr. Groh has arranged them alphabetically by states, towns, and individuals. He finds that Cincinnati is superior to any other city in the number of its varieties, no fewer than 768 having thence derived their origin. New York City claims 544. Philadelphia has only 17. The farther we go to the eastward, the less frequent they become, though even Bangor, so near the borders of "the Province," had 2 to exhibit. Assembled in mass, these pieces are beautiful to the eye; they are interesting geographically, historically, and as memorials of business enterprise in troubled days; and they must certainly increase in value with the lapse of time.

Groh was in the tobacco business and also traded in coins. In the *AJN* in December 1869, the earlier-mentioned Joseph N.T. Levick stated that Groh with no fewer than 4,700 pieces had the very finest collection of Civil War tokens in existence, with the runners up being George B. Davis and John Hanna. Levick had about 2,000. The Davis tokens were sold at auction on May 31, 1869, in New York City at the auction rooms of Bangs, Merwin & Co. Hanna compiled a manuscript list of his holdings and gave it to the American Numismatic Society.

In the late 1870s Groh retired from business and moved from Manhattan to Williamsburg across the East River. On October 21, 1901, the *New York Times* published an interview with Groh. Concerning an 1804 copper cent, by then worth $200, he recalled, "I remember finding a half dozen of those very coins when I was a boy, simply by examining the change that passed through my hands. It paid one to examine change then. I never let a single piece slip by unnoticed."

On the subject of Civil War tokens, Groh reported that his collection was acquired in every instance by gathering them at the very time they were issued, and by trading with other interested collectors. Not a single piece was bought from a dealer, he stated proudly. Groh's collection, by then totaling 5,286 pieces including duplicates, and the cabinet in which it was stored, was given to the American Numismatic Society. He passed away on January 2, 1905, at which time he was the last surviving founder of the Society.

Charles W. Idell

The Charles W. Idell Collection of Civil War and other tokens crossed the auction block at Bangs & Co., New York, January 8 and 9, 1878, cataloged by Emmanuel J. Attinelli, one of the best-informed numismatists of the era. A resident of Hoboken, New Jersey, and well known in horticultural circles as a commission merchant and dealer in fruit, Idell was an active collector in the early days and on April 26, 1866, joined the American Numismatic and Archaeological Society. His interest must have faded, for in April 1870 he resigned from the group. In the *American Journal of Numismatics*, December 1868, J.N.T. Levick called Idell's collection of store cards one of the best in the country.

In the Idell auction catalog this information was given preceding lot 53, the beginning of a large offering of numismatic strikes by various makers, primarily in New York City:

> The next 56 lots are Rebellion tokens or Copperheads in the finest condition. These sets in the metals are rare, but from 4 to 10 sets of each being struck for, and at the special request of Messrs. Idell and Groh, after which many of the dies were destroyed. The following abbreviations will be used: S. silver, C. copper, B. brass, G. German silver, N. nickel. T. tin.

Many of the tokens were by Emil Sigel and William H. Bridgens, but other engravers were represented as well. Lot 95, "Minerva with Flag, Reverse 'America,'" is the famous token by Mossin & Marr of Milwaukee, today called the Amazonian die. It seems likely that Idell was an active correspondent with many of the token makers.

In the Auction Room

Patriotic Civil War tokens and Civil War store cards were an important feature of many coin auctions from 1863 onward. Although such pieces had relatively little value, W. Elliot Woodward in particular often devoted descriptions sufficiently detailed that they can be translated to Fuld numbers today. Sometimes prices for a token described and listed as a single lot were as low as six cents!

There were no agreed-upon grading standards, and one person's Very Fine might be another's Uncirculated. For that reason bidders either attended in person or placed bids with a commission agent (for Woodward, Edward D. Cogan was listed in catalogs as a suggested contact).

CATALOGUE

OF

American and Foreign

COINS, MEDALS, TOKENS, &c.,

CONTAINED IN THE COLLECTIONS OF

MESSRS. A. V. JENCKS AND GEORGE T. PAINE,
OF PROVIDENCE, R. I.,

TO BE SOLD BY AUCTION,

AT THE

BOOK TRADE SALES ROOMS,
498 BROADWAY, NEW YORK,

BY

MESSRS. LEAVITT, STREBEIGH & CO.,
AUCTIONEERS,

On Monday, December 10th, and following Evenings,
COMMENCING EACH DAY AT FIVE O'CLOCK, P. M.

CATALOGUE BY W. ELLIOT WOODWARD.

Orders entrusted to EDWARD COGAN, Esq., 101 William Street, New York, to the Auctioneers, or to W. ELLIOT WOODWARD, Roxbury, Mass., promptly and faithfully executed.

Text on the catalog title page of W. Elliot Woodward's 1866 sale of the A.V. Jencks and George T. Paine collections. Many rare Civil War patriotic tokens and store cards were included. The two men were prominent in the Rhode Island Numismatic Association.

Viewing of lots was usually done on the morning and afternoon of the sale when the items offered were displayed on tables in the front of the auction room. At the sale itself it was usual practice for a runner to take each lot as it was sold and deliver it to the buyer, while a clerk tallied invoices for later payment. In other instances a box was filled for buyers who were especially active.

The market price of a typical Civil War token was less than ten cents for scarce issues, hardly inspiring anyone to list them individually. Common tokens retailed for two or three cents each. Even Woodward, who often enjoyed giving detailed descriptions of inexpensive numismatic items in the 1860s, in the 1870s presented only rare Civil War tokens, and not often for these. In May 1871 E.L. Mason Jr., a leading Philadelphia dealer, made this offer: "100 store cards, all different, Fine $3; Rebellion tokens, all different, Fine, $3."

In 1878 in Germany, dealer Adolph Weyl issued an auction catalog, *Die Jules Fonrobert'sche Sammlung überseeischer Münzen und Medaillen* (the Jules Fonrobert Collection of Overseas [Transatlantic] Coins and Medals), which contained extremely detailed descriptions of many Civil War tokens interspersed with tokens of other eras, arranged geographically when known. As an example a common bronze Yankee Robinson token (Fuld IL-692-A-1a) was given. No auction catalog before or since has been so comprehensive. Amazing! The publication contained 558 pages comprising 6,205 lots. Civil War tokens were indexed by state and town at the end! Fonrobert, a resident of Berlin, assembled an incredible cabinet of coins, tokens, and medals of the Americas. The catalog remains a prime reference today. Up to that time, nothing comparable had ever been published.

Civil War tokens continued to diminish in American auction listings, continuing into the early 20th century. Collecting interest continued apace, but there was virtually nothing useful in print save for the aforementioned Fonrobert catalog—which was a listing with no information about rarity or any other aspects. Further, few people in America were aware of these tokens.

The American Numismatist

The American Numismatist, September 1886, a magazine published by Charles E. Leal, of Paterson, New Jersey, gave this commentary:[14]

War Cents

Small change became so scarce in 1862 that storekeepers and other persons began to issue this private currency to supply the deficiency; and they continued to coin them in immense quantities until 1864, when the government, to protect itself, was compelled to prohibit their further coinage or circulation. The first coinage of War Cents, or Tokens, or Store Cards, as they are sometimes called, took place in Cincinnati where nearly 900 varieties were issued, fully three times as many varieties as any other city issued except New York.

A number of other Western cities soon followed the example of Cincinnati, but it was not until the early part of 1863 that New York began to issue the famous Lindenmueller cents, of which there were more than a million coined; these were followed by the Knickerbocker tokens, consisting of many varieties. Altogether there were between 600 and 700 varieties issued from New York City. Ohio issued about 1,300 varieties from 100 different cities and towns, more than any other state issued; New York State comes next after Ohio, with over 900 varieties.

When the government stopped the coinage of these tokens there were upward of 20,000,000 of them in circulation, but there are in all probability not more than

1,000,000 in existence at the present time. In my estimation War Cents comprise one of the principal branches of numismatics and should occupy a prominent place in the cabinet of every American collector. It is impossible now to obtain a complete collection for any sum of money; but $24 or $30 should buy a very good collection for an amateur.

Continuing Interest

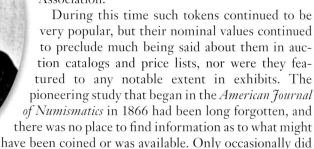

In August 1890, a reader of *The Numismatist*, a magazine launched in 1888 by Dr. George F. Heath of Monroe, Michigan, could order 100 different varieties of Civil War tokens for $2.50 for the group. The seller was Heath himself, who in 1891 would be instrumental in the founding of the American Numismatic Association.

During this time such tokens continued to be very popular, but their nominal values continued to preclude much being said about them in auction catalogs and price lists, nor were they featured to any notable extent in exhibits. The pioneering study that began in the *American Journal of Numismatics* in 1866 had been long forgotten, and there was no place to find information as to what might have been coined or was available. Only occasionally did intellectual curiosity come to the fore, as in this May 1901 comment by Farran Zerbe, of Tyrone, Pennsylvania. Zerbe, later the official distributor for several commemoratives and president of the

George F. Heath, M.D., was publisher of *The Numismatist* commencing in 1888 and founder of the American Numismatic Association in 1891.

ANA, had just purchased a hoard of 4,000 patriotic and store card tokens: "A hurried glance at them shows many varieties, some perhaps uncommon."

In this era Chicago brewing magnate Virgil M. Brand was busy forming what would become the world's largest privately held collection of coins, tokens, medals, and paper money. One account had it that he owned tens of thousands of Civil War tokens, including countless duplicates, stored in "three barrels," per an unlikely recollection. After his death in 1926 his collection was dispersed privately and at auction over a long period of years. On November 17, 1969, the "Million Dollar Sale" held by Harmer Rooke in New York City included some of his rarer pieces including Civil War tokens.

Every now and again a feature article on Civil War tokens would appear in the pages of *The Numismatist*. Waldo C. Moore, an Ohio banker, was one of the most important contributors in this regard. Year by year interest grew.

The Hetrich-Guttag Book

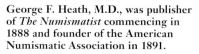

Civil War tokens continued to be a passion for many numismatists, but there was still no guide to consult. That changed in 1924 when Dr. George Hetrich, of Birdsboro, Pennsylvania, formed an arrangement with well-to-do New York City dealer Julius Guttag to publish his manuscript. *Civil War Tokens and Tradesmen's Cards* was soon available and caused a sensation among enthusiasts. Listed were 1,194 patriotic tokens and 7,241 store cards for a total of 8,345. The store cards were issued from 296 cities and towns in 23 states. Patriotic dies were illustrated as were stock dies used for store card reverses. The obverses of the store cards were not shown, probably as the authors felt that the written descriptions would suffice. However, for dies having portraits, flags, shields, wreaths, eagles, and the like, a picture was indeed worth many words, thus the stock die pictures.

In a paper read before the New York Numismatic Club on April 14, 1922, Dr. Hetrich described how he entered numismatics and later focused on tokens as a specialty:

> I believe that a speaker should at least give a reason for the faith that is within him, and I shall frankly tell you why my love for collecting has become centered upon Civil War tokens. I wish to say before going any further that when I use the word "token" I use it in a generic sense, meaning both token and store cards. I shall never forget the day about 47 years ago when the latent spirit of collecting was fully aroused within me upon seeing a fine copy of a 1794 cent, and I had no peace of mind until I became the owner of that coin upon the payment of 25 cents; and I question very much if that coin would bring more than the original price at present.
>
> I slowly added to this possession until I had a complete collection of United States cents. However, upon taking up the collecting of the silver and gold coins it was not very long before I discovered that it took a millionaire to satisfy the cravings of a collector whose ambition was to get together an Uncirculated collection of these coins. I, however, was bound to collect something, when eventually I decided upon this inexpensive line of token collecting—a series whose numbers are unlimited and at present unknown—enough varieties to satisfy the most avaricious collector.[15]

H&G numbers became the standard and endured into the 1960s and 1970s, when the works of George and Melvin Fuld came into use. The Fulds did not work alone, and their two books, *Patriotic Civil War Store Cards* and *U.S. Civil War Store Cards*, credit dozens of contributors.

Among those who took up dealing in these tokens after the H&G book became available was Joseph Barnet, of Brooklyn, who was a familiar face at regional club meetings. He also studied and wrote about them, such as an article bearing the title of the Hetrich-Guttag book and published in *The Numismatist* in November 1932. A list of the various states and towns with the number of store cards issued by each was given. For example, in Illinois 32 towns issued a total of 285 token varieties, while in New York 24 towns produced 1,296 issues, and in Ohio 104 towns produced 2,646. Virginia, however, saw just two tokens produced by two towns, Alexandria and Norfolk. Totally, 396 towns and cities and 23 different states issued a total of 8,435 varieties according to knowledge of the time.[16]

At the May 14, 1937, meeting of the New York Numismatic Club at Keen's Chop House (where the club had met ever since its founding in 1909) Barnet played "show and tell" with some items from his collection:

> 862 different varieties of Civil War tokens and cards of which the tokens were 56 in brass, 48 in nickel, 58 in copper-nickel, 51 in white metal, seven in silver, six in German silver, five in lead, three gold-plated and one silver-plated. Of the cards there were 419 in brass, 42 in nickel, 59 copper-nickel, 48 white metal, eight silver, one German silver, nine zinc, one tin, one iron, one rubber and two silver-plated.
>
> Quite a number of the cards struck in copper-nickel were struck over copper-nickel eagle and Indian Head cents, and many of them plainly show the date of the pieces they were struck on. A number of the brass cards are brass on obverse

Detail of a photographic plate of female heads in the deluxe leather-bound edition of the Hetrich-Guttag *Civil War Tokens and Tradesmen's Cards* book. Only patriotic and "stock" store card reverse dies were illustrated. There were no pictures of dies with advertisements of merchants.

Various motifs are shown on part of another H&G plate.

	INDIANA—Continued			
	New Paris			
3029	A M Davis Dry Goods Groceries			
3030	Crockery Drugs &c New Paris Ind	Variation of 150	C	Pl
	North Vernon			
3031	John Wentzel/Dealer / in/Stoves/ &/Tin Ware/North Vernon Ind	521	C	Pl
	Oldenburg			
3032	J Holker / good for / 1—drink / at the/bar/Oldenburg Ind	664	Br	R
	Peru			
3033	J Kreutzer / Dealer / in / Glass /			
3034	Queensware/&/Crockery/Peru Ind	560	C	Pl
3035	J S Queeby/Dealer/in/Dry Goods/ &/Notions/Peru Ind	467	C	Pl
3036	Same	509	C	Pl
3037	Same	518	C	Pl
3038	Same	546	C	Pl
3039	Same	565	C	Pl
3040	Same	589	C	Pl
3041				
3042	Saine & Miller/Groceries/Notions/ Boots & shoes/Peru Ind	534	C	Pl
3043				
	Pierceton			
3044	Murray & Bro/Dry Goods / &/ Groceries/Pierceton/Ind	425	C	Pl
3045				
3046	Reed & Spayde/Dealers in/Dry Goods/&/Groceries / Pierceton Ind	472	C	Pl
	Plainfield			
3047	DRY Goods/&/Clothing/Johnson/ &/Oursler/Plainfield	416	C	R
3048				
3049				
3050	Same	420	C-N	R
3051				
3052	Johnson & Oursler/Dealer/in/ Dry/Goods/Boots & Shoes/Plain- field Ind	420	C-N	R
3053	Same	622	C	R
3054	Same	Same	Br	R
3055				

65

This H&G text page shows Indiana Civil War store cards. At the left is the H&G number, then location, merchant name, and other information. Under "Varieties" is the number used on the photographic plates to identify the reverse. The metal is given next, such as C (copper), Br (brass), and C-N (copper-nickel). The right column describes the edge, Pl (plain) or R (reeded).

and copper on reverse. It seems that when the metal was alloyed and made into strips, one side was brass and the other side copper. The white-metal pieces with the larger planchets and wide borders are trial pieces. The silver Charnley card is struck over a dime.[17]

Barnet maintained a large inventory of Civil War tokens and helped form at least several dozen collections in the greater New York City area in addition to serving mail-order clients.

David C. Wismer, remembered today for his exhaustive study of obsolete bank notes published serially in *The Numismatist* in the 1920s and 1930s, contributed "My Collecting Experience" to that magazine in May 1939:

About 1895 I bought about 3,600 Civil War tokens and store cards. That made me a collector of that type of interesting necessity money. Upon finding quite a variety of die types of "Dix" tokens, I commenced to try to get all the varieties together. In order to get all the die types I bought one lot of "Dixes" of 2,000 and found 19 varieties.

Some years ago Dr. Hetrich accumulated the largest collection of Civil War tokens and store cards. He catalogued them in connection with Mr. Guttag, of

New York, and published it in an interleaved book, listing about 6,000 varieties. He traveled all over Ohio, Pennsylvania, New York and the New England states to see different collections and buy varieties he needed. Just before his demise, three days, in fact, he visited me and showed me a variety of the "Dix" token that I did not have listed in my booklet, entitled "Varieties of Dix Tokens, 1863." Last year I obtained that very much wanted "Dix" token from [Philadelphia dealer James V.] Iannarella for 10 cents.

In 1961 George Fuld and his father Melvin bought the Wismer holding of Civil War tokens by private treaty from the New Netherlands Coin Company, which kept Wismer's main coin collection for sale at auction. There were over 11,000 tokens of which slightly more than 5,000 were Dix tokens vastly duplicated. George sorted through them, kept one of each variety, and then sold them to the Tatham Stamp & Coin Co. in Springfield, Massachusetts. The tokens other than the Dix varieties, which mainly comprised numismatic strikes, he kept for his own collection and for trade.[18]

The continuing popularity of the Hetrich & Guttag text was emphasized by the ANA librarian in a report of April 1946 which told that the most requested book in the library was Beistle's work on half dollar die varieties, followed by *Haseltine's Type Table* on quarters, halves, and dollars, with the Hetrich-Guttag book on Civil War tokens third and Crosby's classic colonial volume fourth in popularity.

One of many die varieties of Dix patriotic Civil War tokens. Fuld 203/412b.

The Early 1960s

On November 19, 1960, the Token and Medal Society was organized, bringing together a group of enthusiasts. The *Token and Medal Society Journal* was inaugurated not long afterward and included many editorial features and contributions about Civil War tokens. George Fuld's *Patriotic Civil War Tokens* was published, a study continuing the work of Hetrich and Guttag, but with many new listings and a new numbering system.

In 1962 *A Guide to Civil War Store Card Tokens*, by George and Melvin Fuld, was released and formed the foundation for enthusiasts who sought to organize their collections. By that time the Hetrich-Guttag book was long out of print, and there was a brisk call for used copies when they could be found.

Later Years

By 1967 there was an active, indeed dynamic, collector interest in Civil War tokens. George and Melvin Fuld had prepared studies that were published in the *Numismatic Scrapbook Magazine*, several dealer specialists had them for sale as part of token and medal displays at conventions, and the Token and Medal Society was going strong. Part of the coverage in the *TAMS Journal* continued to be the field of Civil War tokens.

Seeds for a separate Civil War Token Society were sown on January 17, 1967, by a letter of this date, signed by Chris Mackel Jr. and Earl Rogers, and mailed out to people known to have an interest. Forty-three positive responses were received. A second letter was sent out about a month later with various news, including that Dr. George Fuld was preparing a new reference book on Civil War tokens, but had been delayed by illness. By that time George had done an immense amount of research relating to the issuers. His recognition as an expert in various series had been established when he co-authored with his father, Melvin, "The Token Collector's Page," a popular feature in *The Numismatist* in the 1950s. A letter of April 21 noted that 85 members had signed up.

In August 1968 the first meeting of the society was conducted with the American Numismatic Association's annual convention held that year in San Diego. Attorney and token and medal enthusiast H. Joseph Levine presented articles of incorporation that he had prepared.

From that point growth continued. The society's publication now known as the *Civil War Token Journal* went through name transitions including *The Copperhead Courier*. It became a lively forum for the exchange of ideas, convention news, the listing of newly discovered varieties, and features about various token issuers. Combining the research of the Fulds with contributions from dozens of collectors, dealers, and researchers, the society published *Patriotic Civil War Tokens* and *U.S. Civil War Store Cards* in various editions. These remain the standard references today.

THE CIVIL WAR

19  67

TOKEN SOCIETY

Founded in 1967, the Civil War Token Society is a non-profit organization dedicated exclusively to educational purposes, with the objective of promoting and stimulating the study of Civil War tokens.

The Society issues a quarterly publication, *The Civil War Token Journal.*

For more information or to join the Society, visit our Web site at www.CWTSociety.com

Aspects of Collecting Civil War Tokens

Ways to Collect

The field of Civil War patriotic tokens encompasses over 500 different dies combined with each other to create many more die-pair varieties and even more if metals such as copper, brass, copper-nickel, and other alloys are considered. Merchants issuing Civil War store cards number 1,500 or so, many using more than one reverse die combined with their advertising obverse die. Different metals add even more varieties. All told, the number of different dies, combinations, and metals adds up to well over 10,000!

No one has ever collected all or nearly all of these, although a handful of enthusiasts have acquired between 4,000 and 7,000, such holdings including those of the late Stephen L. Tanenbaum and the present cabinet of the American Numismatic Society.

With such a wide field of opportunity, there are many different ways to collect, including the following.

Patriotic Civil War Tokens

These tokens are a varied assortment with French Liberty Head, Indian Head, and other stock dies combined with reverses with inscriptions such as ARMY & NAVY, NOT ONE CENT, UNION FOREVER and more, often within a wreath. Typically the obverse has a portrait, ship, shield, or other motif. Tokens that combine one portrait die with another, such as Washington on both sides, are called "double headers." Some patriotics are not patriotic at all, but advertise commercial products or services without naming a specific merchant. Properly, these belong among store cards. Chapters 6 and 7 give more information.

A popular way to collect patriotics is to seek one example of each of the more than 500 dies. As dies are combined with each other, such a collection nets to far fewer than 500 tokens needed to illustrate the dies. Most of these dies are readily obtainable and range from Rarity-1 (R-1) to R-7. Even R-7 and R-8 dies can be obtained with some patience. R-9 and R-10 dies tend to be numismatic strikes or special pieces and are very elusive.

The most often seen patriotic tokens are those struck in copper or, occasionally, brass and used in general circulation as monetary substitutes during the Civil War. Most are found easily enough in such grades as EF and AU and are inexpensive. These are the *real* Civil War tokens in the best historical sense. As noted in some of the early accounts given in chapter 4, these give a permanent record of certain aspects of the conflict. Beyond that are those made for the numismatic trade and struck in copper-nickel, white metal, silver, lead (some may be trial strikes as lead is hardly attractive and oxidizes readily), tin, and nickel alloy. These are eminently desirable, for the most part are very elusive, and are enthusiastically collected.

Patriotic tokens can also be collected by topic—such as different heads and portraits, those with inscriptions referring specifically to the Civil War, tokens with political or military figures, weapons and military regalia, and other possibilities. Probably the best formula is "I like it." After you review the designs, history, and other aspects, seek the tokens that appeal to you the most. It is easy enough to compile a "wish list" after you look at die illustrations. More about the specialty of patriotic Civil War tokens is in the next chapter.

CIVIL WAR STORE CARDS

With so many merchants and other issuers to choose from and with such a variety of locations, motifs, trades, and the like, Civil War store cards offer a wonderland of opportunity.

Collecting by states is a popular way to go. Someone living in Ohio, Illinois, Michigan, Pennsylvania, New York, Indiana, or Wisconsin can spend many years seeking an example from each merchant in the state. For some states there are "rare" towns, and these offer a challenge. Many other states had relatively few issuers. New Jersey, Maryland, Kentucky, Rhode Island, Tennessee, and Minnesota are in this category. Enthusiasts are apt to collect a state of residence, but for stimulation and challenge a collection usually expands in other directions as well. The author resides in New Hampshire, which issued just one token, slightly scarce but not hard to find in the marketplace. In neighboring Maine there was just one issuer as well, but two varieties. Rhode Island has its own "personality." Most tokens of that state are special strikes made to the order of the Rhode Island Numismatic Association in 1864 and early 1865. Relatively few varieties were made for circulation.

Collecting by occupation is another popular pursuit. Collectors in the dental and medical professions have many choices among issuers as well as tokens that offer patent medicines, bitters, and other products, some quasi-medical. Transportation-related tokens include bridges, ferries, ships, and trains.

Numismatic rarities are another avenue. There is something quite special about a Civil War token that is plainly struck over a Flying Eagle or Indian Head cent with certain of the cent inscriptions still readable or, better yet, over a Liberty Seated dime. Illogical die combinations are also fun to contemplate, such as the token with the portrait of Lincoln on the obverse and "NO SUBMISSION TO THE NORTH" on the other side.

As with political tokens, the best way is to collect tokens that appeal to you. More comments on such aspects appear in various illustration captions in this book. More about the specialty of Civil War store cards is in chapter 7.

The Marketplace
Grading Civil War Tokens

While no grading standards have been adopted for Civil War tokens, the Official American Numismatic Association Grading Standards, which relate to federal coins, have been adopted by most collectors and dealers. Grading is subjective, and one person's AU-55 might be another's MS-60.[1] Tokens certified by the Numismatic Guaranty Corporation (NGC) or the Professional Coin Grading Service (PCGS) use the ANA numbers and have been popular in recent years.

The listing below is adapted from the ANA Standards for certain federal copper and nickel coins (original text by Kenneth E. Bressett and Q. David Bowers) and is used with the permission of the American Numismatic Association and Whitman Publishing, LLC.

Suggested Grading Standards

MINT STATE • *Absolutely no trace of wear.*

MS-70 • A flawless token exactly as it was minted, with no trace of wear or injury. Must have full mint luster but can show traces of natural toning.

MS-67 • Virtually flawless but with minor imperfections.

MS-65 • No trace of wear; nearly as perfect as MS-67 except for some small weakness or blemish. Has full mint luster, but may be unevenly toned, or lightly fingermarked. A few barely noticeable nicks or marks may be present.

MS-63 • A Mint State token with attractive mint luster, usually brown or red and brown toned, but with noticeable detracting contact marks or minor blemishes.

MS-60 • A strictly Uncirculated token with no trace of wear, but with blemishes more obvious than for MS-63. May lack full mint luster, and surface may be dull or spotted.

The color on copper Civil War tokens is indicated on Mint State coins by BN (brown), RB (red and brown), and RD (mint red). Accordingly, a certain token may be described as MS-65RB. Coins below MS-63 are nearly always with brown toning if in copper.

ABOUT UNCIRCULATED • *Small traces of wear are visible on highest points.*

AU-58 *Very Choice* • Has some signs of abrasion: high points of the design. Shallow or weak spots in the relief are usually caused by improper striking, and not wear.

AU-55 *Choice* • Only a trace of wear shows on high points Some of the mint luster is still present.

AU-50 *Typical* • Traces of wear are more extensive. Traces of mint luster still show.

EXTREMELY FINE • *Very light wear on only the highest points.*

EF-45 *Choice* • Light wear is seen overall, and the highest areas may show flattening, but all lettering and details can be seen.

EF-40 *Typical* • The wear is more extensive, but all details can be seen.

VERY FINE • *Light to moderate even wear. All major features are sharp.*

VF-30 *Choice* • The wear is more extensive, and certain details in highest relief may be absent, but in areas of medium or low relief details will be sharp.

VF-20 *Typical* • Wear is even more extensive, but all lettering and numbers are sharp and clear.

As Civil War tokens, unlike Indian Head cents, did not remain in circulation for decades, nearly all survivors are VF or higher.

In the marketplace, including on the Internet, many Civil War tokens are illustrated but assigned no grades. Unless you buy from a dealer well established in the token specialty caution is urged when making purchases. There are many cleaned coins, counterfeits, and other questionable items, particularly on the Internet.

As a determinant of value, grading is a key factor. A Mint State Civil War token can be worth multiples of one in Very Fine or Extremely Fine grade. In recent years especially nice coins within the Mint State category can bring strong premiums—such as an MS-65 selling for multiples of the price of an MS-60. A token worth, say, $30 in VF grade can be worth several hundred dollars if gem Mint State and rare at that level. For many store cards the finest known grade may be VF or EF. On the other hand numismatic strikes are nearly always seen in Mint State.

Determinants of Value (Patriotic Tokens)

For patriotic Civil War tokens the most important determinant of value is, first, the rarity of the general type. If there is only one die to illustrate a specific motif it will be in greater demand than a type for which many dies are known. Accordingly, the French Liberty Head die, of which quite a few varieties exist, is easy enough to acquire for a type set. The die with an eagle and lettered SILVER MINE (Fuld 287) is one of a kind, not many impressions survive from it, and a Mint State example can sell into the thousands of dollars.

The motif, artistry, inscription, or other appeal of a die are other important determinants. There are various Lincoln portrait dies, and obtaining an example for a type set is not a problem. However, the popularity of Lincoln is such that across the board such tokens are more expensive than, say, miscellaneous French Liberty Head tokens. "Indiana primitive" dies with their crude lettering are not rare in most instances, but they consistently command a premium for their novelty. Although certain such rustically cut dies are also used with store cards, patriotic tokens with these motifs create the most attention.

The rarity of a die combination will add value. Even if two dies are common in other uses, if they are combined to create an R-7 or higher token there will be value added on the part of specialists.

Determinants of Value (Store Cards)

For many Civil War store cards the three most important determinants of value are location, location, and location—as they say in real estate. A token from a tiny town in Wisconsin, Michigan, or another state may be extremely valuable, even into the thousands of dollars, if there was only one issuer in that town and only few tokens are known. An R-9 token in EF-40 grade from a rare location could bring, say, $5,000, while an R-9 variety from Chicago, Detroit, Cincinnati, or New York City might sell in the low hundreds of dollars for the same grade.

Certain states are "rarer" than others. Maine and New Hampshire had only one issuer each, but they issued many tokens. In contrast, Minnesota had more issuers, but no tokens are common, with the result that all are expensive. Looking through this guide, if a state has many tokens R-5 or lower it is "common." If there are only a few issuers and tokens average R-6 or higher, they will be expensive.

Other Aspects That Command a Premium

If a design is deemed to be beautiful or interesting it will sell for more than a token with a motif that is not memorable. Joseph Merriam's die with a dog's head and GOOD FOR A SCENT is not rare, but it is in everlasting demand, and nice examples sell for strong prices and attract a lot of attention. A motif such as a mug of beer, a sewing machine, or a rabbit is more in demand than one with just lettering, if all other aspects such as location, rarity, and grade are equal.

Certain specialties can add value. Tokens issued by doctors and dentists and for patent medicines have been popular for medical professionals to collect. Saloons (available in abundance) are another popular category, and ditto for transportation issuers (boats, trains, coaches), and breweries. In contrast, few have made hotels, oyster houses, milliners, or grocery stores an interest. Tokens depicting Lincoln have a special following as do those with Washington portraits.

The tokens of certain engravers can be valuable. At the quality end of the scale those by William K. Lanphear of Cincinnati are generally well made and have interesting motifs ranging from Indians to mythical creatures to views of products. Dies by Frederick M. Lutz, who worked with Lanphear, are especially attractive. Tokens from the shop of John Stanton, who engaged various engravers, are also highly esteemed. Certain 22 mm tokens of 1860 and 1861, by Benjamin C. True, were issued by Stanton and are widely popular.

Overstrikes on cents, and tokens struck in silver, sell for very strong premiums. Among other metals a token of a given rarity will sell for more if in copper-nickel than in brass or copper. An overstrike on a dime and with the coin's original features still discernible is valued into four figures. For many such overstrikes the opportunity to find them can be more important than the price paid. Often today's high price is tomorrow's bargain in a strong market.

After reviewing offerings in the marketplace you will soon gain insights as to popularity, demand, and price.

Being a Smart Buyer

There are several steps to being a smart buyer and getting more for your money.

The first is to determine what you want. If price is a consideration, determine the grade level you wish to seek for a given variety. Generally, for issues made in quantity for circulation, an AU or lower-grade Mint State coin will do fine, and there may be no sense in paying multiples of, say, an EF price for an MS-63 or higher example. One nice thing about copper metal is that pieces in such grades as VF and EF can be very attractive.[2]

Review this book carefully and, if possible, obtain copies of the Fuld references on patriotic tokens and store cards. This is not absolutely necessary, but it is nice to know what exists. Formulate a "want list." Further, if you have a specialty in mind—say, saloons in Cincinnati—these will be easier to track down.

Second, once you find a token that is appealing, look at it or its image carefully. Is it graded properly? A beautiful EF-40 common token may not be worth buying if it is priced at a MS-60 figure. Be sure the token has excellent eye appeal. Unless a token is of great rarity, let someone else buy it if it is not attractive.

Third, inspect it carefully to be sure it has the best sharpness of strike that can be found (unless the variety is notoriously weak), be sure it hasn't been cleaned, and check the surface for marks, granularity, and other negatives. Looking at pictures in catalogs and on the Internet can tell you what to expect. As an example, among the various Indian Head dies made by the Stanton shop, some nearly always have flat centers on the stars—okay and as expected—while others have sharp stars. In the latter instance, wait until you find one that is sharp.

Fourth and last, be sure that the market price is in the ballpark. Civil War store cards do not have standard values, but for common varieties in Mint State, say R-1 to R-4, the variances are usually not large—$100 in one place, $85 in another, and $115 somewhere else. If a token has good eye appeal and quality, pay the going price and you will own it. On the other hand, if it is R-8 or higher, it may be worth stretching for. As a general rule in the past, the record price of one year can be a bargain years later. Also, if you believe that $100 is the right price for a token, but you have not been able to find a nice one, step up and pay $110 or $120 if you have the chance. A token in the hand is worth two in distant locations.

Insist on a return privilege in case you do not like it. This is sometimes not possible in an auction or Internet bidding contest, but it can usually be worked out if you buy by mail from a dealer's stock.

Dealers and Other Sellers

Nearly all dealers who make Civil War tokens a specialty are knowledgeable and honest. It will pay to establish a relationship, a business friendship, with such a professional. In this way he or she can give you advice, help you find pieces you need, and answer questions.

For your part it is important to pay your way, so to speak, by making occasional purchases and conducting business in the manner you would like to be treated yourself. Be prompt in payments or returns, honor your auction bids, and if you have seen a nice image of a token before buying it, don't return it unless there really is an unseen problem.

If the dealer is a member in good standing in the Token and Medal Society or the Civil War Token Society this is a huge plus.

The above said, you are all set to have many enjoyable years ahead of you.

On the other hand, if the seller is not a professional, be very careful. Civil War tokens offered on the Internet are often overgraded and in more than just a few instances are counterfeit. These are in the minority, fortunately, but buying one bad coin and not being able to return it (or return it easily) is a disappointing experience. Hardly any Internet offerings are vetted for authenticity or quality. Tokens encapsulated by PCGS or NGC are exceptions.

Also, prices can be very erratic in offerings by inexperienced sellers. It is not unusual for some very common Civil War token with an interesting motif to sell on the Internet for several times the price a knowledgeable dealer would charge. If you are bidding without knowledge, don't assume that the underbidder is informed. Sometimes it is the blind leading the blind.

Enjoying Your Civil War Token Collection

A Pleasurable Pursuit

Civil War tokens are inherently interesting. Pity the collector of 20th-century federal coins that differ little except for date and mintmark. In dynamic contrast, each of the patriotic Civil War tokens can lead to an interesting commentary, and among the 1,500 or so issuers of Civil War store cards there is a story for each one.

While no one has ever completed a collection with every patriotic token die—never mind every combination—and no one has ever obtained a store card from each issuing merchant, without much difficulty a nice collection of a thousand or more different varieties can be built. In grades such as VF, EF, and AU these can be very inexpensive. Even with R-8 and R-9 rarities in Mint State the acquisition cost can be from the hundreds to low thousands of dollars—quite a contrast from colonial or federal coins of comparable rarity and grade.

A Civil War store card can furnish, say, one point of enjoyment. Learning about its issuer and history can add one more point, doubling or even tripling or quadrupling your enjoyment. One plus one can equal three or four! Some years ago I became intrigued with the store cards of Yankee Robinson and decided to learn more about his

Civil War store card of Wards Lake Superior Line and the steamer *Planet*. In earlier editions of the Fuld *Store Cards* book it was listed with Cleveland, but in the third edition it is in Detroit as the company's main office was there. MI-225-CJa-2a. Reverse die 1042. Shop of John Stanton of Cincinnati.

Much concerning steamer *Planet* can be found on the Internet, indeed enough to prepare a lengthy article. This printed notice dated 1863 was found in a directory examined by the author at the Massachusetts Historical Society.

The steamer *Planet*.

life. A fascinating and prolonged search led me to the archives of the Circus World Museum in Baraboo, Wisconsin (where curator Fred Dahlinger sent me a large file of notices and articles), to reading back issues of the *New York Clipper* (in the New York City Public Library), and to extensive correspondence. This was in the era before the Internet. In time I published a chapter about him in my *More Adventures With Rare Coins* book.

In nearly countless instances owners of tokens have studied them in detail and have told their fascinating stories in the pages of the *Civil War Token Journal* and its predecessor titles. There are still endless opportunities.

Beyond learning its history, a careful study of a token under magnification or with a high-resolution image can be very rewarding. Such aspects as the order in which certain dies were used in combination with other dies has scarcely been researched, and interesting idiosyncrasies of dies have been touched upon only lightly. There are new discoveries to be made. If you find something interesting the *Civil War Token Journal* is an ideal venue in which to share it with others.

DIRECTORIES, THE INTERNET, AND OTHER SOURCES

Many sources for information beckon. Back issues of the Civil War Token Society magazine are readily available and are a good start. For patriotic tokens, most motifs have a background that can be researched on Wikipedia or elsewhere on the Internet, not to overlook your local library. For store cards, there are several book-length studies of particular states, as well as John Ostendorf's *Civil War Store Cards of Cincinnati*, which deals with a single city (albeit the one that issued more tokens than any other).

Original research—delving into contemporary and other sources outside of numismatics—can be very interesting and challenging, a fine sport.

Directories

For many areas of historical and genealogical research, various city, commercial, and other directories have been found to be useful by many. Indeed, these are the widest and most comprehensive sources. However, such listings must be taken with a very large grain of the proverbial salt as errors and omissions abound. Today, many of these directories, once expensive and hard to find, can be accessed for free on Google Books and other Internet sources. The Cincinnati Public Library web site is the gateway to various Civil War directories of that city and other virtual sources can be found.

In general, city directories of a given date were prepared during the previous year and contain information that may have changed by the directory date. Thus, a directory dated 1860 was likely compiled in 1859. Further, old listings were sometimes continued uncorrected for several years or more, even though a person may have moved or died. Still further, many directories contain unexplained omissions. Thus, a person can be listed at a given address for several years, skipped for a year or two, and then relisted at the same address; obviously, the person has not moved or disappeared in the meantime. Simply stated, the compilers of directories did not check the listings each time a new edition was published.

In many cities (New York City and Cincinnati being important examples), businesses are listed by proprietor, and the shop or trade name is not given. Thus, in a hypothetical instance, if a token of the Jones Restaurant exists with the date 1863, a perusal of the directory for that year will have no listing for such a place. However, unbeknownst to the reader, Joe Jones, of 123 Broadway, who is listed, traded as Jones Restaurant, but there may be dozens of Joneses in the directory. Business trade names such as Eureka, Central, City, National, Washington, etc., are often omitted from directories. The absence of *information* in a directory may not mean that such a business or person did not exist.

Further, sometimes listings are very stale. The writer encountered one instance in which a hotel continued to be listed 17 *years* after it burned down! It was common to list people who had died several years or more earlier.

In connection with a study of Philadelphia Civil War tokens, Charlotte and David Gale encountered an interesting comment by A. McElroy, compiler of directories of that city:

> The "terror" of the draft is more extensively than ever on the people. Every person carrying a City Directory in his hand is suspected of being an enrolling officer, either military or civil, and the very *sight* of this otherwise useful medium of information creates suspicion of ulterior designs and makes it impossible, in most cases, to get correct information. Spurious names are given, and the head of the family said to be in the army or navy, when the *contrary* is the fact.[3]

Because of these considerations, directory listings are not always definitive for a given date, especially for people and businesses in different locations from one year to the next.

In general, useful policies concerning directories are these regarding Civil War tokens:

1. If a person or business is not listed in a directory, the person or business still may have existed in a particular town. There were many people omitted completely, and others were listed intermittently.

2. If a person or business is listed at a given address and trade one year, omitted the next, listed the following year, omitted the next, etc., the listing is simply erratic; the person and business probably were continuous.

3. If a token bears a trade name such as Washington, Atlantic, etc., but not the name of the proprietor, and if the business is a small one, the chances are great that it will not be listed, but the proprietor will be. As the token does not bear the proprietor's name, the connection cannot be made.

4. If a person or business is listed at a certain date, this usually means that such a person or business was active in *or before* the time the directory was *compiled* (which may be significantly earlier than the publication date on the cover). As noted, many listings are stale.

Newspapers

Much more accurate than directory listings are newspaper advertisements. If the Washington Café advertised in a newspaper on April 6, 1863, and gave an address, it is a virtual certainty that the Washington Café existed at that address at that time. If the advertisement listed the proprietor as John Smith, then it is a virtual certainty that this was Smith's business. If there was a misadventure—the place burned down, the proprietor was arrested for thievery, or whatever—no information will be in any directory, but newspapers will have details, sometimes lurid.

Many contemporary newspapers can be found on the Internet with many sources to choose from, such as Chronicling America on the Library of Congress web site. Unfortunately, it is often the rule, not the exception, that resolution ranges from slightly fuzzy to downright poor, especially if the images were made from old microfilms rather than scanning actual copies digitally.

Some genealogy sites offer newspaper access as well, as do certain academic-oriented sites. Some checking will produce good results. In the case of sites that are very expensive to access, often a local or regional college or university can provide entry for you. As each year passes, more and more books and newspapers are digitized for free public access.

Obituaries are also useful, but often contain errors. When such notices are prepared, relatives of the deceased are called upon to furnish birth dates, business dates, etc., often from memory. Accuracy can be lost. There are countless instances in which

The Union Volunteer Refreshment Saloon issued this token in 1863. PA-750-W-3a.

The Union Volunteer Refreshment Saloon was set up in Philadelphia on May 27, 1861, to help feed and entertain soldiers who were on their way to the war. Many arrived in Philadelphia after long train trips and were hungry, tired, and unwashed. Volunteers were urged to provide food and accommodations. Its second annual fair was held on June 15, 1863, and is commemorated on the token. Set up at the foot of Washington Street, it was next door to the Union Volunteer Hospital (Broad Street and Washington Avenue). The structure, made of wood, featured a peaked roof at the center, from front to back, variously shown with a perched eagle or an American flag at the front. By using Internet sites enough information about this saloon can be found to write a monograph!

several or more people in a given town have the same name. Juniors are often not listed as such. Ancestry.com on the Internet, a paid-subscriber service, has a wealth of birth and death dates and related information if you know who to look for. Defining or narrowing a search requires some practice.

Business licenses and municipal records are a great source of useful information. However, sometimes the incorporators or partners in a business may trade under a different name than the business title, or may hire a proprietor, or may simply be investors. Moreover, most require going to a city library or town hall to access them. Hardly any are available on the Internet.

Published town histories are very useful for finding information about businesses. In nearly all instances the information given is of a positive nature, with scandals, bankruptcies, and other problems omitted. On the other hand in various court and law journals there are many records of legal cases that address such. Again, the Internet is a rich source.

Auction Catalogs, Price Lists, and Numismatic References

Auction catalogs have offered Civil War tokens since almost day one. Actually, 1862 is the jumping-off point, after which time such tokens were offered in large numbers through the decade. In the 1860s auction catalogs were often completed just a few weeks prior to the sale. Thus, the information is timely. If an 1864-dated auction catalog lists an 1863 token by John Smith, it is a certainty that the Smith token is of Civil War vintage. On the other hand, if an 1863-dated token by Smith is listed in an 1875 auction catalog (although later listings are very sparse except for rarities), it could have been struck anytime from 1863 to 1875.

Later auction catalogs can be very useful, but relatively few of those of the 20th and early 21st centuries offered tokens singly and carefully described. Exceptions are those issued by dealers in this specialty. Beginning in a large way in the 1960s and with some continuing into later years such dealers as Charles Kirtley, Dorgé (George Fuld and his wife Doris), Jon Harris, C. & D. Gale, Typkoyn, Paul Koppenhaver, Joseph Levine, Steve Hayden, my own firm, and others issued advertisements, auction presentations, and price lists that can yield valuable information today. Historical information is very scarce, however, in such offerings.

There have been many books published with information on Civil War store cards, far fewer on patriotic tokens. New editions render obsolete the older ones, so there is no particular point, for example, in acquiring any but the latest, with the present second edition of *U.S. Civil War Store Cards* being definitive.

MYTHS AND LEGENDS

Numismatic sources can also be unreliable if an auction listing or article was not carefully researched. A poster example is provided by the twice-told tale of a New York City saloonkeeper who issued a million tokens, with 300,000 of them landing in fare boxes in cars of the Fifth Avenue Railroad. The real story can be found in Don Erlenkotter's study, "Gustavus Lindenmueller: The Myth, The Man, The Mystery," the *Civil War Token Journal*, Fall 2010. The dissemination of the myth was aided by its inclusion in the 1924 Hetrich-Guttag book, which was the standard reference from 1924 into the 1960s:

> In the spring of 1863 New York followed [Cincinnati's] example. The first [token] to be made in New York was the Lindenmueller currency, of which a million pieces were struck. . . . These little coins filled the wants of the trades-people, and

were accepted as a means of exchange for the value, which usually was one cent. They undoubtedly were a source of great relief and convenience, but their irresponsible character soon attracted the attention of the federal authorities.

It is said that the Third Avenue Railroad of New York requested Lindenmueller to redeem a large number of his tokens, which they had accepted in the course of business, but this he laughingly refused to do. The railroad had no redress, and it is not improbable that incidents of this character forced the government to put a stop to their issue. This was done by the passage of an act of Congress in 1864, forbidding private individuals to issue any form of money.

Author Erlenkotter found many other such accounts of these particular tokens, some with interesting variations (such as citizens desiring them as they were "as good as gold"), but nothing of the sort published during the 1860s. He verified that Lindenmueller and his beer hall were well known in their time and, of course, that Lindenmueller issued many tokens, for some varieties are common today. There is no evidence that they were the first to be issued in New York City, that anyone considered them to be as good as gold, that the Third Avenue Railroad had accumulated a large quantity, that Lindenmueller refused to redeem them, or that any citizens confused these large (quarter-size) copper tokens with federal copper-nickel Indian Head cents leading to the government to passing a law against them.

A copper 25.5 mm large (quarter size) token, one of 1,000,000 said to have been issued by New York City beer-hall proprietor Gustavus Lindenmueller and also said to have caused a great uproar and commotion when a street railway that had taken in 300,000 found that the issuer would not redeem them. Further, some citizens, perhaps besotted, seem to have confused these with copper-nickel Indian Head cents. This was a factor in the government passing a law against tokens in 1864. *However, read more in the main text.* Per Fuld style the address side is called the obverse and the portrait side the reverse.

Still, tall tales being what they are, likely the scenario will appear again in numismatics.

Among patriotic tokens there is an extensive series of Rhode Island issues beginning with die 481. These were standard in the series until someone guessed they were not contemporary with the Civil War and delisted them. However, modern research, including by George Fuld and the present author, shows that most were struck in 1864 to the order of the Rhode Island Numismatic Association and are indeed contemporary.

Another misconception published in historical accounts is that the Wealth of the South tokens were official issues of the Confederate States of America, never mind that they are dated 1860 and were mostly distributed before the CSA was formed.

Yet another is the conventional wisdom that 1873-dated Indian Head store cards issued by French of Clarksburg, Ohio, Fuld OH-170-A, were struck in the Civil War but misdated 1873 by careless error, rather than the correct 1863. Research compiled by John Ostendorf in connection with revising the Fuld store card book revealed that French started business after the Civil War era.

Similarly, it was found that the drugstore of Fisler & Chance, traditionally listed as a Cincinnati business, was in fact located in Urbana, Ohio. To compound the situation, an advertisement dated July 4, 1866, was found, proclaiming opening day of the business—by which time the Civil War was history.

Diameters and Striking Considerations

If you are of a technical turn of mind you may want to measure your tokens. It is recommended that measurements in millimeters of the diameter of Civil War tokens be done on a vertical axis. Many tokens are out of round and can vary depending upon where it is measured.

Tokens that were struck in a closed steel collar are of constant diameter (unless the dies were used later with a different collar). Also, when viewed edge-on the edge is vertical. Many plain-edge tokens and most reeded edge tokens were struck with a closed collar. Exceptions to the reeded edge are when a token was struck over a dime or other reeded-edge coin, but not using a collar.

Tokens that were struck without a collar can vary, usually only by a small amount but sometimes widely. The diameter can be slightly less if the dies were spaced slightly farther apart. If the dies were closely spaced, more metal would squeeze out from the sides, increasing the width. Diameters of no-collar tokens can vary by a millimeter or two.

As a general rule, tokens in soft metals were sharply struck, these including copper, white metal, and silver. Nickel alloy, being hard, presented difficulties and many if not most such coins have areas of light striking. Often copper-nickel cents were used as planchets after their high rims were filed down. Such file marks remain on the tokens, particularly on the rims, and do not affect their value.

Steel dies, if not carefully preserved, tended to rust, sometimes quickly such as in the humid months of summer. Little appears in literature concerning this, but experiences with die studies show that sometimes dies can rust within a year, and severe rust can take place within two years, perhaps even sooner. For this reason it was good practice to coat the dies with wax, fat, or grease prior to plac-

The reverse die 1247 of OH-165-DE-2a shows severe rust.

ing them in storage. Although certain circulation strikes were made with rusted dies, most often rusted dies are seen on numismatic strikings, particularly among dies made be Emil Sigel and the shop established by John Stanton. If, in fact, these coiners had used 1863 dies in 1865 and 1866, the extensive rust would be explained by their deterioration in the meantime. The dies are not worn or deteriorated, just rusted.

Studying Die States

Die states of Civil War tokens can be fascinating to study. Hardly anything has ever appeared in print about these, although such states can provide a link to the order in which certain tokens were struck. By definition, a token from a perfect die was made before one showing a prominent crack.

In general, a die begins life as a "perfect die" without any cracks or breaks. In early impressions the die may have *raised* die lines, or finish marks. These were prepared when the die was made and are not defects. In time, such die finish lines tended to wear away and disappear or become less prominent.

After use, several things were apt to happen to a die. Cracks sometimes developed, usually starting at the rim and progressing inward (although there are some rare exceptions of interior cracks that do not touch the rim). A crack might begin as a raised ridge, then enlarge, finally resulting in a chip or break out of the die. By studying these features it is possible to determine the sequence in which pieces were made. While die cracks are the most common type seen, so-called "cud" breaks involving a piece of the die falling away from the rim are also often encountered. In some instances, a tiny chip or crack develops into a cud and the progress can be studied by viewing multiple specimens.

As the dies developed cracks and cuds the diesinkers sometimes sought to improve their life by dressing or relapping the die. This was done in several ways. Sometimes the die was simply ground down a tiny fraction of an inch to remove light surface cracks, chips, and marks. When this was done, features in shallow relief disappeared and became part of the general plane or field area. Thus, on dies with Indian portraits, certain areas in the feather veins, or below the feathers, are lost and become part of the flat field; dentils around the border become thinner and more widely spaced as do date numerals and some letters, and inner rings around a plain border can sometimes disappear (as in the instance of an H.M. Lane store card die). In some instances only part of a die was relapped by filing, so careful study is needed. Examples are provided by two dies for Gies of Detroit that were relapped at the top in order to change errors in the name.

In other instances, such as die cuds and rim breaks, the diesinker placed the die in a lathe, and simply trimmed around the rim, smoothing away the cud, and often making the rim area somewhat basined or dished. Sometimes a large cud was reduced to a small one. By means of filing or trimming, a cud with jagged edges was sometimes reduced to one with a rounded or smooth form. An example is provided by treatment given to the Knoop's Cigars & Tobacco store card die of New York City.

The relapping of a die can cause a large die crack to become smaller as parts are ground away. Accordingly, in some instances a token with a shorter crack can represent a later state than one with a slightly larger crack. When a die is relapped some features are lost, as noted, and study can reveal that this is a later use. In the field of studying

This token of Walker & Napier of Nashville, TN-690-7d, shows the obverse die buckled and with a large cud break. Apparently, this die was still kept on hand after it was replaced with another (see discussion in main text). Both dies were used to make numismatic strikes with a late (rusted and relapped) state of reverse die 1018. Notice on the obverse that letters NN (TENN.) are about level with each other.

Walker & Napier token TN-690-E-8d with a replacement obverse die with slightly differing details. Note that the final N (TENN.) is low. Reverse die 1018 is in a late state.

Details of a John Grether error die with IMPORORTER misspelling (OH-200-A die O-1). Part of the die was relapped, and the correct IMPORTER was overpunched. The relapping caused the original error letters to appear very tiny as all but the deepest part of the letters in the die was removed.

large federal copper cents of the 1793–1814 years the study of die states is a major focus for many articles and more than just a few enthusiasts. For Civil War token enthusiasts the field is wide open.

Numismatic adventures through a looking glass are at your beck and call. Studying die states, rust, and other aspects can reveal the order in which certain tokens were struck.

Sometimes a die would come into hard contact with its partner die without a planchet in between. The result would be clash marks manifested by lettering or other features of one die being impressed on the other die. When tokens were later struck from a die with clash marks, such tokens would show evidence of recessed or incuse letters, wreath elements, etc., from the other die. Sometimes (but not at other times; there is great inconsistency) clashed die strikings have been listed as *separate varieties* in the Fuld book. Relative to this, editor David E. Schenkman commented in the Fall 1996 issue of *JCWTS:*

> If minor errors [such as double-struck pieces], most of which are unique, are given separate listings, the variety will be endless. I was prompted to comment on this after noticing in the new book [second edition of the Fuld store card book] two new listings inserted in the regular section, TN-600-B-3a1 and TN-600-E-3a1. These two tokens appear to be nothing more than the product of clashed dies (happening when token 0508/519 was being struck?). . . . If clashed die tokens rate separate listings, why not clipped planchets, off-center strikes, etc. My feeling is that a token of this sort should not be listed based on one person's opinion, but should be first reviewed by a committee of Society members.

In actuality, clashed dies are much more common than the literature indicates. If *all* were to be listed, the Fuld book would have to be expanded tremendously, but for what purpose?

Sometimes a token would be struck but remain in position between the dies. If another blank or planchet was fed in on top of it the result was a *brockage* with one side showing an incuse image of the earlier coin in the die and the other side being in normal relief. Unlike the situation elsewhere in numismatics, the editors of the Fuld store card book have listed brockages as separate varieties with their own numbers. In other series they are called mint errors. Again, there is no end to such things.

D. Peck & Co., Ironton, Missouri, store card, MO-400-1a, with reverse die 1046, one that Stanton combined with many different obverses. The reverse die is in its early or perfect state. MO-400-A-1a.

W.J. Adderly, Detroit grocer, store card with shattered obverse die and with a later state of the reverse die 1046 with a crack linking the first five stars and a crack from the dentils horizontally to the tip of the neck. His surname is misspelled as Adderley. The die below the crack on 1046 is rough and beginning to break up. By studying various uses of die 1046 a chronological sequence of use can be made. MI-225-A-1d.

Often after use and deterioration, dies would be treated to permit further use. To reiterate, such later treatment sometimes included one or more of the following processes.

Cleaning the die. By means of a wire brush, file, or emery paper, a die would be cleaned to remove rust pits. Typically, this would result in such pits being removed from the flat or field areas of the die, but remaining in the recessed areas such as the letters, portrait, and devices.

Relapping the die. A die would be put in a lathe chuck and turned against a file or other abrasive agent, or ground with parallel strokes of a file or a grinding wheel, removing metal from the field or flat surfaces. In the process, low-relief details such as berry stems, dentil features, serifs on letters, and even *light die cracks* would be removed. "Cud" breaks extending into the field of a token from the rim are made smaller as the lower-relief or outer edge areas of the cud break are removed. As noted earlier, because of this, in some instances a token struck from relapped die can have fewer cracks or smaller cud breaks and appear to be an earlier strike than a token from a cracked, un-relapped die! Thus, study of *all* die features, in addition to cracks, is necessary to determine the die state and sequence of striking.

In instances in which certain dies were relapped on a lathe, sometimes just a portion of the die—such as the outer areas at and near the dentils—would be relapped. In instances in which a file or grinding wheel were used, nearly always the entire die was relapped.

Altering the die. There are some instances in which a die was used to strike tokens, sometimes in large quantities, and then was altered by punching one letter over another or by changing some other feature, after which additional tokens were struck of this "new" variety. This process is called *reworking* a die. One example:

A die for a New York City merchant was made with an erroneous first initial, reading W.S. BROWN. Many tokens were struck. The error was then recognized, and the incorrect W was overpunched with the correct M, creating an M.S. BROWN die, from which many more tokens were struck (Fuld varieties NY-630-N and O).

Cud breaks on the outer rim. In a number of instances among Civil War tokens, mound-like breaks, irregular and extended cud breaks, etc., are seen on the *outer rim* beyond the dentils, and not extending into the dentils. While sometimes this is in the flat rim part of the die beyond the dentils, in some other instances it is a part of a chuck or matrix in which the die is affixed.

Two of many instances in which Emil Sigel used a matrix with two distinctive adjacent cud breaks. H.M. Lane, NY-630-AP-8a, and Story & Southworth, NY-630-BV-15a.

Thus, the Wisconsin store card WI-220-F-2a (J.G. Lowell, Fond du Lac, Wisconsin, druggist) is known with a movable cud break on the obverse rim that is part of the matrix, not the die. Similarly, many Emil Sigel strikings of various merchants have two adjacent, raised mounds on the outer rim, in different positions.

The situation is complicated by the fact that during a given production run, the outer rim cud breaks in the matrix will be in the same position and, thus, will appear alike on multiple examples of a given token variety. However, if the die shifts, or if another production run uses a different matrix, the positions will vary.

If an outer rim cud extends into the dentils or field of the die, then the cud is part of the die. If an outer rim cud is found to vary in its position, then it is definitely a part of the chuck or matrix, not the die.

If an outer cud is not observed to vary in position, it may or may not be a part of the die, and further study—such as the examination of specimens (preferably with different obverse-reverse die rotations or different pairings) is recommended.

As if the preceding were not enough to be confusing, it was sometimes the practice to file down the rims of tokens with cuds immediately after striking. Thus, a token can appear to have a perfect rim, when that is not the case.

Die state observation. The study of die states is best done with high-grade examples in instances in which this is possible. A worn token may have certain features no longer visible. Light die cracks, raised rust pits, and other characteristics may have been worn away.

A token is best checked by bathing it in a strong light from a single source, such as an incandescent bulb, so that the field of the coin will reflect into the viewer's eye. A token must be turned to several different angles during the inspection process, as die cracks are easily seen when they are crosswise to the light source, but may be nearly invisible when parallel to it.

Among higher-grade coins, the ease of checking minute die details varies with the metal and toning. A heavily toned coin may be difficult to inspect.

The ease of checking also varies with the metal of the token. In general, a high-grade token struck in white metal or nickel will reveal delicate cracks more readily than will a piece struck in copper, copper-nickel, or, in particular, brass. For some reason, brass tokens, although struck in an alloy that is softer than nickel alloy, are the most difficult to study. The writer has seen some instances in which brass pieces were struck from a die with tiny hairline cracks, but the full extent of the cracks was not revealed in the finished piece.

Illusions of size. Conditions of observations can vary. A letter, such as the top of an A or the interior of an O, which appears partially filled in a high-grade specimen can appear completely filled in a lower-grade specimen, even though the die state is the same. As letters wear, they tend to appear larger.

Focus on the Styles Used by Several Shops

Relatively little study has been done on the art, letter fonts, workmanship, and other aspects of styles used by the different engraving shops. One formula does not fit all, but for most of the better-known shops, large and small, there are observable characteristics.

The most prolific issuer of Civil War store cards was the shop of John Stanton in Cincinnati with James Murdock Jr. as an associate, continued by Murdock & Spencer. The work of several engravers was used, giving rise to different styles. However, the basic shop style used with-serifs letters, well made, and well aligned on the dies. Often two or three font sizes were used on the same die, the largest at the center, medium around the borders, and the smallest to give the address. If there was a lot of text, just a small font would be used. These dies had well-formed dentils around the border. Many were combined with Indian Head reverses with LIBERTY on the headband, well made and a close match with that on the federal cent. Examination of multiple dies makes the style quite recognizable.

MI-225-BG-3a (ipl) obverse die by Stanton, Randal's Photographic Gallery, Detroit. This uses three font sizes. The surname was misspelled and should have been Randall.

MI-225-AH-3a (ipl) obverse die by Stanton, Tin plated. C.B. Goodrich, Detroit dealer in boots and shoes. This uses three font sizes.

OH-165-BI-10d obverse die by Stanton, Jacob Guth, Cincinnati. This uses two font sizes.

OH-165-FY-5d obverse die by Stanton, D.B.S., Cincinnati grocer. This uses just one font. It may have been done by an apprentice, for there is an erroneous comma after MAIN and the letters are not as well aligned as usual for this shop.

High on the list of numismatic mysteries relating to tokens are the cabalistic inscriptions on OH-165-AD-2d from the Stanton shop. The obverse includes CONSULERE / GENERI / HOMINUM / HO HI / WHANG / B.C. / 129374. The reverse is lettered MAGI GENII / QUBO DAIRI / WHANG.

Many collectors have been mystified by the cabalistic inscriptions on a Civil War token known as OH-165-AD-2. What do you think?

I love a mystery! And, numismatics has more mysteries than anyone can easily count. Among these is a Civil War token issued by the Cincinnati shop of John Stanton. During the war he produced untold millions of cent-sized tokens that were wholesaled to merchants, who passed them along as small change, as we all know.

Collectors scrambled to acquire these copper tokens, and by 1863 interest was intense nationwide. The various coiners accommodated numismatists by making special strikings in other metals, including copper-nickel, white metal, and even silver. It was déjà vu all over again (with a nod to Yogi Berra), reminiscent of the 1790s when in England collectors spent much effort and money to acquire special versions of copper tokens. Now in the 1860s it was America's turn.

The token cataloged as variety OH-165-AD-2 has been a puzzle to many collectors for a long time. The words have no obvious connection with each other. The obverse includes CONSULERE / GENERI / HOMINUM / HO HI / WHANG / B.C. / 129374. The reverse is lettered MAGI GENII / QUBO DAIRI / WHANG. The Fulds considered them to be magicians' tokens. It has also been suggested that these were practice pieces for apprentice diesinkers in the Stanton shop.

Trying to learn more I started browsing around in old catalogs.

In the sale of the C.W. Idell Collection, Bangs & Co., New York, January 8 and 9, 1878, cataloger E.J. Attinelli described under lot 624 the lettering of this token and stated that the token was "a poke at coin collectors." Similarly, in *The Numismatist*, December 1899, Benjamin P. Wright in his "American Store or Business Cards" stated it was "a satirical issue directed against coin collectors."

The words may be mostly nonsense, although *consuleri generi hominum* may mean "mind the interests of mankind." *Dairi* describes a bronze image of Buddha. *Magi* and *genii* have connotations of the origin or source of magic, perhaps inspiring the comment by the Fulds. *B.C.* may relate to the dating of certain ancient coins. *Whang* appears in many contexts in the 1860s and earlier, ranging from a proper name to a large quantity of anything such as a whang of cheese or coal. Perhaps in the 1860s a "whang" of 129,374 tokens was imagined!

For me the mystery is solved: a satire on collectors as stated years ago.

Leaving Stanton behind and going to the leading Chicago maker of Civil War store cards it is seen that most of the dies from the shop of Shubael D. Childs share similar characteristics serving to distinguish them at a glance. Most (but not all) lettering is in a sans-serif font. The border is usually plain, or if there are dentils they are small.

Obverse die by the S.D. Childs shop; for IL-150-AT-2a for W.C. Peck, Chicago grocer. The letters mostly without serifs (GROCER excepted) and the border is plain.

Stock reverse die 111 by the S.D. Childs shop; for IL-150-K-2a. Sans-serif letters, plain border.

STUDYING NUMERALS, LETTERS, AND STARS

Many dies can look alike at first glance or even with casual study, but when examined closely differences can be found. There are many instances in which dies listed in *Patriotic Civil War Tokens* and in *Civil War Store Cards* have been found to vary, creating two varieties. An example is patriotic die 9 listed as such in five editions of the book. Later, it was found that there are actually two different dies (see chapter 6), and today they are designated 9 and 9A.

Numerals. Although there may be exceptions to be researched, it was standard practice for a diesinker to add the numerals individually, yielding differences in the vertical alignment and horizontal spacing. Often the differences are slight, but in many instances they are dramatic. There are variations with the style and shape of most numerals; a 3 can have a rounded top or a flat top, dates can be large or small, etc.

Letters. Letters were usually added individually. Accordingly, there can be differences in spacing and also vertical alignment. Letters are of two main styles: with serifs or plain, the latter called *sans serif* in the printing trade. Some letters are thick, others are heavy, etc. Examining letters in relation to each other and to other die features is a technique leading to the discovery of many varieties. It is also interesting to examine the dies of certain of the larger shops—Stanton and Lanphear are examples—and see how some are lettered very carefully and others have many irregularities and misalignments. Among unascribed patriotic dies of the same general type there can be great variety in workmanship.

Stars. Stars, usually five-pointed or six-pointed, were added by hand. The Stanton Indian Head dies of 1863 furnish an example for contemplation. These used a stock Indian Head punch to which a date was added. The stars were all added by hand. This serves as the "fingerprint" of the die. The first thing to check is the relationship of the

The 1863 date was hand-punched with four numerals to create this part of die 1056. The letters are not carefully aligned, and the 6 is double-punched.

Detail of die with round-top 3.

Small date on die 1088. Flat-top 3.

Large date on die 1089.

Irregularly aligned letters on dies 330 and 331, probably by the same inexperienced hand, or perhaps the diesinker had too much rum.

Stanton die 1021 with one ray of each star pointed toward the border. The star spacing and alignment varies on this and the next two illustrated dies as do other features. • Points of distinction: Date very low, star 13 points to slightly left of the tip of feather 8. Stars 1–3 widely spaced, stars 6–8 closely spaced. Each die has its own "finger-print" to differentiate it from the others.

Stanton die 1030 with most stars with two rays toward the border, stars 6 and 7 slightly tilted, and some other stars at slightly different angles. • Points of distinction: Date about centered between border and portrait, 1 slightly closer to border, curl over 3. Stars 7, 9, 10, 11 slightly tilted. Star 13 just below tip of feather 8. Stars 1 and 2 more closely spaced than any others.

Stanton die 1033 with two rays toward the border. • Points of distinction: Date high, curl centered over right edge of 4. Star 3 double-punched at the top, star 11 slightly double punched. Star 13 just below tip of feather 8. Stars 1–3 closely spaced, stars 3 and 4 widely spaced, stars 7–11 widely spaced. Tiny die crack from border past star 7. This die was earlier called 1035.

This is the relapped version of 1033. The repunching on star 3 is mostly gone, the date numerals are thinner, and the bottom of the headband was ground away and then strengthened by adding a C-shaped ridge at its end. The tiny die crack past star 7 is still visible.

stars to the feather tips (if a die is relapped the stars will be in the same position, but slightly smaller in size and a bit more distant). Then check stars 1 to 13. Some dies have all the stars with one ray pointing to the border and others with two rays. Others have them every which way. By noting each star comparisons can be made. The star spacing, 1 to 2 to 3, etc., there are often differences. With such study, Stanton dies that look quite similar at first glance will be seen to each have a "personality."

Ornaments. To add to the appeal of dies, various ornaments were often added. These include cinquefoils (five-lobed blossom-like decorations), quatrefoils (four lobes), arrow and spear heads, feathers, Maltese crosses, leaves, branches, wreaths, horns and trumpets, berries, shields, Stars of David, rays of glory, all-seeing eyes, beads, pellets, tiny heads (such as of Washington), blossoms, ribbons, and more. Henry D. Higgins, the maker of "Indiana primitives," had a set of various ornaments that he used in profusion.

Die 399 has a wreath, rays of glory, a six-pointed star, and a five-pointed star.

Henry D. Higgins decorated this "Indiana primitive" die with various ornaments.

THE CURIOUS DIES OF THE FAMILY GIES

In Detroit during the Civil War the firm of F. Gies & Co. and also F. Gies proposed to issue tokens. Fred Gies came to America from Neustadt, Germany, in 1830 with his family. In the early 1860s Fred and brothers Paul and John operated a partnership which installed gravel roofing. Fred Gies on his own was a dealer in groceries, provisions, hay, straw, boots, and shoes. The Cincinnati shop of John Stanton was contacted and two dies with each of the trade styles were made.

Something happened along the way, perhaps spoken directions given to a Stanton representative resulted in a misspelling, or there may be another explanation. On the first attempt for Fred Gies the die was lettered F. GEISS (MI-225-AF-2 to 6). The next try, by altering the die, resulted in the correct F. GIES (MI-225-AG-3 to 7).

Similarly, a die was made with the name as F. GEISS & BRO'S (used for Fuld MI-225-AF-1). The error was seen and an attempted correction was made by effacing part of the old inscription and on the same die changing it to F. GEIS & BRO'S (used for MI-225-AE-1 to 4). This was still wrong, and the die was altered to correctly read F. GIES & BRO'S (MI-225-AG-1 and 2). Stanton was bound to get it right and finally did. This resulted in five different obverses with as many different spellings for only two merchants!

Upon their arrival in Detroit the misspellings were noticed, and a counterstamp punch lettered F. GIES was used to stamp many of the pieces for Gies alone and for the partnership, perhaps to inform the public of the correct name. In addition, some unrelated tokens of other issuers were stamped.[4] In ensuing years the family redeemed the tokens as they were presented. In the 1970s a hoard of over 1,000 pieces came to light in the hands of a descendant. Many were Mint State undistributed pieces, but required conservation to remove "green powdery corrosion" due to improper storage. Some others bore the counterstamps.[5]

THE HERO OF PEA RIDGE

Another example of reworking a die is furnished by a patriotic token from dies by Emil Sigel of New York City. Fuld 180/430d features his brother, Union brigadier general Franz Sigel, on horseback with the inscription HERO OF PEA RIDGE.

The general's time of numismatic glory came at the Battle of Pea Ridge, which took place in the northwestern district of Arkansas on March 7 and 8, 1862, as part of action which began on March 5 and ended on the 8th. Engagements are referred to by histo-

The first and earliest state of the obverse for F. Gies, misspelled as F. GEISS. MI-225-AF-3a. While the die in this state was on hand in the Stanton shop, numismatic strikes were made with reverse dies 1042 (shown), 1046, and 1047. Some circulation strikes were made with 1042 as well.

The second and final state with GIES punched over a mostly effaced GEISS, MI-225-AG-8d. Die combinations include 1018, 1042, and 1069 (as here, a new discovery since the second edition).

The first of three die states for the F. Gies & Brothers die, this misspelled GEISS. MI-225-AF-1a. Reverse die 1042.

The second die state with GEISS altered to read GEIS, but still wrong. MI-225-AE-3a. Reverse die 1042. This die was combined with dies 1037, 1042 (as here), 1043, and 1047, mostly numismatic strikes. Circulation strikes were made in quantity using 1043.

The third and final state with the correct GIES spelling. MI-225-AG-1a. Dies 1037 (as here), 1046, and 1047 were used, the last two for numismatic strikes. Die 1037 was used for circulation strikes in copper with reeded edge (the normal edge style on most Detroit pieces by Stanton) plus numismatic strikes with plain edge.

A counterstamped MI-225-AE-3a from the Gies family hoard. Reverse die 1043.

rians as Bentonville (March 6), Leetown (March 7), and Elkhorn Tavern (March 8). The Confederates generally designated the several days' action under the inclusive title of Battle of Elkhorn Tavern, after a local stopping place which had a pair of elk horns mounted on the front. Sigel's troops, under the overall command of General Samuel R. Curtis, came into battle and, on March 8, routed the Confederates, who had run low on spirit and ammunition. Sigel is said to have seized the opportunity to parade forward on his horse, saber at the fore, in a statuesque pose later memorialized on this token.

The obverse die went through two later reworkings as described below.

NEW DISCOVERIES

The study of die states and characteristics among Civil War store cards is in its infancy, and many discoveries await those with a magnifying glass, intellectual curiosity, and patience. "You can see a lot by just looking," to again quote baseball star and philosopher Yogi Berra.

Since the publication of the second edition of the *U.S. Civil War Store Cards* book in 1975 several hundred new major die varieties have been found—these being hitherto undescribed dies or die combinations. Many but hardly all have been reported in the *Civil War Token Journal*.

This commentary does not include known tokens and medalets described in Russell Rulau's *The Standard Catalog of U.S. Store Cards 1700–1900* or elsewhere, some of which are to be moved into the third edition of *U.S. Civil War Store Cards*.

Emil Sigel's patriotic token 180/430d in its original obverse die state. Reverse die 430 was also combined with patriotic dies 54 and 151; all examples seen by the author show extensive rust as does the illustrated 180/430d.

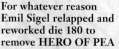 

For whatever reason Emil Sigel relapped and reworked die 180 to remove HERO OF PEA RIDGE (except for a tiny trace of DGE) and to shorten and alter the ground beneath the horse, creating 180/389b. New beads were added to the border. In the process his F. SIGEL caption (for Franz Sigel) became lighter. Reverse die shows slight crumbling on the rim at the upper right.

The relapped obverse die 180 deteriorated and rust developed on the motif, prominent on the horse's mane, the rider's cape, and elsewhere. The die was further reworked, Sigel added his signature deeply into the die, and seven stars were added to the top field to create what is known as 181/343d, with the same reverse die as preceding, now in a later state with more crumbling of the rim and with several small cuds.

Some years ago I was studying the dies made by Joseph Merriam, the Boston diecutter, looking for variations in punches and arrangements. In viewing a series of four store cards issued by C.F. Tuttle's Restaurant in Boston I noticed that the letters around the reverse die were identical on each of the four denominations, 5, 10, 25, and 50 cents. I also noticed that there was a tiny raised circle around the center number visible on some examples. It was but a short leap to conclude that these were *modular* dies. The reverse die with the denomination was placed on the bottom in the coining press and became the anvil die, so called. The obverse die with the steer's head was the hammer or top die.

The reverse die had a perfectly circular hole cut at the center, extending in for a short distance. Into this hole was placed a small circular shallow die with the number 5, 10, 25, or 50 as desired. The denomination could be changed at will. I examined the different denominations of sutler's tokens made for Harvey Lewis, sutler to the 23rd Massachusetts Regiment, and found that the same method had been used. This modular die arrangement is familiar in other numismatic venues such as for inserting names in the official award medals for the World's Columbian Exposition, but this is the first time it had been recognized in the Civil War store card and sutler token series.

Four different denominations made by Joseph Merriam for Tuttle's Restaurant using a common obverse die combined with a modular reverse die into which a small insertion bearing the denomination could change the value. MA-115-G-1a to 4a.

Shortly after the turn of the 21st century Steve Hayden discovered a distinctively different obverse die for H. Dobson, proprietor of the Arcade House in Providence, RI. Although other dies were known for the Arcade House and, separately, Dobson, this is the first time the two names were seen on a single die. Because of this find the third edition of the Fuld book will combine RI-700-A into RI-700-D, the latter being Dobson cards. Adding to the excitement was the pairing with reverse stock die 1147, one of the most popular in the Rhode Island series, said by some to represent Abraham Lincoln. RI-700-A-5a.

Upon discovery a new variety is presumed to be R-10, unique, one and only. However, in many instances the publication of such a variety, especially if from a variant new die (rather than a die combination) will prompt collectors to examine their coins, with the result that an R-10 token often becomes R-9 or even R-8. The finding of a new die sometimes can result in a token being valued into four figures, especially if it "stays rare." The attribution of a new token to a Civil War merchant or, better yet, a town not reported can create a token worth many thousands of dollars, again if it "stays rare."

New discoveries of metallic varieties are important, but do not cause as much excitement. Such can occur when a die combination is known in copper, copper-nickel, and nickel alloy, and one is discovered in white metal.

The Tokens of Yankee Robinson

That each token issuer can have an interesting story is further exemplified by Yankee Robinson, a famous entertainer I have studied for a long time. As noted earlier, a chapter about him appeared in my *More Adventures With Rare Coins* (2002). His Civil War tokens are quite varied, and close study has unraveled some mysteries.

Fayette Lodawick Robinson was born on May 2, 1818, near Avon Mineral Spring in Livingston County, New York. While a teenaged student in his native town, he made his first stage appearance in a school play, essaying the role of Jonathan Doolittle in *A Yankee in England*. This may have inspired his nickname. Seeking a trade he learned shoemaking, but this was not satisfying to him. He loved the circus and on occasion would help with itinerant troupes in the area. In Danville, New York, he set up a traveling show in August 1845, after which he was a circus man for the rest of his life. He was a gifted actor and comedian as well and could take almost any role. For the next decade he usually traveled with his own troupe or another show in the warmer months and was on stage in the winter.

In the winter of 1852–1853 he leased Frank's Museum in Cincinnati and added "Yankee" before his surname, forever after being known as Yankee Robinson. The first Yankee Robinson circus opened in 1854, after which it continued for years, sometimes under different names and with various partners. For several early years the company presented circus acts in the afternoon and *Uncle Tom's Cabin* at nights, becoming the first of hundreds of tent shows to feature the stirring melodrama.

In the meantime the showman developed comic monologues and routines. In 1854 and 1855 he counterstamped thousands of American silver coins, especially half dollars, with the inscription: FREE TICKET TO / YANKEE / ROBINSON'S / QUADRUPLE-SHOW. Anyone finding them could have "free admission" by surrendering this "ticket" at the gate!

In the season of 1859 he started from Charleston, S.C., and went on the road with a large retinue of performers and 60 horses. All went well more or less, but with a name like "Yankee" he met with many complaints. The end came after John Brown's raid on Harper's Ferry, Virginia, in October. After some difficulties, including severe illness of his second wife, Robinson fled to the North. "I had to run away and leave an outfit which cost me $40,000," he stated.[6]

A counterstamped half dollar was a "free ticket" to the Yankee Robinson show, representative of the humor of the showman who called himself "the Great Comedian."

In 1862 Yankee Robinson's Circus incorporated "Three Great Epochs," the past, present, and future, including Civil War battle themes. Late in the year he appeared at the New National Theatre, Washington, D.C., in a military comic drama, *The Times of '76, or The Days That Tried Men's Souls.* This was a great favorite.

In 1863, the year he had John Stanton make store cards, he began the season with newly painted backdrops, a team of 40 horses, and other equipment, and headed west from New York state. All went well at many stops in the Northeast and Midwest.

The "Triad," past, present, and future, was a popular theme and was mentioned on his tokens. Certain varieties were made by the thousands and were popular in their time.

Yankee Robinson store card IL-692-A-1a with his portrait on the obverse and mention of his Triad show on the reverse.

Yankee Robinson store card IL-692-A-12a with 1863 date on another Triad die with the finger pointing to the viewer's right.

The *New York Clipper,* June 6, 1863:

> Yankee Robinson's "Triad" gave a one day show at Watkins, Schuyler Co., N.Y., on the 29th ult.

New York Clipper, July 25, 1863:

> Yankee Robinson's "Triad" was at Valparaiso, Ind. 21st inst., Crown Point 22d, and Momence 23d.

New York Clipper, June 27, 1863:

> Yankee Robinson writes us that his wife is fast recovering from her late severe illness. Yankee says that business is first rate with the "Triad." He has a fine set of scenery, including a handsome drop curtain painted by Hielge and a present from P.T. Barnum. He gives dramatic performances in conjunction with gymnastic and various other kinds of entertainments. On the 16th, he was at Trumansburg, N.Y., steering for the far West.

The very successful season ended with a stand in Peoria, Illinois, where equipment was put into storage. This was as close as a "home base" for the peripatetic Robinson as any location during the Civil War token era.

New York Clipper, November 14, 1863:

> Yankee Robinson, having closed up the season of the "Triad," is now making preparations for a speedy departure to Havana, where he expects to spend the winter, for the benefit of his wife's health, which of late has become very much impaired.

New York Clipper, March 20, 1864:

> The Yankee Robinson goes out as bright and as happy as any of 'em. The Yankee says that he is not at liberty to give a list of his company at present. He says he

starts from Peoria, Ill., about the last of April, with a complete new outfit, and a new chariot built by Quimby & Co., of Newark, N.J. One of his principal features in the ring will be the military equestrian drama of the "Battle of Chattanooga, or, the Storming of Lookout Mountain," in which twenty men and horses take an active part. Twelve Tableaux Vivants will also be performed. Yankee Robinson notifies his company through our columns this week that he expects to meet them at Peoria, Ill., on the 26th of April.

By all accounts the season of 1864 was a success as well. In ensuing years he traveled with his own circus and sometimes with others in the warmer months and was on stage in the winter. In 1867 sheet music for *Yankee Robinson at Bull Run. Grand Skedaddle,* was published. The dedication read, "To my sisters Mary and Fannie, Old Homestead, Richmond, Ontario County, NY."

In 1869 it seems that Robinson took delivery of more cent-sized tokens from William W. Spencer, successor to the John Stanton and Murdock & Spencer businesses. One die dated 1863 was altered to read 1869 by punching a 9 over the last digit. Another token of this year showed a profile portrait of the showman. Circus historians John and Ariel Grant stated that in 1869 "the show took in more money than any other show up to that time."[7]

Robinson continued as a circus man and entertainer for the rest of his life, with his business ranging from insolvency to great success. Such was the story of many American people in the circus. He died in Jefferson, Iowa, on September 4, 1884. The Yankee Robinson name remained in use by others into the 20th century.[8]

The cover of *Yankee Robinson at Bull Run. Grand Skedaddle,* "An original comic Yankee song written and sung thousands of times by the Great Yankee."

Detail from the cover.

Yankee Robinson store card IL-592-A-18d with another Triad die, this dated 1869 and with the finger pointed to the viewer's left. Numismatic strike in copper-nickel.

Yankee Robinson store card IL-692-A-17d with 1869 date on another Triad die with the finger pointing to the viewer's left. The reverse is Stanton's extensively used die 1047 dated 1864, here in die state II with a cud break on the rim below the date. This was a "Rosetta Stone" discovery—revealing that tokens with the 1047 die in later states III to V, which are numerous, were struck no earlier than 1869.

IL-682-A-22d, a numismatic strike with the 1869 Triad die (the 1863 die overdated) in what may be its final die state combined with die 1047 in die state II, another tell-tale token. In its several 1869 combinations all seen have the die cracked.

Store card IA-930-A-2a of H. & G. Goodhue of Waterloo, Iowa, with reverse 1047 in die state V with cancellation cuts in the headdress. This is a numismatic strike rated R-9.

In 1869 a new obverse die with a portrait of Yankee Robinson was combined with several reverses, including some for the numismatic trade. IL-692-A-15d uses a rusted late state of Stanton's reverse die 1018, indicating that it was still in use at that time.

A new Yankee Robinson die with the showman wearing his stovepipe hat and carrying a gun, date 18/69. The illustrated example is a mint error brockage in iron, an unusual metal. It is not known if this die was used to make circulating tokens.

6

PATRIOTIC CIVIL WAR TOKENS

Introduction

As earlier noted, patriotic Civil War tokens comprise one of two large sections in this series, the other being the more numerous store cards. The standard reference is *Patriotic Civil War Tokens* by George Fuld, whose numbers are used in this chapter and elsewhere throughout the text.

Patriotic tokens were front-row center among the new issues of 1863. Although some were made earlier and a few later, this was the year for by far the largest outpouring. Most production was centered in the East with the Scovill Manufacturing Company (presumably), Emil Sigel, and other shops involved. Stanton and Lanphear, the two largest and most important Cincinnati minters, mainly concentrated on store cards and left most patriotic production to others. Only a few tokens were signed with the names or initials of the diesinkers. As most were anonymous, after Civil War tokens were no longer needed in commerce and many merchants redeemed theirs, holders of patriotics had nowhere to go. Accordingly, many remained in circulation for a long time.

Today patriotic tokens are arranged into two main classes. The first and largest is tokens that have portraits or other motifs on the obverse and slogans, emblems, and the like on the reverse, and reflected loyalty to the Union. The other category comprises tokens with a patriotic motif on one side and an inscription or emblem on the other relating to commerce, sometimes referring to a product or service but without the name of a specific merchant. These are sometimes called "half cards." More logically, they belong with store cards. However, they are listed in *Patriotic Civil War Cards* but not in *U.S. Civil War Store Cards*. Many of the half card dies were indeed used with store cards and thus have two Fuld numbers. Both series were arranged by George and Melvin Fuld many years ago with major contributions from Jack Detwiler, Stephen Tanenbaum, and others. The assignments, as illogical as some may seem today, are now part of numismatic tradition.

The French centime design was copied by Robert Lovett Jr. in 1859 and was later used on Civil War tokens by Lovett and other shops.

92

The Fuld text commences with varieties featuring the French Liberty Head as earlier used in France on centimes, an especially popular motif on patriotic Civil War tokens, much more so than on store cards. Several different makers turned out versions of the design. Other feminine heads used included the Conical Cap, Indian Princess, and many variations on the Indian Head.

The very first listing in the *Patriotic Civil War Tokens* book is 1/105 by Emil Sigel combining the French Liberty Head with a reverse showing Washington. The engraver's signature, crude, is below, with E. SIGEL on the left under a star ray, and the incomplete address 177 WILLI under a ray to the right. N.Y. is below. At the time his shop was at 177 William Street. As there are portraits on both sides, tokens of this nature are sometimes nicknamed "double headers." This example is struck in brass.

Patriotic token 20/303a by Emil Sigel. French Liberty Head obverse. On the reverse at the bottom the die is signed ES.

Patriotic token 25/418a is ascribed to George J. Glaubrecht, 95 Fulton Street, New York City, based on study by David Gladfelter.

French Liberty Head token 2/270. The 1864 date is unusual for this design; most are 1863.

The shop of S.D. Childs in Chicago used this familiar S.D. Childs portrait to create political token 31A/375a in copper.

Patriotic Civil War token 3/273 from dies ascribed to Francis X. Koehler of Baltimore, Maryland.

Patriotic token 36/340a is ascribed to George J. Glaubrecht.

Patriotic token 41/337a is thought to be by Charles D. Hörter. Conical Cap Head facing right. The cap is made of a wrapped sash or ribbon. The dies were lightly rusted when the illustrated token was struck. For want of a better descriptive term, Jack R. Detwiler in an article in *JCWTS*, Summer 1969, suggested that this design be called the "Marco Polo" head; the same writer, in the Winter 1970 issue, pointed out that the portrait might have been adapted from American gold coins of the 1795–1807 type.

73/84a combines two popular Stanton Indian Head dies, an illogical muling. The "reverse" is the only die to be dateless and having stars completely encircling the portrait. When used for store cards these two dies are 1028 and 1045.

Patriotic Civil War token 43/387a is boldly signed L. LEICHTWEIS under the distinctively styled portrait.

75/459a, a "half card" with Stanton's Indian Head obverse 75 (a.k.a. 1042 as one of the most popular store card dies). The reverse is die 459 in patriotic use and 1370 when used on a store card.

The Indian Princess design by James B. Longacre, introduced on federal $3 gold coins in 1854, was the inspiration for the obverse of 50/335a from dies ascribed by David Gladfelter to Charles D. Hörter.

91/303a Indian Head with plain headband, probably by either Emil Sigel or Charles D. Hörter.

The Indian Princess 56/161a token is ascribed to Emil Sigel.

96/144a Indian Head with KEY PHILA in the headband. The reverse shows Ulysses S. Grant. This was listed among patriotics for years but is now considered to be NC (non-contemporary). Although Grant was a famous Civil War general, his portrait is not known to have been used on Civil War–related tokens until after the war.

Silver striking over an 1854 Liberty Seated dime for the numismatic trade of 97/389f, an Indian Head with FORT LAFAY in the headband. Ascribed to Emil Sigel. The obverse and reverse when read in combination are a political statement, MILLIONS FOR CONTRACTORS, NOT ONE CENT FOR THE WIDOWS.

Fort Lafayette in New York City harbor was made of stone with a center courtyard and had two levels of openings or windows on the sides, with chimneys protruding from the peaked roofs that covered the quarters on various sides. Many dissidents to the Northern cause were imprisoned in Fort Lafayette during the Civil War in what many complained were overcrowded, unhealthy conditions. During the war the largest number of prisoners at any

one time was 135, of which on at least one occasion, 119 were civilians. Those confined included newspapermen who were viewed as disloyal, privateers for the Confederacy, former Union Army officers who defected to the Southern cause and who were captured, defrauders of the federal government, and a category known as "Maryland prisoners." The latter included Baltimoreans, members of the Maryland State Legislature, and others who were viewed as being dangerous. At the time, the affections of certain Marylanders seemed to waver between North and South.

104/521a is by an unknown issuer. The COPPER MINE TOKEN die may have referred to a mining operation at a location not recorded. The story of this token is a mystery waiting to be solved.

Portraits of presidents, political candidates, military leaders, and other notable figures past and present form another category of patriotic token dies. A few were employed on store cards as well. Washington tokens in particular were made in many combinations.

106/432a (dies 1133 and 1275 when used on store cards) is perhaps by Louis Roloff, if the LR initials below Washington's portrait are his. These dies were used by F.C. Key and Sons, 329 Arch Street, Philadelphia, to strike tokens. The reverse in particular was muled with many dies to create tokens for the numismatic trade.

Patriotic token 113/114a is from dies made and first used before the Civil War.

117/420a has not been ascribed to a specific engraver.

111/340a is from dies ascribed by David Gladfelter to George J. Glaubrecht.

119/360d is ascribed to Emil Sigel. Struck in copper-nickel on a planchet made from a filed-down federal cent with file marks visible on the rim.

126/248a is another Lincoln token for the 1864 campaign, again possibly by Burr.

175/403a is a "primitive" struck by Henry D. Higgins of Mishawaka, Indiana. The obverse depicts Henry K. Brown's equestrian statue of Washington erected in Union Square, New York City, on July 4, 1856. Related dies showing the statue were made by other engravers. Multiple numbers could be assigned to what is now 175 as there are several variations that differ minutely from each other.

133/458b made for the 1864 campaign features Lincoln the railsplitter, evoking his activity as a young man. GOOD FOR ANOTHER HEAT is a horse-track term referring to another race.

Robert Lovett Jr. of Philadelphia made the dies for this 1864 campaign token, 138A/150, featuring General George Brinton McClellan for president and the Honorable J.H. Pendleton for vice president.

Lincoln token 124/295a refers to his 1864 reelection campaign. The issuer has not been confirmed. When used on store cards these dies are known as 1144 and 1245. Obverse dies 124 (a.k.a. store card die 1144) and 125 (not shown here) are different states of the same die; the former has a beaded border and is the earlier state, the latter is a later state with the border beading ground away with a lathe, yielding a plain border.

McClellan token 140/394a notes on the reverse that this is a medal costing one cent, avoiding any criticism that it was intended to pass as a coin. Die 104 is known as 1153 when used with store cards. The letter S below the bust is unattributed (Emil Sigel is not known to have signed dies with S).

This related McClellan "medal," 143/261b, has a reverse very closely approximating a federal cent, perhaps more so than any other Civil War token die. The obverse and reverse inscriptions if read together price the medal at one cent.

Benjamin Franklin token 151/430a is from dies by Emil Sigel and includes one of the subject's sayings on the reverse. When used for store cards the obverse die is known as 1149. The reverse was used only on patriotics.

146-283d. General Ambrose Burnside of Rhode Island, who led troops in the Battle of Antietam, is shown on the obverse in a rare facing-forward portrait style. The letters are by an unknown die cutter who engraved each by hand. The reverse is a stock die. When used for store cards these dies are known as 1159 and 1191. The reverse die was probably made for a button.

Stephen A. Douglas, a popular figure who in 1860 had run for president, is featured on 154/417a by Mossin & Marr of Milwaukee. When used for store cards the dies are known as 1155 and 1272. The reverse was one of the most-used dies in the series and was combined with many obverses to create numismatic specimens.

Military motifs were very popular on Civil War store cards. Subjects include flags, cannon, regalia, the historic USS *Monitor* ironclad, and various inscriptions and slogans.

209/414a features the Union flag and a saying adapted from John Adams Dix, secretary of the Treasury, who on January 21, 1861, wrote to Hemphill Jones, agent for the Treasury in New Orleans, instructing Jones to tell Lieutenant Caldwell, captain of a revenue cutter, "If any one attempts to haul down the American flag, shoot him on the spot." Not long afterward the city was taken over by the Confederacy.

The Union forces were back in command of the city on June 1, 1862, after it had been occupied by Louisiana and Confederate troops for a year. In 1922 David C. Wismer published a booklet, "Varieties of Dix Tokens, 1863," describing 19 known to him. The variety illustrated here, not a rarity, has the humorous SPOOT misspelling.

223/328a is representative of another extensive patriotic series. The illustrated variety has BY instead of the correct BE in the inscription. The saying by Andrew Jackson dates back to the early 19th century when Senator John C. Calhoun of South Carolina threatened to have his state secede from the Union.

229/359d in copper-nickel (dies 1236 and 1252 when used for store cards). Another patriotic token by Emil Sigel, a prolific issuer. He also did a lively business in making off-metal strikes, as here, for the numismatic trade.

OUR LITTLE MONITOR token 239/422b is one of several patriotics featuring the famous Union ironclad.

230/352a with cannon, flags, and regalia on the reverse die. This token is thought to have been made by the Scovill Manufacturing Co. of Waterbury, Connecticut.

The USS *Monitor* ironclad depicted on a die signed C.D.H. for Charles D. Hörter. The obverse die was kept in use for a long time and after having rusted was relapped, only to rust again. It was combined with dies 18, 40, 178, 240, 241, 336, and 350.

233/312a features the United States Capitol. Die 213 is designated 1237 when used with a store card. The reverse was used only on patriotics. Tentatively ascribed to the Scovill Manufacturing Co.

Hörter made another *Monitor* die, this one unsigned, 241. This proved to be a sturdy performer, was used, then rusted (above left), relapped, then rusted again (upper right).

234/431 by Henry D. Higgins, maker of "Indiana primitives," shows his version, but with the misspelled CAPITAL below the building. The details are weak as made. The reverse is one of Higgins's dies with various sayings; this copied from a Higley copper threepence of 1737.

Certain of the higher die numbers among patriotic tokens are quite *miscellaneous*. The legend on this translates from the German to "Remembrance of 1863."

Beyond *miscellaneous* is *completely irrelevant* obverse die 253 combined with a Latin-American plantation token valued at one real (about 12½¢). This obverse was also mated with 125, 127, 248, 294, 295, and 432 to create numismatic pieces. Its original purpose was to fill a foreign order for tokens to be used on a tropical plantation.[1]

332/336d combines two patriotic dies most often used as reverses. Made by Charles D. Hörter.

Charles D. Hörter made the dies for 286/382a (dies known as 1199 and 1263 when used on store cards). The obverse die was made for use on an apothecary scale weight, the unit being equal to 1/16th of an ounce (27.34 grains), which is slightly more than half of the weight of a typical copper Civil War token.

Patriotic Civil War token 433/434b combines two dies by William Bridgens that were most often used as reverses for store cards, in that context as dies 1214 and 1215.

Another scale weight die by Hörter, this for 2 Dwt (2 pennyweight equal to 1/20th of a troy ounce or 24 grains). The obverse SILVER MINE TOKEN die was combined with dies from at least three engravers, and it is not known who created it, another unsolved mystery. The present token is a numismatic strike from a late obverse die state.

449/471b uses two stock reverse dies, the first also known as store card die 1406. The second die was obviously made for a store card, but none are known using it—a mystery.

Francis X. Koehler of Baltimore created this 451C/532b token by combining two dies normally used as reverses. Die 451C was used as the obverse for several Baltimore tokens. Die 532 is also known as store card die 1296 and shows a mug of beer surrounded by a hops vine.

474/475a combines two dies by Henry D. Higgins, maker of "Indiana primitives." These would seem to have been intended as reverses for merchants' tokens, but none are known today. The legends are hardly patriotic—another example of the patriotic category being a catch-all for miscellany.

Rhode Island medalet 481/482a, part of a series combining obverse 481, the seal of Rhode Island, with more than a dozen different reverses, dies 482 to 493C. Most of the dies, including those with hunting and sporting scenes, were probably originally used to make buttons. The Rhode Island Numismatic Association commissioned these to be struck late in 1864 or in early 1865.

Made by an unknown engraver this rare 478/480b token combines dies with motifs of Rhode Island. Neither die is known in any other patriotic combination.

The curious 520/521a is lettered COPPER MINE TOKEN on the obverse, with a value of 1 cent. The reverse takes its design from a Capped Bust silver coin of the early 19th century. The issuer of this enigmatic and rare token is unknown.

Patriotic Civil War Token Varieties

Each die is listed in Fuld number order followed by a brief description. Nearly all are illustrated. If there is an equivalent store card that number is given. The other dies with which the dies are combined are listed. An example is given of the most common or one of the most common varieties using that die, with approximate market values in EF to AU grade and MS-63. The rarity rating is given as well.

Examples with superb eye appeal can bring higher prices, often much higher, and impaired tokens will bring less. Within the Mint State grade MS-60 to MS-62 tokens will bring less. Choice and gem pieces in higher grades can sell for much more as can rarities in metals such as copper-nickel, white metal, nickel alloy, silver, and others, as well as overstrikes, mint errors, and other varieties.

The market for many Civil War tokens is undocumented in some instances, especially for scarce and rare dies and combinations and tokens in very high grades. Accordingly, for a given transaction the market price may vary, even widely. The price estimates are as of late 2014 and will necessarily change as time goes on.

If only circulated examples are known, Mint State listings are not given, and vice-versa.

Omitted numbers, of which there are many, are dies that have been determined by the Civil War Token Society to be non-contemporary, duplicates of other dies, not patriotic, or deleted for other reasons.

The listings are organized as follows:

Patriotic die 0 • *Blank die* • True blank reverse dies with raised rim or with raised rim and beads and dentils in the 519 number series are few and far between. *Caveat:* Most "0" listings I have encountered, including in a stint as the CWTS verification officer, are one or another of these: (1) A mint error caused when an un-struck blank planchet is resting on the anvil die; this has plain surfaces. When another planchet is inserted at the anvil die comes down, the result is a wavy reverse and the first blank planchet is now forced into the anvil die and creates another token with a blank reverse. (2) When a blank planchet is put on a flat surface and struck with a die, such as to test the die. (3) A regular token that has had one side ground off. This is the most often seen "blank reverse" and is of no numismatic value. These are slightly lower weight. *There is no reliable listing of dies that have true blank reverses in the 519 series. Some "0" attributions may be in this category but in-person verification is necessary.*

Patriotic die 1 • *1863 French Liberty Head (13 border stars)* • Die ascribed to Emil Sigel[2] • Same as store card die 1000 • Combined with dies 0 (blank on cent), 105, 198, 229, 359, 360, 391 (some overstruck on cents), 436 (some overstruck on cents) • 1/391 (R-1): EF–AU $25–$40 • MS-63 $50–$75.

Patriotic die 3 • *1863 French Liberty Head (13 border stars, LIBERTY on headband)* • Die ascribed to Francis X. Koehler • Same as store card die 1001 • Combined with dies 273, 464A, 529A • 3/273b (R-6): EF–AU $250–$375 • MS-63 $700–$1,000.

Patriotic die 4 • *1863 French Liberty Head (13 border stars)* • Combined with die 288 • 4/354g (R-7): EF–AU $700–$1,000 • In lead. Only one variety.

Patriotic die 2 • *1864 French Liberty Head (14 border stars)* • Combined with die 270 • 1/270 (R-7): EF–AU $600–$900 • MS-63 $1,500–$2,250.

Patriotic die 5 • *1863 French Liberty Head (13 border stars)* • Combined with 588 • 5/288a (R-2): EF–AU $30–$45 • MS-63 $60–$90 • Also metals b, g, j.

Patriotic die 6B • *1863 French Liberty Head (13 border stars)* • Die ascribed to Frederick B. Smith • Combined with die 308 • 6B/308a (R-4): EF–AU $25–$40 • MS-63 $75–$100 • Only one variety.

Patriotic die 6 • *1863 French Liberty Head (13 border stars)* • Die ascribed to Frederick B. Smith • Combined with die 268 • 6/268a (R-1): EF–AU $25–$40 • MS-63 $50–$75 • Only one variety.

Patriotic die 6C • *1863 French Liberty Head (13 border stars)* • Die ascribed to Frederick B. Smith • Combined with die 314 • 6C/314a (R-5): EF–AU $30–$45 • MS-63 $75–$100 • Only one variety.

Patriotic die 6A • *1863 French Liberty Head (13 border stars)* • Die ascribed to Frederick B. Smith • Combined with die 269 • 6A/269a (R-4): EF–AU $35–$50 • MS-63 $100–$150 • Only one variety.

Patriotic die 6D • *1863 French Liberty Head (13 border stars)* • Die ascribed to Frederick B. Smith • Combined with die 310 • 6D/310a (R-3): EF–AU $35–$50 • MS-63 $100–$150 • Also metal b (R-9).

Patriotic die 7 • *1863 French Liberty Head (13 border stars)* • Die ascribed to Frederick B. Smith • Combined with dies 313 and 315 • 7/313a (R-2): EF–AU $25–$40 • MS-63 $50–$75 • Also 7/315a (R-3).

Patriotic die 8 • *1863 French Liberty Head (13 border stars)* • Die ascribed to Frederick B. Smith • Combined with dies 268 (not confirmed), 309, 314 • 8/314a (R-1): EF–AU $25–$40 • MS-63 $50–$75 • Also 8/309a (R-3).

Patriotic die 7A • *1863 French Liberty Head (13 border stars)* • Die ascribed to Frederick B. Smith • Combined with dies 316 and 317 • 7A/316a (R-3): EF–AU $25–$40 • MS-63 $50–$75.

Patriotic die 8A • *1863 French Liberty Head (13 border stars)* • Combined with die 317 • 8A/317a (R-2): EF–AU $25–$40 • MS-63 $50–$75 • Only one variety.

Patriotic die 7B • *1863 French Liberty Head (13 border stars)* • Die ascribed to Frederick B. Smith • Combined with dies 313 and 315 • 7B/315a (R-7): EF–AU $35–$50 • MS-63 $75–$100 • Also 7B/313a (R-8).

Patriotic die 8B • *1863 French Liberty Head (13 border stars)* • Combined with die 309 • 8B/309a (R-2): EF–AU $25–$40 • MS-63 $50–$75 • Only one variety.

Patriotic die 8C • *1863 French Liberty Head (13 border stars)* • Combined with die 313 • 8C/313a (R-3): VF–EF $25–$40 • MS-63 $50–$75 • Only one variety.

Patriotic die 10 • *1863 French Liberty Head (13 border stars)* • Die by the Scovill Manufacturing Co. (?) • Same as store card die 1002 • Combined with dies 298 and 312 • 10/312a (R-1): EF–AU $25–$40 • MS-63 $50–$75.

Patriotic die 9 • *1863 French Liberty Head (13 border stars; some border beads missing at upper left)* • Die ascribed to Henry D. Higgins ("Indiana primitive") • Same as store card die 1003.[3] • Combined with dies 85, 211, 238, 298A, 400, 405, 431 • 9/211a (R-6): EF–AU $150–$225 • MS-63 $400–$600 • This is the die illustrated as 9 by Fuld.

Patriotic die 11 • *1863 French Liberty Head (13 border stars)* • Die by the Scovill Manufacturing Co. (?) • Combined with dies 298 and 312 • 11/298a (R-1): EF–AU $25–$40 • MS-63 $50–$75.

Patriotic die 9A • *1863 French Liberty Head (13 border stars, border beads complete)* • Combined with dies 404, 406, 407, and to strike IN-530-B-1 • 9A/406a (R-6): EF–AU $250–$375 • MS-63 $700–$1,000 • 9A/407a is also R-6 • This variety is not illustrated in the fifth edition of Fuld and is now designated as 9A.

Patriotic die 12 • *1863 French Liberty Head (13 border stars)* • Die by the Scovill Manufacturing Co. (?) • Combined with dies 297 and 351 • 12/297a (R-2): EF–AU $25–$40 • MS-63 $50–$75.

Patriotic die 13 • *1863 French Liberty Head (13 border stars)* • Die by the Scovill Manufacturing Co. (?) • Combined with die 297 • 12/297a (R-2): EF–AU $25–$40 • MS-63 $50–$75 • Also metals b, g.

Patriotic die 16 • *1863 French Liberty Head (13 border stars)* • Die ascribed to Louis Leichtweis • Combined with dies 300, 301, 353 • 16/300a (R-3): EF–AU $25–$40 • MS-63 $60–$90.

Patriotic die 14 • *1863 French Liberty Head (13 border stars)* • Combined with die 297 • Die by the Scovill Manufacturing Co. (?) • 14/297a (R-5): EF–AU $50–$75 • MS-63 $125–$175 • Also metals b, g.

Patriotic die 17 • *1863 French Liberty Head (13 border stars)* • Die ascribed to Louis Leichtweis • Combined with die 388 • 17/388 (R-2): EF–AU $25–$40 • MS-63 $50–$75 • Only one variety.

Patriotic die 15 • *1863 French Liberty Head (13 border stars)* • Combined with die 319 • 15/319a (R-2): EF–AU $25–$40 • MS-63 $50–$75 • Also metals b, d, e, f (including over a dime), i.

Patriotic die 18 • *1863 French Liberty Head (13 border stars)* • Die ascribed to Louis Leichtweis • Same as store card die 1004 • Combined with dies 300, 304, 305, 337, 353 • 18/300a (R-2): EF–AU $25–$40 • MS-63 $50–$75.

Patriotic die 19 • *1863 French Liberty Head (13 border stars)* • Same as store card die 1005A. Combined with die 396 • 19/396a (R-2): EF–AU $25–$40 • MS-63 $50–$75 • Also metal b (R-4).

Patriotic die 22 • *1863 French Liberty Head (13 border stars)* • Same as store card die 1005 • Combined with dies 418 and 422 • 22/422a (R-2): EF–AU $25–$40 • MS-63 $50–$75.

Patriotic die 23 • *1863 French Liberty Head (13 border stars)* • Combined with dies 271 and 306 • 23/306a (R-2): EF–AU $25–$40 • MS-63 $50–$75.

Patriotic die 20 • *1863 French Liberty Head (13 border stars)* • Die ascribed to Emil Sigel • Combined with dies 303, 318, 384 • 20/303a (R-3): EF–AU $30–$50 • MS-63 $125–$175.

Patriotic die 24 • *1863 French Liberty Head (13 border stars)* • Combined with die 246 • 24/246a (R-2): EF–AU $30–$50 • MS-63 $100–$150 • Also metal b (R-6).

Patriotic die 21 • *French Liberty Head (undated; 13 border stars)* • Combined with die 170 • 21/170a (R-10): VF $10,000–$15,000 • Also metal e (R-10) • Only two known (Fuld, fifth edition, p. 288).

Patriotic die 25 • *1863 French Liberty Head (13 border stars)* • Combined with die 418 • 25/418s (R-4): EF–AU $30–$50 • MS-63 $90–$135 • Also metal b (R-7) and over a copper-nickel cent (R-10).

Patriotic die 26 • *1863 French Liberty Head (13 border stars)* • Combined with die 418 • 26/418a (R-2): EF–AU $25–$40 • MS-63 $60–$90 • Also metals b, do (on copper-nickel cent), g, j.

Patriotic die 29 • *1863 French Liberty Head (13 border stars)* • Die ascribed to Emil Sigel • Combined with die 303 • 29/303a (R-2): EF–AU $25–$40 • MS-63 $50–$75 • Also metal b (R-6).

Patriotic die 27 • *1863 French Liberty Head (13 border stars)* • Die ascribed to Emil Sigel • Combined with die 365 • 27/365a (R-3): EF–AU $25–$40 • MS-63 $75–$110 • Only one variety.

Patriotic die 30 • *1863 Coronet Head (13 border stars)* • Same as store card die 1101 • Combined with die 280 • 30/280j (R-9; two known, both VF): VF $4,000–$6,000 • Although this die is exceedingly rare on a political token it is easily enough found on a store card.

Patriotic die 28 • *1863 French Liberty Head (13 border stars)* • Die ascribed to Emil Sigel • Combined with die 303 • 28/303a (R-2): EF–AU $25–$40 • MS-63 $50–$75 • Also metal b (R-5).

Patriotic die 30A • *1863 Coronet Head (13 border stars)* • Same as store card die 1097 • Combined with die 277 • 30A/277Ab (R-10): VF $4,000–$6,000, such an estimate being theoretical • Although this die is rare on a political token it is easily enough found on a store card.

Patriotic die 31 • *1863 Coronet Head (13 border stars)* • Same as store card die 1094 • Combined with dies 183A, 279, 447A • 31/279a (R-6): EF–AU $100–$150 • MS-63 $250–$375.

Patriotic die 33 • *1863 Coronet Head (13 border stars UNION above)* • Same as store card die 1105 • Combined with dies 275 and 534 • 33/275a (R-7): EF–AU $125–$200 • MS-63 NA.

Patriotic die 31A • *1863 Coronet Head (13 border stars)* • Same as store card die 1099 • Combined with die 275 and 280A • 31A/275a (R-7): EF–AU $250–$375 • Also 31A/280Aa (R-10).

Patriotic die 34 • *1863 Coronet Head (14 border stars UNION)* • Same as store card die 1106 • Combined with dies 275, 276, 277, 278, 279 • 34/277a (R-3): EF–AU $30–$50 • MS-63 $60–$90.

Patriotic die 32 • *1863 Coronet Head (13 border stars)* • Same as store card die 1095 • Combined with die 275 • 32/275a (R-6): EF–AU $50–$75 • Only one variety.

Patriotic die 35 • *1864 Coronet Head (13 border stars UNION in field)* • Die ascribed to S.D. Childs • Same as store card die 1107 • Combined with dies 265, 274, 277, 278 • 35/265a (R-4): EF–AU $30–$50 • MS-63 $100–$150.

Patriotic die 36 • *1863 Cloaked Head Left (LIBERTY AND NO SLAVERY)* • Die ascribed to George J. Glaubrecht • Combined with dies 271, 340, 432 • 36/340a (R-2): EF–AU $50–$75 • MS-63 $125–$200.

Patriotic die 38A • *1863 Mercury Head (12 border stars)* • Ascribed to the shop of William K. Lanphear, die by Frederick W. Lutz • Same as store card die 1123 • Combined with die 0 • 38A/0 (R-9): EF–AU $2,500–$3,700 • Although this die is rare on a political token it is easily enough found on a store card.

Patriotic die 37 • *1863 French Liberty Head (FOR PUBLIC ACCOMODATION)* • Die ascribed to William H. Bridgens. Should be spelled ACCOMMODATION • Same as store card die 1006 • Combined with dies 0, 255, 256, 434 • 37/434a (R-1): EF–AU $25–$40 • MS-63 $50–$75.

Patriotic die 38B • *1863 Mercury Head (14 border stars)* • Ascribed to the shop of William K. Lanphear, die by Frederick W. Lutz • Same as store card die 1126 • Combined with die 424 • 38B/424a (R-10) • MS-63 $6,000–$9,000 • Although this die is rare on a political token it is easily enough found on a store card.

Patriotic die 38 • *1863 Mercury Head (13 border stars)* • Ascribed to the shop of William K. Lanphear, die by Frederick W. Lutz • Same as store card die 1124 • Combined with dies 0 and 438 • 38/438a (R-9): EF–AU $3,500–$5,000 • MS-63 $6,000–$9,000 • Also 38/0a (R-10), 38/438d (R-9). Although this die is rare on a political token it is easily enough found on a store card.

Patriotic die 39 • *1863 Mercury Head (13 border stars)* • Die Ascribed to the shop of William K. Lanphear, die by Frederick W. Lutz • Same as store card die 1127 • Combined with die 448 • 39/448a (R-9): EF–AU $4,000–$6,000 • MS-63 $8,000–$12,000 • Although this die is rare on a political token it is easily enough found on a store card.

Patriotic die 40 • *Mercury Head (13 border stars)* • Ascribed to the shop of William K. Lanphear, die by Frederick W. Lutz • Same as store card die 1122 • Combined with die 193 • 40/193a (R-9): EF–AU $4,000–$6,000 • MS-63 $8,000–$12,000 • Also metal b (R-9). Although this die is rare on a political token it is easily enough found on a store card.

Patriotic die 43 • *1863 Leichtweis Head (13 border stars)* • Dies by Louis Leichtwis • Combined with dies 387 and 388 • 43/388a (R-2): EF–AU $25–$40 • MS-63 $50–$75.

Patriotic die 41 • *1863 Conical Cap Head (14 border stars)* • Dies by Charles D. Hörter • Combined with dies 178, 240, 267, 337, 341, 342 • 41/337a (R-2): EF–AU $25–$40 • MS-63 $50–$75.

Patriotic die 45 • *1863 Conical Cap Head (12 border stars; LIBERTY)* • Dies by Charles D. Hörter • Combined with dies 332, 350, 432 • 45/332a (R-1): EF–AU $25–$40 • MS-63 $50–$75.

Patriotic die 42 • *1864 Conical Cap Head (14 border stars)* • Charles D. Hörter • Combined with dies 0 and 336 • 42/336a (R-4): EF–AU $35–$50 • MS-63 $100–$150 • 42/0 (R-10), 42/336 also metals b, d, e, f.

Patriotic die 46 • *1864 Conical Cap Head (10 border stars [5x5]; LIBERTY)* • Dies by Charles D. Hörter • Combined with dies 335 and 339 • 46/339a (R-1): EF–AU $25–$40 • MS-63 $50–$75.

Patriotic die 47 • *1864 Conical Cap Head (12 border stars [6x6]; LIBERTY)* • Dies by Charles D. Hörter • Combined with die 332 • 47/332a (R-1): EF–AU $25–$40 • MS-63 $50–$75 • Also metals ao (over CWT), b, d, e, f, j.

Patriotic die 50 • *Indian Princess (12 border stars)* • Dies by Charles D. Hörter • Combined with dies 179, 335, 342 • 50/335a (R-2): EF–AU $25–$40 • MS-63 $50–$75.

Patriotic die 51 • *Indian Princess (13 border stars)* • Dies by Charles D. Hörter • Combined with dies 0, 333, 334, 342, 342A • 51/334a (R-1): EF–AU $25–$40 • MS-63 $50–$75 • 51/342a is also R-1.

Patriotic die 48 • *1863 Conical Cap Head (UNITED WE STAND DIVIDED WE FALL)* • Dies by Charles D. Hörter • Combined with die 299 • 48/299a (R-1): EF–AU $25–$40 • MS-63 $50–$75 • Only one variety.

Patriotic die 53 • *Indian Princess (12 border stars)* • Dies by Charles D. Hörter • Combined with dies 179 and 336 • 53/336a (R-1): EF–AU $25–$40 • MS-63 $50–$75.

Patriotic die 49 • *Indian Princess (12 border stars)* • Dies by Charles D. Hörter • Combined with die 343 • 49/343a (R-1): EF–AU $25–$40 • MS-63 $50–$75 • Also metals b, c.

Patriotic die 54 • *Indian Princess (12 border stars)* • Dies by Charles D. Hörter • Combined with dies 179, 296, 335, 342, 343, 343A, 430 • 54/342a (R-1): EF–AU $25–$40 • MS-63 $50–$75.

Patriotic die 57 • *1862 Indian Head left (13 border stars; LIBERTY on headband)* • From the shop of John Stanton • Same as store card die 1009 • Combined with dies 185, 467, 473 • 57/467a (R-7): EF–AU $1,000–$1,500 • MS-63 $2,000–$3,000 • 57/473a is also R-7 • Although this die is rare on a political token it is easily enough found on a store card.

Patriotic die 55 • *1864 Indian Princess (12 border stars)* • Die ascribed to Emil Sigel • Combined with die 162 • 55/162 (R-1): EF–AU $25–$40 • MS-63 $50–$75 • Only one variety.

Patriotic die 57A • *1862 Indian Head left (13 border stars; LIBERTY on headband)* • From the shop of John Stanton • Same as store card die 1008 • Combined with dies 444 and 473 • 57A/473a (R-9): EF–AU $3,000–$4,500 • MS-63 $5,000–$7,500 • Although this die is rare on a political token it is easily enough found on a store card.

Patriotic die 56 • *1864 Indian Princess (13 border stars)* • Die ascribed to Emil Sigel • Same as store card die 1073 • Combined with dies 161, 162, 229, 436 • 56/161a (R-5): EF–AU $100–$150 • MS-63 $200–$300.

Patriotic die 57B • *1862 Indian Head left (13 border stars; LIBERTY on headband)* • From the shop of John Stanton • Same as store card die 1007 • Not known with another die; the single example is a mint error with incuse reverse • 57B (R-10): EF–AU $5,000–$7,500 • Although this die is rare on a political token it is easily enough found on a store card.

Patriotic die 58 • *1863 Indian Head left (13 border stars; LIBERTY on headband; L. ROLOFF)* • Die ascribed to Louis Roloff • Same as store card die 1010 • Combined with dies 439 and 439A • 58/439a (R-3): EF–AU $75–$110 • MS-63 $200–$300.

Patriotic die 60 • *1863 Indian Head left (21 beads on headband; E.S. above 18)* • Die ascribed to Emil Sigel • Same as store card die 1015 • Combined with dies 0, 200, 346 • 60/346a (R-5): EF–AU $100–$150 • MS-63 $250–$375.

Patriotic die 58A • *1863 Indian Head left (13 border stars; LIBERTY on headband; L. ROLOFF)* • Die ascribed to Louis Roloff • Combined with dies 255 and 434 • 58A/255a (R-10): EF–AU $4,000–$6,000 • MS-63 $6,000–$9,000 • The other variety, 58A/434a, is also R-10 • Classic rarities in the patriotic series.

Patriotic die 61 • *1863 Indian Head left (13 border stars; 17 beads on headband; E.S. faint below last feather)* • Die ascribed to Emil Sigel • Same as store card die 1016 • Combined with dies 105, 198, 355 • 61/198a (R-3): EF–AU $30–$50 • MS-63 $60–$90 • 61/355a is also R-3.

Patriotic die 59 • *1863 Indian Head left (13 border stars; 6 stars on headband)* • Combined with dies 385 to 453 • 59/385a (R-2): EF–AU $40–$60 • MS-63 $125–$175.

Patriotic die 62 • *1863 Indian Head left (13 border stars; 16 beads on headband; E.S. above right of 3)* • Die ascribed to Emil Sigel • Combined with dies 367 and 369 • 62/367a (R-3): EF–AU $25–$40 • MS-63 $50–$75 • *Former die 62A, now delisted, is the same as die 62.*

Patriotic die 63 • *1863 Indian Head left (13 border stars; 17 beads on headband)* • Die ascribed to Emil Sigel • Combined with dies 366 and 443 • 63/366a (R-1): EF–AU $25–$40 • MS-63 $50–$75.

Patriotic die 66 • *1863 Indian Head left (13 border stars; 16 beads on headband)* • Die ascribed to Emil Sigel • Combined with die 370 • 66/370a (R-2): EF–AU $25–$40 • MS-63 $50–$75 • Also 66/370b (R-8).

Patriotic die 64 • *1863 Indian Head left (12 border stars; 16 beads on headband)* • Die ascribed to Emil Sigel, struck by Charles D. Hörter • Combined with die 362 • 64/362a (R-4): EF–AU $60–$90 • MS-63 $200–$300 • Also metals b, d.

Patriotic die 67 • *1863 Indian Head left (13 border stars; 14 beads on headband)* • Die ascribed to Emil Sigel • Combined with dies 0 and 372 • 67/372d (R-5): EF–AU $90–$135 • MS-63 $200–$300 • Usually well worn, one of only a handful of circulating copper-nickel Civil War tokens. Many are struck over other tokens. Several unique overstrikes are in the collection of the American Numismatic Society.

Patriotic die 65A • *1863 Indian Head left (13 border stars; 12 beads on headband)* • Die ascribed to Emil Sigel • Combined with die 65A • 65A/371a (R-6): EF–AU $60–$90 • MS-63 $125–$175 • Only one variety.

Patriotic die 68 • *1863 Indian Head left (13 border stars; 16 beads on headband)* • Die ascribed to Emil Sigel • Same as store card die 1017 • Combined with dies 105, 119, 198, 199, 355, 359, 350, 371 • 68/198a (R-4): EF–AU $35–$50 • MS-63 $100–$150 • 68/355a is also R-4.

Patriotic die 68A • *1863 Indian Head left (13 border stars; 17 beads on headband; truncation of bust scarcely exceeds necklace)* • Die ascribed to Emil Sigel • Combined with die 371 • 68A/371 (R-3): EF–AU $30–$50 • MS-63 $90–$135 • Also metal d (R-8).

Patriotic die 70A • *1863 Indian Head left (13 border stars; LIBERTY on headband)* • From the shop of John Stanton • Same as store card die 1043 • Combined with die 475A • 70A/475a (R-10): EF–AU $6,000–$9,000 • Although this die is rare on a political token it is easily enough found on a store card.

Patriotic die 69 • *1863 Indian Head left (13 border stars; 17 beads on headband)* • Combined with dies 261, 269, 367, 369 • 69/369a (R-3): EF–AU $25–$40 • MS-63 $50–$75.

Patriotic die 71 • *1863 Indian Head left (13 border stars; LIBERTY on headband)* • From the shop of John Stanton • Same as store card die 1019 • Combined with dies 72A, 148, 182, 183, 281, 444, 452, 455, 456, 469, 473 • 71/467a (R-9): EF–AU $1,500–$2,250 • MS-63 $3,000–$4,500 • Many other varieties, mostly R-9, some R-10. Although this die is rare on a political token it is easily enough found on a store card.

Patriotic die 70 • *1863 Indian Head left (13 border stars; LIBERTY on headband)* • From the shop of John Stanton • Same as store card die 1038 • Combined with dies 281, 444, 452, 456 • 70/281a (R-6): EF–AU $250–$375 • MS-63 $600–$900.

Patriotic die 71A • *1863 Indian Head left (13 border stars; LIBERTY on headband)* • From the shop of John Stanton • Same as store card die 1018 • Combined with dies 71 (as reverse) 76, 76A • 71A/76d (R-10): MS-63 $6,000–$9,000 • Other combinations are also R-10 • Although this die is rare on a political token it is easily enough found on a store card.

Patriotic die 72A • *1863 Indian Head left (13 border stars; LIBERTY on headband)* • From the shop of John Stanton • Combined with dies 0 and 71 (as reverse) • 72A/0 (R-10): EF–AU $3,000–$4,500 • Also 71/72Aa (R-10).

Patriotic die 73A • *1863 Indian Head left (13 border stars; LIBERTY on headband)* • From the shop of John Stanton • Used as reverse with dies 71, 72B, 76 • 72B/73A (R-10): EF–AU $4,000–$6,000 • Also 71/73Aa (R-10).

Patriotic die 72B • *1863 Indian Head left (13 border stars; LIBERTY on headband)* • From the shop of John Stanton • Combined with die 73A • 72B/73A (R-10): EF–AU $4,000–$6,000.

Patriotic die 74 • *1863 Indian Head left (13 border stars; LIBERTY on headband)* • From the shop of John Stanton • Same as store card die 1030 • Combined with dies 0, 73 (as reverse), 84 • 73/74a (R-8): EF–AU $5,000–$7,500 • Although this die is rare on a political token it is easily enough found on a store card.

Patriotic die 73 • *1863 Indian Head left (13 border stars; LIBERTY on headband)* • From the shop of John Stanton • Same as store card die 1028 • Combined with dies 74, 84. 525 (formerly OH-175-C-13a) • 73/525a (R-4): EF–AU $100–$150 • MS-63 $250–$375.

Patriotic die 75 • *1863 Indian Head left (13 border stars; LIBERTY on headband)* • From the shop of John Stanton • Same as store card die 1042 • Combined with dies 459 and 467 • 75/459a (R-8): EF–AU $300–$450 • MS-63 $900–$1,350 • Other varieties are R-8 or R-9 • Although this die is rare on a political token it is easily enough found on a store card.

Patriotic die 76 • *1864 Indian Head left (13 border stars; LIBERTY on headband)* • From the shop of John Stanton or successors • Same as store card die 1046 • Combined with dies 444, 456A, 456B, 473, 522 (was OH-74-A-14a reeded edge), 523 (was OH-175-O-5a reeded edge), • 76/523a (R-4): EF–AU $125–$175.

Patriotic die 78 • *1863 Indian Head left (9 border stars; 7 diamonds on headband)* • Same as store card die 1051 • Combined with die 330 • 78/330a (R-4): EF–AU $40–$60 • MS-63 $125–$175 • Only one variety.

Patriotic die 76A • *1864 Indian Head left (13 border stars; LIBERTY on headband)* • From the shop of John Stanton or successors • Same as store card die 1047 • Combined with dies 71A (as reverse), 522 (was OH-74-A-15a reeded edge) • 71A/76Ad (R-10): MS-63 $6,000–$9,000 • Although this die is rare on a political token it is easily enough found on a store card.

Patriotic die 79 (early state of die 81) • *1863 Indian Head left (13 border stars; LIBERTY on headband)* • Die by the Scovill Manufacturing Co. (?) • Combined with dies 0, 297, 351 • 79/351a (R-1): EF–AU $25–$40 • MS-63 $50–$75.

Patriotic die 80 • *1863 Indian Head left (13 border stars; LIBERTY on headband)* • Die by the Scovill Manufacturing Co. (?) • Combined with die 351 • 80/351a (R-2): EF–AU $25–$40 • MS-63 $60–$90 • Also metals b (R-8), d (R-10).

Patriotic die 77 • *1863 Indian Head left (10 border stars; 7 diamonds on headband)* • Combined with die 331 • 77/331a (R-4): EF–AU $35–$50 • MS-63 $100–$150.

Patriotic die 81 (late state of die 79; altered die) • *1863 Indian Head left (13 border stars; 17 beads on headband)* • Die by the Scovill Manufacturing Co. (?) • Combined with die 351 • 81/351a (R-2): EF–AU $25–$40 • MS-63 $50–$75 • Also 81/351b (R-8).

Patriotic die 84 • *Indian Head left (undated; 18 stars in border; LIBERTY on headband)* • Die ascribed to the shop of John Stanton • 74 (as reverse), 84 (as reverse), 148, 444 • 84/148a (R-7): EF–AU $600–$900 • MS-63 $1,500–$2,250.

Patriotic die 82 • *1863 Indian Head left (13 border stars; 13 beads in headband)* • Die by the Scovill Manufacturing Co. (?) • Combined with dies 351 and 352A • 82/351a (R-2): EF–AU $25–$40 • MS-63 $50–$75 • Also 81/352a (R-2).

Patriotic die 85 • *1863 Indian Head left (12 border stars; wavy line on headband)* • Die ascribed to Henry D. Higgins ("Indiana primitive") • Same as store card die 1049 • Combined with dies 9 (as reverse) and 431 • 85/431 (R-8): EF–AU $600–$900 • Although this die is rare on a political token it is easily enough found on a store card.

Patriotic die 83 • *Indian Head (13 border stars; LIBERTY on headband; L below neck)* • Combined with die 264 • 83/264a (R-5): EF–AU $75–$125 • MS-63 $250–$375 • Also metal b (R-9).

Patriotic die 86 • *1863 Indian Head left (13 border stars; plain headband)* • Dies by Charles D. Hörter • Same as store card die 1053 • Combined with dies 357A and 357B • 86/357a (R-2): EF–AU $25–$40 • MS-63 $50–$75.

Patriotic die 87 • *1863 Indian Head left (13 border stars; plain headband)* • Dies by Charles D. Hörter • Combined with die 356 • 87/356a (R-1): EF–AU $25–$40 • MS-63 $50–$75 • Also metal b (R-7).

Patriotic die 91 • *1863 Indian Head left (13 border stars; plain headband)* • Dies by Charles D. Hörter, struck by Emil Sigel) • Combined with dies 303, 373, 432, and 435 • 91/303a (R-3): EF–AU $25–$40 • MS-63 $60–$90.

Patriotic die 88 • *1863 Indian Head left (13 border stars; two rows of beads on headband)* • Same as store card die 1054 • Combined with dies 361 and 362 • 388/361a (R-3): EF–AU $25–$40 • MS-63 $100–$150.

Patriotic die 92 • *1863 Indian Head left (13 border stars; plain headband)* • Dies by Charles D. Hörter, struck by Emil Sigel) • Same as store card die 1052 • Combined with dies 105, 119, 198, 199, 440 • 92/199a (R-3): EF–AU $30–$50 • MS-63 $100–$150.

Patriotic die 90 • *1863 Indian Head left (13 border stars; plain headband)* • Dies by Charles D. Hörter • Combined with die 364 • 90/364a (R-1): EF–AU $30–$50 • MS-63 $60–$90 • Also metals b (R-8), g (R-9).

Patriotic die 93 • *1863 Indian Head left (13 border stars; plain headband; H above date)* • Dies by Charles D. Hörter • Combined with dies 362 and 364 • 93/362a (R-2): EF–AU $25–$40 • MS-63 $50–$75 • Also 93/394a (R-3).

Patriotic die 94 • *1863 Indian Head left (13 border stars; plain headband)* • Dies by Charles D. Hörter • Combined with die 363 • 94/363a (R-6): EF–AU $150–$225 • MS-63 $350–$500 • Only one variety.

Patriotic die 96A • *Indian Head left (undated; 13 border stars; KEY PHILA)* • From the shop of F.C. Key & Sons • Combined with die 131A • 96A/131Aa (R-8): MS-63 $1,000–$1,500 • Also metals b and j, each R-8 • Numismatic strikes.

Patriotic die 95 • *1863 Indian Head left (13 stars on raised band at border)* • Die ascribed to Emil Sigel • Combined with dies 0 and 368 • 95/368a (R-2): EF–AU $25–$40 • MS-63 $50–$75.

Patriotic die 97 • *1863 Indian Head left (MILLIONS FOR CONTRACTORS in field; FORT LAFAYE on headband)* • Die ascribed to Emil Sigel • Combined with dies 261 and 389 • 97/389a (R-2): EF–AU $40–$60 • MS-63 $110–$175.

Patriotic die 96 • *1864 Indian Head left (13 border stars; KEY PHILA on headband)* • From the shop of F.C. Key & Sons • Same as store card die 1048 • Combined with dies 116, 129, 284, 368 • 96/116a (R-8): EF–AU $300–$450 • MS-63 $750–$1,000 • Others are R-8 and R-9 • Although this die is rare on a political token it is easily enough found on a store card.

Patriotic die 98 • *1863 Indian Head left (UNION AND LIBERTY; 14 beads on headband; 2 stars at border)* • Die ascribed to Emil Sigel • Combined with die 291 • 98/291a (R-5): EF–AU $50–$75 • MS-63 $125–$175 • Only one variety.

Patriotic die 99 • *1863 Indian Head left (UNION AND LIBERTY)* • Combined with die 292 • 99/292a (R-3): EF–AU $50–$75 • MS-63 $150–$225 • Also metal b (R-8).

Patriotic die 100B • *1863 Indian Head left (UNITED WE STAND)* • Dies by Charles D. Hörter • Combined with die 0 • 100B/0a (R-10): MS-63 $2,000–$3,000.

Patriotic die 100 • *1863 Indian Head left (UNITED WE STAND; plain headband)* • Dies by Charles D. Hörter • Combined with die 341 • 100/341a (R-7): EF–AU $100–$150 • MS-63 $250–$375 • Only one variety.

Patriotic die 101 • *1861 Indian Head (BUSINESS CARD)* • Die ascribed to A.W. Escherich • Same as store card die 1072 • Combined with die 263 • 101/263 (R-7): EF–AU $1,000–$1,500 • Only one variety.

Patriotic die 101A • *Description not available* • Combined with die 0 • 101A/0a (R-10) • Not illustrated in Fuld nor is any die description given.

Patriotic die 100A • *1863 Indian Head left (UNITED WE STAND)* • Dies by Charles D. Hörter • Unique strike in ANS with obverse and reverse being the same, per Fuld.

Patriotic die 102A • *1863 Indian Head left (13 border stars)* • Combined with die 345A • 102A/345A (R-9): MS-63 $6,000–$9,000 • Ex Stephen L. Tanenbaum Collection.

Patriotic die 103 • *Indian Head left (undated; plain field; 17 beads on headband?)* • Die ascribed to Emil Sigel • Same as store card die 1074 • Combined with dies 293 and 375 • 103/293a (R-6): EF–AU $60–$90 • MS-63 $200–$300 • Also 103/375a (R-4).

Patriotic die 103A • *Indian Head left (undated; plain field; plain headband)* • Known only as a mint error brockage with incuse reverse • 103A/103Aa (R-10): MS-63 $6,000–$9,000.

Patriotic die 104 • *Indian Head left (undated; plain field; LIBERTY on headband)* • Die ascribed to A.W. Escherich • Combined with dies 263 and 521 • 104/263 (R-5): EF–AU $125–$175 • MS-63 $350–$500 • Also 104/521a (R-9).

Patriotic die 105 • *Washington portrait within five-pointed star (Sigel signature and address below)* • Die ascribed to Emil Sigel • Combined with dies 1 (as reverse), 61 (as reverse), 68 (as reverse), 92 (as reverse), 196, 198, 199, 229, 355, 358, 359, 360, 391, 436 • 105/355a (R-3): EF–AU $35–$50 • MS-63 $100–$150 • Many varieties, mostly rare numismatic strikes.

Patriotic die 106 • *Washington portrait facing right (13 border stars; L.R)* • Same as store card die 1133 • Combined with die 432 • 106/432do (R-4): EF–AU $125–$175 • MS-63 $300–$450 • The copper-nickel variety struck over a Brimelow store card is a circulation strike. Also metals b, e, do (multiples), e, f, these being rare numismatic strikes.

Patriotic die 107 • *1863 Washington portrait facing right (13 border stars); shallow relief, contemporary copy die* • Combined with dies 108, 271, 432 • 107/432a (R-1): EF–AU $30–$45 • MS-63 $60–$90.

Patriotic die 108 • *1863 Washington portrait facing right (13 border stars)* • Combined with dies 107 (as reverse) and 201 • 108/201a (R-3): EF–AU $25–$40 • MS-63 $50–$75.

Patriotic die 110 • *1863 Washington portrait facing right (12 border stars)* • Die ascribed to George J. Glaubrecht • Combined with dies 271 and 442 • 110/442a (R-1): EF–AU $25–$40 • MS-63 $50–$75 • Also 110/271a (R-9).

Patriotic die 113 • *Washington portrait facing left (PATER PATRIÆ)* • Die by George H. Lovett. Used on an 1860 store card issued by Augustus B. Sage (Baker-571) • Combined with dies 0 (thick planchet, possibly a die trial?), 114A, 127, 294, 432, and 537 • 113/114Aa (R-8): MS-63 $1,000–$1,500 • Numismatic strikes, some pre-war.

Patriotic die 111 • *1863 Washington portrait facing right (13 border stars)* • Die ascribed to George J. Glaubrecht • Combined with dies 271 and 340 • 111/271a (R-3): EF–AU $25–$40 • MS-63 $50–$75 • 111/340a is also R-3.

Patriotic die 114 • *Washington portrait facing left (plain field)* • Combined with die 432 • 114/432a (R-9): MS-63 $5,000–$7,500 • Also metal f (R-9). Numismatic strikes. Estimated 8 known (Fuld, fifth edition).

Patriotic die 112 • *Washington portrait facing right (12 border stars)* • Dies by Charles D. Hörter • Combined with die 396a • 112/396a (R-1): EF–AU $25–$40 • MS-63 $50–$75 • Also metal b (R-9).

Patriotic die 114A • *Washington portrait facing left (GEORGE WASHINGTON BORN 1732 DIED 1799)* • Also used elsewhere including on a Baltimore Monument token (Baker-323) • Reverse with die 113 • 113/114Aa (R8): MS-63 $1,000–$1,500 • Also metal b (R-9). Electrotypes exist. Dies by George H. Lovett.

Patriotic die 114B • *Washington portrait facing left (GEORGE WASHINGTON, THE CINCINNATUS OF AMERICA / B. 1732 D. 1799)* • Medalet, numismatic strikes by George H. Lovett. 31.3 mm • Combined with dies 227 and 228 • 114B/227a (R-7): MS-63 $1,000–$1,500.

Patriotic die 115 (early state of die that later became 115B) • *Washington portrait facing right (GEORGE WASHINGTON)* • Die ascribed to Robert Lovett Jr. • Signed LOVETT under portrait. Baker-208. Also used on an 1860 store card issued by William K. Idler • Combined with dies 0 and 115A • 115/115A (R-8): MS-63 $300–$450 • Numismatic strikes.

Patriotic die 115A (early state of die that later became 115C) • *Martha Washington portrait facing left (MARTHA WASHINGTON)* • Dies made by George H. Lovett and first used in 1860. Baker-208 • Combined with die 115 (as reverse) • 115/115Ae (R-7): MS-63 $300–$450 • Numismatic strikes, some probably pre-war.

Patriotic die 115B (late state of die 115 a.k.a. 1140) • *1792 Washington portrait facing right (GEORGE WASHINGTON)* • Combined with die 115C • 115B/115Ca (R-9): MS-63 $1,000–$1,500 • Also metal f (R-9). Numismatic strikes.

Patriotic die 115C (late state of die 115A) • *1792 Martha Washington portrait facing left (MARTHA WASHINGTON)* • Combined with die 115B (as reverse) • 115B/115Ca (R-9): MS-63 $1,000–$1,500 • Also metal f (R-9). Repeat of preceding listing. Numismatic strikes.

Patriotic die 116 • *Washington portrait facing forward and slightly left (BORN FEB. 22 1732. DIED DEC. 14 1799.)* • From the shop of F.C. Key & Sons • Same as store card die 1134 • Die by William Key. Also used on 1870-dated store cards issued by E.L. Mason Jr. (Baker 559) • Combined with dies 96 (as reverse), 129, 153, 282, 349, 477 • 116/129e (R-8): EF–AU $300–$450 • MS-63 $800–$1,200 • Also 116/153a and b are both R-8 • Numismatic strikes.

Patriotic die 117 • *1863 Washington portrait facing right, above two crossed flags (13 border stars)* • Combined with die 420 • 117/420a (R-1): EF–AU $25–$40 • MS-63 $50–$75 • Also metals b (R-4), d (R-9), f (R-9), fo (R-8), g (R-9), j (R-9).

Patriotic die 120 • *1863 Washington portrait facing right (THE WASHINGTON TOKEN)* • Die ascribed to William H. Bridgens • Same as store card die 1137 • Combined with dies 255, 256, 434 • 120/255b (R-7): EF–AU $100–$150 • MS-63 $300–$450 • Various numismatic strikes. 120/434d is also R-7.

Patriotic die 118 • *1863 Washington portrait facing right, two crossed flags behind (13 stars at top border)* • Die ascribed to George J. Glaubrecht • Combined with dies 418 and 419 • 118/418a (R-2): EF–AU $30–$45 • MS-63 $60–$90.

Patriotic die 121 • *Washington portrait facing right (GEO. WASHINGTON PRESIDENT; 8 stars at border)* • Same as store card die 1138 • Combined with dies 0 and 531 (was NY-630-K-4) • 121/531a (R-9): MS-63 $3,000–$4,500 • Also metals b, e, f, j (all R-9), 121/0 (R-10) • Die is a Philadelphia Mint product, probably by assistant engraver Anthony C. Paquet.

Patriotic die 119 • *1863 Washington portrait facing right above two crossed oak branches (13 stars at top border)* • Die ascribed to Emil Sigel • Combined with dies 0, 68 (as reverse), 92 (as reverse), 199, 360, 398 • 119/398a (R-1): EF–AU $25–$40 • MS-63 $50–$75.

Patriotic die 123 • *Washington portrait facing right in plain field* • Die made at the Philadelphia Mint, hub portrait punch entered individually in multiple dies with some variation as to spacing • Same as store card die 1135 (earlier also 1136) • Combined with die 0 • 123/0f, modern restrike from extant die (R-5): MS-63 $200–$300 • Also double-headed impression, date unknown.

Patriotic die 124 (early state of die 125) • *18/64 Lincoln portrait facing left (ABM. LINCOLN PRESIDENT)* • Same as store card die 1144 • Combined with dies 177, 201, 252, 294 • 124/294a (R-7): EF–AU $300–$450 • MS-63 $750–$1,000 • Numismatic strikes except for 124/294a.

Patriotic die 127 • *1864 Lincoln portrait facing left (13 border stars)* • Same as store card die 1145 • Combined with dies 1660, 177, 185A, 201, 248, 252, 253, 294, 295, 428, 432 • 127/248a (R-3): EF–AU $75–$110 • MS-63 $200–$300 • Many varieties, all but a few being numismatic strikes.

Patriotic die 125 (late state of die 124, a.k.a. 1144) • *18/64 Lincoln portrait facing left (ABM. LINCOLN PRESIDENT)* • Combined with dies 0, 160, 185, 201, 248, 253, 294, 295, 427, 448, 432 • 125/248a (R-6): EF–AU $150–$225 • MS-63 $400–$600 • Many numismatic strikes likely made postwar during the great demand for Lincolniana.

Patriotic die 128 • *1864 Lincoln portrait facing right (35 stars around border)* • From the shop of F.C. Key & Sons • Combined with dies 289 and 290 • 128/289b (R-3): EF–AU $75–$110 • MS-63 $225–$350.

Patriotic die 126 • *1864 Lincoln portrait facing left (THE RIGHT MAN IN THE RIGHT PLACE)* • Combined with dies 248, 294, 295, 406A, 432 • 126/295a (R-5): EF–AU $150–$225 • MS-63 $400–$600 • Most varieties are numismatic strikes.

Patriotic die 129 • *1864 Lincoln portrait facing right (ABRAHAM LINCOLN; K below bust, rope border)* • From the shop of F.C. Key & Sons • Same as store card die 1146 • Combined with dies 0, 130, 137A, 142, 153, 282, 347, 348, 349, 477 • 129/347e (R-7): EF–AU $200–$350 • MS-63 $600–$750 • Many varieties, mostly numismatic strikes made after Lincoln's April 1865 death. F.C. Key & Sons muled obverse 129 with various dies on hand • This die exists and has been used to make modern strikings.

Patriotic die 130 • *1864 Lincoln portrait facing right (ABRAHAM LINCOLN; K below bust, dentils)* • From the shop of F.C. Key & Sons • Combined with dies 142, 347, 348, 349 • 130/349a (R-9): MS-63 $1,250–$1,750 • Various other R-9 numismatic strikes plus an R-10.

Patriotic die 132 • *Lincoln portrait facing right (FOR PRESIDENT ABRAHAM LINCOLN; 2 stars at border; R.L.)* • Die ascribed to Robert Lovett Jr. • Combined with die 149 • 132/149a (R-5): EF–AU $200–$300 • MS-63 $500–$750 • Also metals ao (R-9), b (R-7).

Patriotic die 131 • *1864 Lincoln portrait facing right (ABRAHAM LINCOLN; dentils)* • From the shop of F.C. Key & Sons • Combined with dies 217 and 479 • 131/217a (R-8): MS-63 $900–$1,350 • Various other R-8 numismatic strikes.

Patriotic die 132A • *Lincoln portrait facing right (FOR PRESIDENT ABRAHAM LINCOLN; 2 stars at border)* • Die ascribed to Robert Lovett Jr. • Combined with die 149 • 132A/149a (R-5): EF–AU $200–$300 • MS-63 $500–$750 • Also metal b (R-8).

Patriotic die 131A • *1864 Lincoln portrait facing right in circle (ABRAHAM LINCOLN)* • From the shop of F.C. Key & Sons • Combined with die 349 • 131A/349b (R-7): EF–AU $350–$550 • MS-63 $700–$1,000.

Patriotic die 133 • *Lincoln portrait facing left (LINCOLN. AND LIBERTY.)* • Combined with die 458 • 133/458b (R-5): EF–AU $125–$175 • MS-63 $300–$450 • Also metal a (R-8). Almost always holed for suspension.

Patriotic die 134 • *Bearded portrait facing left (14 border stars; REDEEMED)* • Same as store card die 1147 • Combined with dies 184, 283, 472, 481 • 134/472d (R-9): EF–AU $1,000–$1,500 • MS-63 $2,000–$3,000 • Also other varieties, all R-9 (a generic guess; some may be R-10). Numismatic strikes to the order of the Rhode Island Numismatic Association. Over the years there has been much debate as to if the portrait is of Abraham Lincoln; bearded men were common in the 1860s.

Patriotic die 137 • *Andrew Jackson portrait facing left (THE UNION MUST AND SHALL BE PRESERVED; star at border; S)* • Die ascribed to Frederick B. Smith • Combined with dies 309 and 395 • 137/395a (R-1): EF–AU $30–$45 • MS-63 $60–$90 • Two other varieties are both R-9.

Patriotic die 135 • *Andrew Jackson portrait facing left (FOR OUR COUNTRY A COMMON CAUSE)* • Die ascribed to Emil Sigel • Combined with dies 0, 199, 432, 440, 441 • 135/441a (R-2): EF–AU $25–$40 • MS-63 $50–$75 • Many other combinations are all R-9 and R-10.

Patriotic die 137A • *Andrew Jackson portrait facing left (plain field)* • Combined with die 129 • 137a/129 (R-10): MS-63 $9,000–$12,000 • Only four known (Fuld, fifth edition), but recent scholarship (Tanenbaum, Hayden, Glazer) suggests that the Zabriskie specimen is unique.

Patriotic die 136 • *Andrew Jackson portrait facing left (THE UNION MUST AND SHALL BE PRESERVED; star at border; S)* • Die ascribed to Frederick B. Smith • Combined with die 397 • 136/397a (R-1): EF–AU $40–$60 • MS-63 $150–$175 • Also metals do (R-10), g (R-9).

Patriotic die 138 • *McClellan portrait facing left (GENERAL G.B. McCLELLAN)* • Die ascribed to William H. Bridgens • Same as store card die 1152 • Combined with dies 0, 255, 256, 434 • 138/434a (R-1): EF–AU $30–$45 • MS-63 $75–$125.

Patriotic die 138A • *McClellan portrait facing left (FOR PRESIDENT GEO. B. McCLELLAN)* • Die ascribed to Robert Lovett Jr. • Combined with dies 149 and 150 • 138A/150a (R-6): EF–AU $200–$300 • MS-63 $500–$750 • Also 138A/149a (R-9).

Patriotic die 142 • *McClellan portrait facing left (MAJ. GEN. GEO. B. M'CLELLAN U.S.A.; K on shoulder)* • From the shop of F.C. Key & Sons • Combined with dies 282, 347, 348, 349 • 142/347b (R-7): EF–AU $125–$175 • MS-63 $300–$450.

Patriotic die 140 • *1863 McClellan portrait facing left, in open wreath (13 border stars LITTLE MACK, S above date)* • Same as store card die 1153 • Combined with dies 187 and 394 • 140/394a (R-1): EF–AU $30–$45 • MS-63 $100–$150.

Patriotic die 143 • *McClellan portrait facing right (THIS MEDAL OF G.B. McCLELLAN PRICE; 2 stars at border)* • Same as store card die 1153A • Combined with die 261 • 143/261a (R-1): VF–EF $25–$35 • MS-63 $75–$110 • Also metals b (R-7), e (R-9), g plain edge (R-8), g reeded edge (R-9), j (R-9).

Patriotic die 141 • *1863 McClellan portrait facing left (GEO. B. McCLELLAN)* • Combined with die 307 • 141/307a (R-1): EF–AU $30–$45 • MS-63 $75–$125 • Also metals B (R-8), d (R-9).

Patriotic die 146 • *Burnside portrait (Rhode Island First In The Field; 1864)* • Same as store card die 1159 • Combined with dies 184, 283, 472 • 146/472j (R-0) • 134/472d (R-9): EF–AU $500–$750 • MS-63 $1,500–$2,250 • Also other varieties, all R-9 (a generic guess; some may be R-10). Numismatic strikes to the order of the Rhode Island Numismatic Association.

Patriotic die 147 • *1861 Bust of soldier facing slightly to viewer's left (I AM READY.)* • Medalet • Combined with dies 227 and 228 • 147/227b (R-6): EF–AU $400–$600 • MS-63 $1,000–$1,500 • Often seen silver-plated in higher grades.

Patriotic die 150 • *Johnson portrait facing right (FOR VICE PRESIDENT HON J.H. PENDLETON; 2 stars at border)* • Used as reverse with die 138A • 138A/150a (R-6): EF–AU $200–$300 • MS-63 $500–$750 • Only one variety.

Patriotic die 148 • *Portrait of bearded man facing left (plain field)* • From the shop of John Stanton • Same as store card die 1160 • Used as reverse with dies 71 and 84 • 84/148a (R-7): EF–AU $600–$900 • MS-63 $1,500–$2,250 • Also 71/148a (R-9).

Patriotic die 151 • *Franklin portrait facing right (BENJAMIN FRANKLIN; E. SIGEL)* • Die ascribed to Emil Sigel • Same as store card die 1149 • Combined with die 430 • 151/430a (R-1): EF–AU $25–$40 • MS-63 $60–$90 • Also metals b (R-9), e (R-9), f (R-8).

Patriotic die 149 • *Johnson portrait facing right (FOR VICE PRESIDENT ANDREW JOHNSON; 2 stars at border; R.L.) [overstrike]* • Die ascribed to Robert Lovett Jr. • Used as reverse with dies 132, 132A, 138A • 149/132a (R-5): EF–AU $200–$300 • MS-63 $500–$750 • 149/132Aa is also R-5.

Patriotic die 153 • *Franklin portrait facing left (BENJAMIN FRANKLIN)* • From the shop of F.C. Key & Sons • Same as store card die 1150 • Combined with dies 0, 116, 129, 199, 282, 519B • 153/0ao over large cent (R-7): EF–AU $400–$600 • MS-63 $1,250–$1,750 • Numismatic strikes • This die exists and has been used to make modern strikings.

Patriotic die 154 • *Douglas portrait facing right (STEPHEN A. DOUGLAS; MARR)* • Same as store card die 1155 • Combined with dies 154, 218, 417, 469B • 154/218a (R-5): EF–AU $175–$250 • MS-63 $500–$750.

Patriotic die 156 • *1863 Flying eagle, head at right (12 border stars)* • Ascribed to the shop of William K. Lanphear • Same as store card die 1170 • Combined with dies 519C and 524 • 156/524a R-8 EF–AU $500–$750 • MS-63 $1,250–$1,750 • 156/519C is R-10.

Patriotic die 154A • *Douglas portrait facing left (S.A.D. below bust)* • Die ascribed to John Marr of Mossin & Marr • Same as store card die 1156 • Mint error brockage of obverse die • 154A brockage (R-9): MS-63 $4,000–$6,000 • The store card use is rare.

Patriotic die 157 • *1863 Flying eagle, head at right (13 border stars)* • Ascribed to the shop of William K. Lanphear • Same as store card die 1172 • Combined with die 425 • 157/425a (R-9): MS-63 $6,000–$9,000 • 157/425 e thick planchet ANS (R-10).

Patriotic die 155 • *1863 Perched eagle, head facing left (16 stars at border; UNION)* • Die ascribed to Henry D. Higgins ("Indiana primitive") • Same as store card die 1165 • Combined with dies 400 and 431 • 155/431a (R-4): EF–AU $100–$150 • MS-63 $300–$450 • Also 155/431a (R-4).

Patriotic die 158 • *1863 Flying eagle, head at left (12 border stars)* • Ascribed to the shop of William K. Lanphear • Same as store card die 1166 • Combined with die 424 • 158/424a (R-9): MS-63 $5,000–$7,500 • Only one variety.

Patriotic die 159 • *1863 Flying eagle, head at left (12 border stars)* • Ascribed to the shop of William K. Lanphear • Same as store card die 1169 • Combined with die 469 • 159/469a (R-8): MS-63 $750–$1,250 • Only one variety.

Patriotic die 162 • *Perched eagle, head facing left (OUR ARMY)* • Die ascribed to Emil Sigel • Same as store card die 1175 • Combined with dies 55 (as reverse), 56 (as reverse), 338 • 55/162a (R-1): EF–AU $25–$40 • MS-63 $50–$75.

Patriotic die 160 • *1864 Eagle perched on cannon (LIBERTY FOR ALL)* • Die ascribed to John Marr of Mossin & Marr • Same as store card die 1174 • Combined with dies 125 and 127 • 160/417a (R-4): MS-63 $175–$250 • 127/160a is also R-8 • Others are R-9 • Many are numismatic strikes.

Patriotic die 163 • *Open wreath (shield inscribed UNION, with eagle on top, flags to sides)* • Die by the Scovill Manufacturing Co. (?) • Same as store card die 1201 • Combined with die 352 • 162/352a (R-2): EF–AU $25–$40 • MS-63 $50–$75 • Only one variety.

Patriotic die 161 • *Perched eagle, head facing left (OUR ARMY)* • Die ascribed to Emil Sigel • Same as store card die 1175A • Used as reverse with 56 • 56/161a (R-5): EF–AU $100–$150 • MS-63 $200–$300.

Patriotic die 164 • *Open wreath (shield inscribed UNION, with eagle on top, flags to sides)* • Die by the Scovill Manufacturing Co. (?) • Same as store card die 1200 • Combined with die 312 • 164/312a (R-1): EF–AU $25–$40 • MS-63 $50–$75 • Also metals b (R-9), j (R-8).

Patriotic die 165 • *Open wreath (shield inscribed UNION, with eagle on top, flags to sides)* • Die ascribed to Henry D. Higgins ("Indiana primitive") • Same as store card die 1202 • Combined with dies 400 and 431 • 165/400a (R-5). EF–AU $100–$150 • MS-63 $300–$450 • 165/431a is also R-5.

Patriotic die 168 • *1863 Cannon facing left (13 stars at the border)* • Combined with die 311 • 168/311a (R-1): EF–AU $40–$60 • MS-63 $100–$150 • Also metal b (R-6).

Patriotic die 166 • *Open wreath (shield inscribed UNION, with eagle on top, flags to sides, stars at border above)* • Combined with die 432 • 166/432a (R-6): EF–AU $100–$150 • MS-63 $250–$375 • Only one variety.

Patriotic die 169 • *Cannon facing left (13 border stars; PEACE MAKER)* • Combined with die 213 • 269/213a (R-2): EF–AU $50–$75 • MS-63 $150–$225 • Also metal b (R-6).

Patriotic die 167 • *1863 Shield with eagle to each side, liberty cap above (UNION)* • Combined with dies 318 and 435 • 167/318a (R-5): EF–AU $75–$125 • MS-63 $200–$300.

Patriotic die 170 • *Wreath enclosing cannon facing right (6 cannonballs below barrel)* • Used as reverse with die 21 • 21/170a (R-10): VF $10,000–$15,000 • Also metal e (R-10). Similarly, only 2 known (Fuld, fifth edition, p. 288).

Patriotic die 171 • *1863 Cannon facing right, with flag (THE PEACEMAKER; G.G.)* • Die ascribed to George J. Glaubrecht • Combined with dies 340 and 428 • 171/428a (R-7): EF–AU $1,000–$1,500 • MS-63 $2,250–$3,250.

Patriotic die 174 • *1863 Washington on horseback statue (FIRST IN WAR, FIRST IN PEACE)* • Die by the Scovill Manufacturing Co. (?) • Baker-477 • Combined with dies 189, 233, 272 • 174/272a (R-1): EF–AU $25–$40 • MS-63 $50–$75.

Patriotic die 175 • *1863 Washington on horseback statue (FIRST IN WAR, FIRST IN PEACE)* • Die ascribed to Henry D. Higgins ("Indiana primitive") • Same as store card die 1161 • Combined with dies 232, 400, 401, 403 • 175/400a (R-3): EF–AU $50–$75 • MS-63 $250–$375 • There are at least five slightly differing dies grouped as die 175.[4]

Patriotic die 172 • *1863 Crossed cannons, star above (12 border stars)* • Die ascribed to Alexander Gleason • Same as store card die 1221 • Combined with die 429 • 172/429a (R-5): EF–AU $75–$125 • MS-63 $250–$375 • Only one variety.

Patriotic die 173 • *1863 Washington on horseback statue (FIRST IN WAR, FIRST IN PEACE)* • Die by the Scovill Manufacturing Co. (?) • Baker-476 • Combined with die 272 • 173/292a (R-2): EF–AU $25–$40 • MS-63 $50–$75 • Also metal f (R-9). Also non-contemporary strikes from the obverse die; reverse blank. This die survives and has been used to make modern uniface restrikes.

Patriotic die 176 • *1863 Washington on horseback statue (FIRST IN WAR, FIRST IN PEACE)* • Die ascribed to George J. Glaubrecht • Combined with die 271 • 176/271a (R-1): EF–AU $25–$40 • MS-63 $50–$75 • Also metals b (R-7), e (R-9), e (R-8), j (R-7).

Patriotic die 177 • *1863 Washington on horseback statue (FIRST IN WAR, FIRST IN PEACE)* • Various Baker numbers • Combined with dies 124 (as reverse), 177 (as reverse), 271, 294, 295, 432 • 177/271a (R-4): EF–AU $30–$45 • MS-63 $90–$135.

Patriotic die 180 • *Franz Sigel on horseback (HERO OF PEA RIDGE F. SIGEL)* • Die ascribed to Emil Sigel, brother of Franz Sigel • Combined with dies 341, 343, 430 • 180/341 (R-1): EF–AU $25–$40 • MS-63 $50–$75. • Only when combined with reverse 430 is the full legend visible.

Patriotic die 178 • *1863 Andrew Jackson on horseback (THE FEDERAL UNION IT MUST BE PRESERVED)* • Combined with dies 41 (as reverse), 266, 267, 337 • 178/367a (R-1): EF–AU $25–$40 • MS-63 $50–$75.

Patriotic die 181 • *Franz Sigel on horseback (7 stars at border; F. SIGEL)* • Die ascribed to Emil Sigel • Combined with die 343 • 181/343a (R-7): EF–AU $250–$375 • MS-63 $600–$900 • Metal j is also R-7 • Later reworked state of die 180.

Patriotic die 179 • *1864 Andrew Jackson on horseback (THE FEDERAL UNION IT MUST BE PRESERVED)* • Dies by Charles D. Hörter • Used as reverse with dies 50, 53, 54 • 54/179a (R-2): EF–AU $25–$40 • MS-63 $50–$75.

Patriotic die 182 • *Small image of male lion standing, facing left* • From the shop of John Stanton • Same as store card die 1282 • Used as reverse with die 71 • 71/182 m(pl) (R-10): MS-63 $6,000–$9,000 • Although this die is rare on a political token it can be found on a store card, although it is hardly common.

Patriotic die 183 • *Small image of bison standing, facing right* • From the shop of John Stanton • Same as store card die 1283 • Used a reverse with die 71 • 71/183a (R-9): MS-63 $6,000–$9,000 • Metal b is also R-9 • The store card use is scarce.

Patriotic die 185 • *Bull standing, facing right (plain field)* • From the shop of John Stanton • Same as store card die 1288 • Used as reverse with die 185 • 57/185a (R-9): EF–AU $3,000–$4,500 • MS-63 $6,000–$9,000 • Also 57/185do over cent (R-9).

Patriotic die 183A • *1863 Male lion couchant, facing left (SIGN OF THE LION.)* • Same as store card die 1281 • Used as reverse with die 31 • 31/183Aa (R-10) • ANS.

Patriotic die 185A • *1863 Group of fruit and vegetables (LIVE AND LET LIVE; signed G. GL.)* • Die ascribed to George J. Glaubrecht, possibly struck in another shop • Same as store card die 1353 • Combined with dies 125 (as reverse) 295, 432 • 125/185Aa (R-9): EF–AU $4,000–$6,000 • MS-63 $7,000–$10,000 • Also three other varieties each R-9.

Patriotic die 184 • *Two hunting dogs in field, heading to left* • From the shop of John Stanton • Same as store card die 1285 • Combined with dies 134 (as reverse), 146 (as reverse), 427 • 134/184j (R-8): EF–AU $1,500–$2,250 • MS-63 $4,000–$6,000 • 146/184j and 184/427j are also R-8.

Patriotic die 185B • *1863 Hippocampus facing left (13 border stars)* • Ascribed to the shop of William K. Lanphear • R-10 • MS-63 $2,500–$3,750 • Although this die is rare on a political token it can be found on a store card, although it is hardly common.

Patriotic die 186 • *1863 Rooster, standing and facing left (13 border stars)* • Die ascribed to Emil Sigel • Same as store card die 1293 • Pictured but not listed as a variety in Fuld.

Patriotic die 188A • *1864 Beehive (INDUSTRY)* • Ascribed to the shop of William K. Lanphear • Same as store card die 1350 • Illustrated but not listed in the Fuld text.

Patriotic die 187 • *1863 Horse and rider facing right (TIME IS MONEY EXIGENCY)* • Same as store card die 1162 • Combined with dies 140 (as reverse), 214, 450 • 187/214g (R-8): EF–AU $300–$450. • This is likely a contemporary counterfeit.

Patriotic die 189 • *1863 Crossed flags, UNION and rays above (13 border stars)* • Die by the Scovill Manufacturing Co. (?) • Combined with dies 174A (as reverse), 239, 399 • 189/399a (R-1): EF–AU $25–$40 • MS-63 $60–$90.

Patriotic die 188 • *1863 Beehive (INDUSTRY; C.D.H.)* • Dies by Charles D. Hörter, struck by Emil Sigel • Combined with dies 384 and 435 • 188/384a (R-3): EF–AU $40–$60 • MS-63 $125–$175 • 188/384b is also R-3.

Patriotic die 191 • *1863 Star with shield (PRO BONO PUBLICO)* • Die ascribed to Emil Sigel • Combined with die 443 • 191/443a (R-1): EF–AU $25–$40 • MS-63 $50–$75.

Patriotic die 192 • *1863 Shield inscribed UNION (ONE COUNTRY; 2 stars at border)* • Ascribed to the shop of William K. Lanphear • Same as store card die 1224 • Combined with die 470A • 192/470Aa (R-9): EF–AU $4,000–$6,000 • MS-63 $8,000–$12,000 • Although this die is rare on a political token it is easily enough found on a store card.

Patriotic die 194 • *1863 Shield inscribed UNION (TOYS AND CONFECTION-ERY)* • Same as store card die 1227 • "Half card" die • Combined with die 424 • 194/424a (R-9): EF–AU $3,000–$4,500 • MS-63 $6,000–$9,000 • Although this die is rare on a political token it is easily enough found on a store card.

Patriotic die 193 • *1863 Shield inscribed UNION (THE ARMY & NAVY; 2 stars at border)* • Ascribed to the shop of William K. Lanphear • Same as store card die 1226 • Used as reverse with die 40 • 40/193a (R-9): EF–AU $4,000–$6,000 • MS-63 $8,000–$12,000 • Also metal b (R-9).

Patriotic die 195 • *1863 Eagle perched on shield (UNITED STATES OF AMERICA)* • Die ascribed to Emil Sigel • Combined with dies 247, 376, 378 • 195/378a (R-3): EF–AU $40–$60 • MS-63 $100–$150.

Patriotic die 193A • *1864 Shield inscribed UNION (ONE COUNTRY; 2 stars at border)* • Ascribed to the shop of William K. Lanphear • Same as store card die 1228 • Combined with die 470A • 193A/470Aa (R-8): EF–AU $1,250–$1,750 • MS-63 $2,500–$3,750 • Only one variety. Although this die is rare on a political token it is easily enough found on a store card.

Patriotic die 196 • *1863 Eagle perched on shield (UNITED STATES OF AMERICA; E.S.)* • Die ascribed to Emil Sigel • Same as store card die 1216 • Combined with dies 105 (as reverse), 355, 360 • 196/355a (R-3): EF–AU $25–$40 • MS-63 $60–$90.

Patriotic die 197 • *1863 Eagle perched on shield (UNITED STATES OF AMERICA; E.S.)* • Die ascribed to Emil Sigel • Same as store card die 1217 • Combined with dies 378 and 380 • 197/380a (R-2): EF–AU $25–$40 • MS-63 $50–$75.

Patriotic die 198 • *1863 Eagle perched on shield (UNITED STATES OF AMERICA)* • Die ascribed to Emil Sigel • Same as store card die 1218 • Combined with dies 1 (as reverse), 61 (as reverse), 68 (as reverse), 92 (as reverse), 105 (as reverse), 360, 436 • 61/198a (R-3): EF–AU $30–$45 • MS-63 $75–$125.

Patriotic die 199 • *1863 Eagle perched on shield (UNITED STATES MEDAL)* • Die ascribed to Emil Sigel • Same as store card die 1219 • Combined with dies 68 (as reverse), 92 (as reverse), 105 (as reverse), 119 (as reverse), 135 (as reverse), 359, 360, 440 • 92/199a (R-3): EF–AU $30–$45 • MS-63 $90–$135.

Patriotic die 200 • *18/63 Shield with anchor (NEW-YORK; 2 stars at border)* • Die ascribed to Emil Sigel • Same as store card die 1230 • Combined with dies 60 (as reverse), 346 • 200/346a (R-8): EF–AU $150–$225 • MS-63 $350–$500 • Also metals ao (R-8), e (R-9). Although this die is rare on a political token it is easily enough found on a store card.

Patriotic die 201 • *Shield (OUR UNION; 2 stars at border)* • Combined with dies 108 (as reverse), 124 (as reverse), 127 (as reverse), 101 (as reverse), 271, 294, 295, 432 • 201/432a (R-3): EF–AU $25–$40 • MS-63 $50–$75.

Patriotic die 202 • *Shield with GOOD FOR ONE CENT (TRADESMENS CURRENCY; 2 stars at border)* • Die ascribed to William H. Bridgens • Same as store card die 1232 • Combined with die 434 • 202/434a (R-1): EF–AU $25–$40 • MS-63 $50–$75 • Only one variety.

Patriotic die 203 • *1863 flag (THE FLAG OF OUR UNION; 13 stars around flag)* • Combined with dies 412 and 413 • 203/412 (R-3): EF–AU $30–$45 • MS-63 $100–$150 • 203/413a is also R-3.

Patriotic die 206 • *1863 flag (THE FLAG OF OUR UNION; 13 stars around flag)* • Same as store card die 1233 • Combined with dies 320, 323, 326 • 206/320a (R-1): EF–AU $25–$40 • MS-63 $50–$75.

Patriotic die 204 • *1863 flag (THE FLAG OF OUR UNION; 13 stars around flag)* • Combined with die 413 • 204/413 (R-5): EF–AU $150–$225 • MS-63 $350–$500 • Only one variety.

Patriotic die 207 • *1863 flag (THE FLAG OF OUR UNION; 13 stars around flag)* • Combined with dies 323, 324, 325, 327, 409. 410, 412 • 207/410a (R-1): EF–AU $25–$40 • MS-63 $50–$75.

Patriotic die 205 • *1863 flag (THE FLAG OF OUR UNION; 13 stars around flag)* • Combined with dies 410 and 411 • 205/410a (R-3): EF–AU $25–$40 • MS-63 $50–$75 • Only one variety.

Patriotic die 208 • *1863 flag (THE FLAG OF OUR UNION; 13 stars around flag)* • Combined with die 410 • 208/410a (R-1): EF–AU $25–$40 • MS-63 $50–$75 • Only one variety.

Patriotic die 209 • *1863 flag (THE FLAG OF OUR UNION; 13 stars around flag)* • Combined with dies 409, 410, 412, 414 • 209/414a (R-2): EF–AU $40–$60 • MS-63 $125–$175.

Patriotic die 212 • *1863 flag (THE FLAG OF OUR UNION; 13 stars around flag)* • Combined with die 415 • 212/415a (R-2): EF–AU $25–$40 • MS-63 $50–$75 • Only one variety.

Patriotic die 210 • *1863 flag (THE FLAG OF OUR UNION; 13 stars around flag)* • Same as store card die 1233A • Combined with dies 323, 408, 413A, 415, 416 • 210/323a (R-3): EF–AU $25–$40 • MS-63 $50–$75 • 210/408a is also R-3.

Patriotic die 213 • *1863 flag (STAND BY THE FLAG)* • Used as reverse with die 169 • 169/213a (R-2): EF–AU $50–$75 • MS-63 $150–$225 • Only one variety.

Patriotic die 211 • *1863 flag (THE FLAG OF OUR UNION; 13 stars around flag)* • Die ascribed to Henry D. Higgins ("Indiana primitive"). Believed to have been made by impacting a struck 210 token with a soft steel blank, then hardening to make a die. • Same as store card die 1234A • Combined with dies 400 and 402 (almost certainly does not exist) • 211/400a (R-4): EF–AU $75–$125 • MS-63 $200–$300.

Patriotic die 214 • *Flag (THE FLAG OF OUR UNION; 13 stars around flag)* • Same as store card die 1235 • Combined with dies 187 (as reverse), 415, 416 • 214/416 (R-1): EF–AU $25–$40 • MS-63 $50–$75.

Patriotic die 216 • *Flag within closed wreath (13 stars around flag)* • Die ascribed to Emil Sigel • Combined with die 293 • 216/293a (R-3): EF–AU $40–$60 • MS-63 $100–$150 • Only one variety.

Patriotic die 217 • *Flag (LONG MAY IT WAVE; 13 border stars)* • From the shop of F.C. Key & Sons • Combined with dies 131 (as reverse) and 479 • 217/479a (R-7): EF–AU $200–$300 • MS-63 $600–$900 • 217/479 b and e are also R-7.

Patriotic die 218 • *1863 Amazon maiden with flag* • Same as store card die 1220 • Combined with dies 154 (as reverse), 160 (as reverse), 417 • 154/218a (R-5): EF–AU $175–$250 • MS-63 $500–$750 • One of the more popular motifs.

Patriotic die 219 • *THE FEDERAL UNION IT MUST AND SHALL BE PRESERVED (13 border stars)* • Combined with dies 320 and 323 • 219/320a (R-1): EF–AU $25–$40 • MS-63 $50–$75 • The sentiment is attributed to President Andrew Jackson, who on April 13, 1830, was a guest at a dinner party in Washington to honor Thomas Jefferson's birthday. After multiple toasts, including by Senator John Calhoun, well-known for suggesting that his state, South Carolina, was at divergence on various issues with the government, Jackson uttered the quoted phrase.

Patriotic die 220 • *THE FEDERAL UNION IT MUST AND SHALL BE PRESERVED (13 border stars)* • Combined with dies 322 and 327 • 220/327a (R-1): EF–AU $25–$40 • MS-63 $50–$75.

Patriotic die 221 • *THE FEDERAL UNION IT MUST AND SHALL BE PRESERVED (13 border stars)* • Combined with dies 324 and 327 • 221/324 (R-1): EF–AU $25–$40 • MS-63 $50–$75.

Patriotic die 222 (late version of die 223) • *THE FEDERAL UNION IT MUST AND SHALL BE [E over Y] PRESERVED (13 border stars)* • Combined with die 325 • 222/325a (R-2): EF–AU $25–$40 • MS-63 $50–$75 • Also metal b (R-3).

Patriotic die 225 • *THE FEDERAL UNION IT MUST AND SHALL BE PRESERVED (13 border stars)* • Combined with dies 321 and 327 • 225/327a (R-1) • EF–AU $25–$40 • MS-63 $50–$75 • One in ANS.

Patriotic die 223 (early version of die 222) • *THE FEDERAL UNION IT MUST AND SHALL BY PRESERVED (13 border stars)* • Combined with dies 325 and 328 • 223/328a (R-1): EF–AU $25–$40 • MS-63 $50–$75.

Patriotic die 225A • *THE FEDERAL UNION IT MUST AND SHALL BE PRESERVED (13 border stars)* • Combined with die 327 • 225A/327a (R-3): EF–AU $25–$40 • MS-63 $50–$75 • Also metal b (R-7).

Patriotic die 224 • *THE FEDERAL UNION IT MUST AND SHALL BE PRESERVED (13 border stars)* • Combined with dies 322, 325, 326, 327 • 224/322a (R-2): EF–AU $25–$40 • MS-63 $50–$75 • 224/326a is also R-2.

Patriotic die 226 • *THE FEDERAL UNION IT MUST AND SHALL BE PRESERVED (13 border stars)* • Combined with die 321 • 226/321a (R-4): EF–AU $25–$40 • MS-63 $75–$125 • Also metal b (R-8).

Patriotic die 226A • *THE FEDERAL UNION IT MUST AND SHALL BE PRESERVED (13 border stars)* • Combined with die 322A • 226A/322A (R-10⁵): EF–AU $5,000–$7,500 • MS-63 $8,000–$12,000.

Patriotic die 227 • *THE UNION MUST & SHALL BE PRESERVED (35 stars at border)* • Die ascribed to John D. Lovett • Medalet, numismatic strike • Combined with dies 114B (as reverse) and 147 (as reverse) • 147/227b (R-6) • EF–AU $400–$600 • MS-63 $1,000–$1,500.

Patriotic die 228 • *All-seeing eye surrounded by glory of rays ('THE UNION MUST AND SHALL BE PRESERVED;)* • Die ascribed to John D. Lovett • Medalet, numismatic strike • Combined with dies 114B (as reverse), 147 (as reverse), 493C • 147/228 (R-7): EF–AU $750–$1,250 • MS-63 $2,000–$3,000.

Patriotic die 229 • *Closed wreath (shield with crossed branches, OUR COUNTRY, star, 2 arrowheads)* • Die ascribed to Emil Sigel • Same as store card die 1236 • Combined with dies 1 (as reverse), 56 (ass reverse with), 105 (as reverse), 359, 360, 391 • 1/229a (R-1): EF–AU $25–$40 • MS-63 $50–$75.

Patriotic die 230 • *Closed wreath (shield with crossed branches, OUR COUNTRY, star, 2 arrowheads)* • Combined with die 352B • 230/352B (R-2): EF–AU $25–$40 • MS-63 $50–$75 • Also metal b (R-8).

Patriotic die 231 • *Closed wreath (shield with crossed branches, OUR COUNTRY, star, 2 arrowheads)* • Die by the Scovill Manufacturing Co. (?) • Combined with dies 189 (as reverse), 352A, 399 • 231/352Aa (R-1): EF–AU $25–$40 • MS-63 $50–$75.

Patriotic die 232 • *Closed wreath (shield with crossed branches, OUR COUNTRY, star, 2 arrowheads)* • Die ascribed to Henry D. Higgins ("Indiana primitive") • Used as reverse with die 175 • 75/232a (R-6): EF–AU $100–$150 • MS-63 $300–$450.

Patriotic die 234 • *1863 Capitol building (UNITED STATES CAPITAL 8 stars at border)* • Combined with die 431 • 234/431a (R-6): EF–AU $175–$250 • MS-63 $700–$1,000 • Only one variety.

Patriotic die 232A • *1864 Closed wreath (shield with crossed branches, OUR COUNTRY, star, 2 arrowheads)* • Die ascribed to Henry D. Higgins ("Indiana primitive") • Combined with die 403 • 232A/403a (R-9): EF–AU $8,000–$12,000 • Only one variety.

Patriotic die 235 • *1863 Open wreath (LIBERTY)* • Die ascribed to Frederick B. Smith • Combined with die 269 • 235/269a (R-2): EF–AU $25–$40 • MS-63 $75–$125 • Also metal d (R-9).

Patriotic die 236 • *1863 Open wreath (LIBERTY)* • Die ascribed to Frederick B. Smith • Combined with die 426 • 236/426a (R-1): EF–AU $25–$40 • MS-63 $50–$75 • Also metal b (R-7).

Patriotic die 233 • *1863 Capitol building (UNITED STATES 8 stars at border)* • Same as store card die 1237 • Combined with dies 9 (as reverse), 174 (as reverse), 312 • 233/312a (R-1): EF–AU $25–$40 • MS-63 $50–$75.

Patriotic die 237 • *Monitor (OUR LITTLE MONITOR)* • Combined with die 432 • 237/423a (R-2): EF–AU $50–$75 • MS-63 $200–$300 • Also metal b (R-9).

Patriotic die 240 • *1863 Monitor (13 stars in field; C.D.H.)* • Dies by Charles D. Hörter • Combined with dies 0 (as reverse), 41 (as reverse), 337, 341 • 240/337a (R-1): EF–AU $40–$60 • MS-63 $125–$175 • Also 240/341a (R-1).

Patriotic die 238 • *Monitor (OUR LITTLE MONITOR)* • Die ascribed to Henry D. Higgins ("Indiana primitive") • Combined with dies 9, 402, and 405 • 238/405a (R-3): EF–AU $250–$350 • MS-63 $700–$1,000.

Patriotic die 241 • *1864 Monitor (12 stars in field)* • Dies by Charles D. Hörter • Combined with dies 296, 336, 337, 338 • 241/336a (R-1): EF–AU $50–$75 • MS-63 $150–$225.

Patriotic die 239 • *Monitor (OUR LITTLE MONITOR)* • Combined with dies 421 and 422 • 239/422a (R-2): EF–AU $50–$75 • MS-63 $200–$300.

Patriotic die 241A • *Monitor (UNION FOREVER)* • Combined with die 417A • 241A/417Aao (R-10): EF–AU $10,000–$15,000 • 241A/41Ag also R-10.

Patriotic die 242 • *CONSTITUTION FOR EVER (2 stars at border)* • Die ascribed to Emil Sigel • Combined with dies 338 and 374 • 242/374a (R-2): EF–AU $25–$40 • MS-63 $50–$75.

Patriotic die 245 • *REMEMBRANCE OF 1863* • Die ascribed to Emil Sigel • Combined with dies 375 (may not exist per Fuld who also called it R-8) and 375A • 245/375Aa (R-3): EF–AU $50–$75 • MS-63 $200–$300.

Patriotic die 243 • *ERINNERUNG an 1863* • Die ascribed to Emil Sigel • Same as store card die 1240 • Combined with dies 247, 378, 380 • 243/247a (R-3): EF–AU $25–$40 • MS-63 $50–$75 • 243/378 is also R-3.

Patriotic die 246 • *REMEMBRANCE OF THE WAR OF 1861 '62 '63* • Die ascribed to George J. Glaubrecht • Used as reverse with die 24 • 24/246a (R-2): EF–AU $30–$50 • MS-63 $100–$150 • Also metal b (R-6).

Patriotic die 244 • *REMEMBRANCE OF 1863* • Die ascribed to Emil Sigel • Same as store card die 1239 • Combined with dies 0 (as reverse), 291, 375A, 381 • 244/291a (R-2): EF–AU $25–$40 • MS-63 $50–$75 • 244/381a is also R-2.

Patriotic die 246A • *A TOKEN OF THE WAR FOR THE UNION. 1863* • Dies by Charles D. Hörter • Mint error brockage; earlier was known as NY-630-BC-2a (R-10): EF–AU $3,000–$4,500.

Patriotic die 247 • *CONSTITUTION FOR EVER* • Die ascribed to Emil Sigel • Combined with dies 195 (as reverse), 247 (as reverse), 377, 379, 380 • 247/377a (R-2): EF–AU $25–$40 • MS-63 $50–$75.

Patriotic die 251 • *Masonic emblems of compass and square (13 border stars)* • Die ascribed to William Johnston • Same as store card die 1386 • Combined with die 345 • 251/345a (R-5): EF–AU $150–$225 • MS-63 $400–$600 • Only one variety.

Patriotic die 248 • *O.K. within 13 chain links* • Same as store card die 1241 • Combined with dies 126 (as reverse), 125 (as reverse), 127 (as reverse), 271, 295, 428, 432, 436 • 127/248a (R-3): EF–AU $75–$110 • MS-63 $200–$300 • 248/432a is also R-3.

Patriotic die 252 • *Masonic emblems of compass, square, and G* • Combined with dies 124 (as reverse), 127 (as reverse), 248 (as reverse), 271, 294, 295, 432 • 252/271a (R-4): VF–EF $75–$110 • MS-63 $150–$225.

Patriotic die 250 • *Large star NORTH STAR (18 stars at border, 10 stars in field, 1 large star at center)* • Ascribed to the shop of William K. Lanphear • Same as store card die 1242 • Combined with die 437 • 250/437a (R-5): EF–AU $150–$225 • MS-63 $350–$500 • Only one variety.

Patriotic die 252A • *Masonic emblems of compass, square, and G with rays* • Ascribed to the shop of William K. Lanphear • Same as store card die 1387 • Illustrated in Fuld but not listed.

Patriotic die 253 • *1864 Palmetto tree (YNGENIO ECUADOR)* • Combined with dies 125 (as reverse), 294, 295, 432 • 125/253a (R-9): MS-63 $6,000–$9,000 • Other combinations are also R-9. Reverse die for a Latin America plantation token! Curious numismatic strikes.

Patriotic die 256 • *1863 Portrait of woman in wreath (HORRORS OF WAR BLESSINGS OF PEACE)* • Die ascribed to William H. Bridgens • Combined with dies 37 (as reverse), 120 (as reverse), 138 (as reverse), 433 • 37/256a (R-2): EF–AU $40–$60 • MS-63 $125–$175.

Patriotic die 254 • *1863 Man with backpack (MONEY MAKES THE MARE GO)* • Die ascribed to William H. Bridgens • Same as store card die 1243 • Combined with dies 255 and 434 • 254/255a (R-1): EF–AU $25–$40 • MS-63 $50–$75.

Patriotic die 257 • *Man standing at dockside, ironclad in background (13 panels at border)* • Combined with die 311 • 257/311a (R-3): EF–AU $50–$75 • MS-63 $125–$175 • Also metal b (R-7).

Patriotic die 255 • *Standing man (KNICKERBOCKER CURRENCY)* • Die ascribed to William H. Bridgens • Combined with dies 0 (as reverse), 37 (as reverse), 58A (as reverse), 120 (as reverse), 138 (as reverse), 254 (as reverse), 390, 392, 393, 433 • 254/255a (R-1): EF–AU $25–$40 • MS-63 $50–$75 • 255/390a, 255/393a, and 255/433a, are also R-1. This die was used by Bridgens to create many numismatic strikes.

Patriotic die 258 • *1863 Seated goddess facing left, mountains in background* • Die ascribed to Emil Sigel • 19 mm, 20 mm, 23 mm, and 26 mm diameters, see Fuld • Combined with dies 0 and 446 • 258/446a 23 mm (R-3): EF–AU $50–$75 • MS-63 $150–$225 • Die used mostly for numismatic strikes including over a variety of other coins.

Patriotic die 259 • *Sailing ship (TRADE AND COMMERCE; 6 stars at border)* • Combined with die 445 • 259/445a (R-2): EF–AU $50–$75 • MS-63 $150–$225 • Also metal j (R-9).

Patriotic die 263 • *Open oak wreath, shield at apex (OUR CENT)* • Used as reverse with dies 101, 104, 248 • 104/263a (R-5): EF–AU $125–$175 • MS-63 $350–$500.

Patriotic die 264 • *1863 Wreath with shield at apex, PAY TO THE BEARER (ONE CENT)* • Used as reverse with die 83 • 83/264a (R-5): EF–AU $75–$125 • MS-63 $250–$375 • Also metal b (R-9).

Patriotic die 260 • *1861 CONSTITU-TION (Scroll; 6 stars at border)* • Combined with die 447 • 260/447a (R-7): EF–AU $300–$450 • MS-63 $800–$1,100 • Metals b and j are also R-7, others are rarer.

Patriotic die 265 • *Open laurel wreath (THE UNION)* • Die ascribed to S.D. Childs • Used as reverse with die 35 • 35/265 (R-4): EF–AU $30–$50 • MS-63 $100–$150 • Only one variety.

Patriotic die 261 • *Open oak wreath, shield (ONE CENT), copy of federal cent* • Die ascribed to Emil Sigel • Used as reverse with dies 69, 97, 143 • 143/261 (R-1): EF–AU $30–$45 • MS-63 $90–$135.

Patriotic die 266 • *Open wreath, shield and spears (OUR UNION)* • Dies by Charles D. Hörter • Used as reverse with dies 0 and 178 • 178/266a (R-3): EF–AU $25–$40 • MS-63 $50–$75.

Patriotic die 269 • *Open wreath (UNION FOR EVER)* • Die ascribed to Frederick B. Smith • Used as reverse with dies 6A, 69, 235 • 235/269a (R-2): EF–AU $25–$40 • MS-63 $75–$125.

Patriotic die 267 • *Open wreath, shield and spears (OUR UNION)* • Dies by Charles D. Hörter • Used as reverse with dies 41 and 178 • 178/267a (R-1): EF–AU $25–$40 • MS-63 $50–$75.

Patriotic die 270 • *Open wreath (UNION star FOREVER)* • Used as reverse with die 2 • 2/270a (R-7): EF–AU $600–$900 • MS-63 $1,500–$2,250 • Also metal b (R-9).

Patriotic die 268 • *Open wreath (UNION FOR EVER)* • Die ascribed to Frederick B. Smith • Used as reverse with dies 6 and 8 (may not exist) • 6/268a (R-1): EF–AU $25–$40 • MS-63 $50–$75.

Patriotic die 271 • *Open wreath, shield and flags (UNION FOR EVER)* • Die ascribed to George J. Glaubrecht • Same as store card die 1246 • Used as reverse with dies 23, 36, 107, 110, 111, 176, 177, 201, 248, 252 • 176/271a (R-1): EF–AU $25–$40 • MS-63 $50–$75 • Many numismatic strikes.

Patriotic die 272 • *Open wreath, shield and flags (UNION FOR EVER)* • Die by the Scovill Manufacturing Co. (?) • Used as reverse with dies 173 and 174 • 174/272a (R-1): EF–AU $25–$40 • MS-63 $50–$75.

Patriotic die 275 • *Open laurel wreath (OUR CARD)* • Die ascribed to S.D. Childs • Same as store card die 1357 • Used as reverse with dies 31A, 32, 33, 34, 279A • 32/275a (R-6): EF–AU $50–$75 • 34/275a is also R-6.

Patriotic die 273 • *Open wreath, swords and ribbon (THE UNION FOR EVER)* • Die ascribed to Francis X. Koehler • Used as reverse with die 3 • 3/273a (R-6): EF–AU $250-375 • MS-63 $700–$1,000.

Patriotic die 276 • *Open laurel wreath (OUR CARD)* • Die ascribed to S.D. Childs • Same as store card die 1357A (unlisted) • Combined with dies 34 (as reverse) and 278 • 34/276a (R-6): EF–AU $50–$75 • Also 276/278a (R-6).

Patriotic die 274 • *Open laurel wreath (OUR CARD)* • Die ascribed to S.D. Childs • Used as reverse with die 35 • 35/274a (R-6): EF–AU $40–$60 • MS-63 $125–$175 • Only one variety.

Patriotic die 277 • *Open laurel wreath (OUR CARD)* • Die ascribed to S.D. Childs • Used as reverse with dies 34 and 35 • 34/277a (R-3): EF–AU $30–$50 • MS-63 $60–$90.

Patriotic die 277A • *1861 Perched eagle, head to viewer's left (UNION; 2 stars at border)* • Die ascribed to S.D. Childs • Same as store card die 1207 • Used as reverse with die 30A • 30A/277A (R-10): VF $6,000–$9,000 • Although this die is rare on a political token it is easily enough found on a store card.

Patriotic die 279A • *1863 Perched eagle, head to viewer's left (UNION; 2 stars at border)* • Die ascribed to S.D. Childs • Same as store card die 1212 • Used as reverse with die 275 • 275/279Aa (R-10): VF–EF $6,000–$9,000 • Only one variety. Although this die is rare on a political token it is easily enough found on a store card.

Patriotic die 278 • *1863 Perched eagle, head to viewer's left (UNION)* • Die ascribed to S.D. Childs • Same as store card die 1205A • Used as reverse with dies 34, 35, 276 • 34/278a (R-5): EF–AU $75–$125.

Patriotic die 280 • *1863 Perched eagle, head to viewer's left (13 border stars)* • Die ascribed to S.D. Childs • Same as store card die 1203 • Used as reverse with die 30 • 30/280j (R-9): VF $4,000–$6,000 • Only one variety. Although this die is rare on a political token it is easily enough found on a store card.

Patriotic die 279 • *1863 Perched eagle, head to viewer's left (UNION; 2 stars at border)* • Die ascribed to S.D. Childs • Same as store card die 1205 • Used as reverse with dies 31 and 34 • 31/279a (R-6): EF–AU $100–$150 • MS-63 $300–$450.

Patriotic die 280A • *1863 Perched eagle, head to viewer's left (13 border stars)* • Die ascribed to S.D. Childs • Same as store card die 1204 • Used as reverse with die 31A • 31A/280Aa (R-10): EF–AU $8,000–$12,000 • Only one variety. Although this die is rare on a political token it is easily enough found on a store card.

Patriotic die 281 • *Perched eagle, head to viewer's right (no date)* • From the shop of John Stanton • Same as store card die 1192 • Combined with dies 70 (as reverse), 71 (as reverse), 468 • 70/281a (R-6): EF–AU $250–$375 • MS-63 $500–$750.

Patriotic die 284 • *Perched eagle. head to viewer's left, with shield on breast (no date)* • From the shop of F.C. Key & Sons • Same as store card die 1182 • Used as reverse with die 96 • 96/284b R-9): EF–AU $1,000–$1,500 • MS-63 $2,000–$3,000 • Only one variety. Although this die is rare on a political token it is easily enough found on a store card.

Patriotic die 282 • *1863 Flying eagle, head at left is turned to face date (13 stars in field)* • From the shop of F.C. Key & Sons • Same as store card die 1193 • Used as reverse with dies 116, 129, 142, 153 • 153/282a (R-8): EF–AU $1,000–$1,500 • MS-63 $2,500–$3,750 • Mostly numismatic strikes. This die is rare on a political token and nearly as rare on a store card.

Patriotic die 285 • *1863 Perched eagle, head to viewer's left (13 border stars)* • Die ascribed to Alexander Gleason • Same as store card die 1183 • Combined with dies 0 and 383a • 285/383a (R-7): EF–AU $600–$900.

Patriotic die 283 • *Eagle perched on anchor (ribbed background; 16 stars at border)* • Same as store card die 1191 • Combined with dies 134 (as reverse), 146 (as reverse), 427 • 134/283j (R-8): EF–AU $1,500–$2,250 • MS-63 $4,000–$6,000 • Other varieties are R-8 and R-9; numismatic strikes. Rare as well on a store card.

Patriotic die 285A • *1863 Perched eagle, head to viewer's left* • Ascribed to the shop of William K. Lanphear • Combined with dies 0 and 519B (the last a true blank reverse) • 285A/0a (R-9): EF–AU $2,000–$3,000.

Patriotic die 286 • *1863 Perched eagle and branches (APOTH. WEIGHT ONE DRAM)* • Dies by Charles D. Hörter • Same as store card die 1197 • "Half card" die • Combined with die 382 • 286/382a (R-7): EF–AU $150–$225 • MS-63 $350–$500 • Also metals ao (R-7) and b (R-7). Often found struck over another token.

Patriotic die 288 • *Open wreath (star GOD star PROTECT THE UNION)* • Used as reverse with die 5 • 5/288a (R-2): EF–AU $30–$45 • MS-63 $60–$90 • Also metals b (R-3), g (R-9), j (R-8).

Patriotic die 286A • *Perched eagle and branches (GOLD WEIGHT 2 DWT NEW YORK)* • Same as store card die 1199 • "Half card" die • Combined with die 287 • 287A/287a (R-9): MS-63 $2,500–$3,750 • Also metals b, d, e, j (all R-9).

Patriotic die 289 • *Perched eagle above open wreath (LINCOLN AND UNION)* • From the shop of F.C. Key & Sons • Used as reverse with die 128 • 128/289b (R-3): EF–AU $75–$110 • MS-63 $200–$300 • Also metal a (R-9).

Patriotic die 287 • *Perched eagle (SILVER MINE TOKEN E)* • Same as store card die 1213 • "Half card" die • Combined with dies 286A (as reverse), 417, 520 • 286A/287a (R-9): MS-63 $2,500–$3,750 • Other varieties are R-9 (mostly) and R-10.

Patriotic die 290 • *LINCOLN AND UNION* • From the shop of F.C. Key & Sons • Used as reverse with die 128 • 128/290s (R-3): EF–AU $100–$150 • MS-63 $300–$450 • Also other varieties, R-7 to R-9, numismatic strikes.

Patriotic die 291 • *Closed wreath (ONE COUNTRY)* • Dies by Charles D. Hörter, struck by Emil Sigel • Used as reverse with dies 98 and 244 • 244/291a (R-2): EF–AU $25–$40 • MS-63 $60–$90.

Patriotic die 294 • *Open wreath, shield and flags, star at apex (FREE DOM)* • Same as store card die 1244 • Combined with dies 113 (as reverse), 124 (as reverse), 125 (as reverse), 127 (as reverse), 428, 432 • 124/294a (R-7): EF–AU $300–$450 • MS-63 $700–$1,000.

Patriotic die 292 • *Closed wreath (ONE COUNTRY)* • Used as reverse with die 99 • 99/292a (R-3): EF–AU $50–$75 • MS-63 $150–$225 • Also metal b (R-8).

Patriotic die 295 • *Open wreath, shield and flags, star at apex (FREE DOM)* • Same as store card die 1245 • Combined with dies 125, 126, 127, 177, 185A, 201, 248, 252, 253 (as reverse), 428, 432 • 126/295a (R-5): EF–AU $150–$225 • MS-63 $400–$600 • Many numismatic strikes.

Patriotic die 293 • *ONE COUNTRY. with rays surrounding (at border, NO WEST [star] NO NORTH [star] NO EAST [star] NO SOUTH [star])* • Die ascribed to Emil Sigel • Used as reverse with dies 103 and 216 • 216/293a (R-3): EF–AU $40–$60 • MS-63 $100–$150.

Patriotic die 296 • *Open wreath, crossed swords (ARMY & NAVY)* • Dies by Charles D. Hörter • Used as reverse with dies 54 and 241 • 54/296a (R-5): EF–AU $30–$45 • MS-63 $75–$125.

Patriotic die 297 • *Open wreath, crossed swords (ARMY & NAVY)* • Die by the Scovill Manufacturing Co. (?) • Used as reverse with dies 12, 13, 14, 79 • 13/297a (R-2): EF–AU $25–$40 • MS-63 $50–$175.

Patriotic die 299 • *Open wreath, crossed swords (ARMY & NAVY)* • Dies by Charles D. Hörter • Combined with die 48 (as reverse) and 350 • 48/299a (R-1): EF–AU $25–$40 • MS-63 $50–$75.

Patriotic die 298 • *Open wreath, crossed swords (ARMY & NAVY)* • Die by the Scovill Manufacturing Co. (?) • Used as reverse with dies 10 and 11 • 11/298a (R-1): EF–AU $25–$40 • MS-63 $50–$75.

Patriotic die 300 • *Open wreath, crossed swords, star at apex (ARMY & NAVY)* • Die ascribed to Louis Leichtweis • Used as reverse with dies 16 and 18 • 18/300a (R-2): EF–AU $25–$40 • MS-63 $60–$90.

Patriotic die 301 • *Open wreath, crossed swords, star at apex (ARMY & NAVY)* • Die ascribed to Louis Leichtweis • Used as reverse with die 16 • 16/301a (R-4): EF–AU $30–$45 • MS-63 $100–$150 • Only one variety.

Patriotic die 298A • *Open wreath, crossed swords (ARMY & NAVY)* • Die ascribed to Henry D. Higgins ("Indiana primitive") • Used as reverse with die 9 • 9/298A (R-7): EF–AU $175–$250 • MS-63 $500–$750 • Also metal b (R-8).

Patriotic die 303 • *Open wreath, crossed swords, star at apex (ARMY & NAVY)* • Die ascribed to Emil Sigel • Used as reverse with dies 20, 28, 29, 91 • 28/303a (R-2): EF–AU $25–$40 • MS-63 $50–$75 • 29/303a is also R-2.

Patriotic die 306 • *Open wreath, crossed swords (ARMY & NAVY)* • Used as reverse with die 23 • 23/306a (R-2): EF–AU $25–$40 • MS-63 $50–$75 • Also metals b (R-5), d (R-9), e (R-9), j (R-8).

Patriotic die 307 • *Open wreath, crossed swords (ARMY & NAVY)* • Used as reverse with die 141 • 141/307a (R-1): EF–AU $30–$45 • MS-63 $70–$100 • Also metals b (R-8), d (R-9).

Patriotic die 304 • *Open wreath, crossed swords (ARMY & NAVY)* • Die ascribed to Louis Leichtweis • Used as reverse with die 18 • 18/304a (R-6): EF–AU $40–$60 • MS-63 $100–$150 • Only one variety.

Patriotic die 308 • *Open wreath, crossed swords (ARMY & NAVY)* • Die ascribed to Frederick B. Smith • Used as reverse with die 6B • 6B/308a (R-4): EF–AU $30–$45 • MS-63 $70–$100 • Only one variety.

Patriotic die 305 • *Open wreath, star at apex (ARMY & NAVY)* • Die ascribed to Louis Leichtweis • Used as reverse with dies 18 and 350 • 18/305a (R-9): EF–AU $700–$1,000 • Only one variety.

Patriotic die 309 • *Open wreath, crossed swords (ARMY & NAVY)* • Die ascribed to Frederick B. Smith • Used as reverse with dies 8, 8B, 137 • 8B/309a (R-2): EF–AU $25–$40 • MS-63 $50–$75.

Patriotic die 312 • *Open wreath, crossed swords (ARMY & NAVY)* • Die by the Scovill Manufacturing Co. (?) • Used as reverse with dies 10, 11, 164, 233 • 10/312s (R-1): EF–AU $25–$40 • MS-63 $50–$75 • 164/213a and 233/312a are also R-1.

Patriotic die 310 • *Open wreath, crossed swords (ARMY & NAVY)* • Die ascribed to Frederick B. Smith • Used as reverse with die 6D • 6D/310a (R-3): EF–AU $40–$60 • MS-63 $100–$150 • Also metal b (R-9).

Patriotic die 313 • *Open wreath, crossed swords (ARMY & NAVY)* • Die ascribed to Frederick B. Smith • Used as reverse with dies 7 and 7B • 8/314a (R-1): EF–AU $40–$60 • MS-63 $100–$150.

Patriotic die 311 • *Open wreath, crossed swords (ARMY & NAVY)* • Used as reverse with dies 168 and 257 • 168/311a (R-1): EF–AU $40–$60 • MS-63 $100–$150.

Patriotic die 314 • *Open wreath, crossed swords (ARMY & NAVY)* • Die ascribed to Frederick B. Smith • Used as reverse with die 8 • 8/314a (R-1): EF–AU $25–$40 • MS-63 $50–$75 • Only one variety.

Patriotic die 315 • *Open wreath, crossed swords (ARMY & NAVY)* • Die ascribed to Frederick B. Smith • Used as reverse with dies 7 and 7B • 7/315a (R-3): EF–AU $25–$40 • MS-63 $50–$75.

Patriotic die 318 • *Open wreath, crossed swords (ARMY & NAVY)* • Die ascribed to Emil Sigel • Used as reverse with dies 20 and 167 • 167/318a (R-5): EF–AU $70–$100 • MS-63 $200–$300.

Patriotic die 316 • *Open wreath, crossed swords (ARMY & NAVY)* • Die ascribed to Frederick B. Smith • Used as reverse with die 7A • 7A/316 (R-3): EF–AU $25–$40 • MS-63 $60–$90 • Only one variety.

Patriotic die 319 • *Open wreath, crossed swords (ARMY & NAVY)* • Used as reverse with die 15 • 15/319a (R-2): EF–AU $25–$40 • MS-63 $50–$75 • Also metals b (R-7), d (R-7), e (R-7), fo over dime (R-8), j (R-6).

Patriotic die 317 • *Open wreath, crossed swords (ARMY & NAVY)* • Die ascribed to Frederick B. Smith • Used as reverse with dies 0 and 8A • 8A/317a (R-2): EF–AU $25–$40 • MS-63 $50–$75 • Also 0/317a (R-10).

Patriotic die 320 • *Open wreath, swords and anchor star at apex (ARMY AND NAVY)* • Used as reverse with dies 206 and 209 • 206/320a (R-1): EF–AU $25–$40 • MS-63 $50–$75 • 219/320a is also R-1.

Patriotic die 321 • *Open wreath, swords and anchor star at apex (ARMY AND NAVY)* • Used as reverse with dies 225 and 226 • 226/321a (R-4): EF–AU $25–$40 • MS-63 $70–$100.

Patriotic die 323 • *Open wreath, swords and anchor star at apex (ARMY AND NAVY)* • Used as reverse with dies 206, 207, 210, 219 • 219/323a (R-2): EF–AU $25–$40 • MS-63 $50–$75.

Patriotic die 322 • *Open wreath, swords and anchor star at apex (ARMY AND NAVY)* • Used as reverse with dies 220 and 224 • 220/322a (R-1): EF–AU $25–$40 • MS-63 $50–$75.

Patriotic die 324 • *Open wreath, swords and anchor, star at apex (ARMY AND NAVY)* • Used as reverse with dies 207 and 221 • 221/324a (R-1): EF–AU $25–$40 • MS-63 $50–$75.

Patriotic die 322A • *Open wreath, swords and anchor star at apex (ARMY AND NAVY)* • Used as reverse with die 226A • 226A/322Aa (R-10): EF–AU $5,000–$7,500 • MS-63 $8,000–$12,000.

Patriotic die 325 • *Open wreath, swords and anchor star at apex (ARMY AND NAVY)* • Used as the reverse die with 207, 222, 223, 224 • 222/325a (R-2): EF–AU $25–$40 • MS-63 $50–$75.

Patriotic die 326 • *Open wreath, swords and anchor star at apex (ARMY AND NAVY)* • Used as reverse with dies 207 and 224 • 224/326a (R-2): EF–AU $25–$40 • MS-63 $50–$75.

Patriotic die 330 • *Open wreath (ARMY. & NAVY.)* • Used as reverse with die 78 • 78/330a (R-4): EF–AU $40–$60 • MS-63 $125–$175 • Only one variety.

Patriotic die 327 • *Open wreath, swords and anchor star at apex (ARMY AND NAVY)* • Used as reverse with dies 220, 221, 224, 225, 225A • 225/327a (R-1): EF–AU $25–$40 • MS-63 $50–$75.

Patriotic die 331 • *Open wreath, crossed cannons (ARMY & NAVY)* • Used as reverse with die 77 • 77/331a (R-4): EF–AU $40–$60 • MS-63 $100–$150 • Only one variety.

Patriotic die 328 • *Open wreath, swords and anchor star at apex (ARMY AND NAVY)* • Used as reverse with die 223 • 223/328a (R-2): EF–AU $25–$40 • MS-63 $50–$75 • Only one variety.

Patriotic die 332 • *Closed wreath (star OUR ARMY star)* • Dies by Charles D. Hörter • Used as reverse with dies 0, 45, 47 and obverse with 336 • 47/332a (R-1): EF–AU $25–$40 • MS-63 $50–$75.

Patriotic die 333 • *Closed wreath (star OUR ARMY star)* • Dies by Charles D. Hörter • Used as reverse with die 51 • 51/333a (R-6): EF–AU $400–$600 • MS-63 $800–$1,200 • Only one variety.

Patriotic die 336 • *Open wreath (OUR NAVY)* • Dies by Charles D. Hörter • Used as reverse with dies 0, 42, 53, 241, 332, obverse with 337 • 53/336a (R-1): EF–AU $25–$40 • MS-63 $50–$75 • 241/336a is also R-1.

Patriotic die 334 • *Closed wreath (star OUR ARMY diamond)* • Dies by Charles D. Hörter • Used as reverse with die 51 • 51/334a[6] (R-1): EF–AU $25–$40 • MS-63 $50–$75 • Also metals b (R-8), d (R-7), e (R-7), f (R-9), fo over dime (R-9), j (R-6).

Patriotic die 337 • *Open wreath (OUR NAVY)* • Dies by Charles D. Hörter • Used as reverse with dies 18, 41, 178, 240, 241, 336, obverse with die 350 • 240/337a (R-1): EF–AU $40–$60 • MS-63 $125–$175.

Patriotic die 335 • *Open wreath (OUR ARMY)* • Dies by Charles D. Hörter • Used as reverse with dies 46, 50, 54 • 46/336a (R-2): EF–AU $25–$40 • MS-63 $50–$75 • 50/335a is also R-2.

Patriotic die 338 • *Closed wreath (star OUR NAVY diamond)* • Dies by Charles D. Hörter • Used as reverse with dies 162, 241, 242 • 241/338a (R-2): EF–AU $50–$75 • MS-63 $150–$225.

Patriotic die 339 • *1864 Shield (13 border stars)* • Dies by Charles D. Hörter • Used as reverse with die 46 • 46/339a (R-1): EF–AU $25–$40 • MS-63 $50–$75 • Also metals b (R-7), d (R-8), e (R-8), f (R-7), j (R-7).

Patriotic die 342 • *1864 Shield (UNION FOR EVER; 2 stars at border)* • Dies by Charles D. Hörter • Combined with dies 41, 50, 51, 54 • 51/342a (R-1): EF–AU $25–$40 • MS-63 $50–$75 • 54/342a is also R-1.

Patriotic die 342A • *1864 Shield (UNION FOR EVER; 2 stars at border)* • Dies by Charles D. Hörter • Used as reverse with die 51 • 51/342A (R-2): EF–AU $25–$40 • MS-63 $50–$75 • Also mint error a (R-9), e (R-9), e oversized planchet (R-10).

Patriotic die 340 • *Open wreath enclosing shield, flag to each side, liberty cap encircled by 13 stars above* • Die ascribed to George J. Glaubrecht • Combined with dies 36 (as reverse), 111 (as reverse), 171 (as reverse), 432 • 36/340a (R-2): EF–AU $40–$60 • MS-63 $125–$175.

Patriotic die 343 • *1864 Shield (UNION FOR EVER; 2 stars at border)* • Dies by Charles D. Hörter • Used as reverse with dies 49, 54, 142, 180, 181 • 49/343a (R-1): EF–AU $25–$40 • MS-63 $50–$75.

Patriotic die 341 • *1863 Shield (UNION FOR EVER; 2 stars at border)* • Dies by Charles D. Hörter • Used as reverse with dies 0, 41, 100, 180, 240 • 180/341a (R-1): EF–AU $25–$40 • MS-63 $50–$75 • 240/341a is also R-1.

Patriotic die 343A • *1864 Shield (UNION FOR EVER)* • Used as reverse with die 54 • 54/343A (R-6): EF–AU $100–$150 • MS-63 $300–$450 • Only one variety.

Patriotic die 345 • *Shield (13 border stars; UNION)* • Die ascribed to William Johnston • Same as store card die 1247 • Used as reverse with die 251 • 251/345a (R-5): EF–AU $150–$225 • MS-63 $400–$600 • Only one variety.

Patriotic die 347 • *Open wreath enclosing shield, etc.* • From the shop of F.C. Key & Sons • Combined with dies 129 (as reverse), 130 (as reverse), 142 • 129/347e (R-7): EF–AU $200–$300 • MS-63 $500–$750.

Patriotic die 345A • *Shield (13 border stars; UNION)* • Die ascribed to William Johnston • Same as store card die 1248 • Used as reverse with die 102A • 102A/345Aa (R-10): EF–AU $4,000–$6,000 • Only one variety. Although this die is rare on a political token it can be found on a store card, although it is hardly common.

Patriotic die 347A • *Open oak wreath enclosing spade-shaped shield* • Same as store card die 1352A. Combined with die 451A • 347A/451Ab (R-9): EF–AU $2,000–$3,000.

Patriotic die 346 • *Shield within closed wreath; E.S. (CONSTITUTION AND THE UNION; star at border)* • Die ascribed to Emil Sigel • Same as store card die 1249 • Used as reverse with dies 60 and 200 • 60/346a (R-5): EF–AU $75–$125 • MS-63 $250-375.

Patriotic die 348 • *Drums, rifles, cannons, flags, etc.* • From the shop of F.C. Key & Sons • Used as reverse with dies 129, 130, 142 • 129/348e (R-9): EF–AU $300–$500 • MS-63 $700–$1,000 • Also other R-9 varieties.

Patriotic die 349 • *1864 Drums, rifles, cannons, flags, etc.* • From the shop of F.C. Key & Sons • Same as store card die 1250 • Combined with dies 116 (as reverse), 129 (as reverse), 130 (as reverse), 477 • 129/349a (R-9): EF–AU $300–$450 • MS-63 $750–$1,250 • Also other R-9 numismatic strikes and an R-10.

Patriotic die 351 • *Open wreath enclosing crossed cannons, drum, flags, liberty cap* • Die by the Scovill Manufacturing Co. (?) • Used as reverse with dies 12, 79, 80, 81, 82 • 79/351a (R-1): EF–AU $25–$40 • MS-63 $50–$75.

Patriotic die 352 • *Open wreath enclosing crossed cannons, drum, flags, liberty cap* • Die by the Scovill Manufacturing Co. (?) • Used as reverse with die 163 • 163/352a (R-2): VF–EF $25–$40 • MS-63 $50–$75 • Also metals b (R-9), j (R-9).

Patriotic die 349A • *Drums, rifles, cannons, flags, etc. (OUR COUNTRY AND OUR FLAG NOW & FOREVER)* • From the shop of F.C. Key & Sons • Used as reverse with die 131A • 131A/349Ab (R-7): VF–EF $250–$375 • MS-63 $600–$900 • Also metals a (R-8), f (R-9). Numismatic strikes.

Patriotic die 352A • *Open wreath enclosing crossed cannons, drum, flags, liberty cap* • Die by the Scovill Manufacturing Co. (?) • Used as reverse with dies 82 and 231 • 231/252A (R-1): EF–AU $25–$40 • MS-63 $50–$75.

Patriotic die 350 • *Open wreath enclosing crossed cannons, drum, flags, liberty cap* • Dies by Charles D. Hörter • Used as reverse with dies 0, 45, 299, 305, 337 • 45/350a (R-2): VF–EF $25–$40 • MS-63 $50–$75 • 229/350a and 337/350a are also R-2.

Patriotic die 352B • *Open wreath enclosing crossed cannons, drum, flags, liberty cap* • Die by the Scovill Manufacturing Co. (?) • Used as reverse with die 230 • 230/352Ba (R-2): EF–AU $25–$40 • MS-63 $50–$75 • Also metal b (R-8).

Patriotic die 355 • *Open wreath (NOT ONE CENT)* • Die ascribed to Emil Sigel • Same as store card die 1251 • Used as reverse with dies 61, 68, 105, 196 • 61/355a (R-3): EF–AU $30–$45 • MS-63 $60–$90 • 105/355a and 196/355a are also R-3.

Patriotic die 353 • *Crossed cannons, drum, flags, liberty cap* • Die ascribed to Louis Leichtweis • Used as reverse with dies 16 and 18 • 18/353a (R-3): EF–AU $25–$40 • MS-63 $50–$75.

Patriotic die 356 • *Open wreath (NOT ONE CENT)* • Dies by Charles D. Hörter • Used as reverse with die 87 • 87/356a (R-1): EF–AU $25–$40 • MS-63 $50–$75 • Also metal b (R-7).

Patriotic die 354 • *Open wreath (NOT ONE CENT)* • Used as reverse with die 4 • 4/354g (R-7): EF–AU $700–$1,000 • Only one variety.

Patriotic die 357 • *Open wreath (NOT ONE CENT)* • Dies by Charles D. Hörter • Used as reverse with dies 0 and 86 • 86/357a (R-2): EF–AU $25–$40 • MS-63 $50–$75.

Patriotic die 358 • *Open wreath (NOT ONE CENT)* • Die ascribed to Emil Sigel • Used as reverse with die 105 • 105/358a (R-4): EF–AU $50–$75 • MS-63 $125–$175 • Only one variety.

Patriotic die 361 • *Open wreath (NOT ONE CENT; H)* • Dies by Charles D. Hörter • Same as store card die 1254 • Used as reverse with die 88 • 88/361a (R-3): EF–AU $25–$40 • MS-63 $100–$150 • Also metals b (R-8), d (R-9), do over cent (R-9), f (R-9), fo over dime (R-9).

Patriotic die 359 • *Open wreath (NOT ONE CENT)* • Die ascribed to Emil Sigel • Same as store card die 1252 • Used as reverse with dies 0, 68, 105, 199, 229, and as obverse with die 436 • 1/359a (R-7): EF–AU $75–$125 • MS-63 $250–$375 • 1/359j is also R-7.

Patriotic die 362 • *Open wreath (NOT ONE CENT; J.G.W.)* • Used as reverse with dies 64, 88, 93 • 93/362a (R-2): EF–AU $25–$40 • MS-63 $50–$75.

Patriotic die 363 • *Open wreath (NOT ONE CENT)* • Dies by Charles D. Hörter • Used as reverse with die 94 • 94/363a (R-6): EF–AU $150–$225 • MS-63 $350–$500 • Only one variety.

Patriotic die 360 • *Open wreath (NOT ONE CENT)* • Die ascribed to Emil Sigel • Same as store card die 1253 • Used as reverse with dies 1, 68, 105, 119, 196, 198, 199, 229 and obverse with 436 • 1/360a (R-7): EF–AU $75–$125 • MS-63 $250–$375 • 1/360b, e, and j are also R-7.

Patriotic die 364 • *Open wreath (NOT ONE CENT; eagle's head facing left)* • Dies by Charles D. Hörter • Used as reverse with die 90 • 90/364a (R-1): EF–AU $25–$40 • MS-63 $50–$75 • Also metals b (R-8), g (R-9).

Patriotic die 367 • *Open wreath (NOT ONE CENT)* • Die ascribed to Emil Sigel • Used as reverse with dies 62 and 69 • 62/367a (R-3): EF–AU $25–$40 • MS-63 $50–$75.

Patriotic die 365 • *Open wreath (NOT ONE CENT)* • Die ascribed to Emil Sigel • Used as reverse with die 27 • 27/365a (R-3): EF–AU $25–$40 • MS-63 $75–$110 • Only one variety.

Patriotic die 368 • *Open wreath (NOT ONE CENT)* • Die ascribed to Emil Sigel • Used as reverse with dies 95 and 96 • 95/368a (R-2): EF–AU $25–$40 • MS-63 $50–$75.

Patriotic die 369 • *Open wreath (NOT ONE CENT)* • Die ascribed to Emil Sigel • Used as reverse with die 69 • 69/369a (R-3): EF–AU $25–$40 • MS-63 $50–$75.

Patriotic die 366 • *Open wreath (NOT ONE CENT)* • Die ascribed to Emil Sigel • Used as reverse with die 63 • 63/366a (R-1): EF–AU $25–$40 • MS-63 $50–$75 • Also metal j (R-9).

Patriotic die 370 • *Open wreath (NOT ONE CENT)* • Die ascribed to Emil Sigel • Used as reverse with die 66 • 66/370a (R-2): EF–AU $25–$40 • MS-63 $50–$75 • Also metal b (R-8).

Patriotic die 373 • *Open wreath (NOT ONE CENT)* • Die ascribed to Emil Sigel • Used as reverse with die 91 • 91/373a (R-7): EF–AU $600–$900 • Only one variety.

Patriotic die 371 • *Open wreath (NOT ONE CENT)* • Die ascribed to Emil Sigel • Used as reverse with dies 65A and 68A • 68A/371a (R-3): EF–AU $30–$45 • MS-63 $75–$125.

Patriotic die 374 • *Open wreath, star at apex (NOT ONE CENT star)* • Die ascribed to Emil Sigel • Used as reverse with die 242 • 242/374a (R-2): EF–AU $25–$40 • MS-63 $50–$75 • Also metals d (R-9), do over cent (R-9).

Patriotic die 372 • *Open wreath (NOT ONE CENT)* • Die ascribed to Emil Sigel • Used as reverse with dies 0 and 67 • 67/372d (R-5): EF–AU $75–$125 • MS-63 $250–$375 • Also many overstrikes and other numismatic issues.

Patriotic die 375 • *1863 Closed wreath (NOT ONE CENT)* • Die ascribed to Emil Sigel • Used as reverse with dies 103 and 245 (may not exist) • 103/375 (R-4): EF–AU $35–$50 • MS-63 $150–$225.

Patriotic die 375A • *1863 Closed wreath (NOT ONE CENT)* • Die ascribed to Emil Sigel • Used as reverse with dies 244 and 245 • 245/375Aa (R-3): EF–AU $60–$90 • MS-63 $200–$300.

Patriotic die 378 • *Closed wreath (NOT ONE CENT L. ROLOFF)* • Die ascribed to Louis Roloff, struck by Emil Sigel • Same as store card die 1257 • Used as reverse with dies 195, 197, 243 • 195/378a (R-3): EF–AU $25–$40 • MS-63 $50–$75 • 243/378a is also R-3.

Patriotic die 376 • *Closed wreath (NOT ONE CENT E.S.)* • Die ascribed to Emil Sigel • Used as reverse with die 195 • 195/376a (R-4): EF–AU $40–$60 • MS-63 $100–$150 • Only one variety.

Patriotic die 379 • *Closed wreath (NOT ONE CENT)* • Die ascribed to Emil Sigel • Same as store card die 1258 • Used as reverse with die 247 • 247/379a (R-3): EF–AU $25–$40 • MS-63 $50–$75 • Also metal do over cent (R-9).

Patriotic die 377 • *Closed wreath (NOT ONE CENT L. ROLOFF)* • Die ascribed to Louis Roloff, struck by Emil Sigel • Same as store card die 1256 • Used as reverse with die 247 • 247/377a (R-2): EF–AU $25–$40 • MS-63 $50–$75.

Patriotic die 380 • *Closed wreath (NOT ONE CENT)* • Same as store card die 1259 • Used as reverse with dies 197, 243, 247 • 197/380a (R-2): EF–AU $25–$40 • MS-63 $50–$75.

Patriotic die 381 • *Closed wreath (NOT ONE CENT)* • Die ascribed to Emil Sigel • Used as reverse with dies 0 and 244 • 244/381a (R-2): EF–AU $25–$40 • MS-63 $50–$75 • Only one variety if you discard die 0 (really not a die).

Patriotic die 384 • *Closed wreath (NOT ONE CENT)* • Die ascribed to Emil Sigel • Used as reverse with dies 20 and 188 • 188/384a (R-3): EF–AU $40–$60 • MS-63 $125–$175.

Patriotic die 385 • *Open wreath (NOT ONE CENT)* • Used as reverse with die 59 • 59/385a (R-2): EF–AU $40–$60 • MS-63 $125–$175 • Also metal b (R-4).

Patriotic die 382 • *Closed wreath (NOT ONE CENT)* • Dies by Charles D. Hörter • Same as store card die 1263 • Used as reverse with die 286 • 286/382a (R-7): EF–AU $150–$225 • MS-63 $350–$500 • Also R-7 are ao and b, the other two combinations.

Patriotic die 386 • *Open wreath (GOOD FOR ONE CENT 1863 Redeem.ed)* • Same as store card die 1264 • Combined with die 427 • 386/427j (R-7): EF–AU $500–$750 • MS-63 $1,250–$1,750 • Also metals a, b, d, e, f, g (all R-8).

Patriotic die 383 • *Open wreath (NOT ONE CENT; 13 stars in field)* • Die ascribed to Alexander Gleason • Same as store card die 1262 • Used as reverse with die 285 • 285/383a (R-7): EF–AU $600–$900 • Primitive die by Alexander Gleason.

Patriotic die 387 • *MILLIONS FOR DEFENCE; open wreath, 3 stars below wreath (NOT ONE CENT FOR TRIBUTE)* • Die ascribed to Louis Leichtweis • Used as reverse with die 43 • 43/387a (R-4): EF–AU $50–$75 • MS-63 $150–$225 • Also metal g (R-9).

Patriotic die 390 • *I-O-U two small Washington portraits; CENT; at center, 1 PURE COPPER* • Die ascribed to William H. Bridgens • Same as store card die 1265 • Used as reverse with dies 0, 255, 434 • 255/390a (R-1): EF–AU $25–$40 • MS-63 $50–$75.

Patriotic die 388 • *MILLIONS FOR DEFENCE; open wreath, beaver below wreath (NOT ONE CENT FOR TRIBUTE)* • Die ascribed to Louis Leichtweis • Used as reverse with dies 17 and 43 • 17/388a (R-2): EF–AU $25–$40 • MS-63 $50–$75 • 43/388a is also R-2.

Patriotic die 390A • *I-O-U 2 small female portraits; CENT; at center, 1 PURE COPPER* • Die ascribed to William H. Bridgens • Same as store card die 1266 • Brockage error (R-9): EF–AU $3,000–$4,500 • Only one variety (if you consider a mint error to be a separate variety) as a patriotic token.

Patriotic die 389 • *Open wreath (NOT ONE CENT FOR THE WIDOWS)* • Die ascribed to Emil Sigel • Used as reverse with die 97 • 97/389a (R-2): EF–AU $40–$60 • MS-63 $110–$175 • Also metals b (R-7), d (R-6), do over cent (R-8), e (R-9), f (R-9), fo over dime (R-8).

Patriotic die 391 • *Open wreath; I O.U. 1 CENT* • Die ascribed to Emil Sigel • Same as store card die 1267 • Used as reverse with dies 1, 105, 229, 255 and obverse with 434 • 1/391a (R-1): EF–AU $25–$40 • MS-63 $50–$75.

Patriotic die 392 • *GOOD FOR 1 CENT (2 stars at border)* • Die ascribed to William H. Bridgens • Same as store card die 1268 • Combined with dies 255 (as reverse) and 434 • 255/392a (R-2): EF–AU $25–$40 • MS-63 $50–$75.

Patriotic die 395 • *Open wreath; THIS MEDAL PRICE ONE CENT* • Die ascribed to Frederick B. Smith • Used as reverse with die 137 • 137/395a (R-1): EF–AU $30–$45 • MS-63 $60–$90 • Also metal b (R-9).

Patriotic die 393 • *GOOD FOR 1 CENT (2 stars at border)* • Die ascribed to William H. Bridgens • Same as store card die 1269 • Used as reverse with die 255 • 255/393a (R-1): EF–AU $25–$40 • MS-63 $50–$75 • Also metals b (r-3), do over cent (R-9), j (R-9).

Patriotic die 396 • *Open wreath (H; WILSON'S 1 MEDAL / H)* • Same as store card die 1271 • Used as reverse with dies 19 and 112 • 112/396a (R-1): EF–AU $25–$40 • MS-63 $50–$75.

Patriotic die 394 • *Mc CLELLAN MEDAL FOR ONE CENT; 2 stars* • Dies by Charles D. Hörter • Used as reverse with dies 93 and 140 • 140/394a (R-1): EF–AU $30–$45 • MS-63 $100–$150.

Patriotic die 397 • *1863 Rattlesnake (BEWARE; 34 stars inside border)* • Die ascribed to Frederick B. Smith • Used as reverse with die 136 • 136/397a (R-1): EF–AU $40–$60 • MS-63 $150–$225 • Also metals do mint error and over cent (R-10), g (R-9).

Patriotic die 398 • *Open wreath; six-pointed star with shield* • Die ascribed to Emil Sigel • Used as reverse with die 119 • 119/398a (R-1): EF–AU $25–$40 • MS-63 $50–$75 • Also metals b (R-8), g (R-9).

Patriotic die 399 • *Open wreath; six-pointed star with five-pointed star at center, rays surrounding.* • Used as reverse with dies 189 and 231 • 189/399a (R-1): EF–AU $25–$50 • MS-63 $60–$90.

Patriotic die 400 • *THE UNION MUST AND SHALL BE PRESERVED JACK-SON; ornaments* • Die ascribed to Henry D. Higgins ("Indiana primitive") • Used as reverse with dies 9, 155, 165, 175, 211 • 175/400a (R-3): EF–AU $50–$75 • MS-63 $250–$375.

Patriotic die 401 • *THE UNION MUST AND SHALL BE PRESERVED JACK-SON; ornaments* • Die ascribed to Henry D. Higgins ("Indiana primitive") • Used as reverse with die 175 • 175/401a (R-5): EF–AU $50–$75 • MS-63 $250–$375 • Only one variety.

Patriotic die 402 • *THE UNION MUST, AND SHALL BE PRESERVED JACK-SON; ornaments* • Die ascribed to Henry D. Higgins ("Indiana primitive") • Used as reverse with dies 211 (almost certainly does not exist) and 238 • 238/403a (R-4): EF–AU $250–$350 • MS-63 $700–$1,000.

Patriotic die 403 • *THE UNION MUST & SHALL BE PRESERVED JACKSON; ornaments* • Die ascribed to Henry D. Higgins ("Indiana primitive") • Used as reverse with dies 175 and 232A • 175/403a (R-4): EF–AU $50–$75 • MS-63 $250–$375.

Patriotic die 404 • *THE UNION MUST AND SHALL BE PRESERVED JACK-SON; ornaments* • Die ascribed to Henry D. Higgins ("Indiana primitive") • Used as reverse with die 9A • 9A/404a (R-9): EF–AU $2,500–$3,750 • MS-63 $5,000–$7,500 • Only four known (Fuld, fifth edition). Only one variety.

Patriotic die 405 • *THE CONSTITU-TION MUST AND SHALL BE PRE-SERVED; leaves and ornaments* • Die ascribed to Henry D. Higgins ("Indiana primitive") • Used as reverse with dies 9 and 238 • 238/405a (R-3): EF–AU $250–$350 • MS-63 $700–$1,000.

Patriotic die 406 • *PROCLAIM LIB-ERTY. THROUGH OUT. THE LAND; leaves, three linked rings; etc.* • Die ascribed to Henry D. Higgins ("Indiana primi-tive") • Used as reverse with die 9A • 9A/406a (R-6): EF–AU $250–$375 • MS-63 $700–$1,000 • Only one variety.

Patriotic die 406A • ? • Used as reverse with die 126 • 126/406A (R-10 Non-collectible).

Patriotic die 407 • *PROCLAIM LIB-ERTY LINCOLN around star THROUGH OUT THE LAND; ornaments* • Die ascribed to Henry D. Higgins ("Indiana primitive") • Used as reverse with die 9A • 9A/407a (R-6): EF–AU $150–$225 • Only one variety.

Patriotic die 408 • *IF ANYBODY ATTEMPTS . . . SPOT (stars as punctua-tion)* • Used as reverse with die 210 • 210/408a (R-3): EF–AU $25–$40 • MS-63 $50–$75 • Only one variety. Although most tokens in this design series are called copper, the appearance of many is more like brass.

Patriotic die 409 • *IF ANYBODY ATTEMPTS . . . SPOT (stars as punctua-tion)* • Used as reverse with dies 207 and 209 • 207/409a (R-1): EF–AU $25–$40 • MS-63 $50–$75.

Patriotic die 410 • *IF ANYBODY ATTEMPTS . . . SPOT (stars as punctuation)* • Used as reverse with dies 205, 207, 208, 209 • 207/410a (R-1): EF–AU $25–$40 • MS-63 $50–$75 • 208/410a is also R-1.

Patriotic die 413 • *IF ANYBODY ATTEMPTS . . . SPOT (stars as punctuation)* • Used as reverse with dies 203 and 204 • 203/413a (R-3): EF–AU $30–$45 • MS-63 $100–$150.

Patriotic die 411 • *IF ANYBODY ATTEMPTS . . . SPOT (stars as punctuation)* • Used as reverse with die 205 • 205/411a (R-9): EF–AU $2,500–$3,750 • MS-63 $4,000–$6,000 • Only four known (Fuld, fifth edition). Only one variety.

Patriotic die 413A • *IF ANYBODY ATTEMPTS . . . SPOT (stars as punctuation)* • Used as reverse with die 210 • 210/413Ab (R-9): EF–AU $2,500–$3,750 • Only four known (Fuld, fifth edition). Only one variety.

Patriotic die 412 • *IF ANYBODY ATTEMPTS . . . SPOT (stars as punctuation)* • Used as reverse with dies 203, 207, 209 • 203/412a (R-3): EF–AU $30–$45 • MS-63 $100–$150 • 207/412a and 109/412a are also R-3.

Patriotic die 414 • *IF ANYBODY ATTEMPTS . . . SPOOT (stars as punctuation)* • Used as reverse with die 209 • 209/414a (R-2): EF–AU $40–$60 • MS-63 $125–$175 • Also metal ao over NY-10-F (R-10).

Patriotic die 415 • *IF ANYBODY ATTEMPTS . . . SPOT (star at border)* • Used as reverse with dies 210, 212, 214 • 212/415a (R-2): EF–AU $25–$40 • MS-63 $50–$75.

Patriotic die 417A • *Many six-pointed stars in field* • Used as reverse with die 241A • 214A/417Ag (R-10): EF–AU $10,000–$15,000 • Only one variety.

Patriotic die 416 • *IF ANYBODY ATTEMPTS . . . SPOT (star at border)* • Used as reverse with dies 210 and 214 • 214/416a (R-1): EF–AU $25–$40 • MS-63 $50–$75.

Patriotic die 418 • *Open wreath (PEACE clasped hands with SOUT and NORT on cuffs FOREVER, wreath tips distant)* • Used as reverse with dies 0, 22, 25, 26, 118 • 26/418a (R-2): EF–AU $25–$40 • MS-63 $60–$90 • 118/418a is also R-2.

Patriotic die 417 • *Open wreath (13 stars in field; AMERICA)* • Die ascribed to John Marr of Mossin & Marr • Same as store card die 1272 • Used as reverse with dies 125, 154, 160, 218, 417 • 160/417a (R-4): EF–AU $50–$75 • MS-63 $175–$250 • Also many numismatic strikes.

Patriotic die 419 • *Open wreath (PEACE clasped hands with SOUT and NORT on cuffs FOREVER, wreath tips close)* • Die ascribed to George J. Glaubrecht • Used as reverse with die 118 • 118/419a (R-5): EF–AU $60–$90 • MS-63 $150–$225 • 118/419b is also R-5.

Patriotic die 420 • *Open wreath; drum, crossed cannons, etc. (EXCHANGE)* • Used as reverse with die 117 • 117/420a (R-1): EF–AU $25–$40 • MS-63 $50–$75 • Also metals b (R-4), d (R-9), e (R-8), f (R-9), fo over dime (R-8), g (R-9), j (R-9).

Patriotic die 423 • *1863 Open wreath, crossed cannons, anchor at apex* • Used as reverse with die 237 • 237/423a (R-1): EF–AU $50–$75 • MS-63 $200–$300 • Also metal b (R-9).

Patriotic die 424 • *1863 Open oak wreath* • Same as store card die 1273 • Used as reverse with dies 38B, 158, 194 and as obverse with 451 • 158/424a (R-9): MS-63 $5,000–$7,500 • 194/424a is also R-9.

Patriotic die 421 • *1863 Open wreath, crossed cannons, anchor at apex* • Used as reverse with die 239 • 239/421 (R-3): EF–AU $50–$75 • MS-63 $200–$300 • Only one variety.

Patriotic die 425 • *1863 Open oak wreath* • Same as store card die 1274 • Used as reverse with die 157 • 157/425a (R-9): MS-63 $6,000–$10,000 • Also metal e thick planchet (R-10).

Patriotic die 422 • *1863 Open wreath, crossed cannons, anchor at apex* • Used as reverse with die 239 • 239/422a (R-2): EF–AU $50–$75 • MS-63 $200–$300 • Only one variety.

Patriotic die 426 • *Open laurel wreath (UNION)* • Die ascribed to Frederick B. Smith • Used as reverse with dies 0 and 236 • 326/426a (R-1): EF–AU $25–$40 • MS-63 $50–$75.

Patriotic die 429 • *MILITARY NECESITY (2 stars at border; one at center)* • Die ascribed to Alexander Gleason • Used as reverse with die 172 • 172/429a (R-5): EF–AU $75–$125 • MS-63 $250–$375 • Only one variety.

Patriotic die 427 • *Wreath (UNION; 1863; C)* • Same as store card die 1374 • Used as reverse with dies 184, 283, 386 and obverse with 472 and 480A • 386/427j (R-7): EF–AU $500–$750 • MS-63 $1,250–$1,750.

Patriotic die 430 • *Open wreath, star at apex (PENNY SAVED IS A PENNY EARNED)* • Die ascribed to Emil Sigel • Used as reverse with dies 54, 151, 180 • 151/430 (R-1): EF–AU $25–$40 • MS-63 $60–$90.

Patriotic die 428 • *Open wreath, crossed swords and anchor, star at apex (C.L.R.)* • Used as reverse with dies 125, 127, 171, 248, 294, 295, 340 and obverse with 432 • 171/428a (R-7): EF–AU $1,000–$1,500 • MS-63 $2,250–$3,250 • Many numismatic strikes.

Patriotic die 431 • *Closed "wreath" of 14 leaves (VALUE ME AS YOU PLEAS; ornaments)* • Die ascribed to Henry D. Higgins ("Indiana primitive") • Used as reverse with dies 9, 85, 155, 165, 234 • 155/431a (R-4): EF–AU $100–$150 • MS-63 $300–$450.

Patriotic die 432 • *Open wreath, crossed cannons (NO COMPROMISE WITH TRAITORS)* • Same as store card die 1275 • Used as reverse with dies 36, 45, 91, 106, 107, 113, 125, 126, 127, 135, 177, 185a, 201, 248, 252, 253, 294, 295, 428 • 107/432a (R-1): EF–AU $30–$45 • MS-63 $60–$90 • To create numismatic strikes this die was combined with more others than any die in the patriotic series.

Patriotic die 435 • *UNITED WE STAND DIVIDED WE FALL; within open wreath is a fasces surmounted by a liberty cap* • Die ascribed to Emil Sigel • Same as store card die 1276 • Used as reverse with dies 91, 167, 188 • 91/435a (R-7): EF–AU $125–$175 • MS-63 $300–$450 • 188/435j and 167/435a are also R-7.

Patriotic die 433 • *Eagle perched on top of globe (UNION FOR EVER at top border)* • Die ascribed to William H. Bridgens • Same as store card die 1214 • Used as reverse with dies 255 and 434 • 255/433a (R-1): EF–AU $25–$40 • MS-63 $50–$75.

Patriotic die 436 • *UNITED COUNTRY in ellipse; 34 stars around border* • Die ascribed to Emil Sigel • Same as store card die 1277 • Used as reverse with dies 1, 56, 105, 198, 248, 359, 360 • 1/436a (R-5): EF–AU $40–$60 • MS-63 $125–$175.

Patriotic die 434 • *Eagle perched on the top of globe inscribed COPPER (UNITED STATES at top border)* • Die ascribed to William H. Bridgens • Same as store card die 1215 • Used as reverse with dies 37, 58A, 120, 138, 202, 254, 390, 392, 433 • 37/434a (R-1): EF–AU $25–$40 • MS-63 $50–$75 • 138/434a and 202/434a are also R-1.

Patriotic die 437 • *1863 Stocking (13 border stars)* • Same as store card die 1278 • "Half card" die • Die ascribed to the shop of William Lanphear • Used as reverse with die 250 • 250/437a (R5): EF–AU $150–$225 • MS-63 $350–$500.

Patriotic die 438 • *Liberty head ("Phoenician Head"; 13 border stars; LUTZ)* • Same as store card die 1131 • Used as reverse with die 38 • 38/438 (R-9): EF–AU $3,500–$5,000 • MS-63 $6,000–$9,000 • Also metal d (R-9). The store card use is scarce.

Patriotic die 439 • *All-seeing eye with rays, bow, crossed arrows, hand holding a heart, three linked rings* • Die ascribed to Louis Roloff • Used as reverse with die 58 • 58/439a (R-3): EF–AU $70–$100 • MS-63 $175–$250 • Also metal e (R-9).

Patriotic die 439A • *All-seeing eye with rays, bow, crossed arrows, hand, three linked rings; E.S* • Used as reverse with die 58 • 58/439A (R-10): MS-63 $8,000–$12,000 • Only one variety.

Patriotic die 440 • *NOW AND FOR EVER* • Die ascribed to Emil Sigel • Used as reverse with dies 92, 135, 199 • 135/440a (R-2): EF–AU $25–$40 • MS-63 $50–$75.

Patriotic die 441 • *NOW AND FOR EVER* • Die ascribed to Emil Sigel • Used as reverse with die 135 • 135/441a (R-2): EF–AU $25–$40 • MS-63 $50–$75 • Only one variety.

Patriotic die 442 • *Open laurel wreath (NEW YORK; star)* • Die ascribed to George J. Glaubrecht • Used as reverse with dies 22 and 110 • 110/442 (R-1): EF–AU $25–$40 • MS-63 $50–$75.

Patriotic die 443 • *Open laurel wreath (NEW YORK)* • Die ascribed to Emil Sigel • Used as reverse with dies 63 and 191 • 191/443a (R-1): EF–AU $25–$40 • MS-63 $50–$75.

Patriotic die 444 • *Grouping of fruit and vegetables (20 stars around border)* • From the shop of John Stanton • Same as store card die 1279 • "Half card" die • Used as reverse with dies 57, 71, 76, 84, 70 • 84/444a (R-8): EF–AU $700–$1,000 • MS-63 $1,750–$2,500.

Patriotic die 447 • *CONCESSION BEFORE SECESSION* • Used as reverse with die 260 • 260/447a (R-7): EF–AU $300–$450 • MS-63 $800–$1,200 • Also metals b (R-7), d (R-8), e (R-9), f (R-9), g (R-9), j (R-7).

Patriotic die 447A • *Sewing machine* • Ascribed to the shop of William K. Lanphear • Same as store card die 1298 • "Half card" die • Used as reverse with die 31 • 31/447A (R-10): MS-63 $6,000–$9,000 • The store card use is scarce but obtainable.

Patriotic die 445 • *COPPERS 20 Pr Ct PREMIUM, in square* • Used as reverse with die 259 • 259/445a (R-2): EF–AU $50–$75 • MS-63 $150–$225 • Also metal j (R-9).

Patriotic die 446 • *Ship sailing to right (TRADE AND COMMERCE)* • Die ascribed to Emil Sigel • Used as reverse with die 258 • 258/446a 23 mm (R-3): EF–AU $50–$75 • MS-63 $150–$225 • Various planchet sizes 19 mm to 26 mm, numismatic strikes.

Patriotic die 448 • *Saddle (SADDLES, BRIDLES, &C.)* • Ascribed to the shop of William K. Lanphear • Same as store card die 1341 • "Half card" die • Used as reverse with die 39 • 39/448a (R-9): EF–AU $4,000–$6,000 • MS-63 $8,000–$12,000 • Elusive but available as a store card.

Patriotic die 449 • *Thistle (UNITED WE STAND DIVIDED WE FALL; 2 stars at border)* • Same as store card die 1406 • 449/471a (R-3): EF–AU $30–$45 • MS-63 $75–$125.

Patriotic die 450 • *Thistle (UNITED WE STAND DIVIDED WE FALL; 2 stars at border)* • Same as store card die 1407 • Used as reverse with die 471 • 450/471a (R-1): EF–AU $25–$40 • MS-63 $50–$75 • Readily available in its store card use.

Patriotic die 451 • *1863 Hat (FURNISH-ING GOODS; 6 stars at border)* • Ascribed to the shop of William K. Lanphear • Same as store card die 1342 • "Half card" die • Used as reverse with die 424 • 424/451a (R-10): MS-63 $6,000–$9,000 • Readily available in its store card use.

Patriotic die 451A • *GOOD FOR 4 CENTS* • Raised line in field opposite border tips. 4 leans right; upright, if extended, would pass clear of the right of the D (GOOD) above.• "Half card" die • Used as reverse with die 347A • 347A/451Ab (R-9): EF–AU $2,000–$3,000.

Patriotic die 451B • *GOOD FOR / 4 / CENTS* • 4 is vertical; upright, if extended, would impact or graze the right side of the D (GOOD) above. S (CENTS) slightly high. Combined with die 532 • 451B/532b (R-10): EF–AU $2,000–$3,000.

Patriotic die 451C • *GOOD FOR / CENT* • Combined with die 532 • 451C/532b (R-10): EF–AU $2,000–$3,000.

Patriotic die 452 • *10 in beaded circle (24 stars around border)* • From the shop of John Stanton or his successors • Same as store card die 1393 • "Half card" die • Used as reverse with dies 70 and 71 • 70/452 (R-9): MS-63 $3,000–$4,500 • Also other R-9 varieties.

Patriotic die 452A • *10 CENTS (12 border stars)* • *Store card die equivalent:* 1394 • "Half card" die • Used as reverse with die 444 • 444/452Ab (R-9): EF–AU $4,000–$6,000 • Also elusive in its store card use.

Patriotic die 452B • *10 CENTS (12 border stars)* • Same as store card die 1396 • "Half card" die • Used as reverse with die 519 • 452B/519j (R-9): MS-63 $4,000–$6,000.

Patriotic die 453 • *10 CENTS (open wreath)* • Used as reverse with die 59 • 59/453b (R-8): EF–AU $300–$450 • Also metal a (R-8).

Patriotic die 453A • *15 CENTS (11 border stars)* • Combined with die 464C • 453A/464Cb (R-10): Fine $4,000–$6,000 • Unlisted in Fuld.

Patriotic die 454 • *15 in otherwise plain field* • From the shop of John Stanton or his successors • Same as store card die 1397 • Brockage mint error • (R-9): MS-63 $3,000–$4,500.

Patriotic die 454A • *50 in otherwise plain field* • From the shop of John Stanton or his successors • "Half card" die • Combined with die 0 • 454A/0a (R-10): MS-63 $4,000–$6,000.

Patriotic die 454B • *50 CENTS (11 border stars)* • Combined with die 464C • 454B/464Cb (R-10): EF $4,000–$6,000 • Unlisted in Fuld.

Patriotic die 454E • *45 CENTS (10 border stars)* • Combined with die 464E • 454C/464Eb (R-10): EF $4,000–$6,000 • 19.2 mm. Unlisted in Fuld.

Patriotic die 455 • *GOOD FOR 25 CENTS PAYABLE IN BANK BILLS; 3 stars* • From the shop of John Stanton • Same as store card die 1400 • "Half card" die • Used as reverse with die 71 • 71/455a (R-9): MS-63 $6,000–$9,000 • Also metal b (R-9). The store card use is rare.

Patriotic die 456B • *25 in otherwise plain field* • From the shop of John Stanton or his successors • "Half card" die • Used as reverse with die 76 • 76/456Bb (R-9): EF–AU $5,000–$7,500 • Only one variety. The store card use is scarce.

Patriotic die 456 • *1862; GOOD FOR 25 CENTS; 2 maple leaves* • From the shop of John Stanton • Same as store card die 1401 • "Half card" die • Used as reverse with dies 70 and 71 • 70/456a (R-9): MS-63 $5,000–$7,500 • 71/456a is also R-9. The store card use is rare.

Patriotic die 457 • *1863 Crossed flags over sunrise (13 border stars)* • Same as store card die 1381 • Used as reverse with die 0 • Brockage mint error (R-9): MS-63 $3,000–$4,500 • Also 0/457do over cent (R-10).

Patriotic die 456A • *25 CENTS (11 border stars)* • From the shop of John Stanton or his successors • Same as store card die 1399 • "Half card" die • Used as reverse with die 76 • 76/456Aa (R-9): EF–AU $5,000–$7,500 • Also metal b (R-9). The store card use is scarce.

Patriotic die 458 • *Axe and log (GOOD FOR ANOTHER HEAT)* • Used as reverse with die 133 • 133/458b (R-5): EF–AU $125–$175 • MS-63 $300–$450 • Also metal a (R-8).

Patriotic die 459 • *A BUSINESS CARD (10 stars near center)* • From the shop of John Stanton • "Half card" die • Same as store card die 1370 • Used as reverse with die 75 • 75/459a (R-8): EF–AU $300–$450 • MS-63 $900–$1,350 • Also metal b (R-9).

Patriotic die 464E • *"No" in plain field, two dots under o* • Combined with die 454C • 454C/464Eb (R-10): EF $4,000–$6,000 • Die intended for counterstamping with a number. 19.2 mm. Unlisted in Fuld.

Patriotic die 464B • *"No" in plain field (top of o slightly high)* • Combined with die 453A • 453A/464Bb (R-10): EF $4,000–$6,000 • Die intended for counterstamping with a number. Unlisted in Fuld.

Patriotic die 467 • *THE FEDERAL GOVERNMENT, etc.* • From the shop of John Stanton • Store card die equivalent: None, but there should be (as it was used as a reverse with *several* store cards) • Used as reverse with dies 57, 71, 75 • 57/467a (R-7): EF–AU $1,000–$1,500 • MS-63 $2,000–$3,000.

Patriotic die 464C • *"No" in plain field (tops of N and o even)* • Combined with die 453A • 453A/464Cb (R-10): Fine $4,000–$6,000 • Die intended for counterstamping with a number. Unlisted in Fuld.

Patriotic die 464D • *"No" in plain field, two dots under o* • Combined with die 454B • 454B/464Cb (R-10): EF $4,000–$6,000 • Die intended for counterstamping with a number. Unlisted in Fuld.

Patriotic die 468 • *GOOD FOR 1 LOAF OF BREAD* • "Half card" die • Used as reverse with die 281 • 281/468b (R-8 per Fuld, p. 167): EF–AU $600–$900.

Patriotic die 469 • *DRY GOODS AND GROCERIES* • Ascribed to the shop of William K. Lanphear • "Half card" die • Used as reverse with die 159 • 159/469a (R-8): EF–AU $750–$1,250 • Only one variety.

Patriotic die 470 • *Mortar and pestle (DEALERS IN DRUGS HARDWARE & SADDLERY)* • From the shop of John Stanton • Same as store card die 1313 • "Half card" die • Used as reverse with die 76 • 76/470a (R-7): EF–AU $300–$450 • Only one variety.

Patriotic die 469A • *DRY GOODS GRO-CERIES & PROVISIONS* • Die ascribed to John Marr of Mossin & Marr • "Half card" die • Used as reverse with die 154A • 154A/469Aa (R-9): EF–AU $6,000–$9,000 • Only one variety.

Patriotic die 470A • *DEALER IN DRUGS MEDICINES & GROCERIES* • Ascribed to the shop of William K. Lanphear • "Half card" die • Used as reverse with dies 192 and 193A • 193A/470A (R-8): EF–AU $1,250–$1,750 • MS-63 $2,500–$3,750.

Patriotic die 469B • *HARDWARE, IRON, NAILS, GLASS, & STOVES. 1863* • Die ascribed to John Marr of Mossin & Marr • As a store card die used as the reverse of WI-510-AG • Used as reverse with die 154 • 154/469Ba (R-9): EF–AU $4,000–$6,000 • Only one variety.

Patriotic die 471 • *DRUGS DRY GOODS GROCERIES HARDWARE & NOTIONS (4 stars at border)* • "Half card" die • Used as reverse with dies 449 and 450 • 450/471a (R-1): EF–AU $25–$40 • MS-63 $50–$75.

Patriotic die 472 • *EAST BOSTON 1837* • Same as store card die 1428, a left-over 1837 Hard Times token die • Used as reverse with dies 134, 146, 427 • 134/472j (R-8): EF–AU $1,000–$1,500 • MS-63 $2,000–$4,000 • Other R-8 and R-9 numismatic strikes.

Patriotic die 475 • *ONE QUART MILK (11 stars round border, etc.)* • Die ascribed to Henry D. Higgins ("Indiana primitive") • "Half card" die • Used as reverse with die 474 • 474/475a (R-8): EF–AU $1,250–$1,750 • MS-63 $3,000–$4,500 • Only one variety. Estimated 10 known (Fuld, fifth edition).

Patriotic die 473 • *REDEEMED IN PAR FUNDS IN SUMS OF ONE DOLLAR* • Same as store card die 1470 • From the shop of John Stanton • "Half card" die • Used as reverse with dies 57, 57A, 71, 76 • 57/473a (R-7): EF–AU $750–$1,250 • MS-63 $2,000–$3,000 • Other R-9 numismatic strikes.

Patriotic die 475A • *ONE QUART OF MILK* • From the shop of John Stanton • Same as store card die 1465 • "Half card" die • Used as reverse with die 70A • 70A/475Aa (R-10): EF–AU $6,000–$9,000 • Only one variety.

Patriotic die 474 • *Border of leaves (MILK CHECK; stars, etc.)* • Die ascribed to Henry D. Higgins ("Indiana primitive") • "Half card" die • Combined with die 475 • 474/475a (R-8): EF–AU $1,250–$1,750 • MS-63 $3,000–$4,500 • Only one variety. Estimated 10 known (Fuld, fifth edition).

Patriotic die 477 • *PROCESE* • Used as reverse with dies 116, 129, 349 • 349/349e (R-9): EF–AU $350–$500 • MS-63 $700–$1,000 • Also two other R-9 varieties. Estimated 10 known (Fuld, fifth edition).

Patriotic die 478 • *1863 Anchor (14 border stars)* • Combined with die 480 • 478/480b (listed as a by Fuld) (R-9): EF–AU $10,000–$15,000 • Only four known (Fuld, fifth edition).

Patriotic die 479 • *1863 Shield above wreath; NATIONAL UNION LEAGUE OF THE UNITED STATES* • From the shop of F.C. Key & Sons • Used as reverse with dies 131 and 217 • 217/479a (R-7): EF–AU $200–$300 • MS-63 $600–$900 • 271/479b and e are also R-7.

Patriotic die 480 • *HOPE; curlicues above and below* • Used as reverse with die 478 • 478/480b (listed as a by Fuld) (R-9): EF–AU $10,000–$15,000 • Only four known (Fuld, fifth edition).

Patriotic die 480A • *EUREKA, GOOD FOR 10 / X, stars* • Thought by Steven L. Tanenbaum to be a die of the Eureka Saloon, Providence, RI • Used as reverse with die 427 • 427/480Aa (R-9): EF–AU $600–$900 • Also metal b (R-9).

Patriotic die 481 • *Arms of Rhode Island, modified (shield, stars, HOPE, 1844)* • Same as store card die 1429 • Medalet, numismatic strike • Used as reverse with dies 134 (showing only the center) and 483 to 493C • 481/482a (R-9): MS-63 $600–$900 • The medalets 481 to 493C (except 493) were made in late 1864 or early 1865 for the Rhode Island Numismatic Society. Many other tokens R-9, a few R-10. When seen in collections nearly all are Mint State. • An impression of the center of this die, small diameter, was combined with patriotic dies 134, 146, 427 and with store card dies RI-700-D and E.

Patriotic die 482 • *Hunting dogs in meadow* • Same as store card die 1285 • Medalet, numismatic strike circa 1864 • Used as reverse with die 481 • 481/482a (R-9): MS-63 $600–$900 • Also metals b (R-9), g (R-9 or R-10), j (R-9), i (R-9 or R-10) .

Patriotic die 483 • *Standing eagle holding shield (16 stars around border)* • 481/483a (R-9): MS-63 $600–$900 • Also metals b (R-9), g (R-9 or R-10), j (R-9), i (R-9 or R-10).

Patriotic die 484 • *Standing hunter aiming gun at flying bird* • 481/484a (R-9): MS-63 $600–$900 • Also metals b (R-9), g (R-9 or R-10), j (R-9), i (R-9 or R-10).

Patriotic die 485 • *Leaping stag, to left* • 481/485a (R-9): MS-63 $600–$900 • Also metals b (R-9), g (R-9 or R-10), j (R-9), i (R-9 or R-10).

Patriotic die 486 • *Militiaman facing to viewer's left (V.T. MILITIA)* • 481/486a (R-9): MS-63 $600–$900 • Also metals b (R-9), g (R-9 or R-10), j (R-9), i (R-9 or R-10).

Patriotic die 487 • *Hare running toward the right* • 481/487a (R-9): MS-63 $600–$900 • Also metals b (R-9), g (R-9 or R-10), j (R-9), i (R-9 or R-10).

Patriotic die 488 • *Wolfhound standing, facing to left* • 481/488a (R-9): MS-63 $600–$900 • Also metals b (R-9), g (R-9 or R-10), j (R-9), i (R-9 or R-10).

Patriotic die 489 • *Two standing game birds facing right, in meadow* • 481/489a (R-9): MS-63 $600–$900 • Also metals b (R-9), g (R-9 or R-10), j (R-9), i (R-9 or R-10).

Patriotic die 490 • *Huntsman on horse running to the left with pack of dogs* • /490a (R-9): MS-63 $600–$900 • Also metals b (R-9), g (R-9 or R-10), j (R-9), i (R-9 or R-10).

Patriotic die 491 • *Dog near duck at edge of marsh* • 481/491a (R-9): MS-63 $600–$900 • Also metals b (R-9), g (R-9 or R-10), j (R-9), i (R-9 or R-10).

Patriotic die 492 • *Three standing grouse* • 481/492a (R-9): MS-63 $600–$900 • Also metals b (R-9), g (R-9 or R-10), j (R-9), i (R-9 or R-10).

Patriotic die 493 • *Wreath (WAR OF 1861 ENGAGED IN THE ABOVE BATTLES)* • Civil War soldier's "dog tag" to be filled in with stamped letters when used • Used as reverse with die 481 • 481/493 (R-9): EF–AU $500–$750 • Also metals a (R-9 or R-10), b (R-9 or R-10), g (R-9 or R-10), j (R-9 or R-10). Not widely studied.

Patriotic die 493A • *Soldier on running horse (BOSTON LIGHT DRAGOON)* • Medalet, numismatic strike • Used as reverse with die 481 • 481/493Aa (R-9): MS-63 $1,500–$2,250 • Also metals b (R-9 or R-10), g (R-9 or R-10), i (R-9 or R-10), j (R-9 or R-10). Not widely studied.

Patriotic die 493B • *Perched eagle (FREMONT & DAYTON THE PEOPLES CHOICE; 2 stars)* • Numismatic medalet using an old campaign die • Used as reverse with die 481 • 481/493Bb (R-9): MS-63 $1,000–$1,500 • Also metals a (R-9 or R-10), g (R-9 or R-10), i (R-9 or R-10), j (R-9 or R-10). Not widely studied.

Patriotic die 493C • *1844 Henry Clay, 26 stars* • Used as reverse with die 481, restrikes circa 1864 • 481/493Cb (R-9): MS-63 $600–$900 • Also metals a (R-9 or R-10), g (R-9 or R-10), i (R-9 or R-10), j (R-9 or R-10). Not widely studied. Originals are known to have been made in copper and brass, 26.9 mm, and are not part of the Civil War token series. The restrikes are slightly wider and are part of the series.

Patriotic die 502 • *PEACE (elliptical wreath surrounding)* • Combined with die 503 • 502/503b (R-8): EF–AU $2,000–$3,000.

Patriotic die 506A • *Lincoln portrait facing left (FOR PRESIDENT ABRAHAM LINCOLN OF ILL, coat ends over I)* • From the shop of John Stanton, die by Benjamin C. True • Combined with dies 507 and 512 (perhaps more as this is a new discovery) • 506A/507a (R-10): EF–AU $1,100–$1,600 • MS-63 $2,700–$3,900 • 506A/512b (ipl) (R-10).

Patriotic die 503 • *Circular band with 7 raised dots* • Used as the reverse for die 502 • 502/503b (R-8): EF–AU $2,000–$3,000.

Patriotic die 507 • *Lincoln portrait facing left (FOR PRESIDENT ABRAHAM LIN-COLN OF ILL.)* • From the shop of John Stanton, die by Benjamin C. True • Same as store card die 1419 • Combined with dies 506 (as reverse), 506A (as reverse), 508, 509, 510, 510A, 511, 513, 514, 519 • 507/508a (R-8): EF–AU $700–$1,000 • MS-63 $1,750–$2,500 • Many R-8 and R-9 varieties.

Patriotic die 506 • *Lincoln portrait facing left (FOR PRESIDENT ABRAHAM LIN-COLN OF ILL, coat ends over L)* • From the shop of John Stanton, die by Benjamin C. True • Same as store card die 1418 • Combined with dies 507, 508, 509, 510, 510A, 511, 512, 513, 514, 519 • 506/507a (R-8): EF–AU $1,000–$1,500 • MS-63 $2,500–$3,750 • Many R-8 and R-9 varieties.

Patriotic die 508 • *Breckinridge portrait facing left (FOR PRESIDENT JOHN C. BRECKINRIDGE OF KY.)* • From the shop of John Stanton, die by Benjamin C. True • Same as store card die 1420 • Combined with dies 506 (as reverse), 507 (as reverse), 508, 509, 510, 510A, 510B, 511, 512, 513, 514, 529 • 508/509a (R-8): EF–AU $400–$600 • MS-63 $800–$1,200 • Many R-8 and R-9 varieties.

Patriotic die 509B • *Bell portrait facing left (FOR PRESIDENT JOHN BELL OF TENNESSEE.)* • From the shop of John Stanton, die by Benjamin C. True • Combined with die 510B • 509B/510Ba (R-9): EF–AU $3,000–$4,500 • MS-63 $6,000–$9,000 • Also metals b plain edge (R-9), b reeded edge (R-9).

Patriotic die 509 • *Bell portrait facing left (FOR PRESIDENT JOHN BELL OF TENNESSEE)* • From the shop of John Stanton, die by Benjamin C. True • Same as store card die 1158 • Combined with b dies 506, 507, 508 (as reverse) and o dies 510, 510A, 510B, 511, 512, 513, 514, 519 (as obverse) • 509/510Aa (R-8): EF–AU $400–$600 • MS-63 $800–$1,200 • Many R-8 and R-9 varieties.

Patriotic die 510 • *Douglas portrait facing left (FOR PRESIDENT STEPHEN A. DOUGLAS OF ILL.)* • From the shop of John Stanton, die by Benjamin C. True • Same as store card die 1422 • Combined with dies 506, 507, 508, 509 (as reverse) and 510A, 510B, 510C, 511, 512, 513, 514, 519 (as obverse) • 510/510Aa (R-8): EF–AU $400–$600 • MS-63 $800–$1,200 • Many R-8 and R-9 varieties.

Patriotic die 509A • *Bell portrait facing left (FOR PRESIDENT JOHN BELL OF TENNESSEE.)* • From the shop of John Stanton, die by Benjamin C. True • Combined with dies 510A and 510B • 509A/510Ab (R-9): EF–AU $500–$750 • MS-63 $1,000–$1,500 • 509A/510Bb is also R-9.

Patriotic die 510A • *White House (PRES-IDENTS HOUSE; T in lawn)* • From the shop of John Stanton, die by Benjamin C. True • Same as store card die 1421 • Combined with dies 506, 507, 508, 509, 510 (as reverse) and 511, 512, 513, 514, 519 (as obverse) • 510A/511 (R-8): EF–AU $400–$600 • MS-63 $800–$1,200 • Many R-8 and R-9 varieties.

Patriotic die 510B • *White House (PRES-IDENTS HOUSE)* • From the shop of John Stanton, die by Benjamin C. True • Combined with dies 508, 509, 509A, 509B, 509A, 509B (as reverse) • 508/510Ba (R-9): EF–AU $600–$900 • MS-63 $1,500–$2,250 • Several other varieties are R-9 and R-10. Usually show wear.

Patriotic die 510C • *Douglas portrait facing left (FOR PRESIDENT STEPHEN A. DOUGLAS OF ILL.)* • From the shop of John Stanton, die by Benjamin C. True • Combined with die 510 (as reverse) • 510/510C (R-10): MS-63 $3,000–$4,500 • New discovery.

Patriotic die 511 • *Agricultural products (THE WEALTH OF THE SOUTH, etc.)* • From the shop of John Stanton, die by Benjamin C. True • Same as store card die 1423 • Combined with dies 506, 507, 508, 509, 510, 510A (as reverse), 512, 513, 514, 515, 516, 517, 518, 519 (as obverse) • 511/514b (R-5): EF–AU $500–$750 • MS-63 $1,250–$1,750.

Patriotic die 512 • *Shield (THE UNION MUST AND SHALL BE PRESERVED)* • From the shop of John Stanton, die by Benjamin C. True • Same as store card die 1424 • Combined with dies 506, 608, 509, 510, 510a, 511 (as reverse), 513, 514, 519 (as obverse) • 506/512a (R-8): EF–AU $1,000–$1,500 • MS-63 $2,500–$3,750 • Many R-8 and R-9 varieties.

Patriotic die 513 • *Shield (OUR RIGHTS, THE CONSTITUTION AND THE UNION)* • From the shop of John Stanton, die by Benjamin C. True • Same as store card die 1425 • Combined with dies 506, 507, 508, 509, 510, 510A, 511, 512 (as reverse) and 514, 519 (as obverse) • 509a/513 (R-8): EF–AU $600–$900 • MS-63 $1,250–$1,750 • Many R-8 and R-9 varieties.

Patriotic die 514 • *1860 Palmetto, cannon, 15 stars, etc. (NO SUBMISSION TO THE NORTH)* • From the shop of John Stanton, die by Benjamin C. True • Same as store card die 1426 • Combined with dies 506, 507, 508, 509, 510, 510A, 511, 512, 513 (as reverse) and 516, 519 (as obverse) • 511/514b (R-5): EF–AU $500–$750 • MS-63 $1,250–$1,750 • Many R-8 and R-9 varieties.

Patriotic die 515 • *1860 Palmetto, cannon, 15 stars, etc. (NO SUBMISSION TO THE NORTH)* • From the shop of John Stanton, die by Benjamin C. True • Used as reverse with die 511 • 511/515b (ipl) (R-7): EF–AU $500–$750 • MS-63 $1,250–$1,750 • Also metals a (R-9), e (R-9).

Patriotic die 518 • *1860 Palmetto, cannon, 15 stars, etc. (NO SUBMISSION TO THE NORTH)* • From the shop of John Stanton, die by Benjamin C. True • Used as reverse with die 511 • 511/518b (R-8): EF–AU $750–$1,250 • MS-63 $2,000–$3,000 • Only one variety, a classic rarity.

Patriotic die 516 • *1860 Palmetto, cannon, 15 stars, etc. (NO SUBMISSION TO THE NORTH)* • From the shop of John Stanton, die by Benjamin C. True • Used as reverse with dies 511 and 514 • 511/516b (R-5): EF–AU $500–$750 • MS-63 $1,250–$1,750.

Patriotic die 519 • *Blank reverse with raised rim and dentils* • *Generic listing as diameters vary* • One is the same as store card die 1427 from the shop of John Stanton, die by Benjamin C. True when used with another True die; used as reverse with dies 506, 507, 508, 509, 510, 510A, 511, 512, 513, 514 • 506/519a (R-8): EF–AU $800–$1,200 • MS-63 $1,750–$2,500 • Many R-8 varieties.

Patriotic die 517 • *1860 Palmetto, cannon, 15 stars, etc. (NO SUBMISSION TO THE NORTH)* • From the shop of John Stanton, die by Benjamin C. True • Used as reverse with die 511 • 511/517b (R-6): EF–AU $500–$750 • MS-63 $1,500–$2,500 • Also metals a (R-8), e (R-9).

Patriotic die 519A • *Blank reverse with raised rim and beaded border* • *Generic listing as diameters vary* • One such die is ascribed to Francis X. Koehler when used with another Koehler die; used as reverse with die 3 • 3/519Aa (R-9): EF–AU $500–$750 • Also metal b (R-9). Estimated 8 known (Fuld, fifth edition).

Patriotic die 519B • *Blank reverse with raised rim and plain border* • *Generic listing as diameters vary* • One was used as reverse with dies 153 and 285A • 153/519Be (R-10): EF–AU $1,000–$1,500 • MS-63 $2,500–$3,750 • 285A/519B is also R-10.

Patriotic die 519C • *Blank reverse with raised rim; mound in center* • Used as reverse with die 156 • 156/519Ca (R-10): EF–AU $2,000–$3.000.

Patriotic die 520 • *1860 Capped Bust facing left (13 border stars)* • Used as reverse with die 287 and 521 • EF–AU $750–$1,250 • 520/521a (R-7).

Patriotic die 521 • *COPPER MINE TOKEN (C 1; star at bottom border)* • Same as store card die 1213 • Used as reverse with dies 104 and 520 • 520/521a (R-7): EF–AU $750–$1,250.

Patriotic die 522 • *FAMILY / & / SHIP / REAPER, etc.* • From the shop of John Stanton • "Half card" die • Used as reverse with dies 76 and 76A • 76A/522a (R-9): MS-63 $5,000–$7,500 • Earlier listed under OH-74-A and OH-175-O • Although this is not assigned a store card stock die number it was used with OH-74-A.

Patriotic die 523 • *GRIND STONES / FLAGGING / & / BUILDING / STONES* • From the shop of John Stanton • "Half card" die • 76/523a (R-4): MS-63 $5,000–$7,500 • Although this is not assigned a store card stock die number it was used with OH-175-O.

Patriotic die 524 • *1863; SEWING / MACHINES / NEATLY / REPAIRED; 2 stars at border* • Ascribed to the shop of William K. Lanphear • "Half card" die • Used as reverse with die 156 • 156/524a (R-8): EF–AU $500–$750 • MS-63 $1,250–$1,750 • Only one variety • Although this is not assigned a store card stock die number it was used with OH-175-FC.

Patriotic die 525 • *$100 BOUNTY / PENSIONS, etc.* • Same as store card die 1451 • "Half card" die • Used as reverse with die 73 • 73/525a (R-4): EF–AU $100–$150 • MS-63 $250–$375 • Only one variety.

Patriotic die 532 • *Beer mug within continuous hops vine wreath* • "Half card" die • Same as store card die 1296 • Used as reverse with dies 451A and 451B • 451A/532b (R-9): EF–AU $2,000–$3,000.

Patriotic die 533 • *Spectacles (2 pairs) and attachment (PERISCOPIC SPECTACLES; 2 stars in field)* • "Half card" die • Same as store card die 1327 • Used as reverse with die 85 • 85/533a (R-9): MS-63 $8,000–$12,000 • Only one variety. The store card use is available but scarce.

Patriotic die 530 • *Rattlesnake (DONT TREAD ON ME)* • Used as reverse with dies 115, 115A (R-0) • 115/530g (apl) (R-7): EF–AU $700–$1,000.

Patriotic die 531 • *GOOD FOR ONE GLASS OF SODA (31 stars at border)* • "Half card" die • Used as reverse with die 121 • 121/531a (R-9): MS-63 $3,000–$4,500 • Also metals b, e, f, j (all R-9).

Patriotic die 534 • *Jacket (MANUFACTURERS OF CLOTHING)* • "Half card" die • *Store card die equivalent:* 1338 • Used as reverse with die 33 • 33/534a (R-10): EF–AU $6,000–$9,000 • Only one variety. Available with its store card use.

Patriotic die 535 • *Pocket watch* • Same as store card die 1319 • "Half card" die • Combined with die 536 • 535/536a (R-10): MS-63 $6,000–$9,000 • Available on store cards.

Patriotic die 537 • *1864 general on horseback (Mc PHERSON)* • Used as reverse with die 113 • 113/537b (R-9): MS-63 $2,000–$3,000 • Non-contemporary despite its 1864 date.

Patriotic die 536 • *Open wreath of laurel leaves; blank center* • Used as reverse with die 535 • 535/536a (R-10): MS-63 $6,000–$9,000 • A major rarity in the series.

CIVIL WAR STORE CARDS

Introduction

Civil War store cards comprise the class of tokens with at least one, sometimes both dies bearing the name of a specific merchant, product, service, or other commercial aspect. A strict definition places such tokens as having been issued from April 1861 to April 1865 during the period of the war. As noted earlier, some store cards dating back to 1859 were adopted into the series generations ago and were given Fuld numbers.

The tokens issued by John Stanton from dies cut by Benjamin C. True for the four presidential candidates of 1860 were muled in 1861 and 1862 with dies advertising various merchants and services. Similarly, the several Wealth of the South dies by True for the 1860-dated NO SUBMISSION TO THE NORTH tokens, popular in 1860 and early 1861, were combined with various merchant dies in 1861 and 1862 and are part of the Civil War token series.

In 1861 S.D. Childs of Chicago issued many store cards with this date, seemingly keeping the dies in use in 1862 (assumed as no 1862-dated tokens are known) and then in 1863 issued many more. In 1862 John Stanton produced several Indian Head dies that were combined with commercial reverses, and 1862-dated tokens also appeared elsewhere.

A great flood of Civil War store cards spread across commerce in 1863, continuing in reduced scale in 1864. New York City was the focal point for issuers of patriotic tokens although millions of store cards were made there as well. Cincinnati was the main center for store card issuers plus a relatively small output of patriotics. Shops in Chicago, Philadelphia, Waterbury (Connecticut), and other locations contributed to the stream. By 1864 tens of millions of tokens had been placed in circulation. This era is discussed in detail in chapter 4.

In ensuing years many merchants redeemed tokens when they were presented. Probably most tokens, however, remained in circulation for years afterward and simply disappeared.

Today in the Fuld references these circulation strikes account for nearly all varieties listed with rarity ratings from R-1 to R-6. In addition there are many that were produced for circulation but in small quantities, perhaps from only 500 to a few thousand, which are R-7 or higher now. The vast majority of circulation strikes in collections today show wear, sometimes extensive.

In 1989, Dale Cade estimated that over 95 percent of all known examples of Civil War tokens were struck in copper.[1] These were mostly circulation strikes. Brass tokens make up about 4 percent, again with many circulation strikes but far fewer than in copper, with the tiny remainder of 1 percent consisting of other metals such as copper-nickel, white metal, etc., for the numismatic market.

TOKENS MADE FOR COLLECTORS

Varieties in both the patriotic and store card series were made to order for numismatists who collected them at the time. These were often in copper-nickel (d) or nickel alloy (j), less often in white metal or pewter (e), and only rarely in silver (f). Some were over-struck on federal coins such as copper-nickel Flying Eagle and Indian Head cents and silver dimes and quarters. As desirable as these overstrikes are to numismatists today, it seems that no particular effort was made by the coiners to strike them in a way that the undertype coin motifs would remain clear. As a matter of chance some designs are quite clear in outline form and others require careful examination to detect.

Such producers as William K. Lanphear (Cincinnati), John Stanton (Cincinnati), Emil Sigel (New York City), William H. Bridgens (New York City), and Mossin & Marr (Milwaukee), among others, were pleased to accommodate numismatic buyers. Today all of these special strikings are elusive, typically R-7 and higher and are nearly always found in Mint State.

Among Civil War store cards of Ohio, OH-895-A has always been considered a prime rarity. The token inscription tells us that it was issued by C. McCarty of the Washington House in Urbana. At the same time this die and its combinations have curious aspects. In the course of selling two varieties to the author on August 6, 1998, Steve Tanenbaum wrote:

This is a mysterious merchant. The R-8 variety with reverse 1047 is not a circulation strike and six R-10s are listed plus OH-895-A-3e1 (plain edge) and OH-895-A-3eo over a token with a large 3 on reverse.

The shop of Murdock & Spencer (successor to John Stanton) took die 1069, THE PRAIRIE FLOWER, dated 1863, and produced strikings in copper-nickel by filing down the rims of federal cents. Obverse dies from merchants were combined with the die, resulting in at least these many varieties (per the research of Larry Dziubek): Alabama 1, Illinois 6, Indiana 2, Michigan 13, Missouri 1, New York 1, Ohio 101, Pennsylvania 9, Tennessee 4, and Wisconsin 1.

Steve Tanenbaum concluded that only a single example was struck of most varieties, with two for a few. Stanton used the same Indian Head hub punch to make these dies, mostly dated 1863, for which the stars and dates were punched in by hand, creating different varieties: 1018 to 1045, 1046 (dated 1864), 1046A (dated 1864), 1047 (dated 1864), 1068 (undated), and 1069 (1863).

C. McCarty (should be McCarthy) OH-895-A-01a token with reverse 1047 in its latest state with die cancellation cuts in the headdress.

Years later, while writing the present book, Steve's comment piqued my interest. The variety with reverse 1047 is in late Die State V, known to date from the late 1860s (also see Yankee Robinson's use of this late die state). This was a workhorse die that the shop of John Stanton, later Murdock & Spencer, combined with many other dies to make rarities for collectors. As known specimens are all Mint State or close, it is evident these were not made for general circulation.

In my 2012 investigation I had a tool not generally used in 1998: the Internet with thousands of old directories, newspaper accounts, and the like available with a few keystrokes. Lo and behold! I came across this account from the *Urbana Union*, January 29, 1868:

> WASHINGTON HOUSE: This hotel is located near the Sandusky, Cincinnati and Cleveland Railroad Depot at Urbana and is convenient to travelers. We can assure the traveling public that it is conducted in first-class style and the comfort of guests is properly considered. The building is new, having been lately erected, and the rooms are all heated by steam and furnished in elegant style. The proprietor, Mr. Chas. McCarthy, is a clever and affable, and few landlords know how to render their guests as comfortable as he does, We know we are not exaggerating when we say is the best hotel in Urbana, which together with its convenience to the railroad depots which renders it as the most desirable hotel to stop at.

This was an exchange article picked up from the *Kenton Democrat*. The McCarthy spelling is different from that on the token. Some more investigation found that Charles McCarthy is the proper name, and he is found in other citations of the era.[2]

There are several characteristics which, if present on a given token singly or in combination, serve to suggest that it may be a numismatic or specimen strike. There are exceptions to these rules, but they are few.

1. Struck in a metal other than copper (the usual metal of choice for circulation strikes) or brass. Nearly all tokens in nickel alloy, copper-nickel, white metal, silver, and various metals with tin plating are numismatic strikes.

2. Struck in any metal (including copper and brass) with a reeded edge, if it is now R-8 or higher, and if the same combination is known with a plain edge and is R-7 or lower with a plain edge.

3. If one or both dies are known to have been made after the Civil War (e.g., Stoner & Shroyer store cards with a reverse die made in 1868 featuring presidential candidate Ulysses S. Grant).

4. If one or both dies are severely rusted or severely relapped.

5. If, among store cards, the die combination is incongruous, and each die relates to a different merchant or topic.

6. If it is struck over a federal coin such as a copper-nickel cent or a silver denomination.

As noted, most numismatic strikes in existence today are in higher grades, typically Mint State or close to it. These special numismatic strikes are highly attractive to collectors. Many, if not most, are expensive.

The corollary to the above is that circulation strikes are typically:

1. Made of copper (usually) or brass.

2. Struck from dies made during the 1861–1865 Civil War period.

3. Are from dies that are logical combinations of obverse and reverse.

4. Most are known in worn grades (except for those from hoards).

The preceding differences are interesting to study. However, in the marketplace for Civil War tokens, just about all issues listed in the Fuld patriotic and store card texts are eagerly sought. From the standpoint of value and demand the listing of a token in one or the other of these two books is a more important determinant of market popularity than is its true Civil War or other status.

In the shop of John Stanton die 1042 was used to make many numismatic strikes. Many of those, as here, were tin plated.

LINDESMITH ON MULINGS

One of the leading scholars in the token field in the 1960s was Robert J. Lindesmith, who wrote this:

> It may be in order to mention that while there has been a great deal of criticism aimed at the muling of the Rhode Island Civil War tokens, the same practice was carried on in New York, Cincinnati and Philadelphia, although not quite on such an extensive a scale. Just as examples: In New York City, the Bridgens dies were used to create close to 300 varieties of the patriotic and Civil War cards. Cincinnati has the mulings of the "Wealth of the South" series and the muling of John Stanton dies. In Philadelphia there are the mulings of Key and Robert Lovett dies.
>
> As this practice was encouraged by the majority of the prominent token and medal collectors of that period, it would hardly seem necessary at present to keep this subject clouded in mystery. From my own investigation in to this subject it is apparent that once this mystery is removed, there is a logical explanation for all the listings that appear in the Civil War series.[3]

As most mulings range from rare to very rare and can be expensive, a very nice collection of Civil War store cards can be made by specializing only in the varieties actually made for circulation during the Civil War. Most are in copper, some in brass, and except for some rare merchants nearly all are affordable.

Numismatic strikes can be very fascinating to collect. Over the years a number of enthusiasts have endeavored to acquire representative examples. Even though they are very rare, most such pieces sell for tiny fractions of the cost of comparable federal coin rarities and even for far less than rarities in the Hard Times token series (1832–1844) collected by far fewer people.

Early Store Cards
The 1859 Business Card Tokens

The first significant group of store cards to be adopted into the Civil War series had the advertisement of a merchant on the obverse and on the reverse BUSINESS / CARD within an agricultural wreath copied from the back of the federal Flying Eagle cent. Frederick N. Dubois of Chicago was the diesinker and minter. Distribution was in three states:

Iowa: IA-570-A-1 Gage, Lyall & Keeler (Lyons)

Illinois: IL-25-B-1 Gates & Trask (Aurora), IL-150-B-1 Barker & Ilsley (Chicago), IL-150-H-1a J.J. Brown (Chicago), IL-150-M-1 R.H. Countiss (Chicago), IL-150-M-2 R.H. Countiss (Chicago), IL-150-P-2 F.N. Dubois (Chicago), IL-150-Q-1 Edwards (Chicago), IL-150-S-1 Flaggs Cheap Store (Chicago), IL-150-T-2 Flagg & Mac Donald (Chicago), • IL-150-W-1 and IL-150-W-1 Freedman, Goodkind & Co. (Chicago), IL-150-X-1 P. Gaffney (Chicago), • IL-150-Z-1 G.E. Gerts & Co. (Chicago) IL-150-AD-1 R. Heilbroner (Chicago), IL-150-AE-1 W.A. Hendrie (Chicago), IL-150-AH-1 Judd & Corthell (Chicago), IL-150-AJ-1 and IL-150-AJ-2 F.A. Leavitt (Chicago), IL-150-AQ-1 Oppenheimer & Metzger (Chicago), IL-150-AU-1 W.R. Prentice (Chicago), IL-150-BE-1 W. Treleaven (Chicago)

New York: NY-80-B-1 Herschman Bros. & Co. (Binghamton), NY-80-A-1 • Evans & Allen (Binghamton), and NY-105-M-1 Reilly's Bazaar (Buffalo)

Certain of these were listed in the January 1860 *Catalogue of American Store Cards &c., With Space for Marking the Condition, Price, Rarity, &c., of Each Piece, Designed for the Use and Convenience of Collectors.* Copper was the usual metal with many examples being struck for general circulation. Most are common today. Some nickel-alloy tokens were also made. Ed. Frossard's March 1881 sale, *American and Foreign Coins*, included this:

Lot 158: Tokens: Obv., Business Card, within a wreath. Rev., Different names of firms, mostly in Chicago, Ill. Struck in nickel, extremely rare, as only one other set was struck, and the pieces forming it sold in the Mickley Sale. 9 pieces.

In his era Frossard was one of the more highly acclaimed catalogers. His direct statement that just two sets were struck in nickel is controverted today by nickel impressions being rated as R-8, or 5 to 10 known.

IA-570-A-01a by Dubois for Gage, Lyall & Keeler, Lyons, Iowa grocers. As a class Iowa store cards are scarce.

IL-025-B-01j by Dubois for Gates & Trask, Aurora, Illinois jewelers. This is a numismatic strike in nickel alloy. This metal was used for fewer than half of the Dubois die combinations. Such tokens are all R-8.

THE 1861–1862 STORE CARDS
FROM BENJAMIN C. TRUE DIES

In 1860 before the Civil War began, the shop of John Stanton issued 22 mm tokens picturing the four presidential candidates of the year—Lincoln, Breckinridge, Bell, and Douglas—with the standard President's House reverse. In addition Stanton issued Wealth of the South tokens with reverses dated 1860 and showing a palmetto tree with the inscription, NO SUBMISSION TO THE NORTH. These are discussed under patriotic tokens.

In early 1861 a store card for *Steamer Lancaster No. 4*, launched in January of that year, was combined with the Wealth of the South die (no. 511 in the political series and 1423 if used with a store card as here). This initiated an extensive series of mulings in which dies for the 1860 candidates, the Wealth of the South die, several different SUBMISSION TO THE NORTH dies, and several other 22 mm dies with patriotic motifs were combined with those of merchants. The store cards featured the following enterprises (in Fuld-number order).

Store card with the obverse of 516 combined with an advertising die for the Excelsior Tobacco Works of Cincinnati, listed as Fuld OH-165-AMa. Struck in copper.

Excelsior Tobacco Works • OH-165-AMb, Cincinnati. John Weighell and John T. Weighell, father and son, operated the Excelsior Tobacco Works at 210 and 212 Elm Street in downtown Cincinnati.

OH-165-GI-3a in copper. Lincoln reverse die 1419 with advanced crack, as often seen, from the border at the upper right.

Weighell & Son • OH-165-GI, Cincinnati. Given two numbers in the Fuld text, perhaps in error as the same company is involved. Tokens of the firm may not have been issued until 1862. All varieties are exceedingly rare today.

Steamer Lancaster No. 4 OH-165-FX, a ship based in Cincinnati, one of a series of Lancaster sidewheelers in passenger and freight service in and out of Cincinnati. No. 4, of 218 tons, was built at Dan Morton's shipyard in Cincinnati and launched in January 1861. See illustration in chapter 5.

TN-600-A-7a. Cossitt, Hill & Co. die combined with The Union Must and Shall Be Preserved. The reverse is a late state with a crack from the border through O (UNION) as always seen, plus a crack from the right of the circle at the top of the die. Certain letters are filled in at their centers.

Cossitt, Hill & Co. • TN-600-A, Memphis importers and jobbers in staple and fancy dry goods, and dealers in boots, shoes, hats, caps, and saddlery at 210 and 212 Main Street, corner of Jefferson Street.

TN-600-B-4a. Elliott, Vinson & Co. die combined with irrelevant die 1421 showing the Presidents House, a die first used on campaign tokens of 1860.

Elliott, Vinson & Co. • TN-600-B, Memphis steamboat agents located at the corner of Promenade and Jefferson Street.

TN-600-F-6a. Stockman & Co. die combined with the famous Wealth of the South die 1423.

Stockman & Co. • TN-600-F, Memphis wholesale dealers in foreign and domestic liquors, rectified whisky, fancy groceries, tobacco, groceries, etc., per advertisements in the *Memphis Daily Appeal.*

A SELECTION OF STORE CARDS

IN-770-D-5a by Tansey & Ballard, druggists in Plainfield, Indiana, from dies from the Stanton shop. The reverse 1213 is a stock die and was used by other merchants as well.

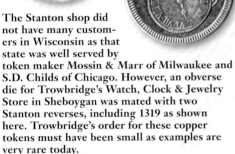

The Stanton shop did not have many customers in Wisconsin as that state was well served by token maker Mossin & Marr of Milwaukee and S.D. Childs of Chicago. However, an obverse die for Trowbridge's Watch, Clock & Jewelry Store in Sheboygan was mated with two Stanton reverses, including 1319 as shown here. Trowbridge's order for these copper tokens must have been small as examples are very rare today.

OH-165-DU-3b with a copper-colored obverse and brass reverse. The reverse is a Murdock & Spencer backstamp by the successors to the Stanton business. The obverse die has light trisecting cracks. "S-B-Monarch" may refer to a ship that operated on the Ohio River. From the *Cincinnati Daily Enquirer*, May 30, 1862: "The Sanitary Commission, last night, ordered the payment of $6,146.83, including payment of $2,450 to steamer *Monarch* for two trips to the Tennessee River."

Two very extensive series for the numismatic trade were made by the Stanton shop. One, as illustrated here, combined many different merchants' obverses with a tin-plated striking of reverse die 1042, giving the tokens the appearance of a mirrored silver Proof, except that the tin retains its brightness. Shown is MI-225-AR-3a (ipl) of P.N. Kneeland, a dealer in "STOEVS" (a rare misspelling on a Stanton die) a Detroit dealer in stoves and tinware. The other lengthy series used die 1047.

Stanton reverse 1047 as shown here with MI-225-Z-4d of William Eisenlord, Peninsular Hotel, Detroit, was combined with hundreds of obverses to create numismatic rarities. This is in copper-nickel, a metal used only for numismatic strikes and not circulating issues. Die state of 1047 has the signature rim cud below the date and is fairly early. At least three later die states exist.

Civil War Store Card Stock Reverse Dies

Each die is listed in Fuld-number order followed by a brief description. Nearly all are illustrated. For store card dies that were also used to strike patriotics, the equivalent patriotic die number is given. The numbers are those that will be used in the third edition of *U.S. Civil War Store Cards*.

CIVIL WAR CARD REVERSE DIES

Store card die 1000 • *1863 French Liberty Head (13 border stars)* • **Same as patriotic die 1.**

Store card die 1003 • *1863 French Liberty Head (13 border stars)* • **Same as patriotic die 9.**

Store card die 1005A • *1863 French Liberty Head (13 border stars)* • **Same as patriotic die 19.**

Store card die 1001 • *1863 French Liberty Head (13 border stars, LIBERTY on headband)* • **Same as patriotic die 3.**

Store card die 1004 • *1863 French Liberty Head (13 border stars)* • **Same as patriotic die 18.**

Store card die 1006 • *1863 French Liberty Head (FOR PUBLIC ACCOMODATION)* • **Same as patriotic die 37.**

Store card die 1002 • *1863 French Liberty Head (13 border stars)* • **Same as patriotic die 10.**

Store card die 1005 • *1863 French Liberty Head (13 border stars)* • **Same as patriotic die 22.**

Store card die 1007 • *1862 Indian Head left (13 border stars; LIBERTY on headband)* • **Same as patriotic die 57B.**

Store card die 1008 • *1862 Indian Head left (13 border stars; LIBERTY on headband)* • Same as patriotic die 57A.

Store card die 1011 • *1863 Indian Head left (13 border stars; LIBERTY on headband; L. ROLOFF).*

Store card die 1015 • *1863 Indian Head left (21 beads on headband; E.S. above 18)* • Same as patriotic die 60.

Store card die 1009 • *1862 Indian Head left (13 border stars; LIBERTY on headband)* • Same as patriotic die 57.

Store card die 1012 • *1863 Indian Head left (13 border stars; 15 beads on headband; L. ROLOFF).*

Store card die 1016 • *1863 Indian Head left (13 border stars; 17 beads on headband; E.S.)* • Same as patriotic die 61.

Store card die 1009A • *1862 Indian Head left (13 border stars; beads on headband).*

Store card die 1013 • *1863 Indian Head left (13 border stars; 10 stars on headband; E.S.).*

Store card die 1017 • *1863 Indian Head left (13 border stars; 16 beads on headband)* • Same as patriotic die 68.

Store card die 1010 • *1863 Indian Head left (13 border stars; LIBERTY on headband; L. ROLOFF)* • Same as patriotic die 58.

Store card die 1014 • *1863 Indian Head left (13 border stars; LIWERTY on headband).*

Store card die 1018 • *1863 Indian Head left (13 border stars; LIBERTY on headband)* • Same as patriotic die 71A.

Store card die 1019 • *1863*
Indian Head left (13 border
stars; LIBERTY on headband)
• Same as patriotic die 71.

Store card die 1023 • *1863*
Indian Head left (13 border
stars; LIBERTY on headband).

Store card die 1027 • *1863*
Indian Head left (13 border
stars; LIBERTY on headband).

Store card die 1020 • *1863*
Indian Head left (13 border
stars; LIBERTY on headband)
• Same as patriotic die 72.

Store card die 1024 • *1863*
Indian Head left (13 border
stars; LIBERTY on headband).

Store card die 1028 • *1863*
Indian Head left (13 border
stars; LIBERTY on headband)
• Same as patriotic die 73.

Store card die 1021 • *1863*
Indian Head left (13 border
stars; LIBERTY on headband).

Store card die 1025 • *1863*
Indian Head left (13 border
stars; LIBERTY on headband).

Store card die 1029 • *1863*
Indian Head left (13 border
stars; LIBERTY on headband).

Store card die 1022 • *1863*
Indian Head left (13 border
stars; LIBERTY on headband).

Store card die 1026 • *1863*
Indian Head left (13 border
stars; LIBERTY on headband).

Store card die 1030 • *1863*
Indian Head left (13 border
stars; LIBERTY on headband)
• Same as patriotic die 74.

Store card die 1031 • *1863 Indian Head left (13 border stars; LIBERTY on headband).*

Store card die 1034 • *1863 Indian Head left (13 border stars; LIBERTY on headband).*

Store card die 1039 • *1863 Indian Head left (13 border stars; LIBERTY on headband).*

Store card die 1032 (same as 1030) • *1863 Indian Head left (13 border stars; LIBERTY on headband).*

Store card die 1036 • *1863 Indian Head left (13 border stars; LIBERTY on headband).*

Store card die 1039A • *1863 Indian Head left (13 border stars; LIBERTY on headband)* • Discovered since the publication of the second edition of the Fuld book. Used as the reverse for MI-45-A-1.

Store card die 1033 • *1863 Indian Head left (13 border stars; LIBERTY on headband)* • Two former numbers, 1033 and 1035, are the same die. This die was relapped in later use and in that state has thin numerals in the date. All have a tiny die crack from the border down to the right of star 7. All former 1035 varieties are now consolidated under 1033.

Store card die 1037 • *1863 Indian Head left (13 border stars; LIBERTY on headband).*

Store card die 1040 • *1863 Indian Head left (13 border stars; LIBERTY on headband).*

Store card die 1038 • *1863 Indian Head left (13 border stars; LIBERTY on headband)* • Same as patriotic die 70.

Store card die 1042 • *1863 Indian Head left (13 border stars; LIBERTY on headband)* • Same as patriotic die 75.

Store card die 1043 • *1863 Indian Head left (13 border stars; LIBERTY on headband) • Same as patriotic die 70A.*

Store card die 1046 • *1864 Indian Head left (13 border stars; LIBERTY on headband).*

Store card die 1049 • *1863 Indian Head left (only 12 border stars; wavy line on headband) • Same as patriotic die 85.*

Store card die 1044 • *1863 Indian Head left (13 border stars; LIBERTY on headband).*

Store card die 1046A • *1864 Indian Head left (13 border stars; LIBERTY on headband)* • This was first described in "New 1864 Indian Head Die," Byron Johnson, *Journal of the Civil War Token Society*, Spring 1976.

Store card die 1050 • *1863 Indian Head left (13 border stars; no inscription on headband?).*

Store card die 1045 • *Indian Head left (undated; 18 stars in border; LIBERTY on headband) • Same as patriotic die 84.*

Store card die 1047 • *1864 Indian Head left (13 border stars; LIBERTY on headband)* • Same as patriotic die 76A.

Store card die 1050A • *1863 Indian Head left (11 border stars; wavy line on headband).*

Store card die 1045A • *Indian Head left (undated; stars 7 left and 6 right; four ornaments below head in place of a date; beads on headband).*

Store card die 1048 • *1864 Indian Head left (13 border stars; KEY PHILA incuse on headband) • Same as patriotic die 96.*

Store card die 1051 • *1863 Indian Head left (9 border stars; 7 diamonds on headband) • Same as patriotic die 78.*

Store card die 1052 • *1863 Indian Head left (13 border stars; plain headband)* • Same as patriotic die 92.

Store card die 1056 • *1863 Indian Head left (13 border stars; LIBERTY on headband).*

Store card die 1060 • *1863 Indian Head left (UNITED WE STAND; plain headband).*

Store card die 1053 • *1863 Indian Head left (13 border stars; plain headband)* • Same as patriotic die 86.

Store card die 1057 • *1863 Indian Head left (13 border stars; plain headband).*

Store card die 1061 • *1863 Indian Head left (UNITED WE STAND; plain headband; H).*

Store card die 1054 • *1863 Indian Head left (13 border stars; two rows of beads on headband)* • Same as patriotic die 88.

Store card die 1058 • *1863 Indian Head left (13 border stars; plain headband).*

Store card die 1062 • *1863 Indian Head left (UNITED WE STAND; plain headband).*

Store card die 1059 • *1873 Indian Head (error date; 13 border stars; LIBERTY on headband)* • Non-contemporary made in 1873 (earlier thought to be a misdated 1863 die). Illustrated here for reference only.

Store card die 1062A • *1863 Indian Head left (UNITED WE STAND; plain headband).*

Store card die 1055 • *1863 Indian Head left (13 border stars; two rows of beads on headband; H).*

Store card die 1063 • *1863 Indian Head left (UNITED WE STAND; plain headband).*

Store card die 1063A • *1863 Indian Head left (UNITED WE STAND; plain headband).*

Store card die 1064 • *1863 Indian Head left (UNITED WE STAND; plain headband; CDH).*

Store card die 1065 • *1863 Indian Head left (UNITED WE STAND; plain headband).*

Store card die 1066 • *Indian Head (13 border stars; ANN ARBOR; 17 beads on headband).*

Store card die 1067 • *1863 Indian Head left (13 border stars; ANN ARBOR; 15 stars on headband).*

Store card die 1068 • *Indian Head left (undated; THE PRAIRIE FLOWER; LIBERTY on headband).*

Store card die 1069 • *1863 Indian Head left (THE PRAIRIE FLOWER; LIBERTY on headband).*

Store card die 1072 • *1861 Indian Head left (BUSINESS CARD; plain headband) • Same as patriotic die 101.*

Store card die 1073 • *1864 Indian Princess left (13 border stars) • Same as patriotic die 56.*

Early state of die 1075 with 6 stars.

Late state of die 1075 with 5 stars. Store card die 1075 • *Indian Head left (undated; plain field; 6 stars in headband) • A later state of this die with the first star gone, the center of each feather strengthened, and with the beads redone was earlier known as die 1076 with 5 stars.*

Store card die 1077 • *1863 Indian Head left (8 stars at border; BUSINESS CARD.; 5 stars on headband).*

Store card die 1078 • *1863 Indian Head left (12 border stars; BUSINESS CARD.; vertical lines in headband).*

Store card die 1082 • *1863 Capped Head right (13 border stars; LUTZ).*

Store card die 1087 • *1863 Capped Head right (13 border stars; LUTZ).*

Store card die 1079 • *3981 (backward date) Indian Head left (4 stars at border; BUSINESS CARD.; backward D; 5 stars on headband).*

Store card die 1083 • *1863 Capped Head right (13 border stars).*

Store card die 1088 • *1863 Capped Head right (plain field).*

Store card die 1080 • *Indian Head left (undated; 8 stars at border; BUSINESS CARD).*

Store card die 1084 • *1863 Capped Head right (13 border stars; Lutz)* • The die earlier listed as 1086 is a relapped version of 1084 with the Lutz signature ground away. Intermediate states exist.

Store card die 1089 • *1863 Capped Head right (14 border stars).*

Store card die 1090 • *1864 Capped Head right (13 border stars).*

Store card die 1081 • *Indian Head left (undated; 2 stars at border; BUSINESS CARD.; 5 stars in headband).*

Store card die 1085 • *1863 Capped Head right (13 border stars; LUTZ).*

Store card die 1091 • *1864 Capped Head right (plain field).*

Store card die 1093A • *French Liberty Head (undated; RL).*

Store card die 1097 • *1863 Coronet Head (13 border stars)* • Same as patriotic die 30A.

Store card die 1092 • *Longacre-style Coronet Head, JACOBUS [retrograde] (13 stars).*

Store card die 1094 • *1863 Coronet Head (13 border stars)* • Same as patriotic die 31.

Store card die 1098 • *1863 Coronet Head (13 border stars).*

Store card die 1092A • *Longacre-style Coronet Head (13 stars).*

Store card die 1095 • *1863 Coronet Head (13 border stars)* • Same as patriotic die 32.

Store card die 1099 • *1863 Coronet Head (13 border stars)* • Same as patriotic die 31A.

Store card die 1093 • *French Liberty Head (13 border stars; RL).*

Store card die 1096 • *1863 Coronet Head (13 border stars).*

Store card die 1101 • *1863 Coronet Head (13 border stars)* • Same as patriotic die 30.

Store card die 1102 • *1863 Coronet Head (13 border stars).*

Store card die 1108 • *1863 Coronet Head (13 border stars UNION in field).*

Store card die 1113 • *1861 Coronet Head (CHILDS MANFR. CHICAGO)*

Store card die 1105 • *1863 Coronet Head (13 border stars UNION above)* • **Same as patriotic die 33.**

Store card die 1110 • *1863 Coronet Head (13 border stars UNION in field).*

Store card die 1114 • *1861 Coronet Head (CHILDS MANFR. CHICAGO).*

Store card die 1106 • *1863 Coronet Head (14 border stars UNION)* • **Same as patriotic die 34.**

Store card die 1111 • *1861 Coronet Head (CHILDS MANFR. CHICAGO).*

Store card die 1115 • *1861 Coronet Head (CHILDS MANFR. CHICAGO).*

Store card die 1107 • *1864 Coronet Head (13 border stars UNION in field)* • **Same as patriotic die 35.**

Store card die 1112 • *1861 Coronet Head (CHILDS MANFR. CHICAGO).*

Store card die 1116 • *1861 Coronet Head (CHILDS MANFR. CHICAGO).*

Store card die 1117 • *1861 Coronet Head (CHILDS MANFR. CHICAGO).*

Store card die 1118 • *1861 Coronet Head (BUSINESS CARD; star to each side).*

Store card die 1119 • *1861 Coronet Head (BUSINESS CARD; star to each side).*

Store card die 1120 • *1861 Coronet Head (SHOP RIGHTS FOR SALE IN WESTN STS.).*

Store card die 1121 • *Conical Cap Head (undated; UNITED WE STAND DIVIDED WE FALL).*

Store card die 1121A • *Conical Cap Head (undated; UNITED WE STAND DIVIDED WE FALL).*

Store card die 1122 • *Mercury Head (13 border stars)* • Same as patriotic die 40.

Store card die 1123 • *1863 Mercury Head (12 border stars)* • Same as patriotic die 38A.

Store card die 1124 • *1863 Mercury Head (13 border stars; LUTZ)* • Same as patriotic die 38.

Store card die 1125 • *1863 Mercury Head (13 border stars; LUTZ).*

Store card die 1126 • *1863 Mercury Head (14 border stars)* • Same as patriotic die 38B.

Store card die 1127 • *1863 Mercury Head (13 border stars)* • Same as patriotic die 39.

Store card die 1128 • *1863 Mercury head (no stars; LUTZ).*

Store card die 1130 • *1863 Mercury Head (13 border stars; LUTZ).*

Store card die 1131 • *Liberty head ("Phoenician Head"; 13 border stars; LUTZ)* • Same as patriotic die 438.

Store card die 1132 • *Washington portrait within five-pointed star (Sigel signature and address below)* • Same as patriotic die 105.

Store card die 1133 • *Washington portrait, 7 stars left, 6 stars right, LR below neck truncation* • Same as patriotic die 106.

Store card die 1133A • *Washington portrait (6 stars left, 6 stars right)* • Large date with round-top 3.

Store card die 1134 • *Washington portrait facing forward and slightly left (BORN FEB. 22 1732. DIED DEC. 14 1799.)* • Same as patriotic die 116.

Store card die 1135 • *Washington portrait facing right in plain field* • Same as patriotic die 123 • Dies are Philadelphia Mint products,

probably by assistant engraver Anthony C. Paquet • Melvin and George Fuld, "The Tokens of the Great Central Fair of Philadelphia," *The Numismatist*, September 1952, described 28 Great Central Fair die and metal (bronze and silver) varieties; scarcely any attention is paid to these today. The obverse dies were individually made as well and have variations in spacing. These tokens were struck at the Fair on a Mint press and offered for 10 cents copper and 50 cents silver.

Store card die 1136 • *Washington portrait in plain field* • Same as patriotic die 123.

Store card die 1137 • *1863 Washington portrait (THE WASHINGTON TOKEN)* • Same as patriotic die 120.

Store card die 1138 • *Washington portrait facing right (GEO. WASHINGTON PRESIDENT; 8 stars at border)* • Same as patriotic die 121.

Store card die 1139 • *Washington portrait facing left (GEO. WASHINGTON PRESIDENT; 13 border stars).*

Store card die 1140 (early state of die that later became 0115B) • *Washington portrait facing right (GEORGE / WASHINGTON)* • Same as patriotic die 115.

Store card die 1142 • *1863 Washington portrait facing right, within continuous wreath (DRY GOODS, GROCERIES &c. star / G.G. N.Y.).*

Store card die 1143 • *1863 Washington portrait facing right, above two crossed flags (UNITED WE STAND).*

Store card die 1144 (early state of what became die patriotic 125) • *18/64 Lincoln portrait facing left (ABM. LINCOLN PRESIDENT)* • Same as patriotic die 124.

Store card die 1145 • *1864 Lincoln portrait facing left (13 border stars)* • Same as patriotic die 127.

Store card die 1146 • *1864 Lincoln portrait facing right (ABRAHAM LINCOLN; K below bust)* • Same as patriotic die 129 • This die exists and has been used to make modern strikings.

Store card die 1147 • *Bearded portrait facing left (14 border stars; REDEEMED)* • Same as patriotic die 134.

Store card die 1148 • *1861 Franklin portrait facing left (BENJAMIN FRANKLIN; LOVETT)* • Same as patriotic die 152.

Store card die 1149 • *Franklin portrait facing right (BENJAMIN FRANKLIN; E. SIGEL)* • Same as patriotic die 151.

Store card die 1150 • *Franklin portrait facing left (BENJAMIN FRANKLIN)* • Same as patriotic die 153 • This die exists and has been used to make modern strikings.

Store card die 1150A • *Franklin portrait.*

Store card die 1151 • *Grant portrait facing left (KEY F.)* • Same as patriotic die 144 (now delisted).

Store card die 1155 • *Douglas portrait facing left (STEPHEN A. DOUGLAS.; MARR)* • Same as patriotic die 154.

Store card die 1159 • *1864 Burnside portrait (Rhode Island First In The Field)* • Same as patriotic die 146.

Store card die 1152 • *McClellan portrait facing left (GENERAL G.B. McCLELLAN)* • Same as patriotic die 138.

Store card die 1156 • *Douglas portrait facing left (S.A.D. below bust; MARR on truncation)* • Same as patriotic die 154A.

Store card die 1160 • *Portrait of bearded man facing left (plain field)* • Same as patriotic die 148.

Store card die 1153 • *1863 McClellan portrait facing left, in open wreath (13 border stars LITTLE MACK, S above date)* • Same as patriotic die 140.

Store card die 1157 • *Horatio Seymour portrait facing right (KEY F.)* • Same as patriotic die 145 (now delisted).

Store card die 1161 • *1863 Washington on horseback statue (FIRST IN WAR, FIRST IN PEACE)* • Same as patriotic die 175.

Store card die 1153A • *THE MEDAL OF G.B. McCLELLAN / PRICE* • Same as patriotic die 143.

Store card die 1158 • *Bell portrait facing left (FOR PRESIDENT JOHN BELL OF TENNESSEE)* • Same as patriotic die 509.

Store card die 1162 • *1863 Horse and rider facing right (TIME IS MONEY EXIGENCY)* • Same as patriotic die 187.

Store card die 1163 • *1863 Horse and rider facing right (TIME IS MONEY EXPEDIENCY).*

Store card die 1164 • *1863 Seated goddess facing left, mountains in background (E. SIGEL NEW YORK).*

Store card die 1165 • *1863 Perched eagle, head facing left (16 stars at border; UNION)* • Same as patriotic die 155.

Store card die 1166 • *1863 Flying eagle, head at left (12 border stars)* • Same as patriotic die 158 • Die 1167 is simply a later state of 1166.

Store card die 1168 • *1863 Flying eagle, head at left (12 border stars).*

Store card die 1169 • *1863 Flying eagle, head at left (12 border stars)* • Same as patriotic die 159.

Store card die 1170 • *1863 Flying eagle, head at right (12 border stars)* • Same as patriotic die 156.

Store card die 1171 • *1864 Flying eagle, head at left.*

Store card die 1172 • *1863 Flying eagle, head at right (13 border stars)* • Same as patriotic die 157.

Store card die 1173 • *1864 Flying eagle, head at left (A. BUTTON).*

Store card die 1174 • *1864 Eagle perched on cannon (LIBERTY FOR ALL)* • Same as patriotic die 160.

Store card die 1175A • *Perched eagle, head facing left (OUR ARMY)* • Same as patriotic die 161.

Store card die 1176 • *Eagle perched on shield, head right.*

Store card die 1180 • 1863 *Perched eagle, head to viewer's left.*

Store card die 1183 • *1863 Perched eagle, head to viewer's left (13 border stars)* • **Same as patriotic die 285.**

Store card die 1177 • *Eagle perched on shield, head right.*

Store card die 1180A • 1863 *Perched eagle, head to viewer's left.*

Store card die 1183A • *1863 Perched eagle, head to viewer's left (13 border stars).*

Store card die 1178 • 1863 *Perched eagle, head to viewer's left.*

Store card die 1181 • *Perched eagle (no date)* • This die became 1179 when a date was added to it.

Store card die 1184 • *1863 Perched eagle, head to viewer's left (13 border stars).*

Store card die 1179 • 1863 *Perched eagle, head to viewer's left* • Die 1181 now with 1863 date added.

Store card die 1182 • *Perched eagle. head to viewer's left, with shield on breast (no date)* • Same as patriotic die 284.

Store card die 1185 • *1863 Perched eagle, head to viewer's left (A. GLEASON MANUF'R. HILLSDALE MICH.).*

Store card die 1185A • *1863*
*Perched eagle, head to viewer's
left (A. GLEASON MANUF'R.
HILLSDALE, MICH.).*

Store card die 1189 • *Eagle
perched on rock in sea, holding
serpent (NO NORTH NO
SOUTH ONE FLAG ONE
UNION).*

Store card die 1193 • *1863
Flying eagle, head curved to
face date (13 border stars) •
Same as patriotic die 282.*

Store card die 1186 • *1863
Perched eagle, head to viewer's
left (A. GLEASON
HILLSDALE; 2 stars at
border).*

Store card die 1190 • *Perched
eagle, head to viewer's left (NO
NORTH NO SOUTH ONE
FLAG ONE UNION; star at
border).*

Store card die 1194 • *1863
Perched eagle, head turned to
viewer's right.*

Store card die 1187 • *1863
Perched eagle, head to viewer's
left (A. GLEASON MANUF'R.
HILLSDALE, MICH.; 12 stars
in field).*

Store card die 1191 • *Eagle
perched on anchor (ribbed
background; 16 stars at border)
• Same as patriotic die 283.*

Store card die 1195 • *1863
Perched eagle, head turned to
viewer's right.*

Store card die 1196 • *1863
Perched eagle, head turned to
viewer's right.*

Store card die 1188 • *Perched
eagle with shield in open wreath
(10 border stars).*

Store card die 1192 • *Perched
eagle, head to viewer's right (no
date) • Same as patriotic die
281.*

Store card die 1197 • *1863 Perched eagle and branches (APOTH. WEIGHT ONE DRAM) • Same as patriotic die 286.*

Store card die 1201 • *Open wreath (shield inscribed UNION, with eagle on top, flags to sides) • Same as patriotic die 163.*

Store card die 1205 • *1863 Perched eagle, head to viewer's left (UNION; 2 stars at border) • Same as patriotic die 279.*

Store card die 1198 • *Perched eagle and branches (GOLD WEIGHT TROY 2 PENNYWEIGHT NEW YORK).*

Store card die 1202 • *Open wreath (shield inscribed UNION, with eagle on top, flags to sides) • Same as patriotic die 165.*

Store card die 1206 • *1861 Perched eagle, head to viewer's left (UNION; 2 stars at border).*

Store card die 1199 • *Perched eagle and branches (GOLD WEIGHT 2 DWT NEW YORK) • Same as patriotic die 286A.*

Store card die 1203 • *1863 Perched eagle, head to viewer's left (13 border stars) • Same as patriotic die 280.*

Store card die 1207 • *1861 Perched eagle, head to viewer's left (UNION; 2 stars at border) • Same as patriotic die 277A.*

Store card die 1200 • *Open wreath (shield inscribed UNION, with eagle on top, flags to sides) • Same as patriotic die 164.*

Store card die 1204 • *1863 Perched eagle, head to viewer's left (13 border stars) • Same as patriotic die 280A.*

Store card die 1208 • *1861 Perched eagle, head to viewer's left (UNION; 2 stars at border).*

Store card die 1209 • *1863*
Perched eagle, head to viewer's
left (UNION; 2 stars at
border).

Store card die 1210 • *1863*
Perched eagle, head to viewer's
left (UNION; 2 stars at
border).

Store card die 1211 • *1863*
Perched eagle, head to viewer's
left (UNION; 2 stars at
border).

Store card die 1212 • *1863*
Perched eagle, head to viewer's
left (UNION; 2 stars at border)
• *Same as patriotic die 279A.*

Store card die 1212A • *Childs*
eagle, no date.

Store card die 1213 • *Perched*
eagle (SILVER MINE TOKEN
E) • Same as patriotic die 287.

Store card die 1214 • *Eagle*
perched on top of globe (UNION
FOR EVER at top border) •
Same as patriotic die 433.

Store card die 1215 • *Eagle*
perched on the top of globe
inscribed COPPER (UNITED
STATES at top border) • Same
as patriotic die 434.

Store card die 1216 • *1863*
Eagle perched on shield
(UNITED STATES OF
AMERICA; E.S.) • Same as
patriotic die 196.

Store card die 1217 • *1863*
Eagle perched on shield
(UNITED STATES OF
AMERICA; E.S.) • Same as
patriotic die 197.

Store card die 1218 • *1863*
Eagle perched on shield
(UNITED STATES OF
AMERICA) • Same as
patriotic die 198.

Store card die 1219 • *1863*
Eagle perched on shield
(UNITED STATES MEDAL)
• Same as patriotic die 199.

Store card die 1220 • *1863 Amazon maiden with flag •* Same as patriotic die 218.

Store card die 1221 • *1863 Crossed cannons, star above (12 border stars) •* Same as patriotic die 172.

Store card die 1222 • *1863 Shield inscribed UNION (13 border stars).*

Store card die 1223 (a.k.a. 1229) • *1864 Shield inscribed UNION (13 border stars).*

Store card die 1224 • *1863 Shield inscribed UNION (ONE COUNTRY; 2 stars at border) •* Same as patriotic die 192.

Store card die 1225 • *1863 Shield inscribed UNION (ONE COUNTRY).*

Store card die 1226 • *1863 Shield inscribed UNION (THE ARMY & NAVY; 2 stars at border) •* Same as patriotic die 193.

Store card die 1227 • *1863 Shield inscribed UNION (TOYS AND CONFECTIONERY) •* Same as patriotic die 194.

Store card die 1228 • *1864 Shield inscribed UNION (ONE COUNTRY; 2 stars at border) •* Same as patriotic die 193A.

Store card die 1230 • *18/63 Shield with anchor (NEW-YORK; 2 stars at border) •* Same as patriotic die 200.

Store card die 1231 • *1863 NEW YORK (13 stars around border).*

Store card die 1232 • *Shield with GOOD FOR ONE CENT (TRADESMENS CURRENCY; 2 stars at border) •* Same as patriotic die 202.

Store card die 1233 • *1863 flag (THE FLAG OF OUR UNION; 13 stars around flag)* • Same as patriotic die 206.

Store card die 1235 • *Flag (THE FLAG OF OUR UNION; 13 stars around flag)* • Same as patriotic die 214.

Store card die 1239 • *REMEMBRANCE OF 1863* • Same as patriotic die 244.

Store card die 1233A • *1863 flag (THE FLAG OF OUR UNION; 13 stars around flag)* • Same as patriotic die 210.

Store card die 1236 • *Closed wreath (shield with crossed branches, OUR COUNTRY, star, 2 arrowheads)* • Same as patriotic die 229.

Store card die 1240 • *ERINNERUNG an 1863* • Same as patriotic die 243.

Store card die 1234 • *1863 flag (THE FLAG OF OUR UNION; 13 stars around flag)*.

Store card die 1237 • *1863 Capitol building (UNITED STATES 8 stars at border)* • Same as patriotic die 233.

Store card die 1241 • *O.K. within 13 chain links* • Same as patriotic die 248.

Store card die 1234A • *1863 flag (THE FLAG OF OUR UNION; 13 stars around flag)* • Same as patriotic die 211 • H.D. Higgins impact copy die with some details missing. Used on IN-710-A-3a, IN-915-A-1a.

Store card die 1238 • *1863 Capitol building (UNITED STATES CAPITAL 8 stars at border)* • Similar to, but not the same as, patriotic die 234.

Store card die 1242 • *Large star NORTH STAR (28 stars in field)* • Same as patriotic die 250.

Store card die 1243 • *1863 Man with backpack (MONEY MAKES THE MARE GO)* • Same as patriotic die 254.

Store card die 1247 • *Shield (13 border stars; UNION)* • Same as patriotic die 345.

Store card die 1250A • *Eagle on drum, flags to left and right, rays above.*

Store card die 1244 • *Open wreath, shield and flags, star at apex (FREE DOM)* • Same as patriotic die 294.

Store card die 1248 • *Shield (13 border stars; UNION)* • Same as patriotic die 345A.

Store card die 1251 • *Open wreath (NOT ONE CENT)* • Same as patriotic die 355.

Store card die 1245 • *Open wreath, shield and flags, star at apex (FREE DOM)* • Same as patriotic die 295.

Store card die 1249 • *Shield within closed wreath; E.S. (CONSTITUTION AND THE UNION; star at border)* • Same as patriotic die 346.

Store card die 1252 • *Open wreath (NOT ONE CENT)* • Same as patriotic die 359.

Store card die 1246 • *Open wreath, shield and flags (UNION FOR EVER)* • Same as patriotic die 271.

Store card die 1250 • *1864 Drums, rifles, cannons, flags, etc.* • Same as patriotic die 349.

Store card die 1253 • *Open wreath (NOT ONE CENT)* • Same as patriotic die 360.

Store card die 1254 • *Open wreath (NOT ONE CENT; H)* • Same as patriotic die 361.

Store card die 1255 • *Open wreath, star at apex (NOT ONE CENT star)* • Same as patriotic die 374.

Store card die 1256 • *Closed wreath (NOT ONE CENT L. ROLOFF)* • Same as patriotic die 377.

Store card die 1257 • *Closed wreath (NOT ONE CENT L. ROLOFF)* • Same as patriotic die 378.

Store card die 1258 • *Closed wreath (NOT ONE CENT)* • Same as patriotic die 379.

Store card die 1259 • *Closed wreath (NOT ONE CENT)* • Same as patriotic die 380.

Store card die 1260 • *Closed wreath (NOT ONE CENT L. ROLOFF).*

Store card die 1261 • *Closed wreath (NOT ONE CENT; L. ROLOFF).*

Store card die 1262 • *Open wreath (NOT ONE CENT; 13 stars in field)* • Same as patriotic die 383.

Store card die 1263 • *Closed wreath (NOT ONE CENT)* • Same as patriotic die 382.

Store card die 1264 • *Open wreath (GOOD FOR ONE CENT 1863 Redeem.ed)* • Same as patriotic die 386.

Store card die 1265 • *I-O-U 2 small Washington portraits; CENT; at center, 1 PURE COPPER* • Same as patriotic die 390.

Store card die 1266 • *I-O-U 2 small female portraits; CENT; at center, 1 PURE COPPER* • Same as patriotic die 390A.

Store card die 1267 • *Open wreath; I O.U. 1 CENT* • Same as patriotic die 391.

Store card die 1268 • *GOOD FOR 1 CENT (2 stars at border)* • Same as patriotic die 392.

Store card die 1269 • *GOOD FOR 1 CENT (2 stars at border)* • Same as patriotic die 393.

Store card die 1270. *GOOD FOR 1 CENT (2 stars at border, CENT closer to dentils than to beads).*

Store card die 1270A • *GOOD FOR 1 CENT (2 stars at border, CENT closer to beads than to dentils).*

Store card die 1270B • *GOOD FOR 1 CENT, CENT closer to beads than to dentils).*

Store card die 1271 • *Open wreath (H; WILSON'S 1 MEDAL)* • Same as patriotic die 396.

Store card die 1272 • *Open wreath (13 stars in field; AMERICA)* • Same as patriotic die 417.

Store card die 1273 • *1863 Open oak wreath* • Same as patriotic die 424.

Store card die 1274 • *1863 Open oak wreath* • Same as patriotic die 425.

Store card die 1275 • *Open wreath, crossed cannons (NO COMPROMISE WITH TRAITORS)* • Same as patriotic die 432.

Store card die 1276 • *UNITED WE STAND / DIVIDED WE FALL; within open wreath is a fasces surmounted by a liberty cap* • Same as patriotic die 435.

Store card die 1277 • *UNITED COUNTRY in ellipse; 34 stars around border* • Same as patriotic die 436.

Store card die 1278 • *1863 Stocking (13 border stars)* • **Same as patriotic die 437** • **Die ascribed to the shop of William Lanphear.**

Store card die 1279 • *Grouping of fruit and vegetables (20 stars around border)* • **Same as patriotic die 444.**

Store card die 1280 • *1863 Male lion couchant, facing right (SIGN OF THE LION; 2 stars).*

Store card die 1281 • *1863 Male lion couchant, facing left (SIGN OF THE LION)* • **Same as patriotic die 183A.**

Store card die 1282 • *Small image of male lion standing, facing left* • **Same as patriotic die 182.**

Store card die 1283 • *Small image of male bison standing, facing right* • **Same as patriotic die 183.**

Store card die 1284 • *1863 Dog's head (GOOD FOR A SCENT; 2 stars at border).*

Store card die 1285 • *Two hunting dogs running to left in meadow (ribbed background)* • **Same as patriotic die 184.**

Store card die 1286 • *Steer head with two flags.*

Store card die 1287 • *Bull standing, facing right.*

Store card die 1288 (early state of what became die 1289) • *Bull standing, facing right (plain field)* • **Same as patriotic die 185.**

Store card die 1289 (modification of die 1288) • *Bull standing, facing right (BRIGHTON HOUSE).*

Store card die 1290 • *1863 Hippocampus facing left (13 border stars)* • Same as patriotic die 185B.

Store card die 1291 • *1863 Stag's head; 26 & 28 EXCHANGE PLACE N.Y.; G. GL.*

Store card die 1292 • *1863 Stag's head; 26 & 28 EXCHANGE PLACE N.Y.; G. GL.*

Store card die 1293 • *1863 Rooster, standing and facing left (13 border stars)* • Same as patriotic die 186.

Store card die 1294 • *1864 beer mug (12 border stars).*

Store card die 1295 • *Beer mug in open wreath, star at apex.*

Store card die 1296 • *Beer mug within continuous hops vine wreath* • Same as patriotic die 532.

Store card die 1297 • *Coffee pot (HOUSE FURNISHING GOODS).*

Store card die 1298 • *Sewing machine* • Same as patriotic die 447A.

Store card die 1299 • *1863 Kitchen stove.*

Store card die 1300 (*altered from die 1302*) • *1863 Kitchen stove (PEACE MAKER 1863).*

Store card die 1301 • *1864 Kitchen stove.*

Store card die 1302 (*die later altered to create 1300*) • *Kitchen stove (PEACE MAKER 1863).*

Store card die 1303 • *1863*
Kitchen stove (13 border stars).

Store card die 1304 • *1863*
Kitchen stove (13 border stars).

Store card die 1305 • *1863*
GOOD SAMARITAN kitchen
stove (13 border stars).

Store card die 1306 • *1863*
THE TRIUMPH kitchen stove
(13 border stars).

Store card die 1307 • *1862*
GOOD SAMARITAN kitchen
stove.

Store card die 1307A • *1862*
GOOD SAMARITAN kitchen
stove • Discovered as a new
reverse die with MI-370-D-4b.
ANS has the only known
example.

Store card die 1308 • *1862*
GOOD SAMARITAN kitchen
stove.

Store card die 1309 • *Mortar*
and pestle (PRESCRIPTIONS
ACCURATELY
COMPOUNDED).

Store card die 1310 • *Mortar*
and pestle (DRUGS AND
MEDICINES).

Store card die 1311 • *Mortar*
and pestle.

Store card die 1312 • *Mortar*
and pestle (PERFUMERIES,
NOTIONS, AND FANCY
ARTICLES).

Store card die 1313 • *Mortar*
and pestle (DEALERS IN
DRUGS HARDWARE &
SADDLERY) • Same as
patriotic die 470.

Store card die 1314 • *Mortar*
and pestle (DRUGGISTS ANN
ARBOR MICH; 2 stars at
border).

Store card die 1315 • *Mortar and pestle (DRUGGISTS ANN ARBOR MICH; 2 stars at border).*

Store card die 1319 • *Pocket watch* • Same as patriotic die 535.

Store card die 1323 • *1863 Book (BOOKS & STATIONERY; 2 stars at border).*

Store card die 1316 • *1863 Mortar and pestle (DRUGS AND MEDICINES).*

Store card die 1320 • *1863 Pocket watch (ALL WORK WARRANTED; 2 stars at border).*

Store card die 1324 • *1863 Book (BOOKS STATIONERY &C; 2 stars at border).*

Store card die 1317 • *Boot (BOOTS AND SHOES MADE TO ORDER).*

Store card die 1321 • *Pocket watch (WATCHES & JEWELRY REPAIRED).*

Store card die 1324A • *1863 Book (BOOKS, STATIONERY &C; 2 stars at border).*

Store card die 1318 • *1864 Boot (BOOTS & SHOES MADE TO ORDER).*

Store card die 1322 • *1863 Book (BOOKS & STATIONERY; 6 stars at border).*

Store card die 1325 • *1864 Book (BOOKS AND STATIONERY; star divides date 18 64).*

Store card die 1326 • *1863 Padlock inscribed HARDWARE DEALER (at border, IRON NAILS AND GLASS; 2 stars at border).*

Store card die 1330 • *Coining press; 18/63; B&K* • The initials **B&K** have not been attributed.

Store card die 1334 • *Anvil (HARDWARE AND TOOLS.).*

Store card die 1327 • *Spectacles (2 pairs) and attachment (PERISCOPIC SPECTACLES; 2 stars in field)* • Same as patriotic die 533.

Store card die 1331 • *Open wreath (scale, box of cigars, etc.)* • Same as patriotic die 526.

Store card die 1335 • *Barrel on its side (WINES & LIQUORS).*

Store card die 1328 • *Spectacles (2 pairs) and attachment (PERISCOPIC SPECT [space] ACLES).*

Store card die 1332 • *Anvil.*

Store card die 1336 • *Barrel on its side (CHILD'S ONE PENNY BARREL; 2 stars at border).*

Store card die 1329 • *Spectacles (PERISCOPIC SPECTACLES).*

Store card die 1333 • *Anvil (HARDWARE, IRON & STOVES; 3 stars at border).*

Store card die 1337 • *Jacket and pants (QUICK SALES AND SMALL PROFITS).*

Store card die 1338 • *Jacket (MANUFACTURERS OF CLOTHING).*

Store card die 1342 • *1863 Hat (FURNISHING GOODS; 6 stars at border)* • **Same as patriotic die 451.**

Store card die 1346 • *Anchor with rope.*

Store card die 1339 • *Jacket (GENTLEMENS FURNISING GOODS).*

Store card die 1343 • *Two cue sticks and four billiard balls.*

Store card die 1347 • *1863 SIGN OF THE 8 (10 border stars).*

Store card die 1340 • *Tombstone (IN MEMORY OF).*

Store card die 1344 • *EXCELSIOR on ribbon above human teeth, dental tools below; LUTZ.*

Store card die 1348 • *1863 Face (BULLY FOR YOU).*

Store card die 1341 • *Saddle (SADDLES, BRIDLES, &C.)* • **Same as patriotic die 448.**

Store card die 1345 • *Crossed rifles, crossed pistols, etc. (PISTOLS, GUNS etc.).*

Store card die 1349 • *1864 Face (BULLY FOR YOU).*

Store card die 1350 • *1864 Beehive (INDUSTRY)* • Same as patriotic die 188A.

Store card die 1353 • *1863 Group of fruit and vegetables (LIVE AND LET LIVE; signed G. GL.)* • Same as patriotic die 185A.

Store card die 1357 • *Open laurel wreath (OUR CARD)* • Same as patriotic die 275.

Store card die 1351 • *1863 Beehive (TYLER'S BEE HIVE STORE INDUSTRY).*

Store card die 1354 • *Gambrinus astride a barrel marked BIER, etc.*

Store card die 1357A. (Unlisted as a store card die) • *Open laurel wreath (OUR CARD)* • Same as patriotic die 276.

Store card die 1352 • *Open wreath enclosing a shield lying on its side.*

Store card die 1355 • *Gambrinus astride a barrel marked BEER, etc.*

Store card die 1358 • *1861 Open wreath (BUSINESS CARD)* • This is a reworked later state of die 1367. A light crack at the top of the wreath was nearly completely relapped away, and the date 1861 was added.

Store card die 1352A • *Open oak wreath enclosing spade-shaped shield* • Same as patriotic die 347A.

Store card die 1356 • *1863 Justice seated at seashore.*

Store card die 1359 • *Open wreath (BUSINESS CARD).*

Store card die 1360 • *Open wreath (BUSINESS CARD)* • Although leaf treatments and some other details differ, 1360 and 1363 are closely related topologically.

Store card die 1361 • *Open wreath (BUSINESS CARD)*.

Store card die 1362 • *Open wreath (BUSINESS CARD)*.

Store card die 1363 • *Open wreath (BUSINESS CARD)* • Although leaf treatments and some other details differ, 1360 and 1363 are closely related topologically.

Store card die 1364 • *Open wreath (MINER'S CARD)*.

Store card die 1365 • *Open wreath (BUSINESS CARD)*.

Store card die 1366 • *Open wreath (BUSINESS CARD)*.

Store card die 1367 • *Open wreath (BUSINESS CARD)* • This die was reworked, a light crack at the top of the wreath was nearly completely relapped away, and the date 1861 was added to create die 1358.

Store card die 1368 • *Open wreath (BUSINESS CARD)* • Same as patriotic die 461.

Store card die 1369 • *Wreath with shield at apex (BUSINESS CARD)*.

Store card die 1370 • *A BUSINESS CARD (10 stars near center)* • Same as patriotic die 459.

Store card die 1371 • *Open wreath, star at apex (UNION & LIBERTY)*.

Store card die 1373 • *LIBERTY & LAW (13 stars around border).*

Store card die 1374 • *Wreath (UNION; 1863; C) • Same as patriotic die 427.*

Store card die 1374A • *Ornate 3 within C, 13 stars around border.*

Store card die 1375 • *18/63 Shield with E PLURIBUS UNUM on ribbon.*

Store card die 1376 • *18/63 Shield with E PLURIBUS UNUM on ribbon (L. ROLOFF).*

Store card die 1377 • *1863 Arms of Philadelphia (PHILADA.; 13 border stars).*

Store card die 1378 • *1863 Arms of Philadelphia (PHILADA.; 13 border stars).*

Store card die 1379 • *1863 Arms of Philadelphia (PHILADA.; 13 border stars; signature JACOBUS and small PHILA).*

Store card die 1380 • *1863 Arms of Philadelphia (PHILADA.; 13 border stars; signature JACOBUS and small PHILA).*

Store card die 1381 • *1863 Crossed flags over sunrise (13 border stars) • Same as patriotic die 457.*

Store card die 1382 • *1863 Tree (signed HORTER; 13 border stars).*

Store card die 1383 • *Large five-pointed star with U N I O N between rays (10 border stars).*

Store card die 1383A • *Large five-pointed star with U N I O N between rays (10 border stars)* • Different alignment; note, for example, the position of the N at lower right in relation to the two stars.

Store card die 1384 • *Open wreath of oak-like leaves, star at apex (large five-pointed star at center; ornaments).*

Store card die 1385 • *1862 Open wreath (enclosing superimposed stars).*

Store card die 1386 • *Masonic emblems of compass and square (13 border stars)* • Same as patriotic die 251.

Store card die 1387 • *Masonic emblems of compass, square, and G with rays* • Same as patriotic die 252A.

Store card die 1388 • *Masonic emblems of compass and square (13 border stars).*

Store card die 1389 • *Arm and hammer (23 four-bladed ornaments at border).*

Store card die 1390 • *1861 Arm and hammer (CHILDS MANFR. CHICAGO; 2 stars at border).*

Store card die 1391 • *5 CENTS (11 border stars).*

Store card die 1391A (unlisted) • *5 CENTS (11 border stars).*

Store card die 1391B (unlisted) • *5 CENTS (11 border stars)* • Used as the reverse of IN-280-C and OH-165-GY-32.

Store card die 1391C (unlisted) • *5 CENTS in thin letters (11 border stars).*

Store card die 1392 • *10 in otherwise plain field.*

Store card die 1396 • *10 CENTS (12 border stars)* • Same as patriotic die 452B.

Store card die 1398 • *25 in otherwise plain field.*

Store card die 1393 • *10 in beaded circle (24 stars around border)* • Same as patriotic die 452.

Store card die 1396A • *GOOD FOR 10 CENTS, 1862.*

Store card die 1399 • *25 CENTS (11 border stars)* • Same as patriotic die 456A.

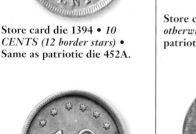

Store card die 1394 • *10 CENTS (12 border stars)* • Same as patriotic die 452A.

Store card die 1397 • *15 in otherwise plain field* • Same as patriotic die 454.

Store card die 1400 • *GOOD FOR 25 CENTS PAYABLE IN BANK BILLS; 3 stars* • Same as patriotic die 455.

Store card die 1395 • *10 CENTS (12 stars around border).*

Store card die 1397A • *20 in otherwise plain field.*

Store card die 1401 • *1862; GOOD FOR 25 CENTS; 2 maple leaves* • Same as patriotic die 456.

Store card die 1401A • *30 in otherwise plain field.*

Store card die 1402 • *35 in otherwise plain field.*

Store card die 1402A • *45 CENTS; 10 stars at border.*

Store card die 1403 • *50 in otherwise plain field.*

Store card die 1404 • *50 CENTS (11 border stars).*

Store card die 1404A • *100 in otherwise plain field.*

Store card die 1405 • *500 with M C K A in tiny letters at right border* • The letters are vestiges of MC KAY. This die was used for the reverse of TN-690-D-9b, McKay & Lapsley, and may have had more lettering, removed by relapping. It was used for other merchants as well.

Store card die 1405A • *10 / DOLLARS curved at bottom.*

Store card die 1406 • *Thistle (UNITED WE STAND DIVIDED WE FALL; 2 stars at border)* • Same as patriotic die 449.

Store card die 1407 • *Thistle (UNITED WE STAND DIVIDED WE FALL; 2 stars at border)* • Same as patriotic die 450.

Store card die 1408 • *Thistle (UNITED WE STAND DIVIDED WE FALL; 2 stars at border).*

Store card die 1409 • *Thistle (UNITED WE STAND DIVIDED WE FALL; 2 stars at border).*

Store card die 1410 • *1863; REDEEMED AT OUR STORE.*

Store card die 1413 • *Open wreath (Bunker Hill Monument).*

Store card die 1414 • *Open wreath (Bunker Hill Monument).*

Store card die 1415 • *Open wreath (Bunker Hill Monument).*

Store card die 1416 • *Open wreath (large five-pointed star).*

Store card die 1417 and 1417A • *Eight-pointed star made of lines (beer glass; signed EMIL SIGEL; 24 stars around border).*

Store card die 1418 • *Lincoln portrait facing left (FOR PRESIDENT ABRAHAM LINCOLN OF ILL) • Same as patriotic die 506.*

Store card die 1419 • *Lincoln portrait facing left (FOR PRESIDENT ABRAHAM LINCOLN OF ILL.) • Same as patriotic die 507.*

Store card die 1420 • *Breckinridge portrait facing left (FOR PRESIDENT JOHN C. BRECKINRIDGE OF KY.) • Same as patriotic die 508.*

Store card die 1421 • *White House (PRESIDENTS HOUSE; T in lawn) • Same as patriotic die 510A.*

Store card die 1422 • *Douglas portrait facing left (FOR PRESIDENT STEPHEN A. DOUGLAS OF ILL.) • Same as patriotic die 510.*

Store card die 1423 • *Agricultural products (THE WEALTH OF THE SOUTH, etc.) •* From the shop of John Stanton, die by Benjamin C. True • *Same as patriotic die 511.*

Store card die 1426A • *1860 Palmetto, cannon, 15 stars, etc. (NO SUBMISSION TO THE NORTH) • Same as patriotic die 516.*

Store card die 1427 • *Blank with raised rim and dentils. 22 mm* • Same as patriotic die 519 (generic).

Store card die 1427A • *Blank with raised rim and dentils. 18 mm* • Reverse of OH-165-BWa-09a illustrated.

Store card die 1428 • *EAST BOSTON 1837 [Hard Times token die]* • Same as patriotic die 472, a leftover 1837 Hard Times token die.

Store card die 1429 • *Arms of Rhode Island, modified (shield, stars, HOPE, 1844)* • Same as patriotic die 481.

Store card die 1430 • *J.A. HUGHES / METALIC / CARDS / CINCINNATI, O.* • This and the following stock dies are new to the third edition of the Fuld text.

Store card die 1431 • *H. MILLER CO. / LOUISVILLE / Hand holding mug / 5C.*

Store card die 1432 • *MURDOCK & SPENCER / 139 / W' FIFTH / STREET / CINCINNATI.*

Store card die 1433 • *MURDOCK & SPENCER / 139 / W' 5' ST / CIN. O.* • Usually struck over an 1864 presidential campaign token and used for a jewelry check.

Store card die 1434 • *W.K. LANPHEAR / MANU'FR / OF / METALIC / CARDS / CINCINNATI, O. Open wreath.*

Store card die 1435 • *W.K. LANPHEAR / GENERAL ENGRAVER . . .*

Store card die 1436 • *W.K. LANPHEAR MANUF'R OF METALIC CARDS CINTI OHIO, 6 stars.*

Store card die 1437 • *W.K. LANPHEAR / MANUFACTURER / OF / STORE CARDS . . .*

Store card die 1438 •
*PILKINGTON / MAKER / 83
/ EXCHANGE PLACE /
BALTIMORE.*

Store card die 1439 • *Wm.
Senour (in script).*

Store card die 1440 • *JOHN
STANTON / STAMP / &
BRAND / CUTTER /
CINCINNATI.*

Store card die 1451 • *$100
BOUNTY / PENSIONS /
BACK PAY /&C /
COLLECTED / & / CASHED*
• Same as patriotic die 525.

Store card die 1452 • *ALSO /
CUTLERY,/ NOTIONS / &C.*

Store card die 1453 • *ARCTIC
/ SODA WATER . . .*

Store card die 1454 • *BOOTS,
/ SHOES / AND / YANKEE /
NOTIONS.*

Store card die 1455 •
*CLOTHING / AT /
WHOLESALE.*

Store card die 1456 •
*DEALER / IN / CLOCKS /
WATCHES / & / JEWELRY.*

Store card die 1457 •
*DEALER IN / IRON. / NAILS.
& / STOVES. / CROCKERY /
& PAINTS.*

Store card die 1458 •
*DEALER IN / IRON / NAILS
/ STOVES / CROCKERY / & /
PAINTS.*

Store card die 1459 •
*DEALERS / IN / HOOP /
SKIRTS / HATS CAPS/ AND
/ NOTIONS.*

Store card die 1460 • *DRY GOODS, CLOTHING, BOOTS & SHOES . . .*

Store card die 1460A • *GOOD FOR / ONE GLASS / BEER.*

Store card die 1461 • *GROCERIES. / PROVISIONS / & / DRY GOODS / 1863.*

Store card die 1461A • *DRY GOODS, / GROCERIES / & / PROVISIONS.*

Store card die 1462 • *LEATHER / AND / SHOE FINDINGS / WOOL, / SHEEP PELTS, / SHIPPING / FURRS / &C. / & C.* • FURRS is a misspelling.

Store card die 1463 • *ONE / HALF / PINT / OF / MILK.*

Store card die 1464 • *1 / PINT / OF / MILK.*

Store card die 1465 • *ONE / QUART / OF / MILK* • Same as patriotic die 475A.

Store card die 1466 • *ONE / HALF / GALL / OF / MILK.*

Store card die 1467 • *ONE / GALL / OF / MILK.*

Store card die 1468 • *PAYABLE / IN / MERCHANDISE.*

Store card die 1469 • *RAIL ROAD / 1863 / WARE HOUSE.*

Store card die 1470 • REDEEMED / IN / PAR FUNDS / IN SUMS OF / ONE / DOLLAR • Same as patriotic die 473.

Store card die 1472 • THE / FEDERAL / GOVERNMENT / A / NATIONAL / CURRENCY . . . • Same as patriotic die 467.

Store card die 1474 • TRY / ALLEN'S / BLACKLEAD / COMPOUND / BABBITT / METAL / 1863.

Store card die 1471 • THE CELEBRATED / TEA / ESTABLISHMENT.

Store card die 1473 • Try / ALLEN'S / BLACKLEAD / COMPOUND / BABBITT / METAL / 1862.

Store card die 1475 • STEREOSCOPIC / PICTURES / AND / INSTRUMENTS / FOR / SALE / P.O. BOX 2566.

Civil War Store Card Varieties

Civil War store cards are arranged in order by state, town, and merchant. An example is given of the most common or one of the most common varieties issued by a merchant or other entity, with approximate market values in EF to AU grade and MS-63. The rarity rating is given. In instances in which more than one obverse die exists, nearly all such dies are illustrated. Stock reverse dies are listed, described, and illustrated above. For illustrations of other obverse dies see *U.S. Civil War Store Cards.*

ALABAMA

Only one issuer is recorded for Alabama, and tokens of White & Swann are all rarities. These are in great demand from those who desire one token from each issuing state.

AL, Huntsville • White & Swann • AL-425-A • ? • Ascribed to the shop of Murdock & Spencer • Reverse dies: 1047, 1069, 1392, 1394, 1397, 1398, 1399, 1402, 1403, 1404, and 1405 • AL-425-A-3a Rev-1392 (R-8): VF-EF $2,000–$3,000 • MS-63 $6,000–$9,000 • No records have been found of this partnership. Some of the reverse dies postdate 1865. Many of these tokens, widely discussed in the lit-erature, were probably made for the numismatic trade. Others likely circulated as evidenced by worn examples in exis-tence today.

CONNECTICUT

Tokens of several different issuers are known from Connecticut. Most are very collectible as types, although certain vari-eties are rare. Orrin Rudd, Arch Saloon is a rarity and the token of Dr. O.G. Keit-teridge is one of the most famous rarities in the store card series.

CT, Bridgeport • E.W. Atwood • CT-035-A • *Dealer in books and newspapers •* Ascribed to the Scovill Manufacturing

Co. • Reverse dies: 1002 and 1237 • CT-035-A-1a Rev-1002 (R-3): VF–EF $25–$40 • MS-63 $50–$75.

CT, Bridgeport • A.W. Wallace • CT-035-B • *Bakery* • Ascribed to Scovill? • Reverse die: 1201 • CT-035-B-1a Rev-1201 (R-1): VF–EF $25–$40 • MS-63 $50–$75.

CT, Montville • Arch Saloon, O. Rudd • CT-600-B • *Saloon* • Ascribed to unknown RI diesinker • Reverse die: 1147 • CT-600-B-1b(fpl) Rev-1147 (R-8): VF–EF $2,500–$3,750 • Formerly attributed to Willimantic, Connecticut. Just one die pair and metal. Only token-issuing merchant of this town.

CT, Norwich • City of New York • CT-345aA • *Steamship* • Ascribed to Louis Roloff[4] • Reverse dies: 1011, 1164, custom • CT-345aA-1a Rev-1011 (R-1): VF–EF $30–$45 • MS-63 $90–$135 • Earlier listed as NY-630-Q and thought to be an issue of that city. Some unusual overstrikes exist including over a copper-nickel cent, 1858 Canadian 20¢, Liberty Seated 25¢, and others. See the Fuld catalog. Only token-issuing merchant of this town.

CT, Waterbury • New York Store • CT-560-A • *Millinery and fancy goods* • ? • Reverse dies: Two different custom dies • CT-560-A-1a Rev-1st custom (R-4): VF–EF $50–$75 • MS-63 $125–$175 • Only token-issuing merchant of this town.

CT, Willimantic • Dr. O.G. Keitteridge • CT-600-A • *Physician* • Ascribed to unknown RI diesinker • Reverse die: 1147 • CT-600-A-1a (R-9): VF–EF $20,000–$25,000 • Two known, one in the American Numismatic Society. Value theoretical. Only token-issuing merchant of this town.

IDAHO

Only one Civil War store card is known from Idaho.

ID, Idaho City • Miners Brewery & Bakery • ID-600-A • *Brewery and bakery*

• ? • Reverse die: Custom • ID-600-A-1a (R-7): VG-F $500–$750, VF–EF $1,000–$1,500 • This 24.9 mm token was classified as a Civil War store card at the turn of the 20th century. On Saturday, May 20, 1865, the *Idaho World* reported that nearly the entire downtown district of Idaho City had been burned the preceding Thursday night. Under the losses listed was the Main Street establishment of "Knauer & Co., Miners Brewery, $15,000."

ILLINOIS

The Civil War tokens of Illinois are a vast panorama of towns (dominated by Chicago) and issuers. Although some are scarce, most are readily collectible as types. Illinois tokens are often collected by towns, with many having just one issuer. Numismatic strikes are rare. Many were struck by the shop of S.D. Childs of Chicago. F.N. Dubois of Chicago produced many tokens using reverse die 1368, most of which were issued by Illinois merchants. These are listed in the Philadelphia Numismatic Society's January 1860 *Catalogue of American Store Cards &c.* indicating they were made by 1859.

IL-10-A-1b •
Walter & Smith •
10 cents obverse die.

IL-10-A-2b •
Walter & Smith •
25 cents obverse die.

IL, Alton • Walter & Smith • IL-010-A • *Prison sutlers (?)* • Ascribed to the shop of John Stanton • Reverse die: Stanton advertising die • IL-010-A-1b (R-9): VF–EF $10,000–$15,000 • This is one of the greatest rarities in the Illinois series. Two varieties, 10 cents and 25 cents, each R-9. Only token-issuing merchant of this town.

IL, Aurora • Ira H. Fitch • IL-025-A • *Dealer in leather, harnesses, etc.* • Ascribed to the shop of S.D. Childs • Reverse die: 1207 • IL-025-A-1a (R-4): VF–EF $50–$75 • MS-63 $150–$225 • Only one variety for this issuer.

IL, Aurora • Gates & Trask • IL-025-B • *Dealers in jewelry, watches, silverware* • Dies by F.N. Dubois • Reverse die: 1368 • IL-025-B-1a (R-4): 20 mm • VF–EF $30–$45 • MS-63 $125–$175 • Struck in or before 1859. In nickel this die combination is R-9.

IL, Belvidere • George B. Ames • IL-045-A • *Dealer in drugs, books, etc.* • ? • Reverse die: Custom • IL-045-A-1b (R-2): VF–EF $25–$40 • MS-63 $60–$90 • Only token-issuing merchant of this town.

IL, Bloomingdale • C.P. Sedgwick & Co. • IL-065-A • *General merchandise* • ? • Reverse dies: 1144, 1145, 1241, 1244, 1245, 1275 • IL-065-A-6a Rev-1275 (R-4): VF–EF $30–$45 • MS-63 $100–$150 • Only token-issuing merchant of this town.

IL, Cairo • R.C. Culley • IL-095-A • *Watchmaker, jeweler* • ? • Reverse die: Blank • IL-095-A-1b (R-8): VF–EF $2,000–$3,000 • MS-63 $5,000–$7,500 • This is watchmaker's check. In copper it is R-9, in brass R-8.

IL, Cairo • D. Ford • IL-095-B • *Watchmaker and jeweler* • Ascribed to the shop of W.K. Lanphear • Reverse dies: blank, 1122, 1248 • IL-095-B-1a Rev-1122 (R-4): VF–EF $50–$75 • MS-63 $250–375 • Watchmaker's check sometimes stamped with a number.

IL, Cairo • William H. Schutter • IL-095-C • *Merchant* • ? • Reverse die: Liberty Head similar to that on the American quarter eagle, LIBERTY on headband. 13 six-pointed stars surrounding • IL-095-C-1b (R-9): Rossa & Tanenbaum sold an F-12 example for $560 in August 1997 • Schutter was a merchant in Cairo in 1864. He also served in the Civil War.

IL, Chemung • William Moore • IL-140-A • *Dry goods, groceries, drugs* • Ascribed to the shop of S.D. Childs • Reverse dies: 1099 and 1105 • IL-140-A-1a Rev-1099 (R-7): VF–EF $400–$600 • MS-63 $1,250–$1,750 • One of the rarer Illinois merchants.

IL, Chemung • B.A. Wade & Co. • IL-140-B • *Dry goods, groceries, etc.* • Ascribed to the shop of S.D. Childs • Reverse dies: 1099, 1357, 1390 • IL-140-B-2a Rev-1357 (R-5): VF–EF $200–$300 • MS-63 $600–$900.

IL, Chicago • Baierle's Saloon • IL-150-A • *Saloon* • Reverse die: Custom • IL-150-A-1b (R-9): VF–EF $1,500–$2,250 • MS-63 $N/A • This token is very small, about 14 mm. Just one variety. A landmark Illinois rarity.

IL, Chicago • Barker & Ilsley • IL-150-B • *Hardware, nails, stoves* • Ascribed to the shop of F.N. Dubois • Reverse die: 1368 • IL-150-B-1a (R-3): 20 mm • VF–EF $25–$40 • MS-63 $50–$75 • Struck in or before 1859.

IL, Chicago • Ira Brown • IL-150-G • *Book dealer* • Ascribed to the shop of S.D. Childs • Reverse dies: 1196. 1105, 1107 • IL-150-G-1a Rev-1196 (R-6): VF–EF $40–$60 • MS-63 $150–$225.

IL, Chicago • J.H. Brown • IL-150-H • *Grocer* • Dies by F.N. Dubois • Reverse die: 1368 • IL-150-H-1a (R-4): 20 mm • VF–EF $30–$45 • MS-63 $100–$150 • Struck in or before 1859. Just one variety. Certain tokens with reverse 1368 and known today only in copper likely were struck in nickel alloy as well.

IL, Chicago • Adolph Candler • IL-150-I • *Clocks and jewelry* • Ascribed to the shop of S.D. Childs • Reverse dies: 1105, 1203, 1207 1356 • IL-150-I-4a Rev-1356 (R-5): VF–EF $40–$60 • MS-63 $125–$175.

IL-150-J •
Childs Die Sinker &
Engraver •
O-1 used with
150-J-1 to 7.

IL-150-M •
R.H. Countiss •
O-1 used on
IL-150-M-1.

IL-150-M •
R.H. Countiss •
O-2 used on
IL-150-M-2.

IL-150-J •
Childs Die Sinker
& Engraver •
O-2 used with
150-J-8 to 14.

IL-150-J •
Childs Manufacturer •
O-3 used with former
150-K-1 to 7.

IL, Chicago • Childs Die Sinker & Engraver • IL-150-J & K • *Diesinker, engraver* • Ascribed to the shop of S.D. Childs • Reverse dies: 1097, 1099, 1111, 1113, 1206, 1208, and 1356 (with O-1); 1111, 1113, 1114, 1115, 1116, 1118, and 1356 (with O-2) • IL-150-J-1a Rev-1097 (R-5): VF–EF $30–$45 • MS-63 $100–$150.

IL, Chicago • Childs Manufacturer / Manufr • IL-150-K • *Diesinker, engraver* • Ascribed to the shop of S.D. Childs • Reverse dies: 1097, 1099, 1111, 1113, 1208, 1208, and 1356 (with O-1, see above); 1111, 1113, 1114, 1115, 1116, 1118, 1084, 1098, 1102, 1203, 1204, 1205, and 1357 (with O-3) • IL-150-K-4a Rev-1203 (R-5): VF–EF $30–$45 • MS-63 $100–$150 • Will be merged into IL-150-J in the third edition of the Fuld book.

IL, Chicago • R.H. Countiss • IL-150-M • *Grocer and tea dealer* • Ascribed to the shop of F.N. Dubois • Reverse die: 1368 • IL-150-M-1a (R-3): 20 mm • VF–EF $25–$40 • MS-63 $50–$75 • Struck in or by 1859.

IL, Chicago • Dodd's Elgin Dairy • IL-150-N • *Dairy* • Ascribed to the shop of S.D. Childs • Reverse dies: 1105, 1111, 1206, 1208 • IL-150-N-2a Rev-1111 (R-4): VF–EF $30–$45 • MS-63 $100–$150 • Operated by Louisa Dodd, widow of Miles Dodd.

IL, Chicago • D. Dryer & Co. • IL-150-O • *Groceries and provisions* • Ascribed to A.W. Escherich • Reverse die: 1080 • IL-150-O-1a Rev-1080 (R-7): VF–EF $400–$600 • MS-63 $1,250–$1,750 • Only one variety.

IL, Chicago • Frederick N. Dubois • IL-150-P • *Silverware, token manufacturer* • Dies by F.N. Dubois • Reverse die: 1368 • IL-150-P-2a reverse 1368 (R-8): VF–EF $400–$600 • 20 mm • Copper tokens were issued by 1859. Nickel alloy numismatic strikes may have been made later.

IL, Chicago • John T. Edwards • IL-150-Q • *Watches and jewelry* • Dies by F.N. Dubois • Reverse die: 1368 • IL-150-Q-1a Rev 1368 (R-6): VF–EF $40–$60 • MS-63 $150–$225 • 20 mm • Only one variety. Issued by 1859.

IL-150-R •
A.W. Escherich •
O-1 used on
IL-150-R-1 and 2.

IL-150-T •
Flagg & MacDonald •
O-1 used on
IL-150-T-2.
Address: 181 Lake St.

IL-150-T •
Flagg & MacDonald •
O-2 used on
IL-150-T-1.
Address: 189 Lake St.

IL-150-R •
A.W. Escherich •
O-2 used on
IL-150-R-3.

IL-150-R •
A.W. Escherich •
O-3 used on
IL-150-R-4.

**IL, Chicago • August W. Escherich •
IL-150-R •** *Engraver, engineer, wire worker*
• ? • Reverse dies: 1080, 1369, 1188, 1369 •
IL-150-R-1a Rev-1080 with die O-1 (R-4):
VF–EF $50–$75 • MS-63 $250–$375 •
Escherich had three different obverse dies
used with stock reverses and also for merchants. Listed in directories 1860–1863.[5] In
1861 he is listed as a gun maker, in 1862 he
appears as a wire worker, and in 1863 his
profession is given as an engineer. In 1864
he is not listed, but his widow Louisa is
listed at her home, 363 Wells.

**IL, Chicago • Flaggs Cheap Store •
IL-150-S •** *Boots and shoes* • Dies by F.N.
Dubois • Reverse die: 1368 • IL-150-S-1a
Rev 1368 (R-3): VF–EF $25–$40 • MS-63
$50–$75 • 20 mm • Made in or by 1859.

**IL, Chicago • Flagg & MacDonald •
IL-150-T •** *Boots and shoes* • Dies by F.N.
Dubois • Reverse die: 1368 • IL-150-T-1a
Rev 1368 (R-4): VF–EF $25–$40 • MS-63
$50–$75 • 20 mm • Made in or by 1859.
Two obverse dies.

**IL, Chicago • James J Foster Jr. & Co.
• IL-150-U •** *Optician* • Ascribed to the
shop of John Stanton • Reverse dies:
1046, 1047 • IL-150-U-2a Rev 1047 (R-9):
VF–EF $2,000–$3,000 • MS-63 $4,000–
$6,000.

**IL, Chicago • Freedman & Goodkind
• IL-150-V •** *Dry goods and millinery* •
Ascribed to the shop of S.D. Childs •
Reverse dies: 1111, 1118, 1207, 1357 •
IL-150-V-2a Rev 1118 (R-3): VF–EF $30–
$45 • MS-63 $75–$125 • Joseph Freedman, Louis Goodkind, and Henry
Goodman. Later issues than the related
IL-150-W tokens. Die with 171 Lake
Street address. An unusual instance of a
merchant ordering tokens from more than
one maker, no doubt because Dubois was
no longer in this trade after 1860.

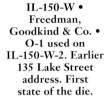

IL-150-W •
Freedman,
Goodkind & Co. •
O-1 used on
IL-150-W-2. Earlier
135 Lake Street
address. First
state of the die.

IL-150-W •
Freedman,
Goodkind & Co. •
O-2 used on
IL-150-W-1. Nickel
alloy striking. Die
crack at bottom. This
is die O-1 reworked
to change the
address from 135
to 171 Lake Street.

IL, Chicago • Freedman, Goodkind & Co. • IL-150-W • *Dry goods and millinery* • Dies by F.N. Dubois • Reverse die: 1368 • IL-150-W-1a Rev 1368 (R-4): VF–EF $25–$40 • MS-63 $50–$75 • 20 mm • Made in or by 1859. The obverse die in its original form was reworked to create a second variety or state of the same die.

IL, Chicago • Patrick Gaffney • IL-150-X • *Grocer and tea dealer* • Dies by F.N. Dubois • Reverse die: 1368 • IL-150-X-1a Rev 1368 (R-4): VF–EF $25–$40 • MS-63 $50–$75 • 20 mm • Made in or by 1859.

IL, Chicago • Frederick Gall / New York Meat Market • IL-150-Y • *Butcher* • Unknown diesinker who created dies for IL-150-Y, IL-150-AY, and IL-150-BB. Some have suggested Escherich • Reverse dies: 1286, 1286 • IL-150-Y-1a Rev 1286 (R-4): VF–EF $75–$125 • MS-63 $250–$375.

IL, Chicago • G.E. Gerts & Co. • IL-150-Z • *Brush factory and store* • Dies by F.N. Dubois • Reverse die: 1368 • IL-150-Z-1a Rev 1368 (R-4): VF–EF $25–$40 • MS-63 $50–$75 • 20 mm • Made in or by 1859.

IL, Chicago • Haas & Powell • IL-150-AA • *Butchers* • Ascribed to the shop of S.D. Childs • Reverse dies: 1111, 1205, 1207 • IL-150-AA-1a Rev 1111 (R-4): VF–

EF $30–$45 • MS-63 $100–$150 • Joseph Haas, Simon Haas, and Simon Powell.

IL, Chicago • R. Heilbroner • IL-150-AD • *Fancy dry goods* • Dies by F.N. Dubois • Reverse die: 1368 • IL-150-AD-1a Rev 1368 (R-3): VF–EF $25–$40 • MS-63 $50–$75 • 20 mm • Made in or by 1859.

IL, Chicago • William A. Hendrie • IL-150-AE • *Watches, clocks, and jewelry* • Dies by F.N. Dubois • Reverse die: 1368 • IL-150-AE-1a Rev 1368 (R-7): VF–EF $50–$75 • MS-63 $125–$175 • 20 mm • Made in or by 1859.

IL, Chicago • S.A. Ingram • IL-150-AG • *Watches and clocks* • Ascribed to James A. Hughes, dies made by the shop of W.K. Lanphear • Reverse dies: 1007, 1172, 1274, 1430, 1131, 20690, 34690 • IL-150-AG-2a (R-8): VF–EF $750–$1,250 • MS-63 $2,500–$3,750 • Numismatic strikings. This is the only Hughes-Lanphear token in Chicago. No information about the Ingram business has been located. Not listed in Chicago directories 1858–1866.[6]

IL, Chicago • Judd & Corthell • IL-150-AH • *Boots and shoes* • Dies by F.N. Dubois • Reverse die: 1368 • IL-150-AH-1a Rev 1368 (R-6): VF–EF $30–$45 • MS-63 $100–$150 • 20 mm • Made in or by 1859.

IL-150-AI •
O. Kendall's
Sons & Co. •
O-1 used on
IL-150-AI-1 and 4.

IL-150-AI •
O. Kendall's
Sons & Co. •
O-2 used on
IL-150-AI-2 and 3.

IL, Chicago • O. Kendall's Sons & Co. • IL-150-AI • *Bread sellers* • Ascribed to the shop of S.D. Childs • Reverse dies: 1094, 1098, 1390, 1203 • IL-150-AI-3b Rev 1390 (R-6): VF–EF $150–$225 • MS-63 $400–$600.

IL, Chicago • Klare & Friedrick • IL-150-AIa • *Billiard hall owners* • Ascribed to the shop of S.D. Childs • Reverse die: 1205 • IL-150-AIa-2b Rev 1205 (R-9): VF–EF $1,000–$1,500 • MS-63 $2,500–$3,750 • Klare & Friedrich's (the correct spelling) billiard hall was listed in the Chicago directory of 1865–1866 as being owned by Henry Klare and Andrew Friedrich, at 214 and 216 Indiana Street.

IL-150-AJ • Frank A. Leavitt • O-1 used on IL-150-AJ-1.

IL-150-AJ • Frank A. Leavitt • O-2 used on IL-150-AJ-2. This was probably the earlier of the two reverse dies.

IL, Chicago • Frank A. Leavitt • IL-150-AJ • *Family grocery* • Dies by F.N. Dubois • Reverse die: 1368 • IL-150-AJ-1a (R-4): VF–EF $20–$30 • MS-63 $60–$90 • 20 mm • Made in or by 1859. Two obverse dies by Dubois are each stylistically different.

IL, Chicago • Marsh & Miner • IL-150-AK • *Clothier* • Ascribed to the shop of John Stanton • Reverse dies: 1023, 1030, 1042, 1047, 1069 • IL-150-AK-2a (R-6): VF–EF $30–$45 • MS-63 $125–$175 • This represents an unusual instance of a Cincinnati maker preparing tokens for a Chicago merchant, deep in "Childs territory."

IL, Chicago • A. Meyer • IL-150-AL • *Rag store* • Ascribed to A.W. Escherich • Reverse die: 1080 • IL-150-AL-1a Rev 1080 (R-6): VF–EF $125–$175 • MS-63 $400–$600 • "Primitive" letter alignment.

IL, Chicago • Charles E. Meyer • IL-150-AM • *Saloonkeeper* • Reverse die: 1860A • IL-150-AM-1b (R-8): VF–EF $1,000–$1,500 • MS-63 $2,500–$3,750.

IL, Chicago • G.R. Meyer • IL-150-AN • **?** • Reverse die: 20780 with a mansion on a hill • IL-150-AN-1a Rev 20780 (R-8): VF–EF $1,200–$2,000 • This is one of the most scenic, detailed dies in the Civil War series. The Fuld reference notes that "the reverse of this piece is most unusual and attractive."

IL, Chicago • J.U. Mingers Saloon • IL-150-AO • *Saloon and boarding house* • Ascribed to A.W. Escherich • Reverse die: 1080 • IL-150-AO-1a Rev 1080 (R-6): VF–EF $300–$450 • "Primitive" die work.[7]

IL, Chicago • Oppenheimer & Metzger • IL-150-AQ • *Jewelry and watch materials* • Dies by F.N. Dubois • Reverse die: 1368 • IL-150-AQ-1a Rev 1368 (R-5): VF–EF $30–$45 • MS-63 $100–$150 • 20 mm • Made in or by 1859. Listed in directories 1859–1862. Henry Oppenheimer and Isaac Metzger.

IL, Chicago • William Ostendorf • IL-150-AR • *Saloonkeeper* • Dies by F.N. Dubois • Reverse die: 1860A • IL-150-AR-1b Rev 1860A (R-7): VF–EF $300–$450 • MS-63 $1,000–$1,500 • Listed in directories 1859–1863.

IL, Chicago • Passage Certificates [George Whitney] • IL-150-AS • *Passage agent, broker* • Ascribed to the shop of S.D. Childs • Reverse dies: 20830, 1111 • IL-150-AS-1a (R-5): VF–EF $70–$100 • MS-63 $200–$300 • John Ostendorf in "IL-150-AS Identified," *CWTJ*, Winter 2007, located George Whitney as a passenger agent, emigration agent, and banker at 6 South Clark St. during the Civil War—the same address that appears on the token, which lacks the name of the issuer.

IL, Chicago • Willis G. Peck IL-150-AT • *Grocer* • Ascribed to the shop of S.D. Childs • Reverse dies: 1105, 1111, 1113, 1114, 1115, 1116, 1207, 1356 • IL-150-AT-4 (rev. 1114), AT-6 (rev 116), and AT-8 (rev 1356) are all R-6 • VF–EF $30–$45 • MS-63 $100–$150.

IL, Chicago • William R. Prentice • IL-150-AU • *Family grocer* • Dies by F.N. Dubois • Reverse die: 1368 • IL-150-AU-1a Rev 1368 (R-4): VF–EF $25–$40 • MS-63 $50–$75 • 20 mm • Made in or by 1859. Listed in directories 1859–1860. Listed differently 1861–1864.[8]

IL, Chicago • N. Henry Regensburg • IL-150-AX • *Grocery and bakery* • Ascribed to A.W. Escherich • Reverse die: 1080 • IL-150-AX-1a Rev 1080 (R-5): VF–EF $40–$60 • MS-63 $200–$300.

IL, Chicago • William Reinhardt / Great West Market • IL-150-AY • *Fresh and salt meat* • Unknown diesinker who created dies for IL-150-Y, IL-150-AY, and IL-150-BB. Said by some to be by Escherich • Reverse die: 1286 • IL-150-AY-1a Rev 1286 (R-3): VF–EF $60–$90 • MS-63 $200–$300.

IL, Chicago • Francis E. Rigby • IL-150-AZ • *Wallpaper* • Ascribed to the shop of S.D. Childs • Reverse dies: 1111, 1206, 1208, 1356, 1357 • IL-150-AZ-4a (R-3): VF–EF $30–$45 • MS-63 $100–$150.

| IL-150-BB • John F. Siehler / Deutsches Gast & Boarding Haus • O-1 used on IL-150-BB-1 to 3. | IL-150-BB • John F. Siehler / Deutsches Gast & Boarding Haus • O-2 used on IL-150-BB-4 to 6. |

IL, Chicago • John F. Siehler / Deutsches Gast & Boarding Haus • IL-150-BB • *German guest and boarding house* • Unknown diesinker who created dies for IL-150-Y, IL-150-AY, and IL-150-BB • Reverse dies: 1072, 1080, 1354, 1355, 1213 by more than one maker • IL-150-BB-3a Rev 1354 (R-4): VF–EF $50–$75 • MS-63 $300–$450 • Partners included John Siehler (1858–1859), Charles F. Siehler

(1860–1861 and 1866), Fritz Siehler (1863), John F. Siehler (1865), and Frederick J. Siehler (1864). Two obverse dies.

IL, Chicago • C. & S. Stein • IL-150-BC • *Dry goods store* • Ascribed to the shop of S.D. Childs • Reverse dies: 1111, 1116, 1118, 1205, 1207, 1356 • IL-150-BC-3a Rev 1118 (R-4): VF–EF $30–$45 • MS-63 $75–$125 • Charles and Solomon Stein. Listed with address on token in directories 1861–1863.

IL, Chicago • Walter Treleaven • IL-150-BE • *Gold pen maker* • Dies by F.N. Dubois • Reverse die: 1368 • IL-150-BE-1a Rev 1368 (R-6): VF–EF $60–$90 • 20 mm • Made in or by 1859. Surname incorrectly listed as "Trefaven" in certain 19th-century catalogs. Gold pens, often made of brass or gold-colored non-gold alloys such as oroide, were all the rage in the 1860s and were widely advertised by many manufacturers and sellers.

IL, Chicago • Caspar Winsauer • IL-150-BG • *Gunsmith* • ? • Reverse die: 1345 • IL-150-BG-1a Rev 1345 (R-4): VF–EF $90–$135 • MS-63 $500–$750 • Listed in directories 1861–1862. His primary business seems to have been gunsmithing.

| IL-200-A • Isaac Leonard Elwood • O-1 used on IL-200-A-1 to 3. Die by Bridgens. | IL-200-A • Isaac Leonard Elwood • O-2 used on IL-200-A-4. |

IL, De Kalb • Isaac Leonard Ellwood • IL-200-A • *Hardware, tin, stoves* • Dies by William H. Bridgens and, separately, the shop of S.D. Childs • Reverse dies: 1137 by Bridgens, and 1105, 1207, 1356 by Childs • IL-200-A-1a Rev 1137 (R-5): VF–EF $125–$175 • MS-63 $400–$600 •

Two obverse dies by two different makers.[9] Only token-issuing merchant of this town.

IL, Dixon • Edward Weibezahn • IL-210-A • *Groceries and dry goods* • Ascribed to the shop of S.D. Childs[10] • Reverse dies: 1105, 1390 • IL-210-A-1a Rev 1105 (R-6): VF–EF $200–$300 • Only token-issuing merchant of this town.

IL-215-A •
J. Hayes & Bro. •
O-1 used on
IL-215-A-1.

IL-215-A •
J. Hayes & Bro. •
O-2 used on
IL-215-A-2 to 4.
E (HAYES) over
erroneous S.

IL, Du Quoin • J. Hayes & Bro. • IL-215-A • *Saloonkeeper* • Ascribed to the shop of W.K. Lanphear • Reverse dies: 1169, 1181, 1295 • IL-215-A-1a Rev 1169 (R-7): VF–EF $400–$600 • MS-63 $1,000–$1,500 • Only token-issuing merchant of this town. Earlier listed as OH-165-BP. Two obverse dies.

IL, Dunleith • J.M. Daggett & Co., Bates House • IL-220-A • *Hotel keeper* • Ascribed to the shop of John Stanton • Reverse dies: 1046, 1047 • IL-220-A-1a Rev 1046 (R-9): VF–EF $1,500–$2,250 • MS-63 $3,000–$4,500 • Only token-issuing merchant of this town. Earlier listed as a Cincinnati merchant.

IL, Durand • H.L. Mosely • IL-225-A • *Groceries, hardware, crockery, and notions* • Reverse die: 20990 • IL-225-A-1a Rev 20990 (R-3): VF–EF $40–$60 • MS-63 $125–$175 • Only token-issuing merchant of this town.

IL, El Paso • P.H. Tompkins • IL-275-A • *Dry goods, groceries, etc.* • Ascribed to the shop of S.D. Childs • Reverse dies: 1108, 1390 • IL-275-A-1a Rev 1108 (R-6):

VF–EF $125–$175 • MS-63 $300–$450 • Only token-issuing merchant of this town.

IL, Elgin • M. McNeil • IL-270-A • *Dry goods, groceries, boots, and shoes* • Ascribed to the shop of S.D. Childs • Reverse die: 1209 • IL-270-A-1a Rev 1209 (R-5): VF–EF $125–$175 • MS-63 $400–$600 • Only token-issuing merchant of this town. Elgin is listed out of alphabetical order in the Hetrich-Guttag and Fuld texts (it is listed before El Paso).

IL, Freeport • D.S. Bogar / Farmers Store • IL-320-A • *Dry goods and groceries* • Ascribed to the shop of S.D. Childs • Reverse dies: 1095, 1098, 1105, 1209 • IL-320-A-1a Rev 1095 (R-6): VF–EF $50–$75.

IL, Freeport • D.S. Brewster • IL-320-B • *Dealer in butter, eggs, etc.* • Ascribed to the shop of S.D. Childs • Reverse dies: 1209, 1390 • IL-320-B-1a Rev 1209 (R-5): VF–EF $60–$90 • MS-63 $250–$375.

IL, Freeport • J.D. Diffenbaugh • IL-320-C • *Confectioner and dealer in fruit* • Ascribed to the shop of S.D. Childs • Reverse dies: 1095, 1357 • IL-320-C-1a Rev 1095 (R-3): VF–EF $40–$60 • MS-63 $150–$225.

IL, Freeport • W.P. Emmert • IL-320-D • *Hardware, stoves, iron, and tinware* • Ascribed to the shop of S.D. Childs • Reverse dies: 1205, 1357 • IL-320-D-2a Rev 1357 (R-8): VF–EF $150–$225 • MS-63 $500–$750.

IL, Freeport • Helena Hertrich / Freeport Brewery • IL-320-E • *Brewery* • Ascribed to Mossin & Marr • Reverse dies: 1196, 1220 • IL-320-E-2a Rev 1220 (R-5): VF–EF $150-225 • MS-63 $600–$900.

IL, Lacon • Ellsworth & Halsey • IL-472-A • *General merchandise and goods for ladies' wear* • Ascribed to the shop of John Stanton • Reverse dies: 1046, 1047 • IL-472-A-1a Rev 1046 (R-6): VF–EF $200–$300 • MS-63 $600–$900 • Only token-issuing merchant of this town.

IL, La Salle • **Adams & Hatch** • **IL-495-A** • *Dry goods, carpets, boots, and shoes* • Ascribed to the shop of S.D. Childs • Reverse dies: 1105, 1205 • IL-495-A-1a Rev 1105 (R-4): VF–EF $40–$60 • MS-63 $200–$300 • Only token-issuing merchant of this town.

IL-500-A • W.J. Bollinger • O-1 used on IL-500-A-1. Narrow padlock.

IL-500-A • W.J. Bollinger • O-2 used on IL-500-A-2. Wide padlock.

IL, Lena • **W.J. Bollinger** • **IL-500-A** • *Dealer in hardware, iron, and steel* • Ascribed to the shop of S.D. Childs • Reverse die: 1357 • IL-500-A-1a Rev 1357 (R-6): VF–EF $50–$75 • MS-63 $200–$300 • Two obverse dies.

IL-500-B • M. Weaver • O-1 used on IL-500-B-1 to 4.

IL-500-B • M. Weaver • O-2 used on IL-500-B-5.

IL, Lena • **M. Weaver** • **IL-500-B** • *Dry goods and groceries* • Ascribed to the shop of S.D. Childs, lettering irregularly arranged • Reverse dies: 1106, 1107, 1205, 1357, 1205 • IL-500-B-1a Rev 1106 (R-4): VF–EF $40–$60 • MS-63 $200–$300 • Two obverse dies.

IL, Lodi • **C.H. Taylor** • **IL-520-A** • *Stoves & cutlery dealer* • Ascribed to the shop of S.D. Childs • Reverse dies: 1107, 1205 • IL-520-A-1a Rev 1107 (R-7): VF–EF $1,500–$2,250 • MS-63 $3,000–$4,500 • Only token-issuing merchant of this town. There were three towns named Lodi in Illinois; this one is now a part of Maple Park in Kane County (known as Kendall County at the time).

IL, Macomb • **T. Adcock** • **IL-535-A** • *Keeper of a billiard saloon* • Ascribed to the shop of S.D. Childs • Reverse die: 1205 • IL-535-A-1b Rev 1205 (R-9): VF–EF $4,000–$6,000 • Only token-issuing merchant of this town. Earlier known as SNL-1.

IL, Macomb • **IL-535-B** • **Smith's Billiard Saloon** • *Billiard saloon* • Ascribed to the shop of S.D. Childs • Reverse die: 1205 • IL-535-B-1a Rev 1205 (R-9): VF–EF $2,500–$3,750 • Also b, same rarity. Earlier known as SNL-3. Also known with 1106 reverse.

IL, Marengo • **H.G. Skinner** • **IL-540-A** • *Groceries and provisions* • Ascribed to the shop of S.D. Childs • Reverse die: 1357 • IL-540-A-1a Rev 1357 (R-4): VF–EF $60–$90 • MS-63 $200–$300 • Only token-issuing merchant of this town.

IL, Mendota • **A. Erlenborn** • **IL-560-A** • *Groceries* • Ascribed to the shop of S.D. Childs • Reverse die: 1205 • IL-560-A-1a Rev 1205 (R-4): VF–EF $60–$90 • MS-63 $200–$300.

IL, Naperville • **Robert Naper** • **IL-615-A** • *Dry goods, groceries* • Ascribed to the shop of John Stanton • Reverse dies: 1046, 1047 • IL-615-A-1a Rev 1046 (R-6): VF–EF $150–$225 • MS-63 $400–$600 • Only token-issuing merchant of this town.

IL, Ottawa • **A. & H. Alschuler** • **IL-660-A** • *Men's clothier* • Ascribed to the shop of S.D. Childs • Reverse dies: 1205, 1338 • IL-660-A-2a Rev 1338 (R-3): VF–EF $60–$90 • MS-63 $175–$250 • Only token-issuing merchant of this town.[11]

IL, Palatine • **Dean & Slade** • **Il-680-A** • *Dry goods and hardware* • Ascribed to Mossin & Marr • Reverse die: 1195 • IL-680-A-1a Rev 1195 (R-5): VF–EF $75–$125 • MS-63 $300–$450.

IL, Paris • Collins Brothers • IL-690-A • *Druggists* • Ascribed to the shop of John Stanton • Reverse dies: 1036, 1042, 1045, 1046, 1047, 1069, 1021 • IL-690-A-1a Rev 1036 (R-7): VF–EF $60–$90 • MS-63 $200–$300.

IL, Paris • A.C. Connely • IL-690-B • *Dry goods* • Ascribed to the shop of John Stanton • Reverse dies: 1026, 1042, 1045, 1047, 1069, 1341, 1027 • IL-690-B-1a Rev 1026 (R-4): VF–EF $40–$60 • MS-63 $150–$225.

IL, Paris • James Miller • IL-690-C • *Dry goods* • Ascribed to the shop of John Stanton • Reverse dies: 1026, 1029, 1042, 1047, 1069 • IL-690-C-2a Rev 1029 (R-7), IL-690-C-3a Rev 1042 (R-7): VF–EF $50–$75 • MS-63 $200–$300.

IL, Paris • Penoyer & Larkin • IL-690-D • *Grocers, provision dealers* • Ascribed to the shop of John Stanton • Reverse dies: 1028, 1029, 1042, 1045, 1047, 1069 • IL-690-D-1a Rev 1028 (R-7), IL-690-D-3a Rev 1042 (R-7), IL-690-D-3b Rev 1042 (R-7): VF–EF $50–$75 • MS-63 $200–$300.

IL, Paris • Sisk & Whalen Restaurant • IL-690-E • *Restaurant* • Ascribed to the shop of John Stanton • Reverse dies: 1026, 1028, 1042, 1047, 1069 • IL-690-E-2a Rev 1042 (R-7): VF–EF $200–$300 • MS-63 $600–$900 • Obverse die with irregular alignment and repunching of some letters.

IL-692-A •
Yankee Robinson •
O-3 used on
IL-692-A-18.
Non-contemporary.

IL-692-A •
Yankee Robinson •
O-4 used on
IL-692-A-17d.
Non-contemporary.

IL, Peoria • Yankee Robinson • IL-692-A • *Comedian, entertainer, circus owner* • Ascribed to the shop of John Stanton • Reverse dies: 1018, 1028, 1034, 1069, 34050, 34060, 34070 • IL-692-A-1a Rev 34050 (R-4), IL-692-A-3a Rev 34070 (R-4), IL-692-A-9a Rev 1028 (R-4): VF–EF $30–$45 • MS-63 $100–$150 • Only token-issuing merchant of this city, although for Robinson Peoria was headquarters for just a short time. For illustrations see earlier narrative. In the third edition of the Fuld text the non-contemporary varieties will be listed in the NC section.

IL, Peru • Lininger & Bro. • IL-695-A • *Dry goods, notions, boots and shoes* • Ascribed to the shop of S.D. Childs • Reverse dies: 1357, 1390 • IL-695-A-1a Rev 1357 (R-4): VF–EF $50–$75 • MS-63 $175–$250 • Only token-issuing merchant of this town.

IL, Pontiac • Dehner & Maples • IL-700-A • *Dry goods and groceries* • Ascribed to the shop of S.D. Childs • Reverse die: 1105 • IL-700-A-1a Rev 1105 (R-5): VF–EF $90–$135 • MS-63 $300–$450 • Only token-issuing merchant of this town.

IL-692-A •
Yankee Robinson •
O-1 used on
IL-692-A-1 to 7.

IL-692-A •
Yankee Robinson •
O-2 used on
IL-692-A-8 to 13.

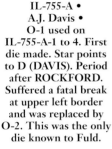

IL-755-A •
A.J. Davis •
O-1 used on
IL-755-A-1 to 4. First
die made. Star points
to D (DAVIS). Period
after ROCKFORD.
Suffered a fatal break
at upper left border
and was replaced by
O-2. This was the only
die known to Fuld.

IL-755-A •
A.J. Davis •
O-2 used on
IL-755-A-5. Second
die. Star points
to period. Comma
after Rockford.

IL, Rockford • A.J. Davis • IL-755-A •
Grocer • Ascribed to the shop of S.D.
Childs • Reverse dies: 1095, 1105, 1106,
1205 • IL-755-A-1a Rev 1095 (R-6),
IL-755-A-2a Rev 1105 (R-6): VF–EF
$40–$60 • MS-63 $200–$300 • Two
obverse dies, O-1 and O-2.[12]

IL, Rockford • Holmes & Norton •
IL-755-B • *Druggists* • Ascribed to the
shop of S.D. Childs • Reverse dies: 1209,
1357 • IL-755-B-1a Rev 1209 (R-4): VF–
EF $60–$90 • MS-63 $250–$375.

**IL, Rockford • Hope & Clow • IL-
755-C** • *Stoves, hardware, iron, etc.* •
Ascribed to the shop of S.D. Childs •
Reverse dies: 1094, 1098, 1205 • IL-755-C-
1a Rev 1094 (R-6), IL-755-C-2a Rev 1098
(R-6): VF–EF $60–$90 • MS-63 $250–
$375.

**IL, Rockford • William Knapp • IL-
755-D** • *Artesian well driller* • Ascribed to
the shop of S.D. Childs • Reverse die:
1107 • IL-755-D-1a Rev 1107 (R-4): VF–
EF $50–$75 • MS-63 $200–$300.

IL, Rockton • V.A. Lake • IL-762-A •
Grain dealer • Ascribed to the shop of
John Stanton • Reverse dies: 1018, 1047,

1069 • IL-762-A-1a Rev 1018 (R-6): VF–
EF $175–$250 • MS-63 $600–$900 •
Only token-issuing merchant of this town.

**IL, Sandwich • M.B. Castle / Sandwich
Bank • IL-775-A** • *Bank* • Ascribed to
the shop of W.K. Lanphear • Reverse
dies: 21320, 21340 • IL-775-A-1a Rev
21320 (R-3), IL-775-A-2a Rev 21340 (R-3):
VF–EF $30–$45 • MS-63 $125–$175 • M
(M.W.) cut over erroneous W.[13]

**IL, Sandwich • W.B. Castle / Sandwich
Bank • IL-775-B** • *Druggist and banker* •
Ascribed to the shop of W.K. Lanphear •
Reverse die: 1316 • IL-775-B-1a Rev 1316
(R-5): VF–EF $40–$60 • MS-63 $150–
$225 • Error die; should be M.B. Castle.

**IL, Sandwich • A.G. Greenman • IL-
775-C** • *Druggist* • Ascribed to the shop
of W.K. Lanphear • Reverse die: 1316 •
IL-775-C-1a Rev 1316 (R-6): VF–EF
$60–$90 • MS-63 $250–$375.

IL, Springfield • J.C. Yager • IL-795-A
• *Trunk maker* • Ascribed to the shop of
W.K. Lanphear • Reverse dies: 1172,
1274, 28060, 34690 • IL-795-A-2a Rev
1274 (R-4): VF–EF $40–$60 • MS-63
$125–$175 • Only token-issuing merchant
of this town.

**IL, Sycamore • Lott & Warner • IL-
825-A** • *Dry goods, groceries, etc.* • Ascribed
to the shop of S.D. Childs • Reverse dies:
1111, 1117, 1205, 1207 • IL-825-A-2a Rev
1117 (R-5): VF–EF $200–$300 • MS-63
$600–$900. Only token-issuing merchant
of this town.

**IL, Waukegan • Kingsley & Whipple •
IL-890-A** • *Groceries and provisions* •
Ascribed to the shop of S.D. Childs •
Reverse die: 1106 • IL-890-A-1106-1a
Rev 1106 (R-7): VF–EF $150–$225 •
MS-63 $500–$750.

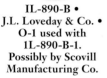

IL-890-B •
J.L. Loveday & Co. •
O-1 used with
1L-890-B-1.
Possibly by Scovill
Manufacturing Co.

IL-890-B •
J.L. Loveday & Co. •
O-2 used with
1L-890-B-2. Die by
George J. Glaubrecht
who signed the
reverse die used
with this obverse.

IL, Waukegan • J.L. Loveday & Co. •
IL-890-B • *Dry goods and groceries* • Scovill Manufacturing Co (?) and separately George J. Glaubrecht • Reverse dies: 1142, 1408 • IL, 890-B-1b Rev 1408 (R-4): VF–EF $25–$35 • MS-63 $60–$90 • Two different obverse dies by two different makers.

IL, Waukegan • D.P. Millen • IL-890-C • *Boots and shoes* • Ascribed to the shop of S.D. Childs • Reverse dies: 1106, 1107 • IL-890-C-1a Rev 1106 (R-6): VF–EF $125–$175 • MS-63 $400–$600.

IL, Woodstock • M.D. Stevers • IL-920-A • *Grain dealer* • Ascribed to Mossin & Marr • Reverse die: 1195 • IL-920-A-1a Rev 1195 (R-6): VF–EF $400–$600 • MS-63 $1,000–$1,500 • Only token-issuing merchant of this town.

Indiana

Civil War store cards attributed to Indiana are at once diverse and extensive. Located between the token-manufacturing centers of Chicago (Shubael D. Childs) and Cincinnati (the shops of W.K. Lanphear and John Stanton), the merchants of Indiana were good customers of these three firms. Mishawaka was home to entrepreneur Henry D. Higgins, creator of the "Indiana primitive" token dies, some tokens from which were struck by Childs.

Several small and medium-size towns rise to importance in the chronicle of the Civil War series, with Bowling Green, Columbia City, Corunna, Danville, Goshen, Kendallville, LaPorte, Ligonier, Plainfield, and Richmond each with enough merchant issuers that separate studies could be prepared on each. Among larger cities, Fort Wayne and South Bend each were home to multiple token issuers, and over two dozen merchants in Indianapolis issued more than 125 die combinations and varieties. All told, 69 different Indiana municipalities were home to token distributors.

Indiana merchants were early in the Civil War token-issuing arena, and certain varieties made for them by Childs circulated as early as 1861, a year or two before such pieces were widely issued in eastern cities such as New York City and Boston. John Stanton stated that seeing such tokens in circulation in Indiana gave him the idea of producing his own Civil War store cards.

An important study by William E. Hamm, *Indiana Merchant Issuers of Civil War Tokens: Business History from City Directories and County Histories*, is the source for much information known today about Indiana token issuers.[14]

IN, Albany • Allegre & Wroughton • IN-005 • *Dry goods and groceries* • Ascribed to the shop of W.K. Lanphear • Reverse die: 1122 • IN-005-A-1a Rev 1122 (R-5): VF–EF $60–$90 • MS-63 $250–$375 • Only token-issuing merchant of this town. 1858–1864 directories: Allegre & Manning, general merchandise. The token, identified as Allegre & Wroughton, is circa 1863, thus the partnership must have existed. Perhaps, directory listings were not updated. 1866: The Allogree [*sic*] & Martin partnership listed as proprietors of a general store. Separately, Cyrus Wroughton is listed as a general-store operator as well.

IN, Alexandria • Wolfe & Sherman • IN-010-A • *Dry goods* • Ascribed to the shop of John Stanton • Reverse dies: 1037, 1046, 1047 • IN-010-A-1a Rev 1037 (R-6): VF–EF $75–$125 • MS-63 $300–$450 • Only token-issuing merchant of this town. 1860–1862 directories: Wolfe & Sherman, general merchants and manufacturers of pumps. 1864–1866: Wolfe & Sherman, general merchants.

IN, Anderson • J.P. Barnes • IN-020-A • *Dealer in stoves and tinware* • Ascribed to the shop of W.K. Lanphear • Reverse dies: 1299, 1346 • IN-020-A-1a Rev 1299 (R-4): VF–EF $40–$60 • MS-63 $150–$225.

IN, Anderson • T. & N.C. McCullough • IN-020-B • *Dealers in hardware* • Ascribed to the shop of W.K. Lanphear • Reverse die: 1326 • IN-020-B-1a Rev 1326 (R-5): VF–EF $50–$75 • MS-63 $200–$300.

IN, Avilla • Baum Walter & Co. • IN-070-A • *Dry goods, groceries* • Ascribed to the shop of John Stanton • Reverse dies: 1037, 1046, 1047 • IN-070-A-1a Rev 1037 (R-6): VF–EF $100–$150 • MS-63 $400–$600 • Only token-issuing merchant of this town.

IN, Bethel • Thompson & Wiley • IN-100-A • *Dry goods and groceries* • Ascribed to the shop of W.K. Lanphear • Reverse dies: 1124, 1180 • IN-100-A-1a Rev 1124 (R-5), IN-100-A-2a Rev 1180 (R-5): VF–EF $60–$90 • MS-63 $300–$450 • Only token-issuing merchant of this town.

IN, Bowling Green • O.H.P. Ash's Cheap Cash Store • IN-120-A • *Cash store* • Ascribed to the shop of John Stanton • Reverse dies: 1021, 1038, 1042, 1046, 1047, 1069 • IN-120-A-3a Rev 1042 (R-6), IN-120-A-3b Rev 1042 (R-6): VF–EF $40–$60 • MS-63 $150–$225.

IN, Bowling Green • Ash & Black • IN-120-B • *Cash store* • Ascribed to the shop of John Stanton • Reverse dies: 1030, 1042, 1046, 1047, 1069 • IN-120-B-1a Rev 1030 (R-4): VF–EF $40–$60 • MS-63 $150–$225 • Listed out of alphabetical order in the Fuld book.

IN, Brazil • Connely's New York Store • IN-130-A • *Store* • Ascribed to the shop of John Stanton • Reverse dies: 1018, 1022, 1026, 1036, 1042, 1047, 1069, 32705 • IN-130-A-2a Rev 1022 (R-5): VF–EF $60–$90 • MS-63 $200–$300 • Only token-issuing merchant of this town.

IN, Brooklyn • Cox & Landers • IN-135-A • *Dry goods, clothing, boots, etc.* • Ascribed to the shop of John Stanton • Reverse dies: 1046, 1047 • IN-135-A-1a Rev 1046 (R-7): VF–EF $300–$450.

IN, Brookville • H. Linck • IN-140-A • *Groceries, hardware* • Ascribed to the shop of John Stanton • Reverse dies: 1019, 1026, 1029, 1042, 1045, 1047, 1069 • IN-140-A-3a Rev 1042 (R-6), IN-140-A-4a Rev 1045 (R-6): VF–EF $60–$90 • MS-63 $250–$375 • Only token-issuing merchant of this town.

IN, Brownsburg • G.W. Nash • IN-145-A • *Drugs, wine, liquor, notions, etc.* • Ascribed to the shop of John Stanton • Reverse die: 1311 • IN-145-A-1a Rev 1311 (R-7): VF–EF $200–$300 • MS-63 $1,000–$1,500 • Only token-issuing merchant of this town.

IN, Brownstown • S.S. Early & Co. • IN-150-A • *Dry goods, groceries* • Ascribed to the shop of W.K. Lanphear • Reverse die: 1088 • IN-150-A-1a Rev 1088 (R-5): VF–EF $75–$125 • MS-63 $300–$450 • Only token-issuing merchant of this town.

IN, Butler • J. Lutes • IN-155-A • *Dry goods, groceries* • Ascribed to the shop of W.K. Lanphear • Reverse die: 1122 • IN-155-A-1a Rev 1122 (R-5): VF–EF $75–$125 • MS-63 $250–$375 • Only token-issuing merchant of this town.

IN, Cadiz • C. Bond • IN-160-A • *Druggist* • Ascribed to the shop of John Stanton • Reverse dies: 1037, 1046, 1047 • IN-160-A-1a Rev 1037 (R-5): VF–EF $50–$75 • MS-63 $200–$300.

IN, Cadiz • Hiatt & Showalter • IN-160-B • *Dry goods and groceries* • Ascribed to the shop of John Stanton • Reverse dies: 1037, 1046, 1047 • IN-160-B-1a Rev 1037 (R-7), IN-160-B-1a-1 Rev 1037 (R-7): VF–EF $50–$75 • MS-63 $200–$300.

IN, Centerville • Gentrys • IN-165-A • *Grocers* • Ascribed to the shop of John Stanton • Reverse dies: 1037, 1047 • IN-165-A-1a Rev 1037 (R-8): VF–EF $750–$1,250 • MS-63 $2,500–$3,750 • Only token-issuing merchant of this town.

IN, Columbia City • Gaffney & McDonnell • IN-175-A • *Groceries, liquor, cigars* • Ascribed to the shop of W.K. Lanphear • Reverse die: 1226 • IN-175-A-1a Rev 1226 (R-6): VF–EF $60–$90 • MS-63 $200–$300.

IN, Columbia City • Harley & Linvill • *Hardware, stoves, tinware* • Ascribed to the shop of W.K. Lanphear • Reverse dies: 1088, 1299, 1302 • IN-175-B-1a Rev 1088 (R-5), IN-175-B-2a Rev 1299 (R-5): VF–EF $35–$50 • MS-63 $125–$175.

IN, Columbia City • W.W. Kepner & Son • IN-175-C • *Dry goods and groceries* • Ascribed to the shop of W.K. Lanphear • Reverse die: 1088 • IN-175-C-1a Rev 1088 (R-6): VF–EF $75–$125 • MS-63 $250–$375.

IN, Columbia City • Dr. C. Kindermann • IN-175-D • *Druggist, bookseller* • Ascribed to the shop of John Stanton • Reverse dies: 1047, 1373 • IN-175-D-2a Rev 1373 (R-4): VF–EF $75–$125 • MS-63 $400–$600.

IN, Columbia City • S.S. Lavey • IN-175-E • *Watchmaker, jeweler, etc.* • Ascribed to the shop of John Stanton • Reverse dies: 1456, 1047 • IN-175-E-1a Rev 1456 (R-6): VF–EF $75–$125 • MS-63 $400–$600.

IN, Columbia City • John C. Washburn • IN-175-F • *Dry goods and groceries* • Ascribed to the shop of W.K. Lanphear

• Reverse dies: 1168, 1169 • IN-175-F-1a Rev 1169 (R-5): VF–EF $40–$60 • MS-63 $200–$300.

IN, Como • Jacob Groyen • IN-185-A • *Grocer* • Ascribed to the shop of W.K. Lanphear • Reverse dies: 1176, 1295, 1331 • IN-185-A-1a Rev 1176 (R-5): VF–EF $75–$125 • MS-63 $250–$375 • Only token-issuing merchant of this town.

IN, Corunna • Samuel Beck • IN-190-A • *Dealer in butter, eggs, hides, and pelts* • Ascribed to the shop of W.K. Lanphear • Reverse dies: 1127, 1130 • IN-190-A-1a Rev 1127 (R-6): VF–EF $60–$90 • MS-63 $200–$300.

IN, Corunna • Ira W. Bowen • IN-190-B • *Drugs, medicine, groceries, hardware* • Ascribed to the shop of W.K. Lanphear • Reverse dies: 1084, 1085, 1181, 1316 • IN-190-B-4a Rev 1316 (R-5): VF–EF $50–$75 • MS-63 $200–$300.

IN, Corunna • John Childs • IN-190-C • *Dry goods and groceries* • Ascribed to the shop of W.K. Lanphear • Reverse die: 1089 • IN-190-C-1a • Rev 1089 (R-5): VF–EF $60–$90 • MS-63 $200–$300.

IN, Corunna • J.L. & G.F. Rowe • IN-190-D • *Dry goods and groceries* • Ascribed to the shop of W.K. Lanphear • Reverse dies: 1088, 1089, 1090, 1128, 1168 • IN-190-D-2a Rev 1089 (R-6), IN-190-D-3a Rev 1090 (R-6), IN-190-D-4a Rev 1128 (R-6): VF–EF $40–$60 • MS-63 $150–$225.

IN, Danville • R.K. Carter • IN-230-A • *Dry goods, groceries, shoes* • Ascribed to the shop of John Stanton • Reverse dies: 1046, 1047 • IN-230-A-1a Rev 1046 (R-6): VF–EF $175–$250.

IN, Danville • Craddick & Homan • IN-230-B • *Books, stationery, tobacco* • Ascribed to the shop of John Stanton • Reverse dies: 1046, 1047 • IN-230-B-1a Rev 1046 (R-5): VF–EF $100–$150.

IN, Danville • S.A. Russell • IN-230-C
• *Merchant* • Ascribed to the shop of John
Stanton • Reverse dies: 1046, 1047 (same
as two preceding) • IN-230-C-1a Rev
1046 (R-7): VF–EF $175–$250 • MS-63
$600–$900.

IN, Dublin • A. Jenks • IN-250-A •
Dry goods, groceries • Ascribed to the shop
of John Stanton • Reverse dies: 1037,
1046, 1047 • IN-250-A-1a Rev 1037 (R-7):
VF–EF $600–$900 • MS-63 $1,500–
$2,250 • Only token-issuing merchant of
this town.

**IN, Elkhart • J. Davenport & Son •
IN-260-B** • *Dry goods* • Dies by Henry D.
Higgins • IN-260-B-1a Rev 1003 (R-8):
VF–EF $750–$1,250.

IN-260-C •   IN-260-C •
C.T. Greene & Co. •   C.T. Greene & Co. •
O-1 used with   O-2 used with
IN-260-C-1 and 2.   IN-260-C-3.

**IN, Elkhart • C.T. Greene & Co. • IN-
260-C** • *Groceries, provision dealers* • Dies
by Henry D. Higgins • Reverse dies:
1003, 1161 (found with both obverses) •
IN-260-C-1a Rev 1003 (R-6): VF–EF
$175–$250 • MS-63 $600–$900 • Two
obverse dies.

IN, Elkhart • John Guipe • IN-260-D
• *Dealer in boots and shoes* • Ascribed to the
shop of S.D. Childs • Reverse dies: 1114,
1205, 1207 • IN-260-D-1a Rev 1114 (R-5):
VF–EF $75–$125 • MS-63 $400–$600.

**IN, Evansville • Bittroloff & Geisler •
IN-280-A** • *Jewelers* • ? • Reverse die: 0
• IN-280-A-1a Rev 0 (R-10): VF–EF
$6,000–$9,000 • Jeweler's check intended
to be stamped on the reverse. Ron Vore in

JCWTS, Winter 1996, advertised:
"Wanted Dead or Alive, Evansville, Indiana, 280-A. Reward $300."

**IN, Evansville • P.L. Geissler • IN-
280-B** • *Watch maker* • Ascribed to the
shop of Murdock & Spencer • Reverse
die: 0 • IN-280-B-1b Rev 0 (R-9): MS-63
$10,000–$15,000 • Watchmaker's check
intended to be stamped on the reverse.
Some over 1864 McClellan campaign
tokens.

IN, Evansville • C. Habbe • IN-280-C
• *Saloonkeeper* • ? • Reverse die: 1391B •
IN-280-C-1e Rev 1391B (R-10): VF–EF
$5,000–$7,500.

**IN, Evansville • Monroe House /
Mertens & Krueger • IN-280-D** • *Hotel*
• ? • Reverse die: 1391C • IN-280-D-1e
Rev 1391C (R-10): VF–EF $5,000–$7,500.

**IN, Fort Wayne • C. Anderson • IN-
290-A** • *Groceries and provisions* • Ascribed
to the shop of W.K. Lanphear • Reverse
die: 1228 • IN-290-A-1a Rev 1228 (R-4):
VF–EF $30–$45 • MS-63 $150–$225.

**IN, Fort Wayne • Anderson & Evans •
IN-290-B** • *Grocers* • Ascribed to the
shop of W.K. Lanphear • Reverse die:
1226 • IN-290-B-1a Rev 1226 (R-5): VF–
EF $40–$60 • MS-63 $150–$225.

**IN, Fort Wayne • T.K. Brackenridge /
Phœnix Grocery • IN-290-C** • *Groceries* • Ascribed to the shop of W.K. Lanphear • Reverse dies: 1222, 1226 •
IN-290-C-2a Rev 1226 (R-4): VF–EF
$60–$90 • MS-63 $200–$300 • Œ
(PHŒNIX) made as a ligature, but from
separate O and E punches.

**IN, Fort Wayne • A.D. Brandiff & Co.
• IN-290-D** • *Hardware, stoves* • Ascribed
to the shop of W.K. Lanphear • Reverse
die: 1299 • IN-290-D-1a Rev 1299 (R-6):
VF–EF $75–$125 • MS-63 $300–$450.

IN-290-E •
W.H. Brooks Jr. •
O-1 used with
IN-290-E-1
to 6 and 7.

IN-290-E •
W.H. Brooks Jr. •
O-2 used with
IN-290-E-7.

IN, Fort Wayne • W.H. Brooks Jr. • IN-290-E • *Wall and window paper* • Ascribed to the shop of W.K. Lanphear • Reverse dies: 1089, 1091, 1171, 1223, 1226, 1323, 1350 • IN-290-E-5a Rev 1323 (R-5): VF–EF $30–$45 • MS-63 $125–$175.

IN, Fort Wayne • I. Lauferty • IN-290-F • *Clothier(?)* • Ascribed to the shop of W.K. Lanphear • Reverse die: 1337 • IN-290-F-1a Rev 1337 (R-5): VF–EF $60–$90 • MS-63 $250–$375.

IN, Fort Wayne • P. Pierr • IN-290-G • *Dry goods and groceries* • Ascribed to the shop of W.K. Lanphear • Reverse die: 1088 • IN-290-G-1a Rev 1088 (R-5): VF–EF $60–$90 • MS-63 $200–$300.

IN, Fort Wayne • C. Schoerpf & Co. • IN-290-H • *Wholesale druggists* • Ascribed to the shop of W.K. Lanphear • Reverse die: 1316 • IN-290-H-1a Rev 1316 (R-4): VF–EF $60–$90 • MS-63 $250–$375.

IN, Fortville • J.H. Thomas • IN-285-A • *Dry goods and groceries* • Ascribed to the shop of W.K. Lanphear • Reverse dies: 1088, 1122, 1168, 1350 • IN-285-A-1a Rev 1088 (R-4): VF–EF $30–$45 • MS-63 $200–$300 • Only token-issuing merchant of this town. Listed far out of alphabetical order in the Fuld text.

IN, Franklin • Hulsman & Alexander • IN-295-A • *Saloon, sale and livery stable* • Ascribed to the shop of John Stanton • Reverse dies: 1046, 1047 • IN-295-A-1a Rev 1046 (R-6): VF–EF $125–$175 • MS-63 $400–$600 • Only token-issuing merchant of this town.

IN, Fremont • G.W. Follett • IN-305-A • *Dry goods, groceries, boots, hardware* • Ascribed to the shop of John Stanton • Reverse dies: 1037, 1046, 1047 • IN-305-A-1a Rev 1037 (R-5): VF–EF $175–$250 • Only token-issuing merchant of this town.

IN, Goshen • W.A. Beane / Democrat Job Printing Office • IN-350-A • *Printing, newspaper* • Ascribed to the shop of S.D. Childs • Reverse die: 1111 • IN-350-A-1a Rev 1111 (R-6): VF–EF $125–$175 • MS-63 $400–$600.

IN, Goshen • Hascall, Alderman & Brown • IN-350-B • *Dry goods and groceries* • Reverse dies: 1111, 1114 • IN-350-B-1a Rev. 1111 (R-6): VF–EF $50–$75 • MS-63 $200–$300.

IN, Goshen • J.L. Kindig • IN-350-C • *Dry goods* • Ascribed to the shop of John Stanton • Reverse dies: 1037, 1046, 1047 • IN-350-C-2a Rev 1046 (R-5): VF–EF $50–$75 • MS-63 $200–$300.

IN, Goshen • William H. Lash & Co. • IN-350-D • *Dry goods and groceries* • Ascribed to the shop of S.D. Childs • Reverse die: 1111 • IN-350-D-1a Rev 1111 (R-6): VF–EF $60–$90 • MS-63 $250–$375.

IN, Goshen • Joseph Lauferty • IN-350-E • *Clothier* • Ascribed to the shop of S.D. Childs • Reverse dies: 1111, 1339 • IN-350-E-2a Rev 1339 (R-6), IN-350-E-2b Rev 1339 (R-6): VF–EF $60–$90 • MS-63 $300–$450.

IN, Goshen • Lawrence & Noble • IN-350-F • *Stoves, hardware* • Ascribed to the shop of S.D. Childs • Reverse die: 1114 • IN-350-F-1a Rev 1114 (R-5), IN-350-F-1b Rev 1114 (R-5): VF–EF $60–$90 • MS-63 $200–$300.

IN, Goshen • C.G. Marsh • IN-350-G • *Wholesale grocer and druggist* • Ascribed to the shop of S.D. Childs • Reverse die: 1111 • IN-350-G-1a Rev 1111 (R-6): VF–EF $75–$125 • MS-63 $300–$350.

IN, Granville • Calvin Crooks & Co. • IN-355-A • *Dry goods, hardware, shoes* •

Ascribed to the shop of John Stanton[15] • Reverse dies: 1037, 1046, 1047 • IN-355-A-1a Rev 1037 (R-6): VF–EF $150–$225 • MS-63 $500–$750 • Only token-issuing merchant of this town.

IN, Greencastle • Brattin • IN-357-A • *Jeweler* • Dies by Murdock & Spencer • Reverse dies: 1047, 1319 • IN-357-A-1a Rev 1319 (R-9): MS-63 $6,000–$9,000 • Only token-issuing merchant of this town. Jeweler's check meant to be counter-stamped on the reverse. Earlier known as OH-175-B.[16]

IN, Greenfield • Carr Ryon & Co • **IN-360-A** • *Dry goods* • Ascribed to the shop of John Stanton • Reverse dies: 1046, 1047 • IN-360-A-1a Rev 1046 (R-6): VF–EF $175–$250 • MS-63 $600–$900 • Only token-issuing merchant of this town.

IN, Greensboro • Baldwin & Sweet • **IN-365A** • *Groceries* • Ascribed to the shop of W.K. Lanphear • Reverse die: 1387 • IN-365-A-1a Rev 1387 (R-6): VF–EF $250–$375 • MS-63 $1,000–$1,500 • Only token-issuing merchant of this town.

IN, Hagerstown • E. & L. Small • IN-370-A • *Dry goods, shoes* • Ascribed to the shop of John Stanton • Reverse dies: 1007, 1018, 1019, 1028, 1042, 1047, 1069 • IN-370-A-1a Rev 1007 (R-6): VF–EF $60–$90 • MS-63 $250–$375 • Only token-issuing merchant of this town.

IN, Hartford City • Jas. Lyon • IN-395-A • *Dry goods, groceries, shoes* • Ascribed to the shop of John Stanton • Reverse dies: 1037, 1046, 1047 • IN-395-A-1a Rev 1037 (R-6), IN-395-A-2a Rev 1046 (R-6): VF–EF $90–$135 • MS-63 $250–$375 • Only token-issuing merchant of this town.

IN, Huntington • William Bickle • IN-430-A • *Dealer in books, toys, and notions* • Ascribed to the shop of W.K. Lanphear • Reverse dies: 1226, 1387 • IN-430-A-2a Rev 1387 (R-8): VF–EF $100–$150.

IN, Huntington • Bippus & Morgan • IN-430-B • *Dealers in hardware* • Ascribed to the shop of W.K. Lanphear • Reverse dies: 1301, 1350 • IN-430-B-1a Rev 1301 (R-6), IN-430-2a Rev 1350 (R-6): VF–EF $60–$90.

IN, Huntington • Sam Buchanan IN-430-C • *Dealer in agricultural implements* • Ascribed to the shop of W.K. Lanphear • Reverse die: 1169 • IN-430-C-1a Rev 1169 (R-7): VF–EF $150–$225.

IN, Huntington • Jesse Davies • IN-430-D • *Drugs and medicines* • Ascribed to the shop of W.K. Lanphear • Reverse dies: 1166, 1316, 1323 • IN-430-D-2a Rev 1316 (R-5): VF–EF $60–$90.

IN, Huntington • J.W. Griffith • IN-430-E • *Dealer in drugs and medicines* • Ascribed to the shop of W.K. Lanphear • Reverse die: 1316 • IN-430-E-1a Rev 1316 (R-6): VF–EF $150–$225.

IN, Huntington • J.H. Insworth & Co. • IN-430-F • *Dry goods and groceries* • Ascribed to the shop of W.K. Lanphear • Reverse die: 1169 • IN-430-F-1a Rev 1169 (R-5): VF–EF $60–$90.

IN, Huntington • J.S. Ream • IN-430-G • *Groceries and provisions* • Ascribed to the shop of W.K. Lanphear • Reverse die: 1171 • IN-430-G-1a Rev 1171 (R-7): VF–EF $200–$300.

IN, Huntington • Schafer & Bro. • IN-430-H • *Druggists and apothecaries* • Ascribed to the shop of W.K. Lanphear • Reverse die: 1316 • IN-430-H-1a Rev 1316 (R-8): VF–EF $400–$600.

IN, Indianapolis • Alvord, Caldwell & Alvord • IN-460-A • *Wholesale grocers* • Ascribed to the shop of John Stanton • Reverse dies: 1037, 1042, 1043 • IN-460-A-1a Rev 1037 (R-6): VF–EF $50–$75 • MS-63 $175–$250.

IN, Indianapolis • Boston Store • IN-460-B • *Dry goods* • Ascribed to the shop of John Stanton • Reverse dies: 1037, 1042, 1046, 1047 • IN-460-B-1a Rev 1037 (R-7): VF–EF $60–$90 • MS-63 $200–$300.

IN, Indianapolis • Frost's Medicine (J.M. Frost) • IN-460-Ba • *Medicine* • Ascribed to the shop of John Stanton • Reverse dies: 1037, 1042, 1046, 1047 (same as preceding, interestingly enough) • IN-460-Ba-3a Rev 1046 (R-5): VF–EF $50–$75 • MS-63 $250–$375 • Formerly OH-165-AZ.

IN, Indianapolis • C.E. Geisendorff & Co. / Hoosier Woolen Factory • IN-460-C • *Wool dealers and manufacturers* • Ascribed to the shop of W.K. Lanphear • Reverse die: 22260 • IN-460-C-2a Rev 22260 (R-5): VF–EF $40–$60 • MS-63 $200–$300 • 1863: G.W. Geisendorff & Co. owned by George W. Geisendorff and Christian E. Geisendorff. C.E. Geisendorff lived on North West Street. In May 1863 George W. Geisendorff was a captain in the Rome City Zouaves unit in the Civil War.

| IN-460-D • G.W. Geisendorff & Co. / Hoosier Woolen Factory • O-1 used with former IN-460-D-1. | IN-460-D • G.W. Geisendorf & Co. / Hoosier Woolen Factory • Surname misspelled • O-2 used with former IN-460-D-2. |

IN, Indianapolis • G.W. Geisendorff & Co. / Hoosier Woolen Factory • IN-460-D • *O-1; Wool dealers and manufacturers; O-2: Domestic staple and fancy goods* • Ascribed to the shop of W.K. Lanphear • Reverse dies: 22260, 22290 • IN-460-D-1a Rev 22260 (R-4): VF–EF $30–$45 • MS-63 $150–$225 • Two obverse dies, two surname spellings • In the 3rd edition of the Fuld book IN-460-D will be merged into IN-460-C.

IN, Indianapolis • M.H. Good • IN-460-E • *Dry goods* • Ascribed to the shop of John Stanton • Reverse dies: 1028, 1037, 1043, 1046, 1047 • IN-460-E-2a Rev 1037 (R-6): VF–EF $60–$90 • MS-63 $200–$300.

IN, Indianapolis • J.B. Grout / City Shoe Store • IN-460-F • *Shoe store* • Ascribed to the shop of John Stanton • Reverse dies: 1028, 1037, 1043, 1046, 1047 • IN-460-F-2a Rev 1037 (R-6): VF–EF $60–$90 • MS-63 $200–$300.

IN, Indianapolis • J.C. Hareth • IN-460-G • *Saddler* • Ascribed to the shop of John Stanton • Reverse dies: 1037, 1043, 1047 • IN-460-G-1a Rev 1037 (R-3): VF–EF $60–$90 • MS-63 $200–$300.

IN, Indianapolis • C.L. Holmes / City Grocery • IN-460-H • *Grocery* • Ascribed to the shop of John Stanton • Reverse dies: 1037, 1043, 1046, 1047 • IN-460-H-1a Rev 1037 (R-6), IN-460-H-2a Rev 1043 (R-6): VF–EF $50–$75 • MS-63 $200–$300.

IN, Indianapolis • J.B. Johnson • IN-460-I • *Grocer, produce dealer* • Ascribed to the shop of John Stanton • Reverse dies: 1037, 1043, 1046, 1047 • IN-460-I-1a Rev 1037 (R-6): VF–EF $50–$75 • MS-63 $150–$225.

IN, Indianapolis • Charles Kuhn • IN-460-J • *Butcher* • Ascribed to the shop of John Stanton • Reverse dies: 1037, 1047 • IN-460-J-1a Rev 1037 (R-5): VF–EF $50–$75 • MS-63 $200–$300.

IN, Indianapolis • J.F. Lenour • IN-460-K • *Druggist* • Ascribed to the shop of John Stanton • Reverse dies: 1047, 1311 • IN-460-K-2a Rev 1311 (R-6): VF–EF $75–$125 • MS-63 $250–$375 • Error die for J.F. Senour (see next page). In the third edition of the Fuld book IN-460-K will disappear and will be merged into IN-460-R.

IN, Indianapolis • Joseph McCreery • IN-460-L • *Stoves, cutlery, glass, queensware • ?* • Reverse die: 22380 • IN-460-L-1a Rev 22380 (R-4): VF–EF $50–$75 • MS-63 $200–$300.

IN, Indianapolis • Moritz, Bro. & Co • IN-460-M • *Clothiers, cloth sales* • Ascribed to the shop of John Stanton • Reverse dies: 1037, 1043, 1047 • IN-460-M-1a Rev 1037 (R-7), IN-460-M-1b Rev 1037 (R-7): VF–EF $75–$125 • MS-63 $250–$375.

IN, Indianapolis • R.R. Parker • IN-460-N • *Ladies' and gents' clothing* • Lanphear? • Reverse dies: 22410, 47130 • IN-460-N-1a Rev 22410 (R-5): VF–EF $75–$125 • MS-63 $250–$375.

IN, Indianapolis • Pomeroy, Fry & Co. • IN-460-O • *Iron merchants* • Ascribed to the shop of John Stanton • Reverse dies: 1037, 1046, 1047 • IN-460-O-1a Rev 1037 (R-6): VF–EF $50–$75 • MS-63 $175–$250.

IN, Indianapolis • Roll & Smith • IN-460-P • *Carpets and wallpaper* • Ascribed to the shop of John Stanton • Reverse dies: 1037, 1046, 1047 • IN-460-P-1a Rev 1037 (R-5): VF–EF $50–$75 • MS-63 $200–$300.

IN, Indianapolis • Roos & Schmalzried • IN-460-Q • *Butchers* • Ascribed to the shop of John Stanton • Reverse dies: 1037, 1043, 1047 • IN-460-Q-1a Rev 1037 (R-6): VF–EF $60–$90 • MS-63 $200–$300.

IN-460-R •
J.F. Senour •
O-1 used with
IN-260-1 to 3.

IN-460-R •
J.F. Senour •
O-2 used with
IN-260-4.

IN, Indianapolis • J.F. Senour • IN-460-R • *Druggist* • Ascribed to the shop of John Stanton • Reverse dies: 1037, 1047, 1311, 1316 • IN-460-R-1a Rev 1037 (R-7), IN-460-R-3a Rev 1311 (R-7), IN-460-R-4a Rev 1316 (R-7): VF–EF $75–$125 • MS-63 $250-375 • The earlier-listed

"Lenour" cards, IN-460-K, are intended for Senour, but were cut with an erroneous inscription. In the third edition of the Fuld book IN-460-K will disappear and will be merged into IN-460-R.

IN, Indianapolis • Smith & Taylor • IN-460-S • *Toy store* • Ascribed to the shop of W.K. Lanphear • Reverse dies: 1084, 1086 • IN-460-S-1a Rev 1084 (R-5): VF–EF $50–$75 • MS-63 $200–$300.

IN, Indianapolis • M. Spencer • IN-460-T • *Grocer* • Ascribed to the shop of John Stanton • Reverse dies: 1037, 1043, 1046, 1047 • IN-460-T-1a Rev 1037 (R-6): VF–EF $60–$90 • MS-63 $200–$300.

IN, Indianapolis • Mrs. A. Thomson & Son • IN-460-U • *Stationers* • Ascribed to the shop of John Stanton • Reverse dies: 1037, 1042, 1043, 1047 • IN-460-U-3a Rev 1043 (R-6): VF–EF $125–$175 • MS-63 $500–$750.

IN-460-V •
Tyler •
O-1 used with
IN-460-V-1.

IN-460-V •
Tyler •
O-2 used with
IN-460-V-2 and 3.

IN, Indianapolis • Tyler's Bee Hive • IN-460-V • *Dry goods dealer* • Ascribed to the shop of W.K. Lanphear • Reverse dies: 0016N, 1436, 22505 • IN-460-V-1a Rev 22505 (R-6): VF–EF $75–$125 • MS-63 $250–$375 • Certain tokens with O-2 were earlier attributed to Ohio as the die was used in combination with Ohio merchants.

IN, Indianapolis • Voegtle & Metzger • IN-460-W • *Manufacturers of stove, tinware, stamped wear, etc.* • Ascribed to the shop of W.K. Lanphear • Reverse die: 22520 • IN-460-W-1a Rev 22520 (R-6): VF–EF $75–$125 • MS-63 $300–$450.

IN, Indianapolis • Weaver & Maguire • IN-460-X • *Grocers* • Ascribed to the shop of John Stanton • Reverse dies: 1037, 1043, 1046, 1047 • IN-460-X-1a Rev 1037 (R-6): VF–EF $50–$75 • MS-63 $200–$300.

IN, Indianapolis • J.B. Wilson • IN-460-Y • *Hardware, cutlery, bread* • Ascribed to the shop of John Stanton • Reverse dies: 1037, 1047 • IN-460-Y-1a Rev 1037 (R-5): VF–EF $50–$75 • MS-63 $175–$250.

IN, Indianapolis • A.D. Wood • IN-460-Z • *Hardware merchant* • Ascribed to the shop of John Stanton • Reverse dies: 1037, 1043, 1047 • IN-460-Z-1a Rev 1037 (R-7), IN-460-Z-1b Rev 1037 (R-7), IN-460-Z-2a Rev 1043 (R-7): VF–EF $60–$90 • MS-63 $250–$375.

IN, Jamestown • G.W. Wayland • IN-470-A • *Drugs, medicines, notions* • Ascribed to the shop of John Stanton • Reverse dies: 1046, 1047 • IN-470-A-1a Rev 1046 (R-8): VF–EF $1,250–$1,750 • MS-63 $3,500–$5,000 • Only token-issuing merchant of this town.

IN, Jonesboro • Robert Cooder • IN-495-A • *Dry goods, groceries* • Ascribed to the shop of John Stanton • Reverse dies: 1046, 1047 • IN-495-A-1a Rev 1046 (R-6): VF–EF $300–$450 • MS-63 $1,000–$1,500 • Only token-issuing merchant of this town.

IN, Kendallville • Beyer, Meyer & Bro. • IN-500-A • *Druggists* • Ascribed to the shop of W.K. Lanphear • Reverse dies: 1310, 1316 • IN-500-A-1a Rev 1316 (R-8): VF–EF $300–$450 • MS-63 $1,000–$1,500 • Of all small Indiana towns, Kendallville is especially remarkable for the number of merchants who issued store cards during the Civil War. As certain reverses are common among multiple merchants, it is presumed that the orders for such pieces were all placed at the same time. W.K. Lanphear of Cincinnati was the provider.

IN, Kendallville • Bosworth & Whitford • IN-500B • *Groceries and provisions* • Ascribed to the shop of W.K. Lanphear • Reverse dies: 1091, 1223, 1227 • IN-500-B-3a Rev 1223 (R-7): VF–EF $150–$225 • MS-63 $600–$900.

IN, Kendallville • M.M. Bowen • IN-500-C • *Groceries, provisions, and cigars* • Ascribed to the shop of W.K. Lanphear • Reverse die: 1127 • IN-500-C-1a Rev 1127 (R-6): VF–EF $60–$90 • MS-63 $250–$375.

IN, Kendallville • W & J.R. Bunyan • IN-500-D • *Drugs, medicines, paints, and oils* • Ascribed to the shop of W.K. Lanphear • Reverse dies: 1130, 1226 • IN-500-D-1a Rev 1130 (R-7), IN-500-D-2a Rev 1226 (R-7): VF–EF $60–$90 • MS-63 $300–$450.

IN, Kendallville • J.F. Corle • IN-500-E • *Dry goods and groceries* • Ascribed to the shop of W.K. Lanphear • Reverse dies: 1171, 1181 • IN-500-E-2a Rev 1181 (R-5): VF–EF $50–$75 • MS-63 $250–$375.

IN, Kendallville • S.C. Evans & Co. • IN-500-F • *Dry goods and groceries* • Ascribed to the shop of W.K. Lanphear • Reverse dies: 1082, 1089, 1226 • IN-500-F-1a Rev 1082 (R-6): VF–EF $50–$75 • MS-63 $250–$375.

IN, Kendallville • G.C. Glatte • IN-500-G • *Groceries and provisions* • Ascribed to the shop of W.K. Lanphear • Reverse dies: 1122, 1181 • IN-500-G-2a Rev 1181 (R-5): VF–EF $50–$75 • MS-63 $200–$300.

IN, Kendallville • J.H. Gotsch • IN-500-H • *Dealer in clocks, watches, and jewelry* • Ascribed to the shop of W.K. Lanphear • Reverse die: 1321 • IN-500-H-1a Rev 1321 (R-8): VF–EF $250–$375 • MS-63 $600–$900.

IN, Kendallville • E. Graden • IN-500-I • *Livery and sale stable* • Ascribed to the shop of W.K. Lanphear • Reverse die: 1127 • IN-500-I-1a Rev 1127 (R-5): VF–EF $60–$90 • MS-63 $200–$300.

IN, Kendallville • Jacobs & Co. • IN-500-J • *Dry goods and clothing dealer* • Ascribed to the shop of W.K. Lanphear • Reverse dies: 1083, 1181 • IN-500-J-2a Rev 1181 (R-7): VF–EF $100–$150 • MS-63 $300–$450.

IN, Kendallville • Jones & Mosher's Bakery & Provision Store • IN-500-K • *Bakery and provision store* • Ascribed to the shop of W.K. Lanphear • Reverse die: 1223 • IN-500-K-1a Rev 1223 (R-6): VF–EF $75–$125 • MS-63 $250–$375.

IN, Kendallville • J.J. Joyce • IN-500-L • *Groceries and provisions* • Ascribed to the shop of W.K. Lanphear • Reverse die: 1335 • IN-500-L-1a Rev 1335 (R-7): VF–EF $150–$225 • MS-63 $500–$750.

IN, Kendallville • J. Lants • IN-500-M • *Dealer in boots and shoes* • Ascribed to the shop of W.K. Lanphear • Reverse die: 1318 • IN-500-M-1a Rev 1318 (R-6): VF–EF $100–$150 • MS-63 $400–$600.

IN, Kendallville • S.J.M. Loomis • IN-500-N • *Dry goods and groceries* • Ascribed to the shop of W.K. Lanphear • Reverse dies: 1083, 1089, 1127, 1128 • IN-500-N-1a Rev 1083 (R-6), IN-500-N-2a Rev 1089 (R-6): VF–EF $50–$75 • MS-63 $150–$225.

IN, Kendallville • F.W. Mesing • IN-500-O • *Dealer in groceries and liquors* • Ascribed to the shop of W.K. Lanphear • Reverse die: 1335 • IN-500-O-1a Rev 1335 (R-6): VF–EF $125–$175 • MS-63 $500–$750 • In the past often quoted as F.W. Messing; token reads Mesing.

IN, Kendallville • Miller & Crow • IN-500-P • *Groceries and provisions* • Ascribed to the shop of W.K. Lanphear • Reverse die: 1350 • IN-500-P-1a Rev 1350 (R-6): VF–EF $75–$125 • MS-63 $250–$375.

IN, Kendallville • G.S. Rowell & Son • IN-500-Q • *Produce dealers* • Ascribed to the shop of W.K. Lanphear • Reverse dies: 1091, 1130 • IN-500-Q-1a Rev 1091 (R-5), IN-500-Q-2a Rev 1130 (R-5): VF–EF $40–$60 • MS-63 $175–$250.

IN, Kendallville • Steer & Bowen • IN-500-R • *Dealers in hardware* • Ascribed to the shop of W.K. Lanphear • Reverse die: 1326 • IN-500-R-1a Rev 1326 (R-5): VF–EF $75–$125 • MS-63 $300–$450.

IN, Kendallville • Joseph Thew • IN-500-S • *Manufacturer of and dealer in boots and shoes* • Ascribed to the shop of W.K. Lanphear • Reverse die: 1318 • IN-500-S-1a Rev 1318 • (R-7): VF–EF $125–$175 • MS-63 $500–$750.

IN, Kendallville • W.S. Thomas • IN-500-T • *Dry goods and groceries* • Ascribed to the shop of W.K. Lanphear • Reverse dies: 1122, 1181 • IN-500-T-1a Rev 1122 (R-7), IN-500-T-2a Rev 1181 (R-7): VF–EF $60–$90 • MS-63 $200–$300.

IN, Kendallville • D.S. Welch • IN-500-U • *Dry goods and groceries* • Ascribed to the shop of W.K. Lanphear • Reverse dies: 1127, 1168, 1181, 1226 • IN-500-U-1a Rev 1127 (R-6), IN-500-U-2a Rev 1168 (R-6), IN-500-U-4a Rev 1226 (R-6): VF–EF $50–$75 • MS-63 $200–$300.

IN, Kokomo • J.V. Cullen • IN-510-A • *Groceries* • Ascribed to the shop of W.K. Lanphear • Reverse die: 1122 • IN-510-A-1a Rev 1122 (R-6): VF–EF $125–$175 • MS-63 $500–$750.

IN, Kokomo • D.P. Florer • IN-510-Aa • *Watchmaker* • Ascribed to the shop of John Stanton • Reverse die: 1440 • IN-510-Aa-1b Rev 1440 (R-10): VF–EF $5,000–$7,500.

IN, Kokomo • Haskett & Co. Prairie Store • IN-510-B • *Dry goods* • Ascribed to the shop of W.K. Lanphear • Reverse die: 22810 • IN-510-B-1a Rev 22810 (R-6): VF–EF $150–$225 • MS-63 $400–$600.

IN, Kokomo • I.N. Pattison • IN-510-C • *Druggist* • Ascribed to the shop of W.K. Lanphear • Reverse die: 1316 • IN-510-C-1a Rev 1316 (R-6): VF–EF $150–$225 • MS-63 $500–$750.

IN, La Porte • L. Eliel • IN-530-A • *Clothier* • Ascribed to the shop of S.D. Childs • Reverse die: 1114 • IN-530-A-1a Rev 1114 (R-6): VF–EF $100–$150 • MS-63 $400–$600.

IN-530-B •
J.B. Faller & Son •
O-1 used with
IN-530-B-1 to 3.

IN-530-B •
J.B. Faller & Son •
O-2 used with
IN-530-B-4.

IN, La Porte • J. Faller & Son • IN-530-B • *Watchmakers and jewelers* • Dies by Henry D. Higgins • Reverse dies: 1003, 1165, 1202 • IN-530-B-2a Rev 1165 (R-6): VF–EF $100–$150 • MS-63 $500–$750.

IN, La Porte • Jas. Lewis & Co. • IN-530-C • ? • Ascribed to the shop of S.D. Childs • Reverse dies: 1112, 1114, 1115, 1116 • IN-530-C-2a Rev 1114 (R-3): VF–EF $50–$75 • MS-63 $250–$375.

IN, La Porte • Neuburger & Hamburger • IN-530-E • *Clothiers* • Ascribed to the shop of S.D. Childs • Reverse dies: 1115, 1119 • IN-530-E-1a Rev 1119 (R-6): VF–EF $150–$225.

IN, La Porte • J.M. Neuburger • IN 530-D • *Clothier* • Ascribed to the shop of S.D. Childs • Reverse dies: 1357, 1357A • IN-530-D-2a Rev 1357A (R-7): VF–EF $60–$100.

IN, La Porte • W.W. Wallace • IN-530-F • *Wholesale and retail grocer* • Ascribed to the shop of S.D. Childs • Reverse dies: 1115, 1119 • IN-530-F-2a Rev 1119 (R-7): VF–EF $250–$375.

IN, La Porte • L.D. Webber • IN-530-G • *Stoves and hardware* • Ascribed to the shop of S.D. Childs • Reverse dies: 1112, 1115, 1118, 1119 • IN-530-G-3a Rev

1119 (R-5): VF–EF $50–$75 • MS-63 $250–$375.

IN, Ligonier • O. Arnold • IN-550-A • *Druggist and grocer* • Ascribed to the shop of W.K. Lanphear • Reverse die: 1316 • IN-550-A-1a Rev 1316 (R-5): VF–EF $50–$75 • MS-63 $200–$300 • Multiple merchants of this town issued tokens made by Lanphear.

IN, Ligonier • Barney Bro. • IN-550-B • *Dry goods* • Ascribed to the shop of W.K. Lanphear • Reverse dies: 1091, 1222, 1224, 1225 • IN-550-B-1a Rev 1091 (R-6), IN-550-B-2a Rev 1222 (R-6), IN-550-B-3a Rev 1224 (R-6): VF–EF $30–$45 • MS-63 $150–$225.

IN, Ligonier • J.C. Best • IN-550-C • *Hardware, stoves, tinware, etc.* • Ascribed to the shop of W.K. Lanphear • Reverse dies: 1299, 1326 • IN-550-C-1a Rev 1299 (R-6): VF–EF $40–$60 • MS-63 $150–$225.

IN, Ligonier • J. Decker • IN-550-D • *Groceries and provisions* • Ascribed to the shop of W.K. Lanphear • Reverse dies: 1085, 1088, 1223 • IN-550-D 1 Rev 1085 (R-6), IN-550-D-2a Rev 1085 (R-6): VF–EF $50–$75 • MS-63 $200–$300.

IN, Ligonier • S. Mier & Co. • IN-550-E • *Dry goods, clothing, and produce* • Ascribed to the shop of W.K. Lanphear • Reverse dies: 1083, 1089, 1091 • IN-550-E-2a Rev 1089 (R-5), IN-550-E-3a Rev 1091 (R-5): VF–EF $30–$45 • MS-63 $150–$225.

IN, Ligonier • George C. Nill • IN-550-F • *Drugs, groceries, and stationery* • Ascribed to the shop of W.K. Lanphear • Reverse dies: 1169, 1310 • IN-550-F-2a Rev 1310 (R-6): VF–EF $40–$60 • MS-63 $150–$225.

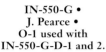

IN-550-G •
J. Pearce •
O-1 used with
IN-550-G-D-1 and 2.

IN-550-G •
J. Pearce •
O-2 used with
IN-550-G •
The state is
incorrectly given as
LIGONIER / MICH.
on the token!

IN, Ligonier • J. Pearce • IN-550-G • *Drugs, groceries, and notions* • Ascribed to the shop of W.K. Lanphear • Reverse dies: 1169, 1310 • IN-550-G-1a Rev 1169 (R-6), IN-550-G-2a Rev 1310 (R-6), IN-550-G-3a Rev 1310 (R-6): VF–EF $60–$90 • MS-63 $250–$375 • Two obverse dies.[17]

IN, Ligonier • E. Reeve • IN-550-H • *Groceries, crockery, and glassware* • Ascribed to the shop of W.K. Lanphear • Reverse dies: 1088, 1310 • IN-550-H-1a Rev 1088 (R-6): VF–EF $50–$75 • MS-63 $200–$300.

IN, Ligonier • Straus Brothers • IN-550-I • *Dry goods, clothing, and produce* • Ascribed to the shop of W.K. Lanphear • Reverse dies: 1085, 1088, 1171 • IN-550-I-2a Rev 1088 (R-5), IN-550-I-3a Rev 1171 (R-5): VF–EF $30–$45 • MS-63 $125–$175.

IN, Ligonier • C.G. Vail • IN-550-J • *Dry goods and groceries* • Ascribed to the shop of W.K. Lanphear • Reverse die: 1088 • IN-550-J-1a Rev 1088 (R-6): VF–EF $50–$75 • MS-63 $200–$300.

IN, Ligonier • J.C. Zimmerman • IN-550-K • *Dry goods, clothing, etc.* • Ascribed to the shop of W.K. Lanphear • Reverse dies: 1088, 1224 • IN-550-K-2a Rev 1224 (R-2): VF–EF $50–$75 • MS-63 $200–$300.

IN, Lisbon • G.D. Baughman & Bro. • IN-560-A • *Dry goods and groceries* • Ascribed to the shop of W.K. Lanphear • Reverse die: 1318 • IN-560-A-1a Rev 1318 (R-6): VF–EF $200–$300 • MS-63 $600–$900 • Only token-issuing merchant of this town.

IN, Logansport • Booth & Sturges • IN-570-A • *Boots and shoes* • Ascribed to the shop of W.K. Lanphear • Reverse die: 1318 • IN-570-A-1a Rev 1318 (R-7): VF–EF $150–$225 • MS-63 $600–$900.

IN, Logansport • H.C. Eversole • IN-570-B • *Dealer in clocks and watches* • Ascribed to the shop of John Stanton • Reverse die: 1456 • IN-570-B-1b Rev 1456 (R-9): VF–EF $6,000–$9,000 • MS-63 $10,000–$15,000.

IN, Logansport • M.H. Gridley • IN-570-C *Watchmaker, jeweler* • Ascribed to the shop of W.K. Lanphear • Reverse die: 1320 • IN-570-C-1a Rev 1320 (R-6): VF–EF $125–$175 • MS-63 $400–$600.

IN, Logansport • A. Kendall • IN-570-D • *Dealer in groceries and flour* • Ascribed to the shop of W.K. Lanphear • Reverse die: 1171 • IN-570-D-1a Rev 1171 (R-7): VF–EF $90–$135.

IN, Logansport • King & Reed • IN-570-E • *Dealers in stoves and tinware* • Ascribed to the shop of W.K. Lanphear • Reverse dies: 1171, 1304 • IN-570-E-2a Rev 1304 (R-5): VF–EF $60–$90 • MS-63 $300–$450 • This is an error die. The correct surname spelling is Krug. See IN-570-F. In the third edition of the Fuld book IN-570-E will disappear and will be merged into IN-570-F.

IN, Logansport • Krug & Reed • IN-570-F • *Dealers in stoves and tinware* • Ascribed to the shop of W.K. Lanphear • Reverse die: 1304 • IN-570-F-2a Rev 1304 (R-7): VF–EF $60–$90 • MS-63 $300–$450 • See comments in previous listing (IN-570-E).

IN, Logansport • McDonald & Co. • IN-570-G • *Dry goods, carpets* • Ascribed to the shop of W.K. Lanphear • Reverse dies: 1122, 1349 • IN-570-G-1a Rev 1122 (R-7): VF–EF $75–$125 • MS-63 $300–$450.

IN, Logansport • A.J. Murdock • IN-570-H • *Dry goods, groceries* • Ascribed to the shop of W.K. Lanphear • Reverse die: 1171 • IN-570-H-1a Rev 1171 (R-6): VF–EF $100–$150 • MS-63 $500–$750.

IN, Lynn • Elliott & Hinshaw • IN-580-A • *Dry goods, groceries* • Ascribed to the shop of John Stanton • Reverse dies: 1046, 1047 • IN-580-A-1a Rev 1046 (R-7): VF–EF $75–$125 • MS-63 $250-375.

IN, Lynn • J.A. Hinshaw • IN-580-B • *Dry goods and groceries* • Ascribed to the shop of John Stanton • Reverse dies: 1026, 1027, 1037, 1042, 1045, 1046, 1047 • IN-580-B-2a Rev 1027 (R-6), IN-580-B-3a Rev 1042 (R-6): VF–EF $50–$75 • MS-63 $200–$300.

IN, Mechanicsburg • Elliott & Swain • IN-600-A • *Dry goods, groceries, hardware, etc.* • Ascribed to the shop of W.K. Lanphear • Reverse dies: 1124, 1127 • IN-600-A-1a Rev 1124 (R-7): VF–EF $200–$300 • MS-63 $750–$1,250.

IN, Mechanicsburg • Ezra Swain • IN-600-B • *Dry goods, groceries, and hardware* • Ascribed to the shop of W.K. Lanphear • Reverse dies: 1124, 1180 • IN-600-B-1a Rev 1124 (R-6): VF–EF $150–$225 • MS-63 $500–$750.

IN, Middlebury • C. Stutz • IN-615-A • *Dry goods, clothing, shoes* • Ascribed to the shop of John Stanton • Reverse dies: 1037, 1047 • IN-615-A-1a Rev 1037 (R-6): VF–EF $150–$225 • MS-63 $500–$750 • Only token-issuing merchant of this town.

IN, Middletown • W.W. Cotterall, P.M. • IN-620-A • *Postmaster and insurance agent* • Ascribed to the shop of John Stanton • Reverse dies: 0, 1037, 1046, 1047 • IN-620-A-2a Rev 1046 (R-5): VF–EF $75–$125 • MS-63 $300–$450 • Only token-issuing merchant of this town.

IN-630-A •
Henry D. Higgins •
O-1 used with
IN-630-A-1 and 2.

IN-630-A •
Henry D. Higgins •
O-2 used with
IN-630-A-3.

IN-630-A •
Henry D. Higgins •
O-3 used with
IN-630-A-4 and 5.

IN-630-A •
Henry D. Higgins •
O-4 used with
IN-630-A-6 to 9.

IN-630-A •
Henry D. Higgins •
O-5 used with
IN-630-A-10 to 12.

IN-630-A •
Henry D. Higgins •
O-6 used with
IN-630-A-13 and 14.

IN, Mishawaka • H.D. Higgins • IN-630-A • *Jeweler, optician, token maker, barometer maker* • "Primitive" obverse dies ascribed to Henry D. Higgins, others to the shop of S.D. Childs • Reverse dies: 1003, 1049, 1050, 1050A, 1097, 1111, 1327, 1328, 1329, 1383, 1383A • IN-630-A-5a Rev 1328 (R-3), IN-630-A-6a Rev 1049 (R-3): VF–EF $40–$60 • MS-63 $200–$300.

IN, Mishawaka • B. Holcomb • IN-630-B • *Groceries, stoneware, oil, etc.* • Dies by Henry D. Higgins • Reverse dies: 1049, 1097, 23200 & 23210 • IN-630-B-1a Rev 1049 (R-3): VF–EF $30–$45 • MS-63 $150–$225.

IN, Mishawaka • S.H. Judkins • IN-630-C • *Groceries and provisions* • Ascribed to the shop of S.D. Childs • Reverse die: 1114 • IN-630-C-1a Rev 1114 (R-6): VF–EF $100–$150 • MS-63 $400–$600.

IN, Mooresville • W.H.P. Woodward • IN-640-A • *Dry goods, etc. goods* • Ascribed to the shop of John Stanton • Reverse dies: 1046, 1047 • IN-640-A-1a Rev 1046 (R-6): VF–EF $90–$135 • MS-63 $300–$450 • Only token-issuing merchant of this town.

IN, New Albany • J.F. Larwell • IN-680-A • *Watchmaker* • Ascribed to the shop of John Stanton • Reverse dies: 0, 1046, 1047, 1319 • IN-680-A-1a Rev 1046 (R-8): VF–EF $750–$1,250 • MS-63 $2,500–$3,750 • Only token-issuing merchant of this town.

IN, New Castle • M.L. Powell • IN-690-A • *Dealer in stoves and tinware* • Ascribed to the shop of W.K. Lanphear • Reverse dies: 1125, 1180, 1180A, 1299, 1300, 1380A • IN-690-A-2a Rev 1180 (R-6), IN-690-A-4a Rev 1304 (R-6): VF–EF $90–$135 • MS-63 $400–$600 • Only token-issuing merchant of this town.

IN, New Paris • A.M. Davis • IN-710-A • *Dry goods, groceries, crockery, drugs, etc.* Dies by Henry D. Higgins • Reverse dies: 1003, 1161, 1234 • IN-710-A-2a Rev 1161 (R-7): VF–EF $750–$1,250 • MS-63 $2,500–$3,750 • Only token-issuing merchant of this town.

IN, North Vernon • John Wenzel • IN-715-A • *Dealer in stoves and tinware* • Ascribed to the shop of W.K. Lanphear • Reverse die: 1299 • IN-715-A-1a Rev 1299 (R-7): VF–EF $125–$175 • MS-63 $500–$750.

IN, Peru • J. Kreutzer • IN-740-A • *Dealer in glass, queensware, and crockery* • Ascribed to the shop of W.K. Lanphear • Reverse die: 1346 • IN-740-A-1a Rev 1346 (R-5): VF–EF $50–$75 • MS-63 $200–$300.

IN, Peru • J.S. Queeby • IN-740-B • *Dry goods, notions* • Ascribed to the shop of W.K. Lanphear • Reverse dies: 0, 1176, 1290, 1295, 1331, 1352, 1384, 23320, 40965 • IN-740-B-6a Rev 1384 (R-2): VF–EF $30–$45 • MS-63 $75–$125.

IN, Peru • Saine & Miller • IN-740-C • *Groceries, notions, boots, and shoes* • Ascribed to the shop of W.K. Lanphear • Reverse die: 1318 • IN-740-C-1a Rev 1318 (R-5): VF–EF $50–$75 • MS-63 $200–$300.

IN, Pierceton • Murray & Bro. • IN-760-A • *Dry goods and groceries* • Ascribed to the shop of W.K. Lanphear • Reverse die: 1088 • IN-760-A-1a Rev 1088 (R-5): VF–EF $75–$125 • MS-63 $300–$450.

IN, Pierceton • Reed & Spayde • IN-760-B • *Dry goods and groceries* • Dies by Alexander Gleason • Reverse die: 1183 • IN-760-B (R-6): VF–EF $200–$300 • MS-63 $600–$900 • Town name misspelled as Peirceton on die. This is Gleason's only Indiana token.

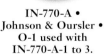

IN-770-A • Johnson & Oursler • O-1 used with IN-770-A-1 to 3.

IN-770-A • Johnson & Oursler • O-2 used with IN-770-A-4 and 5.

IN, Plainfield • Johnson & Oursler • IN-770-A • *Dry goods, clothing, shoes* • Ascribed to the shop of John Stanton • Reverse dies: 1018, 1037, 1047, 23380 • IN-770-A-1a Rev 1037 (R-7), IN-770-A-3a Rev 23380 (R-7), IN-770-A-4a Rev 1018 (R-7): VF–EF $75–$125 • MS-63 $300–$450 • Two obverse dies are completely different in their layouts.

IN, Plainfield • M. Osborn • IN-770-B • *Groceries, notions, toys, fancy articles* • Ascribed to the shop of John Stanton •

Reverse dies: 1046, 1047, 1069, 23400 • IN-770-B-2a Rev 23400 (R-7), IN-770-B-2b Rev 23400 (R-7): VF–EF $75–$125 • MS-63 $300–$450.

IN, Plainfield • Isaac M. Shidler • IN-770-C • *Dry goods, clothing, shoes, notions* • Ascribed to the shop of John Stanton • Reverse dies: 1018, 1047, 1069, 23420 • IN-770-C-1a Rev 23420 (R-6): VF–EF $75–$125 • MS-63 $300–$450.

IN, Plainfield • Tansey & Ballard • IN-770-D • *Drugs, medicines* • Ascribed to the shop of John Stanton • Reverse dies: 1018, 1019, 1047, 1069, 1311, 1312 • IN-770-D-5a Rev 1312 (R-5): VF–EF $75–$125 • MS-63 $300–$450.

IN, Plymouth • J.M. Dale • IN-780-A • *Dry goods, groceries, crockery, boots, shoes, etc.* • Ascribed to the shop of W.K. Lanphear • Reverse die: 1342 • IN-780-A-1a Rev 1342 (R-6): VF–EF $60–$90 • MS-63 $250–$375.

IN, Plymouth • H.B. Dickson & Co. • IN-780-B • *Hardware, stoves, and tinware* • Ascribed to the shop of W.K. Lanphear • Reverse die: 1299 • IN-780-B-1a Rev 1299 (R-4): VF–EF $30–$45 • MS-63 $125–$175.

IN, Plymouth • H. Humrichouser • IN-780-C • *Grain and produce dealer* • Ascribed to the shop of W.K. Lanphear • Reverse die: 1222 • IN-780-C-1a Rev 1222 (R-5): VF–EF $50–$75 • MS-63 $200–$300.

IN, Richmond • C.C. Buhl • IN-800-A • *Stoves and tinware* • Ascribed to the shop of W.K. Lanphear • Reverse dies: 1168, 1299 • IN-800-A-2a Rev 1299 (R-5): VF–EF $60–$90 • MS-63 $200–$300.

IN, Richmond • G.P. Emswiler & Co. • IN-800-B • *Fancy goods and toys* • Ascribed to the shop of John Stanton • Reverse dies: 1023, 1030, 1042, 1046, 1047, 1068, 1192 • IN-800-B-3a Rev 1042 (R-7): VF–EF $60–$90 • MS-63 $200–$300.

IN, Richmond • E.F. Hirst • IN-800-C • *Watchmaker, jeweler* • Ascribed to the shop of John Stanton • Reverse dies: 1008, 1028, 1042, 1046, 1047 • IN-800-C-1a Rev 1008 (R-6): VF–EF $60–$90 • MS-63 $200–$300.

IN, Rochester • D.S. Gould • IN-810-A • *Dry goods, groceries* • Ascribed to the shop of John Stanton • Reverse dies: 1046, 1047 • IN-810-A-1a Rev 1046 (R-5): VF–EF $100–$150 • MS-63 $500–$750 • Only token-issuing merchant of this town.

IN, Seymour • J.F. Johnson • IN-830-A • *News dealer* • Ascribed to the shop of W.K. Lanphear • Reverse dies: 1091, 1223 • IN-830-A-1a Rev 1091 (R-8), IN-830-A-2b Rev 1223 (R-8): VF–EF $300–$450 • MS-63 $1,000–$1,500 • Only token-issuing merchant of this town.

IN, South Bend • W.W. Bement • IN-860-A • *Edge tool manufacturer* • Dies by Henry D. Higgins • Reverse die: 23220 • IN-860-A-1a Rev 23220 (R-8): VF–EF $10,000–$15,000 • Steve Tanenbaum comment, March 26, 1998: "The rarest 'primitive' merchant is W.W. Bement, South Bend, single variety, six known."

IN, South Bend • Blowney & Johnson • IN-860-B • *Manufacturers of composition roofing* • Dies by Henry D. Higgins • Reverse dies: 1161, 1202 • IN-860-B-1a Rev 1161 (R-8), IN-860-B-2a Rev 1202 (R-8): VF–EF $150–$225 • MS-63 $600–$900.

IN, South Bend • S.M. Chord • IN-860-C • *Dry goods, groceries, crockery, carpets* • ? • Reverse die: 1233A • IN-860-C-1a Rev 1233A (R-4): VF–EF $50–$75 • MS-63 $175–$250.

IN-860-D •
Hammonds
Shoe Store •
O-1 used with
IN-860-D-1.

IN-860-D •
Hammond's
Stove Store •
O-2 used with
IN-860-D-2.

IN, South Bend • Hammond's Shoe Store / Hammond's Stove Store • IN-860-D • *Shoe store (with stove store error)* • Ascribed to the shop of S.D. Childs • Reverse die: 1106 • IN-860-D-1a Rev 1106 (R-5): VF–EF $70–$125 • MS-63 $300–$450 • Two different obverse dies were used with a single reverse die. The Fuld text suggests that "apparently the word STOVE is an error on the second die, as apparently the correct usage is SHOE." This may be supportive of the fact that the STOVE die was used first (as evident from the die state of the common reverse). Contemporary directories list J. Oliver Hammond as a seller of shoes, with no mention of stoves.

IN, South Bend • J.C. Knoblock • IN-860-E • *Agent, baker. and grocer* • Ascribed to the shop of S.D. Childs • Reverse dies: 1099, 1114, 1207 • IN-860-E-2a Rev 1114 (R-4): VF–EF $50–$75 • MS-63 $200–$300.

IN, South Bend • A.M. Purdy • IN-860-F • *Nurseryman and fruit grower* • Ascribed to the shop of S.D. Childs • Reverse dies: 1108, 1357 • IN-860-F-1a Rev 1108 (R-5): VF–EF $50–$75 • MS-63 $225–$350.

IN, South Bend • George Wyman • IN-860-G • *Fancy dry goods* • Ascribed to the shop of S.D. Childs • Reverse dies: 0, 1097, 1098, 1101, 1102, 1205, 1211 • IN-860-G-3a Rev 1101 (R-6): VF–EF $60–$75 • MS-63 $300–$450.

IN, Sullivan • Price Brothers • IN-870-A • *Dry goods, clothing, shoes* • Ascribed to the shop of John Stanton • Reverse dies: 1025, 1030, 1042, 1047, 1069 • IN-870-A-2a Rev 1042 (R-6): VF–EF $125–$175 • MS-63 $500–$750 • Only token-issuing merchant of this town.

IN, Swan • D.H. Haines & Bro. • IN-880-A • *Dry goods and groceries* • Ascribed to the shop of W.K. Lanphear • Reverse die: 1223 • IN-880-A-1a Rev 1223 (R-6): VF–EF $125–$175 • MS-63 $500–$750 • Only token-issuing merchant of this town.

IN, Tipton • A.A. Budd • IN-900-A • *Watchmaker* • Dies by Murdock & Spencer • Reverse die: 0 • IN-900-A-1a Rev 0 (R-9): VF–EF $2,500–$3,750 • MS-63 $4,000–$6,000 • Only token-issuing merchant of this town.

IN-915-A •
Bartholomew
& McClelland •
O-1 used with
IN-915-A-1.
"Valpariso"
misspelling.

IN-915-A •
Bartholomew
& McClelland •
O-2 used with
IN-915-A-2.

IN, Valparaiso • Bartholomew & McClelland • IN-915-A • *Dry goods, boots, shoes* • Dies by Henry D. Higgins[18] • Reverse dies: 1234, 1238 • IN-915-A-2a Rev 1238 (R-5): VF–EF $100–$150 • MS-63 $400–$600 • Only token-issuing merchant of this town.

IN, Wabash • Gordon & Thurston • IN-940-A • *Drugs, books, jewelry • ?* • Reverse dies: 0, 23650 • IN-940-A-1a Rev 23650 (R-5): VF–EF $125–$175 • MS-63 $400–$600 • Only token-issuing merchant of this town.

IN, Warsaw • D. Carlile • IN-950-A • *Oysters, confectionery, cigars, etc.* • Ascribed to the shop of John Stanton • Reverse dies: 1008, 1047, 1069, 1400 • IN-950-A-4b Rev 1400 (R-7): VF–EF $250–$375 • MS-63 $750–$1,250.

IN, Warsaw • John Lane • IN-950-B • *Watchmaker and jeweler* • Ascribed to the shop of W.K. Lanphear • Reverse die: 0 • IN-950-B-1b Rev 0 (R-8): VF–EF $750–$1,250 • MS-63 $2,000–$3,000.

IN, Warsaw • D.R. Pottenger & Co, • IN-950-C • *Druggists* • Ascribed to the shop of W.K. Lanphear • Reverse die: 1316 • IN-950-C-1a Rev 1316 (R-6): VF–EF $150–$225 • MS-63 $500–$750.

IN, Wheeling • J.G. Williams & Co. • IN-970-A • *Dry goods, hardware, boots dealer* • Ascribed to the shop of John Stanton • Reverse dies: 1046, 1047 • IN-970-A-1a Rev 1046 (R-6): VF–EF $200–$300 • MS-63 $600–$900 • Only token-issuing merchant of this town.[19] There are three Wheelings in Indiana; this one is in Washington Township, a part of Delaware County.[20]

Iowa

There were four issuers of Civil War store cards in Iowa. Representative tokens from each are collectible but scarce.

IA, Cedar Rapids • Reynolds & Co. New York Store • IA-150-A • *Retail store* • Ascribed to the shop of S.D. Childs • Reverse dies: 1105, 1205 & 23730 • IA-150-A-1a Rev 23730 (R-6): VF–EF $750–$1,250 • MS-63 $2,000–$3,000 • Only token-issuing merchant of this town.

IA, Lansing • William Flemming & Bro. • IA-560-A • *Lumber, lath, and shingles* • Ascribed to the shop of John Stanton • Reverse dies: 1037, 1043, 1046, 1047 • IA-560-A-1a Rev 1037 (R-7), IA-560-A-3a Rev 1043 (R-7): VF–EF $500–$750 • MS-63 $2,000–$3,000 • Only token-issuing merchant of this town.

IA, Lyons • Gage, Lyall & Keeler • IA-570-A • *Grocers* • Dies by F.N. Dubois • Reverse die: 1368 • IA-570-A-1a Rev 1368 (R-6): VF–EF $400–$600 • MS-63 $1,500–$2,250 • Only token-issuing merchant of this town.

IA, Waterloo • H. & G. Goodhue • IA-930-A • *Lath, shingles, doors, etc., factory* • Ascribed to the shop of John Stanton • Reverse dies: 1046, 1047 • IA-930-A-1a Rev 1946 (R-7): VF–EF $600–$900 • MS-63 $2,000–$3,000 • Only token-issuing merchant of this town.

Kansas

Alabama, Idaho, Kansas, Maine, and New Hampshire are states with but a single token-issuing merchant. The Kansas merchant was A. Cohen of Leavenworth, for whom two metal varieties exist from the same pair of dies. At the time, Leavenworth was an important depot for supplies and a point of departure for travelers to the West, including to the gold fields in Colorado Territory.

KS, Leavenworth • A. Cohen • KS-550-A • *Clothing and gents' furnishing goods* • Ascribed to the shop of W.K. Lanphear • Reverse die: 1085 • KS-550-A-1a Rev 1085 (R-6): VF–EF $2,000–$3,000 • MS-63 $6,000–$9,000 • Only token-issuing merchant of this state.[21]

Kentucky

Civil War tokens issued by Kentucky merchants include an interesting series from dies by H. Miller & Co., Louisville, using Miller stock dies (the best-known of which shows a hand holding a beer mug) combined with dies for various Louisville liquor dispensaries. For the third edition of *U.S. Civil War Store Cards* the entire Louisville section has been recataloged beginning with the letter C to avoid confusion from prior listings.

Among other Kentucky tokens are varieties made in Cincinnati (across the Ohio River from Newport and Covington, KY) in the shop of John Stanton, including the cards of John W. Lee denominated in various quantities of milk such as ONE HALF PINT, 1 PINT, ONE QUART, ONE HALF GALL, and ONE GALL.

KY, Covington • Arbeiter Halle • KY-150-A • *Saloon* • Ascribed to the shop of John Stanton • Reverse dies: 1023, 1028, 1030, 1042, 1047, 1069 • KY-150-A-1a Rev 1023 (R-6): VF–EF $150–$225 • MS-63 $500–$750 • "Arbeiter Halle" is German for "Workers' Hall," no doubt a social gathering place where beer flowed profusely.

KY, Covington • Covington & Cincinnati Ferry Co. • KY-150-B • *Ferry* • Ascribed to the shop of John Stanton • Reverse dies: 1042, 1046, 1047, 1069 • KY-150-B-1a Rev 1042 (R-8), KY-150-B-1b Rev 1042 (R-8): VF–EF $300–$450 • MS-63 $750–$1,250.

KY, Covington • J. Dolman • KY-150-C • *Stocking manufacturer* • Ascribed to the shop of W.K. Lanphear but somewhat crudely done • Reverse die: 1278 • KY-150-C-1a Rev 1278 (R-4): VF–EF $90–$135 • MS-63 $300–$450 • 1861: James Dolman, stocking manufacturer, east side of Madison Street between 5th and 6th streets.

KY, Covington • V.C. Engert, Germania Saloon • KY-150-D • *Saloon* • Ascribed to the shop of John Stanton • Reverse dies: 1019, 1026, 1028, 1042, 1047, 1069 • KY-150-D-2a Rev 1026 (R-5): VF–EF $125–$175 • MS-63 $400–$600 • 1861: Victor Engert, grocer and Germania Saloon, south side of 6th between Russell and Washington streets.

KY, Lexington • J.L. Keiningham • KY-480-A • *Grocer* • Ascribed to the shop of John Stanton • Reverse dies: 1047, 1391A, 23874 • KY-480-A-1a Rev 1047 (R-9), KY-480-A-3b Rev 1391A (R-8): VF–EF $2,500–$3,750 • MS-63 $6,000–$9,000.

KY, Lexington • John W. Lee • KY-480-B • *Baker and confectioner per inscrip-*

tion on token • Ascribed to the shop of John Stanton • Reverse dies: 1463, 1464, 1465, 1466, 1467, 1047, 1068, 1069 • KY-480-B-1a Rev 1047 (R-8), KY-480-B-3a Rev 1463 (R-8), KY-480-B-3b Rev 1463 (R-8), KY-480-B-4a Rev 1464 (R-8), KY-480-B-4b Rev 1464 (R-8), KY-480-B-5a Rev 1465 (R-8), KY-480-B-5b Rev 1465 (R-8), KY-480-B-6a Rev 1466 (R-8), KY-480-B-6b Rev 1466 (R-8), KY-480-B-7a Rev 1467 (R-8), KY-480-B-7b Rev 1467 (R-8): VF–EF $200–$300 • MS-63 $600–$900.

KY, Louisville • J G R B • KY-510-C • ? • Reverse die: 1431 • KY-510-C-1a Rev 1431 (R-9): VF–EF $1,000–$1,500 • MS-63 $2,000–$3,000.

KY, Louisville • George Brucklacher • KY-510-D • *Saloonkeeper* • Ascribed to H. Miller & Co. • Reverse die: 1431 • KY-510-D-2b Rev 1431 (R-7): VF–EF $300–$450 • MS-63 $900–$1,360.

KY, Louisville • S.S. Clarke • KY-510-E • *Whiskey wholesale and retail* • Ascribed to H. Miller & Co. • Reverse die: 1431 • KY-510-E-1b Rev 1431 (R-9), KY-510-E-2a Rev 1431 (R-9): VF–EF $1,500–$2,250 • MS-63 $4,000–$6,000.

KY, Louisville • M. Egelhoff • KY-510-F • *Saloonkeeper* • Ascribed to H. Miller & Co. • Reverse die: 1431 • KY-510-F-1a Rev 1431 (R-9): VF–EF $1,500–$2,500 • MS-63 $4,000–$6,000.

KY, Louisville • A. Huber • KY-510-G • ? • Ascribed to H. Miller & Co. • Reverse die: 1431 • KY-510-G-1a Rev 1431 (R-9): VF–EF $1,500–$2,250 • MS-63 $4,000–$6,000.

KY, Louisville • J. Kuntz • KY-510-H • *Saloonkeeper* • Ascribed to H. Miller & Co. • Reverse die: 1431 • KY-510-H-1a Rev 1431 (R-9), KY-510-H-1b Rev 1431 (R-9): VF–EF $1,000–$1,500 • MS-63 $2,000–$3,000.

KY, Louisville • H.P. Opfeld • KY-510-I • ? • Reverse die: 1009A • KY-510-I-1a Rev 1009A (R-9): VF–EF $4,000–$6,000.

KY, Louisville • H. Preissler • KY-510-J • *Druggist* • Ascribed to H. Miller & Co. • Reverse die: 24010 • KY-510-J-1a Rev 24010 (R-7), KY-510-J-1a(fp) Rev 24010 (R-9): VF–EF $750–$1,250 • MS-63 $2,000–$3,000.

KY, Louisville • Roehrs & Bryant • KY-510-K • ? • Ascribed to H. Miller & Co. • Reverse die: 1431 • KY-510-K-1a Rev 1431 (R-9): VF–EF $1,500–$2,250.

KY, Louisville • Schöne Aussicht • KY-510-L • *H. Miller & Co. good-luck token? Name of a saloon?* • Ascribed to H. Miller & Co. • Reverse die: 1431 • KY-510-L-1a Rev 1431 (R-8): VF–EF $750–$1,250 • *Schöne aussicht* means "pretty view" in German. David Gladfelter comments: "My theory: 'schöne aussicht' did not refer to a specific merchant, but was an expression of well-wishing similar in meaning to 'success' or 'good luck' because 'aussicht' by extension means 'prospect,' that is to say, Miller hopes that his customers have favorable business prospects (which they will, of course, if they buy advertising tokens from him)."[22]

KY, Louisville • F.C. Stump / T.T.S. • KY-510-M • *Saloonkeeper* • Ascribed to H. Miller & Co. • Reverse die: 1431 • KY-510-M-1a Rev 1431 (R-9): VF–EF $750–$1,250.

KY, Louisville • S-B Tempest (Steamboat Tempest) • *Steamboat* • Dies by H. Miller & Co. • Reverse die: 99340 • KY-510-Ma-2b Rev 99340 (R-9): $3,000–$4,500 • Attribution tentative. The *Tempest* was based in Louisville and ran on the Ohio River.

KY, Louisville • Garrett Townsend • KY-510-N • *Saloonkeeper* • Ascribed to H. Miller & Co. • Reverse die: 1431 • KY-510-N-1b Rev 1431 (R-8): VF–EF $400–$600 • MS-63 $1,250–$1,750.

KY-510-O •
A. Weber •
O-1 used with
KY-510-O-1 and 2.

KY-510-O •
A. Weber •
O-2 used with
KY-510-O-3.

KY, Louisville • A. Weber • KY-510-O • *Saloonkeeper?* • Ascribed to H. Miller & Co. • Reverse dies: 1431, 24070 • KY-510-O-1b Rev 24070 (R-7), KY-510-O-2b Rev 1431 (R-8): VF–EF $400–$600 • MS-63 $1,250–$1,750.

KY, Newport • J. Butcher • KY-640-A • *Dry goods* • Ascribed to the shop of John Stanton • Reverse dies: 1026, 1030, 1042, 1047, 1069 • KY-640-A-2a Rev 1030 (R-6): VF–EF $200–$300 • MS-63 $500–$750.

KY, Newport • Newport & Covington Bridge Co. • *Toll bridge* • Ascribed to the shop of John Stanton • Reverse dies: 1029, 1034, 1042, 1044, 1047, 1069, 1400 • KY-640-B-2a Rev 1034 (R-8), KY-640-B-3a Rev 1042 (R-8), KY-640-B-3b Rev 1042 (R-8): VF–EF $250–$375 • MS-63 $750–$1,250 • 1860: Newport & Covington Bridge Company. Office at east end of the bridge. Chartered January 1st, 1852. Capital $75,000. J.M. Caldwell, president; Charles Southgate, secretary and treasurer. Directors in Covington: John T. Levis, B.W. Foley. Directors in Newport: Peter Constans and M. King.

KY, Newport • H.B. Xelar • KY-640-C • *Saloonkeeper* • Ascribed to the shop of W.K. Lanphear • Reverse dies: 1430, 1033, 1124, 1131, 1274, 1452 & 35300 • KY-640-C-3a Rev 1274 (R-3): VF–EF $50–$75 • MS-63 $125–$175 • Earlier listed as OH-165-GT. The correct spelling of his surname was probably Exeler or Exler.

LOUISIANA

Although no Civil War tokens are known to have been struck in or for the state of Louisiana, a counterstamped cent made by J.B. Schiller as emergency money is contemporary with the Civil War token series. J.B. SCHILLER counterstamped across the obverse of a contemporary federal cent. Sans serif letters. Counterstamp goes from border to border. On the reverse an X for 10¢ is stamped. Russell Rulau has written that before New Orleans fell back into the hands of the Union on May 1, 1862, these pieces were issued as small change. Schiller also produced paper scrip notes dated April 3, 1862, in the denominations of 25¢ and 50¢.

LA, New Orleans • J.B. Schiller • LA-670-A • *Saloonkeeper* • J.B. Schiller • Reverse die: 24092 • LA-670-A-1d Rev 24092 (R-7): F-VF $2,500–$3,750.

MAINE

There are only two token die combinations from Maine and they are from the same issuer, R.S. Torrey. One of them, ME-100-A-01a, is from dies by S.D. Childs of Chicago, Illinois, a long way from Maine. The other die may be by the Scovill Manufacturing Co.

ME-100-A •
R.S. Torrey •
O-1 used with
ME-100-A-1.
Die from the shop
of S.D. Childs.

ME-100-A •
R.S. Torrey •
O-2 used with
ME-100-A-2. Die
possibly by the Scovill
Manufacturing Co.

ME, Bangor • R.S. Torrey • ME-100-A • *Inventor, dealer in bees and honey* • Dies by two makers: S.D. Childs and possibly by Scovill Manufacturing Co. • Reverse dies: 1105, 1200 • ME-100-A-2a

Rev 1200 (R-3): VF–EF $100–$150 • MS-63 $300–$450 • Only token-issuing merchant of this state. Two obverse dies from two different makers.[23] *A Business Directory of the Subscribers to the New Map of Maine*, J. Chace Jr., Portland, 1862: "R.S. Torrey, patentee of Torrey's Me. State Bee Hive and dealer in bees and honey, No. 49 Fifth Street."

MARYLAND

The present corpus of Civil War tokens attributed to Maryland includes many brass tavern checks earlier listed under Chicago, Illinois, following revisions in the third edition of *U.S. Civil War Store Cards*.[24] The entire Baltimore section has been recataloged beginning with the letter C to avoid confusion from prior listings. These seem to have been made by counterstamping letters into otherwise blank brass checks made by Francis X. Koehler, Baltimore diesinker best known for his sutler tokens. Examples are named (Bauernschmidt and Odenwald), or are letters counterstamped on three die varieties of tokens (provisionally called patriotic dies 0451A, 0451B, and 0451C). These letters perhaps represent saloonkeepers, or perhaps servers, or perhaps control letters. Unless directory listings can be found for the initials and/or names counterstamped on these pieces, I am not inclined to consider them as separate merchants; in any event, they are counterstamps, not varieties of token *dies*.

Perhaps the best-known regularly struck token issued within the state is that of G.R. Bowman, Hagerstown confectioner, which illustrates a telescope on the reverse. Certain tokens earlier listed under Snow Hill, Maryland, have been relocated to Snow Hill, West Virginia.

MD, Baltimore • CLA • MD-060-C • *Counterstamped tavern check* • Possibly made by F.X. Koehler • Reverse die: 1352A • MD-060-C-1b Rev 1352A (R-9), MD-060-C-2b Rev 1352A (R-9): VF–EF $250–$375.

MD, Baltimore • PRA/MK • MD-060-Ca • *Counterstamped tavern check* • Possibly made by F.X. Koehler • Reverse die: 1352A • MD-060-Ca-1b Rev 1352A (R-9): VF–EF $250–$375.

MD, Baltimore • GA • MD-060-D • *Counterstamped tavern check* • Possibly made by F.X. Koehler • Reverse die: 1352A • MD-060-D-1b Rev 1352A (R-9): VF–EF $250–$375.

MD, Baltimore • W.S. Ahern & J.F. Broadbent • MD-060-E • *Oyster & fruit packers*[25] • ? • Reverse die: 1296A • MD-060-E-1b Rev 1296A (R-9): VF–EF $500–$750.

MD, Baltimore • AB • MD-060-F • *Counterstamped tavern check* • Possibly made by F.X. Koehler • Reverse die: 1296 • MD-060-F-1b Rev 1296 (R-9): VF–EF $250–$375.

MD, Baltimore • DB • MD-060-G • *Counterstamped tavern check* • Possibly made by F.X. Koehler • Reverse die: 1296 • MD-060-G-1b Rev 1296 (R-10): VF–EF $250–$375.

MD, Baltimore • FB • MD-060-H • *Counterstamped tavern check* • Possibly made by F.X. Koehler • Reverse dies: 1001, 1296 • MD-060-H-1b Rev 1296 (R-9), MD-060-H-2b Rev 1296 (R-9): VF–EF $250–$375.

MD, Baltimore • I.B. • MD-060-I • *Counterstamped tavern check* • Possibly made by F.X. Koehler • Reverse die: 1296 • MD-060-I-1b Rev 1296 (R-9): VF–EF $250–$375.

MD, Baltimore • George Bauernschmidt • MD-060-J • *Brewer* • Possibly made by F.X. Koehler • Reverse die: 1296 • MD-060-J-1b Rev 1296 (R-8): VF–EF $600–$900 • Earlier attributed to Chicago, Illinois as IL-150-C-01.[26]

MD, Baltimore • FC • MD-060-K • *Counterstamped tavern check* • Possibly made by F.X. Koehler • Reverse dies: 1001, 1352A • MD-060-K-1b Rev 1001 (R-10), MD-060-K-2b Rev 1352A (R-10): VF–EF $250–$375.

MD, Baltimore • MC • MD-060-L • *Counterstamped tavern check* • Possibly made by F.X. Koehler • Reverse die: 1001 • MD-060-L-1b Rev 1001 (R-9): VF–EF $250–$375.

MD, Baltimore • GAF • MD-060-M • *Counterstamped tavern check* • Possibly made by F.X. Koehler • Reverse die: 1352A • MD-060-M-1b Rev 1352A (R-9): VF–EF $250–$375.

MD, Baltimore • F.G. • MD-060-N • *Counterstamped tavern check* • Possibly made by F.X. Koehler • Reverse die: 1296 • MD-060-N-1b Rev 1296 (R-9): VF–EF $250–$375 • Earlier listed as IL-150-Wa.

MD, Baltimore • FWG • MD-060-O • *Counterstamped tavern check* • Possibly made by F.X. Koehler • Reverse die: 1352A • MD-060-O-1b Rev 1352A (R-9): VF–EF $250–$375.

MD, Baltimore • W. Hild • MD-060-P • *Counterstamped tavern check* • Possibly made by F.X. Koehler • Reverse die: 1296 • MD-060-P-1b Rev 1296 (R-9): VF–EF $400–$600.

MD, Baltimore • PJ • MD-060-Q • *Counterstamped tavern check* • Possibly made by F.X. Koehler • Reverse die: 1352A • MD-060-Q-1b Rev 1352A (R-10): VF–EF $250–$375.

MD, Baltimore • M.K. • MD-060-R • *Counterstamped tavern check* • Possibly made by F.X. Koehler • Reverse die: 1001 • MD-060-R-1b Rev 1001 (R-9): VF–EF $250–$375.

MD, Baltimore • A. Krebs • MD-060-S • *Tobacconist* • Possibly made by James E. Pilkington • Reverse dies: 1438, 70140, 70150 • MD-060-S-2b Rev 1438 (R-8): VF–EF $1,250–$1,500.

MD, Baltimore • A.L. • MD-060-T • *Counterstamped tavern check* • ? • Reverse die: 1246A • MD-060-T-1b Rev 1246A (R-10): VF–EF $250–$375.

MD, Baltimore • PL • MD-060-U • *Counterstamped tavern check* • Possibly made by F.X. Koehler • Reverse die: 1001 • MD-060-U-1b Rev 1001 (R-10): VF–EF $250–$375.

MD, Baltimore • CM • MD-060V • *Counterstamped tavern check* • Possibly made by F.X. Koehler • Reverse die: 1296, 1352A • MD-060-V-1b Rev 1296 (R-9), MD-060-V-3b Rev 1352A (R-9): VF–EF $250–$375.

MD-060-W • Mount Vernon Club • O-1 used with MD-060-W-1. "5".

MD-060-W • Mount Vernon Club • O-2 used with MD-060-W-2. "25".

MD, Baltimore • Mount Vernon Club • MD-060-W • *Private club* • Ascribed to F.X. Koehler • Reverse dies: 1001, 1092A • MD-060-W-1b Rev 1001 (R-7): VF–EF $400–$600 • MS-63 $1,250–$1,750 • Earlier known as MD-060-A.

MD, Baltimore • EO • MD-060-X • *Counterstamped tavern check* • Possibly made by F.X. Koehler • Reverse die: 1352A • MD-060-X-1b Rev 1352A (R-10): VF–EF $250–$375.

MD, Baltimore • Ph. Odenwald • MD-060-Y • *Brewer* • Possibly made by F.X. Koehler • Reverse die: 1296 • MD-060-Y-1b Rev 1296 (R-8): VF–EF $500–$750 • MS-63 $1,250–$1,750 • Earlier listed as MD-060-N. Philip Odenwald is listed in the 1863 Baltimore directory as a brewer. A tavern was attached to the brewery.[27]

MD, Baltimore • WP • MD-060-Z • *Counterstamped tavern check* • Possibly made by F.X. Koehler • Reverse die: 1001 • MD-060-Z-1b Rev 1001 (R-9): VF–EF $250–$375.

MD, Baltimore • R • MD-060-AA • *Counterstamped tavern check* • Possibly made by F.X. Koehler • Reverse die: 1296 • MD-060-AA-1b Rev 1296 (R-10): VF–EF $250–$375.

MD, Baltimore • F.W.R. • MD-060-AB • *Counterstamped tavern check* • Possibly made by F.X. Koehler • Reverse die: 1296 • MD-060-AB-1b Rev 1296 (R-8): VF–EF $250–$375.

MD, Baltimore • G.R. • MD-060-AC • *Counterstamped tavern check* • Possibly made by F.X. Koehler • Reverse die: 1352A • MD-060-AC-1b Rev 1352A (R-10): VF–EF $250–$375.

MD, Baltimore • LR • MD-060-AD • *Counterstamped tavern check* • Possibly made by F.X. Koehler • Reverse die: 1296 • MD-060-AD-1b Rev 1296 (R-9): VF–EF $250–$375.

MD, Baltimore • LSR • MD-060-AE • *Counterstamped tavern check* • Possibly made by F.X. Koehler • Reverse die: 1296 • MD-060-AE-1b Rev 1296 (R-8): VF–EF $250–$375.

MD, Baltimore • M. Ruben • MD-060-AF • *Counterstamped tavern check* • Possibly made by F.X. Koehler • Reverse die: 1001 • MD-060-AF-1b Rev 1001 (R-10): VF–EF $400–$600.

MD, Baltimore • DS • MD-060-AG • *Counterstamped tavern check* • Possibly made by F.X. Koehler • Reverse die: 1296 • MD-060-A6-1b Rev 1296 (R-10), MD-060-A6-2b (R-10): VF–EF $250–$375.

MD, Baltimore • JS • MD-060-AH • *Counterstamped tavern check* • Possibly made by F.X. Koehler • Reverse die: 1352A • MD-060-AH-1b Rev 1352-A (R-8): VF–EF $250–$375.

MD, Baltimore • F. Schwehr • MD-060-AI • *Counterstamped tavern check* • Possibly made by F.X. Koehler • Reverse die: 1352A • MD-060-AI-1b Rev 1352A (R-9): VF–EF $400–$600 • This is the only Baltimore token with a surname counterstamped in full, in this instance from a prepared counterstamp punch (not individual letters).

MD, Baltimore • S & ST • MD-060-AJ • *Lager beer brewers* • Possibly made by F.X. Koehler • Reverse die: 1296 • MD-060-AJ-1b Rev 1296 (R-10): VF–EF $250–$375.

MD-060-AK •
Shakespeare Club •
O-1 used with
MD-060-AK-1. "5".

MD-060-AK •
Shakespeare Club •
O-2 used with
MD-060-AK-2. "10".

MD-060-AK •
Shakespeare Club •
O-4 used with
MD-060-AK-4. "50".

MD, Baltimore • Shakespeare Club • MD-060-AK • *Private club* • Possibly made by F.X. Koehler • Reverse dies: 1001, 1092A, ? • MD-060-AK-1b Rev 1001 (R-6): VF–EF $500–$750 • MS-63 $1,350–$2,000 • Earlier listed as MD-060-B.

MD, Baltimore • Chas. Stevens • MD-060-AL • *Tobacconist* • Reverse die signed by Pilkington as maker • Reverse dies: 1438, 70410 • MD-060-AL-1b Rev 1438 (R-8): VF–EF $1,500–$2,250.

MD, Baltimore • T • MD-060-AM • *Counterstamped tavern check* • Possibly made by F.X. Koehler • Reverse die: 1001 • MD-060-AM-1b Rev 1001 (R-9): VF–EF $250–$375.

MD, Baltimore • KV • MD-060-AN • *Counterstamped tavern check* • Possibly made by F.X. Koehler • Reverse die: 1001 • MD-060-AN-1b Rev 1001 (R-8): VF–EF $250–$375.

MD, Baltimore • JW • MD-060-AO • *Counterstamped tavern check* • ? • Reverse die: 1246A • MD-060-AO-1b Rev 1246A (R-10): VF–EF $250–$375.

MD, Baltimore • HCW • MD-060-AP • *Counterstamped tavern check* • Possibly made by F.X. Koehler • Reverse die: 1352A • MD-060-AP-1b Rev 1352A (R-10): VF–EF $250–$375.

MD, Baltimore • HEW • MD-060-AQ • *Counterstamped tavern check* • Possibly made by F.X. Koehler • Reverse die: 1296 • MD-060-AQ-1b Rev 1296 (R-10): VF–EF $250–$375.

MD, Hagerstown • G.R. Bowman • MD-560-A • *Confectioner* • ? • Reverse die: 24180 • MD-560-A-1b Rev 24180 (R-8): VF–EF $3,000–$4,500 • Only token issuer of this town.

MASSACHUSETTS

The series of Massachusetts Civil War tokens, centered in Boston but including several other locations as well, is remarkable for its diversity. Joseph H. Merriam, Boston diesinker, created several varieties of tokens bearing his own advertisements and those of others. The typical Merriam die is well cut with deeply impressed letters, and his tokens are boldly struck. Among the best-known Civil War issues from any location or issuer are Merriam's pieces depicting the head of a dog with the punning inscription GOOD FOR A SCENT.

Fall River, Massachusetts, was home to E.P. Francis, who operated the Billiard Room within the City Hotel and issued tokens from rustic hand-cut dies by an unknown person who also made dies for several Providence, Rhode Island, issuers. Harvard, Massachusetts, provides the store card of A. & G.F. Wright, who employed Shubael D. Childs of far-off Chicago to strike the issues, the only instance of a Childs token being issued in Massachusetts. On the island of Nantucket, off the coast of the state, a Washington portrait token was issued for the Sanitary Fair held in August 1864. In Worcester, Massachusetts, diesinker Charles Lang illustrated his advertising token with his own portrait.

MA, Boston • Comer's Commercial College • MA-115-A • *Business college* • Probably by Merriam • Reverse die: 24200 • MA-115-1e Rev 24200 (R-7): VF–EF $200–$300 • Rather than being a circulating substitute for the federal cent, the Comer's Commercial College token was probably used in classes as part of instruction in the handling of money.[28]

MA, Boston • Excelsior Club • MA-115-C • *Private club* • Ascribed to Joseph Merriam • Reverse die: 1284 • MA-115-C-1e Rev 1284 (R-9): VF–EF $15,000–$22,500.

MA-115-D •
Merriam & Co. •
O-1 used with
MA-115-D-1.

MA-115-D •
Merriam & Co. •
O-2 used with
MA-115-D-2.

MA-115-D •
Merriam & Co. •
O-3 used with
MA-115-D-3.

MA, Boston • Merriam & Co. • MA-115-D • *Seal and token maker, engraver* • By Joseph Merriam • Reverse die: 1284 • MA-115-D-1e Rev 1284 (R-8), MA-115-D-2b Rev 1284 (R-8): VF–EF $1,250–$1,750 • MS-63 $3,500–$4,750.

MA-115-E •
Jos. H. Merriam •
O-2 used with
MA-115-E-3.

MA, Boston • Jos. H. Merriam • MA-115-E • *Seal and token maker, engraver* • By Joseph Merriam • Reverse dies: 1284, 1131A, 24290 • MA-115-E-1a Rev 1284 (R-4): VF–EF $400–$600 • MS-63 $1,500–$2,250.

MA, Boston • Pulmonales for Coughs and Colds • MA-115-Ea • *Patent medicine*[29] • ? • Reverse die: 1371 • MA-115-Ea-1a Rev 1371 (R-3): VF–EF $30–$45 • MS-63 $100–$150.

MA, Boston • G.F. Tuttle's Restaurant • MA-115-G • *Restaurant* • Ascribed to Joseph Merriam • Reverse dies: 24330, 24340, 24350, 24360, 24362 • MA-115-G-1a Rev 24330 (R-6), MA-115-G-2a Rev 24340 (R-6), MA-115-G-3a Rev 24350 (R-6), MA-115-G-5e Rev 24362 (R-6): VF–EF $175–$250 • MS-63 $600–$900 • See description of the modular multi-denomination Tuttle die in chapter 5.

MA-200-A •
Dunn & Co.'s
Oyster House •
O-1 used with
MA-200-A-1 and 2.

MA-200-A •
Dunn & Co.'s
Oyster House •
O-2 used with
MA-200-A-3.

MA-200-A •
Dunn & Co.'s
Oyster House •
O-3 used with
MA-200-A-4.

MA, Charlestown • Dunn & Co.'s Oyster House • MA-200-A • *Oyster house* • Ascribed to Joseph Merriam[30] • Reverse dies: 1413, 1414, 1415 • MA-200-A-1a Rev 1413 (R-5): VF–EF $40–$60 • MS-63 $150–$225 • Only token issuer of this town. This brief series includes three different obverse and as many different reverse dies, the latter each featuring the Bunker Hill Monument, although the Monument is not specifically identified.

MA, Fall River • E.P. Francis, Billiard Room and Restaurant • MA-260-A • *Billiard room and restaurant* • Unidentified Rhode Island die cutter • Reverse dies: 1374, 24380, 42060 • MA-260-A-1a Rev 24380 (R-4): VF–EF $30–$45 • MS-63 $125–$200 • Only token issuer of this town.

MA, Harvard • A. & C.F. Wright, Bay State Horse Power • MA-320-A • *Offered shop rights to Bay State Horsepower, a power device* • Ascribed to the shop of S.D. Childs • Reverse die: 1120 • MA-320-A-1a Rev 11120 (R-5): VF–EF

$125–$175 • MS-63 $400–$600 • Only token issuer of this town.

MA, Nantucket • Great Fair in Aid of the U.S. Sanitary Commission • MA-530-A • *Sanitary Fair* • ? • Reverse die: 1138 • MA-530-A-1a Rev 1138 (R-4): VF–EF $90–$135 • MS-63 $300–$450 • Only token issuer of this town. The Nantucket event was one of many sanitary fairs conducted in the North in 1864 for the benefit of Union soldiers and was held on the island on August 3, 1864.[31]

MA, Worcester • Charles Lang • MA-970-A • *Diesinker and engraver* • Reverse die: 24415 • MA-970-A-1a Rev 24415 (R-4): 22.6 mm • VF–EF $75–$125 • MS-63 $250–$375 • Only token issuer of this town.

MICHIGAN

Civil War store cards of Michigan embrace hundreds of varieties. These are enthusiastically collected by towns and merchants. It is a challenge to acquire one of each issuer. Some years ago Steve Tanenbaum gave his view of the availability of certain issues from this state, citing these as the rarest merchants: MI-135-A. Cassopolis. Boyd & Bradly • MI-225-I. Detroit. Fr. Behr • MI-225-BT. Detroit. Seth Smith & Son • MI-595-A. Maple Rapids. Isaac Hewitt • MI-865-A. Saranac. W. Darling.[32]

Tokens of most issuers are readily available, many in higher grades. In addition to circulation issues there were many numismatic strikes made, particularly by the shop of John Stanton, who had a virtual stranglehold on supplying Detroit merchants. The shortage of cents in circulation and perhaps a call for tokens in Detroit in early 1863 is reflected by a notice in the *Detroit Free Press*, April 28, 1863, by S. Freedman & Co. (not a token-issuing firm), dealers in clothing and yardage, which included this paragraph: "WANTED: Five hundred dollars in cents. Highest premium paid."[33] Most Detroit tokens have reeded edges.

In Hillsdale, diesinker Alexander Gleason provided tokens for many local and regional customers. These are generally of a "primitive" or rustic appearance.

MI, Addison • Smith Brothers • MI-003A • *Dry goods, groceries, hardware* • ? • Reverse die: 24430 • MI-003A-1a Rev 24430 (R-4): VF–EF $40–$60 • MS-63 $150–$225 • Only token issuer of this town.

MI, Adrian • Blackman & Dibble • MI-005-A • *Druggists* • Dies by Alexander Gleason • Reverse die: 1183 • MI-005-A-1a Rev 1183 (R-4): VF–EF $50–$75 • MS-63 $200–$300.

MI, Adrian • Buck & Farrar • MI-005-B • *Dealers in hardware, stoves, and tin* • Ascribed to the shop of S.D. Childs • Reverse dies: 1096, 1099, 1390, 27901 • MI-005-B-2a Rev 1099 (R-4): VF–EF $30–$45 • MS-63 $125–$175.

MI, Adrian • J.A. Castle • MI-005-C • *Grocer* • Ascribed to the shop of S.D. Childs • Reverse dies: 1097, 1098, 1099, 1205 • MI-005-C-3a Rev 1098 (R-3), MI-005-C-4a Rev 1099 (R-3): VF–EF $25–$35 • MS-63 $75–$125.

MI-005-D •
Remington
& Bennett •
O-1 used with
MI-005-D-1 to 3.

MI-005-D •
Remington
& Bennett •
O-2 used with
MI-005-D-4.

MI, Adrian • Remington & Bennett • MI-005-D • *Druggists and grocers* • Ascribed to the shop of S.D. Childs • Reverse dies: 1097, 1098, 1105 • MI-005-D-3a Rev 1105 (R-5): VF–EF $30–$45 • MS-63 $125–$175.

MI, Adrian • S. Sammons, Mansion House • MI-005-E • *Innkeeper* • Ascribed to the shop of S.D. Childs • Reverse dies: 1098, 1099, 1211, 1390 • MI-005-E-1a Rev 1098 (R-6), MI-005-E-2a Rev 1099 (R-6): VF–EF $60–$90 • MS-63 $200–$300 • The Mansion House hotel was operated by Sampson Sammons, who was remembered in a "homey novel written by a resident of the area."[34] Sammons was known as "Old Tige," and the motto posted on his hotel was, "Where liberty dwells, there is my country." Adrian was located on a popular route connecting Detroit and Chicago, and the Mansion House was a popular stopover for travelers.

MI, Adrian • William S. Wilcox • MI-005-F • *Hardware dealer* • Ascribed to the shop of S.D. Childs[35] • Reverse dies: 1094, 1098, 1102 • MI-005-F-2a Rev 1097 (R-4): VF–EF $25–$35 • MS-63 $75–$125.

MI, Albion • Albion Commercial College, Ira Mayhew president • MI-025-A • *Business college* • ? • Reverse die: 24520 • MI-025-A-1a Rev 24520 (R-3): VF–EF $20–$30 • MS-63 $50–$75.

MI, Albion • Comstock & Bro • MI-025B • *Druggists* • Ascribed to the shop of S.D. Childs • Reverse dies: 1094, 1203, 1205 • MI-025-B-2a Rev 1203 (R-5): VF–EF $30–$45 • MS-63 $125–$175.

MI, Almont • D.W. Richardson • MI-035-A • *Drugs and books* • Ascribed to the shop of S.D. Childs • Reverse dies: 1099, 1205 • MI-035-A-2a Rev 1099 (R-4): VF–EF $75–$125 • MS-63 $300–$450 • Only token issuer of this town.

MI, Ann Arbor • Philip Bach • MI-040-A • *Dry goods* • Ascribed to Emil Sigel • Reverse dies: 1015, 1066 • MI-040-A-1a Rev 1015 (R-3), MI-040-A-2a Rev 1066 (R-3): VF–EF $25–$35 • MS-63 $60–$90.

MI, Ann Arbor • Dean & Co. • MI-040-B • *Home furnishing goods* • Ascribed to Emil Sigel • Reverse dies: 1015, 1066, 1067 • MI-040-B-1a Rev 1015 (R-3), MI-040-B-2a Rev 1066 (R-3): VF–EF $25–$35 • MS-63 $60–$90.

MI, Ann Arbor • C.H. Millen • MI-040-C • *Dry goods and groceries* • Ascribed to the shop of S.D. Childs • Reverse dies: 1095, 1205 • MI-040-C-1a Rev 1095 (R-4): VF–EF $25–$35 • MS-63 $100–$150.

MI-040-D •
Stebbins & Wilson •
O-1 used with
MI-040-D-1 and 2.

MI-040-D •
Stebbins & Wilson •
O-2 used with
MI-040-D-3.

MI, Ann Arbor • Stebbins & Wilson • MI-040-D • *Dry goods and groceries* • ? • Reverse dies: 1314, 1315 • MI-040-D-1a Rev 1314 (R-2), MI-040-D-3a Rev 1314 (R-2): VF–EF $30–$45 • MS-63 $100–$150.

MI-040-E •
William Wagner •
O-1 used with
MI-040-E-1.

MI-040-E •
William Wagner •
O-2 used with
MI-040-E-2 and 3.

MI, Ann Arbor • William Wagner • MI-040-E • *Merchant tailor, clothing dealer* • Ascribed to the shop of S.D. Childs • Reverse dies: 1095, 1390 • MI-040-E-2a Rev 1095 (R-3): VF–EF $25–$35 • MS-63 $75–$125.

MI, Atlas • F.J. & J. Palmer's Woolen Factory • MI-045-A • *Woolen factory* • Ascribed to the shop of John Stanton • Reverse dies: 1023, 1024, 1031, 1042, 1047 • MI-045-A-2a Rev 1031 (R-3): VF–EF $100–$150 • MS-63 $300–$450 • Only token issuer of this town.

MI, Battle Creek • William Brooks • MI-060aA • *Hardware dealer* • Ascribed to the shop of S.D. Childs • Reverse dies: 1003, 1161, 1202, 1207, 1208 • MI-060-aA-3a Rev 1206 (R-5): VF–EF $90–$135 • MS-63 $300–$450 • Earlier known as IN-260-A. This token has "Battle Creek & Elkhart" as its inscription, Elkhart being in Indiana. Not making matters clearer, per Fuld: "This card is a joint token of Battle Creek, MI, and Elkhart, IN, and was mistakenly listed by Hetrich and Guttag under Battle Creek, Indiana, which does not exist."[36]

MI, Battle Creek • V.P. Collier • MI-060-A • *General hardware* • Dies by Alexander Gleason[37] • Reverse dies: 1184, 1187 • MI-060-A-2a Rev 1187 (R-7): VF–EF $200–$300 • MS-63 $600–$900.

MI, Battle Creek • J.B. Leonard • MI-060-B • *Boot and shoe maker* • Dies by Alexander Gleason • Reverse die: 1186 • MI-060-B-1a Rev 1186 (R-8): VF–EF $500–$750 • MS-63 $1,500–$2,250.

MI, Battle Creek • J. Stuart & Son • MI-060-C • *Stoves, hardware, iron, and nails* • Ascribed to the shop of S.D. Childs • Reverse dies: 1098, 1390 • MI-060-C-1a Rev 1098 (R-5): VF–EF $150–$225 • MS-63 $400–$600.

MI-065-A •
Binder & Co. •
O-1 used with
MI-065-A-1 and 2.

MI-065-A •
Binder & Co. •
O-2 used with
MI-065-A-3 and 4.

MI, Bay City • Binder & Co. • MI-065-A • *Dry goods, groceries, and hardware* • Ascribed to the shop of S.D. Childs • Reverse dies: 1095, 1099, 1101, 1357 • MI-065-A-1a Rev 1095 (R-4), MI-065-A-2a Rev 1357 (R-4): VF–EF $40–$60 •

MS-63 $150–$225 • Only token issuer of this town.

MI, Brighton • Roswell Barnes • MI-085-A • *Maker of and dealer in boots and shoes* • Ascribed to the shop of John Stanton • Reverse dies: 1037, 1042, 1047 • MI-085-A-1a Rev 1037 (R-6): VF–EF $150–$225 • MS-63 $500–$750.

MI, Brighton • William R. Cobb • MI-085-B • *Dry goods and groceries* • Ascribed to the shop of John Stanton • Reverse dies: 1039, 1042, 1046, 1047 • MI-085-B-1a Rev 1039 (R-5): VF–EF $150–$225 • MS-63 $400–$600.

MI, Brighton • W.H. Naylor • MI-085-C • *Dealer in hardware and cutlery* • Ascribed to the shop of John Stanton • Reverse dies: 1039, 1042, 1047 • MI-085-C-1a Rev 1039 (R-5), MI-085-C-2a Rev 1042 (R-5): VF–EF $125–$200 • MS-63 $400–$600.

MI, Buchanan • Weaver & Fox • MI-090-A • *Stoves, tin, and hardware* • Ascribed to the shop of S.D. Childs • Reverse dies: 1105, 1110 • MI-090-A-2a Rev 1110 (R-3): VF–EF $50–$75 • MS-63 $300–$450 • Only token issuer of this town.

MI, Cassopolis • Boyd & Bradly • MI-135-A • *Grocers* • Dies by Henry D. Higgins • Reverse die: 1003 • MI-135-A-1a Rev 1003 (R-8): VF–EF $1,000–$1,500 • Only token issuer of this town.

MI, Charlotte • C. Cummings • MI-160-A • *Dry goods, groceries, boots, and shoes* • Ascribed to the shop of W.K. Lanphear • Reverse dies: 1168, 1225 • MI-160-A-1a Rev 1168 (R-6), MI-160-A-2a Rev 1225 (R-6): VF–EF $60–$90 • MS-63 $175–$250.

MI, Charlotte • Higby & Brother • MI-160-B • *General merchants* • Ascribed to the shop of W.K. Lanphear • Reverse die: 1225 • MI-160-B-1a Rev 1225 (R-6): VF–EF $75–$125 • MS-63 $250–$375.

MI, Charlotte • J. Mikesell & Bro. • MI-160-C • *Groceries and provisions* • Ascribed to the shop of W.K. Lanphear • Reverse die: 1225 • MI-160-C-1a Rev 1225 (R-5): VF–EF $60–$90 • MS-63 $175–$250.

MI, Charlotte • C.J. Piper • MI-160-D • *Groceries, boots, shoes, etc.* • Ascribed to the shop of W.K. Lanphear • Reverse die: 1317 • MI-160-D-1a Rev 1317 (R-5): VF–EF $75–$125 • MS-63 $250–$375.

MI, Chelsea • Congdon Brothers • MI-175-A • *Dry goods, groceries, hardware* • Dies by Alexander Gleason • Reverse dies: 1183A, 1186 • MI-175-A-2a Rev 1186 (R-6): VF–EF $250–$375 • MS-63 $1,000–$1,500 • Only token issuer of this town.[38]

MI, Clarkston • M.H. Clark • MI-180-A • *Dry goods, hardware, shoes* • Ascribed to the shop of John Stanton • Reverse dies: 1039, 1042, 1046, 1047, MI-180-A-1a Rev 1042 (R-5): VF–EF $30–$45 • MS-63 $125–$175.

MI, Clarkston • R. & J.T. Peter • MI-180-B • *Druggists* • Ascribed to the shop of John Stanton • Reverse dies: 1024, 1042, 1047 • MI-180-B-2a Rev 1042 (R-5): VF–EF $50–$75 • MS-63 $150–$225.

MI-185-A •
N.T. Waterman •
O-1 used with
MI-185-A-1.

MI-185-A •
N.T. Waterman •
O-2 used with
MI-185-A-2.

MI, Coldwater • N.T. Waterman • MI-185-A • *Books and jewelry* • Ascribed to the shop of S.D. Childs • Reverse die: 1111 • MI-185-A-1a Rev 1111 (R-8), MI-185-A-2a Rev 1111 (R-8): VF–EF $1,250–$1,750 • Only token issuer of this town.

MI-190-A •
E.H. Sheldon •
O-1 used with
MI-190-A-1 and 2.

MI-190-A •
E.H. Sheldon •
O-2 used with
MI-190-A-3.

MI-225-A •
W.J. Adderly •
O-2 used with
MI-225-A-4 to 8.

MI-225-A •
W.J. Adderly •
O-3 used with
MI-225-A-9.
Surname misspelled
as "Adderley."

MI, Constantine • E.H. Sheldon • MI-190-A • *Hardware dealer* **•** ? **•** Reverse dies: 24810, 24820 • MI-190-A-1a Rev 24810 (R-2): VF–EF $30–$45 • MS-63 $90–$135 • Only token issuer of this town.

MI, Corunna • H.A. Crane • MI-200-A • *Stoves and hardware* **•** Ascribed to the shop of S.D. Childs • Reverse dies: 1094, 1099, 1207 • MI-200-A-1a Rev 1094 (R-5), MI-200-A-3a Rev 1099 (R-5), MI-200-A-4a Rev 1207 (R-5): VF–EF $30–$45 • MS-63 $150–$225.

MI, Corunna • G.W. Goodell • MI-200-B • *Drugs and medicines* **•** Ascribed to the shop of S.D. Childs[39] • Reverse dies: 1094, 1097, 1099, 1357 • MI-200-B-1a Rev 1094 (R-4), MI-200-B-3a Rev 1097 (R-4), MI-200-B-4a Rev 1099 (R-4): VF–EF $30–$45 • MS-63 $150–$225.

MI-225-A •
W.J. Adderly •
O-1 used with
MI-225-A-1 to 3.
Surname misspelled
as "Adderley."

MI, Detroit • W.J. Adderly • MI-225-A • *Grocer* **•** Ascribed to the shop of John Stanton • Reverse dies: 1028, 1039, 1042, 1046, 1047, 1068, 1069 • MI-225-A-3a Rev 1069 (R-4): VF–EF $25–$35 • MS-63 $100–$150.

MI, Detroit • American Coffee Mills • MI-225-B • *Coffee mills* **•** Ascribed to the shop of John Stanton • Reverse dies: 1037, 1039, 1042, 1046, 1047 • MI-225-B-3a Rev 1042 (R-6): VF–EF $40–$60 • MS-63 $125–$175.

MI, Detroit • T.H. Armstrong • MI-225-C • *Dealer in hats, caps, and furs* **•** Ascribed to the shop of John Stanton • Reverse dies: 1025, 1042, 1046, 1047 • MI-225-C-1a Rev 1025 (R-6): VF–EF $50–$75 • MS-63 $175–$250 • *Clark's Annual Directory of . . . the City of Detroit, for 1863–4:* "Thomas H. Armstrong. Hats, caps and furs. 176 Jefferson Avenue; home at 558 Woodward Avenue."[40]

MI, Detroit • Blindbury's Hotel • MI-225-D • *Hotel* **•** Ascribed to the shop of John Stanton • Reverse dies: 1018, 1027, 1042, 1047, 1069 • MI-225-D-1a Rev 1018 (R-3): VF–EF $25–$35 • MS-63 $100–$150.

MI, Detroit • G. Bamlet • MI-225-E • *Grocer and produce dealer* **•** Ascribed to the shop of John Stanton • Reverse dies: 1039, 1042, 1046, 1047 • MI-225-E-1a Rev 1039 (R-6): VF–EF $50–$75 • MS-63 $150–$225.

MI, Detroit • L.W. Barie • MI-225-F • *Baker* • Ascribed to the shop of John Stanton • Reverse dies: 1019, 1024, 1037, 1042, 1046, 1047 • MI-225-F-3a Rev 1037 (R-4): VF–EF $25–$35 • MS-63 $100–$150.

MI, Detroit • George Beard & Son • MI-225-G • *Oyster, fruit, fish, and game depot* • Ascribed to the shop of John Stanton • Reverse dies: 1025, 1042, 1046, 1047 • MI-225-G-1a Rev 1025 (R-6): VF–EF $40–$60 • MS-63 $125–$175 • *Clark's Annual Directory of . . . the City of Detroit, for 1863–4:* "Beard, G. & Son (George and William L.). Oysters, fruit, etc. Russell House." George lived at 96 Michigan Avenue; William L. at 2 Abbott Street.

MI, Detroit • H.W. Beeson • MI-225-H • *Oyster, fruit, fish, and game depot* • Ascribed to the shop of John Stanton • Reverse dies: 1025, 1039, 1042, 1046, 1047 • MI-225-H-2a Rev 1039 (R-4): VF–EF $25–$35 • MS-63 $100–$150 • *Clark's Annual Directory of . . . the City of Detroit, for 1863–4:* "Henry W. Beeson, grocer, at 22 Woodward Avenue. Boarded at 139 Fort Street, West."

MI, Detroit • F.R. Behr • MI-225-I • *Saloon, bowling* • ? • Reverse die: 24940 • MI-225-I-1a Rev 24940 (R-8): VF–EF $3,000–$4,500 • *Clark's Annual Directory of . . . the City of Detroit, for 1863–4:* "94: Frederick Behr, saloon, 926 Jefferson Avenue."

MI, Detroit • Frederick C. Blome • MI-225-J • *Dry goods* • Ascribed to the shop of John Stanton • Reverse dies: 1042, 1047, 1069, 1370 • MI-225-J-4a Rev 1370 (R-5): VF–EF $35–$50 • MS-63 $125–$175.

MI, Detroit • Broeg & Gerber • MI-225-K • *Butchers* • Ascribed to the shop of John Stanton • Reverse dies: 1025, 1027, 1042, 1046, 1047 • MI-225-K-1a Rev 1025 (R-5): VF–EF $40–$60 • MS-63 $150–$225.

MI, Detroit • F.A. Burkhart • MI-225-L • *Butcher* • Ascribed to the shop of

John Stanton • Reverse dies: 1037, 1039, 1042, 1046, 1047 • MI-225-L-2a Rev 1039 (R-4): VF–EF $30–$45 • MS-63 $150–$225.

MI, Detroit • Charles Busch • MI-225-M • *Hardware, stoves, and grates* • Ascribed to the shop of John Stanton • Reverse dies: 1018, 1027, 1042, 1047, 1069 • MI-225-M-1a Rev 1018 (R-4): VF–EF $25–$35 • MS-63 $100–$150 • *Clark's Annual Directory of . . . the City of Detroit, for 1863–4:* "Charles Busch, dealer in hardware, housekeeping articles, mechanics' tools, stoves, nails, grates, tin and Japanned ware. Agent for the sale of the celebrated 'Dispatch' cooking stove. No. 201 Jefferson Ave., Kearsley's Block, Detroit, Mich."

MI, Detroit • Campbell & Calnon • MI-225-MA • *Grocers* • Ascribed to the shop of John Stanton • Reverse dies: 1037, 1039, 1042, 1046, 1047 • MI-225-Ma-2a Rev 1039 (R-5): VF–EF $35–$50 • MS-63 $150–$225.

MI-225-N • Campbell, Linn & Co. / Scotch Store • O-1 used with MI-225-N-1.

MI-225-N • Campbell, Linn & Co. •. / Scotch Store O-2 used with MI-225-N-2 to 4.

MI, Detroit • Campbell, Linn & Co. • MI-225-N • *Dry goods and millinery* • ? • Reverse dies: 25000, 25020, 25030 • MI-225-N-1a Rev 25000 (R-2): VF–EF $25–$35 • MS-63 $60–$90 • *Clark's Annual Directory of . . . the City of Detroit, for 1863–4:* "Scotch Store. Campbell, Linn & Co., wholesale and retail dealers in staple and fancy dry goods and millinery. Corner of Woodward Ave. & Congress St., Detroit."

MI, Detroit • H.A. Christiansen • MI-225-O • *Groceries and provisions* • Ascribed to the shop of John Stanton • Reverse dies: 1018, 1027, 1037, 1042, 1047, 1069 • MI-225-O-1a Rev 1018 (R-5): VF–EF $25–$35 • MS-63 $100–$150 • *Clark's Annual Directory of . . . the City of Detroit, for 1863–4:* "Hans A. Christiansen, grocer, 259 Jefferson Avenue. Home at 97 Larned Street, East."

MI, Detroit • G. & W. Clark • MI-225-P • *Butchers* • Ascribed to the shop of John Stanton • Reverse dies: 1037, 1039, 1042, 1046, 1047 • MI-225-P-2a Rev 1039 (R-5): VF–EF $50–$75 • MS-63 $150–$225 • *Clark's Annual Directory of . . . the City of Detroit, for 1863–4:* "George Clark, meat market, 122 Larned, West. Home at same address."

MI, Detroit • S. Cohen • MI-225-Q • *Clothing dealer* • Ascribed to the shop of John Stanton • Reverse dies: 1027, 1042, 1047, 1069 • MI-225-Q-1a Rev 1027 (R-5): VF–EF $50–$75 • MS-63 $150–$225 • *Clark's Annual Directory of . . . the City of Detroit, for 1863–4:* "Simon Cohen, 155 Jefferson Avenue,; home at 20 Lafayette. Clothier."

MI, Detroit • Alexander W. Copland • MI-225-R • *Steam bakery* • Ascribed to the shop of John Stanton[41] • Reverse dies: 1039, 1042, 1046, 1047 • MI-1a Rev 1039 (R-5): VF–EF $30–$45 • MS-63 $100–$150 • Copland resided at his business address.

MI, Detroit • C.L. Crosby • MI-225-S • *Fruit and produce dealer* • Ascribed to the shop of John Stanton • Reverse dies: 1039, 1042, 1046, 1047 • MI-225-S-1a Rev 1039 (R-5): VF–EF $30–$45 • MS-63 $100–$150 • *Clark's Annual Directory of . . . the City of Detroit, for 1863–4:* "C.L. Crosby & Co. (Charles L. Crosby and James L. Clough), commission and shipping, 160 Woodward Avenue."

MI, Detroit • Geo. E. Curtis • MI-225-T • *Leather and findings* • Ascribed to the shop of John Stanton • Reverse dies: 1027, 1042, 1047, 1069 • MI-225-T-1a Rev 1027 (R-4): VF–EF $25–$35 • MS-63 $100–$150.

MI, Detroit • Godfrey Dean & Co. • MI-225-U • *Painters, picture frame makers* • Ascribed to the shop of John Stanton • Reverse dies: 1037, 1039, 1042, 1047 • MI-225-U-1a Rev 1037 (R-5): VF–EF $25–$35 • MS-63 $100–$150 • *Clark's Annual Directory of . . . the City of Detroit, for 1863–4:* "Godfrey, Dean & Co. (Joseph Godfrey, Horace M. Dean, and Andrew J. Brow). Picture frame painting, etc. 48 Woodward Avenue. Horace M. Dean, partner, lived at 24 Palmer Street."

MI, Detroit • Detroit City Flour Mills • MI-225-V • *Flour mills* • Ascribed to the shop of John Stanton • Reverse dies: 1037, 1038, 1039, 1042, 1046, 1047 • MI-225-V-3a Rev 1039 (R-4): VF–EF $25–$35 • MS-63 $100–$150.

MI, Detroit • D. Dickson • MI-225-W • *Grocer and provision dealer* • Ascribed to the shop of John Stanton • Reverse dies: 1037, 1040, 1042, 1046, 1047 • MI-225-W-2a Rev 1040 (R-6): VF–EF $60–$90 • MS-63 $175–$250.

MI, Detroit • E.A. Drury • MI-225-X • *Grocer* • Ascribed to the shop of John Stanton • Reverse dies: 1025, 1042, 1046, 1047 • MI-225-1a Rev 1025 (R-4): VF–EF $25–$35 • MS-63 $100–$150 • Drury boarded at 231 Woodward Avenue.

MI, Detroit • Francis Eccard • MI-225-Y • *Tobacconist* • Ascribed to the shop of John Stanton • Reverse dies: 1024, 1037, 1039, 1042, 1046, 1047 • MI-225-Y-1a Rev 1024 (R-3): VF–EF $30–$45 • MS-63 $100–$150 • *Clark's Annual Directory of . . . the City of Detroit, for 1863–4:* "Francis Eccard, tobacco manufacturer, 126 and 128 Randolph. Home at 128 Randolph."

MI, Detroit • William Eisenlord, Peninsular Hotel • MI-225-Z • *Hotelkeeper*[42] • Ascribed to the shop of John Stanton • Reverse: dies 1037, 1039, 1042, 1047 •

MI-225-Z-2a Rev 1039 (R-6): VF–EF $40–$60 • MS-63 $150–$225.

MI, Detroit • Farmers Clothing Store (John Schroder & Co.) • MI-225-AA • *Clothing, hats, and caps* • Ascribed to the shop of John Stanton • Reverse dies: 1042, 1046, 1047 • MI-225-AA-1a Rev 1042 (R-7): VF–EF $100–$150 • MS-63 $300–$450 • John Schroder & Co. operated the Farmers Clothing Store at 251 Gratiot during the Civil War. Schroder & Co. (MI-225-BO) and the Farmers Clothing Store (MI-225-AA) are one and the same.[43] In the third edition of the Fuld book MI-225-A will disappear and will be merged into MI-225-BO.

MI, Detroit • C. Fitzsimons & Co. • MI-225-AB • *Grocer* • Ascribed to the shop of John Stanton • Reverse dies: 1039, 1042, 1046, 1047 • MI-225-AB-1a Rev 1039 (R-4): VF–EF $25–$35 • MS-63 $100–$150.

MI, Detroit • L.S. Freeman • MI-225-AC • *News dealer* • Ascribed to the shop of John Stanton • Reverse dies: 1024, 1025, 1036, 1042, 1046, 1047 • MI-225-AC-2a Rev 1025 (R-6): VF–EF $35–$50 • MS-63 $150–$225.

MI-225-AD • Frisbie's • O-1 used with MI-225-AD-1.

MI-225-AD • Frisbie's • O-2 used with MI-225-AD-2.

MI, Detroit • Frisbie's • MI-225-AD • *Dry goods* • ? • Custom reverse die on both varieties • MI-225-AD-2b (R-2): VF–EF $25–$35 • MS-63 $60-$90.

MI, Detroit • F. Geis & Bro's • MI-225-AE • *Roofing, boots and shoes, hay, groceries, etc. (See dies)* • Ascribed to the shop of John Stanton • Reverse dies: 1037,

1042, 1043, 1047 • MI-225-AE-3a Rev 1043 (R-5): VF–EF $30–$45 • MS-63 $100–$150 • See "The Curious Dies of the Family Gies" in chapter 5. Different reworkings of just two different dies resulted in *five* separate entries in the Fuld book. The third edition will consolidate these into just two headings—one for F. Gies and the other for F. Gies & Bros.

MI, Detroit • F. Geiss & Bro's • MI-225-AF • *Roofing, boots and shoes, hay, groceries, etc. (See dies)* • Ascribed to the shop of John Stanton • Reverse dies: 1042, 25240 • MI-225-AF-2a Rev 25240 (R-4): VF–EF $30–$45 • MS-63 $100–$150.

MI, Detroit • F. Geiss • MI-225-AFa • *Roofing, boots and shoes, hay, groceries, etc. (See dies)* • Ascribed to the shop of John Stanton • Reverse dies: 1037, 1042, 1046, 1047 • MI-225-AFa-3a Rev 1042 (R-7): VF–EF $30–$45 • MS-63 $100–$150.

MI, Detroit • F. Gies & Bro's • MI-225-AG • *Roofing, boots and shoes, hay, groceries, etc. (See dies)* • Ascribed to the shop of John Stanton • Reverse dies: 1037, 1046, 1047 • MI-225-AG-1a Rev 1037 (R-4): VF–EF $25–$35 • MS-63 $100–$150.

MI, Detroit • F. Gies • MI-225-AGa • *Roofing, boots and shoes, hay, groceries, etc. (See dies)* • Ascribed to the shop of John Stanton • Reverse dies: 1018, 1042, 1047, 1069 • MI-225-AGa-3a Rev 1018 (R-5): VF–EF $25–$35 • MS-63 $100–$150.

MI, Detroit • C.B. Goodrich • MI-225-AH • *Boots and shoes* • Ascribed to the shop of John Stanton[44] • Reverse dies: 1037, 1040, 1042, 1046, 1047 • MI-225-AH-3a Rev 1042 (R-7): VF–EF $75–$125 • MS-63 $200–$300.

MI, Detroit • F. Hamman & Co. • MI-225-AI • *Liquor store* • Ascribed to the shop of John Stanton • Reverse dies: 1039, 1042, 1047 • MI-225-AI-1a Rev 1039 (R-5): VF–EF $30–$45 • MS-63 $100–$150.

MI, Detroit • Hanna & Co. • MI-225-AJ • *Wholesale tobacconists* • Ascribed to the shop of John Stanton • Reverse dies: 1025, 1037, 1042, 1047 • MI-225-AJ-1a Rev 1025 (R-7), MI-225-AJ-3a Rev 1042 (R-7): VF–EF $60–$90 • MS-63 $250–$375.

MI, Detroit • Heinman's • MI-225 AJa • *Clothing store* • Ascribed to the shop of John Stanton • Reverse dies: 1025, 1042, 1047 • MI-225-AJa-1a Rev 1025 (R-6): VF–EF $75–$125 • MS-63 $250–$375.

MI, Detroit • Herintons Double Thread Sewing Machine • MI-225-AK • *Sewing machine* • Ascribed to the shop of S.D. Childs[45] • Reverse die: 1106 • MI-225-AK-1a Rev 1106 (R-4): VF–EF $30–$45 • MS-63 $150–$225 • Surname should have been spelled Herrinton.[46]

MI, Detroit • Higby & Stearns • MI-225-AL • *Druggists* • Ascribed to the shop of John Stanton • Reverse dies: 1025, 1042, 1047, 25317 • MI-225-AL-1a Rev 1025 (R-4): VF–EF $30–$45 • MS-63 $150–$225 • *Clark's Annual Directory of . . . the City of Detroit, for 1863–4:* "Higby & Stearns, wholesale druggists, dealers in drugs, chemicals, and pharmaceutical preparations, surgical & dental instruments, and miscellaneous articles used by the medical and dental profession. Manufacturers of perfumery and toilet articles, and various goods for domestic and culinary purposes. Priced catalogues sent on application."

MI, Detroit • Hilterscheid Bro's • MI-225-AM • *Meat market* • Ascribed to the shop of John Stanton • Reverse dies: 1039, 1042, 1047 • MI-225-AM-1a Rev 1039 (R-5): VF–EF $30–$45 • MS-63 $100–$150.

MI, Detroit • Jacob Hochstadt • MI-225-AN • *Butcher* • Ascribed to the shop of John Stanton • Reverse dies: 1040, 1042, 1047 • MI-225-AN-1a Rev 1040 (R-7), MI-225-AN-2a Rev 1042 (R-7): VF–EF $50–$75 • MS-63 $150–$225.

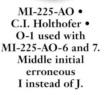

MI-225-AO • C.I. Holthofer • O-1 used with MI-225-AO-6 and 7. Middle initial erroneous I instead of J.	MI-225-AO • C.J. Holthofer • O-1 used with MI-225-AO-1 to 5. Reworked die O-1 now reading correctly.

MI, Detroit • C.J. Holthofer • MI-225-AO • *Dry goods* • Ascribed to the shop of John Stanton[47] • Reverse dies: 1024, 1037, 1039, 1042, 1047 • MI-225-AO-1a Rev 1024 (R-5), MI-225-AO-2a Rev 1037 (R-5): VF–EF $25–$35 • MS-63 $100–$150 • One obverse die with error spelling, reworked. Fuld SC2 issue included incomplete information. *Clark's Annual Directory of . . . the City of Detroit, for 1863–4:* "Caspar J. Holthœfer [oe as a ligature œ, equivalent to ö, pronounced as long o, Anglicized to o on token], dry goods, 120 St. Antoine Street. Home at 28 Fort Street."

MI, Detroit • William B. Howe • MI-225-AP • *Bookseller* • Ascribed to the shop of John Stanton • Reverse dies: 1027, 1042, 1047 • MI-225-AP-1a Rev 1027 (R-5): VF–EF $40–$60 • MS-63 $175–$250.

MI, Detroit • Edward Kanter • MI-225-AQ • *Groceries, produce, ship chandler* • Ascribed to the shop of John Stanton • Reverse dies: 1025, 1042, 1047 • MI-225-AQ-1a Rev 1025 (R-7), MI-225-AQ-2a Rev 1042 (R-7): VF–EF $100–$150 • MS-63 $300–$450 • *Clark's Annual Directory of . . . the City of Detroit, for 1863–4:* "Edward Kanter, wholesale dealer in groceries, produce, and ship chandlery. Manufacturer of twine and cordage, Nos. 4 and 6 Woodward Avenue."

MI, Detroit • P.N. Kneeland • MI-225-AR • *Dealer in stoves and tinware* • ? • Reverse dies: 1037, 1040, 1042, 1047 • MI-225-AR-2a Rev 1040 (R-7), MI-225-AR-3a Rev 1042 (R-7): VF–EF $60–$90 • MS-63 $250–$375.

MI, Detroit • Lapham & Thayer • MI-225-AS • *New and used furniture* • ? • Reverse dies: 1040, 1042, 1047 • MI-225-AS-1a Rev 1040 (R-6): VF–EF $60–$90 • MS-63 $200–$300.

MI, Detroit • Lewis & Moses • MI-225-AT • *Crockery and glassware* • ? • Reverse dies: 1018, 1024, 1025, 1027, 1042, 1047 • MI-225-AT-2a Rev 1024 (R-6), MI-225-AT-3a Rev 1025 (R-6): VF–EF $50–$75 • MS-63 $150–$225.

MI, Detroit • C. Lotz • MI-225-AU • *Grocer* • Ascribed to the shop of John Stanton • Reverse dies: 1037, 1040, 1042, 1047 • MI-225-AU-2a Rev 1040 (R-7), MI-3a Rev 1042 (R-7): VF–EF $90–$135 • MS-63 $250–$375.

MI, Detroit • Martin Bro's • MI-225-AV • *Cheap boot and shoe store* • Ascribed to the shop of John Stanton • Reverse dies: 1042, 1047, 1069 • MI-225-AV-1a Rev 1042 (R-8), MI-225-AV-1b Rev 1042 (R-8): VF–EF $150–$225 • MS-63 $500–$750.

MI, Detroit • M. Marx • MI-225-AW • *Grocer and liquor dealer* • Ascribed to the shop of John Stanton • Reverse dies: 1037, 1039, 1042, 1047 • MI-225-AW-2a Rev 1039 (R-7): VF–EF $75–$110 • MS-63 $200–$300.

MI, Detroit • Mather & Shefferly • MI-225-AX • *Crockery store* • Ascribed to the shop of John Stanton • Reverse dies: 1025, 1037, 1040, 1042, 1047 • MI-225-AX-2a Rev 1037 (R-3): VF–EF $25–$35 • MS-63 $100–$150.

MI, Detroit • Messmore & Lucking • MI-225-AY • *Butchers* • Ascribed to the shop of John Stanton • Reverse dies: 1039, 1042, 1047 • MI-225-AY-1a Rev 1039 (R-6): VF–EF $50–$75 • MS-63 $150–$225.

MI, Detroit • Robert Millar • MI-225-AZ • *Grocer and liquor dealer* • Ascribed to the shop of John Stanton • Reverse dies: 1025, 1042, 1047 • MI-225-AZ-1a Rev 1025 (R-4): VF–EF $25–$35 • MS-63 $100–$150.

MI, Detroit • George Moe • MI-225-BA • *Grocer and liquor dealer* • Ascribed to the shop of John Stanton • Reverse dies: 1037, 1039, 1042, 1047 • MI-225-BA-2a Rev 1039 (R-6): VF–EF $40–$60 • MS-63 $150–$225 • *Clark's Annual Directory of . . . the City of Detroit, for 1863–4:* "George Moe, grocer, 98 Woodward Avenue. Home at 233 Congress Street."

MI, Detroit • George H. Parker • MI-225-BB • *Dealer in hides, leather, and wool* • ? • Reverse dies: 1037, 1040, 1042, 1047 • MI-225-BB-2a Rev 1040 (R-7): VF–EF $100–$150 • MS-63 $300–$450.

MI, Detroit • Perkins Hotel • MI-225-BC • *Hotel* • Ascribed to the shop of John Stanton[48] • Reverse dies: 1042, 1047, 1069 • MI-225-BC-1a Rev 1042 (R-7): VF–EF $100–$150 • MS-63 $350–$500.

MI, Detroit • W. Perkins • MI-225-BD • *Grocer and provision dealer* • Ascribed to the shop of John Stanton • Reverse dies: 1037, 1042, 1047, 25490 • MI-225-BD-4a Rev 25490 (R-6): VF–EF $75–$125 • MS-63 $250–$375 • *Clark's Annual Directory of . . . the City of Detroit, for 1863–4:* "William Perkins, Jr. Groceries and provisions. 102 Grand River. Home at Perkins' Hotel."

MI, Detroit • G.C. Pond • MI-225-BE • *Grocer and provision dealer* • Ascribed to the shop of John Stanton • Reverse dies: 1024, 1025, 1030, 1037, 1039, 1042, 1047 • MI-225-BE-6b Rev 1042 (R-7): VF–EF $60–$90 • MS-63 $200–$300.

MI, Detroit • F. Prouty • MI-225-BF • *Grocer and provision dealer* • Ascribed to the shop of John Stanton • Reverse dies: 1040, 1042, 1047 • MI-225-BF-1a Rev 1040 (R-7), MI-225-BF-2a Rev 1042 (R-7): VF–EF $75–$125 • MS-63 $250–$375.

MI, Detroit • Randal's Photographic Gallery • MI-225-BG • *Photographic gallery* • Ascribed to the shop of John Stanton • Reverse dies: 1037, 1040, 1042, 1047 • MI-225-BG-2a Rev 1040 (R-7), MI-225-BG-3a Rev 1042 (R-7): VF–EF $100–$150 • MS-63 $400–$600 • The surname was misspelled and should have been Randall.[49] Corydon C. Randall, proprietor.

MI, Detroit • Raymond's Photograph Gallery • MI-225-BH • *Photographic gallery* • Ascribed to the shop of John Stanton • Reverse dies: 1040, 1042, 1047 • MI-225-BH-1a Rev 1040 (R-7), MI-225-BH-2a Rev 1042 (R-7): VF–EF $100–$150 • MS-63 $400–$600.

MI, Detroit • Joseph Riggs • MI-225-BI • *Groceries, provisions, flour* • Ascribed to the shop of John Stanton • Reverse dies: 1039, 1042, 1047 • MI-225-BI-1a Rev 1039 (R-4): VF–EF $30–$45 • MS-63 $100–$150 • *Clark's Annual Directory of . . . the City of Detroit, for 1863–4:* "Joseph Riggs. Grocery. 251 Jefferson Avenue and 70 Gratiot Avenue. Residence at 251 Jefferson Avenue."

MI, Detroit • J.A. Rodier • MI-225-BJ • *Boot and shoe dealer* • Ascribed to the shop of John Stanton • Reverse dies: 1037, 1039, 1042, 1047 • MI-225-BJ-3a Rev 1042 (R-7): VF–EF $75–$125 • MS-63 $250–$375 • *Clark's Annual Directory of . . . the City of Detroit, for 1863–4:* "Joseph A. Rodier, boots and shoes, corner of Campus Martius and Michigan Grand Avenue. Home at 46 High Street."

MI, Detroit • Alonzo Rolfe • MI-225-BK • *Produce, fruit, and commission merchant* • Ascribed to the shop of John Stanton • Reverse dies: 1039, 1042, 1047 • MI-225-BK-1a Rev 1039 (R-6): VF–EF $40–$60 • MS-63 $125–$175 • *Clark's*

Annual Directory of . . . the City of Detroit, for 1863–4: "Produce, fruit, and commission merchant. 5 and 6 Russell House Block. Home: 28 Sibley Street."

MI, Detroit • Dr. L.C. Rose • MI-225-BL • *Gynecologist treating "chronic female & venereal diseases."* • Ascribed to the shop of John Stanton • Reverse dies: 1037, 1039, 1042, 1047 • MI-225-BL-2a Rev 1039 (R-6): VF–EF $400–$600 • MS-63 $1,250–$1,750 • Only Civil War token of this medical specialty. Levi C. Rose. Office in his home at 27 Lafayette Street.

MI, Detroit • M. Rosenberger • MI-225-BM • *Ready-made clothing* • Ascribed to the shop of John Stanton • Reverse dies: 1037, 1039, 1040, 1042, 1047 • MI-225-BM-3a Rev 1042 (R-7), MI-225-BM-5a Rev 1040 (R-7): VF–EF $75–$125 • MS-63 $300–$450.

MI, Detroit • J. Schmidt • MI-225-BN • *Grocer* • Ascribed to the shop of John Stanton • Reverse dies: 1025, 1042, 1047 • MI-225-BN-1a Rev 1025 (R-4): VF–EF $25–$35 • MS-63 $100–$150.

MI, Detroit • John Schroder & Co. (Farmers Clothing Store) • MI-225-BO • *Clothing, hats, and caps* • Ascribed to the shop of John Stanton • Reverse dies: 1018, 1042, 1047, 1069, 25160 • MI-225-BO-4a Rev 25160 (R-3): VF–EF $25–$35 • MS-63 $100–$150 • John Schroder & Co. operated the Farmers Clothing Store at 251 Gratiot during the Civil War. Schroder & Co. (MI-225-BO) and the Farmers Clothing Store (MI-225-AA) are one and the same.[50] In the third edition of the Fuld book MI-225-AA will disappear and will be merged into MI-225-BO. *Clark's Annual Directory of . . . the City of Detroit, for 1863–4:* "John Schroder and Christian Kareckel, clothing, hat and boot store. 251 and 253 Gratiot Street."

MI, Detroit • H.A. Sealy • MI-225-BP • *Butcher* • Ascribed to the shop of John Stanton • Reverse dies: 1037, 1040, 1042, 1047 • MI-225-BP-3a Rev 1042 (R-7): VF–EF $40–$60 • MS-63 $125–$175.

MI, Detroit • Cheap John Seeley • MI-225-BQ • *Second-hand furniture* • Ascribed to the shop of John Stanton • Reverse dies: 1037, 1039, 1042, 1047 • MI-225-BQ-2a Rev 1039 (R-6): VF–EF $40–$60 • MS-63 $125–$175 • *Detroit Free Press*, October 15, 1859: "John Seeley, proprietor of a one-horse auction establishment near City Hall Market, was arrested for passing counterfeit money."[51] "The second-hand furniture dealers 'Cheap John' (John Seeley), and the golden-ball rooms have occupied rooms for a long time in the long, low rakish building used as a railroad station, now in the heart of the city." *Clark's Annual Directory of . . . the City of Detroit, for 1863–4:* "John Seeley. Auctions. 11 and 13 Michigan Avenue. Home at same address."

MI, Detroit • J.B. Shagnon • MI-225-BR • *Grocer and provision dealer* • Ascribed to the shop of John Stanton • Reverse dies: 1040, 1042, 1047 • MI-225-BR-2a Rev 1042 (R-7): VF–EF $75–$125 • MS-63 $200–$300.

MI, Detroit • E.B. Smith • MI-225-BS • *Bookseller and stationer* • Ascribed to the shop of John Stanton • Reverse dies: 1025, 1042, 1047 • MI-225-BS-1a Rev 1025 (R-7), MI-225-BS-2a Rev 1042 (R-7): VF–EF $75–$125 • MS-63 $200–$300.

MI, Detroit • Seth Smith & Son • MI-225-BT • *Barrels and tea boxes* • ? • Reverse die: 25670 • MI-225-BT-1a Rev 25670 (R-9): VF–EF $12,500–$17,500.

MI, Detroit • William B. Smith • MI-225-BU • *Butcher* • Ascribed to the shop of John Stanton • Reverse dies: 1040, 1042, 1046, 1047 • MI-225-BU-1a Rev 1040 (R-5): VF–EF $30–$45 • MS-63 $100–$150.

MI, Detroit • Yankee Smith's Saloon • MI-225-BV • *Saloon* • Ascribed to the shop of John Stanton • Reverse dies: 1025, 1037, 1039, 1042, 1047 • MI-225-BV-2a Rev 1039 (R-5): VF–EF $35–$50 • MS-63 $125–$175.

MI, Detroit • George Snooks Fish Depot • MI-225-BW • *Fish dealer* • Ascribed to the shop of John Stanton • Reverse dies: 1037, 1040, 1042, 1047 • MI-225-BW-1a Rev 1040 (R-7), MI-225-BW-2a Rev 1042 (R-7): VF–EF $50–$75 • MS-63 $150–$225.

MI, Detroit • William Snow, Detroit Wire Works • MI-225-BX • *Wire cloth, hardware, cutlery* • Ascribed to the shop of John Stanton • Reverse dies: 1039, 1042, 1047, ? • MI-225-BX-1a Rev 1039 (R-4): VF–EF $30–$45 • MS-63 $125–$175 • *Clark's Annual Directory of . . . the City of Detroit, for 1863-4:* "Detroit Wire Works, Russell House Block, 102 Woodward Avenue. William Snow, manufacturer and dealer in iron, brass & copper wire cloth, brass, copper, steel and iron wire, burr mill stones, bolting cloths, hardware, table and pocket cutlery, nails, glass, pumps, lead pipe, etc."

MI, Detroit • J.D. & C.B. Standish • MI-225-BY • *Pork and wool dealers* • Die is of a high degree of workmanship; unknown maker, possibly in New England • Reverse die: 25725 • MI-225-BY-1a Rev 25725 (R-2): VF–EF $25–$35 • MS-63 $50–$75 • *Clark's Annual Directory of . . . the City of Detroit, for 1863–4:* "John D. Standish. Home: 10 High Street. John D. Standish and David H. Cornell, J.D. Standish & Co., packers, 38 Michigan Grand Avenue."

MI, Detroit • L.J. Staples • MI-225-BZ • *Wholesale grocer and confectioner* • Ascribed to the shop of John Stanton • Reverse dies: 1024, 1025, 1037, 1042, 1047 • MI-225-BZ-1a Rev 1024 (R-7), MI-225-BZ-4a Rev 1042 (R-7): VF–EF $40–$60 • MS-63 $125–$175.

MI, Detroit • Goff Stenton • MI-225-CA • *Meat market* • Ascribed to the shop of John Stanton • Reverse dies: 1039, 1042, 1046, 1047 • MI-225-CA-1a Rev 1039 (R-5): VF–EF $30–$45 • MS-63 $100–$150.

MI, Detroit • Mrs. A. Stringer • MI-225-CB • *Dry goods, millinery, and dress making* • Ascribed to the shop of John Stanton • Reverse dies: 1039, 1042, 1046, 1047 • MI-225-CB-1a Rev 1039 (R-7), MI-225-CB-2a Rev 1042 (R-7): VF–EF $100–$150 • MS-63 $300–$450.

MI, Detroit • G.W. Sutherland • MI-225-CC • *Grocer* • Ascribed to the shop of John Stanton • Reverse dies: 1024, 1025, 1042, 1047 • MI-225-CC-2a Rev 1025 (R-5): VF–EF $25–$35 • MS-63 $100–$150.

MI, Detroit • I. & C. Taylor • MI-225-CD • *Grocers and provision dealers* • Ascribed to the shop of John Stanton • Reverse dies: 1039, 1042, 1047 • MI-225-CD-2a Rev 1042 (R-7): VF–EF $90–$135 • MS-63 $250–$375 • *Clark's Annual Directory of . . . the City of Detroit, for 1863–4:* "Charles Taylor, retail grocer, 86 Grand River; home at same address."

MI, Detroit • The Tea Store • MI-225-CE • *Tea store* • Ascribed to the shop of John Stanton • Reverse dies: 1039, 1042, 1047 • MI-225-CE-1a Rev 1039 (R-6): VF–EF $60–$90 • MS-63 $175–$250.

MI, Detroit • W.E. Tunis • MI-225-CF • *News dealer* • Ascribed to the shop of John Stanton • Reverse dies: 1040, 1042, 1047 • MI-225-CF-1a Rev 1040 (R-6): VF–EF $150–$225 • MS-63 $500–$750 • The token notes that Tunis had branches in Detroit, Clifton C.W. (Canada West), and Milwaukee; attribution to Michigan is per the first city listed on the token.[52]

MI, Detroit • Turner, Hubbell & Co • MI-225-CG • *Boot and shoe manufacturers* • Ascribed to the shop of John Stanton • Reverse dies: 1024, 1027, 1042, 1047 • MI-225-CG-2a Rev 1027 (R-6): VF–EF $60–$90 • MS-63 $225–$350 • W.W. Cogswell and C.C. Tyler, 88 Woodward Avenue.

MI, Detroit • C.C. Tyler & Co. • MI-225-CH • *Boots and shoes* • ? • Reverse die: 25820 • MI-225-CH-1a Rev 25820 (R-6): VF–EF $100–$150 • MS-63 $350–$500.

MI-225-CI •
R.G. Tyler •
O-1 used with
MI-225-CI-1.

MI-225-CI •
R.G. Tyler •
O-2 used with
MI-225-CI-2.

MI, Detroit • R.G. Tyler • MI-225-CI • *Wholesale grocer* • ? • Reverse die: 1367 • MI-225-CI-2a Rev 1367 (R-3): VF–EF $25–$35 • MS-63 $50–$75.

MI, Detroit • Venn & Wreford • MI-225-CJ • *Butchers* • Ascribed to the shop of John Stanton • Reverse dies: 1037, 1039, 1042, 1047 • MI-225-CJ-4a Rev 1039 (R-5): VF–EF $30–$45 • MS-63 $100–$150.

MI, Detroit • Ward's Lake Superior Line. Steamer Planet • MI-225-CJa • *Steamboat* • Ascribed to the shop of John Stanton • Reverse dies: 1024, 1042, 1046, 1047 • MI-225-CJa-1a Rev 1024 (R-6): VF–EF $200–$300 • MS-63 $600–$900 • Earlier listed as OH-175-Q.[53]

MI-225-CK •
Henry Weber •
O-1 used with
MI-225-CK-1 to 5.

MI-225-CK •
Henry Weber •
O-2 used with
MI-225-CK-6 to 8.

MI, Detroit • Henry Weber • MI-225-CK • *Furniture dealer* • Ascribed to the shop of John Stanton • Reverse dies: 1018, 1024, 1037, 1042, 1047 • MI-225-CK-2a Rev 1024 (R-7), MI-225-CK-4a Rev 1042 (R-7), MI-225-CK-6a Rev 1040 (R-7): VF–EF $50–$75 • MS-63 $150–$225 • *Clark's Annual Directory of . . . the City of Detroit, for 1863–4* featured an elaborate full-page spread with much text about the Weber business.

MI, Detroit • B. Webster • MI-225-CL • *Fish dealer* • Ascribed to the shop of John Stanton • Reverse dies: 1039, 1042, 1047 • MI-225-CL-1a Rev 1039 (R-5): VF–EF $40–$60 • MS-63 $150–$225.

MI, Detroit • W.W. Whitlark with Grover & Baker Sewing Machine Co. • MI-225-CM • *Sewing machine dealer* • Ascribed to the shop of John Stanton[54] • Reverse dies: 1039, 1040, 1042, 1047 • MI-225-CM-1a Rev 1039 (R-7), MI-225-CM-3a Rev 1042 (R-7): VF–EF $50–$75 • MS-63 $175–$250 • *Clark's Annual Directory of . . . the City of Detroit, for 1863–4*, front cover, ran a notice for Grover & Baker's showroom at 121 Woodward Avenue, Detroit, without mention of Whitlark.

MI, Detroit • Wilkins & Martins Celebrated Ink & Blacking Depot • MI-225-CN • *Ink and blacking* • Ascribed to the shop of John Stanton • Reverse dies: 1042, 1047, 25420 • MI-225-CN-3a Rev 25420 (R-5): VF–EF $40–$60 • MS-63 $150–$225.

MI, Detroit • J.W. Winckler • MI-225-CO • *Baker* • Ascribed to the shop of John Stanton • Reverse dies: 1037, 1039, 1042, 1047 • MI-225-CO-2a Rev 1039 (R-4): VF–EF $25–$35 • MS-63 $100–$150.

MI, Detroit • F.M. Wing • MI-225-CP • *Grocer and commission merchant* • Ascribed to the shop of John Stanton • Reverse dies: 1037, 1039, 1042, 1047 • MI-225-CP-2a Rev 1039 (R-6): VF–EF $50–$75 • MS-63 $150–$225.

MI, Detroit • G. Winter • MI-225-CQ • *Hatter* • Ascribed to the shop of John Stanton • Reverse dies: 1025, 1042, 1047 • MI-225-CQ-1a Rev 1025 (R-7), MI-225-CQ-2a Rev 1042 (R-7): VF–EF $90–$135 • MS-63 $250–$375.

MI, Detroit • A. Witgen • MI-225-CR • *Groceries, meat market* • Ascribed to the shop of John Stanton • Reverse dies: 1037, 1039, 1042, 1047 • MI-225-CR-2a Rev 1039 (R-4): VF–EF $30–$45 • MS-63 $100–$150 • *Clark's Annual Directory of . . . the City of Detroit, for 1863–4:* "Anthony Witgen, grocer, northeast corner of Hastings and Franklin streets. Home at same address."

MI, Detroit • Henry Wolff • MI-225-CS • *Trunk manufactory* • Ascribed to the shop of John Stanton • Reverse dies: 1018, 1019, 1024, 1027, 1042, 1047, 1069 • MI-225-CS-1a Rev 1018 (R-3): VF–EF $25–$35 • MS-63 $100–$150.

MI, Dowagiac • A.N. Alward • MI-250-A • *Books, stationery, wallpaper* • Ascribed to the shop of S.D. Childs • Reverse dies: 1094, 1357 • MI-250-A-1a Rev 1094 (R-7): VF–EF $150–$225 • MS-63 $600–$900.

MI, Dowagiac • Andrews & Cooper • MI-250-B • *Family groceries and provisions* • Ascribed to the shop of S.D. Childs • Reverse dies: 1105, 1106, 1107, 1205 • MI-250-B2a Rev 1106 (R-6), MI-250-B-4a Rev 1205 (R-6): VF–EF $75–$125 • MS-63 $500–$750.

MI, Dowagiac • A.M. Dickson & Co. • MI-250-C • *Dry goods, clothing, shoes* • Ascribed to the shop of S.D. Childs • Reverse dies: 1099, 1101, 1107, 1205 • MI-250-C-1a Rev 1099 (R-7), MI-250-C-3a Rev 1107 (R-7): VF–EF $100–$150 • MS-63 $500–$750.

MI, Dowagiac • D. Larzelere & Co. • MI-250-D • *Dry goods, groceries, and clothing* • Ascribed to the shop of S.D. Childs • Reverse dies: 1094, 1105 • MI-250-D-1a Rev 1094 (R-5): VF–EF $90–$135 • MS-63 $400–$600.

MI, Dowagiac • D. Pond • MI-250-E • *Grocer and confectioner* • Ascribed to the shop of S.D. Childs • Reverse dies: 1094, 1105 • MI-250-E-1a Rev 1094 (R-8): VF–EF $1,250–$1,750 • MS-63 $4,000–$6,000.

MI, Dowagiac • G.A. Wheelock • MI-250-F • *Groceries and provisions* • Ascribed to the shop of S.D. Childs • Reverse dies: 1094, 1205 • MI-250-F-1a Rev 1094 (R-8), MI-250-F-2a Rev 1205 (R-8): VF–EF $500–$750 • MS-63 $1,500–$2,250.

MI, East Saginaw • Charles W. Bernacki • MI-280-A • *Druggist* • Ascribed to the shop of S.D. Childs • Reverse dies: 1099, 1101, 1390 • MI-280-A-2a Rev 1101 (R-5): VF–EF $100–$150 • MS-63 $500–$750.

MI, East Saginaw • N.W. Clark & Co. • MI-280-B • *Merchants* • Ascribed to the shop of John Stanton • Reverse dies: 1039, 1042, 1046, 1047 • MI-280-B-1a Rev 1039 (R-4): VF–EF $50–$75 • MS-63 $150–$225.

MI, East Saginaw • S.T. Leggett • MI-280-C • *Watchmaker and jeweler* • Ascribed to the shop of S.D. Childs • Reverse die: 1211 • MI-280-C-1a Rev 1211 (R-6): VF–EF $200–$300 • MS-63 $500–$750.

MI, East Saginaw • John McKay • MI-280-D • *Oyster, fruit, and fish depot* • Ascribed to the shop of John Stanton[55] • Reverse dies: 1039, 1042, 1047 • MI-280-D-1a Rev 1038 (R-6): VF–EF $90–$135 • MS-63 $250–$375.

MI, East Saginaw • A. Schmitz • MI-280-E • *Dealer in iron, nails, stoves, crockery, and paint* • Ascribed to the shop of S.D. Childs • Reverse dies: 26070, 1458, 1390 • MI-280-E-1a Rev 26070 (R-4): VF–EF $60–$90 • MS-63 $250–$375.

MI, East Saginaw • Charles Turner • MI-280-G • *Dealer in furs and skins* • Ascribed to the shop of S.D. Childs • Reverse die: 1101 • MI-280-G-1a Rev 1101 (R-7): VF–EF $500–$750.

MI, Eaton Rapids • A.C. Dutton M.D. • MI-300-A • *Books, stationery, and groceries* • Ascribed to the shop of W.K. Lanphear • Reverse die: 1310 • MI-300-A-1a Rev 1310 (R-6): VF–EF $75–$125 • MS-63 $300–$450.

MI, Eaton Rapids • H.M. Frost • MI-300-B • *Druggist and grocer* • Ascribed to the shop of W.K. Lanphear • Reverse die: 1310 • MI-300-B-1a Rev 1310 (R-5): VF–EF $50–$75 • MS-63 $200–$300.

MI, Eaton Rapids • Frost & Daniels • MI-300-C • *Dry goods, groceries, boots, shoes, etc.* • Ascribed to the shop of W.K. Lanphear • Reverse die: 1225 • MI-300-C-1a Rev 1225 (R-5): VF–EF $50–$75 • MS-63 $150–$225.

MI, Eaton Rapids • P. Leonard • MI-300-D • *Dry goods, groceries, boots, and shoes* • Ascribed to the shop of W.K. Lanphear • Reverse die: 1168 • MI-300-D-1a Rev 1168 (R-6): VF–EF $60–$90 • MS-63 $250–$375.

MI, Eaton Rapids • A. Mester & Co. • MI-300-E • *Marble works* • Ascribed to the shop of W.K. Lanphear • Reverse die: 1340 • MI-300-E-1a Rev 1340 (R-5): VF–EF $300–$450 • MS-63 $1,000–$1,500.

MI, Eaton Rapids • William F. Stirling • MI-300-F • *Dry goods, tea* • Ascribed to the shop of W.K. Lanphear • Reverse die: 1471 • MI-300-F-1a Rev 1471 (R-3): VF–EF $40–$60 • MS-63 $150–$225 • Reverse with stock die, "The Celebrated Tea Establishment."

MI, Flint • Giles Bishop • MI-320-A • *Groceries and liquors* • ? • Reverse die: 1315A • MI-320-A-1a Rev 1315A (R-8): VF–EF $30–$45 • MS-63 $125–$175.

MI, Flint • Clark's • MI-320-B • *Drugs, medicines, and groceries* • Ascribed to the shop of S.D. Childs • Reverse dies: 1101, 1205 • MI-320-B-1a (R-5): VF–EF $60–$90 • MS-63 $200–$300.

MI, Grand Haven • H. Brouwer & Co. • MI-360-A • *Dry goods, groceries, boots, and shoes* • Ascribed to the shop of S.D. Childs • Reverse dies: 1094, 1205, 1209, 1210 • MI-360-A-1a Rev 1094 (R-6): VF–EF $50–$75 • MS-63 $300–$450.

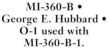

MI-360-B •
George E. Hubbard •
O-1 used with
MI-360-B-1.

MI-360-B •
George E. Hubbard •
O-2 used with
MI-360-B-2.

MI, Grand Haven • George E. Hubbard • MI-360-B • *Dealer in stoves, hardware, iron, etc.* • Ascribed to the shop of W.K. Lanphear • Reverse dies: 1212, 1226 • MI-360-B-1a Rev 1226 (R-5): VF–EF $50–$75 • MS-63 $175–$250.

MI, Grand Haven • G.V. Schelven • MI-360-C • *Dealer in groceries and candy* • Ascribed to the shop of S.D. Childs • Reverse die: 1108 • MI-360-C-1a Rev 1108 (R-6): VF–EF $200–$300 • MS-63 $600–$900.

MI, Grand Rapids • George P. Barnard • MI-370-A • *Book dealer and stationer* • Ascribed to the shop of S.D. Childs • Reverse dies: 1101, 1390 • MI-370-A-1a Rev 1101 (R-5): VF–EF $60–$90 • MS-63 $250–$375.

MI-370-B •
Courlander &
Pressgood / Russian
Clothing Store •
O-1 used with
MI-370-B-1.
"RUSIAN"
error.

MI-370-B •
Courlander &
Pressgood / Russian
Clothing Store •
O-2 used with
MI-370-B-2.
"CLTHING"
error.

MI, Grand Rapids • Courlander & Pressgood, Russian Clothing Store • MI-370-B • *Clothing* • Ascribed to the shop of W.K. Lanphear • Reverse die: 1337 • MI-370-B-2a Rev 1337 (R-6): VF– EF $75–$125 • MS-63 $250–$375 • Two obverse dies, each with a misspelling.

MI-370-C •
Foster & Metcalf •
O-1 used with
MI-370-C-1.

MI-370-C •
Foster & Metcalf •
O-2 used with
MI-370-C-2 and 3.

MI, Grand Rapids • Foster & Metcalf • MI-370-C • *Workers in copper, tin, brass, and heavy sheet iron; plumbing, gas fitting, etc.* • ? • Reverse dies: 1308, 26270 • MI-370-C-1b Rev 26270 (R-3): VF–EF $25–$35 • MS-63 $60–$90.

MI-370-D •
Goodrich & Gay •
O-1 used with
MI-370-D-1.

MI-370-D •
Goodrich & Gay •
O-2 used with
MI-370-D-2 to 4.

MI, Grand Rapids • Goodrich & Gay • MI-370-D • *Dealers in hardware, iron, steel, nails, and glass* • ? • Reverse dies: 1305, 1307, 1307A, 1308 • MI-370-D-1b Rev 1305 (R-3): VF–EF $25–$35 • MS-63 $60–$90 • Two obverse dies.

MI, Grand Rapids • Kruger & Booth • MI-370-E • *Dealers in saddles, harnesses, and trunks* • Ascribed to the shop of S.D. Childs • Reverse dies: 1101, 1357 • MI-370-E-1a Rev 1101 (R-6): VF–EF $40–$60 • MS-63 $200–$300.

| MI-370-F •
C. Kusterer (City
Brewery) •
O-1 used with
MI-370-F-1 to 3. | MI-370-F •
(C. Kusterer) City
Brewery •
O-2 used with
MI-370-F-4. This is
the reverse die used
with MI-370-F-1 to 3. | MI-370-I •
E.K. Powers •
O-1 used with
MI-370-I-1. | MI-370-I •
E.K. Powers •
O-2 used with
MI-370-I-2 and 3. |

MI, Grand Rapids • C. Kusterer, City Brewery • MI-370-F • *Brewer* • Ascribed to the shop of S.D. Childs • Reverse dies: 1105, 1205, 1211, 26330 • MI-370-F-1a Rev 26330 (R-4): VF–EF $300–$450 • MS-63 $800–$1,200 • Two obverse dies.

MI, Grand Rapids • L.A. Merrill • MI-370-G • *Photographic artist* • Ascribed to the shop of S.D. Childs • Reverse dies: 1101, 1105 • MI-370-G-1a Rev 1101 (R-4): VF–EF $150–$225 • MS-63 $400–$600.

| MI-370-H •
J.W. Peirce •
O-1 used with
MI-370-H-1 to 3. | MI-370-H •
J.W. Peirce •
O-2 used with
MI-370-H-4 to 9. |

MI, Grand Rapids • J.W. Peirce • MI-370-H • *Dry goods and groceries* • ? • Reverse dies: 1358, 1359, 1360, 1361, 1362, 1363, 1365 • MI-370-H-2b Rev 1359 (R-2): VF–EF $25–$35 • MS-63 $50–$75.

MI, Grand Rapids • E.K. Powers • MI-370-I • *Confectioner and dealer in soda water* • Ascribed to the shop of S.D. Childs • Reverse dies: 1101, 1205 • MI-370-I-1a Rev 1101 (R-6): VF–EF $75–$125 • MS-63 $250–$375.

MI, Grand Rapids • L.H. Randall • MI-370-J • *Wholesale and retail grocer* • ? • Reverse die: 26700 • MI-370-J-1b Rev 26700 (R-3): VF–EF $25–$35 • MS-63 $75–$125.

MI, Grand Rapids • A. Roberts & Son • MI-370-K • *Dry goods, groceries, crockery* • ? • Reverse dies: 1362, 1365, 1366 • MI-370-K-1b Rev 1362 (R-4): VF–EF $25–$35 • MS-63 $150–$225.

MI, Grand Rapids • Tompkins Photograph and Ambrotype Gallery • MI-370-L • *Photograph gallery* • Ascribed to the shop of S.D. Childs • Reverse dies: 1105, 1205, 1211 • MI-370-L-3a Rev 1211 (R-7): VF–EF $200–$300 • MS-63 $750–$1,250.

MI, Hastings • D.C. Hawley • MI-440-A • *Groceries and provisions* • Ascribed to the shop of S.D. Childs • Reverse dies: 1094, 1101, 1105, 1107, 1205 • MI-440-A-3a Rev 1105 (R-5), MI-440-A-4a Rev 1107 (R-5): VF–EF $50–$75 • MS-63 $200–$300 • Only token issuer of this town.

MI, Hillsdale • J.O. Ames • MI-450-A • *Books and stationery* • Dies by Alexander Gleason • Reverse dies: 1185, 1187 • MI-450-A-1b Rev 1185 (R-8), MI-450-A-2b Rev 1187 (R-8): VF–EF $2,000–$3,000.

MI, Hillsdale • O.S. Betts • MI-450-B
• *Dealer in watches, jewelry, and silverware* • Dies by Alexander Gleason • Reverse dies: 1183, 1186 • MI-450-B-1a Rev 1183 (R-5): VF–EF $50–$75.

MI, Hillsdale • Card, Pearce & Co. • MI-450-C • *Engines and agricultural implements dealer* • Dies by Alexander Gleason • Reverse dies: 1183, 1184, 1186, 1187 • MI-450-C-2a Rev 1194 (R-6): VF–EF $150–$225 • MS-63 $600–$900.

MI, Hillsdale • Farnam's Bronchial Tablets MI-450-D • *Patent medicine* • Dies by Alexander Gleason • Reverse dies: 1185, 1187 • MI-450-D-1a Rev 1185 (R-8), MI-450-D-2b Rev 1187 (R-8): VF–EF $1,250–$1,750.

MI, Hillsdale • French & Parsons • MI-450-E • *Druggists and grocers* • Ascribed to the shop of S.D. Childs • Reverse die: 1111 • MI-450-E-1a Rev 1111 (R-7), MI-450-E-1b Rev 1111 (R-7): VF–EF $200–$300 • MS-63 $600–$900.

MI, Hillsdale • J. Gottlieb • MI-450-F • *Clothier* • Dies by Alexander Gleason • Reverse dies: 1183, 1184, 1185, 1187 • MI-450-F-3b Rev 1187 (R-8): VF–EF $300–$450 • MS-63 $1,000–$1,500.

MI, Hillsdale • Alexander Gleason • MI-450-G • *Diesinker and engraver* • Gleason's own card • Reverse dies: 1183, 1184, 1186, 1187, 1221, 1262 • MI-450-G-7a Rev 1262 (R-2): VF–EF $25–$35 • MS-63 $100–$150.

MI, Hillsdale • E.C. Keating • MI-450-H • *Grocer and produce dealer* • Dies by Alexander Gleason • Reverse dies: 1183, 1185, 1185A, 1186 • MI-450-H-2a Rev 1185 (R-7), MI-450-H-3a Rev 1186 (R-7): VF–EF $75–$125 • MS-63 $400–$600.

MI-450-I • D.H. Lord & Co. • O-1 used with MI-450-I-1.

MI-450-I • D.H. Lord & Co. • O-2 used with MI-450-I-2 and 3.

MI, Hillsdale • D.H. Lord & Co. • MI-450-I • *Dealers in boots and shoes* • Dies by Alexander Gleason • Reverse dies: 1185, 1186 • MI-450-I-2a Rev 1186 (R-7): VF–EF $100–$150.

MI, Hillsdale • C.T. Mitchell & Co. • MI-450-J • *Hardware dealers* • Dies by Alexander Gleason • Reverse dies: 1185, 1186, 1187 • MI-450-J-1a Rev 1185 (R-7): VF–EF $300–$450 • MS-63 $900–$1,350.

MI-450-K • C.H. Mott & Co. • O-1 used with MI-450-K-1.

MI-450-K • C.H. Mott & Co. • O-2 used with MI-450-K-2.

MI, Hillsdale • C.E. Mott & Co. • MI-450-K • *Dry goods and carpeting* • Ascribed to the shop of S.D. Childs • Reverse dies: 1111, 1117 • MI-450-K-1a Rev 1111 (R-5): VF–EF $40–$60 • MS-63 $225–$350 • Listed out of alphabetical sequence in the Fuld text. While Alexander Gleason was the prime supplier of tokens to Hillsdale merchants, the two Mott enterprises went elsewhere.

MI, Hillsdale • Mott & Bro. • MI-450-L • *Druggists and grocers* • Ascribed to the shop of S.D. Childs • Reverse dies: 1111, 1115, 1117, 1185 • MI-450-L-3a Rev 1117 (R-5): VF–EF $50–$75 • MS-63 $300–$450.

MI-450-M •
Samm & Kuhlke •
O-1 used with
MI-450-M-1 and 3.

MI-450-M •
Samm & Kuhlke •
O-2 used with
MI-450-M-3.

MI, Hillsdale • Samm & Kuhlke • MI-450-M • *Grocers* • Dies by Alexander Gleason • Reverse dies: 1185, 1185A, 1186 • MI-450-M-2a Rev 1186 (R-6): VF–EF $100–$150 • MS-63 $500–$750.

MI, Hillsdale • R. Rowe, Union Planing & Stave Mills • MI-450-N • *Lumber mill* • Dies by Alexander Gleason • Reverse dies: 1183, 1186 • MI-450-N-2a Rev 1186 (R-6): VF–EF $150–$225 • MS-63 $600–$900.

MI, Hillsdale • Geo. W. Underwood • MI-450-O • *Druggist and grocer* • Ascribed to the shop of S.D. Childs • Reverse dies: 1115, 1117, 1185 • MI-450-O-2a Rev 1117 (R-4): VF–EF $40–$60 • MS-63 $200–$300 • Another Hillsdale merchant that did not use Gleason.

MI, Hudson • Baker & Brown • MI-480-A • *Dry goods, groceries* • Dies by Alexander Gleason • Reverse dies: 1184, 1186 • MI-480-A-2a Rev 1186 (R-7): VF–EF $400–$600 • MS-63 $1,500–$2,250.

MI, Hudson • A.H. Bowen • MI-480-B • *Baker and grocer* • Dies by Alexander Gleason • Reverse die: 1183 • MI-480-B-1a Rev 1183 (R-6): VF–EF $125–$175.

MI, Hudson • Gillett & Niles • MI-480-C • *Druggists* • Ascribed to the shop of S.D. Childs • Reverse dies: 1099, 1101, 1204, 1390 • MI-480-C-1a Rev 1099 (R-8): VF–EF $400–$600 • MS-63 $1,250–$1,750.

MI, Hudson • Green & Wadsworth • MI-480-D • *Livery* • Dies by Alexander Gleason • Reverse dies: 1183, 1184 •

MI-480-D-1a Rev 1183 (R-6): VF–EF $90–$135.

MI, Hudson • H. Howe & Co. • MI-480-E • *Hardware dealers* • Dies by Alexander Gleason • Reverse dies: 1183, 1184, 1186 • MI-480-E-1a Rev 1183 (R-6): VF–EF $90–$135.

MI, Hudson • Palmer & Goodsall • MI-480-F • *Hardware dealers* • Dies by Alexander Gleason • Reverse dies: 1183, 1186 • MI-480-F-1a Rev 1186 (R-6): VF–EF $60–$90 • MS-63 $300–$450.

MI, Hudson • Tubbs & Spear • MI-480-G • *Grocers* • Dies by Alexander Gleason • Reverse dies: 1183, 1186 • MI-480-G-1a Rev 1183 (R-5): VF–EF $50–$75 • MS-63 $300–$450.

MI-495-A •
James Kennedy •
O-1 used with
MI-495-A-1.

MI-495-A •
James Kennedy •
O-2 used with
MI-495-A-2.

MI, Ionia • James Kennedy • MI-495-A • *Insurance, collection office, war claims* • ? • Reverse die: 26990 • MI-495-A-1a Rev 26990 (R-2): VF–EF $25–$35 • MS-63 $60–$90.

MI, Ionia • F. Sloan • MI-495-B • *Hardware, stoves, steel, and nails* • Ascribed to the shop of S.D. Childs • Reverse dies: 1101, 1211, 1212, 1357 • MI-495-B-1a Rev 1101 (R-5): VF–EF $40–$60 • MS-63 $250–$375.

MI, Jackson • S. Holland & Son • MI-525-A • *Druggists* • Ascribed to the shop of S.D. Childs • Reverse dies: 1098, 1390 • MI-525-A-1a Rev 1098 (R-7): VF–EF $250–$375 • MS-63 $800–$1,200.

MI, Jackson • H.S. Ismon • MI-525-B • *Dry goods* • Ascribed to the shop of S.D. Childs • Reverse die: 1098 • MI-525-B-1a

Rev 1098 (R-5): VF–EF $40–$60 • MS-63 $250–$375.

MI-525-C •
William Jackson •
O-1 used with
MI-525-C-1 and 2.

MI-525-C •
William Jackson •
O-2 used with
MI-525-C-3 to 5.

MI-525-C •
William Jackson •
O-3 used with
MI-525-C-6.

MI-525-C •
William Jackson •
O-4 used with
MI-525-C-7.

MI-525-C •
William Jackson •
O-5 used with
MI-525-C-8.

MI-525-C •
William Jackson •
O-6 used with
MI-525-C-9.

MI-525-C •
William Jackson •
O-7 used with MI-
525-C-10 and 11.

MI, Jackson • William Jackson • MI-525-C • *Groceries* • Ascribed to the shop of W.K. Lanphear • Reverse dies: 1094, 1099, 1105, 1130, 27050, 27060, 27080, 27090, 27120 • MI-525-C-6a Rev 27090 (R-2): VF–EF $25–$35 • MS-63 $60–$90 • In the third edition of the Fuld book MI-525-D will be merged into MI-525-C as the same issuer is involved.

MI-525-D •
W. Jaxon (William
Jackson) •
O-1 used with
MI-535-D-1 to 3.

MI-525-D •
W. Jaxon (William
Jackson) •
O-2 used with
MI-535-D-4.

MI, Jackson • W. Jaxon • MI-525-D • *Groceries* • Ascribed to the shop of W.K. Lanphear • Reverse dies: 1168, 1348, 1349, 1387 • MI-525-D-2a Rev 1348 (R-3), MI-525-D-4a Rev 1349 (R-3): VF–EF $30–$45 • MS-63 $100–$150 • In the third edition of the Fuld book MI-525-D will be merged into MS-525-C as the same issuer is involved.

MI, Jonesville • C.C. Blakeslee • MI-527-A • *Druggist* • Dies by Alexander Gleason • Reverse die: 1187 • MI-527-A-1a Rev 1187 (R-7): VF–EF $150–$225 • MS-63 $600–$900.

MI, Jonesville • A. & H. Gale • MI-527-B • *Manufacturer of agricultural implements* • Dies by Alexander Gleason • Reverse die: 1187 • MI-527-B-1a Rev 1187 (R-8): VF–EF $600–$900 • MS-63 $1,750–$2,500.

MI-527-C •
H.R. Gardner & Co •
O-1 used with
MI-527-C-1 and 2.

MI-527-C •
H.R. Gardner & Co. •
O-2 used with
MI-527-C-3 and 4.

MI, Jonesville • H.R. Gardner & Co. • MI-527-C • *Woolen manufacturers* • Dies by Alexander Gleason • Reverse dies: 1185, 1186 • MI-527-C-1a Rev 1185 (R-6): VF–EF $125–$175.

MI-527-D •
J.S. Lewis •
O-1 used with
MI-527-D-1 and 2.

MI-527-D •
J.S. Lewis •
O-2 used with
MI-527-D-3.

MI, Jonesville • J.S. Lewis • MI-527-D • *Hardware, iron, and nails* • Dies by Alexander Gleason • Reverse dies: 1185, 1186 • MI-527-D-1a Rev 1185 (R-7): VF–EF $175–$250.

MI, Jonesville • Van Ness & Turner • MI-527-E • *Dry goods and groceries* • Dies by Alexander Gleason • Reverse die: 1185 • MI-527-E-1a Rev 1185 (R-5): VF–EF $125–$175.

MI, Jonesville • D.A. Wisner & Son • MI-527-F • *Dry goods and groceries* • Dies by Alexander Gleason • Reverse die: 1185 • MI-527-F-1a Rev 1185 (R-6): VF–EF $150–$225 • MS-63 $400–$600.

MI, Kalamazoo • Babcock & Cobb • MI-530-A • *Dry goods, carpets, and clothing* • Ascribed to the shop of S.D. Childs • Reverse dies: 1108, 1203, 1357 • MI-530-A-1a Rev 1108 (R-6), MI-530-A-2a Rev 1203

(R-6): VF–EF $40–$60 • MS-63 $150–$225.

MI-530-B •
Cobb & Fisher •
O-1 used with
MI-530-B-1.

MI-530-B •
Cobb & Fisher •
O-2 used with
MI-530-B-2 and 3.

MI, Kalamazoo • Cobb & Fisher • MI-530-B • *Dealers in crockery* • Ascribed to the shop of S.D. Childs • Reverse dies: 1094, 1205 • MI-530-B-2a Rev 1094 (R-5): VF–EF $60–$90 • MS-63 $200–$300.

MI-530-C •
Davis & Bates •
O-1 used with
MI-530-C-1 .

MI-530-C •
Davis & Bates •
O-2 used with
MI-530-C-2 to 4.

MI, Kalamazoo • Davis & Bates • MI-530-C • *Cash store* • Ascribed to the shop of S.D. Childs • Reverse dies: 1094, 1095, 1390 • MI-530-C-2a Rev 1094 (R-5): VF–EF $40–$60 • MS-63 $200–$300.

MI, Kalamazoo • R.R. Howard • MI-530-D • *Hardware, cutlery, etc.* • Ascribed to the shop of S.D. Childs • Reverse dies: 1094, 1357 • MI-530-D-1a Rev 1094 (R-4): VF–EF $50–$75 MS-63 $150–$225.

MI, Kalamazoo • Kellogg & Co. • MI-530-E • *Manufacturer of lumber, doors, blinds, and sashes* • Ascribed to the shop of S.D. Childs • Reverse dies: 1094, 1095, 1105, 1357 • MI-530-E-1a Rev 1094 (R-5), MI-530-E-2a Rev 1095 (R-5), MI-530-E-3a Rev 1105 (R-5): VF–EF $40–$60 • MS-63 $150–$225.

MI, Kalamazoo • H.S. Parker & Co. • MI-530-F • *Hats, caps, boots, and shoes* • Ascribed to the shop of S.D. Childs • Reverse dies: 1094, 1108, 1390 • MI-530-F-2a Rev 1108 (R-6): VF–EF $175–$250 • MS-63 $500–$750.

MI-530-G • L.W. Perrin • O-1 used with MI-530-G-1.

MI-530-G • L.W. Perrin • O-2 used with MI-530-G-2 and 3.

MI, Kalamazoo • L.W. Perrin • MI-530-G • *Dry goods, groceries, crockery, carpets* • Ascribed to the shop of John Stanton • Reverse dies: 1037, 1047 • MI-530-G-1a Rev 1037 (R-4): VF–EF $35–$50 • MS-63 $150–$225.

MI, Kalamazoo • Roberts & Hillhouse • MI-530-H • *Druggists* • Ascribed to the shop of S.D. Childs • Reverse dies: 1203, 1357 • MI-530-H-2a Rev 1203 (R-5): VF–EF $175–$225 • MS-63 $600–$900.

MI, Lansing • David Eckstein • MI-560-A • *Groceries and provisions* • Ascribed to the shop of W.K. Lanphear • Reverse dies: 0016N, 1123, 1126, 1166 • MI-560-A-1a Rev 1123 (R-6), MI-560-A-2a Rev 1126 (R-6): VF–EF $75–$125 • MS-63 $300–$450.

MI, Lansing • A.J. Viele • MI-560-B • *Books, stationery, pianos, and sewing machines* • Ascribed to the shop of W.K. Lanphear • Reverse dies: 1123, 1168, 1321, 1322 • MI-560-B-2a Rev 1168 (R-6), MI-560-B-4a Rev 1322 (R-6): VF–EF $60–$90 • MS-63 $400–$600.

MI, Lapeer • H. Griswold & Co. • MI-565-A • *Dry goods and groceries* • Ascribed to the shop of John Stanton • Reverse dies: 1024, 1042, 1046 (shattered die), 1047 • MI-565-A-1a Rev 1024 (R-6): VF–

EF $150–$225 • MS-63 $500–$750 • Only token issuer of this town.

MI, Lawton • Fairbank & Scriver • MI-570-A • *Stoves, hardware, and cutlery* • Ascribed to the shop of S.D. Childs • Reverse dies: 1094, 1098, 1099, 1205 • MI-570-A-3a Rev 1099 (R-5): VF–EF $50–$75 • MS-63 $350–$500 • Only token issuer of this town.

MI, Litchfield • A. Burleson • MI-577-A • *Dry goods, groceries, shoes* • Dies by Alexander Gleason • Reverse die: 1187 • MI-577-A-1b Rev 1187 (R-7): VF–EF $500–$750 • MS-63 $1,250–$1,7500 • Only token issuer of this town.

MI-580-A • W.R. Blaisdell • O-2 used with MI-580-A-2 and 3.

MI, Lowell • W.R. Blaisdell • MI-580-A • *Stoves, tin, and hardware* • Ascribed to the shop of S.D. Childs • Reverse dies: 1101, 1105, 1205 • MI-580-A-2a Rev 1101 (R-7): VF–EF $500–$750 • MS-63 $1,500–$2,250.

MI-580-B • Hatch & Craw • O-1 used with MI-580-B-1 and 2.

MI-580-B • Hatch & Craw • O-2 used with MI-580-B-3 and 4.

MI, Lowell • Hatch & Craw • MI-580-B • *Manufacturers and dealers in flour and grain* • Ascribed to the shop of S.D. Childs • Reverse dies: 1101, 1105, 1108 •

MI-580-B-4a Rev 1108 (R-5): VF–EF $60–$90 • MS-63 $300–$450.

MI, Lyons • Bauder & Button • MI-587-A • *War claim agents and attorneys* • Ascribed to the shop of S.D. Childs • Reverse dies: 1101, 1105 • MI-587-A-1a Rev 1101 (R-8), MI-587-A-2a Rev 1105 (R-8): VF–EF $250–$375 • MS-63 $1,250–$1,750.

MI-587-B •
A. Button •
O-1 used with
MI-587-B-1.

MI-587-B •
A. Button •
O-2 used with
MI-587-B-2.

MI, Lyons • A. Button • MI-587-B • *War claim agent, attorney, insurance* • Ascribed to the shop of W.K. Lanphear • Reverse dies: 1169, 27455 • MI-587-B-2a Rev 27455 (R-6): VF–EF $125–$175 • MS-63 $400–$600.

MI, Lyons • L.F. Heath • MI-587-C • *Watch maker, photographer* • ? • Reverse die: 1321 • MI-587-C-1a Rev 1321 (R-6): VF–EF $200–$300 • MS-63 $600–$900.

MI, Manchester • Van Duyn & Lynch • MI-588-A • *Druggists and grocers* • Ascribed to the shop of W.K. Lanphear • Reverse dies: 1310, 1316 • MI-588-A-1b Rev 1310 (R-7), MI-588-A-2a Rev 1316 (R-7): VF–EF $300–$450 • MS-63 $1,000–$1,500 • Only token issuer of this town.

MI, Maple Rapids • Isaac Hewitt • MI-595-A • *Dry goods and groceries* • Ascribed to the shop of S.D. Childs • Reverse dies: 1101, 1105 • MI-595-A-1a Rev 1101 (R-8): VF–EF $2,000–$3,000 • MS-63 $5,000–$7,500 • Only token issuer of this town.

MI, Marshall • Isaac Beers • MI-610-A • *Stoves, hardware, tools, and tinware* •

Ascribed to the shop of S.D. Childs • Reverse dies: 1098, 1390 • MI-610-A-1a Rev 1098 (R-6): VF–EF $250–$375 • MS-63 $1,000–$1,500.

MI-610-B •
C.M. Brewer •
O-1 used with
MI-610-B-1 to 4.

MI-610-B •
C.M. Brewer •
O-2 used with
MI-610-B-5.

MI, Marshall • C.M. Brewer • MI-610-B • *Dry goods, groceries, and hardware* • Ascribed to the shop of S.D. Childs • Reverse dies: 1095, 1098, 1106, 1205 • MI-610-B-3a Rev 1106 (R-5): VF–EF $30–$45 • MS-63 $125–$175.

MI-610-C •
L.H. Robinson •
O-1 used with
MI-610-C-1 and 2.

MI-610-C •
L.H. Robinson •
O-2 used with
MI-610-C-3 to 7.

MI, Marshall • L.H. Robinson • MI-610-C • *Dealer in groceries and notions* • Ascribed to the shop of John Stanton • Reverse dies: 1018, 1025, 1034, 1042, 1047, 1069 • MI-610-C-3a Rev 1018 (R-4): VF–EF $25–$35 • MS-63 $125–$175.

MI, Mason • J.W. Phelps & Co. • MI-615-A • *Hardware, tin & copper ware, drugs, and medicines* • Ascribed to the shop of John Stanton[56] • Reverse dies: 1024, 1042, 1047 • MI-615-A-1a Rev 1024 (R-4), MI-516-A-2a Rev 1042 (R-4): VF–EF $150–$225 • MS-63 $500–$750 • Only token issuer of this town.

MI, Morenci • J.M. Page & Co. • MI-660-A • *Dealers in hardware* • Dies by Alexander Gleason • Reverse dies: 1184, 1186 • MI-660-A-1a Rev 1186 (R-5): VF–EF $60–$90 • MS-63 $300–$450.

MI, Morenci • Richards & Co. • MI-660-B • *Dealers in dry goods and hardware* • Ascribed to the shop of S.D. Childs • Reverse dies: 1098, 1099, 1205 • MI-660-B-2a Rev 1099 (R-4): VF–EF $30–$45 • MS-63 $200–$300.

MI, Mussey • E.C. Morse • MI-680-A • *Dry goods, groceries, etc.* • Ascribed to the shop of John Stanton • Reverse dies: 1037, 1042, 1047 • MI-680-A-1a Rev 1037 (R-5): $75–$125 MS-63 $250–$375 • Only token issuer of this town.[57]

MI-700-A •
G.A. Colby & Co. •
O-1 used with
MI-700-A-1 and 3.

MI-700-A •
G.A. Colby & Co. •
O-2 used with
MI-700-A-2.

MI, Niles • G.A. Colby & Co. • MI-700-A • *Wholesale groceries and bakery* • Ascribed to the shop of S.D. Childs • Reverse dies: 1203, 1204 • MI-700-A-1a Rev 1203 (R-5): VF–EF $35–$50 • MS-63 $125–$175.

MI, Niles • H. Eastman • MI-700-B • *Dry goods, clothing, boots, and shoes* • Ascribed to the shop of S.D. Childs • Reverse dies: 1099, 1390 • MI-700-B-1a Rev 1099 (R-4): VF–EF $40–$60 • MS-63 $125–$175.

MI-700-C •
E.S. Parker •
O-1 used with
MI-700-C-1 and 2.

MI-700-C •
E.S. Parker •
O-2 used with
MI-700-C-3 and 4.

MI, Niles • E.S. Parker • MI-700-C • *Dealer in hats, caps, and furs* • Ascribed to the shop of S.D. Childs • Reverse dies: 1046, 1047, 1098, 1105 • MI-700-C-2a Rev 1098 (R-5), MI-700-C-3a Rev 1046 (R-5): VF–EF $40–$60 • MS-63 $125–$175.

MI, Niles • G.W. & H.C. Platt • MI-700-D • *Stoves and hardware* • ? • Reverse dies: 1095, 1099, 1101, 1108 • MI-700-D-2a Rev 1101 (R-5): VF–EF $30–$45 • MS-63 $125–$175.

MI, Niles • H.G. Sleight • MI-700-E • *Groceries, seeds, etc.* • Ascribed to the shop of S.D. Childs • Reverse dies: 1095, 1098, 1099, 1101, 1357 • MI-700-E-4a Rev 1101 (R-5): VF–EF $35–$50 • MS-63 $125–$175.

MI, Owosso • C.E. Shattuck • MI-735-A • *Dealer in brick and drain tile* • Ascribed to the shop of W.K. Lanphear • Reverse die: 1122 • MI-735-A-1a Rev 1122 (R-4): VF–EF $50–$75 • MS-63 $200–$300.

MI, Owosso • M.L. Stewart • MI-735-B • *Grocer* • Ascribed to the shop of W.K. Lanphear • Reverse dies: 1127, 1128 • MI-735-B-2a Rev 1128 (R-5): VF–EF $60–$90 • MS-63 $200–$300.

MI, Parma • Glazier's Pharmacy • MI-740-A • *Pharmacy* • ? • Reverse die: 27670 • MI-740-A-1a Rev 27670 (R-5): VF–EF $75–$125 • MS-63 $300–$450 • Only token issuer of this town.

MI, Paw Paw • J.R. Foote • MI-745-A • *Crockery, glassware, groceries* • Ascribed to the shop of S.D. Childs • Reverse dies: 1099, 1101, 1205 • MI-745-A-1a Rev 1099 (R-6): VF–EF $125–$175 • MS-63 $400–$600.

MI, Paw Paw • G.W. Longwell • MI-745-B • *Drugs and groceries* • Ascribed to the shop of S.D. Childs • Reverse dies: 1102, 1105 • MI-745-B-1a Rev 1102 (R-7): VF–EF $400–$600 • MS-63 $1,250–$1,750.

MI, Paw Paw • A. Sherman & Co., Paw Paw Flouring Mills • MI-745-C • *General merchants, flouring mills* • ? • Reverse die: 1003 • MI-745-C-1a Rev 1003 (R-6): VF–EF $200–$300 • MS-63 $1,500–$2,250.

MI, Paw Paw • J.D. Sherman • MI-745-D • *Wholesale groceries and provisions* • Ascribed to the shop of S.D. Childs • Reverse dies: 1105, 1203 • MI-745-D-2a Rev 1203 (R-5): VF–EF $100–$150 • MS-63 $400–$600.

MI, Pontiac • Fox & Smith • MI-770-A • *Produce and commission merchants, dealers in plaster* • Ascribed to the shop of S.D. Childs • Reverse dies: 1105, 1210, 1211 • MI-770-A-2a Rev 1210 (R-4): VF–EF $75–$125 • MS-63 $300–$450.

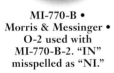

MI-770-B •
Morris & Messinger •
O-2 used with
MI-770-B-2. "IN"
misspelled as "NI."

MI-770-B •
Morris & Messinger •
O-1 used with
MI-770-B-1.
Die O-1 reworked
to correct error.

MI, Pontiac • Morris & Messinger • MI-770-B • *Dealers in hardware, iron, steel, nails, and glass* • ? • Reverse die: 1305 • MI-770-B-1b Rev 1305 (R-4), MI-770-B-2b Rev 1305 (R-4): VF–EF $40–$60 • MS-63 $200–$300.

MI, Pontiac • A. Parker, French's Hair Restorative • MI-770-C • *Dealer in*

drugs, medicines, groceries, and glass • ? • Reverse die: 27760 • MI-770-C-1b Rev 27760 (R-5): VF–EF $150–$225 • MS-63 $500–$750.

MI, Saginaw City • William Binder • MI-845-A • *Dry goods and groceries* • Ascribed to the shop of S.D. Childs • Reverse dies: 1101, 1205 • MI-845-A-1a Rev 1101 (R-6): VF–EF $150–$225 • MS-63 $600–$900.

MI, Saginaw City • Epting & Eaton • MI-845-B • *Drugs and medicines* • Ascribed to the shop of S.D. Childs • Reverse dies: 1095, 1357 • MI-845-B-1a Rev 1095 (R-8): VF–EF $1,250–$1,750 • MS-63 $3,000–$4,500.

MI, Salina • Gallagher & Hess • MI-855-A • *Druggists* • Ascribed to the shop of S.D. Childs • Reverse dies: 1095, 1105, 1211 • MI-855-A-3a Rev 1211 (R-5): VF–EF $90–$135 • MS-63 $300–$450 • Only token issuer of this town.

MI-865-A •
W. Darling •
O-1 used with
MI-865-A-1.

MI-865-A •
W. Darling •
O-2 used with
MI-865-A-2.

MI-865-A •
W. Darling •
O-3 used with
MI-865-A-3.

MI, Saranac • W. Darling • MI-865-A • *Boots and shoes* • ? • Reverse die: 27810 • MI-865-A-1a Rev 27810 (R-8): VF–EF $12,500–$17,500.

MI, Schoolcraft • I. Allen & Son • MI-900-A • *Stoves and hardware* • Ascribed to the shop of S.D. Childs • Reverse dies: 1094, 1095, 1105 • MI-900-A-2a Rev 1095 (R-7): VF–EF $200–$300 • Town listed out of alphabetical order in the Fuld book.

MI-900-B • I.W. Pursel & Co. • Surname misspelled as Prusel • O-1 used with MI-900-B-1 and 2.

MI-900-B • I.W. Pursel & Co. • O-2 used with MI-900-B-3 and 4.

MI, Schoolcraft • I.W. Pursel & Co. • MI-900-B • *Dry goods, groceries, boots, and shoes* • ? • Reverse dies: 1110, 1357, 1390 • MI-900-B-1a Rev 1110 (R-7), MI-900-B-4a Rev 1110 (R-7): VF–EF $200–$300 • MS-63 $750–$1,250.

MI, St. Johns • G.W. Stephenson • MI-915-A • *General merchandise* • Ascribed to the shop of W.K. Lanphear • Reverse die: 1310 • MI-915-A-1a Rev 1310 (R-5): VF–EF $100–$150 • MS-63 $300–$450 • Listed out of alphabetical order in Fuld; should be listed as Saint Johns.

MI, St. Johns • G.W. Stephenson & Son • MI-915-B • *Dry goods, clothing, boots, and shoes* • Ascribed to the shop of S.D. Childs• Reverse die: 1101 • MI-915-B-1a Rev 1101 (R-6): VF–EF $100–$150 • MS-63 $350–$500.

MI, Tecumseh • Fisher & Hendryx • MI-920-A • MI-920-A • *Druggists and grocers* • Ascribed to the shop of W.K. Lanphear[58] • Reverse die: 1310 • MI-920-A-1a Rev 1310 (R-7), MI-920-A-1b Rev 1310 (R-7): VF–EF $250–$375 • MS-63 $750–$1,250.

MI, Tecumseh • Dr. E. Hause • MI-920-B • *Dentist* • Ascribed to the shop of

S.D. Childs[59] • Reverse dies: 1094, 1095, 1099, 1101, 1357 • MI-920-B-1a Rev 1094 (R-6): VF–EF $75–$125 • MS-63 $250–$375.

MI, Tecumseh • G.T. Ketcham • MI-920-C • *News dealer and bookseller*[60] • ? • Reverse dies: 1099, 1357 • MI-920-C-1a Rev 1099 (R-4): VF–EF $30–$45 • MS-63 $200–$300.

MI, Tecumseh • T.S. Patterson • MI-920-D • *Druggist* • Ascribed to the shop of S.D. Childs[61] • Reverse dies: 1099, 1102, 1105, 1316 • MI-920-D-1a Rev 1099 (R-4): VF–EF $40–$60 • MS-63 $150–$175.

MI-960-A • E. Hewitt & Bro. • O-1 used with MI-960-A-1 to 5.

MI-960-A • E. Hewitt & Bro. • O-2 used with MI-960-A-6 to 11.

MI-960-A • E. Hewitt & Bro. • O-3 used with MI-960-A-12 and 13.

MI, Ypsilanti • E. Hewitt and Bro. • MI-960-A • *Dealers in dry goods, manufacturers of boots and shoes* • Ascribed to the shop of S.D. Childs • Reverse dies: 1094, 1095, 1105, 1106, 1107, 1390 • MI-960-A-7a Rev 1095 (R-4): VF–EF $25–$35 • MS-63 $150–$225.

MI-960-B •
Showerman & Bro. •
O-1 used with
MI-960-B-1 to 5.

MI-960-B •
Showerman & Bro. •
O-2 used with
MI-960-B-6 to 11.

MI, Ypsilanti • Showerman & Bro. • MI-960-B • *Dry goods, groceries, caps, boots, and shoes* • Ascribed to the shop of S.D. Childs • Reverse dies: 1105, 1209, 1210 • MI-960-B-2a Rev 1209 (R-4): VF–EF $40–$60 • MS-63 $150–$225.

MINNESOTA

Minnesota is a "rare state" with only six issuers of Civil War cards. Acquiring a representative token from the state will be no problem, such as the watch check of D.C. Greenleaf (MN-760-A which is R-5), but certain of the varieties are major rarities. The shop of W.K. Lanphear in distant Cincinnati was the main coiner.

MN-680-A •
A.W.E. •
O-1 used with
MN-680-A-1 and 2.
19 mm.

MN, Red Wing • A.W.E. (A.W. Esping) • MN-680-A • *Jeweler* • Ascribed to Mossin & Marr • Reverse dies: 1220, 1272, 27936 • MN-680-A-2a Rev 1272 (R-8), MN-680-A-2b Rev 1272 (R-8), MN-680-A-2d Rev 1272 (R-8): VF–EF $2,500–$3,750 • MS-63 $6,000–$9,000 • Only token issuer of this town. A. W. Esping (misspelled Epping) is listed as a dealer in jewelry, watches, clocks, etc. in

Red Wing in the *Wisconsin and Minnesota State Gazetteer, Shippers Guide and Business Directory* for 1865–1866. Mossin & Marr made restrike sets of A.W.E. tokens using reverses 1220 and 1272.[62]

MN, Rochester • F.W. Andrews • MN-720-A • *Dry goods* • Ascribed to the shop of W.K. Lanphear • Reverse dies: 1089, 1128, 1168, 1224, 1284 • MN-720-A-3a Rev 1168 (R-7): VF–EF $450–$650 • MS-63 $1,250–$1,750 • Only token issuer of this town.

MN, St. Paul • D.C. Greenleaf • MN-760-A • *Watch maker* • Ascribed to the shop of W.K. Lanphear • Reverse die: 0 • MN-760-A-1a Rev 0 (R-5): VF–EF $300–$400 • MS-63 $500–$750 • These are watch checks. On the reverse are various numbers individually stamped from 1 to 102 (range presently known). Apparently, two were made of each number, one for Greenleaf to retain with a watch and the other to be given to the watch owner as a receipt. Two tokens are known with additional counterstamps, the so-called MN-760-A-02a, which is numbered 101 and is additionally stamped SENOUR; and MN-760-A-03a, which is numbered 102 and is additionally stamped SENOUR.

MN, St. Paul • F.M. Johnson, Wheeler & Wilson's Sewing Machines • MN-760-B • *Sewing machines* • Ascribed to the shop of W.K. Lanphear • Reverse die: 1298 • MN-760-B-1a Rev 1298 (R-6): VF–EF $450–$700 • MS-63 $1,250–$1,750 • Wheeler & Wilson was a leading maker of the time and had agents in many different towns.

MN, Winona • C. Benson • MN-980-A • *Druggist* • Ascribed to the shop of W.K. Lanphear • Reverse die: 1310 • MN-980-A-1a Rev 1310 (R-7), MN-980-A-1b Rev 1310 (R-7): VF–EF $500–$750 • MS-63 $1,250–$1,750.

MN, Winona • Coe & Hayden, The Regulator • MN-980-B • *Dry goods, crockery, groceries, etc.* • Ascribed to the shop of W.K. Lanphear • Reverse die: 27990 • MN-980-B-1a Rev 27990 (R-6),

MN-980-B-1b Rev 27990 (R-6): VF–EF $400–$600 • MS-63 $1,000–$1,500.

MISSOURI

Missouri is another "rare state," this with just four issuers of metallic tokens. All merchants are collectible. Tokens of the Drovers Hotel in St. Louis, MO-910-A, are the most often seen.

MO, Ironton • D. Peck & Co. • MN-400-A • *Groceries, drugs, and medicines* • Ascribed to the shop of John Stanton • Reverse dies: 1046, 1047 • MN-400-A-1a Rev 1046 (R-7): VF–EF $750–$1,250 • MS-63 $2,000–$3,000 • Only token issuer of this town.

MO, St. Louis • Drovers Hotel • MO-910-A • *Hotel* • Ascribed to the shop of John Stanton • Reverse dies: 1008, 1009, 1038, 1042, 1047, 1288 • MO-910-A-1a Rev 1008 (R-6), MO-910-A-3a Rev 1038 (R-6): VF–EF $200–$300 • MS-63 $1,000–$1,500.

MO-910-B •
Jno. H. Blood
Lallemand's Specific •
O-1 used with
MO-910-B-1 and 2.

MO-910-B •
Jno. H. Blood
Lallemand's Specific •
O-2 used with
MO-910-B-3 to 7.

MO, St. Louis • Jno. H. Blood, Lallemand's Specific • MO-910-B • *Patent medicine* • Ascribed to the shop of John Stanton[63] • Reverse dies: 1018, 1026, 1037, 1047, 1069, 28050 • MO-910-B-1a Rev 28050 (R-6): VF–EF $400–$600 • MS-63 $1,250–$1,750.

MO, St. Louis • Henry Jenkens • MO-910-C • *Clothier* • Ascribed to the shop of W.K. Lanphear • Reverse dies: 1274, 28060, 28070, 34690 • MO-910-C-1a Rev 1274 (R-4): VF–EF $75–$125 • MS-63 $250–$375.

NEW HAMPSHIRE

Alabama, Idaho, Kansas, Maine, and New Hampshire are states with but a single token-issuing merchant. Of these varieties, the tokens of Maine and New Hampshire are the most often found, but on an absolute basis are somewhat scarce.

NH, Concord • A.W. Gale • NH-120-A • *Restaurateur* • Ascribed to Joseph Merriam • Reverse die: 28090 • NH-120-A-1a Rev 28090 (R-4): VF–EF $100–$150 • MS-63 $300–$450 • Only token issuer of this state.[64]

NEW JERSEY

The Civil War store cards of New Jersey include many challenges, but these are primarily among numismatic issues, not among pieces made for circulation, although in the latter category a search for the oversize and quite curious Bodine & Brothers issue of Williamstown can cause an oversize headache. Considering its closeness to such token-issuing centers as New York City and Philadelphia, it is a wonder that the tokens of New Jersey are not more numerous.

NJ-020-A •
Smick's
Neptune House •
O-1 used with
NJ-020-A-1.

NJ-020-A •
Smick's
Neptune House •
O-2 used with
NJ-020-A-2.

NJ, Atlantic City • Smick's Neptune House • NJ-20-A • *Hotel* • ? • Reverse dies: 28110, 28130 • NJ-20-A-1a Rev 28110 (R-3): Only token issuer of this town. The "Smick's" designation is on the side (not illustrated) designated as the reverse, a departure from the usual Fuld style of listing the proprietor first. The owner was John Smick.[65] • VF–EF $25–$35 • MS-63 $60–$90.

NJ, Elizabeth Port • John Engel • NJ-220-A • *Merchant tailor* • Dies by William H. Bridgens • Reverse dies: 1152, 1214, 1265 • NJ-220-A-3a Rev 1265 (R-3): VF–EF $25–$35 • MS-63 $90–$135 • Only token issuer of this town.

NJ, Jersey City • Terhune Brothers • NJ-350-A • *Hardware* • Dies by William H. Bridgens • Reverse die: 1215 • NJ-350-A-1a Rev 1215 (R-4): VF–EF $30–$45 • MS-63 $100–$150 • Only token issuer of this town.

NJ, Newark • J.L. Agens & Co. • NJ-555-A • *Newspapers, cigars, etc.* • Dies by William H. Bridgens • Reverse dies: 1000, 1006, 1137, 1152, 1214, 1265, 1268, 1269 • NJ-555-A-8a Rev 1269 (R-3): VF–EF $25–$35 • MS-63 $50–$75.

NJ, Newark • Charles Kolb • NJ-555-B • *Restaurateur* • ? • Reverse dies: 1014, 28170 • NJ-555-B-1a Rev 1014 (R-3): VF–EF $25–$35 • MS-63 $50–$75.

NJ, Newark • J. Wightman • NJ-555-C • *Grocer* • Ascribed to Emil Sigel • Reverse dies: 1000, 1016, 1017, 1052, 1132, 1218, 1219, 1236, 1252, 1253, 1267, 1277 • NJ-555-C-2a Rev 1016 (R-3): VF–EF $25–$35 • MS-63 $60–$90.

NJ, Perth Amboy • Coutts & Bro. • NJ-690-A • *Dry goods and groceries* • Dies by William H. Bridgens • Reverse dies: 1265, 1269 • NJ-690-A-1a Rev 1265 (R-4), NJ-690-A-2a Rev 1269 (R-4): VF–EF $25–$35 • MS-63 $75–$125 • Only token issuer of this town.

NJ, Trenton • B.W. Titus • NJ-885-A • *Dry goods, oil cloths, carpets, etc.* • ? • Reverse dies: 28210, 28220 • NJ-885-A-1b Rev 28210 (R-2): VF–EF $25–$35 • MS-63 $50–$75 • Only token issuer of this town.

NJ, Williamstown • Bodine & Brothers • NJ-925-A • *Glass manufacturing and sales* • ? • Reverse die: 28230 • NJ-925-A-1b Rev 28230 (R-8): VF–EF $2,500–$3,750 • Only issuer of this town. Not a token, but a thin brass impression, incuse on one side, from a seal press.

NEW YORK

The Civil War tokens attributed to New York state issuers afford an interesting study in themselves and are high on the list of popularity with present-day numismatists. The focal point is New York City, which brings together not only several dozen different merchants and professionals who distributed tokens, but also a number of shops which minted them. Prominent among the latter are such names as William H. Bridgens, Louis Roloff, and, in particular, Emil Sigel, who were the most prolific diecutters. However, the tokens of George Glaubrecht, Albert J. Henning, Charles D. Hörter, and George H. Lovett are important as well. Charles Müller, a medalist, cut the dies for a medal issued by John Matthews, maker of soda fountains, a piece which has been adopted as a "Civil War token," although it is oversize by a large margin and never was intended as a monetary substitute.

Several out-of-state producers had clients in New York. In the western part of the state the shop of John Stanton made inroads and secured a few clients, Sohm & Rohmann and S.B Seward, both of Buffalo, being examples. Shubael D. Childs, the Chicago token issuer, also produced a few New York tokens, an example being that for Langdon's Hardware Store in Belmont. Reverse 1368 by F.N. Dubois is seen on certain Binghamton, New York, tokens. Although the word REDEEMED appears on various tokens scattered throughout the series, nowhere are they more numerous than among the store cards of Albany and Troy; issuers include Benjamin & Herrick (Albany), P.V. Fort (Albany), Straight's Elephantine Shoe Store (Albany), John Thomas, Jr. (Albany), D.L. Wing & Co. (Albany), Charles Babcock (Troy), Oliver Boutwell (Troy), and Robinson & Ballou (Troy). Among these, the Wing, Boutwell, and Robinson & Ballou tokens are especially close cousins, sharing various design and decoration concepts. The ascription for these is not known, although the Scovill Manufacturing Co. is a candidate.

There are a number of "mystery" tokens relative to the authorship of their dies, with none more enigmatic than a cluster of nearly a half dozen issuers of Buffalo whose obverse dies are muled with some of the most "primitive" reverses ever created.

NY-010-A •
Benjamin & Herrick •
O-8 used with
NY-010-A-8. Reverse
of NY-010-A-2.

NY-010-A •
Benjamin & Herrick •
O-9 used with
NY-010-A-9. Reverse
of NY-10-A-04-A.

NY, Albany • Benjamin & Herrick • NY-10-A • *Fruit dealers* • ? • Reverse dies: 1153, 1276, 28250, 28270, 28300, 28335 • NY-10-A-1a Rev 28250 (R-2), NY-10-A-5a Rev 28300 (R-2), NY-10-A-6a Rev 28300 (R-2): VF–EF $25–$35 • MS-63 $50–$75.

NY-010-A •
Benjamin & Herrick •
O-1 used with
NY-010-A-1.

NY-010-A •
Benjamin & Herrick •
O-2 used with
NY-010-A-2.

NY-010-A •
Benjamin & Herrick •
O-4 used with
NY-010-A-4.

NY-010-A •
Benjamin & Herrick •
O-5 used with
NY-010-A-5.

NY-010-B •
P.V. Fort & Co. •
O-1 used with
NY-010-B-1.

NY, Albany • P.V. Fort & Co. • NY-10-B • *Dealers in fruit and nuts* • ? • Reverse die: 28350 • NY-10-B-1a Rev 28350 (R-3): VF–EF $25–$35 • MS-63 $60–$90.

NY, Albany • Jos. McBurney • NY-10-C • *Cigar box manufacturer* • ? • Reverse dies: 28370, 28380 • NY-10-C-1a Rev 28380 (R-3): VF–EF $25–$35 • MS-63 $50–$75.

NY, Albany • New York Central Railroad • NY-10-D • *Railroad* • ? • Reverse die: 28400 • NY-10-D-1a Rev 28400 (R-2): VF–EF $25–$35 • MS-63 $60–$90 • The New York Central Railroad was the main rail carrier between Buffalo and Albany; the Erie Canal served the same

NY-010-A •
Benjamin & Herrick •
O-6 used with
NY-010-A-6.

NY-010-A •
Benjamin & Herrick •
O-7 used with
NY-010-A-7.
Shattered die.

route. The New York Central trains connected with ships of the People's Line (which issued its own Civil War tokens).

NY, Albany • Straight's Elephantine Shoe Store • NY-10-F • *Shoe store* • ? • Reverse die: 28420 • NY-10-F-1a Rev 28420 (R-2): VF–EF $50–$75 • MS-63 $175–$250.

NY, Albany • John Thomas Jr. • NY-10-G • *Premium mills, coffee and spices* • ? • Reverse die: 28440 • NY-10-G-1a Rev 28440 (R-1): VF–EF $25–$35 • MS-63 $50–$75.

NY-010-H •
D.L. Wing & Co. •
O-1 used with
NY-010-H-1.

NY-010-H •
D.L. Wing & Co. •
O-2 used with
NY-010-H-2 and 3.
Early die state
before relapping.

NY-010-H •
D.L. Wing & Co. •
O-3 used with
NY-010-H-3A and 4.

NY-010-H •
D.L. Wing & Co. •
O-4 used with
NY-010-H-5 and 11.

NY-010-H •
D.L. Wing & Co. •
O-5 used with
NY-010-H-6.

NY-010-H •
D.L. Wing & Co. •
O-6 used with
NY-010-H-7 and 12.

NY-010-H •
D.L. Wing & Co. •
O-7 used with
NY-010-H-8 and 9.

NY, Albany • D.L. Wing & Co. • NY-10-H • *Miller*[66] • ? • Reverse dies: 1372, 1372A, 1372B, 1372C, 1372D, 1372E, 1371, 28570 • NY-10-H-8a Rev 1372E (R-1): VF–EF $25–$35 • MS-63 $50–$75.

NY, Almond • H. Dartt • NY-15-A • *Dry goods, groceries, exchange* • Ascribed to the shop of W.K. Lanphear • Reverse die: 1090 • NY-15-A-1a Rev 1090 (R-4): VF–EF $40–$60 • MS-63 $200–$300 • Only token issuer of this town. "Exchange" meant dealing in bank notes, coins, and other money.

NY-077-A •
Langdons
Hardware Store •
O-1 used with
NY-077-A-1 and 2.

NY-077-A •
Langdons
Hardware Store •
O-2 used with
NY-077-A-3.

NY, Belmont • Langdons Hardware Store • NY-77-A • *Hardware, exchange* • S.D. Childs • Reverse die: 1096, 1107, 1228 • NY-77-A-3a Rev 1228 (R-5): VF–EF $50–$75 • MS-63 $175–$250 • Only token issuer of this town. The firm also dealt in exchange. Both Childs and Lanphear made tokens for this merchant.

NY, Binghamton • Evans & Allen • NY-80-A • *Jewelers* • Dies by F.N. Dubois • Reverse die: 1368 • NY-80-A-1a Rev 1368 (R-4): VF–EF $30–$45 • MS-63 $100–$150 • Tokens issued by 1859.

NY, Binghamton • Herschmann Bros. & Co. • NY-80-B • *Dry goods* • Dies by F.N. Dubois • Reverse die: 1368 • NY-80-B-1a Rev 1368 (R-4): VF–EF $30–$45 • MS-63 $100–$150 • Tokens issued by 1859.

NY, Brooklyn • Braun & Schellworth's Pavilion • NY-95-A • *Entertainment* • Dies by William H. Bridgens • Reverse dies: 1243, 1265 • NY-95-A-2a Rev 1265 (R-4): VF–EF $25–$35 • MS-63 $50–$75.

NY, Brooklyn • C.J. Hauck • NY-95-B • • *Inventor* • Ascribed to Louis Roloff • Reverse die: 1256 • NY-95-B-1a Rev 1256 (R-3): VF–EF $25–$35 • MS-63 $60–$90 • Patented an oil can and design in 1866 and 1867, and a flower stand and a tobacco box in 1868.

NY, Brooklyn • M. Ibert • NY-95-C • *Flour dealer* • ? • Reverse die: 1270B • NY-95-C-1g Rev 1270B (R-9): VF–EF $12,500–$17,500.

NY, Brooklyn • T. Ivory • NY-95-D • *Billiards* • Dies by William H. Bridgens • Reverse dies: 1006, 1137, 1152, 1214, 1243, 1265, 1268, 1269 • NY-95-D-6a Rev 1265 (R-5), NY-76-D-8a Rev 1269 (R-5): VF–EF $30–$45 • MS-63 $75–$125.

NY, Brooklyn, E.D. • John Joergers • NY-95-E • *Saloonkeeper* • Ascribed to Louis Roloff • Reverse die: 1256 • NY-95-E-1a Rev 1256 (R-3): VF–EF $25–$35 • MS-63 $60–$90 • "Brooklyn, E.D.," is Brooklyn, Eastern District. In 1855 when Williamsburgh and Bushwick became a part of Brooklyn, this area was called the Eastern District.[67]

NY, Brooklyn • Daniel Williams • NY-95-F • *Grocer* • Dies by William H. Bridgens • Reverse dies: 1005, 1006, 1137, 1265, 1268, 1269 • NY-95-F-5a Rev 1269 (R-3): VF–EF $25–$35 • MS-63 $50–$75.

NY, Buffalo • James Adams & Co. • NY-105-A • *Tobacconist* • ? • Reverse die: 1077 • NY-105-A-1a Rev 1077 (R-4): VF–EF $30–$45 • MS-63 $150–$225.

NY, Buffalo • Alberger's Meat Store • NY-105-B • *Meat store* • Ascribed to the shop of John Stanton • Reverse dies: 1039, 1042, 1047 • NY-105-B-1a Rev 1039 (R-3): VF–EF $25–$35 • MS-63 $125–$175.

NY, Buffalo • E.G. Barrows • NY-105-C • *Brandies, wines, cigars* • Ascribed to the shop of John Stanton • Reverse dies: 1024, 1042, 1046, 1047 • NY-105-C-1a Rev 1024 (R-4): VF–EF $40–$60 • MS-63 $200–$300.

NY, Buffalo • F.J. Bieler • NY-105-D • *Auction and commission merchant* • ? • Reverse dies: 1077, 1079, 1081 • NY-105-D-1a Rev 1077 (R-3): VF–EF $30–$45 • MS-63 $150–$225 • Partner in Bieler & Einsfeld, auction and commission merchants. 338 Main Street.

NY-105-E • T.J. Conry • O-1 used with NY-105-E-1.

NY-105-E • T.J. Conry • O-2 used with NY-105-E-2 to 4. Early state of the die.

NY-105-E • T.J. Conry • O-2, later state with 19 at center beginning to fail. The die has been slightly reworked, including changing the comma after CONRY to a period and adding two dots below T (ST).

NY-105-E • T.J. Conry • O-3 used with NY-105-E-5. This is die O-2 in its final state with the center lettering removed with a lathe, resulting in raised lines on struck examples as shown here.

NY, Buffalo • T.J. Conry • NY-105-E • *Picture frames, newspapers, etc.* • ? • Reverse dies: 1077, 1078, 1079 • NY-105-E-1a Rev

1077 (R-4): VF–EF $25–$35 • MS-63 $100-$150.

NY, Buffalo • A.M. Duburn, Canal Tin Shop • NY-105-F • *Tin shop* • Ascribed to the shop of John Stanton • Reverse dies: 1024, 1042, 1047 • NY-105-F-1a Rev 1024 (R-5): VF–EF $50–$75 • MS-63 $175–$250.

NY, Buffalo • L. Danforth • NY-105-G • *Agent for Howe's scales* • Ascribed to the shop of John Stanton • Reverse dies: 1037, 1042, 1043, 1047 • NY-105-G-3a Rev 1043 (R-6): VF–EF $75–$110 • MS-63 $200–$300 • Listed out of alphabetical order in Fuld.

NY, Buffalo • W.G. Fox • NY-105-H • *Oysters, fruits, liquors* • Ascribed to the shop of John Stanton • Reverse dies: 1024, 1042, 1046, 1047 • NY-105-H-1a Rev 1024 (R-4): VF–EF $30–$45 • MS-63 $100–$150.

NY, Buffalo • Geo. Gage • NY-105-I • *Grocer* • Ascribed to the shop of John Stanton • Reverse dies: 1027, 1030, 1037, 1042, 1043, 1046, 1047 • NY-105-I-5a Rev 1043 (R-3): VF–EF $25–$35 • MS-63 $75–$110.

NY, Buffalo • Hochstetter & Strauss • NY-105-J • *Dry goods* • Ascribed to the shop of John Stanton • Reverse dies; 1024, 1039, 1042, 1046, 1047 • NY-105-J-1a Rev 1024 (R-4): VF–EF $35–$50 • MS-63 $175–$250.

NY, Buffalo • A.M. Johnston • NY-105K • *Grocer* • Ascribed to the shop of John Stanton • Reverse dies: 1039, 1042, 1047 • NY-105-J-1a Rev 1039 (R-3): VF–EF $25–$35 • MS-63 $60–$90.

NY, Buffalo • John C. Post • NY-105-L • *Paints, oils, and glass* • Ascribed to the shop of John Stanton • Reverse dies: 1024, 1042, 1047 • NY-105-L-1a Rev 1024 (R-5): VF–EF $50–$75 • MS-63 $200–$300.

NY, Buffalo • Reilly's Bazaar • NY-105-M • *Merchandise* • F.N. Dubois • Reverse die: 1368 • NY-105-M-1a Rev 1368 (R-6): VF–EF $100–$150.

NY, Buffalo • Robinson & Ball • NY-105-N • *Gents' furnishing goods* • Ascribed to the shop of John Stanton • Reverse dies: 1037, 1042, 1043, 1047 • NY-105-N-4a Rev 1043 ($-5) • VF–EF $40–$60 • MS-63 $150–$225.

NY, Buffalo • Rowe & Co. Oyster & Foreign Fruit Depot • NY-105-O • *Oyster and foreign fruit depot* • Ascribed to the shop of John Stanton • Reverse dies: 1024, 1042, 1047 • NY-105-O-1a Rev 1024 (R-5): VF–EF $40–$60 • MS-63 $150–$225.

NY, Buffalo • S.B. Seward • NY-105-P • *Druggist* • Ascribed to the shop of John Stanton • Reverse dies: 1040, 1042, 1046, 1047 • NY-105-P-1a Rev 1040 (R-5): VF–EF $50–$75 • MS-63 $175–$250.

NY, Buffalo • Sohm & Rohmann • NY-105-Q • *Butchers* • Ascribed to the shop of John Stanton • Reverse dies: 1037, 1042, 1043, 1046, 1047 • NY-105-Q-3a Rev 1043 (R-6): VF–EF $125–$175 • MS-63 $400–$600.

NY, Buffalo • C.R. Walker, Watson's Neuralgia King • NY-105-R • *Patent medicine* • ? • Reverse die: 1077 • NY-105-R-1a Rev 1077 (R-5): VF–EF $90–$135 • MS-63 $300–$450.

NY, Buffalo • Webster & Co. • NY-105-S • *Grocers* • ? • Reverse die: 1077 • NY-105-S-1a Rev 1077 (R-5): VF–EF $30–$45 • MS-63 $110–$175.

NY-140-A •
Alden & Frink •
O-1 used with
NY-140-A-1.

NY-140-A •
Alden & Frink •
O-2 used with
NY-140-A-2.

NY-140-A •
Alden & Frink •
O-3 used with
NY-140-A-3. Reverse
of NY-140-A-1.

NY, Cohoes • Alden & Frink • NY-140-A • *Merchants* • ? • Reverse dies: 0, 28950 • NY-140-A-1a Rev 28950 (R-2), NY-140-A-2a Rev 28950 (R-2): VF–EF $25–$35 • MS-63 $60–$90 • Only token issuer of this town.

NY, Cooperstown • Bingham & Jarvis • NY-145-A • *Drugs, hardware, etc.* • ? • Reverse dies: 1175A, 1236, 1277 • NY-145-A-2a Rev 1236 (R-5): VF–EF $90–$135 • MS-63 $250–$350.

NY, Cooperstown • G.L. Bowne • NY-145-B • *Saloonkeeper* • ? • Reverse dies: 1073, 28970, 28980 • NY-145-B-1j Rev 18970 (R-7), NY-145-B-2a Rev 1073 (R-7), NY-145-B-2j Rev 28980 (R-7): VF–EF $25–$35 • MS-63 $60–$90.

NY, Elmira • Louis Strauss & Co. • NY-230-A • *Dry goods* • Ascribed to the shop of John Stanton • Reverse dies: 1024, 1042, 1047 • NY-230-A-1a Rev 1024 (R-4): VF–EF $40–$60 • MS-63 $200–$300 • Only token issuer of this town.

NY, Fort Edward • Harvey & Co. • NY-270-A • *General store* • ? • Reverse die: 29010 • NY-270-A-1a Rev 29010 (R-2): VF–EF $25–$35 • MS-63 $60–$90 • Only token issuer of this town.

NY, Greenpoint • A. Killeen • NY-330-A • ? • Dies by William H. Bridgens • Reverse dies: 1006, 1137, 1152, 1214, 1232, 1265, 1269 • NY-330-A-5a Rev 1232 (R-4), NY-330-A-7a Rev 1269 (R-4): VF–EF $25–$35 • MS-63 $75–$110 • Only token issuer of this town.

NY, New York City • Atlantic Garden • NY-630-A • *German beer garden* • Ascribed to Louis Roloff • Reverse die: 29040 • NY-630-A-1a Rev 29040 (R-2): VF–EF $25–$35 • MS-63 $50–$75.

NY-630-B •
Cafe Autenreith •
O-1 used with
NY-630-B-1 to 4 and 7.

NY-630-B •
Cafe Autenreith •
O-2 used with
NY-630-B-5 and 6.

NY, New York City • Cafe Autenreith • NY-630-B • *Cafe* • Ascribed to Louis Roloff • Reverse dies: 1075, 1256, 1257, 1259, 1260, 1261, 29800 • NY-630-B-1a Rev 1075 (R-2): VF–EF $25–$35 • MS-63 $50–$75.

NY, New York City • C. Bahr • NY-630-C • *Liquor dealer* • Ascribed to Louis Roloff • Reverse dies: 1075, 1216, 1240, 1256, 1257, 1259, 1260, 1261, 29450, 29460, 29800, 29830 • NY-630-C-4a Rev 1240 (R-2), NY-630-C-6a Rev 1257 (R-2): VF–EF $25–$35 • MS-63 $50–$75.

NY, New York City • H.J. Bang • NY-630-D • *Wine importer, restaurateur* • Dies by George Glaubrecht • Reverse die: 29130 • NY-630-D-1a Rev 29130 (R-1): VF–EF $25–$35 • MS-63 $50–$75.

NY, New York City • Thos. Bennett [NJ] / J.C. Bailey {NJ} • NY-630-E • *Hotel keeper [Bailey] / liquor and cigar dealer [Bennett]* • Attributed to Albert J. Henning • Reverse die: 29150 • NY-630-E-1a Rev 29150 (R-3): VF–EF $25–$35 • MS-63 $90–$135 • Should have been listed under NJ by Fuld as this precedes NY in the alphabet.

NY-630-F •
V. Benner and Ch.
Bendinger •
O-1 used with
NY-630-F-1.

NY-630-F •
V. Benner and Ch.
Bendinger •
O-2 used with
NY-630-F-2.

NY, New York City • V. Benner & Ch. Bendinger • NY-630-F • *Liquor dealers* • ? • Reverse die: 29170 • NY-630-F-1a Rev 29170 (R-3), NY-630-F-2a Rev 29170 (R-3): VF–EF $25–$35 • MS-63 $75–$110.

NY, New York City • Samuel H. Black • NY-630-Fa • *Electrotyper* • ? • Reverse die: 29186 • NY-630-Fa-1a Rev 29186 (R-?): VF–EF $1,500–$2,250 • Lead token copper plated resembling a copper large cent.

NY-630-G •
I.W. Blain •
O-2 used with
NY-630-G-2.

NY, New York City • I.W. Blain • NY-630-G • *Restaurateur* • ? • Reverse die: 0 • NY-630-G-1b Rev 0 (R-9): VF–EF $12,500–$17,500 • Miller NY-98.

NY, New York City • J.L. Bode • NY-630-H • *Taxidermist and glassware dealer* • Ascribed to Louis Roloff • Reverse dies: 0, 1010, 1011, 29210, NY-630-H-1a Rev 29210 (R-1): VF–EF $25–$35 • MS-63 $100–$150.

NY, New York City • J.M. Bradstreet and Sons, and Bradstreet, Hoffman & Co. • NY-630-Ha • *Mercantile agency* • ? • Reverse dies: 1145A, 29214 • NY-630-Ha-1a (R-8): VF–EF $200–$300 • MS-63 $700–$1,000 • The medalets of J.M. Bradstreet & Sons and Bradstreet, Hoffman & Co. are related and are by the same diesinker. These are indexed and listed in Rulau's *Standard Catalog of U.S. Tokens 1700–1900*, but not under the Civil War series, although these pieces were issued 1862–1863.

NY, New York City • Jas. Brennan • NY-630-I • *Stamp dealer* • Dies by William H. Bridgens • Reverse dies: 1152, 1214, 1243 • NY-630-I-1a Rev 1152 (R-3): VF–EF $30–$45 • MS-63 $100–$150.

NY, New York City • William H. Bridgens • NY-630-J • *Diesinker & engraver* • Bridgens' own store card • Reverse dies: 1006, 1137, 1152, 1243 • NY-630-J-2b Rev 1137 (R-5): VF–EF $40–$60 • MS-63 $150–$225.

NY-630-K •
T. Brimelow •
O-1 used with
NY-630-K-1
to 3 and 11.

NY-630-K •
T. Brimelow •
O-2 used with
NY-630-K-4. Stock
reverse die of
NY-630-K-3 here used
as an obverse; no
mention of Brimelow.

NY-630-K •
T. Brimelow •
O-3 used with
NY-630-K-5 to 7.

NY-630-M •
Broas Brothers •
O-1 used with
NY-630-M-1, 4, 5, 14.

NY-630-M •
Broas Brothers •
O-2 used with
NY-630-M-2, 7, 11, 12.

NY-630-M •
Broas Brothers •
O-3 used with
NY-630-M-8.

NY-630-K •
T. Brimelow •
O-4 used with
NY-630-K-8.

NY-630-K •
T. Brimelow •
O-5used with
NY-630-K-9.

NY-630-M •
Broas Brothers •
O-4 used with
NY-630-M-9 and 10.

NY-630-M •
Broas Brothers •
O-5 used with
NY-630-M-13.

NY, New York City • T. Brimelow • NY-630-K • *Druggist* • Dies possibly by the Scovill Manufacturing Co. • Reverse dies: 0, 1133, 1138, 1139, 29240, 29250 • NY-630-K-1a Rev 1138 (R-3): VF–EF $25–$35 • MS-63 $100–$150.

NY, New York City • Broas Brothers • NY-630-M • *Bakers* • Dies by Charles D. Hörter • Reverse dies: 1060, 1061, 1062, 1062A, 1063A, 1064, 1065, 1143, 29315, 29320 • NY-630-M-1a Rev 1060 (R-1), NY-630-M-13a Rev 1143 (R-1): VF–EF $25–$35 • MS-63 $50–$75.

NY-630-L •
Broas Brothers •
O-1 used with
NY-630-L-1 to 4 and 6.

NY-630-L •
Broas Brothers •
O-2 used with
NY-630-L-5.

NY, New York City • Broas Bros. • NY-630-L • *Bakers* • Dies by Charles D. Hörter • Reverse dies: 1004, 1121, 1121A, 1149, 1063 • NY-630-L-2a Rev 1121 (R-2), NY-630-L-5a Rev 1063 (R-2): VF–EF $25–$35 • MS-63 $50–$75.

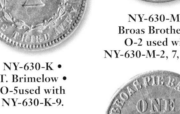
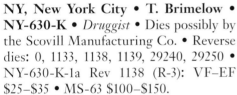

NY-630-N •
M.S. Brown •
O-2 used with
NY-630-N-2.

NY-630-P •
Carland's •
O-1 used with
NY-630-P-1.

NY-630-N •
M.S. Brown •
O-3 used with
NY-630-N-3.

NY-630-N •
M.S. Brown •
O-4 used with
NY-630-N-4.

NY-630-P •
Carland's •
O-2 used with
NY-630-P-2.

NY-630-P •
Carland's •
O-3 used with
NY-630-P-3.

NY, New York City • M.S. Brown • NY-630-N • *Saloonkeeper* • Ascribed to Louis Roloff • Reverse dies: 29360, 29380 • NY-630-N-4a Rev 29380 (R-2): VF–EF $25–$35 • MS-63 $50–$75 • In the third edition of the Fuld book NY-630-N and O will be consolidated under NY-630-N.

NY, New York City • W.S. Brown (M.S. Brown) • NY-630-O • *Saloon-keeper* • Ascribed to Louis Roloff • Reverse dies: 1011, 29380 • NY-630-O-1a Rev 29380 (R-6): VF–EF $100–$200 • MS-63 $300–$450 • Error die; should be M.S. Brown. In the third edition of the Fuld book NY-630-N and O will be consolidated under NY-630-N.

NY, New York City • Carland's • NY-630-P • *Liquor dealer* • ? • Reverse die: 29430 • NY-630-P-1a Rev 29430 (R-2): VF–EF $25–$35 • MS-63 $50–$75.

NY, New York City • Tom Cullen • NY-630-S • *Liquor dealer* • Ascribed to Louis Roloff • Reverse dies: 1240, 1255, 1256, 1257, 29800, 29830 • NY-630-S-3a Rev 1256 (R-4), NY-630-S-4a Rev 1257 (R-4): VF–EF $25–$35 • MS-63 $60–$90.

NY, New York City • J.J. Diehl • NY-630-T • *Undertaker* • Dies by Louis Roloff • Reverse die: 1011 • NY-630-T-1a Rev 1011 (R-2): VF–EF $30–$45 • MS-63 $110–$175.

NY, New York City • Carl Diem, Constanzer Brauerei • NY-630-U • *Brewer* • Dies by Emil Sigel[68] • Reverse die: 1417 • NY-630-U-1a Rev 1417 (R-3): VF–EF $30–$45 • MS-63 $150–$225.

NY-630-V •
C. Doscher •
O-1 used with
NY-630-V-1 to 5.

NY-630-Z •
Fr. Freise •
O-1 used with
NY-630-Z-1.

NY-630-Z •
Fr. Freise •
O-2 used with
NY-630-Z-2 as
the obverse and
Z-1 as the reverse.

NY-630-V •
C. Doscher •
O-2 used with
NY-630-V-6.

NY-630-V •
C. Doscher •
O-3 used with
NY-630-V-7 and 8.

NY, New York City • C. Doscher • NY-630-V • *Grocer, liquor seller* • Dies by Charles D. Hörter • Reverse dies: 0, 1005, 1053, 1054, 1055, 1254, 1254A • NY-630-V-2a Rev 1053 (R-3): VF–EF $25–$35 • MS-63 $50–$75.

NY, New York City • Felix Dining Saloon • NY-630-W • *Restaurant* • Dies by Emil Sigel • Reverse dies: 1015, 1249 • NY-630-W-1a Rev 1015 (R-4): VF–EF $75–$110 • MS-63 $250–$375 • Undistributed tokens were used in quantity as planchets for other varieties. This is the only Civil War store card with the word "kosher" expressed in Hebrew letters.[69]

NY, New York City • Lewis Feuchtwanger • NY-630-X • *Chemist, metallurgist, merchant, etc.* • ? • Reverse die: 29550 • NY-630-X-1j Rev 29550 (R-5): VF–EF $1,750–$2,500 • MS-63 $4,000–$6,000.

NY, New York City • J. Fisher • NY-630-Y • *Cigar store* • Dies by William H. Bridgens • Reverse die: 1214 • NY-630-Y-1a Rev 1214 (R-4): VF–EF $40–$60 • MS-63 $135–$200.

NY, New York City • Fr. Freise • NY-630-Z • *Undertaker* • Dies by Emil Sigel • Reverse die: 29580 • NY-630-A-1a Rev 29580 (R-2): VF–EF $35–$50 • MS-63 $150–$225.

NY, New York City • J.F. Gardner • NY-630-AA • Dies by Emil Sigel • *Leather goods* • Reverse die: 1015 • NY-630-AA-1a Rev 1015 (R-5): VF–EF $30–$45 • MS-63 $90–$135.

NY, New York City • A. Gavron • NY-630-AB • *Butcher* • Dies by William H. Bridgens • Reverse dies: 1006, 1137, 1152, 1214, 1243, 1265, 1268, 1269 • NY-630-AB-8a Rev 1269 (R-3): VF–EF $25–$35 • MS-63 $50–$75 • This is one of the most extensive numismatic series among Bridgens die combinations.

NY, New York City • Charles Gentsch, Café Restaurant du Commerce • NY-630-AC • *Restaurant* • ? • Reverse die: 29620 • NY-630-AC-1a Rev 29620 (R-3): VF–EF $25–$35 • MS-63 $50–$75.

NY, New York City • H.D. Gerdts • NY-630-AD • *Coin dealer, broker* • Dies by William H. Bridgens • Reverse dies: 1137, 1243 • NY-630-AD-1a Rev 1137 (R-3): VF–EF $30–$45 • MS-63 $100–$150.

NY, New York City • G. Graham • NY-630-AE • *Liquor dealer* • Dies by Charles D. Hörter • Reverse dies: 1257, 1263 • NY-630-AE-1a Rev 1263 (R-2): VF–EF $25–$35 • MS-63 $50–$75.

NY, New York City • J.A.C. Grube • NY-630-AF • *Tobacconist* • Dies by Louis Roloff • Reverse dies: 1240, 1257, 1258, 1259, 29800 • NY-630-AF-2a Rev 1257 (R-4), NY-630-AF-3a Rev 1258 (R-4): VF–EF $25–$35 • MS-63 $50–$75.

NY-630-AG •
John P. Gruber •
O-1 used with
NY-630-AG-1.

NY-630-AG •
John P. Gruber •
O-2 used with
NY-630-AG-3 to 7.

NY, New York City • John P. Gruber • NY-630-AG • *Manufacturer of scales* • Dies by Charles D. Hörter and others in combinations • Reverse dies: 1015, 1197, 1198, 1199, 1213, 1230, 1249, 30530 • NY-630-AG-1a Rev 1197 (R-1): VF–EF $25–$35 • MS-63 $50–$75.

NY, New York City • William Hastings • NY-630-AI • *Liquor dealer* • Dies by Charles D. Hörter • Reverse die: 29730 • NY-630-AI-1g Rev 29730 (R-2): VF–EF $25–$35.

NY, New York City • James Havens • NY-630-AIa • *Hat dealer* • ? • Reverse die: 29734 • NY-630-AIa-1a Rev 29734 (R-6): VF–EF $100–$150 • MS-63 $300–$450.

NY, New York City • A.J. Henning • NY-630-AH • *Diesinker and engraver* • Reverse die: 29710 • NY-630-AH-1a Rev 29710 (R-4): VF–EF $50–$75 • MS-63 $200–$300 • Listed out of order by Fuld.

NY, New York City • Chr. F. Hetzel • NY-630-AJ • *Roofer* • ? • Reverse die: 1330 • NY-630-AJ-1a Rev 1330 (R-3): VF–EF $25–$35 • MS-63 $50–$75.

NY-630-AK •
Hussey's Special
Message Post •
O-1 used with
NY-630-AK-1.

NY-630-AK •
Hussey's Special
Message Post •
O-2 used with
NY-630-AK-2.

NY, New York City • Hussey's Special Message Post • NY-630-AK • *Message delivery service*[70] • ? • Reverse dies: 1162, 1163 • NY-630-AK-1a Rev 1162 (R-1): VF–EF $25–$35 • MS-63 $50–$75.

NY, New York City • George Hyenlein • NY-630-AL • *Liquor dealer* • ? • Reverse dies: 1016, 1017, 1132, 1253, 1257, 1258, 1259, 31130 • NY-630-AL-1a Rev 1016 (R-3), NY-630-AL-3a Rev 1132 (R-3), NY-630-AL-7a Rev 1259 (R-3): VF–EF $25–$35 • MS-63 $50–$75.

NY, New York City • Christoph Karl • NY-630-AM • *Liquor dealer* • ? • Reverse dies: 0, 1164 • NY-630-AM-1a Rev 1164 (R-2): VF–EF $25–$35 • MS-63 $50–$75.

NY-630-AMa •
H.M. Kayser •
O-1 used with
NY-630-AMa-1.

NY-630- AMa •
H.M. Kayser •
O-2 used with
NY-630-AMa-2 and 3.

NY, New York City • H. & M. Kayser & Co. • NY-630-AMa • *Fancy goods importer* • Ascribed to the well-known maker of brass spielmarken (play money), Ludwig Christoph Lauer, Nuremberg, Germany • Reverse dies: 1189, 1190, 29785 • NY-630-AMa-1b Rev 1190 (R-7): VF–EF $500–$750 • MS-63 $1,500–$2,250 • Strasburger & Nuhn issued other brass tokens in the 1850s. Nuhn resided in Europe and was the buyer for the New York City firm bearing his name.

NY, New York City • R.T. Kelly • NY-630-AN • *Hatter* • Dies by Emil Sigel • Reverse dies: 1230, 1249 • NY-630-AN-1a Rev 1249 (R-3): VF–EF $25–$35 • MS-63 $75–$110.

NY-630-AQ • Gustavus Lindenmueller • O-1 used with NY-630-AQ-1 to 3, 7, 9.

NY-630-AO • Knoops Segars & Tobacco • O-1 used with NY-630-AO-1 to 5.

NY-630-AO • Knoops Segars & Tobacco • O-2 used with NY-630-AO-6.

NY, New York City • Knoops Segars & Tobacco • NY-630-AO • *Tobacconist* • Dies by Louis Roloff • Reverse dies: 1075, 1240, 1257, 1258, 1259, 1260, 1261 • NY-630-AO-3a Rev 1257 (R-5), NY-630-AO-5a Rev 1261 (R-5): VF–EF $25–$35 • MS-63 $50–$75.

NY, New York City • H.M. Lane • NY-630-AP • *Lamp and kerosene oil dealer* • Certain dies by Louis Roloff, others by Emil Sigel • Reverse dies: 1000, 1016, 1017, 1052, 1132, 1216, 1218, 1219, 1236, 1240, 1251, 1252, 1253, 1257, 1258, 1259, 1277 • NY-630-AP-6a Rev 1216 (R-2): VF–EF $25–$35 • MS-63 $50–$75 • A comparison of obverse die states indicates relative time of striking. The Fuld number listings bear little relation to the striking sequence.

NY-630-AQ • Gustavus Lindenmueller • O-2 used with NY-630-AQ-4 and 5.

NY-630-AQ • Gustavus Lindenmueller • O-3 used with NY-630-AQ-6.

NY, New York City • Gustavus Lindenmueller • NY-630-AQ • *Beer hall and theatre* • Dies by Louis Roloff[71] • Reverse dies: 29840, 29850, 29860, 29870, 29890, 29900 • NY-630-AQ-4a Rev 29850 (R-2): VF–EF $25–$35 • MS-63 $60–$90.

NY-630-AR • Charles A. Lührs • O-1 used with NY-630-AR-1 and 2.

NY-630-AR • Charles A. Lührs • O-2 used with NY-630-AR-3. Reverse die of the preceding.

NY, New York City • Charles A. Lührs, Pike Slip Shades • NY-630-AR • *Saloon* • Dies by Emil Sigel • Reverse dies: 1293, 29920 • NY-630-AR-1a Rev 29920 (R-2): VF–EF $25–$35 • MS-63 $50–$75.

NY, New York City • C. Magnus, National Printing Establishment • NY-630-AS • *Printer, publisher* • Dies by Emil Sigel • Reverse die: 29940 • NY-630-AS-1b Rev 29940 (R-3): VF–EF $25–$35 • MS-63 $75–$110 • 1861 New York City directory: Charles Magnus & Co. Publishers. 12 Frankfort Street. National Printing Establishment. The firm was a leading publisher of patriotic envelopes and other printed items relating to the war.[72]

NY, New York City • J. Mahnken • NY-630-AT • *Liquor, cigars* • Dies by William H. Bridgens • Reverse dies: 1006, 1152, 1214, 1256, 1265, 1269 • NY-630-AT-5a Rev 1269 (R-3): VF–EF $25–$35 • MS-63 $50–$75.

NY, New York City • B. Maloney, National • NY-630-AU • *Saloon* • Dies possibly by the Scovill Manufacturing Co. • Reverse die: 29970 • NY-630-AU-1a Rev 29970 (R-1): VF–EF $25–$35 • MS-63 $50–$75.

NY, New York City • John Matthews • NY-630-AV • *Soda water apparatus* • Dies by Charles Müller • Reverse die: 29990 • NY-630-AV-1a Rev 29990 (R-4): VF–EF $60–$90 • MS-63 $200–$300 • This large-diameter 27.7 mm MATTHEWS MEDAL, as it is lettered, has been adopted into the CWT series ever since the time of its issue.[73]

NY, New York City • H.B. Melville • NY-630-AW • *Jeweler* • ? • Reverse die: 30010 • NY-630-AW-1a Rev 30010 (R-4): VF–EF $30–$45 • MS-63 $110–$175.

NY, New York City • Edward Miehling • NY-630-AX • *Meat market* • Dies by Louis Roloff • Reverse dies: 1010, 1011, 1012 • NY-630-AX-1a Rev 1010 (R-3): VF–EF $25–$35 • MS-63 $50–$75.

NY-630-AY •
Use Miller's 50 Cents
N.Y. Hair Dye
(relief letters) •
O-1 used with
NY-630-AY-1. A
struck token.

NY-630-AY •
Use Miller's
50 Cent Hair Dye
(incuse letters) •
O-2 used with
NY-630-AY-2. Made
by counterstamping
each side separately
with the same die.

NY-630-AZ •
Use L. Miller's
Hair Invigorator
(incuse letters) •
O-1 used with
NY-630-AZ-1. Various
types of coins were
counterstamped on
each side separately
with the same die.

NY, New York City • Louis Miller, Miller's Hair Dye and Invigorator • NY-630-AY and AZ • *Barber, hair preparations* • ? • Reverse dies: 30040, 30050 • NY-630-AY-1a Rev 30040 (R-2): VF–EF $25–$35 • MS-63 $50–$75 • In the third edition of the Fuld book NY-630-AY and AZ will be consolidated under NY-630-AY as here.

NY-630-BA •
G.M. Mittnacht's
Eagle Safe •
O-1 used with
NY-630-BA-1.

NY-630-BA •
G.M. Mittnacht's
Eagle Safe •
O-2 used with
NY-630-BA-2.

NY, New York City • G.M. Mittnacht • NY-630-BA • *Safe maker* **•** ? **•** Reverse die: 30080 **•** NY-630-BA-2a Rev 30080 (R-2): VF–EF $25–$35 **•** MS-63 $50–$75.

NY, New York City • Monks Metal Signs • NY-630-BB • *Metal signs* **•** Dies by Emil Sigel **•** Reverse dies: 1000, 1218, 1219, 1236, 1252, 1253, 1267, 1277, 30110 **•** NY-630-BB-7a Rev 30110 (R-4): VF–EF $25–$35 **•** MS-63 $50–$75 **•** 1861 New York City directory: Charles Monks. Signs. 399 Broadway at the corner of Walker Street. Home: 99 Franklin Street.

NY, New York City • Henry C. Montz • NY-630-BC • *Beer garden* **•** Dies by Charles D. Hörter **•** Reverse die: 30130 **•** NY-630-BC-1a Rev 30130 (R-4): VF–EF $30–$45 **•** MS-63 $75–$110.

NY, New York City • G. Parsons • NY-630-BE • *Fireworks, fancy goods* **•** Dies by Emil Sigel **•** Reverse die: 000, 1017, 1052, 1132, 1218, 1219, 1236, 1252, 1253, 1267, 1277 **•** NY-630-BE-2a Rev 1017 (R-4): VF–EF $25–$35 **•** MS-63 $50–$75 **•** Listed out of order by Fuld.

NY, New York City • Peoples Line • NY-630-BD • *Passenger steamships* **•** ? **•** Reverse die: 30150 **•** NY-630-BD-1a Rev 30150 (R-2): VF–EF $25–$35 **•** MS-63 $50–$75 **•** These tokens served as both advertisements and time tables.

NY, New York City • Chas. Pfaff • NY-630-BF • *Restaurant* **•** ? **•** Reverse die: 30180 **•** NY-630-BF-1a Rev 30180 (R-3): VF–EF $25–$35 **•** MS-63 $50–$75 **•** This was a famous establishment for many years.[74]

NY, New York City • John Quinn • NY-630-BG • *Grocer* **•** Dies by William H. Bridgens **•** Reverse dies: 0, 1006, 1137, 1152, 1214, 1243, 1265, 1268 **•** NY-630-BG-6a Rev 1265 (R-4): VF–EF $25–$35 **•** MS-63 $50–$75.

NY-630-BH •
Christian Rauh •
O-1 used with
NY-630-BH-1 and 3.

NY-630-BH •
Christian Rauh •
O-2 used with
NY-630-BH-2.

NY, New York City • Christian Rauh • NY-630-BG • *Confectioner* **•** Dies by Emil Sigel **•** Reverse dies: 1293, 29920 **•** NY-630-BG-2a Rev 1293 (R-3): VF–EF $25–$35 **•** MS-63 $50–$75.

NY-630-BI •
Frederick
Rollwagen Jr. •
O-1 used with
NY-630-BI-1.

NY-630-BI •
Frederick
Rollwagen Jr. •
O-2 used with
NY-630-BI-2.

NY, New York City • Frederick Rollwagen Jr. • NY-630-BI • *Butcher* **•** Dies possibly by the Scovill Manufacturing Co. **•** Reverse die: 30230 **•** NY-630-BI-2a Rev 30230 (R-2): VF–EF $25–$35 **•** MS-63 $50–$75.

NY, New York City • St. Charles Billiard Rooms • NY-630-BT • *Billiard rooms* **•** Dies by Louis Roloff **•** Reverse dies: 1075, 1257, 1258, 1259 **•** NY-630-BT-1a Rev 1075 (R-3): VF–EF $25–$35 **•** MS-63 $60–$90 **•** Listed out of order in the Fuld reference; St. should be alphabetized as Saint.

NY, New York City • Sanitary Commission (Great Fair for the Sanitary Commission) • NY-630-BJ • *Sanitary fair* **•** Dies possibly by the Scovill Manufacturing Co. **•** Reverse die: 1138 **•** NY-630-BJ-1a Rev 1138 (R-7): VF–EF

$500–$750 • MS-63 $1,500–$2,250 • The Nantucket, Massachusetts, Sanitary Fair tokens (MA-530-A) and the New York City Sanitary Fair tokens (NY-630-BJ) share die 1138 and were probably made about the same time; both varieties seem to have been made after the same reverse die was used to strike the Brimelow tokens (NY-630-K).[75]

NY-630-BK •
Edward Schaaf •
O-1 used with
NY-630-BK-1.

NY-630-BK •
Edward Schaaf •
O-2 used with
NY-630-BK-2 to 4.

NY, New York City • Ed. Schaaf • NY-630-BK • *Grocer* • Dies by Emil Sigel • Reverse dies: 1230, 1231, 30270 • NY-630-BK-1a Rev 1230 (R-2), NY-630-BK-2a Rev 1230 (R-2): VF–EF $20–$30 • MS-63 $50–$75.

NY, New York City • George D. Schmidt • NY-630-BN • *Restaurant, saloon* • Dies by Emil Sigel • Reverse die: 1015 • NY-630-BN-1a Rev 1015 (R-5), NY-630-BN-1b Rev 1015 (R-5): VF–EF $25–$35 • MS-63 $60–$90 • Listed out of order by Fuld.

NY, New York City • J. Schork • NY-630-BL • *Jeweler, clock retailer* • Crude die stamped on lead planchet • Reverse die: 30290 • NY-630-BL-1a Rev 30290 (R-7): VF–EF $1,750–$2,500 • 1863: Had clock shop at the corner of Broadway and 52nd Street.

NY, New York City • John Schuh • NY-630-BM • *Saloon* • Dies by Louis Roloff • Reverse dies: 1010, 29450 • NY-630-BM-1a Rev 1010 (R-1): VF–EF $25–$35 • MS-63 $50–$75.

NY, New York City • Edwd. Schulze's Restaurant • NY-630-BO • *Restaurant* •

Dies by George Glaubrecht • Reverse dies: 30325, 30326 • NY-630-BO-2a Rev 30326 (R-1): VF–EF $25–$35 • MS-63 $60–$90.

NY, New York City • S.H. Scripture • NY-630-BP • *Liquor dealer* • Hard rubber token listed here as it was one of three in the second edition of the Fuld text • Reverse dies: 30330, 30335 • NY-630-BP-2h bla Rev 30335 (R-6): VF–EF $400–600 • MS-63 $1,000–$1,500 • NY-630-BP-4h bla is also R-6.

NY-630-BQ •
Ph. J. Seiter •
O-1 used with
NY-630-BQ-1, 3, 6.

NY-630-BQ •
Ph. J. Seiter •
O-2 used with
NY-630-BQ-2.

NY-630-BQ •
Ph. J. Seiter •
O3 used with
NY-630-BQ-4 and 5.
This die was used
as the reverse of
NY-630-BQ-1 and 2.

NY, New York City • Ph. J. Seiter • NY-630-BQ • *Provisions, meats* • ? • Reverse dies: 0, 1052, 1219, 30370 • NY-630-BQ-1b Rev 30370 (R-1): VF–EF $25–$35 • MS-63 $50–$75.

NY, New York City • I. Sommers, Jones Wood Hotel • NY-630-BR • *Hotel* • Dies by Charles D. Hörter[76] • Reverse die: 1382 • NY-630-BR-1a Rev 1382 (R-2): VF–EF $25–$30 • MS-63 $50–$75.

 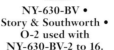 

NY-630-BS •
Staudinger's •
O-1 used with
NY-630-BS-1.

NY-630-BS •
Staudinger's •
O-2 used with
NY-630-BS-2.

NY-630-BV •
Story & Southworth •
O-2 used with
NY-630-BV-2 to 16.

NY-630-BV •
Story & Southworth •
O3 used with
NY-630-BV-17 to 31.

NY, New York City • Staudinger's • NY-630-BS • *Confectioner* • Dies by Louis Roloff • Reverse dies: 1375, 1376 • NY-630-BS-2a Rev 1376 (R-1): VF–EF $25–$35 • MS-63 $50–$75.

NY-630-BU •
S. Steinfeld •
O-1 used with
NY-630-BU-1 and 4.

NY-630-BU •
S. Steinfeld •
O-2 used with
NY-630-BU-2, 3, 5.

NY, New York City • S. Steinfeld • NY-630-BU • *Liquors* • Dies by Emil Sigel • Reverse dies: 1010, 30435, 30445, patriotic 439 • NY-630-BU-3a Rev 30435 (R-2): VF–EF $25–$35 • MS-63 $50–$75 • Steinfeld issued encased postage stamps (John Gault, patent) as advertisements.

NY-630-BV •
Story & Southworth •
O-1 used with
NY-630-BV-1.

NY, New York City • Story & Southworth • NY-630-BV • *Grocers* • Dies by Emil Sigel • Reverse dies: 1000, 1016, 1017, 1052, 1132, 1216, 1217, 1218, 1219, 1236, 1251, 1252, 1252, 1253, 1257, 1259, 1267, 1268, 1277, 1330 • NY-630-BV-6a Rev 1216 (R-2): VF–EF $25–$35 • MS-63 $50–$75.

NY, New York City • Strasburger & Nuhn • NY-630-BW • *Importers* • Ascribed to the well-known maker of brass spielmarken (play money), Ludwig Christoph Lauer, Nuremberg, Germany • Reverse die: 1189 • NY-630-BW-1a Rev 1189 (R-4): VF–EF $90–$135 • MS-63 $300–$450 • Strasburger & Nuhn issued other brass tokens in the 1850s. Nuhn resided in Europe and was the buyer for the New York City firm bearing his name.

 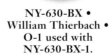 

NY-630-BX •
William Thierbach •
O-1 used with
NY-630-BX-1.

NY-630-BX •
William Thierbach •
O-2 used with
NY-630-BX-2.

NY, New York City • William Thierbach • NY-630-BX • *Grocer* • Dies by Charles D. Hörter • Reverse dies: 30490, 30500 • NY-630-BX-1g Rev 30490 (R-2): VF–EF $25–$35.

NY, New York City • C. Tollner & Hammacher • NY-630-BY • *Hardware dealers* • Dies by Louis Roloff • Reverse dies: 1256, 1258 • NY-630-BY-1a Rev 1256 (R-2): VF–EF $25–$35 • MS-63 $50–$75.

NY-630-BZ •
Peter Warmkessel •
O-1 used with
NY-630-BZ-1 to 3.

NY-630-BZ •
Peter Warmkessel •
O-2 used with
NY-630-BZ-4 and 5.

NY, New York City • Peter Warmkessel • NY-630-BZ • *Beer hall* • Dies by Charles D. Hörter • Reverse dies: 1197, 1263, 30530 • NY-630-BZ-1a Rev 30530 (R-3): VF–EF $25–$35 • MS-63 $50–$75.

NY, New York City • James H. Warner • NY-630-CA • *Liquor dealer* • ? • Reverse die: 1385 • NY-630-CA-1a Rev 1385 (R-7), NY-630-CA-1b Rev 1385 (R-7), NY-630-CA-1d Rev 1385 (R-7), NY-630-CA-1e Rev 1385 (R-7): VF–EF $200–$300 • MS-63 $600–$900.

NY, New York City • William F. Warner • NY-630-CB • *Butcher* • Dies by William H. Bridgens • Reverse dies: 1006, 1265 • NY-630-CB-1a Rev 1006 (R-3): VF–EF $25–$35 • MS-63 $60–$90.

NY, New York City • Washington Market Exchange • NY-630-CC • *Farmers' market* • Dies by George Glaubrecht • Reverse dies: 1144, 1245, 1275, 1353 • NY-630-CB-4a Rev 1353 (R-2): VF–EF $30–$45 • MS-63 $125–$175.

NY, New York City • Washington Restaurant • NY-630-CD • *Restaurant* • Dies by William H. Bridgens • Reverse dies: 1006, 1265 • NY-630-CD-1a Rev 1265 (R-3): VF–EF $25–$35 • MS-63 $60–$90 • The hotel opened in 1848 at an address steeped in city history back to Revolutionary War days.[77]

NY, New York City • John Watson • NY-630-CE • *Tea dealer* • Dies by Charles D. Hörter • Reverse dies: 1219, 30590 • NY-630-CE-1a Rev 30590 (R-4): VF–EF $30–$45 • MS-63 $90–$135.

NY, New York City • Watson's "T" Store • NY-630-CF • *Tea dealer* • Crude dies • Reverse die: 30610 • NY-630-CF-1g Rev 30610 (R-5): VF–EF $125–$175.

NY, New York City • Hugo Wellencamp Colosseum • NY-630-CFa • *Beer hall* • ? • Reverse die: 30612 • NY-630-CFa-1b Rev 30612 (R-6): VF–EF $150–$225 • All letters incuse and deeply stamped. Flat disc without raised rim.

NY, New York City • George W. White • NY-630-CG • *Hatter* • ? • Reverse die: 1051 • NY-630-CG-1a Rev 1051 (R-3): VF–EF $25–$35 • MS-63 $75–$125 • During the time this token was issued, White had ground-floor premises in the P.T. Barnum's American Museum. White issued encased postage stamps (John Gault, patent) as advertisements.

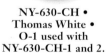

NY-630-CH •
Thomas White •
O-1 used with
NY-630-CH-1 and 2.

NY-630-CH •
Thomas White •
O-2 used with
NY-630-CH-3 to 5.

NY, New York City • Thomas White • NY-630-CH • *Butcher* • Dies possibly by the Scovill Manufacturing Co. • Reverse dies: 0, 30640, 30650, 30670, 30685 • NY-630-CH-1a Rev 30640 (R-2), NY-630-CH-3a Rev 30670 (R-2): VF–EF $25–$35 • MS-63 $50–$75.

NY-630-CI •
Willard & Jackson's
Oyster House •
O-1 used with
NY-630-CI-1 to 3.

NY-630-CI •
Willard & Jackson's
Oyster House •
O-2 used with
NY-630-CI-4.

NY, New York City • Willard & Jackson's Oyster House • NY-630-CI • *Oyster house* • ? • Reverse dies: 30690, 30700, 30710, 30720 • NY-630-CI-1a Rev 30700 (R-3): VF–EF $25–$35 • MS-63 $60–$90.

NY, Niagara Falls • M. Walsh & Sons • NY-640-A • *Dry goods* • Ascribed to the shop of John Stanton • Reverse dies: 1037, 1042, 1043, 1047 • NY-640-A-1a Rev 1042 (R-6): VF–EF $150–$225 • MS-63 $500–$750 • Only token-issuing merchant of this town.

NY, Norwich • John W. Weller • NY-660-A • *News dealer* • Dies by William H. Bridgens • Reverse die: 1266 • NY-660-A-1a Rev 1266 (R-3): VF–EF $40–$60 • MS-63 $250–$375 • Only token-issuing merchant of this town. Earlier listed as CT-345-A.[78]

NY, Ogdensburg • G. Idler • NY-665-A • *Meat market* • Ascribed to the shop of John Stanton • Reverse dies: 1042, 1043, 1047 • NY-665-A-1a Rev 1042 (R-7): VF–EF $60–$90 • MS-63 $200–$300.

NY, Ogdensburg • A.M. Sherman, Johnson House • NY-665-B • *Hotel* • Ascribed to the shop of John Stanton • Reverse dies: 1037, 1042, 1043, 1047 • NY-665-B-1a Rev 1042 (R-6): VF–EF $40–$60 • MS-63 $200–$300.

NY, Oswego • Morgan L. Marshall • NY-695-A • *Variety store, coin dealer*[79] • ?

• Reverse die: 30790 • NY-695-A-2a Rev 30790 (R-1): VF–EF $30–$45 • MS-63 $125–$175 • Only token-issuing merchant of this town.[80] In addition to the Civil War token, Marshall issued a large 29 mm advertising medalet.

NY, Poughkeepsie • Eastman National Business College • NY-760-A • *Business college* • ? • Reverse die: 30810 • NY-760-A-1d Rev 30810 (R-5): VF–EF $125–$175 • MS-63 $250–$375 • Only token-issuing merchant of this town.[81]

NY, Seneca Falls • D. Skidmore, Skidmore's Head Quarters • NY-845-A • *Hotel* • Dies by William H. Bridgens • Reverse dies: 30820, 30830 • NY-845-A-1a Rev 30830 (R-6), NY-845-A-1b Rev 30830 (R-6): VF–EF $250–$375 • MS-63 $900–$1,350 • Only token-issuing merchant of this town.

NY-890-A •
Charles Babcock •
O-1 used with
NY-890-A-1.

NY-890-A •
Charles Babcock •
O-2 used with
NY-890-A-2.

NY-890-A •
Charles Babcock •
O-3 used with
NY-890-A-3.

NY, Troy • Charles Babcock • NY-890-A • *Jeweler* • ? • Reverse die: 1013, 30860, 30880 • NY-890-A-1a Rev 1013 (R-3): VF–EF $25–$35 • MS-63 $75–$125.

NY-890-B •
Oliver Boutwell •
O-1 used with
NY-890-B-1 and 2.

NY-890-B •
Oliver Boutwell •
O-2 used with
NY-890-B-3 and 4.

NY-890-B •
Oliver Boutwell •
O-9 used with
NY-890-B-17 and 18.

NY-890-B •
Oliver Boutwell •
O-10 used with
NY-890-B-19 to 22.

NY-890-B •
Oliver Boutwell •
O-3 used with
NY-890-B-5.

NY-890-B •
Oliver Boutwell •
O-4 used with
NY-890-B-6 to 8.

NY-890-B •
Oliver Boutwell •
O-11 used with
NY-890-B-23.

NY-890-B •
Oliver Boutwell •
O-12 used with
NY-890-B-24.

NY-890-B •
Oliver Boutwell •
O-5 used with
NY-890-B-9.

NY-890-B •
Oliver Boutwell •
O-6 used with
NY-890-B-10 and 11.

NY-890-B •
Oliver Boutwell •
O-13 used with
NY-890-B-25.

NY-890-B •
Oliver Boutwell •
O-14 used with
NY-890-B-26.

NY-890-B •
Oliver Boutwell •
O-7 used with
NY-890-B-12.

NY-890-B •
Oliver Boutwell •
O-8 used with
NY-890-B-13 to 16.

NY-890-B •
Oliver Boutwell •
O-15 used with
NY-890-B-27.

NY-890-B •
Oliver Boutwell •
O-16 used with
NY-890-B-28 and 29.

NY-890-B •
Oliver Boutwell •
O-17 used with
NY-890-B-30.

NY-890-B •
Oliver Boutwell •
O-18 used with
NY-890-B-31.

NY-890-B •
Oliver Boutwell •
O-19 used with
NY-890-B-32.

NY-890-B •
Oliver Boutwell •
O-20 used with
NY-890-B-33.

NY-890-B •
Oliver Boutwell •
O-21 used with
NY-890-B-34.

NY-890-B •
Oliver Boutwell •
O-22 used with
NY-890-B-35.

NY, Troy • Oliver Boutwell • NY-890-B • *Miller*[82] • ? • Reverse dies: 30900A, 30900D, 30900G, 30900I, 30910A, 30910B, 30910C, 30910C, 30910D, 30910E, 30910F, 30910G, 30910H, 30910I, 30910J, 30910K, 30910L, 30910M, 30910N, 30910O, 30910P, 30910Q, 30910R, 30910S, 30910T, 30910U, 30920A, 30920B, 30925 • NY-890-B-1b Rev 30910-A (R-1), NY-890-B-10a Rev 30910I (R-1): VF–EF $20–$30 • MS-63 $50–$75.

NY, Troy • Fred A. Plum • NY-890-C • *Rubber goods* • Hard rubber token listed here as it was one of three in the second edition of the Fuld text • Reverse dies:

30940, 30950 • NY-890-C-1h bla Rev 30940 (R-5): VF–EF $100-150 • MS-63 $300-450 • NY-890-C-2h bla is also R-5.

NY, Troy • W.E. Hagan • NY-890-D • *Druggist* • Hard rubber token listed here as it was one of three in the 2nd edition of the Fuld text • Reverse die: 30970 • NY-890-D-1h bla (R-5): VF–EF $250-375• MS-63 $750-1,250.

NY-890-E •
Robinson & Ballou •
O-1 used with
NY-890-E-1 to 3.

NY-890-E •
Robinson & Ballou •
O-2 used with
NY-890-E-4 to 6.

NY-890-E •
Robinson & Ballou •
O-3 used with
NY-890-E-7.

NY-890-E •
Robinson & Ballou •
O-4 used with
NY-890-E-8.

NY-890-E •
Robinson & Ballou •
O-5 used with
NY-890-E-9 to 11.

NY-890-E •
Robinson & Ballou •
O-6 used with
NY-890-E-12.

NY, Troy • Robinson & Ballou • NY-890-E • *Grocers* • ? • Reverse dies: 31010A, 31010B, 31010C, 31010D, 31010E, 31010F, 31010G • NY-890-E-1b Rev 31010A (R-1), NY-890-E-5b Rev 31010D (R-1): VF–EF $20–$30 • MS-63 $50–$75.

NY, Utica • Dickinson Comstock & Co. • NY-905-A • *Druggists and grocers* • Dies by William H. Bridgens • Reverse die: 1266 • NY-905-A-1a Rev 1266 (R-5): VF–EF $60–$90 • MS-63 $300–$450.

NY, Utica • I.J. Knapp • NY-905-B • *Wines and liquors* • Dies by William H. Bridgens • Reverse dies: 1265, 1266 • NY-905-B-2a Rev 1266 (R-2): VF–EF $25–$35 • MS-63 $75–$125.

NY, Utica • Sherwood & Hopson • NY-905-C • *China emporium* • WBC • Reverse die: 1233 • NY-905-C-1a Rev 1233 (R-2): VF–EF $25–$35 • MS-63 $50–$75.

NY-940-A •
Henry C. Welles •
O-1 used with
NY-940-A-1 and 2.

NY-940-A •
Henry C. Welles •
O-2 used with
NY-940-A-3.

NY, Waterloo • Henry C. Welles • NY-940-A • *Druggist, bookseller*[83] • ? • Reverse dies: 1358, 1367 • NY-940-A-1a Rev 1358 (R-2): VF–EF $25–$35 • MS-63 $60–$90 • Only token-issuing merchant of this town.

NY, Watertown • Hart's Arcade Gallery • NY-945-A • *Photographer* • ? • Reverse dies: 1407, 1408 • NY-945-A-1a Rev 1407 (R-3): VF–EF $30–$45 • MS-63 $100–$150 • Only token-issuing merchant of this town.

NY, Whitehall • E.W. Hall, Atherton's Pills, Atherton's Wild Cherry Syrup • NY-985-A • *Chemist, druggist, bookseller, stationer* • ? • Reverse die: 31100 • NY-985-A-1a Rev 31100 (R-1): VF–EF $25–$35 • MS-63 $50–$75 • Only token-issuing merchant of this town.[84]

NY, Williamsville • Williamsville Exvpress • NY-990-A • *Railroad* • ? •

Reverse die: 31120 • NY-990-A-1a Rev 31120 (R-5): VF–EF $125–$175 • MS-63 $500–$750 • Only token-issuing merchant of this town.

NY, Yonkers • E.E. Hasse • NY-995-A • *Saloonkeeper* • Dies by Louis Roloff • Reverse dies: 1075, 1240, 1257 • NY-995-A-1a Rev 1075 (R-3): VF–EF $30-45 • MS-63 $100-150 • Only token issuer of this town.

OHIO

The store cards attributed to Ohio are the most numerous among the state series. Over 100 towns and cities yielded over 3,100 different die and metal combinations. Particularly extensive is the series relating to Cincinnati, this being the home of two especially important makers of tokens, the shops of W.K. Lanphear and John Stanton. In addition, several other diesinkers and/or token makers produced varieties of such pieces, some working with the aforementioned Lanphear and Stanton facilities.

OH, Adamsville • Stoner & Shroyer • OH-005-A • *Dry goods dealer* • Dies by the shop of F.C. Key & Son • Reverse dies: 1048, 1134, 1146, 1150, 1193, 1250 • OH-005-A-1a Rev 1048 (R-3): VF–EF $35–$50 • MS-63 $125–$175 • Only token issuer of this town. Many if not most are probably slightly postwar.[85]

OH, Adelphi • D.H. Strous • OH-010-A • *Flour and woolen manufacturers* • Ascribed to the shop of W.K. Lanphear • Reverse dies: 1091, 1171 • OH-010-A-2a Rev 1171 (R-5): VF–EF $70–$135 • MS-63 $300–$450 • Only token issuer of this town.

OH, Ashland • Ella Buchanan • OH-25-A • *Watchmaker* • Dies by Murdock & Spencer • Reverse die: 1432 • OH-25-A-1b Rev 1432 (R-9): VF–EF $5,000–$7,500 • MS-63 $12,500–$17,500 • Only token issuer of this town. Watch repair check. Most are struck over 1864 presidential campaign tokens. Ashland is one of the "rarest towns" in the Civil War store card series.

OH, Barnesville • N. Patterson • OH-050-A • *Saddlery, hardware, leather and shoe findings, wool, sheep pelts, furs, etc.* • Ascribed to the shop of W.K. Lanphear • Reverse dies: 1126, 1462 • OH-050-A-2a Rev 1126 (R-3): VF–EF $50–$75 • MS-63 $150–$225.

OH, Barnesville • W.A. Talbot & Son • OH-050-B • *Dry goods* • Ascribed to the shop of W.K. Lanphear • Reverse dies: 1091, 1126, 1127, 1128, 1223, 1332 • OH-050-B-2a Rev 1126 (R-4): VF–EF $25–$35 • MS-63 $75–$125.

OH, Bellaire • Bellaire Ferry Ticket • OH-060-A • *Ferry ticket* • Ascribed to the shop of W.K. Lanphear • Reverse die: 1168 • OH-060-A-1a Rev 1168 (R-7): VF–EF $250–$375 • MS-63 $750–$1,250.

OH, Bellaire • J.S. Bonbright • OH-060-B • *Hardware and stove dealer* • Ascribed to the shop of W.K. Lanphear • Reverse dies: 1084, 1123, 31270 • OH-060-B-1a Rev 1084 (R-7), OH-060-B-2a Rev 1123 (R-7): VF–EF $75–$125 • MS-63 $250–$375.

OH-060-C •
Richardson & Bro. •
O-2 used with
OH-060-C-3 to 5.

OH, Bellaire • Richardson & Bro. • OH-060-C • *Dry goods, notions, drugs, and medicines* • Ascribed to the shop of W.K. Lanphear • Reverse dies: 1178, 1179, 1180 • OH-060-C-4a Rev 1178 (R-8), OH-060-C-5a Rev 1179 (R-8): VF–EF $60–$90 • MS-63 $200–$300.

OH, Bellaire • E.B. Winans & Co. • OH-060-D • *Dry goods, notions, drugs, and medicine* • Ascribed to the shop of W.K. Lanphear • Reverse dies: 1091, 1166, 1168, 1180, 1181, 1224, 1310 • OH-060-D-2 Rev 1166 (R-6): VF–EF $50–$75 • MS-63 $200–$300.

OH, Bellevue • Applegate & Co. Cheap Cash Store • OH-065-A • *Stove and home furnishings dealer* • Ascribed to the shop of W.K. Lanphear • Reverse die: 1181 • OH-065-A-1a Rev 1181 (R-5): VF–EF $50–$75 • MS-63 $200–$300.

OH-065-B • P. Brady • O-1 used with OH-065-B-1 and 2.	OH-065-B • P. Brady • O-2 used with OH-065-B-3 to 5.

OH, Bellevue • P. Brady • OH-065-B • *Dealer in stoves, tinware, etc.* • Ascribed to the shop of W.K. Lanphear • Reverse dies: 0, 1122, 1297, 1300, Pat 143 • OH-065-B-1a Rev 1122 (R-6), OH-065-B-3a Rev 1297 (R-6): VF–EF $50–$75 • MS-63 $200–$300.

OH, Bellevue • C.A. Willard • OH-65-C • *Dry goods dealer* • Ascribed to the shop of W.K. Lanphear • Reverse die: 1127 • Reverse 065-C-1a Rev 1127 (R-6): VF–EF $60–$90 • MS-63 $200–$300.

OH, Belmont • O.G. Metcalf • OH-070-A • *Dry goods dealer* • Ascribed to the shop of W.K. Lanphear • Reverse die: 1090 • Reverse 070-A-1a Rev 1090 (R-8): VF–EF $2,000–$3,000 • Only token issuer of this town.

OH-074-A •
D.E. Stearns •
O-1 used with
OH-074-A-1 to 10.

OH-074-A •
D.E. Stearns •
O-2 used with
OH-074-A-11
to 13, 17, 18.

OH-074-A •
D.E. Stearns •
O-3 used with
OH-074-A-14 and 15.

OH-074-A •
D.E. Stearns •
O-4 used with
OH-074-A-16, 18. The
reverse is the obverse
of OH-165-BJ-12.

OH, Berea • D.E. Stearns • OH-074-A
• *Grindstones, harvester knives* • Ascribed
to the shop of John Stanton[86] • Reverse
dies: 1018, 1019, 1037, 1042, 1046, 1047,
1069, 1203, 31360, 31370, 32490, 32705 •
OH-074-A-1a Rev 31370 (R-3): VF–EF
$25–$35 • MS-63 $75–$125 • Only token
issuer of this town.

OH, Beverly • P. Burkholter • OH-076-A • *Groceries, provisions, confectionery, and produce* • Ascribed to the shop of W.K.
Lanphear • Reverse die: 1082 • OH-076A-1a Rev 1082 (R-5): VF–EF $75–110
• MS-63 $300–450 • Only token issuer of
this town.

**OH, Birmingham • Craig & Foy •
OH-079-A** • *Dry goods* • Ascribed to the
shop of W.K. Lanphear • Reverse dies:
1082, 1089 • OH-079-A-2a Rev 1089
(R-5): VF–EF $75–$125 • MS-63 $225–
$350 • Only token issuer of this town.

OH, Bryan • Jeff Miller • OH-100-A •
Hardware dealer • Ascribed to the shop of

W.K. Lanphear • Reverse die: 1326 •
OH-100-A-1a Rev 1326 (R-3): VF–EF
$30–$45 • MS-63 $100–$150.

OH-100-B •
E.G. Selby & Co. •
O-1 used with
OH-100-B-1 and 2.

OH-100-B •
E.G. Selby & Co. •
O-2 used with
OH-100-B-5 and 6.

OH, Bryan • E.G. Selby & Co. • OH-100-B • *Hardware dealer* • Ascribed to the
shop of W.K. Lanphear • Reverse dies:
011N, 1122, 1228, 1334, 31450 •
OH-100-B-2a Rev 1334 (R-4): VF–EF
$25–$35 • MS-63 $100–$150.

OH, Cadiz • G.B. Barrett • OH-110-A
• *Dealer in watches, jewelry, fancy goods, etc.*
• Ascribed to the shop of John Stanton •
Reverse dies: 1018, 1019, 1025, 1028, 1042,
1046, 1047, 1069 • OH-110-A-1a Rev 1018
(R-7): VF–EF $40–$60 • MS-63 $125–
$175.

OH, Cadiz • J.M. Robinson • OH-110-B • *Dealer in hardware, stoves, fire
fronts, etc.* • Ascribed to the shop of John
Stanton • Reverse dies: 1018, 1025, 1042,
1047, 1069 • OH-110-B-1a Rev 1018 (R-5):
VF–EF $25–$35 • MS-63 $125–$175.

OH, Cambridge • A.C. Cochran • OH-115-A • *Hardware dealer* • Ascribed to the
shop of W.K. Lanphear • Reverse dies: 0,
1166, 1178, 1179, 1303, 1304, 1180, 31500,
31510 • OH-115-A-2a Rev 1178 (R-6),
OH-115-A-3a Rev 1179 (R-6): VF–EF
$40–$60 • MS-63 $175–$250.

OH, Cambridge • J.J. Squier • OH-115-B • *Dry goods dealer* • Ascribed to the
shop of W.K. Lanphear • Reverse dies:
1084, 1085, 1087, 1088, 1122, 1126, 1130,
1166, 1168, 1179, 1228 • OH-115-B-6a
Rev 1126 (R-4): VF–EF $25–$35 • MS-63
$100–$150.

OH, Camden • C. Chadwick • OH-120-A • *Dry goods dealer* • Ascribed to the shop of W.K. Lanphear • Reverse dies: 1171, 1223 • OH-120-A-2a Rev 1223 (R-6): VF–EF $60–$90 • MS-63 $200–$300.

OH, Camden • J.P. Fornshell • OH-120-B • *Grocer and oyster dealer* • Ascribed to the shop of John Stanton • Reverse dies: 1038, 1042, 1047, 1069 • OH-120-B-1a Rev 1038 (R-6): VF–EF $60–$90 • MS-63 $200–$300.

OH, Canaan • Grimes & Griner • OH-122-A • *Dry goods, notions, etc.* • Ascribed to the shop of W.K. Lanphear • Reverse die: 1123 • OH-122-A-1a Rev 1123 (R-5): VF–EF $75–$125 • MS-63 $250–$375 • Only token-issuing merchant of this location.

OH, Canton • J.A. Meyer • OH-125-A • *Watches, clocks, and jewelry* • Ascribed to the shop of John Stanton • Reverse dies: 1028, 1042, 1045, 1046, 1047, 1069 • OH-125-A-1a1 Rev 1028 (R-5): VF–EF $50–$75 • MS-63 $150–$225.

OH, Canton • C. Oberly • OH-125-B • *Groceries, provisions, confectionery, utensils* • Ascribed to the shop of W.K. Lanphear • Reverse dies: 1122, 1346 • OH-125-B-1a Rev 1122 (R-6): VF–EF $90–$135 • MS-63 $300–$450.

OH, Centerville • James Mathews • OH-135-A • *Dry goods and groceries* • Ascribed to the shop of W.K. Lanphear • Reverse dies: 1085, 1227 • OH-135-A-1a Rev 1085 (R-6): VF–EF $175–$250 • MS-63 $500–$750 • Only token issuer of this town.

OH, Chesterville • Bartlett Goble & Co. • OH-150-A • *Dry goods and groceries* • Ascribed to the shop of John Stanton • Reverse dies: 1046, 1047 • OH-150-A-1a Rev 1046 (R-6): VF–EF $75–$110 • MS-63 $250–$375.

OH, Chesterville • Miles & Sperry • OH-150-B • *Dry goods and groceries* •

Ascribed to the shop of John Stanton • Reverse dies: 1046, 1047 • OH-150-B-1a Rev 1046 (R-7): VF–EF $60–$90 • MS-63 $250–$375.

OH-160-A • John Bohn • O-1 used with OH-160-A-1.

OH-160-A • John Bohm • Surname given as "Bohm." O-2 used with OH-160-A-2.

OH, Chillicothe • John Bohn • OH-160-A • *Grocery and saloon* • Dies possibly by Murdock & Spencer[87] • Reverse die: 1391 • OH-160-A-1b Rev 1391 (R-8): VF–EF $200–$300 • MS-63 $600–$900.

OH, Chillicothe • Jno F. Bier & Co. • OH-160-B • *Groceries, boots, and shoes* • Ascribed to the shop of W.K. Lanphear • Reverse dies: 1084, 1123, 1166, 1178, 1179 • OH-160-B-2a Rev 1123 (R-6): VF–EF $60–$90 • MS-63 $250–$375.

OH, Chillicothe • H. Keim • OH-160-D • *Grocer* • Ascribed to the shop of W.K. Lanphear • Reverse die: 1171 • OH-160-D-1a Rev 1171 (R-6): VF–EF $75–$125.

OH, Chillicothe • John Kirchenschlager • OH-160-Da • *Saloon* • Ascribed to the shop of W.K. Lanphear[88] • Reverse die: 1295 • OH-160-Da-1a Rev 1295 (R-6): VF–EF $150–$225 • MS-63 $300–$450.

OH, Chillicothe • M. Kirsch, Phoenix House • OH-160-E • *Hotel, tavern, etc.* • ? • Reverse die: 31660 • OH-160-E-1b Rev 31660 (R-9): VF–EF $300–$450.

OH, Chillicothe • Adam S. Kramer • OH-160-F • *Confectionery, toys, notions* • Ascribed to the shop of W.K. Lanphear • Reverse dies: 1126, 1166, 1227 • OH-160-E-3a Rev 1227 (R-6): VF–EF

$50–$75 • MS-63 $200–$300 • Adam S. Kramer threw open the doors of his new confectionery shop on September 17, 1861.

OH, Chillicothe • Rufus Motter • OH-160-G • *Books, periodicals, cigars, etc.* • Ascribed to the shop of W.K. Lanphear • Reverse dies: 1125, 1176, 1177, 1180, 1322, 1323, 1324 • OH-160-G-5a Rev 1322 (R-4): VF–EF $30–$45 • MS-63 $135–$200 • Motter operated the Valley House News Depot. In 1864 he sold it to Augustus Wallace (see listing below), who kept it only for a short time.

OH, Chillicothe • T. Rupel & Co. • OH-160-H • *Grocers* • Ascribed to the shop of W.K. Lanphear • Reverse dies: 1125, 1178, 1180, 1181, 1327 • OH-160-H-1a Rev 1125 (R-6), OH-160-H-4a Rev 1181 (R-6): VF–EF $50–$75 • MS-63 $150–$225 • On April 11, 1865, Rupel placed this notice: "T. Rupel & Co., No. 52 Fourth Str. Groceries, provisions, dry goods, boots and shoes, back in business."

OH, Chillicothe • William M. Sosman • OH-160-I • *Baker and grocer* • Ascribed to the shop of W.K. Lanphear • Reverse dies: 1125, 1126, 1166 • OH-160-I-1a Rev 1125 (R-5): VF–EF $40–$60 • MS-63 $100–$150.

OH, Chillicothe • Augustus Wallace • OH-160-J • *News depot, tobacco, cigars, and notions* • ? • Reverse dies: 1168, 1223, 1323, 1324 • OH-160-J-1a Rev 1168 (R-5): VF–EF $30–$45.

OH, Cincinnati • Martin Adleta • OH-165-A • *Coffee house* • Ascribed to the shop of John Stanton[89] • Reverse dies: 1026, 1029, 1033, 1036, 1039, 1042, 1047, 1069 • OH-165-A-1a Rev 1026 (R-5): VF–EF $25–$35 • MS-63 $100–$150.

OH, Cincinnati • W. Alenburg • OH-165-B • *Meat store* • Dies by W. Johnston • Reverse die: 1386 • OH-165-B-1a Rev 1386 (R-7): VF–EF $135–$200 • MS-63 $400–$600.

OH, Cincinnati • B.B. Armstrong, Black Bear Hotel • OH-165-C • *Hotel* • Ascribed to the shop of John Stanton • Reverse dies: 1018, 1019, 1022, 1042, 1046, 1047, 1069, 34280 • OH-165-C-3a Rev 1022 (R-6), OH-165-C-4a Rev 1042 (R-6): VF–EF $40–$60 • MS-63 $150–$225.

OH, Cincinnati • F. Arnold, Gruhlers Garden Concert Saloon • OH-165-E • *Coffeehouse* • Ascribed to the shop of John Stanton • Reverse dies: 1019, 1021, 1038, 1042, 1047, 1069, 1192 • OH-165-E-2a Rev 1021 (R-5): VF–EF $30–$45 • MS-63 $100–$150.

OH, Cincinnati • James S. Austin • OH-165-F • *Staple and fancy groceries* • Ascribed to the shop of John Stanton • Reverse dies: 1009, 1019, 1042, 1047 • OH-165-F-1a Rev 1009 (R-5): VF–EF $25–$35 • MS-63 $100–$150 • James S. Austin, grocer, north east corner of 5th and Elm streets. Home at southwest corner of 4th and Elm streets.

OH, Cincinnati • H. Avermaat • OH-165-G • *Dealer in butter and eggs* • Ascribed to the shop of John Stanton • Reverse dies: 1008, 1019, 1020, 1038, 1042, 1047, 1069 • OH-165-G-1a Rev 1008 (R-4): VF–EF $25–$35 • MS-63 $100–$150.

OH, Cincinnati • Samuel Bacciocco • OH-165-H • *Confectionery, ice cream saloon* • Ascribed to the shop of W.K. Lanphear • Reverse dies: 1131, 1172, 1274, 34690 • OH-165-H-3a Rev 1274 (R-5): VF–EF $25–$35 • MS-63 $100–$150.

OH, Cincinnati • W. Baker & Co. • OH-165-Ia • *Omnibus line operator* • Ascribed to the shop of John Stanton • Reverse die: 1440 • OH-165-Ia-1b Rev 1440 (R-8): VF–EF $400–$600 • MS-63 $1,000–$1,500.

OH, Cincinnati • R. Bathgate • OH-165-J • *Boots, shoes, and groceries* • Ascribed to the shop of John Stanton • Reverse dies: 1008, 1019, 1042, 1047, 1069 •

OH-165-J-1a Rev 1008 (R-6): VF–EF $30–$45 • MS-63 $125–$175.

OH, Cincinnati • John Bauer • OH-165-K • *Coffeehouse* • Ascribed to the shop of John Stanton • Reverse dies: 1022, 1028, 1029, 1030, 1031, 1033, 1034, 1042, 1043, 1047, 1069 • OH-165-K-5a Rev 1031 (R-5): VF–EF $25–$35 • MS-63 $100–$150.

OH-165-L •
C.H. Beer's Saloon •
Should be Beers' •
O-1 used with
OH-165-L-1 to 7.

OH-165-L •
C.H. Beers •
O-2 used with
OH-165-L-8.
"Revolvers,
cutlery, notions."

OH-165-L •
C.H. Beers •
O-3 used with
OH-165-L-9. This is
O-2 slightly reworked
by changing the
circles at the side
of 55 by adding a
star to their centers.

OH, Cincinnati • C.H. Beer's Saloon / C.H. Beers • OH-165-L • *Coffeehouse / revolvers, cutlery, notions* • Ascribed to the shop of W.K. Lanphear • Reverse dies: 0, 1432, 1124, 1170, 1176, 1177, 1295, 1331, 31870 • OH-165-L-1a Rev 31870 (R-4): VF–EF $25–$35 • MS-63 $90–$135.

OH, Cincinnati • B.P. Belknap • OH-165-M • *Dentist* • Ascribed to the shop of W.K. Lanphear • Reverse die: 1346 • OH-165-M-1a Rev 1346 (R-6): VF–EF

$175–$250 • MS-63 $600–$900 • Surname misspelled as "Belknp." Office and residence at 137 West 4th St.

OH, Cincinnati • C.H. Bennett • OH-165-O • *Steam bakery* • Ascribed to the shop of John Stanton • Reverse dies: 1022, 1024, 1029, 1030, 1033, 1034, 1037, 1042, 1069 • OH-165-O-2a Rev 1029 (R-5): VF–EF $25–$35 • MS-63 $100–$150 • Charles H. Bennett, bakery, 89 West Court Street; home at 175 Laurel Street.

OH-165-N •
Dr. Bennett's
Medicines •
O-1 used with
OH-165-N-1 to 7.

OH-165-N •
Dr. Bennett's
Medicines •
O-3 used with
OH-165-N-9.

OH-165-N •
Dr. Bennett's
Medicines •
O-4 used with
OH-165-N-10
to 19, 27, 28.

OH-165-N •
Dr. Bennett's
Medicines •
O-5 used with
OH-165-N-21
to 26, 29.

OH, Cincinnati • Dr. D.M. Bennett / Dr. Bennett's Medicines • OH-165-N • *Medical doctor, patent medicine compounder* • Ascribed to the shops of W.K. Lanphear (1 to 9) and John Stanton (the other dies) • Reverse dies: 1435, 1018, 1023, 1026, 1027, 1030, 1033, 1034, 1038, 1039, 1042, 1044, 1045, 1047, 1069, 1124, 1176, 1290, 1295, 1331, 1352, 31920, 31940, 31960, 32470 • OH-165-N-9a Rev 1352 (R-3): VF–EF $20–$30 • MS-63 $60–$90.

OH-165-P •
Frank Beresford •
O-1 used with
OH-165-P-1 to 5, 9.

OH-165-P •
Frank Beresford •
O-2 used with
OH-165-P-6 to 8.
Used as the reverse
die of the preceding.

OH-165-R •
Lew Boman •
O-3 used with
OH-165-R-13 to 18.

OH-165-R •
Lew Boman •
O-4 used with
OH-165-R-19 to 22.
This die was used as
the *reverse* of certain
other varieties.

OH, Cincinnati • Frank Beresford • OH-165-P • *Meat market* • Ascribed to the shop of John Stanton • Reverse dies: 0, 1018, 1019, 1042, 1047, 1069, 31990 • OH-165-P-1a1 Rev 31990 (R-4): VF–EF $25–$35 • MS-63 $100–$150.

OH, Cincinnati • Frederick Billiods • OH-165-Q • *Brewer* • Ascribed to the shop of John Stanton • Reverse die: 1440 • OH-165-Q-1b Rev 1440 (R-8): VF–EF $25–$35 • MS-63 $100–$150 • Frederick Billiods, Lafayette Brewery, No. 184 on north side of Hamilton Road between Vine and Race streets. Home at 721 Vine Street.

OH-165-R •
Lew Boman •
O-1 used with
OH-165-R-1
to 7, 23, 25.

OH-165-R •
Lew Boman •
O-2 used with
OH-165-R-8
to 12, 24, 26.

OH, Cincinnati • Lew Boman • OH-165-R • *Restaurant* • Ascribed to the shop of John Stanton[90] • Reverse dies: 1009, 1018, 1019, 1030, 1036, 1042, 1045, 1046, 1047, 1069, 1192, 1288, 1289, 1393, 33430 • OH-165-R-11a Rev 1192 (R-6): VF–EF $30–$45 • MS-63 $125–$175.

OH, Cincinnati • A. Bruggemann • OH-165-S • *Grocer* • Dies by W. Johnston • Reverse dies: 1056, 1386 • OH-165-S-2a Rev 1386 (R-6): VF–EF $60–$90 • MS-63 $300–$450.

OH, Cincinnati • J. Campbell • OH-165-T • *Grocer and provision dealer* • Ascribed to the shop of John Stanton • Reverse dies: 1023, 1028, 1030, 1034, 1042, 1047, 1069, 35010 • OH-165-T-1a Rev 1023 (R-5), OH-165-T-4a Rev 1034 (R-5): VF–EF $25–$35 • MS-63 $100–$150.

OH, Cincinnati • Cincinnati & Covington Ferry Co. • OH-165-W • *Ferry across the Ohio River* • Ascribed to the shop of John Stanton • Reverse dies: 1022, 1026, 1033, 1036, 1039, 1042, 1047, 1069, 34615 • OH-165-W-1a Rev 1022 (R-5), OH-165-W-3a Rev 1033 (R-5): VF–EF $30–$45 • MS-63 $100–$150.

OH, Cincinnati • City Hosiery Store • OH-165-X • *Hosiery* • Ascribed to the shop of John Stanton • Reverse dies: 1021, 1042, 1046, 1047, 1069 • OH-165-X-1a Rev 1021 (R-5): VF–EF $35–$50 • MS-63 $125–$175 • Trade style of Gabriel Simon & Son who otherwise advertised as wholesale clothiers.[91]

OH, Cincinnati • C.E. Clark's Lightning Hair Dyeing Room • OH-165-Y • *Barber* • Ascribed to the shop of John Stanton • Reverse dies: 1019, 1942, 1047, 1068, 1069, 1393 • OH-165-Y-2a Rev 1042 (R-7), OH-165-Y-2b Rev 1042 (R-7), OH-165-Y-4b Rev 1068, Oh-165-Y-5j Rev 1393 (R-7): VF–EF $75–$125 • MS-63 $300–$450.

OH, Cincinnati • M.A. Cohn • OH-165-Ya • *Coffeehouse* • Ascribed to the shop of John Stanton • Reverse die: 0 • OH-165-Ya-1b Rev 0 (R-9): VF–EF $500–$750 • MS-63 $1,000–$1,500.

OH, Cincinnati • Cole's Bakery • OH-165-Z • *Bakery* • Ascribed to the shop of John Stanton • Reverse die: 1470, 1009, 1022, 1026, 1031, 1038, 1042, 1046, 1047 • OH-165-Z-3a Rev 1026 (R-5): VF–EF $30–$45 • MS-63 $125–$175.

OH, Cincinnati • Commission Boots & Shoes • OH-165-AA • *Boots and shoes* • Ascribed to the shop of John Stanton • Reverse dies: 1008, 1019, 1042, 1047, 1069 • OH-165-AA-1a Rev 1008 (R-5): VF–EF $30–$45 • MS-63 $100–$150 • In the third edition of the Fuld book OH-165-AA and GJ will be consolidated under OH-165-GJ.

OH, Cincinnati • Connecticut Mutual Life Insurance Co. • OH-165-AB • *Life insurance* • Ascribed to the shop of John Stanton • Reverse die: 1047 • OH-165-AB-1a Rev 1047 (R-8): VF–EF $1,000–$1,500 • MS-63 $2,000–$3,000.

OH, Cincinnati • Chas. Conroy • OH-165-AC • *Grocer and liquor dealer* • Ascribed to the shop of John Stanton • Reverse dies: 1026, 1039, 1042, 1046, 1047, 1069 • OH-165-AC-1a Rev 1026 (R-5): VF–EF $40–$60 • MS-63 $125–$175.

OH, Cincinnati • Costello's Trimmings and Fancy Goods • OH-165-AE • *Fancy goods dealer* • Ascribed to the shop of John Stanton • Reverse dies: 1007, 1008, 1019, 1020, 1021, 1023, 1026, 1029, 1030, 1032, 1034, 1042, 1047, 1069 • OH-165-AE-3a Rev 1019 (R-6), OH-165-AE-5a Rev 1021 (R-6), OH-165-AE-6a Rev 1023 (R-6), OH-165-AE-9a Rev 1030 (R-6): VF–EF $25–$35 • MS-63 $75–$125.

OH, Cincinnati • Crittenden Shades • OH-165-AF • *Saloonkeeper* • Dies by W. Johnston • Reverse die: 1056 • OH-165-AF-1a Rev 1056 (R-5): VF–EF $50–$75 • MS-63 $200–$300 • In *Civil War Tokens of Cincinnati* John Ostendorf suggests that this somewhat mysterious token (the inscription has few clues) may refer to a wine cellar conducted by S.E. Chittenden in the Burnet House.

OH-165-AH •
George R.
Dixon & Co. •
O-1 used with
OH-165-AH-1,
2, 4 to 10.

OH, Cincinnati • George R. Dixon & Co. • OH-165-AH • *Ohio Mustard and Spice Mills* • Ascribed to the shop of John Stanton • Reverse dies: 1007, 1008, 1009, 1019, 1021, 1042, 1047, 1068, 1069, 1192 • OH-165-AH-1a Rev 1007 (R-5), OH-165-AH-2a Rev 1008 (R-5): VF–EF $25–$35 • MS-63 $100–$150.

OH, Cincinnati • J.N. Doniphan • OH-165-AI • *Furniture dealer?* • Ascribed to the shop of John Stanton • Reverse dies: 0, 1032, 1042, 1044, 1047, 1069 • OH-165-AI-1a Rev 1032 (R-5): VF–EF $25–$35 • MS-63 $75–$125.

OH, Cincinnati • Garrett T. Dorland • OH-165-AJ • *Importer of watches and jewelry* • Ascribed to the shop of John Stanton • Reverse dies: 1008, 1019, 1029, 1042, 1047, 1068, 1069 • OH-165-AJ-1a Rev 1008 (R-5): VF–EF $25–$35 • MS-63 $75–$125.

OH, Cincinnati • Robert Downing • OH-165-AK • *Publisher of sheet songs and dealer in old coins* • Ascribed to the shop of John Stanton • Reverse dies: 1046, 1047, 1069, 1192, 1279, 1283, 1370 • OH-165-AK-7b Rev 1370 (R-7): VF–EF $600–$900 • MS-63 $1,750–$2,250 • See information about Downing in chapter 4.

OH, Cincinnati • Lorenz Eckert • OH-165-AL • *Bookbinder, stationer, and fancy goods* • Ascribed to the shop of John Stanton • Reverse dies: 1007, 1019, 1020, 1026, 1030, 1036, 1038, 1039 • OH-165-AL-4a Rev 1026 (R-5): VF–EF $25–$35 • MS-63 $75–$125 • Lorenz Eckert, books and stationery, northwest corner Walnut and 13th streets. Sometimes anglicized as Lawrence Eckert.

OH, Cincinnati • C.W. Ellis, Connecticut Mutual Life Insurance Co. • OH-165-AM • *Insurance agent* • Ascribed to the shop of John Stanton • Reverse dies: 1047, 1069, 32190 • OH-165-AM-1a Rev 32190 (R-6): VF–EF $90–$135 • MS-63 $300–$450.

OH, Cincinnati • E.W. Evans • OH-165-AMc • *Watchmaker* • Dies by Murdock & Spencer • Reverse die: 0 • OH-165-AMc Rev 0 (R-9): VF–EF $1,750–$2,500 • MS-63 $4,000–$6,000 • Jeweler's repair check.

OH, Cincinnati • Platt Evens Jr. • OH-165-AMa • *Sewing machine sales and repairs* • Ascribed to the shop of John Stanton • Reverse dies: 0, 1440 • OH-165-AMa-2a Rev 1440 (R-7): VF–EF $150–$225 • MS-63 $400–$600 • Evens was also a diesinker, but this is not noted on the token.

OH, Cincinnati • Excelsior Tobacco Works (Weighell & Son) • OH-165-AMb • *Tobacco products factory* • Dies probably by Benjamin C. True, struck by John Stanton • Reverse dies: 1418, 1426A, 1423 • OH-165-AMb-1a Rev 1418 (R-9), Oh-165-AMb-2i Rev 1426A (R-9), OH-165-AMb-3a Rev 1423 (R-9): VF–EF $1,500–$2,250 • MS-63 $3,000–$4,500 •

Also see OH-165-GI • In the third edition of the Fuld book OH-165-AMb and GI will be consolidated under OH-165-GI.

OH, Cincinnati • Fenton & Beck • OH-165-AN • *Meat market* • Ascribed to the shop of John Stanton • Reverse dies: 1030, 1034, 1042, 1047, 1069 • OH-165-AN-1a Rev 1030 (R-5): VF–EF $25–$35 • MS-63 $75–$125.

OH, Cincinnati • John Ferguson • OH-165-AO • *Grocer* • Ascribed to the shop of John Stanton • Reverse dies: 1008, 1019, 1021, 1042, 1047, 1068, 1069 • OH-165-AO-3a Rev 1021 (R-5): VF–EF $25–$35 • MS-63 $100–$150.

OH-165-AP •
E. Fiedler's
Beer Hall •
O-1 used with
OH-165-AP-1 to 11.

OH, Cincinnati • E. Fiedler's Beer Hall / Eduard Fiedler • OH-165-AP and AQ • *Beer hall* • Ascribed to the shop of John Stanton • OH-165-AP: Reverse dies: 1022, 1026, 1029, 1030, 1033, 1036, 1042, 1044, 1047, 1069 • OH-165-AP-5a Rev 1033 (R-5): VF–EF $20–$30 • MS-63 $100–$150 • OH-165-AQ Reverse die: 0013N, 32400 • OH-165-AQ-1e Rev 0013N (R-9), OH-165-AQ-2e Rev 32400 (R-9): VF–EF $1,500–$2,250 • MS-63 $4,000–$6,000 • In the third edition of the Fuld book OH-165-AP and AQ will be consolidated under OH-165-AP as here.

OH, Cincinnati • F. Fischer • OH-165-AS • *Coffee house* • Ascribed to the shop of John Stanton • Reverse dies: 1033, 1042, 1047, 1069, 32490 • OH-165-AS-1a Rev 1033 (R-5): VF–EF $25–$35 • MS-63 $100–$150.

OH, Cincinnati • W.C. Fithian • OH-165-AU • *Painter and grainer* • Dies by Murdock & Spencer • Reverse die: 1432 • OH-165-AU-1a Rev 1432 (R-8): VF–EF $300–$450 • MS-63 $900–$1,350.

OH, Cincinnati • James W. Fitzgerald • OH-165-AV • *Grocer* • Ascribed to the shop of W.K. Lanphear • Reverse dies: 0, 1127, 1384 • OH-165-AV-2a Rev 1384 (R-6): VF–EF $50–$75 • MS-63 $175–$225.

OH-165-AW •
Charles Flach •
O-1 used with
OH-165-AW-1.

OH-165-AW •
Charles Flach •
O-2 used with
OH-165-AW-2 to 10.

OH, Cincinnati • Charles Flach • OH-165-AW • *Dealer in provisions* • Ascribed to the shop of John Stanton • Reverse dies: 1026, 1033, 1036, 1039, 1042, 1047, 1069, 31400 • OH-165-AW-2a Rev 1026 (R-6), OH-165-AW-3a Rev 1033 (R-6): VF–EF $25–$35 • MS-63 $75–$125.

OH-165-AX •
James Foster Jr.
& Co. •
O-1 used with
OH-165-AX-1, 2, 5.

OH-165-AX •
James Foster Jr.
& Co. •
O-2 used with
OH-165-AX-3.
This is a repair check.

OH, Cincinnati • James Foster Jr. & Co. • OH-165-AX • *Optician, laboratory and scientific equipment* • Ascribed to the shop of John Stanton; O-2 dies by Murdock & Spencer • Reverse dies: 0, 1432, 1046, 1047, 32510 • OH-165-AX-1a Rev

1047 (R-8), OH-165-AX-3b Rev 1432 (R-8): VF–EF $600–$900 • MS-63 $1,500–$2,500.

OH, Cincinnati • John Galvagni • OH-165-BA • *Fancy goods and toys* • Ascribed to the shop of John Stanton • Reverse dies: 1007, 1019, 1019, 1042, 1047, 1069, 1273 • OH-165-BA-1a Rev 1007 (R-4): VF–EF $25–$35 • MS-63 $75–$100.

OH-165-BB •
L. Geilfus •
O-1 used with
OH-165-BB-1.

OH-165-BB •
L. Geilfus •
O-2 used with
OH-165-BB-2 and 3.

OH, Cincinnati • Louis Geilfus • OH-165-BB • *Grocer* • Dies by Johnston • OH-165BB • Reverse dies: 1247, 1386 • OH-165-BB-3a Rev 1247 (R-5): VF–EF $75–$125 • MS-63 $250–$375.

OH, Cincinnati • F. Geiser • OH-165-BBa • *Cigar maker* • ? • Reverse die: 0013N • OH-165-BBa-1e Rev 0013N (R-10): VF–EF $1,500–$2,250.

OH, Cincinnati • J. Geiser • OH-165-BC • *Coffee house* • Dies by W. Johnston • Reverse die: 1386, 1388 • OH-165-BC-1a Rev 1386 (R-7), OH-165-BC-2a Rev 1388 (R-7): VF–EF $200–$300 • MS-63 $600–$900.

OH, Cincinnati • W. Gentsch • OH-165-BD • *Wine and beer saloon* • Ascribed to the shop of John Stanton • Reverse dies: 1026, 1029, 1042, 1047, 1069 • OH-165-BD-1a Rev 1026 (R-6): VF–EF $35–$50 • MS-63 $125–$175.

OH, Cincinnati • Gibson House • OH-165-BEa • *Hotel* • Murdock & Spencer? • Reverse die: 0 • OH-165-BEa-1b Rev 0 (R-10): VF–EF $1,500–$2,250 • MS-63 $4,000–$6,000.

OH, Cincinnati • John Grossius • OH-165-BH • *Tinner* • Dies by W. Johnston • Reverse dies: 1056, 33790 • OH-165-BH1aa Rev 1056 (R-7): VF–EF $125–$175 • MS-63 $300–$450.

OH, Cincinnati • Jacob Guth • OH-165-BI • *Barkeeper* • Ascribed to the shop of John Stanton • Reverse dies: 1021, 1022, 1026, 1031, 1036, 1039, 1042, 1047, 1069, 32680 • OH-165-BI-5a Rev 1036 (R-5): VF–EF $25–$35 • MS-63 $75–$125.

OH-165-BJ •
Carl Haas •
O-1 used with
OH-165-BJ-1 to 8, 26.

OH-165-BJ •
Carl Haas •
O-2 used with
OH-165-BJ-9 to 11.
Large letters.

OH-165-BJ •
Carl Haas •
O-3 used with
OH-165-BJ-12 to 25.
CARL HAAS
mostly repunched.
Small letters.

OH, Cincinnati • Carl Haas • OH-165-BJ • *Coffee house* • Ascribed to the shop of John Stanton • Reverse dies: 1019, 1020, 1021, 1022, 1023, 1026, 1029, 1032, 1033, 1034, 1036, 1038, 1039, 1042, 1044, 1045, 1047, 32700, 32705 • OH-165-BJ-12a Rev 1020 (R-2): VF–EF $30–$45 • MS-63 $100–$150 • Haas = "rabbit" in German.

OH, Cincinnati • C. Hahnemann's Bakery • OH-165-BK • *Bakery* • ? •

Reverse die: 0013N • OH-165-BK-1e Rev 0013N (R-8): VF–EF $500–$750 • MS-63 $2,000–$3,000.

OH, Cincinnati • W.W. Hanley • OH-165-BL • *Wholesale grocer* • Ascribed to the shop of John Stanton • Reverse dies: 1472, 1008, 1009, 1038, 1042, 1047 • OH-165-BL-1a Rev 1008 (R-5): VF–EF $30–$45 • MS-63 $100–$150.

OH-165-BM •
Luther M. Harpel •
O-1 used with
OH-165-BM-1 to 3.

OH-165-BM •
Luther M. Harpel •
O-2 used with
OH-165-BM-4.

OH, Cincinnati • Luther M. Harpel • OH-165-BM • *Printer* • Ascribed to the shop of John Stanton • Reverse dies: 1009, 32750, 33850 • OH-165-BM-1a Rev 1009 (R-5): VF–EF $35–$50 • MS-63 $100–$160.

OH, Cincinnati • C.G. Hartmann • OH-165-BN • *Grocer* • Dies by W. Johnston • Reverse die: 1248 • OH-165-BN-1a Rev 1248 (R-5): VF–EF $75–$125 • MS-63 $250–$375.

OH, Cincinnati • M. Hartzel • OH-165-BO • *Grocer and commission merchant* • Ascribed to the shop of John Stanton • Reverse dies: 1009, 1019, 1020, 1042, 1047 • OH-165-BO-1a Rev 1009 (R-3): VF–EF $25–$35 • MS-63 $75–$100.

OH, Cincinnati • Elizabeth Heinzmann • OH-165-BR • *Dining saloon* • Dies by W. Johnston[92] • Reverse die: 1386, 1388 • OH-165-BR-1a Rev 1386 (R-7), OH-165-BR-2a Rev 1388 (R-7): VF–EF $60–$90 • MS-63 $200–$300.

OH, Cincinnati • J. Helmig • OH-165-BS • *Grocer* • Ascribed to the shop of

John Stanton • Reverse die: 1022, 1029, 1042, 1047 • OH-165-BS-2a Rev 1029 (R-4): VF–EF $25–$35 • MS-63 $90–$135.

OH, Cincinnati • B. Hempelman • OH-165-BT • *Dealer in groceries and feed* • Ascribed to the shop of John Stanton • Reverse dies: 1019, 1020, 1021, 1022, 1032, 1033, 1034, 1036, 1038, 1042, 1047, 1069, 1274, 34405 • OH-165-BT-1a Rev 1019 (R-3): VF–EF $25–$35 • MS-63 $90–$135.

OH, Cincinnati • Herancourt's Brewery • OH-165-BU • *Brewery* • Ascribed to the shop of John Stanton • Reverse die: 1440 • OH-165-BT-1b Rev 1440 (R-8): VF–EF $1,000–$1,500 • MS-63 $2,500–$3,750.

OH-165-BV • V. Heyl, Farmers Hotel • O-1 used with OH-165-BV-1 to 14.

OH-165-BV • V. Heyl, Farmers Hotel • O-2 used with OH-165-BV-15 to 21.

OH, Cincinnati • V. Heyl, Farmers Hotel • OH-165-BV • *Hotel* • Ascribed to the shop of John Stanton • Reverse dies: 1435, 1008, 1018, 1019, 1022, 1026, 1029, 1030, 1032, 1033, 1034, 1038, 1039, 1042, 1046, 1047, 1192 • OH-165-BV-4a Rev 1026 (R-3), OH-165-BV-17a Rev 1033 (R-3): VF–EF $25–$35 • MS-63 $75–$125.

OH, Cincinnati • Dr. H.H. Hill & Co. • OH-165-BW • *Drugs, medicines* • Ascribed to the shop of John Stanton • Reverse dies: 0, 1008, 1030, 1038, 1042, 1047, 1311, 1312, 1313, 33455 • OH-165-BW-2a Rev 1030 (R-3), OH-165-BW-4b Rev 1042 (R-3): VF–EF $25–$35 • MS-63 $75–$125.

OH, Cincinnati • B. Hintrick & C. Glaser • OH-165-BX • *Line of trade unknown* • Ascribed to the shop of John Stanton • Reverse dies: 1020, 1036, 1042, 1047, 1069 • OH-165-BX-1a Rev 1020 (R-5): VF–EF $30–$45 • MS-63 $100–$150.

OH, Cincinnati • James A. Hughes • OH-165-BZ • *Numismatist* • Ascribed to the shop of W.K. Lanphear • Reverse dies: 1473, 1131, 1172, 1419, 34690 • OH-165-BZ-1a Rev 1131 (R-9), OH-165-BZ-1d Rev 1131 (R-9), OH-165-BZ-2a Rev 1172 (R-9), OH-165-BZ-5e Rev 34690 (R-9), OH-165-BZ-5f Rev 34690 (R-9): VF–EF $750–$1,250 • MS-63 $2,250–$3,500 • Hughes issued a number of numismatic strikes. Hughes, the numismatist, is also believed to have been a diecutter, possibly with the Lanphear shop. Circa 1867–1874 he was a stationer and printer in Cincinnati; also known as Hughes Brothers.[93]

OH, Cincinnati • C.C. Hyatt • OH-165-CB • *Grocer* • Ascribed to the shop of John Stanton • Reverse dies: 1007, 1019, 1042, 1047 • OH-165-CB-1a Rev 1007 (R-4): VF–EF $40–$60 • MS-63 $125–$175.

OH, Cincinnati • Bernard Jahr • OH-165-CC • *Baker* • Dies by Murdock & Spencer • Reverse dies: 1046, 1047, 1392 • OH-165-CC-2a Rev 1047 (R-9): VF–EF $500–$750 • MS-63 $1,500–$2,250.

OH, Cincinnati • B. Jahr & Co. • OH-165-CD • *Baker* • Dies by Murdock & Spencer • Reverse dies: 1047, 1392, 1397 • OH-165-CD-1a Rev 1047 (R-9), OH-165-CD-2a Rev 1392 (R-9), OH-165-CD-3a Rev 1397 (R-9): VF–EF $500–$750 • MS-63 $1,500–$2,250.

OH, Cincinnati • H. Johnston (W. Johnston) • OH-165-CE • *Diesinker* • Dies by W. Johnston • Reverse dies: 1386, 1388 • OH-165-CE-1a Rev 1388 (R-8): VF–EF $1,000–$1,500 • H is thought to be an error instead of the correct W.

OH-165-CF •
W. Johnston •
O-1 used with
OH-165-CF-1 and 2.

OH-165-CF •
W. Johnston •
O-2 used with
OH-165-CF-3 and 4.
Rusted die used with
165-CF-3a illustrated.

OH-165-CF •
W. Johnston •
O-3 used with
OH-165-CF-5.

OH, Cincinnati • W. Johnston • OH-165-CF • *Diesinker* • Johnston's own store card • Reverse dies: 1056, 1247, 1248, 1386, 1388 • OH-165-CF-1a Rev 1056 (R-3), OH-165-CF-2a Rev 1248 (R-3): VF–EF $25–$35 • MS-63 $60–$90.

OH, Cincinnati • C. Kahn & Co. • OH-165-CG • *Meat store* • Dies by W. Johnston • Reverse dies: 1056, 1386 • OH-165-CG-1a Rev 1056 (R-7), OH-165-CG-2a Rev 1386 (R-7): VF–EF $100–$150 • MS-63 $400–$600.

OH, Cincinnati • Andrew Karman • OH-165-CH • *Coffeehouse* • Dies by W. Johnston • Reverse dies: 1247, 1386 • OH-165-CH-1a Rev 1247 (R-6), OH-165-CH-2a Rev 1386 (R-6): VF–EF $50–$75 • MS-63 $200–$300.

OH-165-CJ •
Warren Kennedy •
O-1 used with
OH-165-CJ-1 to 5.

OH-165-CJ •
Warren Kennedy •
O-2 used with
OH-165-CJ-6 to 11.

OH, Cincinnati • Warren Kennedy • OH-165-CJ • *News depot* • Ascribed to the shop of John Stanton • Reverse dies: 1022, 1026, 1042, 1047, 1069, 1124, 1176, 1290, 1295, 1331, 33860 • OH-165-CJ-7a Rev 1176 (R-2): VF–EF $25–$35 • MS-63 $75–$125.

OH, Cincinnati • Frank Kern • OH-165-CK • *Grocer* • Ascribed to the shop of John Stanton • Reverse dies: 1018, 1029,1033, 1042, 1047 • OH-165-CK-2a Rev 1029 (R-4): VF–EF $25–$35 • MS-63 $100–$150.

OH, Cincinnati • J. Kirker & Co. • OH-165-CM • *Grocers and produce dealers* • Ascribed to the shop of W.K. Lanphear • Reverse dies: 1227, 1295, 1352 • OH-165-CM-3a Rev 1352 (R-5): VF–EF $40–$60 • MS-63 $135–$200.

OH-165-CN •
B. Kittredge & Co. •
O-1 used with
OH-165-CN-1. The
French Liberty Head
on this and the next,
from a hub punch, are
perhaps the most finely
crafted of this motif in
the Civil War series.

OH-165-CN •
B. Kittredge & Co. •
O-2 used with
OH-165-CN-2.

OH, Cincinnati • B. Kittredge & Co. • OH-165-CN • *Sporting and military goods* • Dies possibly by the Scovill Manufacturing Co. • Reverse die: 33150 • OH-165-CN-1a Rev 33150 (R-2): VF–EF $25–$35 • MS-63 $100–$150 • Scovill, the die and token maker, was also a supplier of buttons and certain accessories, and it may have been that Kittredge contacted Scovill through this connection. Both obverse dies had the portrait added to the die by means of a portrait transfer lathe; the lathe lines are continuous from the portrait into the surrounding field, and on each die are slightly different; thus, a portrait punch was not used. 1861 *Williams' Cincinnati Directory:* B. Kittredge & Co. B. Kittredge and A.A. Bennett. Importers of guns and sporting apparatus and dealers in gunpowder. 134 Main Street. B. Kittredge, home, Madisonville.[94]

OH, Cincinnati • J. Klein • OH-165-CP • *Grocer* • Ascribed to the shop of John Stanton • Reverse die: 1026, 1029, 1042, 1047, ? • OH-165-CP-2a Rev 1029 (R-6): VF–EF $30–$45 • MS-63 $125–$175.

OH, Cincinnati • Jacob Knauber • OH-165-CQ • *Butcher* • Ascribed to the shop of John Stanton • Reverse dies: 1007, 1019, 1038, 1042, 1047, 1192 • OH-165-CQ-1a Rev 1007 (R-3): VF–EF $25–$35 • MS-63 $75–$110.

OH, Cincinnati • William Knecht • OH-165-CR • *Grocer* • Ascribed to the shop of John Stanton • Reverse dies: 1026, 1030, 1033, 1034, 1042, 1047 • OH-165-CR-4a Rev 1034 (R-3): VF–EF $25–$35 • MS-63 $75–$110.

OH, Cincinnati • John Koch • OH-165-CS • *Coffeehouse* • Ascribed to the shop of John Stanton • Reverse dies: 1026, 1042, 1047 • OH-165-CS-1a Rev 1026 (R-5): VF–EF $30–$45 • MS-63 $90–$135.

OH, Cincinnati • Koos Restaurant • OH-165-CT • *Restaurant and coffeehouse* • Ascribed to the shop of John Stanton • Reverse dies: 1192, 1391A • OH-165-CT-1a Rev 1192 (R-9), OH-165-CT-2a Rev 1391A (R-9): VF–EF $500–$750 • MS-63 $2,000–$3,000 • Beer check for restaurant.

OH, Cincinnati • B. Kreager • OH-165-CU • *Grocer* • Ascribed to the shop of John Stanton • Reverse dies: 1026, 1030, 1031 1032, 1033, 1034, 1042, 1047 • OH-165-CU-1a Rev 1026 (R-4): VF–EF $25–$35 • MS-63 $90–$135.

OH, Cincinnati • H. Kreber • OH-165-CV • *Grocer* • Ascribed to the shop of W.K. Lanphear • Reverse dies: 1176, 1177, 1242, 1331 • OH-165-CV-1a Rev 1176 (R-4): VF–EF $30–$45 • MS-63 $75–$110.

OH, Cincinnati • A. Krengel's Union Exchange • OH-165-CW • *Coffeehouse* • Ascribed to the shop of John Stanton • Reverse dies: 1019, 1021, 1025, 1026, 1028, 1029, 1032, 1033, 1034, 1038, 1039, 1042, 1045, 1047 • OH-165-CW-4a Rev 1026 (R-4), OH-165-CW-8a Rev 1033 (R-4): VF–EF $25–$35 • MS-63 $75–$110.

OH, Cincinnati • Jacob Krick • OH-165-CX • *Huckster* • Ascribed to the shop of John Stanton • Reverse dies: 1047, 1391A • OH-165-CX-1a Rev 1047 (R-8), OH-165-CX-2a Rev 1391A (R-8): VF–EF $500–$750 • MS-63 $1,500–$2,250.

OH-165-CY •
W.K. Lanphear •
O-1 used with
OH-165-CY-1
to 46. 110 to 113.

OH-165-CY •
W.K. Lanphear •
O-2 used with
OH-165-CY-47 to 96.

OH-165-CY •
W.K. Lanphear •
O-3 used with
OH-165-CY-97 and 98.

OH-165-CY •
W.K. Lanphear •
O-3 used with
OH-165-CY-99 to 102.

OH-165-CY •
W.K. Lanphear •
O-5 used with
OH-165-CY-103
to 106.

OH-165-CY •
W.K. Lanphear •
O-6 used with
OH-165-CY-107
and 108.

OH-165-CY •
W.K. Lanphear •
O-7 used with
OH-165-CY-114.
Earlier known as
OH-100-B-4. Actually
a reverse die.

**OH, Cincinnati • William K. Lanphear
• OH-165-CY •** *Diesinker* • Dies by the

Lanphear shop • Reverse dies: 0, 1475, 0016N, 1436, 1437, 1083, 1084, 1087, 1088, 1089, 1091, 1122, 1124, 1125, 1127, 1128, 1166, 1168, 1169, 1176, 1179, 1180, 1181, 1222, 1223, 1225, 1226, 1227, 1228, 1247, 1273, 1274, 1280, 1290, 1295, 1298, 1299, 1300, 1302, 1303, 1304, 1310, 1311, 1316, 1320, 1321, 1323, 1324, 1326, 1331, 1332, 1336, 1337, 1340, 1341, 1342, 1344, 1346, 1348, 1349, 1387, 1452, 1459, 1454, 1462, 33310, 33320 • OH-165-CY-97a Rev 33310 (R-2): VF–EF $25–$35 • MS-63 $50–$75.

OH-165-CZ •
Lanphear's •
O-1 used with
OH-165-CZ-1.

OH, Cincinnati • Lanphear's • OH-165-CZ • *Tobacconist* • Dies by the W.K. Lanphear shop, but of different style • Reverse die: 0 • OH-165-CZ-1b Rev 0 (R-4): VF–EF $25–$35 • MS-63 $75–$110 • The D.C. Wismer estate had 400 of these tokens. A side venture by W.K. Lanphear.

OH, Cincinnati • S. Lasurs • OH-165-DB • *Dealer in rags and metals* • Dies by Johnston or Linderman • Reverse dies: 1057, 1247 • OH-165-DB-1a Rev 1057 (R-2): VF–EF $25–$35 • MS-63 $50–$75.

OH-165-DC •
H. Lazaress •
O-1 used with
OH-165-DC-1.

OH-165-DC •
H. Lazaress •
O-2 used with
OH-165-DC-2.

OH, Cincinnati • H. Lazaress • OH-165-DC • *Dealer in rags and metals* • Dies by Johnston or Linderman • Reverse dies: 1058, 1247 • OH-165-DC-1a Rev 1247 (R-5), OH-165-DC-2a Rev 1058 (R-5): VF–EF $25–$35 • MS-63 $60–$90 • OH-165-DB (S. Lasurs) and 165-DC (H. Lazaress) are both at the same address, 16 15th Street; the two token types must refer to the same person or at least the same business. Both are probably misspellings of Lazarus. Perhaps the orders for the tokens were given verbally.

OH-165-DD •
Leavitt & Bevis •
O-1 used with
OH-165-DD-1 to 6.

OH-165-DD •
Leavitt & Bevis •
O-2 used with
OH-165-DD-7 to 11.

OH, Cincinnati • Leavitt & Bevis • OH-165-DD • *Hosiery and gloves* •

Ascribed to the shop of John Stanton • Reverse dies: 1009, 1019, 1042, 1047, 1069, 33430 • OH-165-DD-1a Rev 1009 (R-3): VF–EF $25–$35 • MS-63 $75–$110 • This firm issued shell cards in the late 1860s.

OH, Cincinnati • M. Lindermann • OH-165-DE • *Check maker (token maker)* •

Lindermann's own card • Reverse dies: 1057, 1247, 1416 • OH-165-DE-1a Rev 1057 (R-3), OH-165-DE-3a Rev 1416 (R-3): VF–EF $25–$35 • MS-63 $60–$90.

OH, Cincinnati • Hy Loewenstein • OH-165-DF • *Butcher* • Ascribed to the

shop of John Stanton • Reverse dies: 1028, 1029, 1032, 1033, 1036, 1037, 1042, 1044, 1047, 1069 • OH-165-DF-5a Rev 1036 (R-4): VF–EF $25–$35 • MS-63 $75–$110.

OH, Cincinnati • F.W. Lutz • OH-165-DG • *Engraver* • Lutz made dies for

the shop of W.K. Lanphear • Reverse dies: 1068, 1298 • OH-165-DG-1a Rev 1298 (R-8): VF–EF $750–$1,250 • MS-63 $2,500–$3,750.

OH, Cincinnati • R.E. Macauley • OH-165-DH • *Bread seller* • Ascribed to

the shop of John Stanton • Reverse die: 1440 • OH-165-DH-1a Rev 1440 (R-8): VF–EF $1,500–$2,250.

OH-165-DJ •
Marsh & Miner •
O-1 used with
OH-165-DJ-1 to 4.

OH-165-DJ •
Marsh & Miner •
O-2 used with
OH-165-DJ-15 to 22.

OH, Cincinnati • Marsh & Miner • OH-165-DJ • *Vest manufacturers* •

Ascribed to the shop of John Stanton • Reverse dies: 1008, 1009, 1019, 1020, 1021, 1026, 1030, 1031, 1038, 1042, 1047, 1069 • OH-165-DJ-2a1 Rev 1009 (R-2), OH-165-DJ-15a Rev 1008 (R-2): VF–EF $25–$35 • MS-63 $60–$90.

OH, Cincinnati • Martin's Grocery • OH-165-DK • *Grocery* • Ascribed to the

shop of John Stanton • Reverse dies: 1022, 1026, 1031, 1042, 1047, 1069 • OH-165-DK-1a Rev 1022 (R-3), OH-165-DK-2a Rev 1026 (R-3): VF–EF $30–$45 • MS-63 $100–$150.

OH, Cincinnati • W.C. McClenahan & Co. • OH-165-DL • *Grocer* • Ascribed to

the shop of W.K. Lanphear • Reverse dies: 1089, 1123, 1124, 1290 • OH-165-DL-3a Rev 1124 (R-6), OH-165-DL-4a Rev 1290 (R-6): VF–EF $30–$45 • MS-63 $100–$150.

OH, Cincinnati • T.W. McDonald • OH-165-DM • *Boots and shoes* • Ascribed

to the shop of John Stanton • Reverse dies: 1007, 1008, 1019, 1042, 1047, 1069, 1279 • OH-165-DM-2a1 Rev 1008 (R-3): VF–EF $25–$35 • MS-63 $75–$100.

OH, Cincinnati • L. Phil. Meredith and J.N. McClung • OH-165-DN • *Dentists* • Ascribed to the shop of W.K. Lanphear • Reverse dies: 0016N, 1178, 1344 • OH-165-DN-1a Rev 1344 (R-9), OH-165-DN-2a Rev 0016N (R-9): VF–EF $1,500–$2,250 • MS-63 $3,000–$4,500.

OH, Cincinnati • Merchants Hotel • OH-165-DO • *Hotel* • Dies by Murdock & Spencer • Reverse die: 1433 • OH-165-DO-1a Rev 1433 (R-9): VF–EF $1,000–$1,500 • MS-63 $1,750–$2,500 • Actually a hotel key tag or check, not a token. With slot cut at top for strap or cord; space for punching room number. Struck over 1864 campaign tokens.

OH, Cincinnati • Adam Metz • OH-165-DP • *Butcher* • Ascribed to the shop of John Stanton • Reverse dies: 1007, 1008, 1019, 1020, 1038, 1042, 1047, 1068, 1069, 1192 • OH-165-DP-2a Rev 1008 (R-3): VF–EF $25–$35 • MS-63 $75–$110.

OH, Cincinnati • J. & D. Metz • OH-165-DQ • *Pork packers* • Ascribed to the shop of John Stanton • Reverse dies: 1022, 1036, 1042, 1045, 1047, 1069 • OH-165-DQ-1a Rev 1022 (R-5), OH-165-DQ-2a Rev 1036 (R-5), OH-165-4a Rev 1045 (R-5): VF–EF $30–$45 • MS-63 $90–$135 • Packing pork in barrels for shipment downriver was a major Cincinnati industry.

OH, Cincinnati • L. Meyer, West End Saloon • OH-165-DS • *Coffeehouse* • Ascribed to the shop of John Stanton • Reverse dies: 1026, 1039, 1042, 1047, 1069 • OH-165-DS-1a Rev 1026 (R-4): VF–EF $40-60 • MS-63 $125-175.

OH, Cincinnati • H. Miedeking • OH-165-DT • *Grocer* • Ascribed to the shop of John Stanton • Reverse dies: 1019, 1020, 1022, 1042, 1047, 1069 • OH-165-DT-1a Rev 1019 (R-7), OH-165-DT-3a Rev 1042 (R-7), OH-165-DT-3b Rev 1042 (R-7): VF–EF $30–$45 • MS-63 $100–$150.

OH, Cincinnati • S-B-Monarch • OH-165-DU • *Steamship "Steam Boat Monarch"* • Dies by Murdock & Spencer •

Reverse dies: 1432, 1047, 1393 • OH-165-DU-3b Rev 1432 (R-7): VF–EF $1,000–$1,500 • MS-63 $2,500–$3,750 • Thought to be a bar check for use on this steamer that operated out of Cincinnati.

OH, Cincinnati • J.T. Moore • OH-165-DV • *Fruit dealer* • Ascribed to the shop of John Stanton • Reverse dies: 1007, 1019, 1021, 1042, 1043, 1047, 1069, 1279 • OH-165-DV-1a Rev 1007 (R-6): VF–EF $30–$45 • MS-63 $100–$150.

OH-165-DW • Morgan & Ferry • O-1 used with OH-165-DW-1 to 6, 13.

OH-165-DW • Morgan & Ferry • O-2 used with OH-165-DW-7 to 12, 14.

OH, Cincinnati • Morgan & Ferry • OH-165-DW • *Saloon* • Ascribed to the shop of John Stanton • Reverse dies: 1007, 1008, 1022, 1042, 1047, 1069, 1192, 1279, 1393 • OH-165-DW-1a Rev 1007 (R-6), OH-165-DW-5a Rev 1192 (R-6): VF–EF $30–$45 • MS-63 $100–$150.

OH, Cincinnati • L. Meyer, West End the shop of John **OH, Cincinnati • J.B. Morris • OH-165-DWa** • *Jeweler* • Dies by Murdock & Spencer • Reverse die: 0 • OH-165-DWa-1b Rev 0 (R-10): VF–EF $2,000–$3,000 • MS-63 $4,000–$6,000 • Repair check. Struck over an 1864 campaign token.

OH, Cincinnati • H.J. Moser • OH-165-DX • *Watchmaker* • Ascribed to the shop of John Stanton • Reverse die: 1047 • OH-165-DX-1a Rev 1047 (R-9): VF–EF $750–$1,250 • MS-63 $2,000–$3,000 • Made as a watch check die (unknown in this use) muled with 1047 to create a numismatic strike.

OH, Cincinnati • Dies by Murdock & Spencer • OH-165-DZ • *Diesinkers* • Their own store card • Reverse die: 1393 • OH-165-DZ-1a Rev 1393 (R-9): VF–EF

$750–$1,250 • MS-63 $2,000–$3,000 • Listed slightly out of alphabetical order in Fuld.

OH, Cincinnati • James Murdock Jr. • OH-165-DY • *Diesinker* • His own store card • Reverse dies: 1472, 1018, 1047, 1069, 1160, 1192, 1279, 1282, 1283, 1370, 1373 • OH-165-DY-3a Rev 1047 (R-8): VF–EF $250–$375 • MS-63 $600–$900.

OH, Cincinnati • E. Myers & Co. • OH-165-EA • *Dealers in foreign fruit and confectionery* • Ascribed to the shop of John Stanton • Reverse dies: 1019, 1020, 1034, 1036, 1042, 1047, 1069, 1279 • OH-165-EA-4a Rev 1036 (R-5): VF–EF $30–$45 • MS-63 $100–$150.

OH, Cincinnati • E. Niebuhr • OH-165-EB • *Wine and beer saloon* • Ascribed to the shop of W.K. Lanphear • Reverse dies: 1176, 1290, 1295, 1384, 1416, 33760 • OH-165-EB-3a Rev 1295 (R-4): VF–EF $25–$35 • MS-63 $75–$125.

OH, Cincinnati • F.J. Niemer's Hotel • OH-165-EC • *Hotel* • Ascribed to the shop of W.K. Lanphear • Reverse dies: 1124, 1176, 1295, 1331 • OH-165-EC-2a Rev 1176 (R-3): VF–EF $30–$45 • MS-63 $100–$150.

OH, Cincinnati • J.H. Nolwer • OH-165-ED • *Grocer* • Dies by W. Johnston • Reverse dies: 1386, 1388 • OH-165-ED-1a Rev 1388 (R-7): VF–EF $150–$225 • MS-63 $500–$750.

OH, Cincinnati • R.D. Norris • OH-165-EF • *Dry goods* • Ascribed to the shop of John Stanton • Reverse dies: 1019, 1020, 1036, 1042, 1047, 1069 • OH-165-EF-1a Rev 1019 (R-4): VF–EF $25–$35 • MS-63 $75–$110.

OH, Cincinnati • O'Donoghue & Naish • OH-165-EG • *Boots and shoes* • Ascribed to the shop of John Stanton • Reverse dies: 1007, 1008, 1019, 1042, 1047, 1069 • OH-165-EG-3a Rev 1009 (R-3): VF–EF $25–$35 • MS-63 $75–$110.

OH, Cincinnati • O'Reilly Bros. • OH-165-EH • *Dry goods* • Ascribed to the

shop of John Stanton • Reverse dies: 1019, 1020, 1023, 1025, 1042, 1047, 1069, 35920 • OH-165-EF-3a Rev 1023 (R-6): VF–EF $30–$45 • MS-63 $100–$150.

OH, Cincinnati • Joseph R. Peebles • OH-165-EJ • *Grocer* • Ascribed to the shop of John Stanton • Reverse dies: 1007, 1008, 1009, 1019, 1020, 1025, 1026, 1031, 1036, 1038, 1042, 1047, 1069, 1279 • OH-165-EJ-2a Rev 1008 (R-2): VF–EF $25–$35 • MS-63 $60–$90.

OH, Cincinnati • Philip • OH-165-EK • ? • Ascribed to the shop of John Stanton • Reverse dies: 1019, 1022, 1036, 1042, 1047, 1069 • OH-165-EK-2a Rev 1036 (R-3): VF–EF $25–$35 • MS-63 $75–$110.

OH, Cincinnati • J.G. Pleisteiner • OH-165-EL • *Fancy goods and notions* • Reverse dies: 1007, 1019, 1036, 1042, 1047, 1069 • OH-165-EL-1a Rev 1007 (R-7): VF–EF $30–$45 • MS-63 $100–$150.

OH, Cincinnati • Charles Plumb • OH-165-EM • *Huckster* • Ascribed to the shop of John Stanton • Reverse dies: 1029, 1033, 1034, 1042, 1047, 1069 • OH-165-EM-1a Rev 1029 (R-3): VF–EF $25–$35 • MS-63 $75–$110.

OH, Cincinnati • Pogue & Jones • OH-165-EN • *Dry goods* • Ascribed to the shop of John Stanton • Reverse dies: 1028, 1030, 1036, 1042, 1047, 1069, 1192 • OH-165-EN-2a Rev 1036 (R-3): VF–EF $25–$35 • MS-63 $75–$110.

OH, Cincinnati • Henry Porter • OH-165-EO • *Barber* • Dies by Murdock & Spencer • Reverse dies: 1047, 1069, 1397, 1398, 1401A, 1403 • OH-165-EO-1a Rev 1047 (R-8), OH-165-EO-3b Rev 1397 (R-8): VF–EF $1,500–$2,250 • MS-63 $3,000–$4,500.

OH, Cincinnati • H.A. Ratterman • OH-165-EQ • *Agent for the German Mutual Insurance Co. of Cincinnati* • Ascribed to the shop of John Stanton[95] • Reverse dies: 0, 1007, 1008, 1018, 1042, 1047, 1069, 1192 • OH-165-EQ-2a1 Rev 1008 (R-3): VF–EF $25–$35 • MS-63 $75–$110.

OH, Cincinnati • John Ravy • OH-165-ER • *Confectioner* • Ascribed to the shop of John Stanton • Reverse dies: 0, 1007, 1008, 1018, 1019, 1021, 1022, 1038, 1042, 1047, 1068, 1069 • OH-165-ER-2a Rev 1008 (R-2): VF–EF $25–$35 • MS-63 $90–$135.

OH, Cincinnati • Isador Rees • OH-165-ES • *Second hand store* • Ascribed to the shop of W.K. Lanphear • Reverse dies: 1170, 1176 • OH-165-ES-1a Rev 1176 (R-1): VF–EF $25–$35 • MS-63 $50–$75.

OH, Cincinnati • J. Reis & Co. • OH-165-ET • *Meat store* • Dies by W. Johnston • Reverse dies: 1056, 1386 • OH-165-ET-2a Rev 1386 (R-7): VF–EF $100–$150 • MS-63 $400–$600.

OH, Cincinnati • J.F. Resta • OH-165-EU • *Sausage maker* • Ascribed to the shop of John Stanton • Reverse dies: 1018, 1022, 1026, 1029, 1033, 1042, 1047, 1069, 32705 • OH-165-EU-1a Rev 1022 (R-5), OH-165-EU-2a Rev 1026 (R-5): VF–EF $25–$35 • MS-63 $75–$110.

OH, Cincinnati • A. Ricke • OH-165-EV • *Insurance agent?* • Ascribed to the shop of John Stanton • Reverse dies: 1007, 1008, 1018, 1019, 1022, 1032, 1033, 1034, 1036, 1042, 1047, 1069, 1192 • OH-165-EV-5a Rev 1036 (R-3): VF–EF $25–$35 • MS-63 $75–$110.

OH, Cincinnati • B.J. Ricking • OH-165-EW • *Grocer* • Ascribed to the shop of W.K. Lanphear • Reverse dies: 1088, 1090, 1091, 1124, 1170, 1171, 1176, 1223, 1226, 1227, 1295, 1331 • OH-165-EW-1a Rev 1088 (R-2): VF–EF $25–$35 • MS-63 $90–$135.

OH, Cincinnati • George W. Ritter • OH-165-EX • *Meat store* • Ascribed to the shop of W.K. Lanphear • Reverse die: 1290 • OH-165-EX-1a Rev 1290 (R-5): VF–EF $50–$75 • MS-63 $200–$300.

OH, Cincinnati • Ellis Rouse, Elis Rouse's Hair Preservative, Metropolitan Shaving Saloon • OH-165-FB • *Barber* • Ascribed to the shop of John Stanton • Reverse dies: 1047, 1069, 1394 • OH-165-FB-1a Rev 1047 (R-8), OH-165-FB-2a Rev 1394 (R-8): VF–EF $600–$900 • MS-63 $1,500–$2,250 • "Elis" misspelling on token.

OH-165-EV •
A. Ricke •
O-1 used with
OH-165-EV-1 to 8.

OH-165-EV •
A. Ricke •
O-2 used with
OH-165-EV-9 to 16.

OH-165-EV •
A. Ricke •
O-3 used with
OH-165-EV-17 and 18.

OH-165-FC •
John Sacksteder •
O-1 used with
OH-165-FC-1 and 2.

OH-165-FC •
John Sacksteder •
O-2 used with
OH-165-FC-3.
Also known as
patriotic token
156/524. A stock die.

OH, Cincinnati • John Sacksteder • OH-165-FC • *Maker and repairer of sewing machines* • Ascribed to the shop of W.K. Lanphear • Reverse dies: 1170, 34140 • OH-165-FC-2a Rev 1170 (R-2): VF–EF $35–$50 • MS-63 $100–$150.

OH, Cincinnati • Christopher Schloendorn • OH-165-FF • *Paper hangings and fancy goods* • Ascribed to the shop of John Stanton • Reverse dies: 1007, 1018, 1019, 1042, 1047, 1069 • OH-165-FF-1a Rev 1007 (R-5): VF–EF $25–$35 • MS-63 $100–$150.

OH, Cincinnati • G. Sch. (George Scheffel) • OH-165-FG • *Grocer* • Dies by W. Johnston • Reverse die: 1056 • OH-165-FB-1a Rev 1056 (R-9): VF–EF $2,000–$3,000.

OH, Cincinnati • H. Schmidt • OH-165-FH • *Auction and commission goods* • Ascribed to the shop of John Stanton • Reverse dies: 1018, 1026, 1028, 1029, 1031, 1033, 1042, 1047, 1069 • OH-165-FH-5a Rev 1033 (R-4): VF–EF $25–$35 • MS-63 $75–$1,100.

OH, Cincinnati • L. Schneider • OH-165-FI • *Coffeehouse* • Ascribed to the shop of John Stanton • Reverse dies: 1018, 1020, 1022, 1023, 1026, 1029, 1036, 1042, 1047, 1069 • OH-165-FI-6a Rev 1029 (R-3), OH-165-FI-7a Rev 1036 (R-3): VF–EF $25–$35 • MS-63 $60–$90.

OH, Cincinnati • Hy Schott • OH-165-FJ • *Cooper* • Ascribed to James Murdock Jr. • Reverse dies: 0, 1391, 1395 • OH-165-FJ-1b Rev 1391 (R-9), OH-165-FJ-2j Rev 1395 (R-9), OH-165-FJ-3b Rev 0 (R-9): VF–EF $1,250–$1,750.

OH, Cincinnati • William Senour • OH-165-FM • *Engraver* • Associated with the shop of W.K. Lanphear • Reverse dies: 0, 0016N, 1130, 1181, 1298, 1346, 1391 • OH-165-FM-2a Rev 1130 (R-7), OH-165-FM-7a Rev 0016N (R-7): VF–EF $175–$250 • MS-63 $500–$750.

OH, Cincinnati • N. Mendal Shafer • OH-165-FN • *Attorney* • Ascribed to the shop of John Stanton • Reverse dies: 1472, 1009, 1018, 1019, 1021, 1022, 1036, 1042, 1047, 1069, 99050 • OH-165-FN-1a1 Rev 1472 (R-2): VF–EF $25–$35 • MS-63 $90–$135.

OH, Cincinnati • Harry E. Shaw • OH-165-FO • *New and second hand furniture* • Ascribed to the shop of W.K. Lanphear • Reverse dies: 1124, 1176, 1295, 1331 • OH-165-FO-2a Rev 1176 (R-3): VF–EF $30–$45 • MS-63 $100–$150.

OH, Cincinnati • Frederick Sheen • OH-165-FP • *Groceries, breadstuffs* • Ascribed to the shop of John Stanton • Reverse dies: 1018, 1020, 1023, 1025, 1026, 1029, 1031, 1033, 1034, 1036, 1042, 1047, 1069 • OH-165-FP-8a Rev 1033 (R-5), OH-165-FP-10a Rev 1036 (R-5): VF–EF $25–$35 • MS-63 $60–$90.

OH-165-FQ • William E. Sinn • O-1 used with OH-165-FQ-1.

OH-165-FQ • William E. Sinn • O-3 used with OH-165-FQ-3.

OH, Cincinnati • William E. Sinn • OH-165-FQ • *Saloon* • Ascribed to the shop of John Stanton • Reverse die: 1440 • OH-165-FQ-2b Rev 1440 (R-7), OH-165-FQ-3b Rev 1440 (R-7): VF–EF $1,250–$2,000.

OH, Cincinnati • Frank Smith • OH-165-FR • *Grocery and liquor store* • Ascribed to the shop of John Stanton • Reverse dies: 1018, 1023, 1028, 1042, 1043, 1047, 1069, 34340 • OH-165-FR-3a Rev 1028 (R-4): VF–EF $25–$35 • MS-63 $90–$135.

OH, Cincinnati • J. Smith's Meat Store • OH-165-FS • *Meat store* • Ascribed to the shop of John Stanton • Reverse dies: 1018, 1019, 1022, 1026, 1034, 1036, 1042, 1047, 1069 • OH-165-FS-6a Rev 1036 (R-4): VF–EF $25–$35 • MS-63 $75-110.

OH, Cincinnati • S. & L. Smith • OH-165-FT • *Grocers* • Ascribed to the shop of John Stanton • Reverse dies: 1018,

1026, 1033, 1036, 1038, 1042, 1047, 1069, 34540 • OH-165-FT-4a Rev 1036 (R-3): VF–EF $25–$35 • MS-63 $75–$110.

OH, Cincinnati • Frederick Snyder • OH-165-FU • *Grocer* • Dies by W. Johnston • Reverse die: 1247 • OH-165-FU-1a Rev 1247 (R-9): VF–EF $2,000–$3,000.

OH, Cincinnati • Charles Spreen • OH-165-FV • *Grocer and produce dealer* • Ascribed to the shop of John Stanton • Reverse dies: 1018, 1020, 1021, 1026, 1033, 1042, 1047, 1069 • OH-165-FV-2a Rev 1021 (R-4): VF–EF $25–$35 • MS-63 $90–$135.

OH, Cincinnati • Henry Stalkamp • OH-165-FW • *Grocer* • Ascribed to the shop of John Stanton • Reverse dies: 1018, 1030, 1036, 1042, 1047, 1069 • OH-165-FW-2a Rev 1036 (R-3): VF–EF $25–$35 • MS-63 $75–$110.

OH-165-FX •
John Stanton •
O-1 used with
OH-165-FX-1 to 19.

OH-165-FX •
John Stanton •
O-2 used with
OH-165-FX-20 to 24.

OH, Cincinnati • John Stanton • OH-165-FX • *Manufacturer of store cards, stencils, stamps, and brands* • Stanton's own store card • Reverse dies: 1472, 1009, 1018, 1019, 1027, 1033, 1037, 1042, 1045, 1046, 1047, 1068, 1069, 1160, 1192, 1279, 1281, 1282, 1283, 1370, 1373 • OH-165-FX-22a Rev 1046 (R-5): VF–EF $35–$50 • MS-63 $125–$175.

OH, Cincinnati • Steamer Lancaster No. 4 • OH-165-FXa • *Steamship* • Ascribed to the shop of John Stanton • Reverse dies: 1158, 1418, 1419, 1420, 1421, 1422, 1423, 1424, 1425, 1426, 1427, 43130 • OH-165-FXa-7a Rev 1424 (R-6), OH-

165-FXa-7b Rev 1424 (R-6): VF–EF $250–$375 • MS-63 $600–$900.

OH, Cincinnati • Wine Steiner (George Steiner) • OH-165-GN • *Wine seller* • Ascribed to the shop of John Stanton • Reverse dies: 1018, 1019, 1042, 1047, 1069, 1192 • OH-165-GN-5a Rev 1192 (R-4): VF–EF $30–$45 • MS-63 $100–$150 • Alphabetized under W in the Fuld book.

OH, Cincinnati • D.B.S. (David Benjamin Sterrett) • OH-165-FY • *Grocer* • Ascribed to the shop of John Stanton[96] • Reverse dies: 1026, 1029, 1042, 1047 • OH-165-FY-1a Rev 1026 (R-5): VF–EF $30–$45 • MS-63 $100–$150.

OH, Cincinnati • C. Sutton's New Grocery Store • OH-165-FZ • *Grocery* • Ascribed to the shop of John Stanton • Reverse dies: 1018, 1026, 1033, 1042, 1047, 1069 • OH-165-FZ-1a Rev 1026 (R-3): VF–EF $25–$35 • MS-63 $100–$150 • Cornelius Sutton.

OH, Cincinnati • E. Townley • OH-165-GB • *Hives and bees* • ? • Reverse dies: 1018, 1020, 1022, 1023, 1026, 1029, 1030, 1033, 1034, 1042, 1045, 1047, 1069, 34200, 34440 • OH-165-GB-1a Rev 1020 (R-4), OH-165-GB-7a Rev 1034 (R-4): VF–EF $30–$45 • MS-63 $100–$150.

OH, Cincinnati • H. Varwig • OH-165-GD • *Baker* • John Stanton • Reverse die: 1440 • OH-165-GD-1b Rev 1440 (R-8): VF–EF $300–$450 • MS-63 $900–$1,350.

OH, Cincinnati • Jacob Vogel • OH-165-GE • *Butcher* • Ascribed to the shop of John Stanton • Reverse dies: 1018, 1022, 1023, 1028, 1042, 1047, 1069 • OH-165-GE-2a Rev 1023 (R-4): VF–EF $25–$35 • MS-63 $75–$110.

OH, Cincinnati • Weatherby's Cheap Dry Goods Emporium • OH-165-GG • *Dry goods* • Ascribed to the shop of John Stanton • Reverse dies: 1018, 1019, 1030, 1033, 1042, 1045, 1047, 1069 • OH-165-GG-1a Rev 1019 (R-5), OH-165-GG-

2a Rev 1030 (R-5): VF–EF $25–$35 • MS-63 $75–$110 • *Cincinnati Daily Commercial*, October 15, 1864: "Cloaks at Wholesale, Comprising one of the Largest Stocks in the West. The attention of the trade is particularly directed to C.S. Weatherby's, No. 110 Fifth Street, between Vine and Race."

OH, Cincinnati • Henry C. Wehrman • OH-165-GH • *Baker* • Ascribed to the shop of John Stanton • Reverse dies: 1018, 1022, 1026, 1032, 1033, 1036, 1042, 1047, 1069 • OH-165-GH-2a Rev 1026 (R-2): VF–EF $30–$45 • MS-63 $90–$135.

OH, Cincinnati • Weighell & Son • (Excelsior Tobacco Works) • OH-165-GI • *Tobacco products factory* • Ascribed to the shop of John Stanton • Reverse dies: 1158, 1419, 1421, 1422, 1425, 1426A, 1427, 32350 • OH-165-GI-1a Rev 32350 (R-9), OH-165-GI-2a Rev 1419 (R-9), OH-165-GI-3a Rev 1421 (R-9), OH-165-GI-4a Rev 1158 (R-9), OH-165-GI-5a Rev 1425 (R-9), OH-165-GI-6a Rev 1427 (R-9), OH-165-GI-7a Rev 1422 (R-9), OH-165-GI-8a Rev 1426A (R-9): VF–EF $1,250–$1,750 • MS-63 $3,000–$4,500 • Also listed under OH-165-AMb, the same business • In the third edition of the Fuld book OH-165-AMb and GI will be consolidated under OH-165-GI.

OH, Cincinnati • William W. Wert • OH-165-GJ • *Auctioneer; boots and shoes* • Ascribed to the shop of John Stanton • Reverse dies: 1018, 1022, 1023, 1026, 1029, 1030, 1033, 1036, 1039, 1042, 1047, 1069, 35820 • OH-165-GJ-6a Rev 1030 (R-3): VF–EF $25–$35 • MS-63 $60–$90.

OH, Cincinnati • William Tell House • OH-165-GA • *Restaurant or exchange* • Ascribed to the shop of John Stanton • Reverse dies: 1018, 1032, 1034, 1042, 1069 • OH-165-GA-2a Rev 1034 (R-4): VF–EF $30–$45 • MS-63 $100–$150 • Listed out of alphabetical order in Fuld; as a business name it should be under W. Possibly related to the William Tell Exchange, 29 West 7th Street, a restaurant.

OH, Cincinnati • Wilkinson's • OH-165-GK • *Dining saloon and coffeehouse* • Ascribed to the shop of John Stanton • Reverse die: 1470 • OH-165-GK-1a Rev 1470 (R-9): VF–EF $1,000–$1,500 • MS-63 $2,000–$3,000 • William Wilkinson, restaurant, 110 West 4th Street.

OH-165-GL • A.B. Wilson • O-1 used with OH-165-GL-1 to 3, 12.   OH-165-GL • A.B. Wilson • O-2 used with OH-165-GL-4 to 11.

OH, Cincinnati • Adam B. Wilson • OH-165-GL • *Grocer* • Ascribed to the shop of John Stanton • Reverse dies: 1008, 1018, 1019, 1020, 1022, 1026, 1036, 1042, 1047, 1068, 1069 • OH-165-GL-1a Rev 1008 (R-2): VF–EF $25–$35 • MS-63 $60–$90.

OH, Cincinnati • John Woessner's Jefferson Saloon • OH-165-GO • *Coffeehouse and billiard saloon* • Ascribed to the shop of John Stanton • Reverse dies: 1007, 1018, 1019, 1020, 1021, 1027, 1038, 1042, 1047, 1069 • OH-165-GO-1a Rev 1007 (R-3), OH-165-5a Rev 1021 (R-3): VF–EF $25–$35 • MS-63 $90–$135.

OH, Cincinnati • Gustav Wolfer • OH-165-GP • *Tinner* • Ascribed to the shop of John Stanton • Reverse dies: 1018, 1025, 1034, 1042, 1047, 1069 • OH-165-GP-2a Rev 1034 (R-6): VF–EF $25–$35 • MS-63 $75–$110.

OH, Cincinnati • Wright • OH-165-GR • ? • Ascribed to the shop of W.K. Lanphear • Reverse die: 1170 • OH-165-GR-1a Rev 1170 (R-2): VF–EF $25–$35 • MS-63 $60–$90 • Surname not sufficient to attribute the full name. John Ostendorf, *Civil War Store Cards of Cincinnati*, suggests lightning-rod manufacturer Greg G. Wright as a possibility.

OH-165-GS •
Robert Wright •
O-1 used with
OH-165-GS-1 and 2.

OH-165-GS •
Robert Wright •
O-2 used with
OH-165-GS-3
to 11, 26.

OH-165-GS •
Robert Wright •
O-3 used with
OH-165-GS-12
to 25, 27, 28.

**OH, Cincinnati • Robert Wright •
OH-165-GS** • *Dry goods* • Ascribed to the
shop of John Stanton • Reverse dies: 1007,
1008, 1018, 1019, 1020, 1021, 1022, 1023,
1026, 1030, 1032, 1033, 1034, 1038, 1042,
1047, 1068, 1069, 1192, 1274, 34640 • OH-
165-GS-8a Rev 1021 (R-2), OH-165-GS-
9a Rev 1038 (R-2): VF–EF $25–$35 •
MS-63 $60–$90.

**OH, Cincinnati • Van Wunder (Mr.
Vanaken Wunder) • OH-165-GC** •
Butcher in the Findlay Market • Ascribed to
the shop of John Stanton • Reverse dies:
1007, 1008, 1009, 1018, 1019, 1022, 1042,
1045, 1047, 1069, 1288 • OH-165-GC-7a
Rev 1045 (R-5): VF–EF $25–$35 • MS-63
$75–$110 • Alphabetized under V in the
Fuld text.

**OH, Cincinnati • S.Y. (Stephen B. Yeat-
man?) • OH-165-GU** • *Produce broker* •
Ascribed to the shop of John Stanton •
Reverse dies: 1037, 1040, 1042, 1047 • OH-
165-GU-2as Rev 1042 (R-6): VF–EF $50–
$75 • MS-63 $200–$300 • Waldo C. Moore
theorized that S.Y. might be Steven Yeat-
man. As John Ostendorf points out, there
may be other S.Y. people in other cities.

**OH, Cincinnati • Jos. Zandt (Joseph
Zanone) • OH-165-GW** • *Ice-cream
saloon* • ? Ascribed to the shop of W.K.
Lanphear • OH-165-GW-1a Rev 1274
(R-NV) • VF–EF $2,000–$3,000 • The
listing of "Jos. Zandt" as the proprietor of
an ice-cream saloon at 285 Central Avenue,
a die combined with store card die 1274,
represents a typographical error for a token
of Joseph Zanone • In the third edition of
the Fuld book OH-165-GW and GX will be
consolidated under OH-165-GX.

**OH, Cincinnati • Jos. Zanone • OH-
165-GX** • *Ice-cream saloon* • Ascribed to
the shop of W.K. Lanphear • Reverse
dies: 1131, 1172, 1274, 34690 • OH-
165-GX-2a Rev 1172 (R-8): VF–EF $30–
$450 • MS-63 $1,000–$1,500 • In the
third edition of the Fuld book OH-165
GW and GX will be consolidated under
OH-165-GX • Zanone, also spelled
Zanoni, was a well-known numismatist in
this era. On April 24–16, 1867, his collection was auctioned by Edward D. Cogan
at the sale room of Bangs, Merwin & Co.

OH-165-GY •
John Zeltner •
O-1 used with
OH-165-GY-1 to 6.

OH-165-GY •
John Zeltner,
National Hall •
O-2 used with
OH-165-GY-7 to 23.

OH-165-GY •
John Zeltner,
National Hall •
O-3 used with
OH-165-GY-24
to 31, 33, 34.

OH-165-GY •
John Zeltner,
National Hall •
O-4 used with
OH-165-GY-32.

OH, Cincinnati • John Zeltner, National Hall • OH-165-GY • *Restaurant, coffee house, and beer saloon* • Ascribed to the shop of John Stanton • Reverse dies: 1437, 1007, 1008, 1018, 1019, 1020, 1021, 1022, 1026, 1029, 1030, 1031, 1032, 1033, 1036, 1037, 1038, 1042, 1047, 1069, 1283, 1289, 1391B, 1393, 35811 • OH-165-BY-27a Rev 1019 (R-2): VF–EF $25–$35 • MS-63 $60–$90.

OH, Circleville • G.H. Fickardt & Co. • OH-168-A • *Druggist* • Ascribed to the shop of W.K. Lanphear • Reverse dies: 1083, 1124, 1130, 1177, 1179, 1180 • OH-168-A-5a Rev 1179 (R-4): VF–EF $60–$90 • MS-63 $200–$300.

OH, Circleville • J.L. King • OH-168-B • *Grocery and provision store* • Ascribed to the shop of W.K. Lanphear • Reverse dies: 0, 1469, 1124, 1178, 1179, 1180, 1331 • OH-168-B-4a Rev 1331 (R-5): VF–EF $50–$75 • MS-63 $150–$225.

OH, Circleville • Mason & Son • OH-168-C • *Grocers and liquor dealers* • Reverse dies: 1124, 1130, 1178, 1179, 1180, 1295 • OH-168-C-1a Rev 1124 (R-6): VF–EF $50–$75 • MS-63 $200–$300.

OH-175-C •
C.G. Bruce •
O-1 used with
OH-175-C-1 and 2.

OH-175-C •
C.G. Bruce •
O-2 used with
OH-175-C-3 to 5, 15.

OH-175-C •
C.G. Bruce •
O-3 used with
OH-175-C-6.

OH-175-C •
C.G. Bruce •
O-5 used with
OH-175-C-13 and 14.
Also known respectively as patriotic
75/525 and 525/0.

OH-175-C •
C.G. Bruce •
O-6 used with
OH-175-C-16 to 18.

OH, Cleveland • C.G. Bruce • OH-175-C • *War claim agent* • Ascribed to the shop of John Stanton • Reverse dies: 0, 0021N, 1451, 1023, 1024, 1028, 1047, 35020, 35060, 40030 • OH-175-C-1a Rev 0021N (R-2), OH-175-C-7a1 Rev 1451 (R-2): VF–EF $25–$35 • MS-63 $60–$90.

OH, Cleveland • C. Chandler • OH-175-D • *Fruit and seed dealer* • Ascribed to the shop of W.K. Lanphear • Reverse die: 1180A • OH-175-D-Rev 1180A (R-4): VF–EF $35–$50 • MS-63 $175–$250.

OH, Cleveland • Deckand & Englehart • OH-175-E • *Hatters* • Ascribed to the shop of S.D. Childs • Reverse die: 1098, 1205 • OH-175-E-1a Rev 1098 (R-3), OH-175-E-2a Rev 1205 (R-3): VF–EF $30–$45 • MS-63 $90–$135.

OH, Cleveland • Dunn, Goudy & Bro. • OH-175-F • *Groceries* • Ascribed to the shop of W.K. Lanphear • Reverse die: 1125 • OH-175-F-1a Rev 1125 (R-5): VF–EF $30–$45 • MS-63 $125–$175.

OH, Cleveland • D.W. Gage • OH-175-G • *War claim agent* • Ascribed to the shop of John Stanton • Reverse dies: 1451, 1018, 1046, 1047, 1069 • OH-175-G-1a Rev 1451 (R-5): VF–EF $30–$45 • MS-63 $125–$175.

OH, Cleveland • J.H. & A.S. Gorham • OH-175-H • *Grocers, manufacturers of crackers and confectionery* • Ascribed to the shop of W.K. Lanphear • Reverse dies: 1178, 1180A • OH-175-H-1a Rev 1178

(R-4), OH-175-H-2a Rev 1180A (R-4): VF–EF $25–$35 • MS-63 $100–$150.

OH, Cleveland • John Hawkins • OH-175-I • *Ladies' apparel* • ? • Reverse dies: 35130, 35140 • OH-175-I-1a Rev 35140 (R-3): VF–EF $40-$60 • MS-63 $200–$300 • Hawkins, who billed himself on his token as "The Ladies Man" and included his own portrait (rare for a Civil War merchant to do), operated the Newburgh House, a ladies' apparel store at 226 Ontario Street, Cleveland.

OH, Cleveland • J. Langhorn • OH-175-J • *Meat store* • Ascribed to the shop of W.K. Lanphear • Reverse dies: 1125, 1180A • OH-175-J-2a Rev 1180A (R-3): VF–EF $30–$45 • MS-63 $100–$150.

OH, Cleveland • C.L. Marvin • OH-175-K • *Stove and grate depot* • Ascribed to the shop of W.K. Lanphear • Reverse die: 1180A • OH-175K-1a (R-3): VF–EF $50–$75 • MS-63 $150–$225.

OH, Cleveland • T.J. Quinlan • OH-175-L • *Bill poster, news dealer, stationery, etc.* • Ascribed to the shop of W.K. Lanphear • Reverse die: 1168, 1346, 35170, 35180 • OH-175-L-1a Rev 35180 (R-2): VF–EF $25–$35 • MS-63 $100–$150.

OH, Cleveland • I.P. Sherwood • OH-175-M • *Dry goods and millinery* • Ascribed to the shop of John Stanton • Reverse die: 1024, 1037, 1042, 1047 • OH-175-M-1a Rev 1024 (R-4), OH-175-M-2a Rev 1037 (R-4): VF–EF $25–$35 • MS-63 $90–$135 • New obverse die (not OH-175-N reworked) • In the third edition of the Fuld book OH-175-M and N will be consolidated under OH-175-M.

OH, Cleveland • J.P. Sherwood (I.P. Sherwood) • OH-175-N • *Dry goods and millinery* • Ascribed to the shop of John Stanton • Reverse dies: 1018, 1028, 1034, 1037, 1042, 1047, 1069 • OH-175-N-1a Rev 1028 (R-5): VF–EF $25–$35 • MS-63 $100–$150 • Error die intended for I.P. Sherwood • In the third edition of the

Fuld book OH-175-M and N will be consolidated under OH-175-M.

OH, Cleveland • Charles W. Stearns • OH-175-O • *Grindstones, flagstones, etc.* • Ascribed to the shop of John Stanton[97] • Reverse dies: 1018, 1046, 1069, 1160, 35210, 35220 • OH-175-O-1a Rev 35220 (R-2): VF–EF $25–$35 • MS-63 $75–$110.

OH-175-P •
Tages London Yoke
Shirt Manufact'y •
O-1 used with
OH-175-P-1, 3.

OH-175-P •
T Tages London Yoke
Shirs Manufact'y •
O-2 used with
OH-175-P-2.
"Shirs" misspelling.

OH, Cleveland • Tages London Yoke Shirts Manufact'y • OH-175-P • *Shirt factory* • ? • Reverse dies: 1325, 35250 • OH-175-P-1a Rev 35250 (R-5): VF–EF $60–$90 • MS-63 $250–$375.

OH, Cleveland • Joseph Welf • OH-175-R • *Jeweler* • Dies by Murdock & Spencer • Reverse dies: 0, 1319 • OH-175-R-1a Rev 1319 (R-9), OH-175-R-2a Rev 0 (R-9), OH-175-R-2b Rev 0 (R-9): VF–EF $2,000–$3,000 • MS-63 $4,000–$6,000 • Repair claim check.

OH, Cleveland • Western Union Telegraph Co. • OH-175-Ra • *Telegraph company* • OH-175-Ra-1d Rev 0 (R-10): VF–EF $6,000–$9,000 • Name counterstamped on the planed-down reverse of an 1857 Flying Eagle cent. Unique. Tanenbaum collection.

OH-175-S •
George Worthington
& Co. •
O-1 used with
OH-175-S-1.

OH-175-S •
George Worthington
& Co. •
O-2 used with
OH-175-S-4 to 9, 14.

OH-200-A •
John Grether •
O-1 used with
OH-200-A-3, 6.
"Imprororter"
misspelling.

OH-200-A •
John Grether •
O-2 used with
OH-200-A-1, 2, 4, 5.
Reworked O-1 die
with misspelling
corrected.

OH, Cleveland • George Worthington & Co. • OH-175-S • *Hardware dealer* • Ascribed to the shop of W.K. Lanphear[98] • Reverse dies: 1430, 1473, 0016N, 1436, 1474, 1131, 1274, 1310 • OH-175-S-4a Rev 1474 (R-2): VF–EF $25–$35 • MS-63 $100–$150.

OH, Collinsville • P. Carle & Son • OH-185-A • *Grocers and grain dealers* • Ascribed to the shop of John Stanton • Reverse dies: 1019, 1021, 1028, 1038, 1042, 1047, 1192 • OH-185-A-1a Rev 1019 (R-5): VF–EF $75–$110 • MS-63 $300–$450 • Only token-issuing merchant of this town.

OH, Columbiana • Icenhour & Co. • OH-190-A • *Produce and commission merchants* • Ascribed to the shop of John Stanton • Reverse dies: 1046, 1047, 1313 • OH-190-A-3a Rev 1313 (R-5): VF–EF $75–$110 • MS-63 $250–$375.

OH, Columbus • John Grether • OH-200-A • *Importer of china and queensware* • Ascribed to the shop of John Stanton • Reverse dies: 1037, 1042, 1043, 1046, 1047 • OH-200-A-2a Rev 1042 (R-6): VF–EF $50–$75 • MS-63 $150–$225.

OH, Columbus • Heintz & Hinkle • OH-200-B • *Groceries* • Ascribed to the shop of W.K. Lanphear • Reverse dies: 1083, 1125, 1177 • OH-200-B-3a Rev 1177 (R-3): VF–EF $40–$60 • MS-63 $150–$225.

OH, Columbus • J.M. & V. Koerner • OH-200-C • *Grocers* • Ascribed to the shop of W.K. Lanphear • Reverse dies: 1082, 1084, 1125, 1126, 1166, 1168, 1178 • OH-200-C-1a Rev 1082 (R-3): VF–EF $25–$35 • MS-63 $100–$150.

OH-190-B •
G. Kipp •
O-1 used with
OH-190-B-1, 4.

OH-200-D •
S.T. Martin •
O-1 used with
OH-200-D-1 to 5.

OH-200-D •
S.T. Martin •
O-2 used with
OH-200-D-6 to 14.

OH, Columbiana • G. Kipp • OH-190-B • *Produce dealer* • Ascribed to the shop of John Stanton • Reverse dies: 1046, 1047 • OH-190-B-1a Rev 1046 (R-3): VF–EF $25–$35 • MS-63 $100–$150.

OH, Columbus • S.T. Martin • OH-200-D • *Eating house (restaurant)* • Ascribed to the shop of W.K. Lanphear • Reverse dies: 0016N, 1082, 1089, 1123, 1124, 1125, 1126, 1127, 1130, 1166, 1178, 1179 • OH-200-D-2a Rev 1089 (R-1),

OH-200-D-6a Rev 1123 (R-1): VF–EF $25–$35 • MS-63 $75–$100.

OH, Columbus • William H. Restieaux • OH-200-F • *Grocer* • Ascribed to the shop of W.K. Lanphear • Reverse dies: 0016N, 1180A, 1222, 1344 • OH-200-F-2a Rev 1222 (R-3): VF–EF $30–$45 • MS-63 $125–$175.

OH, Columbus • H. Schreiner • OH-200-G • *Groceries, provisions* • Ascribed to the shop of W.K. Lanphear • Reverse dies: 1125, 1180, 1273 • OH-200-G-1a Rev 1125 (R-3): VF–EF $60–$90 • MS-63 $200–$300.

OH, Columbus • Mrs. M.A. Van Houten • OH-200-H • *Milliner* • Ascribed to the shop of W.K. Lanphear • Reverse die: 1127 • OH-200-H-1a Rev 1127 (R-6): VF–EF $150–$225 • MS-63 $400–$600.

OH, Columbus • Wagner's Dining Hall • OH-200-I • *Dining hall* • Ascribed to the shop of W.K. Lanphear • Reverse dies: 1082, 1124, 1178, 1179, 1180, 1342 • OH-200-I-3a Rev 1178 (R-3): VF–EF $30–$45 • MS-63 $90–$135.

OH, Columbus • Wiatt & Bro. • OH-200-J • *Bakers and confectioners* • Ascribed to the shop of W.K. Lanphear • Reverse dies: 1124, 1176, 1177, 1295 • OH-200-J-2a Rev 1176 (R-5): VF–EF $30–$45 • MS-63 $125–$175.

OH, Crestline • Jacob Stump • OH-215-A • *Merchant tailor* • Ascribed to the shop of W.K. Lanphear • Reverse die: 1342 • OH-215-A-1a Rev 1342 (R-5): VF–EF $125–$175 • MS-63 $400–$600 • Only token-issuing merchant of this town.

OH, Dayton • J.C. Cain • OH-230-A • *Notions* • Ascribed to the shop of W.K. Lanphear • Reverse die: 1083 • OH-230-A-1a Rev 1083 (R-4): VF–EF $40–$60 • MS-63 $150–$225.

OH, Dayton • J. Durst • OH-230-B • *Grocer* • Ascribed to the shop of John Stanton • Reverse dies: 1018, 1023, 1042, 1046, 1046A, 1047, 1069 • OH-230-B-1a Rev 1018 (R-4): VF–EF $35–$50 • MS-63 $125–$175.

OH, Dayton • Henry Kline • OH-230-C • *Clocks, watches, and jewelry* • Ascribed to the shop of W.K. Lanphear • Reverse die: 519 • OH-230-C-1a Rev 519 (R-9): VF–EF $3,000–$4,500.

OH, Dayton • Rickey's Book Store • OH-230-D • *Books and newspapers, buyer of rags* • ? • Reverse die: 35520 • OH-230-D-1a Rev 35520 (R-5): VF–EF $30–$45 • MS-63 $135–$200 • 28.5 mm.

OH, Dayton • S. Wild • OH-230-E • *Coffee house* • Ascribed to the shop of John Stanton • Reverse dies: 1046, 1047 • OH-230-E-1a Rev 1046 (R-5): VF–EF $35–$50 • MS-63 $200–$300.

OH, Defiance • Ruhl's Premium Steel Pens • OH-240-A • *Steel pens* • Ascribed to the shop of John Stanton • Reverse dies: 1008, 1018, 1019, 1042, 1045, 1047, 1069 • OH-240-A-1a Rev 1008 (R-3): VF–EF $60–$90 • MS-63 $250–$375 • Only token-issuing merchant of this town.

OH, Delphos • J.W. Hunt • OH-250-A • *Druggist and express agent* • Ascribed to the shop of John Stanton • Reverse dies: 1037, 1046, 1047 • OH-250-A-2a Rev 1046 (R-3): VF–EF $35–$50 • MS-63 $200–$300 • Only token-issuing merchant of this town. 1859–1860 *Hawes' Ohio State Gazetteer and Business Directory:* "Joseph W. Hunt, dealer in all kinds of drugs, medicines, paints, oils, dye stuffs, varnishes, glassy, putty, patent medicines, books, stationery, etc. Canal, three doors north of Upper Bridge."

OH, Edgerton • D. Farnham & Co. OH-270-A • *Dry goods* • Ascribed to the shop of W.K. Lanphear • Reverse dies: 1088, 1091, 1169, 1223, 1337, 1342 • OH-270-A-4a Rev 1223 (R-5): VF–EF $75–$110 • MS-63 $250–$375.

OH-290-A •
W.B. Eager •
O-1 used with
OH-290-A-1. Both
Indian Head dies
are masterpieces,
and each has W.B.
EAGER in tiny letters
on the headband.

OH-290-A •
W.B. Eager •
O-2 used with
OH-290-A-2.

OH-290-A •
W.B. Eager •
O-3 used with
OH-290-A-3 to 9. Die
for Allen's Blacklead,
an Eager product.
Some earlier listed
as OH-175-S, a seller
of this product.

OH, Elyria • W.B. Eager • OH-290-A
• *Wholesale agent, maker of Allen's Blacklead Compound*[99] • ? • Reverse dies: 1473, 1131, 1168, 1172, 1180, 1192, 1242, 1274 • OH-290-A-1b Rev 1473 (R-2): VF–EF $25–$35 • MS-63 $75–$110 • Only token-issuing merchant of this town.

OH, Findlay • E. Bacher, Union Saloon • OH-300-aA • *Eating saloon* • Ascribed to the shop of W.K. Lanphear • Reverse dies: 1348, 35577 • OH-300aA-1a Rev 35577 (R-7), OH-300aA-1b Rev 35577 (R-7): VF–EF $150–$225 • MS-63 $500–$750 • In *JCWTS*, Fall 1984, p. 26, Thomas N. Schade reported that Ernest Bacher was a German immigrant who came to Han-

cock County, OH, in 1858. From 1863 to 1866 he was proprietor of the Union Eating Saloon, 232 South Main Street.

OH, Findlay • Boger & Kimmel • OH-300-A • *Watches* • Dies by Murdock & Spencer • Reverse die: 1433 • OH-300-A-1bo Rev 1433 (R-9), OH-300-A-1bo1 Rev 1433 (R-9): VF–EF $3,000–$4,500 • MS-63 $8,000–$12,000 • Repair check. Struck over an 1864 presidential campaign token.

OH, Findlay • I. Boger • OH-300-B • *Watch maker and jeweler* • Ascribed to the shop of W.K. Lanphear • Reverse dies: 0, 1320 • OH-300-B-1a Rev 1320 (R-8), OH-300-B-2b Rev 0 (R-8): VF–EF $1,000–$1,500 • MS-63 $2,500–$3,750.

OH, Findlay • Osborne & Bro. • OH-300-C • *Grocers and produce dealers* • Ascribed to the shop of John Stanton • Reverse dies: 1024, 1042, 1046, 1047 • OH-300-C-1a Rev 1024 (R-8), OH-300-C-2a Rev 1042 (R-8): VF–EF $200–$300 • MS-63 $600–$900.

OH, Frazeysburg • E.L. Lemert • OH-310-A • *Dry goods and groceries* • Ascribed to the shop of John Stanton • Reverse dies: 1037, 1036, 1047 • OH-310A-1a Rev 1037 (R-6): VF–EF $90–$135 • MS-63 $300–$450 • Only token-issuing merchant of this town.

OH, Fredericktown • Bartlett & Rigby • OH-320-A • *Dry goods and groceries* • Ascribed to the shop of John Stanton • Reverse dies: 1046, 1047 • OH-320-A-1a Rev 1046 (R-6): VF–EF $60–$90 • MS-63 $200–$300.

OH, Fredericktown • Mosure Bro & Lemon • OH-320-B • *Clothing and dry goods* • Ascribed to the shop of W.K. Lanphear • Reverse die: 1346 • OH-320-B-1a Rev 1346 (R-5): VF–EF $90–$135 • MS-63 $300–$450.

OH, Fredericktown • Rogers & Cassell • OH-320-C • *Hardware, iron, and nails* • Ascribed to the shop of W.K. Lanphear • Reverse die: 1304 • OH-320-C-1a Rev 1304 (R-4): VF–EF $100–$150 • MS-63 $400–$600.

OH, Fredericktown • S.S. Tuttle • OH-320-D • *Produce commission and forwarding merchant* • Ascribed to the shop of John Stanton • Reverse dies: 1032, 1037, 1046, 1047 • OH-320-D-3a Rev 1046 (R-4): VF–EF $40–$60 • MS-63 $200–$300.

OH, Fremont • P. Close • OH-330-A • *Groceries, wines, liquor, cigars* • Ascribed to the shop of W.K. Lanphear • Reverse die: 1087 • OH-330-A-1a Rev 1087 (R-4): VF–EF $75–$110 • MS-63 $225–$350 • 1859–1860 *Hawes' Ohio State Gazetteer and Business Directory:* "P. Close, groceries, flour, fish, game, liquors and cigars, wholesale and retail, corner Main and Croghan."

OH-330-B •
Dr. E. Dillon & Son •
O-1 used with
OH-330-B-1.

OH, Fremont • E. Dillon & Son • OH-330-B • *Druggists* • Ascribed to the shop of W.K. Lanphear • Reverse die: 1310 • OH-330-B-1a Rev 1310 (R-5): VF–EF $60–$90 • MS-63 $200–$300.

OH, Fremont • M. Dryfoos • OH-330-C • *Merchant tailor and dealer in ready-made clothing* • Ascribed to the shop of W.K. Lanphear • Reverse die: 1337 • OH-330-C-1a Rev 1337 (R-6): VF–EF $40–$60 • MS-63 $150–$225.

OH, Fremont • Emrich & Co. • OH-330-D • *Dry goods and clothing* • Ascribed to the shop of W.K. Lanphear • Reverse

die: 1087 • OH-330-D-1a Rev 1087 (R-5): VF–EF $50–$75 • MS-63 $200–$300.

OH, Fremont • Hoot & Meng • OH-330-E • *Manufacturers of and dealers in boots and shoes* • ? • Reverse die: 1317 • OH-330-E-1a Rev 1317 (R-4): VF–EF $100–$150 • MS-63 $300–$450.

OH, Fremont • D.W. Krebs & Co. • OH-330-F • *Dry goods and clothing* • Dies by F.W. Lutz for W.K. Lanphear • Reverse dies: 1085 and 1087 • OH-330-F-a Rev 1087 (R-5): VF–EF $75–$110 • MS-63 $225–$350.

Oh, Fremont • Roberts & Sheldon • OH-330-G • *Dealers in stoves, tin, and hardware* • Dies possibly by the Scovill Manufacturing Co. • Reverse die: 1306 • OH-330-G-1a Rev 1306 (R-5): VF–EF $60–$90 • MS-63 $250–$375.

OH, Fremont • Thompson & Spicer • OH-330-H • *Stoves, tin, and house furnishing goods* • Ascribed to the shop of W.K. Lanphear • Reverse die: 1302 • OH-330-H-1a Rev 1302 (R-6): VF–EF $60–$90 • MS-63 $200–$300.

OH, Galion • D. & W. Riblet • OH-340-A • *Hardware dealer* • Dies possibly by the Scovill Manufacturing Co. • Reverse die: 1333 • OH-340-A-1a Rev 1333 (R-4): VF–EF $30–$45 • MS-63 $125–$175 • Only token-issuing merchant of this town.

OH, Gallipolis • J.D. Bailey • OH-345-A • *Dry goods, groceries, and notions* • Ascribed to the shop of John Stanton • Reverse dies: 1037, 1038, 1046, 1047 • OH-345-A-1a Rev 1037 (R-8): VF–EF $75–$110 • MS-63 $250–$375.

OH, Gallipolis • J.J. Cadot & Bro. • OH-345-B • *Grocers* • Ascribed to the shop of W.K. Lanphear • Reverse dies: 1122, 1181 • OH-345-B-1a Rev 1122 (R-5), OH-345-B-2a Rev 1181 (R-5): VF–EF $60–$90 • MS-63 $250–$375.

OH, Greenville • F.H. Hafer & Co. • OH-360-A • *Grocers* • Ascribed to the shop of John Stanton • Reverse dies: 1007,

1038, 1042, 1047, 1192 • OH-360-A-2a Rev 1038 (R-5): VF–EF $40–$60 • MS-63 $150–$225.

OH, Greenville • T.P. Turpen • OH-360-B • *Grocer and tobacco dealer* • Ascribed to the shop of John Stanton • Reverse dies: 1018, 1023, 1042, 1047, 1069 • OH-360-B-3a Rev 1042 (R-7): VF–EF $60–$90 • MS-63 $250–$375.

OH, Hamilton • John Deinzer • OH-385A • *Family grocery* • Ascribed to the shop of John Stanton • Reverse dies: 1021, 1042, 1047, 1069 • OH-385-A-1a Rev 1021 (R-5): VF–EF $40–$60 • MS-63 $150–$225.

OH, Hamilton • H. & W. Frechtling • OH-385-B • *Dry goods and groceries* • Ascribed to the shop of John Stanton • Reverse dies: 1038, 1042, 1047, 1069 • OH-385-B-2a Rev 1042 (R-8), OH-385-B-2b Rev 1042 (R-8), OH-385-B-3a Rev 1047 (R-8): VF–EF $60–$90 • MS-63 $200–$300.

OH, Hamilton • John F. Goller • OH-385-C • ? • Jas. Murdock Jr. • Reverse die: 35851 • OH-385-C-1b Rev 35851 (R-8): VF–EF $500–$750 • MS-63 $1,500–$2,250 • By 1870 he had moved from Hamilton to Cincinnati and requested a license to set up a newsstand.

OH, Hamilton • John Schubert • OH-385-D • *Beer saloon* • Ascribed to the shop of John Stanton • Reverse dies: 1018, 1019, 1021, 1036, 1042, 1047, 1069 • OH-385-D-3a Rev 1021 (R-4), OH-385-D-4a Rev 1036 (R-4): VF–EF $30–$45 • MS-63 $100–$150.

OH, Hillsboro • Black & Kibler • OH-400-A • *Dealers in hardware, iron, and nails* • Ascribed to the shop of W.K. Lanphear • Reverse dies: 1326, 1332, 1334, 1336 • OH-400-A-2a Rev 1332 (R-4): VF–EF $35–$50 • MS-63 $135–$200.

OH, Hillsboro • Chaney & Harris • OH-400-B • *Dry goods* • Ascribed to the shop of W.K. Lanphear • Reverse die: 1122 • OH-400-B-1a Rev 1122 (R-7): VF–EF $125–$175.

OH, Hillsboro • O.J. Eckley • OH-400-C • *Meat market* • Ascribed to the shop of W.K. Lanphear • Reverse die: 1287 • OH-400-C-1a Rev 1287 (R-6): VF–EF $100–$150 • MS-63 $300–$450.

OH, Hillsboro • Herron & Amen • OH-400-D • *Dry goods and notions* • Ascribed to the shop of W.K. Lanphear • Reverse die: 1223 • OH-400-D-1a Rev 1223 (R-3): VF–EF $60–$90 • MS-63 $250–$375.

OH, Hillsboro • George March • OH-400-E • *Dry goods* • Ascribed to the shop of W.K. Lanphear • Reverse dies: 1171, 1223 • OH-400-E-2a Rev 1223 (R-4): VF–EF $35–$50 • MS-63 $150–$225.

OH, Jackson • John Chestnu's Exchange (Jack Chestnut) • OH-415-A • *Grocer* • Ascribed to the shop of John Stanton • Reverse dies: 1046, 1047, 1069, 1396A • OH-415-A-2a Rev 1047 (R-8): VF–EF $3,000–$4,500 • MS-63 $6,000–$9,000.

OH, Kenton • J.M. Brunson • OH-420-A • *Dry goods* • ? • Reverse die: 35951 • OH-420-A-1a Rev 35951 (R-5): VF–EF $30–$45 • MS-63 $100–$150.

OH-440-A • J. Ambruster • O-1 used with OH-440-A-1 to 3.

OH-440-A • J. Ambruster • O-2 used with OH-440-A-4, 5.

OH, Lancaster • J. Ambruster • OH-440-A • *Grocer* • Ascribed to the shop of W.K. Lanphear • Reverse dies: 0, 1084, 1126, 1178, 1344 • OH-440-A-4a Rev 1084 (R-4): VF–EF $60–$90 • MS-63 $150–$225.

OH, Lancaster • J. Block • OH-440-B
• *Ready-made clothing* • Ascribed to the shop of W.K. Lanphear • Reverse dies: 1126, 1337 • OH-440-B-1a Rev 1337 (R-5): VF–EF $150–$225 • MS-63 $400–$600.

OH, Lancaster • Charles Pairan • OH-440-C • *Grocer and liquor dealer* • ? • Reverse dies: 1126, 1127, 1166, 1172, 1227 • OH-440-C-3a Rev 1166 (R-5): VF–EF $50–$75 • MS-63 $200–$300.

OH, Lancaster • Andrew Reid • OH-440-D • *Dry goods and shoes* • Ascribed to the shop of W.K. Lanphear • Reverse die: 1273 • OH-440-D-1a Rev 1273 (R-4): VF–EF $50–$75 • MS-63 $200–$300.

OH, Laurelville • George D. Riegel • OH-445-A • *Dry goods and groceries* • Ascribed to the shop of W.K. Lanphear • Reverse dies: 1082, 1083, 1085, 1223, 1228, 1280 • OH-445-A-1a Rev 1082 (R-3), OH-445-A-6a Rev 1280 (R-3): VF–EF $30–$45 • MS-63 $75–$110 • Only token-issuing merchant of this town.

OH, Lima • R. Boose • OH-450-A • *Dry goods* • Ascribed to the shop of W.K. Lanphear • Reverse dies: 1082, 1091, 1171, 1223 • OH-450-A-2a Rev 1091 (R-3), OH-450-A-4a • VF–EF $25–$35 • MS-63 $90–$135 • Only token-issuing merchant of this town.

OH, Loudenville • F. Schuch • OH-485-A • *Grocer* • Ascribed to the shop of W.K. Lanphear • Reverse dies: 1082, 1083, 1085, 1223, 1228, 1280 • OH-485-A-6a Rev 1280 (R-3): VF–EF $75–$110 • MS-63 $250–$375 • Only token-issuing merchant of this town.

OH, Mansfield • H. Endly • OH-505-A • *Dealer in hats and caps* • Dies by Peter H. Jacobus • Reverse dies: 1270, 1270A • OH-505-A-1a Rev 1270 (R-2), OH-505-A-2a Rev 1270A (R-2): VF–EF $25–$35 • MS-63 $100–$150.

OH, Mansfield • F.B. Orr • OH-505-B • *Dealer in hardware, iron, and nails* • Dies by William H. Bridgens • Reverse dies: 1006, 1137, 1152, 1214, 1243, 1268, 1269 • OH-505-B-7a Rev 1269 (R-3): VF–EF $30–$45 • MS-63 $100–$150.

OH, Marion • A.E. Griffin • OH-520-A • *Dentist* • Ascribed to the shop of W.K. Lanphear • Reverse dies: 1083, 1088 • OH-520-A-1a Rev 1083 (R-5): VF–EF $150–$225 • MS-63 $500–$750 • Only token-issuing merchant of this town.

OH, Martinsburg • A. & W. Barnes • OH-530-A • *Dry goods* • Ascribed to the shop of W.K. Lanphear • Reverse die: 1122 • OH-530-A-1a Rev 1122 (R-2): VF–EF $35–$50 • MS-63 $150–$225.

OH, Martinsburg • M.N. Dayton • OH-530-B • *Dealer in drugs, medicines, and groceries* • ? • Reverse die: 35690 • OH-530-B-1a Rev 35690 (R-6): VF–EF $40–$60.

OH-535-A •
P.G. Albright •
O-1 used with
OH-535-A-1 to 3.

OH-535-A •
P.G. Albright •
O-2 used with
OH-535-A-4 to 6.

OH-535-A •
P.G. Albright •
O-3 used with
OH-535-A-7.

OH-535-A •
P.G. Albright •
O-4 used with
OH-535-A-8 to 10.

OH, Massillon • P.G. Albright • OH-535-A • *Grocer* • Ascribed to the shop of W.K. Lanphear • Reverse dies: 1084, 1087, 1089, 1125, 1127, 1130, 1224, 1225 • OH-535-A-3a Rev 1224 (R-2), OH-535-A-8a Rev 1084 (R-2): VF–EF $25–$35 • MS-63 $75–$110.

OH-535-B •
J.B. Dangler •
O-1 used with
OH-535-B-1 and 2.

OH, Massillon • J.B. Dangler (Isaac B. Dangler) • OH-535-B • *Dry goods* • Ascribed to the shop of W.K. Lanphear • Reverse dies: 1127, 1169 • OH-535-B-1a Rev 1127 (R-6): VF–EF $25–$35 • MS-63 $125–$175 • First initial given as J on token; should be I.

OH, Massillon • G.W. Laughlin • OH-535-Ba • *Jeweler* • Dies by Murdock & Spencer • Reverse die: 0 • OH-535-Ba-1a Rev 0 (R-10): VF–EF $2,500–$3,750 • MS-63 $4,000–$6,000 • Repair check. Struck over an 1864 presidential campaign token.

OH, Massillon • Fred Loeffler • OH-535-C • *Grocer* • Ascribed to the shop of W.K. Lanphear • Reverse dies: 1089, 1130 • OH-535-C-2a Rev 1130 (R-2): VF–EF $30–$45 • MS-63 $125–$175.

OH, Massillon • Henry Knobloch • OH-535-D • *Grocer* • Ascribed to the shop of W.K. Lanphear • Reverse dies: 1082, 1089, 1128, 1224 • OH-535-D-2a Rev 1089 (R-3): VF–EF $25–$35 • MS-63 $90–$135.

OH, Maumee • H. Burritt • OH-540-A • *Drugs, medicines, oils, dyestuffs, etc.* • Ascribed to the shop of W.K. Lanphear • Reverse die: 1310 • OH-540-A-1a Rev 1310 (R-5): VF–EF $100–$150 • MS-63 $400–$600.

OH, Maumee • Maumee & Perrysburg Toll Bridge Co. • OH-540-B • *Toll token* • Ascribed to the shop of W.K. Lanphear • Reverse die: 1128 • OH-540-B-1a Rev 1128 (R-6): VF–EF $150-225 • MS-63 $500–$750.

OH, McConnelsville • H.M. Cochran • OH-550-A • *Tobacco manufacturer* • Ascribed to the shop of W.K. Lanphear • Reverse die: 1331 • OH-550-A-1a Rev 1331 (R-4): VF–EF $60–$90 • MS-63 $200–$300 • Only token-issuing merchant of this town.

OH, Middletown • P.L. Potter • OH-555-A • *Dealer in groceries and queensware* • Ascribed to the shop of John Stanton • Reverse dies: 1019, 1020, 1036, 1042, 1047, 1069, 34640 • OH-555-A-1a Rev 1019 (R-5): VF–EF $50–$75 • MS-63 $200–$300 • Only token-issuing merchant of this town.

OH, Mill Creek Township • John Frank • OH-557 • *Milk seller* • Ascribed to the shop of John Stanton • Reverse dies: 1N to 5N • NY-105-Ha-1a Rev 1N (R-7): VF–EF $175–$250 • MS-63 $500–$750 • The Civil War Token Society moved this listing from Cincinnati (2nd edition) to Mill Creek Township. Possibly related? (*Commercial Advertiser Directory for the City of Buffalo*, 1861, p. 164: "Frank, John. Milk peddler. Home: Steele near Walnut.").

OH-560-A •
R.G. Martin •
O-1 used with
OH-560-A-1 to 4.

OH-560-A •
R.G. Martin •
O-2 used with
OH-560-A-5, 6.

OH-560-A •
R.G. Martin •
O-3 used with
OH-560-A-7.

OH, Monroeville • R.G. Martin • OH-560-A • *Manufacturer of tin, sheet iron, and copper ware* • Ascribed to the shop of W.K. Lanphear • Reverse dies: 1085, 1087, 1128, 1168, 1302 • OH-560-A-5a Rev 1128 (R-3): VF–EF $30–$45 • MS-63 $90–$135.

OH, Monroeville • A.W. Prentiss • OH-560-B • *Dry goods, groceries, boots, and shoes* • Ascribed to the shop of W.K. Lanphear • Reverse dies: 1128, 1169, 1317 • OH-560-B-2a Rev 1169 (R-4): VF–EF $30–$45 • MS-63 $90–$135.

OH, Montgomery County • G. Haines • OH-562-A • ? • Ascribed to the shop of John Stanton • Reverse dies: 1046, 1047 • OH-562-A-1a Rev 1046 (R-5): VF–EF $50–$75 • MS-63 $150–$225 • Only token-issuing merchant of this location description. Formerly known as IN-995-A. Wolf Creek Pike address, no town given. Location attribution still uncertain.

OH, Morristown • P. Lochary New Store • OH-565-A • *Merchant* • Ascribed to the shop of W.K. Lanphear • Reverse dies: 1122, 1128 • OH-565-A-2a Rev 1128 (R-3): VF–EF $40–$60 • MS-63 $175–$250 • Only token-issuing merchant of this town.

OH, Morrow • J.M. Dynes • OH-570-A • *Dry goods and groceries at auction* • Ascribed to the shop of W.K. Lanphear • Reverse die: 1303 • OH-570-A-1a Rev 1303 (R-5): VF–EF $150–$225 • MS-63 $400–$600.

OH, Morrow • E. Levy • OH-570-B • *Dry goods, clothing, boots, and shoes* • Ascribed to the shop of W.K. Lanphear • Reverse die: 1125, 1178 • OH-570-B-1a Rev 1125 (R-6), OH-570-B-2a Rev 1178 (R-6): VF–EF $175–$250 • MS-63 $500–$750.

OH, Mount Eaton • D. Giaugue • OH-585-A • *Groceries and provisions* • Ascribed to the shop of W.K. Lanphear • Reverse dies: 1084, 1086, 1087 • OH-585-A-1a Rev 1086 (R-4): VF–EF $100–$150 • MS-63 $300–$450 • Only token-issuing merchant of this town.

OH, Navarre • Hall & Frymire • OH-597-A • *Dealers in stoves and tinware* • Ascribed to the shop of W.K. Lanphear • Reverse dies: 1300, 1301, 1302 • OH-597-A-1a Rev 1300 (R-5), OH-597-A-3a Rev 1302 (R-5): VF–EF $50–$75 • MS-63 $150–$225 • Only token-issuing merchant of this town.

OH, New London • H.H. Robinson • OH-620-A • *Dry goods, groceries* • Ascribed to the shop of John Stanton • Reverse dies: 0, 1018, 1023, 1028, 1031, 1039, 1042, 1045, 1047, 1069, 1274 • OH-620-A-7a Rev 1045 (R-3): VF–EF $25–$35 • MS-63 $75–$110 • Town listed out of alphabetical order in Fuld.[100]

OH, New London • G.M. Shaw Cheap Cash Store • OH-620-B • *Store* • Ascribed to the shop of W.K. Lanphear • Reverse dies: 1124, 1176, 1177, 1295, 1331 • OH-620-B-2a Rev 1176 (R-7), OH-620-B-3a Rev 1177 (R-7): VF–EF $50–$75 • MS-63 $150–$225 • Town listed out of alphabetical order in Fuld.

OH, Newcomerstown • A.S. Twiford • OH-610-A • *Photograph artist and druggist* • Ascribed to the shop of W.K. Lanphear • Reverse die: 1310 • OH-610-A-1a Rev 1310 (R-7), OH-610-A-1b Rev 1310 (R-7): VF–EF $350–$500 • MS-63 $1,000–$1,500 • Only token-issuing merchant of this town.

OH, North Hampton • M. Hartman • OH-645-A • *Dry goods, hardware, shoes* • Ascribed to the shop of John Stanton • Reverse dies: 1046, 1047 • OH-645-A-2a Rev 1047 (R-7), OH-645-A-2d Rev 1047 (R-7): VF–EF $60–$90 • MS-63 $200–$300.

OH, North Hampton • G.W. McLean • OH-645-B • *Produce dealer* • Ascribed to the shop of John Stanton • Reverse dies: 1037, 1046, 1047 • OH-645-B-1a Rev 1037 (R-7), OH-645-B-2a Rev 1046 (R-7): VF–EF $100–$150 • MS-63 $300–$450.

OH, North Liberty • Samuel Bishop • OH-650-A • *Dry goods and groceries* • Ascribed to the shop of W.K. Lanphear • Reverse dies: 1122, 1225 • OH-650-A-1a Rev 1122 (R-4): VF–EF $60–$90 • MS-63 $200–$300 • Only token-issuing merchant of this town.

OH, Norwalk • P. Timmens • OH-670-A • *Groceries and provisions* • Ascribed to the shop of W.K. Lanphear • Reverse dies: 1082, 1084, 1089 • OH-670-A-3a Rev 1089 (R-6): VF–EF $75–$110 • MS-63 $300–$450 • Only token-issuing merchant of this town.

OH, Oberlin • R.H. Birge • OH-690-A • *Drugs, groceries* • Ascribed to the shop of W.K. Lanphear • Reverse die: 1310 • OH-690-A-1a Rev 1310 (R-6): VF–EF $125–$175 • MS-63 $300–$450.

OH, Oberlin • Frank Hendry • OH-690-B • *Manufacturer of spectacles and eyeglasses* • Ascribed to the shop of W.K. Lanphear • Reverse dies: 1089, 1181 • OH-690-B-1a Rev 1089 (R-6): VF–EF $125–$175 • MS-63 $300–$450.

OH, Orrville • J.F. Seas • OH-695-A • *Hardware, books, paints, and oils* • Ascribed to the shop of John Stanton • Reverse dies: 1007, 1018, 1019, 1042, 1047, 1069 • OH-695-A-1a Rev 1007 (R-5), OH-695-A-3a Rev 1019 (R-5): VF–EF $75–$110 • MS-63 $225–$350 • Only token-issuing merchant of this town.

OH, Oxford • McGaw & Richey • OH-710-A • *Drugs, books, and wallpaper* • Ascribed to the shop of W.K. Lanphear • Reverse dies: 1124, 1180, 1225, 1324A, 1331 • OH-710-A-2a Rev 1180 (R-4): VF–EF $60–$90 • MS-63 $200–$300.

OH, Oxford • Newton & Kumlers • OH-710-B • *Dry goods* • Dies by Johnston or Linderman • Reverse die: 1058 • OH-710-B-1a Rev 1058 (R-6): VF–EF $100–$150.

OH, Perrysburg • G. Beach • OH-725-A • *Dry goods, clothing, boots, and shoes* • Ascribed to the shop of W.K. Lanphear • Reverse dies: 1177, 1181 • OH-725-A-2a Rev 1181 (R-6), OH-725-A-2b Rev 1181 (R-6): VF–EF $100–$150 • MS-63 $400–$600.

OH, Perrysburg • D. Kreps • OH-725-B • *Dealer in agricultural implements, farm tools, steam engines, etc.* • Ascribed to the shop of W.K. Lanphear • Reverse die: 36060 • OH-725-B-1a Rev 36060 (R-6): VF–EF $100–$150 • MS-63 $400–$600.

OH-730-A •
Drs. Brown & Dills •
O-1 used with
OH-730-A-1 to 7, 9.

OH-730-A •
Drs. Brown & Dills •
O-2 used with
OH-730-A-8.

OH, Piqua • Drs. Brown & Dills • OH-730-A • *Dentists* • Ascribed to the shop of W.K. Lanphear • Reverse dies: 1082, 1089, 1123, 1125, 1126, 1127, 1177, 1180, 36090 • OH-730-A-1a Rev 1082 (R-4): VF–EF $50–$75 • MS-63 $175–$250.

OH, Piqua • French & Swonger • OH-730-B • *Meat market* • Ascribed to the shop of W.K. Lanphear • Reverse die: 1287 • OH-730-B-1a Rev 1287 (R-4): VF–EF $125–$175 • MS-63 $400–$600.

OH, Piqua • Martin Hoegner • OH-730-C • *Meat market* • Ascribed to the shop of W.K. Lanphear • Reverse die: 1287 • OH-730-C-1a Rev 1287 (R-6): VF–EF $200–$300 • MS-63 $750–$1,000.

OH, Piqua • Marrow & Parker • OH-730-D • *Dry goods* • Ascribed to the shop of W.K. Lanphear • Reverse die: 1223 • OH-730-D-1a Rev 1223 (R-8): VF–EF $175–$250.

OH, Piqua • Smart & Co • OH-730-E • *Grocers* • Ascribed to the shop of W.K. Lanphear • Reverse dies: 1122, 1166, 1169 • OH-730-E-1a Rev 1122 (R-4): VF–EF $50–$75 • MS-63 $175–$250.

OH, Pomeroy • A.I. Aicher • OH-735-A • *Jeweler* • Dies by Murdock & Spencer • Reverse die: 1433 • OH-735-A-1b Rev 1433 (R-9): VF–EF $3,000–$4,500 • MS-63 $6,000–$9,000 • Repair check struck over an 1864 presidential campaign token.

OH, Pomeroy • J.P. Tou • OH-735-B • *Grocer* • Ascribed to the shop of John Stanton • Reverse dies: 1018, 1023, 1028,

1042, 1045, 1047, 1069 • OH-735-B-5a Rev 1045 (R-5): VF–EF $90–$135 • MS-63 $250–$375.

OH, Portsmouth • Burton's Exchange • OH-745-A • *Saloon* • Ascribed to the shop of John Stanton • Reverse dies: 1047, 1396A, 1401 • OH-745-A-1a Rev 1047 (R-8), OH-745-A-2b Rev 1396-A (R-8): VF–EF $150–$225 • MS-63 $500–$750.

OH, Portsmouth • S.W. Cunning • OH-745-B • *Wholesale liquors* • Ascribed to the shop of John Stanton • Reverse dies: 1009, 1038, 1042, 1047, 1069, 1401 • OH-745-B-2a Rev 1038 (R-8), OH-745-B-3a Rev 1042 (R-8), OH-745-B-3b Rev 1042 (R-8): VF–EF $125–$175 • MS-63 $350–$500.

OH, Putnam • L. Wiles • OH-755-A • *Dry goods* • Ascribed to the shop of W.K. Lanphear • Reverse dies: 1126, 1166, 1178 • OH-755-A-1a Rev 1126 (R-8), OH-755-A-3a Rev 1178 (R-8): VF–EF $100–$150 • MS-63 $400–$600 • Only token-issuing merchant of this town.

OH, Ravenna • Butler Witter & Co. • OH-765-A • *Dealers in "W.R.," butter, cheese, etc.* • Ascribed to the shop of W.K. Lanphear • Reverse dies: 1084, 1123, 1124, 36220 • OH-765-A-1a Rev 36220 (R-3): VF–EF $50–$75 • MS-63 $200–$300.

OH, Ravenna • Dr. D.R. Jennings OH-765-B • *Surgeon and dentist* • Ascribed to the shop of W.K. Lanphear • Reverse dies: 1082, 1084, 1123, 1124, 1344 • OH-765-B-4a Rev 1344 (R-5): VF–EF $200–$300 • MS-63 $600–$900.

OH, Ravenna • C.A. Pease • OH-765-C • *Dealer in groceries and fruits* • Ascribed to the shop of W.K. Lanphear • Reverse dies: 1082, 1168, 1181 • OH-765-C-1a Rev 1082 (R-5): VF–EF $50–$75 • MS-63 $200–$300.

OH, Ravenna • Mrs. Reed • OH-765-D • *Millinery and fancy goods* • Ascribed to the shop of W.K. Lanphear • Reverse die: 1273 • OH-765-D-1a Rev

1273 (R-5): VF–EF $100–$150 • MS-63 $300–$450.

OH-765-E •
William Ward •
O-1 used with
OH-765-E-1.

OH-765-E •
William Ward •
O-2 used with
OH-765-E-2 to 4.
Used as the *reverse*
of OH-765-E-1
and *obverse* of
OH-765-E-02 to 04.

OH, Ravenna • William Ward • OH-765-E • *Dry goods and groceries* • Ascribed to the shop of W.K. Lanphear • Reverse dies: 1084, 1088, 1123, 36270 • OH-765-E-1a Rev 36270 (R-5): VF–EF $100–$150 • MS-63 $300–$450.

OH, Richmond • B.L. Crew • OH-770-A • *Dry goods & grocer* • Ascribed to the shop of John Stanton • Reverse dies: 1028, 1042, 1045, 1046, 1047, 1069 • OH-770-A-3a Rev 1045 (R-5): VF–EF $100–$150 • MS-63 $300–$450 • Only token-issuing merchant of this town.

OH, Ripley • Dunbar & Wolff • OH-780-A • *Watchmakers* • Dies by Murdock & Spencer • Reverse die: 1433 • OH-780-A-1b Rev 1433 (R-9): VF–EF $6,000–$9,000 • MS-63 $10,000–$15,000. Only token-issuing merchant of this town. This is the rarest town in Ohio and one of the very rarest of Civil War store cards. Struck over McClellan token DeWitt GMcC 1864-27.

OH, Sharonville (Hamilton County) • George Metzger • OH-790-A • *Hotel and restaurant* • Ascribed to the shop of John Stanton[101] • Reverse dies: 1029, 1042, 1047, 1069 • OH-790-A-1a Rev 1029 (R-8), OH-790-A-2a Rev 1042 (R-8), OH-790-A-2b Rev 1042 (R-8), OH-790-A-3a Rev 1047 (R-8): VF–EF $150–$225 • MS-63 $600–$900 • Only token-issuing

merchant of this town. Formerly Fuld-OH-165-DR.

OH, Sharonville (Pike County) • W.K. McMillins • OH-800-A • *Merchant* • Ascribed to the shop of John Stanton • Reverse dies: 1028, 1042, 1047, 1069 • OH-800-A-1a Rev 1028 (R-7), OH-800-A-2a Rev 1042 (R-8): VF–EF $100–$150 • MS-63 $300–$450 • Only token-issuing merchant of this town.

OH, Shelby • Cummins & Anderson • OH-805-A • *Dry goods, groceries, and millinery* • Ascribed to the shop of John Stanton • Reverse dies: 1037, 1042, 1043, 1046, 1047 • OH-805-A-3a Rev 1043 (R-5): VF–EF $40–$60 • MS-63 $150–$225.

OH, Shelby • Thomas Mickey • OH-805-B • *Dry goods, groceries, hats, caps, millinery* • Ascribed to the shop of W.K. Lanphear • Reverse die: 36330 • OH-1a Rev 36330 (R-4): VF–EF $40–$60 • MS-63 $150–$225.

OH, Sidney • Fry & Johnston • OH-815-A • *Dry goods, boots, and shoes* • Ascribed to the shop of W.K. Lanphear • Reverse dies: 1090, 1091, 1122, 1225, 1228 • OH-815-A-3a Rev 1122 (R-4): VF–EF $75–$110 • MS-63 $300–$450.

OH, Sidney • Jason McVay • OH-815-B • *Dry goods, boots, and shoes* • Ascribed to the shop of W.K. Lanphear • Reverse die: 1337 • OH-815-B-1a Rev 1337 (R-3): VF–EF $90–$135 • MS-63 $250–$375.

OH, Sidney • S.N. Todd & Co. • OH-815-C • *Druggists and stationers* • Ascribed to the shop of W.K. Lanphear • Reverse die: 1316 • OH-815-C Rev 1316 (R-7): VF–EF $300–$450 • MS-63 $1,250–$1,750.

OH, Sonora • William Leas, Cash Store • OH-820-A • *Merchant* • Ascribed to the shop of W.K. Lanphear • Reverse die: 1091 • OH-820-A-1a Rev 1091 (R-5): VF–EF $60–$90 • MS-63 $250–$375 • Only token-issuing merchant of this town.

OH, Springfield • W.G. Brain • OH-830-A • *Druggist* • Ascribed to the shop of John Stanton[102] • Reverse dies: 1018, 1023, 1025, 1026, 1027, 1028, 1030, 1033, 1034, 1036, 1042, 1047, 1069 • OH-830-A-9a Rev 1034 (R-3): VF–EF $50–$75 • MS-63 $175–$250.

OH, Springfield • Kauffman & Co. • OH-830-B • *Cigars and liquors* • Ascribed to the shop of John Stanton • Reverse dies: 1028, 1034, 1037, 1042, 1044, 1046, 1047 • OH-830-B-1a Rev 1028 (R-4): VF–EF $50–$75 • MS-63 $175–$250.

OH, Springfield • J.W. Low • OH-830-C • *Books and wallpaper* • Ascribed to the shop of John Stanton • Reverse dies: 1022, 1031, 1033, 1037, 1042, 1043, 1046, 1047 • OH-830-C-7a Rev 1046 (R-3): VF–EF $35–$50 • MS-63 $150–$225.

OH, Springfield • Ludlow & Bushnell • OH-830-D • *Druggists* • Ascribed to the shop of John Stanton[103] • Reverse dies: 1018, 1020, 1025, 1036, 1042, 1046, 1046A, 1047, 1069 • OH-830-D-4a Rev 1046 (R-5): VF–EF $50–$75 • MS-63 $175–$250.

OH, Springfield • G.W. McLean • OH-830-E • *Produce dealer* • Ascribed to the shop of John Stanton • Reverse dies: 1042, 1043, 1047 • OH-830-E-1a Rev 1042 (R-5): VF–EF $75–$110 • MS-63 $300–$450.

OH, Springfield • Murphy & Bro. • OH-830-F • *Dry goods* • Ascribed to the shop of John Stanton • Reverse dies: 1026, 1037, 1042, 1047, 1069 • OH-830-F-3a Rev 1042 (R-6): VF–EF $90–$135 • MS-63 $250–$375.

OH, Springfield • C. Runyon • OH-830-G • *Groceries* • ? • Reverse dies: 1037, 1047 • OH-830-G-1a Rev 1037 (R-7): VF–EF $40–$60 • MS-63 $175–$250.

OH, Steubenville • William Dunlap • OH-835-A • *Dry goods and groceries* • Ascribed to the shop of W.K. Lanphear • Reverse dies: 1090, 1166, 1434 •

OH-835-A-2a Rev 1166 (R-3): VF–EF $35–$50 • MS-63 $100–$150.

OH, Steubenville • J.H. Bristor • OH-835-B • *Hotel* • Ascribed to the shop of W.K. Lanphear • Reverse dies: 1084, 1326, 1434 • OH-835-B-2a Rev 1326 (R-3): VF–EF $25–$35 • MS-63 $125–$175.

OH, Steubenville • J.W. Gray • OH-835-C • *Groceries and dry goods* • Ascribed to the shop of W.K. Lanphear • Reverse dies:1127, 1130, 1168, 1181 • OH-835-C-2a Rev 1130 (R-5), OH-835-C-4a Rev 1181 (R-5): VF–EF $25–$35 • MS-63 $90–$135.

OH, Steubenville • J.H. Hind's News Depot • OH-835-D • *News depot* • Ascribed to the shop of W.K. Lanphear • Reverse dies: 1166, 1322, 1434 • OH-835-D-1a Rev 1166 (R-5), OH-835-D-2a Rev 1322 (R-5): VF–EF $35–$50 • MS-63 $125–$175.

OH, Steubenville • C.M. May • OH-835-E • *Merchant tailor and clothier* • Ascribed to the shop of W.K. Lanphear • Reverse dies: 1337, 1342 • OH-835-E-2a Rev 1342 (R-2): VF–EF $50–$75 • MS-63 $150–$225.

OH, Steubenville • J. McCauley • OH-835-F • *Grocer* • Ascribed to the shop of W.K. Lanphear • Reverse die: 1227 • OH-835-F-1a Rev 1227 (R-4): VF–EF $60–$90 • MS-63 $200–$300.

OH, Steubenville • Daniel McConville • OH-835-G • *Dry goods and notions* • Ascribed to the shop of W.K. Lanphear • Reverse dies: 1166, 1178 • OH-835-G-2a Rev 1178 (R-4): VF–EF $75–$110 • MS-63 $200–$300.

OH, Stryker • John S. Kingsland & Bro. • OH-840-A • *Druggists* • Ascribed to the shop of S.D. Childs • Reverse dies: 1094, 1390 • OH-840-A-1a Rev 1094 (R-5): VF–EF $100–$150 • MS-63 $400–$600.

OH, Stryker • G.W. Hamblin • OH-840-B • *General goods* • Ascribed to the shop of S.D. Childs • Reverse dies: 1106, 1107 • OH-840-B-2a Rev 1107 (R-6): VF–EF $150–$225 • MS-63 $500–$750.

OH, Syracuse • H. Bartels • OH-845-A • *Dry goods, groceries, boots, and shoes* • Ascribed to the shop of John Stanton • Reverse dies: 1045, 1046, 1047 • OH-840-A-1a Rev 1045 (R-5): VF–EF $75–$110 • MS-63 $300–$450 • Only token-issuing merchant of this town.

OH, Tiffin • M.J. Kirchner • OH-850-A • *Groceries* • Ascribed to the shop of John Stanton • Reverse dies: 1037, 1046, 1047 • OH-850-A-1a Rev 1037 (R-7): VF–EF $90–$135 • MS-63 $300–$450.

OH-850-B •
Sonder &
Carpenter (Souder
& Carpenter) •
O-1 used with
OH-850-B-1. Error
die with first
surname misspelled.

OH-850-C •
Souder & Carpenter •
O-2 used with
OH-850-C-1.

OH, Tiffin • Sonder & Carpenter (misspelling) • OH-850-B • *Dry goods* • ? • Reverse die: 36570 • OH-850-B-1b Rev 36570 (R-3): VF–EF $40–$60 • MS-63 $175–$250 • In the third edition of the Fuld book OH-850-B and C will be consolidated under OH-850-B.

OH, Tiffin • Souder & Carpenter • OH-850-C • *Dry goods* • ? • Reverse die: 36590 • OH-850-C-1b Rev 36590 (R-3): VF–EF $30–$45 • MS-63 $150–$225 • In the third edition of the Fuld book OH-850-B and C will be consolidated under OH-850-B.

OH, Tippecanoe • E.C. Saylor • OH-855-A • *Meat market* • Ascribed to the shop of W.K. Lanphear • Reverse dies: 1090, 1228, 1287 • OH-855-A-1a Rev 1228 (R-5), OH-855-A-2a Rev 1287 (R-5): VF–EF $60–$90 • MS-63 $225–$350 • Only token-issuing merchant of this town.

OH, Toledo • C.P. Curtis • OH-860-A • *Auction and commission merchant* • Ascribed to the shop of W.K. Lanphear • Reverse dies: 1083, 1085, 1127, 1169, 1181 • OH-860-A-1a Rev 1085 (R-3): VF–EF $25–$35 • MS-63 $75–$110.

OH-860-B •
Hough & Hall •
O-1 used with
OH-860-B-1 and 2.

OH-860-B •
Hough & Hall •
O-2 used with
OH-860-B-3.

OH, Toledo • Hough & Hall • OH-860-B • *Dry goods, carpets, oil cloth, etc.* • Ascribed to the shop of W.K. Lanphear • Reverse dies: 1083, 1168, 1181 • OH-860-B-1a Rev 1168 (R-4), OH-860-B-2a Rev 1181 (R-4), OH-860-B-3a Rev 1083 (R-4): VF–EF $25–$35 • MS-63 $75–$110.

OH, Toledo • Ketcham & Barker • OH-860-C • *Hardware dealer* • Dies possibly by the Scovill Manufacturing Co. • Reverse die: 1305 • OH-860-C-1a Rev 1305 (R-3), OH-860-C-1b Rev 1305 (R-3): VF–EF $25–$35 • MS-63 $100–$150.

OH, Toledo • Plessner & Son • OH-860-D • *Druggists* • Ascribed to the shop of W.K. Lanphear • Reverse die: 1310 • OH-860-D-1b Rev 1310 (R-3): VF–EF $75–$110 • MS-63 $250–$375.

OH, Troy • J. Hall • OH-880-A • *Grain dealer* • Ascribed to the shop of W.K. Lanphear • Reverse die: 1469 • OH-880-A-1a Rev 1469 (R-5): VF–EF $75–$110 • MS-63 $200–$300.

OH-880-B •
S.K. Harter •
O-1 used with
OH-880-B-1.

OH-880-B •
S.K. Harter •
O-2 used with
OH-880-B-2. With
the backward D
(HARDWARE) and
other misalignments
this is perhaps the
crudest die known to
be mated with a
Lanphear reverse.

OH, Troy • S.K. Harter • OH-880-B •
*Dealer in iron, nails, hardware, guns, and
pistols* • Reverse die: 1332 • OH-880-B-1a
Rev 1332 (R-7), OH-880-B-2a Rev 1332
(R-7): VF–EF $125–$175 • MS-63 $300–
$450.

OH, Troy • S.E. Hustler • OH-880-C
• ? • Ascribed to the shop of W.K. Lanphear • Reverse dies: 1089, 1091, 1171,
1223, 1318, 1439 • OH-880-C-4a Rev
1223 (R-3), OH-880-C-5a Rev 1318 (R-3):
VF–EF $25–$35 • MS-63 $75–$110.

OH, Troy • Julian & Co. • OH-880-D
• *Watchmakers and jewelers* • Ascribed to
the shop of W.K. Lanphear • Reverse
dies: 1090, 1320 • OH-880-D-2a Rev
1320 (R-3): VF–EF $40–$60 • MS-63
$150–$225.

OH, Troy • David Kelly • OH-880-E •
Books and stationery • ? • Reverse dies:
1083, 1122, 1124, 1127, 1180, 40930 •
OH-880-E-5a Rev 1180 (R-3), OH-880-E-
6a Rev 40930 (R-3): VF–EF $30–$45 •
MS-63 $90–$135.

**OH, Troy • Pearson & Bro. • OH-
880-F •** *Grocers* • Ascribed to the shop of
W.K. Lanphear • Reverse dies: 1083,
1166, 1171, 1222, 1223, 1228, 1346 •
OH-880-F-3a Rev 1181 (R-3), OH-880-F-
4a Rev 1222 (R-3), OH-880-F-6a Rev
1228 (R-3): VF–EF $25–$35 • MS-63
$90–$135.

**OH, Troy • Rinehart & Gray • OH-
880-G •** *Cash druggists* • Ascribed to the
shop of W.K. Lanphear • Reverse dies:
1126, 1178, 1228, 1223 • OH-880-F-1a
Rev 1126 (R-4): VF–EF $75–$110 •
MS-63 $225–$375.

**OH, Uniontown • Fauley & Brechbill •
OH-890-A •** *Dry goods, clothing, and groceries* • Ascribed to the shop of W.K. Lanphear • Reverse dies: 1091, 1228 •
OH-890-A-1a Rev 1091 (R-5): VF–EF
$75–$110 • MS-63 $250–$375 • Only
token-issuing merchant of this town.

**OH, Urbana • C. McCarthy, Washing-
ton House • OH-895-A •** *Hotel* • Ascribed
to the shop of Murdock & Spencer using
some earlier dies • Reverse dies: 1047,
1069, 1392 • OH-895-A-1a Rev 1047 (R-8):
VF–EF $3,000–$4,500 • MS-63 $5,000–
$7,500 • Surname misspelled "McCarty"
on the token. Non-contemporary.

**OH, Urbana • Walker's Ale Depot •
OH-895-B •** *Liquor* • Ascribed to the
shop of John Stanton • Reverse die: 1018
• OH-895-B-1a Rev 1018 (R-9): VF–EF
$6,500–$10,000 • MS-63 $12,000–
$18.000 • One of the greatest rarities in
the Ohio series.

OH, Van Wert • A. Jacobs • OH-900-A
• *Merchant tailor and ready-made clothing* •
Ascribed to the shop of W.K. Lanphear •
Reverse die: 1342 • OH-900-A-1a Rev
1342 (R-7): VF–EF $175–$250 • MS-63
$400–$600 • Only token-issuing merchant of this town.

OH-905-A •
Davis & Whiteman •
O-1 used with
OH-905-A-1 and 2.

OH-905-A Davis &
Whiteman •
O-2 used with
OH-905-A-3 and 4.

OH, Wapakoneta • Davis & Whiteman • OH-905-A • *Grocers and commission merchants* • Ascribed to the shop of W.K. Lanphear • Reverse dies: 1083, 1226, 1335, 1336 • OH-905-A-4a Rev 1336 (R-4): VF–EF $60–$90 • MS-63 $225–$350.

OH, Wapakoneta • A.C. Miles • OH-905-B • *Groceries and stationery* • Ascribed to the shop of W.K. Lanphear • Reverse die: 1325 • OH-905-B-1a Rev 1325 (R-4): VF–EF $175–$250 • MS-63 $600–$900.

OH, Wapakoneta • Sanitary Fair of Wapakoneta, O. • OH-905-C • *Sanitary fair* • ? • Reverse die: 1250A • OH-905-C-1b Rev 1250A (R-7): VF–EF $600–$900 • MS-63 $1,750–$2,250 • 22 mm.

OH, Wapakoneta • J.H. Timmermeister • OH-905-D • *Dry goods and groceries* • Ascribed to the shop of W.K. Lanphear • Reverse die: 1181 • OH-905-D-1a Rev 1181 (R-3): VF–EF $60–$90 • MS-63 $200–$300.

OH, Warren • Robbins • OH-910-A • *Photographic albums* • Dies possibly by the Scovill Manufacturing Co. • Reverse die: 36840 • OH-910-A-1a Rev 36840 (R-3): VF–EF $40–$60 • MS-63 $150–$225 • Only token-issuing merchant of this town.

OH, Wellsville • Hoover & Camp • OH-915-A • *Pianos, melodions, and musical merchandise* • Ascribed to the shop of W.K. Lanphear • Reverse dies: 1178, 1322 • OH-915-A-2a Rev 1322 (R-6): VF–EF $100–$150 • MS-63 $400–$600.

OH, Wellsville • William Lawrence • OH-915-B • *Clothier and photographic artist* • ? • Reverse dies: 1178, 1179 • OH-915-B-1a Rev 1178 (R-6): VF–EF $100–$150.

OH, West Jefferson • John Tresler • OH-920-A • *Grocery store* • Ascribed to the shop of W.K. Lanphear • Reverse dies: 1336, 1346 • OH-920-A-1a Rev 1336 (R-3): VF–EF $30–$45 • MS-63 $135–$200 • Only token-issuing merchant of this town.

OH, West Newton • C.M. Coffin • OH-925-A • *Dry goods, etc.* • ? • Reverse dies: 1037, 1046, 1047 • OH-925-A-1a Rev 1037 (R-5): VF–EF $75–110 • MS-63 $200–$300 • Only token-issuing merchant of this town.

OH, West Unity • Davies & Maxwell • OH-930-A • *Hardware and agricultural machinery* • Ascribed to the shop of W.K. Lanphear • Reverse dies: 1126, 1178 • OH-930-A-1a Rev 1126 (R-4): VF–EF $50–$75 • MS-63 $200–$300.

OH, West Unity • W.H. McGrew • OH-930-B • *Druggist* • Ascribed to the shop of W.K. Lanphear • Reverse dies: 1089, 1127, 1128 • OH-930-B-2a Rev 1127 (R-4): VF–EF $60–$90 • MS-63 $225–$350.

OH, West Unity • S. Pierce & Son • OH-930-C • *Dry goods, groceries, etc.* • Ascribed to the shop of W.K. Lanphear • Reverse dies: 1083, 1224 • OH-930-C-2a Rev 1224 (R-5): VF–EF $30–$45 • MS-63 $135–$200.

OH, West Unity • S.F. Snow • OH-930-D • *Dentist* • Ascribed to the shop of W.K. Lanphear • Reverse dies: 1127, 1128, 1130 • OH-930-D-3a Rev 1130 (R-6): VF–EF $150–$225 • MS-63 $500–$750.

OH, Wilmington • Mrs. Owens & Taylor • OH-935-A • *Millinery and fancy store* • Ascribed to the shop of W.K. Lanphear • Reverse dies: 1124, 1127, 1178, 1180, 1242, 1278 • OH-935-A-3a Rev 1180 (R-8), OH-935-A-4a Rev 1242 (R-8): VF–EF $250–$375 • MS-63 $750–$1,250.

OH, Wilmington • H. Perrin • OH-935-B • *Hardware and groceries* • Ascribed to the shop of W.K. Lanphear • Reverse die: 1178 • OH-935-B-1a Rev 1178 (R-4): VF–EF $100–$150 • MS-63 $300–$450.

OH, Wilmington • William Preston, Cheap Cash Store • OH-935-C • *Merchant* • ? • Reverse die: 1347 • OH-935-C-1a Rev 1347 (R-4): VF–EF $100–$150 • MS-63 $400–$600.

OH, Wilmington • T.R. Wraith • OH-935-D • *Hardware merchant* • Ascribed to the shop of W.K. Lanphear • Reverse dies: 0, 1178, 38970 • OH-935-D-1a Rev 38970 (R-5): VF–EF $100–$150 • MS-63 $300–$450.

OH, Woodsfield • J.W. Walton • OH-960-A • *Grocer and pension agent* • Ascribed to the shop of W.K. Lanphear • Reverse dies: 0, 1223, 1439, 38990 • OH-960-A-1a Rev 38990 (R-3), OH-960-A-2a Rev 1223 (R-3): VF–EF $25–$35 • MS-63 $90–$135 • Only token-issuing merchant of this town.

OH, Wooster • P.E. Beach • OH-975-A • *Dealer in hats, caps, and fancy goods* • ? • Reverse die: 39010 • OH-975-A-1a Rev 39010 (R-4): VF–EF $40–$60 • MS-63 $175–$250.

OH, Wooster • J.R. Bowman • OH-975-B • *Watches, clocks, jewelry* • Ascribed to the shop of John Stanton • Reverse dies: 1026, 1031, 1036, 1042, 1047, 1069 • OH-975-B-3a Rev 1036 (R-6), OH-975-B-4a Rev 1042 (R-6): VF–EF $40–$60 • MS-63 $150–$225.

OH, Wooster • G. Brumter • OH-975-C • *Groceries* • Ascribed to the shop of W.K. Lanphear • Reverse dies: 1084, 1089, 1178, 1181, 1192 • OH-975-C-3a Rev 1178 (R-5), OH-975-C-4a Rev 1181 (R-5): VF–EF $30–$45 • MS-63 $150–$225.

OH, Wooster • James B. Childs • OH-975-D • *Clothing, hats, caps, and trunks* • Dies possibly by the Scovill Manufacturing Co. • Reverse dies: 1406, 1407 • OH-975-D-1a Rev 1406 (R-3), OH-975-D-2a Rev 1407 (R-3): VF–EF $20–$30 • MS-63 $75–$110.

OH, Wooster • J.S. Duden • OH-975-E • *Groceries and provisions* • Ascribed to the shop of W.K. Lanphear • Reverse die: 1126 • OH-975-E-1a Rev 1126 (R-3): VF–EF $50–$75 • MS-63 $200–$300.

OH, Wooster • Samuel Geitgey • OH-975-F • *Dealer in stoves and tinware* •

Ascribed to the shop of W.K. Lanphear • Reverse dies: 0, 1169, 1180, 1303, 1304, 1309, 31510 • OH-975-F-3a Rev 1303 (R-4), OH-975-F-4a Rev 1304 (R-4): VF–EF $35–$50 • MS-63 $150–$225.

OH, Wooster • John Leis • OH-975-G • *Billiards saloon?* • Ascribed to the shop of W.K. Lanphear • Reverse die: 1343 • OH-975-G-1b Rev 1343 (R-7): VF–EF $1,250–$1,750 • MS-63 $2,000–$3,000.

OH, Wooster • Miller & Co. • OH-975-I • *Queensware, glassware, hoop skirts, and notions* • Ascribed to the shop of W.K. Lanphear • Reverse dies: 1124, 1127, 1177, 1178, 1180, 1331, 1459 • OH-975-I-1a Rev 1459 (R-3), OH-975-I-2a Rev 1124 (R-3): VF–EF $30–$45 • MS-63 $90–$135.

OH, Wooster • Nold & Co. • OH-975-I • *Dealers in pork and beef* • Ascribed to the shop of W.K. Lanphear • Reverse dies: 1084, 1178, 1179 • OH-975-I-1a Rev 1084 (R-5), OH-975-I-2a Rev 1179 (R-5): VF–EF $40–$60 • MS-63 $150–$225.

OH, Wooster • James Patrick • OH-975-K • *Butter packer* • Ascribed to the shop of W.K. Lanphear • Reverse die: 1123 • OH-975-K-1a Rev 1123 (R-2): VF–EF $35–$50 • MS-63 $150–$225.

OH, Wooster • C. Roth • OH-975-L • *Manufacturer of and dealer in boots and shoes* • Ascribed to the shop of W.K. Lanphear • Reverse die: 1317 • OH-975-L-1a Rev 1317 (R-3): VF–EF $60–$90 • MS-63 $250–$375.

OH, Wooster • Rowe & Bro. • OH-975-M • *Watches, clocks, and jewelry* • Ascribed to the shop of W.K. Lanphear • Reverse dies: 1126, 1320, 1343 • OH-975-M-2a Rev 1320 (R-5): VF–EF $100–$150 • MS-63 $300–$450.

OH, Wooster • L. Straub • OH-975-N • *Saloon* • Ascribed to the shop of John Stanton • Reverse die: 1440 • OH-975-N-1b Rev 1440 (R-9): VF–EF $4,000–$6,000.

OH, Wooster • L. Young • OH-975-O • *Billiard saloon* • Ascribed to the shop of

W.K. Lanphear • Reverse dies: 1082, 1343 • OH-975-O-1b Rev 1440 (R-9): VF–EF $300–$450 • MS-63 $750–$1,100 • Earlier listed as OH-165-GV.

OH, Xenia • F.J. Halls • OH-985-A • *Grocery and confectionery store* • Ascribed to the shop of W.K. Lanphear • Reverse die: 1085 • OH-985-A-1a Rev 1085 (R-7): VF–EF $300–$450 • MS-63 $750–$1,100 • Only token-issuing merchant of this town.

OH, Youngstown (and Warren) • W. & A.J. Packard • OH-990-A • *Hardware and iron* • ? • Reverse dies: 39130, 39140 • OH-990-A Rev 39140 (R-2): VF–EF $25–$35 • MS-63 $60–$90 • Only token-issuing merchant of this town.

OH-995-A •
H.G.O. Cary •
O-1 used with
OH-995-A-1.

OH-995-B •
H.G.O. Cary •
O-1 used with
OH-995-B-1 and 2.

OH-995-B •
H.G.O. Cary •
O-2 used with
OH-995-B-3 and 4.
Reverse die of
OH-995-B-1 and 2.

OH, Zanesville • H.G.O. Cary • OH-995-A • *Patent medicines* • Ascribed to the shop of W.K. Lanphear • Reverse die: 39160 • OH-995-A-1a Rev 39160 (R-2): VF–EF $25–$35 • MS-63 $75–$110 • 1859–1860 *Hawes' Ohio State Gazetteer and Business Directory:* "H.G.O. Carey, drug-

gist, western branch office, proprietor Cary's Oil Polish and Leather Preservative." • H.G.O. Carey, dealer in Barrell's Indian Liniment, vermifuge and worm confections, Dr. Blake's Sanitive Pills, and Dr. Stanhopes's Cholagogue Pills. The business later passed to Weller Brothers, 51 Main Street, Zanesville, who continued to advertise extensively • In the third edition of the Fuld book OH-995-A and B will be consolidated under OH-995-A.

OH, Zanesville • H.G.O. Cary • OH-995-B • *Patent medicines* • Ascribed to the shop of W.K. Lanphear • Reverse dies: 1349, 1350, 39160 • OH-995-B-2a Rev 39180 (R-2): VF–EF $25–$35 • MS-63 $75–$110 • Same as preceding business • In the third edition of the Fuld book OH-995-A and B will be consolidated under OH-995-A.

OH, Zanesville • Joseph Crosby • OH-995-C • *Grocer, tea dealer* • ? • Reverse dies: 0016N, 1125, 1126, 1166, 1168, 1178 • OH-995-C-5a Rev 1178 (R-2), OH-995-C-6a Rev 1434 (R-2): VF–EF $25–$35 • MS-63 $75–$110.

OH, Zanesville • Everich & Barton • OH-995-D • *Grocers and liquor dealers* • Ascribed to the shop of W.K. Lanphear • Reverse die: 39200 • OH-995-C-1a Rev 1273 (R-4): VF–EF $60–$90 • MS-63 $200–$300.

OH, Zanesville • Alexander R. Grant • OH-995-E • *Dry goods* • Ascribed to the shop of W.K. Lanphear • Reverse dies: 1125, 1434 • OH-995-E-1a Rev 1125 (R-2): VF–EF $50–$75 • MS-63 $150–$225.

OH, Zanesville • G.W. Griffee • OH-995-F • *News dealer and stationer* • Ascribed to the shop of John Stanton • Grocer • Ascribed to the shop of John Stanton • Reverse dies: 1091, 1322, 1324 • OH-995-F-2a Rev 1322 (R-3), OH-995-F-3a Rev 1324 (R-3): VF–EF $25–$35 • MS-63 $75–$110.

OH, Zanesville • W.B. Harris & Bro. • OH-995-G • *Dry goods and groceries* •

Ascribed to the shop of W.K. Lanphear • Reverse dies: 1082, 1083, 1122, 1126, 1127, 1128, 1168, 1178, 1180, 1434 • OH-995-G-2a Rev 1083 (R-4), OH-995-G-6a Rev 1128 (R-4), OH-995-G-8a Rev 1178 (R-4): VF–EF $25–$35 • MS-63 $75–$110 • W.B. Harris, dealer in dry goods, hardware, &c., Nos. 2 and 3 Pratt's Block, Main Street.

OH, Zanesville • Herendeen & Witter, Singer/s Sewing Machines • OH-995-H • *Sewing machine dealer* • Ascribed to the shop of W.K. Lanphear • Reverse die: 1342 • OH-995-H-1a Rev 1342 (R-3): VF–EF $40–$60 • MS-63 $125–$175.

OH, Zanesville • John Irwin • OH-995-I • *Wholesale wine and liquor* • Ascribed to the shop of W.K. Lanphear • Reverse dies: 1082, 1089, 1130 • OH-995-I-1a Rev 1082 (R-6): VF–EF $60–$90 • MS-63 $150–$225.

OH, Zanesville • C.W. Potwin & Co. • OH-995-J • *Agricultural implements, saddlery, and carriage trimmings* • Ascribed to the shop of W.K. Lanphear • Reverse dies: 1434, 1436, 39270 • OH-995-J-1a Rev 39270 (R-3): VF–EF $50–$75 • MS-63 $150–$225.

OH, Zanesville • Webster, Dumm & Co. • OH-995-K • *Tobacconists* • ? • Reverse dies: 1178, 1181 • OH-995-K-1a Rev 1178 (R-4): VF–EF $30–$45 • MS-63 $90–$135.

PENNSYLVANIA

The state of Pennsylvania offers a rich mixture of tokens. While the number of varieties does not compare to Illinois, Indiana, Michigan, Ohio, New York, and some other states, the designs include Philadelphia die shops that produced motifs not widely represented elsewhere. Among Philadelphia tokens a number have not been ascribed to engravers or shops. In the Western part of the state the shop of John

Stanton had many clients. A basic type set such as one token from each issuer makes a fascinating display to contemplate.

Pittsburg and Pittsburgh are two spellings found for that city on Civil War store cards.

David D. Gladfelter suggested that the Atlantic City, New Jersey, tokens of Smick's Neptune House (NJ-020-A) and the Philadelphia hotel tokens of G.J. Ruelius (PA-750-Q) and Steppacher (PA-750-S) are "linked stylistically and by punches" and may have been made in Philadelphia by an unknown diesinker.[104] The distinctive thin vertical hexagon ornament with spearhead-like points to left and right was used on NJ-020-A (Neptune House, Atlantic City, New Jersey) and four varieties of Philadelphia store cards: PA-750-A (Ton Hall), PA-750-F (M.C. Campbell's Dancing Academy), PA-750-JA (Fox's Casino), PA-750-I (Coombs), and PA-750-Q (G.J. Ruelius, Philadelphia City Hotel).

PA, Allegheny City • William Carson • PA-013-A • *Leather merchant* • Ascribed to the shop of John Stanton • Reverse dies: 1023, 1042, 1047 • PA-013-A-1a Rev 1023 (R-6): VF–EF $40–$60 • MS-63 $175–$250.

PA, Allegheny City • City Tea House (Hahn and Riddle) • PA-013-B • *Tea house* • Ascribed to the shop of John Stanton • Reverse dies: 1042, 1047, 1069 • PA-013-B-1a Rev 1042 (R-8), PA-013-B-1b Rev 1042 (R-8): VF–EF $100–$150 • MS-63 $300–$450 • Operated by George W. Hahn and George D. Riddle, who also issued PA-13-D • In the third edition of the Fuld book PA-013-A and D will be consolidated under PA-013-D.

PA-013-C •
Gregg & Dalzell •
O-1 used with
PA-013-C-1.
Dalzzel
misspelling.

PA-013-C •
Gregg & Dalzell •
O-2 used with
PA-013-C-2 to 6. Die
O-1 reworked by
correcting the
erroneous letters.

PA-013-E •
R. & W. Jenkinson •
O-1 used with
PA-013-E-1 to 5.

PA, Allegheny City • Gregg & Dalzell, National Planing Mill • PA-013-C • *Planing mill* • Ascribed to the shop of John Stanton[105] • Reverse dies: 1028, 1042, 1045, 1047, 1069, 40040 • PA-013-C-1a Rev 1028 (R-8), PA-013-C-2a Rev 40040 (R-8): VF–EF $30–$45 • MS-63 $125–$175.

PA-013-E •
R. & W. Jenkinson •
O-2 used with
PA-013-E-6, 8, 9.

PA-013-E •
R. & W. Jenkinson •
O-3 used with
PA-013-E-7.

PA, Allegheny City • Hahn & Riddell (City Tea House) • PA-013-D • *Tea house and grocers (the last lettered on the token)* • Ascribed to the shop of John Stanton • Reverse dies: 1042, 1047, 40010 • PA-013-D-3a Rev 40010 (R-5): VF–EF $40–$60 • MS-63 $125–$175 • George W. Hahn and George D. Riddle operated the City Tea House advertised on PA-13-B • In the third edition of the Fuld book PA-013-A and D will be consolidated under PA-013-D.

PA, Allegheny City • R. & W. Jenkinson • PA-013-E • *Tobacco dealers* • Ascribed to the shop of W.K. Lanphear • Reverse dies: 1026, 1033, 1042, 1047, 1124, 1176, 1295, 1331, 1352 • PA-013-E-6a Rev 1026 (R-4), PA-013-E-7a Rev 1033 (R-4): VF–EF $25–$35 • MS-63 $90–$135.

PA, Allegheny City • John Sherer • PA-013-F • *Tobacco dealer* • Ascribed to the shop of W.K. Lanphear • Reverse dies: 0, 1124, 1176, 1177, 1180, 1295, 1331, 40965 • PA-013-F-6a Rev 1331 (R-5): VF–EF $30–$45 • MS-63 $100–$150.

PA, Bakerstown • James Maines Gallery • PA-060-A • *Photographic gallery (studio)* • Ascribed to the shop of W.K. Lanphear • Reverse dies: 1125, 1178 • PA-060-A-1a Rev 1125 (R-5): VF–EF $50–$75 • MS-63 $150–$225 • Only token-issuing merchant of this town.

PA, Easton • H. Wind • PA-320-A • *Hotel* • Ascribed to the shop of John Stanton • Reverse dies: 1009, 1018, 1019, 1069, 1192 • PA-320-A-1a1 Rev 1009 (R-8), PA-320-A-5a Rev 1192 (R-8): VF–EF $400–$600 • MS-63 $1,500–$2,250 •

Only token-issuing merchant of this town. Earlier known as OH-165-GM.

PA, Erie • W. Bell • PA-360-A • *Dry goods dealer*[106] • ? • PA-360-A-1d (R-6): VF–EF $100–$150 • MS-63 NA • Only token-issuing merchant of this town. These are 1859 cents with the reverse machined off and counterstamped.

PA, Honesdale (and Scranton and Pittston) • Petersen's • PA-464-A • *Jeweler* • Dies by William H. Bridgens • Reverse dies: 1006, 1137, 1152, 1214, 1243, 1268 • PA-464-A-1a Rev 1006 (R-4): VF–EF $25–$35 • MS-63 $100–$150 • Only token-issuing merchant of this town.

PA, Lancaster • S.H. Zahm • PA-525-A • *Dealer in coins, tokens, and medals* • Dies ascribed to Robert Lovett Jr. • Reverse dies: 0, 1148 • PA-525-A-1a Rev 1148 (R-5), PA-525-A-1b Rev 1148 (R-5), PA-525-A-1e Rev 1148 (R-5): VF–EF $125–$175 • MS-63 $300–$450 • Only token-issuing merchant of this town.

PA, Lawrenceville • William Smith • PA-535-A • *Grocer* • Ascribed to the shop of W.K. Lanphear • Reverse dies: 1177, 1180, 1227, 1295, 1331 • PA-535-A-2a Rev 1180 (R-4): VF–EF $40–$60 • MS-63 $135–$200.

PA, Meadville • G.C. Porter & Co. • PA-615-A • *Dry goods, clothing* • ? • Reverse die: 41055 • PA-615-A-1a Rev 41055 (R-2): VF–EF $25–$35 • MS-63 $60–$90 • Only token-issuing merchant of this town.[107]

PA, Mount Washington • J. McKain • PA-650-A • *Grocer* • ? • Reverse die: 1389 • PA-650-A-1a Rev 1389 (R-2): VF–EF $25–$35 • MS-63 $75–$110 • Only token-issuing merchant of this town.

PA, Philadelphia • Adams / Ton Hall • PA-750-A • *Hotel and tavern* • ? • Reverse die: 40175 • PA-750-A-1b Rev 40175 (R-2): VF–EF $25–$35 • MS-63 $50–$75 • Ton Hall, 457 North 3rd St., was occupied by Frederick Baltz, who was also in the liquor business, later with Baltz & Stilz (Freder-

ick Baltz & John Stilz), wine importers, 333 North 3rd Street. See PA-750-D.

PA, Philadelphia • M.B. Allebach • PA-750-B • *Watchmaker, jeweler* • Dies possibly by Robert Lovett Jr. • Reverse dies: 1093, 1182 • PA-750-B-1d Rev 1093 (R-6): VF–EF $40–$60 • MS-63 $150–$225 • Probably postwar.

PA, Philadelphia • Christian Amon • PA-750-C • *Baker* • ? • Reverse die: 40200 (which was relapped in later use) • PA-750-C-2a Rev 40210 (R-5): VF–EF $50–$75 • MS-63 $200–$300.

PA-750-D • Baltz & Stilz • O-1 used with PA-750-D-1.

PA-750-D • Baltz & Stilz • O-2 used with PA-750-D-2.

PA, Philadelphia • Baltz & Stilz • PA-750-D • *Wine importers* • ? • Reverse die: 1381 • PA-750-D-1a Rev 1381 (R-3): VF–EF $25–$35 • MS-63 $90–$135 • Also see PA-750-A.

PA-750-E • M.F. Beirn, Magnolia Hotel • O-1 used with PA-750-E-1.

PA-750-E • M.F. Beirn, Magnolia Hotel • O-2 used with PA-750-E-2 to 5.

PA, Philadelphia • M.F. Beirn, Magnolia Hotel • PA-750-E • *Hotel* • Dies by Robert Lovett Jr.[108] • Reverse dies: 1093, 1150, 1150A, 1182 • PA-750-E-1a Rev 1093 (R-2): VF–EF $25–$35 • MS-63 $60–$90.

PA, Philadelphia • M.C. Campbell's Dancing Academy • PA-750-F • *Dancing and skating academy* **• ? •** Reverse die: 40270 • PA-750-F-1a Rev 40270 (R-4): VF–EF $30–$40 • MS-63 $135–$200 • 1862 *McElroy's Directory:* "M.C. Campbell, dancing academy, 711 Spring Garden Street. Also, M.C. Campbell, fancy cake store 116 South 8th Street; home at 504 North 8th Street" • Under "Public Halls and Places of Amusement," Washington Hall, home of the academy, is listed at S.W. 8th and Spring Garden streets.

PA, Philadelphia • Chestnut & Walnut Passenger R.R. Co. • PA-750-H • *Street railroad* **•** Dies ascribed to Robert Lovett Jr. • Reverse dies: 1148, 40286 • PA-750-H-1a Rev 1148 (R-9), PA-750-H-1b Rev 1148 (R-9), PA-750-H-1d Rev 1148 (R-9): VF–EF $3,000–$4,500 • MS-63 $9,000–$13,500.

PA, Philadelphia • Nathan Coombs, Exchange Saloon • PA-750-I • *Saloon* **• ? •** Reverse die: 40030 • PA-750-I Rev 40030 (R-3): VF–EF $40–$60 • MS-63 $150–$225.

PA, Philadelphia • Fox's Casino • PA-750-Ja • *Music hall* **• ? •** Reverse die: 40315 • PA-750-Ja-1a Rev 40315 (R-5): VF–EF $30–$45 • MS-63 $125–$175.

PA, Philadelphia • Great Central Fair • PA-750-L • *Sanitary fair* **•** Dies by the U.S. Mint[109] • Reverse die: 1135 • PA-750-L-1a Rev 1135 (R-1): VF–EF $25–$35 • MS-63 $60–$90.

PA, Philadelphia • Hagan's Aromatic Bitters • PA-750-La • *Patent medicine* **• ? •** Reverse die: 40342 • PA-750-La-1a Rev 40342 (R-10): VF–EF $4,000–$6,000 • MS-63 NA.

PA, Philadelphia • William Idler • PA-750-Lb • *Coin dealer* **•** Dies by Robert Lovett Jr. • Reverse dies: 1093, 1093A • PA-750-Lb-1d Rev 1093 (R-7): VF–EF $300–$450 • MS-63 $900–$1,350 • Probably issued in 1860.

PA, Philadelphia • Elwood Ivins • PA-750-Lc • *Metal products, especially for hair styling* **•** Dies by Robert Lovett Jr. (cf. W.E. Woodward's sale of October 18–22, 1864, lots 2536 to 2541) • Reverse die: 40345 • PA-750-Lc-1b (R-6): VF–EF $90–$135 • MS-63 $250–$375 • 25.1 mm. These are more likely advertising medalets, not Civil War tokens in the circulating currency sense.

PA, Philadelphia • F.C. Key & Sons • PA-750-Ld • *Diesinkers and engraver* **•** F.C. Key & Sons • Reverse dies: 40347, 40349, 40350 • PA-750-Ld-2a Rev 40349 (R-9), PA-750-Ld-2e Rev 40349 (R-9), PA-750-Ld-2f Rev 40349 (R-9), PA-750-Ld-3f Rev 40350 (R-9): VF–EF $400–$600 • MS-63 $1,000–$1,500 • Some are post–Civil War.

PA-750-M • M F. & L. Ladner • O-1 used with PA-750-M-1.

PA-750-M • F. & L. Ladner • O-2 used with PA-750-M-2 and 3.

PA, Philadelphia • F. & L. Ladner, North Military Hall • PA-750-M • *Saloon* **•** Peter N. Jacobus • Reverse dies: 1377, 1378, 1379, 1380 • PA-750-M-1a Rev 1377 (R-2), PA-750-M-3a Rev 1379 (R-2): VF–EF $25–$35 • MS-63 $50–$75 • 1861 *McElroy's Directory:* "Frederick Ladner, Military Hall Saloon; home at 532 North 3rd Street. Louis Ladner, tavern, 532 North 3rd Street. William Ladner, clerk, 532 North 3rd Street."

PA, Philadelphia • August Lambert • PA-750-N • *Oyster saloon* **• ? •** Reverse die: 1092 • PA-750-N-1a Rev 1092 (R-4): VF–EF $25–$35 • MS-63 $75–$110.

PA-750-O •
Hugh Mulligan •
O-1 used with
PA-750-O-1.

PA-750-O •
Hugh Mulligan •
O-2 used with
PA-750-O-2.

PA, Philadelphia • Hugh Mulligan PA-750-O • *Jeweler, importer, manufacturer* • ? • Reverse die: 40390 • PA-750-O-1b Rev 40390 (R-5): VF–EF $90–$135 • MS-63 $300–$450.

PA-750-P •
Francis P. Rogers •
O-1 used with
PA-750-P-1.

PA-750-P •
Francis P. Rogers •
O-2 used with
PA-750-P-3.

PA, Philadelphia • Francis P. Rogers • PA-750-P • *Manufacturer of milk cans; metal work* • ? • Reverse dies: 0, 40430 • PA-750-P-3j Rev 40430 (R-5): VF–EF $40–$60 • MS-63 $150–$225.

PA, Philadelphia • George J. Ruelius, Philadelphia City Hotel • PA-750-Q • *Hotel* • ? • Reverse die: 40450 • PA-750-Q-1a Rev 40450 (R-3): VF–EF $25–$35 • MS-63 $50–$75.

PA, Philadelphia • G.A. Schwarz • PA-750-R • *Toys and fancy goods* • Key • Reverse die: 1250 • PA-750-R-1e Rev 1250 (R-9): VF–EF $4,000–$6,000 • MS-63 $10,000–$15,000 • 1865 *McElroy's Directory:* "Gustavus A. Schwarz, fancy goods, 1006 Chestnut. Home at 916 Sergeant." • Another listing, perhaps for a different person: "Gustavus Schwarz, commercial merchant, 144 North Delaware Avenue. Home at 1716 Wallace Street."

PA, Philadelphia • Joseph Steppacher, Orleans House • PA-750-S • *Hotel* • ? • Reverse die: 1381 • PA-750-S-1a Rev 1381 (R-2): VF–EF $25–$35 • MS-63 $50–$75 • 1862 *McElroy's Directory:* "Joseph Steppacher, agent of Orleans House, 531 Chestnut Street." 1863 *McElroy's Directory:* "Joseph Steppacher, hotel keeper, 531 Chestnut Street." 1865 *McElroy's Directory:* "Joseph Steppacher, Orleans House, 531 Chestnut Street. Home at 951 North 10th Street."

PA-750-T •
Granville Stokes •
O-1 used with
PA-750-T-1.

PA-750-T •
Granville Stokes •
O-2 used with
PA-750-T-2.

PA, Philadelphia • Granville Stokes • PA-750-T • *Merchant tailor* • ? • Reverse die: 40500 • PA-750-T-1b Rev 40500 (R-7): VF–EF $100–$150 • MS-63 $400–$600 • 31 mm medalet.

PA, Philadelphia • A.B. Taylor • PA-750-U • *Druggist* • ? • Reverse die: 40520 • PA-750-U-1j Rev 40520 (R-7): VF–EF $175–$250 • MS-63 $500–$750 • Alfred B. Taylor was an enthusiastic numismatist. Over a period of time Taylor's name appeared on the cover of several auction catalogs written by his fellow townsman Edward D. Cogan. Taylor was also a prolific issuer of tokens in the early 1860s; advertised was his apothecary shop at the corner of Walnut and Ninth streets and other locations and two of his compounds: Denticrete and Orilote for the teeth. In 1867 his address was 1015 Chestnut Street, Philadelphia. Taylor remained active in numismatics until at least the early 1870s.

PA-750-V •
N. & G. Taylor Co •
O-1 used with
PA-750-V-1. 1863
above head. 25 mm.

PA-750-V •
N. & G. Taylor Co. •
O-2 used with
PA-750-V-2. 18 / 63 to
sides of head. 38 mm.

PA-750-W •
Union Volunteer
Refreshment Saloon •
O-1 used with
PA-750-W-1.

PA-750-W •
Union Volunteer
Refreshment Saloon •
O-2 used with
PA-750-W-2 and 3.
Similar to preceding
but letters aligned
slightly differently.

PA-750-V •
N. & G. Taylor Co. •
O-1 used with
PA-750-V-3 and 9.
1863 below head,
address in large
letters. 38 mm.

PA-750-V •
N. & G. Taylor Co. •
O-4 used with
PA-750-V-4. 1863
below head, address in
small letters. 38 mm.

PA, Philadelphia • Union Volunteer Refreshment Saloon • PA-750-W • *Refreshment saloon to benefit soldiers • ? •* Reverse dies: 1092, 40680, 40690 • PA-750-W-3a Rev 40680 (R-3): VF–EF $25–$35 • MS-63 $90–$135 • Although this token is dated May 27, 1861, the saloon was open for the next several years.

PA, Pittsburgh • Allegheny Valley Railroad Hotel • PA-765-A • *Hotel •* Ascribed to the shop of John Stanton • Reverse dies: 1023, 1042, 1047, 1069 • PA-765-A-1a Rev 1023 (R-7): VF–EF $100–$150 • MS-63 $400–$600.

PA, Pittsburgh • F. Beilsteine • PA-765-B • *Butcher •* Ascribed to the shop of W.K. Lanphear • Reverse dies: 1124, 1177, 1274 • PA-765-B-2a Rev 1177 (R-4): VF–EF $40–$60 • MS-63 $150–$225.

PA, Pittsburgh • Buffum's Mineral Water • PA-765-C • *Mineral water • ? •* Reverse dies: 1045A, 40740 • PA-765-C-1a Rev 40740 (R-2): VF–EF $20–$30 • MS-63 NA.

PA, Pittsburgh • J.A. Eckert • PA-765-D • *Butcher •* Ascribed to the shop of W.K. Lanphear • Reverse dies: 1124, 1176, 1177, 1295, 1331 • PA-765-D-2a Rev 1176 (R-5): VF–EF $50–$75 • MS-63 $200–$300.

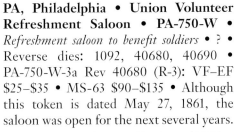 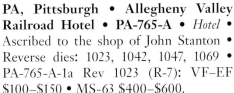

PA-750-V •
N. & G. Taylor Co. •
O-5 used with
PA-750-V-5 to 7, 10.
No date. 38 mm.

PA-750-V •
N. & G. Taylor Co. •
O-6 used with
PA-750-V-8. 38 mm.

PA, Philadelphia • N. & G. Taylor Co. • PA-750-V • *Tin plate, files, metals, etc. •* All dies were made by Peter N. Jacobus[110] • Reverse dies: 40540, 40570, 40590, 40610, 40620, 40630 • PA-750-V-1a Rev 40540 (R-4): VF–EF $25–$35 • MS-63 $100–$150 • The various N. & G. Taylor tokens are of larger than cent diameter and were intended as advertising cards, not as circulating token issues.

PA, Pittsburgh • Joseph Fleming • PA-765-E • *Druggist* • Ascribed to the shop of John Stanton • Reverse dies: 1025, 1026, 1034, 1042, 1046, 1047, 1069 • PA-765-E-2a Rev 1026 (R-3): VF–EF $40–$60 • MS-63 $150–$225.

PA, Pittsburgh • W.A. Gildenfenney • PA-765-F • *Books, paper, stationery* • Ascribed to the shop of John Stanton • Reverse dies: 1032, 1042, 1047, 1069, 1192 • PA-765-F-1a Rev 1032 (R-4): VF–EF $25–$35 • MS-63 $75–$110.

PA, Pittsburgh • D.A. Hall & Co. • PA-765-G • *Tea dealer* • Ascribed to the shop of W.K. Lanphear • Reverse dies: 1124, 1274 • PA-765-G-1a Rev 1124 (R-2): VF–EF $40–$60 • MS-63 $150–$225.

PA, Pittsburgh • John W. Hannah • PA-765-H • *Baker* • Ascribed to the shop of W.K. Lanphear • Reverse dies: 1130, 1177 • PA-765-H-2a Rev 1177 (R-6): VF–EF $40–$60 • MS-63 $200–$300.

PA, Pittsburgh • J.C. & H.W. Lippincott • PA-765-I • *Grocers* • Ascribed to the shop of W.K. Lanphear • Reverse dies: 0, 1124, 1176, 1177 • PA-765-I-2a Rev 1176 (R-4): VF–EF $25–$35 • MS-63 $100–$150.

PA, Pittsburgh • A. Ludewig • PA-765-J • *Dealer in tobacco, snuff, and cigars* • ? • Reverse die: 40820 • PA-765-J-1a Rev 40820 (R-3): VF–EF $30–$45 • MS-63 $200–$300.

PA, Pittsburgh • J.W. McCarthy • PA-765-K • *Bill poster* • Ascribed to the shop of John Stanton • Reverse dies: 1026, 1042, 1047 • PA-765-K-1a Rev 1026 (R-3): VF–EF $40–$60 • MS-63 $200–$300.

PA-765-M • Henry Miner • O-1 used with PA-765-M-1. Dies possibly by the Scovill Manufacturing Co.

PA-765-M • Henry Miner • O-2 used with PA-765-M-2 to 8. Dies ascribed to the shop of W.K. Lanphear.

PA, Pittsburgh • Henry Miner • PA-765-M • *News dealer* • Ascribed to the shop of W.K. Lanphear • Reverse dies: 1124, 1131, 1176, 1180, 1295, 1331, 40855 • PA-765-M-1a Rev 40855 (R-2): VF–EF $25–$35 • MS-63 $60–$90.

PA, Pittsburgh • Pekin Tea Store • PA-765-N • *Tea store* • Ascribed to the shop of John Stanton • Reverse dies: 1023, 1025, 1028, 1029, 1030, 1033, 1034, 1039, 1042, 1047, 1069 • PA-765-N-3a Rev 1028 (R-3): VF–EF $25–$35 • MS-63 $90–$135.

PA, Pittsburgh • A.C. Pentz • PA-765-O • *Metal ware, stoves* • Ascribed to the shop of John Stanton • Reverse dies: 1023, 1042, 1045, 1047, 1069 • PA-765-O-1a Rev 1023 (R-4): VF–EF $25–$35 • MS-63 $150–$225 • The 1a variety nearly always has the 2 in the address, 20 Penn Street, cancelled, likely indicating it was incorrect.

PA-765-P •
Pittock News Dealer •
O-1 used with PA-765-P-1
to 4, 18, 19. Ascribed to
the shop of John Stanton.

PA-765-P •
Pittock's
News Depot •
O-2 used with
PA-765-P-5 to 10.
Ascribed to the shop
of W.K. Lanphear.

PA-765-P •
Pittock News Dealer •
O-4 used with
PA-765-P-13. Dies
possibly by the Scovill
Manufacturing Co.

PA-765-P •
Pittock News Dealer •
O-5 used with
PA-765-P-14 to 17, 20.
Ascribed to the shop
of W.K. Lanphear.

PA-765-Q •
John W. Pittock
News Dealer •
O-1 used with
PA-765-Q-1 to 13.
Ascribed to the shop
of John Stanton.

PA, Pittsburgh • Pittock's News Depot • PA-765-P • *News dealer* • Dies by multiple shops[111] • Reverse dies: 1034, 1042, 1047, 1069, 1124, 1176, 1180, 1192, 1290, 1295, 1324, 1427, 36700, 40920 • PA-765-P-13b Rev 40920 (R-1): VF–EF $25–$35 • MS-63 $60–$90 • In the third edition of the Fuld book PA-765-P and Q will be consolidated under PA-765-P.

PA, Pittsburgh • John W. Pittock • PA-765-Q • *News dealer* • Ascribed to the shop of John Stanton • Reverse dies: 1019, 1020, 1022, 1031, 1033, 1034, 1036, 1042, 1046, 1047, 1069, 34280 • PA-765-Q-2a Rev 1020 (R-3), PA-765-Q-3a Rev 1022 (R-3), PA-765-Q-5a Rev 1033 (R-3): VF–EF $25–$35 • MS-63 $100–$150.

PA-765-R •
Pittsburgh
Dry Goods •
O-1 used with
PA-765-R-1 and 2.

PA-765-R •
Pittsburgh
Dry Goods •
O-2 used with
PA-765-R-3.

PA, Pittsburgh • Pittsburgh Dry Goods • PA-765-R • *Dry goods* • ? • Reverse dies: 1407, 1408, 1409 • PA-765-R-2a Rev 1408 (R-2), PA-765-R-3a Rev 1409 (R-2): VF–EF $25–$35 • MS-63 $60–$90.

PA, Pittsburgh • Pittsburgh Gazette • PA-765-S • *Newspaper* • Ascribed to the shop of W.K. Lanphear • Reverse dies: 1172, 1176, 1177, 1180, 1295, 1331, 23310, 31870 • PA-765-S-2a Rev 1176 (R-3), PA-765-S-3a Rev 1177 (R-3): VF–EF $25–$35 • MS-63 $75–$110.

PA, Pittsburgh • Reymer & Bros. • PA-765-T • *Confectioners* • Ascribed to the shop of W.K. Lanphear • Reverse dies: 1177, 1331, 23310, 31870 • PA-765-T-1a Rev 1177 (R-3): VF–EF $25–$35 • MS-63 $100–$150.

PA, Pittsburgh • Sinclair & Wilson • PA-765-U • *Clothing store* • Ascribed to the shop of W.K. Lanphear • Reverse dies: 1124, 1177 • PA-765-U-1a Rev 1177 (R-4): VF–EF $40–$60 • MS-63 $175–$250.

PA, Pittsburgh • Frank Snyder • PA-765-V • *Tobacco and cigars* • Ascribed to the shop of W.K. Lanphear • Reverse dies: 1124, 1170, 1177, 1273, 1331 • PA-765-V-2a Rev 1177 (R-6), PA-765-V-4a Rev 1331 (R-2): VF–EF $30–$45 • MS-63 $125–$175.

PA, West Greenville • Packard & Co. • PA-967-A • *Hardware, iron, crockery* • ? • Reverse die: 41000 • PA-967-A-1b Rev 41000 (R-3): VF–EF $20–$30 • MS-63 $75–$110 • Only token-issuing merchant of this town. West Greenville, was incorporated in 1837. In 1865 the name was changed to Greenville, Mercer County.[112]

RHODE ISLAND

Among states credited with a large number of Civil War token varieties Rhode Island is unique. As is seen below the number of different issuers was quite small. However, in 1864 the newly formed Rhode Island Numismatic Association commissioned the maker of various Providence store cards to create mulings in nearly every imaginable combination and in many different metals. Today a collection of different Providence merchants can be gathered with ease, but many of the mulings and off-metal strikings are major rarities.

An unknown person created most of the dies for the Providence tokens. These are quite curious in that most of the letters are hand-engraved and not made from punches. Thus, when a letter occurs more than once on a die, its details are slightly different in each instance. The dies have a very rustic and quite interesting appearance. The same diecutter also created dies for two issuers in Connecticut and one in Massachusetts. It seems that more than one unknown engraver was involved, as styles differ slightly.

One of the most famous of all Civil War store cards is that of Theodore Pohle's Elmwood Vineyard in Cranston (which later became part of Providence). When the Steven L. Tanenbaum estate tokens were dispersed beginning in 2012, an example of RI-200-A-1a valued over $20,000 was the most expensive.

RI, Cranston • Theodore Pohle, Elmwood Vineyard • RI-220-A • *Vineyard* • Maker unknown • Reverse dies: 42120, 42122 • RI-220-A-1a Rev 42120 (R-10),

RI-220-A-2b Rev 42122 (R-10), RI-220-A-2g Rev 42122 (R-10): VF–EF $12,000–$16,000 • MS-63 $20,000–$30,000 • Only token-issuing merchant of this town (which later became part of Providence).

RI-700-A •
Arcade House •
O-1 used with
RI-700-A-1 to 4.

RI-700-A •
Arcade House,
H. Dobson •
O-2 used with
RI-700-A-5.

RI-700-A •
Arcade House •
O-3 used with
RI-700-A-6.

RI, Providence • Arcade House • RI-700-A • *Hotel* • ? • Reverse dies: 1147, 1159, 1374, 42055 • RI-700-A-4a Rev 42055 (R-3): VF–EF $25–$35 • MS-63 $60–$90 • Hotel managed by Henry Dobson (see below) • The third edition of the Fuld book will merge RI-700-A into RI-700-D.

RI, Providence • Joseph C. Charnley • RI-700-C • *Saloonkeeper* • ? • Reverse dies: 1147, 1159, 1374, 1429, 42055, 42060 • RI-700-C-3a Rev 1374 (R-3): VF–EF $25–$35 • MS-63 $50–$75.

RI, Providence • Henry Dobson • RI-700-D • *Hotelkeeper* • ? • Reverse dies: 1191, 1285, 1428, 1429, 42090 • RI-700-D-1j Rev 1285 (R-8), RI-700-D-2j Rev 1428 (R-8), RI-700-D-3j Rev 1429 (R-8), RI-300-D-5j Rev 1191 (R-8): VF–EF

$250–$375 • MS-63 $1,250–$1,750 • Dobson managed the Arcade House (see above) • The third edition of the Fuld book will merge RI-700-A into RI-700-D.

RI, Providence • Frank L. Gay • RI-700-E • *Bookseller and stationer* • ? • Reverse dies: 1191, 1264, 1285 • RI-700-E-2a Rev 1264 (R-2): VF–EF $25–$35 • MS-63 $50–$75.

RI, Providence • H.Y. Lefevre, Empire Saloon • RI-700-F • *Saloon* • ?, but different from maker of the Providence tokens listed above and below • Reverse dies: 1294, 42080 • RI-700-F-1a Rev 1294 (R-6), RI-700-F-2a Rev 42080 (R-6): VF–EF $60–$90 • MS-63 $175–$250.

RI, Providence • Phillips, City Fruit Store • RI-700-G • *Fruit store* • ? • Reverse dies: 1147, 1159, 1374, 42100 • RI-700-G-2a Rev 1159 (R-2): VF–EF $40–$60 • MS-63 $175–$250.

RI, Providence • F.W. Shattuck, Burnside Fruit Store • RI-700-I • *Fruit store* • ? • Reverse die: 42140 • RI-700-I-1a Rev 42140 (R-7): VF–EF $300–$450 • MS-63 $900–$1,350.

Tennessee

Civil War tokens of Tennessee are quite varied and, as a class, are somewhat scarce. Certain varieties were used for drayage tokens and are denominated 25 CENTS (tokens B.E. Hammar & Co. and Wm. McDonald, both of Memphis, are examples), while others were made with blank centers to permit later stamping for number punches. These were used extensively in carting goods from Mississippi River docks to merchants in Memphis.

Main makers of dies were Benjamin C. True (originator of many of the to-be-punched-in dies) who worked in the shop of John Stanton and others associated with Stanton's manufactory. Many numismatic delicacies were produced from such dies, with the mulings of the True dies being particularly famous and extensive.

TN-130-A •
Andrew King •
O-1 used with
TN-130-A-1 to 3.

TN-130-A •
Andrew King •
O-2 used with
TN-130-A-4 and 5.

TN, Clarksville • Andrew King • TN-130-A • *Merchant* • Ascribed to the shop of John Stanton • Reverse dies: 1046, 1047, 1069, 43010 • TN-130-A-3a Rev 1047 (R-8): VF–EF $3,000–$4,500 • MS-63 $6,000–$9,000 • Only token-issuing merchant of this town.

TN-180-A •
N.O. Underwood •
O-1 used with
TN-180-A-1 and 2.
25 Cents.

TN-180-A •
N.O. Underwood •
O-2 used with
TN-180-A-3 and 4.
10 Cents.

TN-180-A •
N.O. Underwood •
O-3 used with
TN-180-A-5. 5 Cents.

TN, Dedham • N.O. Underwood • TN-180-A • ? • Ascribed to the shop of W.K. Lanphear • Reverse dies: 1082, 1085, 1168, 1225 • TN-180-A-2b Rev 1085 (R-7): VF–EF $600–$900 • MS-63 $1,500–$2,250 • Only token-issuing merchant of this town.

TN, Knoxville • Barry & McDannel • TN-430-A • *Confectioners* • Ascribed to the shop of John Stanton • Reverse dies: 1012N, 1046, 1047 • TN-430-A-1b Rev 1012N (R-7): VF–EF $1,500–$2,250 • MS-63 $3,000–$4,500.

TN, Knoxville • Chamberlain Bros. • TN-430-B • *Drugs, perfumes, soda fountain, etc.* • Ascribed to the shop of John Stanton • Reverse dies: 1453, 1046, 1047, 1311, 1312 • TN-430-B-4b Rev 1312 (R-7): VF–EF $500–$750 • MS-63 $1,500–$2,250.

TN, Memphis • Cossitt Hill & Co. • TN-600-A • *Importers and jobbers in dry goods, shoes, etc.* • Ascribed to the shop of John Stanton • Reverse dies: 1158, 1418, 1420, 1421, 1422, 1423, 1424, 1425, 1426, 1427, 43070, 43120, 43130 • TN-600-A-7a Rev 1424 (R-6), TN-600-A-7b Rev 1424 (R-6), TN-600-A-8a Rev 1425 (R-6), TN-600-A-8b Rev 1425 (R-6), TN-600-A-10a Rev 1427 (R-6), TN-600-A-10b Rev 1427 (R-6), TN-600-A-11a Rev 43070 (R-6), TN-600-A-12a Rev 43120 (R-6): VF–EF $400–$600 • MS-63 $1,000–$1,500.

TN, Memphis • Elliot, Vinson & Co. • TN-600-B • *Steamboat agents* • Ascribed to the shop of John Stanton • Reverse dies: 1158, 1418, 1420, 1421, 1422, 1423, 1424, 1425, 1426, 1427, 43120, 43130 • TN-600-B-7a Rev 1424 (R-6), TN-600-B-7b Rev 1424 (R-6), TN-600-B-8a Rev 1425 (R-6), TN-600-B-10 Rev 1427 (R-6), TN-600-B-10b Rev 1427 (R-6), TN-600-B-10b (cstp) Rev 1427 (R-6), TN-600-B-11a Rev 43120 (R-6): VF–EF $400–$600 • MS-63 $1,000–$1,500.

TN, Memphis • B.E. Hammar & Co. • TN-600-C • *Grocer* • Ascribed to the shop of John Stanton • Reverse dies: 1042, 1046, 1047, 1401 • TN-600-C-1A Rev 1042 (R-7), TN-600-C-1b Rev 1042 (R-7): VF–EF $400–$600 • MS-63 $1,250–$1,750.

TN, Memphis • Wm. McDonald • TN-600-D • *Drayage* • Ascribed to the shop of John Stanton • Reverse dies: 1042, 1047, 1400, 1401 • TN-600-D-1a Rev 1042 (R-7): VF–EF $400–$600 • MS-63 $1,250–$1,750.

TN, Memphis • Stockman & Co. • TN-600-F • *Wholesale dealers in liquor, tobacco, groceries, etc.* • Ascribed to the shop of John Stanton • Reverse dies: 1158, 1419, 1420, 1421, 1422, 1423, 1424, 1425, 1426, 1427 • TN-600-F-5a Rev 1422 (R-6), TN-600-F-5b Rev 1422 (R-6), TN-600-F-7a Rev 1424 (R-6), TN-600-F-8a Rev 1425 (R-6): VF–EF $400–$600 • MS-63 $1,250–$1,750.

TN, Memphis • Western Foundry • TN-600-G • *Foundry* • ? • Reverse die: 1427 • TN-600-G-1b Rev 1427 (R-9), TN-600-G-2b (cstp) Rev 1427 (R-9): VF–EF $900–$1,350 • MS-63 $2,500–$2,750.

TN, Nashville • Gold Pen Depot • TN-690-A • *Writing pens* • ? • Reverse die: 0 • TN-690-A-1b Rev 0 (R-9): VF–EF $6,000–$9,000 • MS-63 $15,000–$22,500 • Repair check. This is the rarest Tennessee merchant.

TN, Nashville • Harris & Pearl • TN-690-B • *Barbers* • Ascribed to the shop of John Stanton • Reverse dies: 1047, 1397A, 1400, 1403, 1404A • TN-690-B-1a Rev 1047 (R-9), TN-690-B-2e Rev 1397A (R-9), TN-690-B-3a Rev 1400 (R-9), TN-690-B-4a Rev 1404A (R-9), TN-690-B-4e Rev 1404A (R-9), TN-690-B-5a Rev 1403 (R-9): VF–EF $1,500–$2,250 • MS-63 $3,500–$5,000.

TN, Nashville • D.L. Lapsley • TN-690-C • *Barber* • Ascribed to the shop of John Stanton • Reverse dies: 1047, 1069, 1267, 1394, 1397, 1399, 1404 • TN-690-C-1a Rev 1047 (R-9), TN-690-C-4a Rev 1394 (R-9), TN-690-C-5a Rev 1399 (R-9), TN-690-C-6a Rev 1404 (R-9), TN-690-C-7b Rev 1397 (R-9): VF–EF $1,250–$1,750 • MS-63 $3,000–$4,500.

TN-690-D •
McKay & Lapsley •
O-1 used with
TN-690-D-1 to 11.

TN-690-D •
McKay & Lapsley •
O-2 used with
TN-690-D-12.

TN, Nashville • McKay & Lapsley • TN-690-D • *Barbers* • Ascribed to the shop of John Stanton • Reverse dies: 1440, 1018, 1042, 1047, 1069, 1392, 1397, 1397A, 1399, 1403, 1405, 1405A • TN-690-D-2a Rev 1047 (R-8), TN-690-D-9a Rev 1405 (R-8): VF-EF $1,000–$1,500 • MS-63 $2,500–$3,750.

TN, Nashville • N.L. Tarbox & Co. • TN-690-Da • *Watch repairer, jeweler* Ascribed to the shop of John Stanton • Reverse die: 0 • TN-690-Da-1b Rev 0 (R-9): VF-EF $1,500–$2,250 • MS-63 $3,500–$5,000 • Jewelry repair check.

TN-690-E •
Walker & Napier •
O-1 used with
TN-690-E-1 to 7.

TN-690-E •
Walker & Napier •
O-2 used with
TN-690-E-8 and 9.

TN, Nashville • Walker & Napier • TN-690-E • *Barbers* • Ascribed to the shop of John Stanton • Reverse dies: 1453, 1018, 1047, 1069, 1397, 1404A, 1405 • TN-690-E-1a Rev 1047 (R-8): VF-EF $2,000–$3,000 • MS-63 $4,000–$6,000.

WEST VIRGINIA

In 1863 in the middle of the Civil War, West Virginia, which had split away from Virginia, became the 35th state in the Union (if one does not consider that the count had been reduced by the secession of certain states comprising the Confederate States of America). Within the first year of statehood, tokens appeared in circulation, typically from dies made at the shop of William K. Lanphear, Cincinnati.

Today, most West Virginia Civil War store cards show signs of wear, often considerable, indicating that these pieces were used extensively and widely. The vast majority were made for use in commerce. Numismatic delicacies are few. Exceptions are those of Lorena Furnace ("Lorena" was the runaway popular romantic song of the Civil War) and Snow Hill Furnace, rarities today, usually in Mint State and from numismatic cabinets of long ago. Earlier, these had been attributed to Maryland.

WV, Charleston • Lorena Furnace • WV-100-A • *Salt reduction furnace* • Dies by Murdock & Spencer • Reverse die: 1468 • WV-100-A-1a, WV-100-A-2a, WV-100-3a, WV-100-4a, WV-100-5a, WV-100-6a, WV-100-7a Rev 60035 (R-9): VF-EF $1,750–$2,500 • MS-63 $5,000–$7,500 • Furnace to boil brine to obtain crystalline salt.[113]

WV-100-B •
Snow Hill Furnace •
O-1 used with
WV-100-B-1.

WV-100-B •
Snow Hill Furnace •
O-2 used with
WV-100-B-2.

WV-100-B •
Snow Hill Furnace •
O-3 used with
WV-100-B-10.

WV-100-B •
Snow Hill Furnace •
O-4 used with
WV-100-B-4.

WV-100-B •
Snow Hill Furnace •
O-6 used with
WV-100-B-6.

WV-100-B •
Snow Hill Furnace •
O-14 used with
WV-100-B-14.

**WV, Charleston • Snow Hill Furnace •
WV-100-B •** *Salt reduction furnace* • Dies
by Murdock & Spencer • Reverse dies by
Stanton, new CWTS numbering system:
60035 (R-9), WV-100-B-1a1 Rev 60035
(R-9), WV-100-B-2a Rev 60035 (R-9),
WV-100-B-3a Rev 60035 (R-9), WV-B-
100-4a Rev 60035 (R-9), WV-100-B-5a Rev
60035 (R-9), WV-100-B-5d Rev 60035
(R-9), WV-100-B-6a Rev 60035 (R-9),
WV-100-B-6a1 Rev 60035 (R-9),
WV-100-B-7a Rev 60035 (R-9), WV-100-B-
7a1 Rev 60035 (R-9), WV-100-B-7b Rev
60035 (R-9), WV-100-B-8a Rev 1046 (R-9),
WV-100-B-8d Rev 60035 (R-9), WV-100-B-

9d Rev 60035 (R-9), WV-100-B-10d Rev
60035 (R-9), WV-100-B-11d Rev 60035
(R-9), WV-100-B-12d Rev 60035 (R-9),
WV-100-B-13d Rev 60035 (R-9), WV-100-
B-14a Rev 60035 (R-9), WV-100-B-14d Rev
60035 (R-9): VF–EF $1,500–$2,250 •
MS-63 $3,500–$5,000.

**WV, Glen Easton • Bassett's Cheap
Dry Goods, Groceries, Etc. • WV-
220-A •** *Dry goods and groceries* • Ascribed
to the shop of W.K. Lanphear • Reverse
dies: 1084, 1126, 1166, 1225, 1459, 44020
• WV-220-A-2a Rev 1126 (R-7), WV-
100-220-A-5a Rev 44020 (R-7): VF–EF
$250–$375 • MS-63 $1,000–$1,500 • Also
see WV-890-A below. Only token-issuing
merchant of this town.

**WV, Hartford City • Kelly's Store •
WV-260-A •** *Salt furnace company store* •
Murdock? • Reverse dies: 1391, 1395 •
WV-260-A-1b Rev 1391 (R-8),
WV-260-A-2j Rev 1395 (R-8): VF–EF
$400–$600 • MS-63 $1,500–$2,250 •
Only token-issuing merchant of this town.

**WV, Wheeling • Bassett's Cheap Dry
Goods • WV-890-A •** *Dry goods* •
Ascribed to the shop of W.K. Lanphear •
Reverse dies: 1085, 1089, 1126, 1127, 1128,
1166, 1168, 1178, 1222, 1224, 1225, 1226 •
WV-890-A-5a Rev 1128 (R-6), WV-890-
A-11a Rev 1225 (R-6): VF–EF $75–$125 •
MS-63 $600–$900 • Also see WV-220-A
above.

**WV, Wheeling • John Eckhart • WV-
890-B •** *Manufacturer of hosiery* • Ascribed
to the shop of W.K. Lanphear • Reverse
dies: 1126, 1166, 1169, 1346, 1434 •
WV-890-B-1a Rev 1126 (R-5): VF–EF
$100–$150 • MS-63 $600–$900.

**WV, Wheeling • James Graves & Co.
• WV-890-C •** *Wallpaper and news dealers*
• Ascribed to the shop of W.K. Lanphear
• Reverse die: 1322 • WV-890-C-1a Rev
1322 (R-6): VF–EF $125–$175 • MS-63
$750–$1,250.

**WV, Wheeling • R.C. Graves • WV-
890-D •** *Periodical and news dealer* •

Ascribed to the shop of W.K. Lanphear • Reverse dies: 1088, 1122, 1127, 1322, 1348, 1387 • WV-890-D-2a Rev 1122 (R-6), WV-890-D-4a Rev 1322 (R-6): VF–EF $75–$125 • MS-63 $600–$900.

WV, Wheeling • D. Nicoll & Bro. • WV-890-E • *Variety store* • Ascribed to the shop of W.K. Lanphear • Reverse dies: 1126, 1166 • WV-890-E-1a Rev 1126 (R-6): VF–EF $125–$175 • MS-63 $600–$900.

WV, Wheeling • J.W.C. Smith • WV-890-F • *Dealer in leather and findings* • Ascribed to the shop of W.K. Lanphear • Reverse dies: 1169, 1225 • WV-890-F-1a Rev 1169 (R-6): VF–EF $125–$175 • MS-63 $600–$900.

WV, Wheeling • C.E. Stifel • WV-890-G • *Tin and sheet iron ware* • Ascribed to the shop of W.K. Lanphear[114] • Reverse dies: 1166, 1178, 1225, 1227, 1299, 1304, 1434 • WV-890-G-2a Rev 1178 (R-6): VF–EF $600–$900 • MS-63 $90–$135.

Wisconsin

The Civil War tokens of Wisconsin are dominated by issues made by the Milwaukee shop of Mossin & Marr. The typical die of this firm is deeply and boldly cut. Scattered tokens from Childs, Stanton, and Lanphear are also seen. Wisconsin specialist David D. Gladfelter contributed the following:

There are 10 Wisconsin merchants for whom Mossin & Marr produced Civil War tokens and later, one can infer, made up restrike sets of tokens for collectors using the 10 merchant obverses, three stock reverses (1174, 1220 and/or 1272), and four metal varieties (a, b, d, and e). The only merchant for whom a complete restrike set of 12 pieces is known is Ch. Hermann & Co., WI-510-R, using the obverse variety with the large ampersand (&). However, restrike tokens are known from all 10 merchants in all four metals, so a "type set" of 40 tokens is possible to collect. So is a "short" type set of the 10 mer-

chant tokens which includes all four of the metal varieties. The tokens in these collector sets are almost always, if not always, found in Mint State. Mossin & Marr also created many curious "errors" such as brockages, misalignments, and the like.

WI, Appleton • Parsons & Barlow • WI-030-A • *Grocers* • Dies by Mossin & Marr • Reverse dies: 1174, 1195, 1220 • WI-030-A-2a Rev 1195 (R-7): VF–EF $250–$375 • MS-63 $900–$1,350 • Only token issuer of this town.

WI, Baraboo • Peck & Orvis • WI-045-A • *Druggists and grocers* • Burr • Reverse dies: 1145, 1241, 1244, 1245, 1246, 1275, 30560 • [115] WI-045-A-5a Rev 1246 (R-5): VF–EF $50–$75 • MS-63 $150–$225 • Only token issuer of this town.

WI, Barton • John Reisse • WI-050-A • *Dry goods, groceries, and clothing* • Dies by Mossin & Marr • Reverse die: 1194 • WI-050-A-1a Rev 1194 (R-6): VF–EF $400–$600 • MS-63 $1,350–$2,000 • Only token issuer of this town.

WI, Beaver Dam • F. Krueger • WI-055-A • *Dry goods, groceries, footwear, hardware* • Dies by Mossin & Marr • Reverse dies: 1194, 1220 • WI-055-A-1a Rev 1194 (R-5): VF–EF $75–$125 • MS-63 $400–$600.

WI, Beaver Dam • A.P. Redfield • WI-055-B • *Hardware, iron, tin ware, stoves, nails, etc.* • Dies by Mossin & Marr • Reverse die: 1194 • WI-055-B-1a Rev 1194 (R-5): VF–EF $90–$135 • MS-63 NA.

WI, Beaver Dam • O.M. Warren • WI-055-C • *Hardware, iron, tinware, stoves, nails, etc.* • Dies by Mossin & Marr • Reverse dies: 1220, 1272 • WI-055-C-1a Rev 1220 (R-7): VF–EF $100–$150 • MS-63 $500–$750.

WI, Beloit • Peck & Pratt • WI-070-A • *Dealers in wines, liquors, and segars* • Ascribed to the shop of S.D. Childs • Reverse die: 1209 • WI-070-A-1a Rev 1209 (R-6): VF–EF $400–$600 • MS-63 $1,250–$1,750 • Only token issuer of this town.

WI, Columbus • Ph. Carpeles & Co. • WI-120-A • *Dry goods and groceries* • Dies by Mossin & Marr • Reverse die: 1194 • WI-120-A-1a Rev 1194 (R-5): VF–EF $50–$75 • MS-63 $150–$225.

WI, Columbus • Frank Huggins • WI-120-B • *Drugs and medicines* • Dies by Mossin & Marr • Reverse die: 1194 • WI-120-B-1a Rev 1194 (R-5): VF–EF $75–$110 • MS-63 $200–$300.

WI, Columbus • D.F. Newcomb • WI-120-C • *Dry goods and groceries* • Dies by Mossin & Marr • Reverse die: 1194 • WI-120-C-1a Rev 1194 (R-6): VF–EF $75–$110 • MS-63 $250–$375.

WI, Columbus • Williams Brothers • WI-120-D • *Chemists and druggists* • Ascribed to the shop of S.D. Childs • Reverse dies: 1105, 1108, 1110, 1203, 1205 • WI-120-D-1a Rev 1105 (R-5): VF–EF $50–$75 • MS-63 $200–$300.

WI-140-A • C. Dahmen & Son • O-1 used with WI-140-A-1.

WI-140-A • C. Dahmen & Son • O-2 used with WI-140-A-2.

WI, Cross Plains • C. Dahmen & Son • WI-140-A • *Dry goods and groceries* • Ascribed to the shop of S.D. Childs • Reverse die: 1105 • WI-140-A-2a Rev 1105 (R-5): VF–EF $100–$150 • MS-63 $400–$600 • Only token issuer of this town.

WI, East Troy • C.W. Smith • WI-185-A • *Dry goods, groceries, hardware, etc.* • Dies by Mossin & Marr • Reverse dies: 1174, 1194, 1220, 1242, 1272 • WI-185-A-2a Rev 1194 (R-6): VF–EF $60–$90 • MS-63 $200–$300 • Only token issuer of this town.

WI, Edgerton • C.C. Root & Bro. • WI-190-A • *Dry goods, clothing, boots, and shoes* • Ascribed to the shop of W.K. Lanphear • Reverse die: 1222 • WI-190-A-1a Rev 1222 (R-6): VF–EF $75–$125 • MS-63 $250–$375 • Only token issuer of this town.

WI, Fond du Lac • C.L. Alling • WI-220-A • *Grocer* • Ascribed to the shop of W.K. Lanphear • Reverse dies: 1082, 1127, 1168, 1434 • WI-220-A-1a Rev 1082 (R-7): VF–EF $60–$90 • MS-63 $200–$300.

WI, Fond du Lac • A.R. Brass • WI-220-B • *Dealer in produce* • Ascribed to the shop of W.K. Lanphear • Reverse dies: 1089, 1127, 1168 • WI-220-B-1a Rev 1127 (R-7): VF–EF $75–$110 • MS-63 $225–$350.

WI, Fond du Lac • Carpenter & Pier, Farmers Store • WI-220-C • *Merchant* • Ascribed to the shop of W.K. Lanphear • Reverse dies: 1082, 1089 • WI-220-C-1a Rev 1082 (R-6): VF–EF $75–$110 • MS-63 $250–$375.

WI, Fond du Lac • Clarke & Carpenter • WI-220-D • *Dry goods and groceries* • Ascribed to the shop of W.K. Lanphear • Reverse die: 1181 • WI-220-D-1a Rev 1181 (R-6): VF–EF $75–$110 • MS-63 $250–$375.

WI, Fond du Lac • F. Fritz • WI-220-E • *Groceries, crockery, provisions, etc.* • Dies by Mossin & Marr • Reverse dies: 1174, 1194, 1220 • WI-220-E-2a Rev 1194 (R-5): VF–EF $35–$50 • MS-63 $200–$300.

WI, Fond du Lac • J.C. Lowell • WI-220-F • *Druggist and grocer* • Ascribed to the shop of W.K. Lanphear • Reverse dies: 1082, 1089, 1168 • WI-220-F-1a Rev 1082 (R-6): VF–EF $75–$110 • MS-63 $250–$375.

WI, Fond du Lac • T. Mason • WI-220-G • *Grocer & crockery dealer* • Ascribed to the shop of W.K. Lanphear • Reverse die: 45220 • WI-220-G-1a Rev

45220 (R-6): VF–EF $75-110 • MS-63 $250–$375.

WI, Fond du Lac • Nye & Youmans • WI-220-H • *Dealers in groceries and crockery* • ? • Reverse die: 1128 • WI-220-H-1a Rev 1128 (R-2): VF–EF $60–$90 • MS-63 $200–$300.

WI, Fond du Lac • Perkins & Smith • WI-220-J • *Dealers in stoves and tinware* • Ascribed to the shop of W.K. Lanphear[116] • Reverse dies: 1089, 1304 • WI-220-J-2a Rev 1304 (R-6): VF–EF $60–$90 • MS-63 $200–$300.

WI, Fond du Lac • A.T. Perkins, City Bakery • WI-220-I • *Bakery* • Ascribed to the shop of W.K. Lanphear[117] • Reverse dies: 1082, 45250 • WI-220-I-1a Rev 45250 (R-7): VF–EF $65–$100 • MS-63 $200–$300.

WI, Fond du Lac • C.J. Pettibone & Co. • WI-220-K • *Dry goods* • Ascribed to the shop of W.K. Lanphear • Reverse dies: 1082, 45280 • WI-220-K-1a Rev 45280 (R-7): VF–EF $75–$110 • MS-63 $200–$300.

WI, Fond du Lac • A. Raymond • WI-220-L • *Grocer* • Ascribed to the shop of W.K. Lanphear • Reverse dies: 1089, 1168 • WI-220-L-2a Rev 1168 (R-7): VF–EF $75–$110 • MS-63 $250–$375.

WI, Fond du Lac • T.S. Wright • WI-220-M • *Chemist, druggist, and stationer* • Ascribed to the shop of W.K. Lanphear • Reverse die: 45310 • WI-220-M-1a Rev 45310 (R-6): VF–EF $65–$100 • MS-63 $250–$375.

WI, Genesee Station • David L. Edwards • WI-235-A • *Dry goods and groceries* • Ascribed to the shop of S.D. Childs • Reverse die: 1107 • WI-235-A-1a Rev 1107 (R-8): VF–EF $6,000–$9,000 • MS-63 $12,500–$17,500 • Only token issuer of this town. Unknown to earlier catalogers, this store card was first announced by David D. Gladfelter in *JCWTS*, Winter 1972. For some years afterward it was the subject of much discussion.

WI, Green Bay • A. Detrich • WI-250-A • *Groceries, provisions, liquor* • Ascribed to the shop of W.K. Lanphear • Reverse dies: 1127, 1128A (not verified) • WI-250-A-1a Rev 1127 (R-5): VF–EF $35–$50 • MS-63 $135–$200.

WI, Green Bay • Hoffman & Lewis • WI-250-B • *Merchant tailors* • Ascribed to the shop of W.K. Lanphear • Reverse die: 1127 • WI-250-B-1a Rev 1127 (R-6): VF–EF $50–$75 • MS-63 $235–$250.

WI, Green Bay • A. Kimboll • WI-250-C • *Hardware dealer* • Ascribed to the shop of W.K. Lanphear • Reverse die: 1085 • WI-250-C-1a Rev 1085 (R-5): VF–EF $50–$75 • MS-63 $175–$250.

WI, Green Bay • Philipp Klaus • WI-250-D • *Yankee notions and toys* • Ascribed to the shop of W.K. Lanphear • Reverse die: 1089 • WI-250-D-1a Rev 1089 (R-6): VF–EF $60–$90 • MS-63 $250–$375.

WI, Green Bay • Drs. Rhode & Hicks, Eagle Drug Store • WI-250-E • *Drug store* • Ascribed to the shop of W.K. Lanphear • Reverse die: 1316 • WI-250-E-1a Rev 1316 (R-7): VF–EF $150–$225 • MS-63 $500–$750.

WI, Green Bay • F.R. Schettler • WI-250-F • *Hardware dealer* • Ascribed to the shop of W.K. Lanphear • Reverse dies: 1085, 1171, 1223, 1228 • WI-250-F-1a Rev 1085 (R-2): VF–EF $30–$45 • MS-63 $135–$200.

WI, Green Bay • Sam Stern • WI-250-G • *Merchant tailor and dealer in clothing* • Ascribed to the shop of W.K. Lanphear • Reverse die: 1387 • WI-250-G-1a Rev 1387 (R-6): VF–EF $125–$200 • MS-63 $400–$600.

**WI-250-I •
J.J. St. Louis •
O-1 used with
WI-250-I-1 to 3.**

**WI-250-I •
Z.Z St. Louis •
O-2 used with
WI-250-I-4 to 6.
Curious die blunder.**

WI, Green Bay • J.J. St. Louis • WI-250-I • *Hardware dealer* • Ascribed to the shop of W.K. Lanphear • Reverse dies: 1168, 1169, 1346, 1387 • WI-250-I-1a Rev 1168 (R-6), WI-250-I-6a Rev 1387 (R-6): VF–EF $40–$60 • MS-63 $150–$225 • In the *Wisconsin and Minnesota State Gazetteer, Shippers Guide and Business Directory* for 1865–1866 J.J. St. Louis is listed as a "Dealer in hardware, stoves, tin ware, lamps and oils, etc."

WI, Hales Corner • J. Siegel • WI-270-A • *Dry goods and groceries* • Dies by Mossin & Marr • Reverse die: 1194 • WI-270-A-1a Rev 1194 (R-5): VF–EF $65–$100 • MS-63 $250–$375 • Only token issuer of this town.

WI, Janesville • E.S. Barrows • WI-300-A • *Seeds, farming tools, stoves, hardware, etc.* • Ascribed to the shop of S.D. Childs • Reverse die: 45440 • WI-300-A-1a Rev 45440 (R-7): VF–EF $75–$110 • MS-63 $250–$375.

WI, Janesville • L.R. Carswell • WI-300-B • *Confectionery, toys, and groceries* • Ascribed to the shop of S.D. Childs • Reverse die: 1106 • WI-300-B-1a Rev 1106 (R-6): VF–EF $60–$90 • MS-63 $250–$375.

WI, Janesville • Chapmans One Price Store • WI-300-C • *Dry goods, clothing, groceries, etc.* • Ascribed to the shop of S.D. Childs • Reverse dies: 1460, 1111, 1205, 1207 • WI-300-C-1a Rev 1460 (R-5): VF–EF $60–$90 • MS-63 $225–$350.

**WI-300-D •
E, Connell & Co. •
O-1 used with
WI-300-D-1.**

**WI-300-D •
E, Connell & Co. •
O-2 used with
WI-300-D-2 and 3.**

WI, Janesville • E. Connell & Co. • WI-300-D • *Groceries, liquors, lime, and wood* • D-1 ascribed to the shop of S.D. Childs, D-2 ascribed to the shop of W.K. Lanphear. Connell ordered tokens from two different merchants. • Reverse dies: 1106, 1127 • WI-300-D-1a Rev 1106 (R-5), WI-300-D-3a Rev 1127 (R-5): VF–EF $60–$90 • MS-63 $200–$300.

WI, Janesville • M. Harsh, Young America Clothing House • WI-300-E • *Clothing* • Ascribed to the shop of S.D. Childs • Reverse die: 1205 • WI-300-E-1a Rev 1205 (R-7): VF–EF $300–$450 • MS-63 $900–$1,350.

WI, Janesville • H.L. Smith • WI-300-G • *Hardware, wagon stuff, etc.* • Ascribed to the shop of S.D. Childs • Reverse die: 1111 • WI-300-G-1b Rev 1111 (R-6): VF–EF $65–$100 • MS-63 $225–$350.

WI, Jefferson • Philip Johnson • WI-310-A • *Drugs, paints, oils, books, stationery, etc.* • Ascribed to the shop of W.K. Lanphear • Reverse die: 1316 • WI-310-A-1a Rev 1316 (R-6): VF–EF $75–$110 • MS-63 $250–$375.

WI, Jefferson • John Jung • WI-310-B • *Dry goods, groceries, and hardware* • Ascribed to the shop of W.K. Lanphear • Reverse die: 1226 • WI-310-B-1a Rev 1226 (R-6): VF–EF $65–$100 • MS-63 $225–$350.

WI, Jefferson • J.F.W. Meyer • WI-310-C • *Groceries, provisions, and notions* • Ascribed to the shop of W.K. Lanphear • Reverse die: 1088 • WI-310-C-1a Rev 1088 (R-6): VF–EF $60–$90 • MS-63 $200–$300.

WI, Jefferson • D. Ostrander • WI-310-D • *Grocer and insurance agent* • Ascribed to the shop of W.K. Lanphear • Reverse die: 1298 • WI-310-D-1a Rev 1298 (R-7): VF–EF $150–$225 • MS-63 $500–$750.

WI, Jefferson • S. Steinhart • WI-310-E • *Dry goods and groceries* • Ascribed to the shop of W.K. Lanphear • Reverse die: 1337 • WI-310-E-1a Rev 1337 (R-6): VF–EF $90–$135 • MS-63 $250–$375.

WI, Jefferson • Waldo & Brandon • WI-310-F • *Dry goods and groceries* • Ascribed to the shop of W.K. Lanphear • Reverse dies: 1168, 99360, 99370 • WI-310-F-1a Rev 99370 (R-5): VF–EF $125–$175 • MS-63 $400–$600 • Earlier known as OH-165-GF.

WI-320-A •
S.B. Coleman •
O-1 used with
WI-320-A-2. With
curious "Mich" error
instead of "Wis."
Presumably this die
was made first.

WI-320-A •
S.B. Coleman •
O-2 used with
WI-320-A-1.

WI, Juneau • S.H. Coleman • WI-320-A • *Dry goods* • Ascribed to the shop of W.K. Lanphear • Reverse die: 1122 • WI-320-A-1a Rev 1122 (R-7), WI-320-A-2a Rev 1122 (R-7): VF–EF $250–$375 • MS-63 $900–$1,350 • Only token issuer of this town.

WI, Kenosha • N.A. Brown • WI-330-A • *Cream ale, stock porter, and kennet* • Ascribed to the shop of S.D. Childs • Reverse dies: 1101, 1105, 1108 • WI-330-A-2a Rev 1108 (R-7): VF–EF $500–$750 • MS-63 $1,350–$2,000.

WI-330-B •
Gerken & Ernst •
O-1 used with
WI-330-B-1 to 3.

WI-330-B •
Gerken & Ernst •
O-2 used with
WI-330-B-4.

WI, Kenosha • Gerken & Ernst • WI-330-B • *Groceries and provisions* • Ascribed to the shop of S.D. Childs • Reverse dies: 1094, 1095, 1105, 1357 • WI-330-B-1a Rev 1094 (R-7), WI-330-B-2a Rev 1105 (R-7), WI-330-B-4a Rev 1095 (R-7): VF–EF $90–$135 • MS-63 $300–$450.

WI, Kenosha • Hohn Simmons & Co. • WI-330-C • *Boots, shoes, and leather* • Ascribed to the shop of S.D. Childs • Reverse die: 1106 • WI-330-C-1a Rev 1106 (R-6): VF–EF $100–$150 • MS-63 $350–$500.

WI-330-D •
Lyman, Mowry
& Co. •
O-1 used with
WI-330-D-1.

WI-330-D •
Lyman, Mowry
& Co. •
O-2 used with
WI-330-D-2.

WI-330-D •
Lyman, Mowry
& Co. •
O-3 used with
WI-330-D-3.

WI, Kenosha • Lyman, Mowry & Co. • WI-330-D • *Boots, shoes, etc.* • Ascribed to the shop of S.D. Childs • Reverse dies: 1106, 1110 • WI-330-D-1a Rev 1110 (R-7), WI-330-D-2a Rev 1106 (R-7): VF–EF $90–$135 • MS-63 $400–$600.

WI, Kilbourn City • James E. Dixon & Sons • WI-340-A • *Dry goods, groceries, boots, and shoes* • Ascribed to the shop of S.D. Childs • Reverse die: 1205 • WI-340-A-1a Rev 1205 (R-6): VF–EF $135–$200 • MS-63 $500–$750 • Kilbourn City has been known as Wisconsin Dells since February 12, 1894.

WI, Kilbourn City • T. Hofmann (Hofman) • WI-340-B • *Brewer* • Dies by Mossin & Marr • Reverse die: 1194 • WI-340-B-1a Rev 1194 (R-6): VF–EF $135–$200 • MS-63 $500–$750 • Surname should be spelled as Hofman. Brewery established in 1861 at Broadway and Oak St.

WI-360-A •
Mons Anderson •
O-1 used with
WI-360-A-1.

WI-360-A •
Mons Anderson •
O-3 used with
WI-360-A-3.

WI, La Crosse • Mons Anderson • WI-360-A • *Dry goods, clothing, boots, shoes, etc.* • A-1 is ascribed to the shop of W.K. Lanphear, and A-3 is ascribed to the shop of S.D. Childs. Anderon purchased tokens from two different merchants. • Reverse dies: 1280, 1281 • WI-360-A-1a Rev 1280 (R-5): VF–EF $75–$110 • MS-63 $300–$450.

WI, La Crosse • George E. Stanley • WI-360-B • *Jeweler* • Ascribed to the shop of W.K. Lanphear • Reverse die: 1321 • WI-360-B-1a Rev 1321 (R-6): VF–EF $90–$135 • MS-63 $300–$450 • Only token issuer of this town.

WI, Madison • Jas. Fr. Bodtker • WI-410-A • *Photographer* • Ascribed to the shop of S.D. Childs • Reverse dies: 1205, 1357 • WI-410-A-1a Rev 1205 (R-7), WI-410-A-2a Rev 1357 (R-7): VF–EF $200–$300 • MS-63 $600–$900.

WI, Madison • Emigranten Office • WI-410-B • *Norwegian-language newspaper* • Ascribed to the shop of W.K. Lanphear[118] • Reverse die: 45730 • WI-410-B-1a Rev 45730 (R-3): VF–EF $75–$110 • MS-63 $250–$375.

WI, Madison • R.K. Findlay & Co. • WI-410-C • *Druggists and grocers; tea establishment* • Ascribed to the shop of W.K. Lanphear[119] • Reverse dies: 1310, 1471 • WI-410-C-1a Rev 1471 (R-6), WI-410-C-2a Rev 1310 (R-6): VF–EF $60–$90 • MS-63 $225–$350.

WI, Madison • S. Klauber & Co. • WI-410-D • *Dry goods and clothing* • Ascribed to the shop of W.K. Lanphear • Reverse die: 1169 • WI-410-D-1a Rev 1169 (R-5): VF–EF $40–$60 • MS-63 $150–$225.

WI, Madison • Huntley & Steensland • WI-410-E • *Groceries and crockery* • Ascribed to the shop of W.K. Lanphear • Reverse die: 1083 • WI-410-E-1a Rev 1083 (R-3): VF–EF $60–$90 • MS-63 $200–$300.

WI, Madison • J.J. Lawrence • WI-410-F • *Groceries, crockery, glassware* • Ascribed to the shop of W.K. Lanphear • Reverse die: 1222 • WI-410-F-1a Rev 1222 (R-5): VF–EF $50–$75 • MS-63 $175–$250.

WI-410-G • Madison Brewery • O-1 used with WI-410-G-1 to 3.

WI-410-G • Madison Brewery • O-2 used with WI-410-G-4.

WI-410-G • J. Rodermund • O-3 used with WI-410-G-5 and 6.

WI-410-G • J. Rodermund • O-4 used with WI-410-G-7.

WI, Madison • Madison Brewery, J. Rodermund • WI-410-G • *Brewery* • Ascribed to the shop of S.D. Childs • Reverse dies: 1105, 1357, 1390, 45800, 45810 • WI-410-G-2a Rev 45810 (R-6): VF–EF $500–$750 • MS-63 $1,500–$2,250 • Also see WI-410-K below.

WI, Madison • E. Newcomb • WI-410-H • *Meat market* • Ascribed to the shop of W.K. Lanphear • Reverse die: 1169 • WI-410-H-1a Rev 1169 (R-6): VF–EF $40–$60 • MS-63 $175–$250.

WI, Madison • George V. Ott • WI-410-I • *Dealer in leather and hides, tanner* • Ascribed to the shop of W.K. Lanphear • Reverse die: 1205 • WI-410-I-1a Rev 1205 (R-6): VF–EF $60–$90 • MS-63 $250–$375.

WI, Madison • Ramsay & Campbell • WI-410-J • *Stoves, tin, iron, and farming tools* • Ascribed to the shop of W.K. Lanphear • Reverse die: 1332 • WI-410-J-1a Rev 1332 (R-6): VF–EF $50–$75 • MS-63 $150–$225.

WI, Madison • J. Rodermund • WI-410-K • *Dry goods and groceries* • Ascribed to the shop of S.D. Childs • Reverse die: 1105 • WI-410-K-1a Rev 1105 (R-5): VF–EF $50–$75 • MS-63 $175–$250 • Also see WI-410-G above. In the 1866 *Bradstreet Commercial Directory*, J. Rodermund is listed as proprietor of the Madison Brewery.

WI, Madison • William Voight, Capitol Steam Brewery • WI-410-L • *Brewery* • Ascribed to the shop of S.D. Childs[120] • Reverse dies: 1205, 1209, 1357 • WI-410-L-1a Rev 1205 (R-6), WI-410-L-2a Rev 1209 (R-6): VF–EF $75–$110 • MS-63 $250–$375.

WI-420-A • W.H. Horn • O-1 used with WI-420-A-1 to 3.

WI-420-A • W.H. Horn • O-2 used with WI-420-A-4.

WI, Manitowoc • W.H. Horn • WI-420-A • *Produce dealer* • Dies by Mossin & Marr • Reverse dies: 1174, 1194, 1272 • WI-420-A-2a Rev 1194 (R-4), WI-420-A-4a Rev 1194 (R-4): VF–EF $30–$45 • MS-63 $135–$200.

WI-420-B •
Stucke & Co. •
O-1 used with
WI-420-B-1 to 3.
"Dealers."

WI-420-B •
Stucke & Co. •
O-2 used with
WI-420-B-4.
"Dealer."

WI, Manitowoc • Stucke & Co. • WI-420-B • *Produce dealers* • Dies by Mossin & Marr • Reverse dies: 1174, 1194, 1220 • WI-420-B-4a Rev 1194 (R-2): VF–EF $30–$45 • MS-63 $125–$175.

WI, Marshall • I. Livingston • WI-435-A • *Dry goods and groceries* • Dies by Mossin & Marr • Reverse die: 1194 • WI-435-A-1a Rev 1194 (R-7): VF–EF $150–$225 • MS-63 $600–$900.

WI, Marshall • G.W. Vosburgh • WI-435-B • *Hardware, stoves, and tin* • Dies by Mossin & Marr • Reverse die: 1194 • WI-435-B-1a Rev 1194 (R-5): VF–EF $100–$150 • MS-63 $400–$600.

WI, Mauston • D. Campbell • WI-450-A • *Hardware and groceries* • Ascribed to the shop of S.D. Childs • Reverse die: 1107 • WI-450-A-1a Rev 1107 (R-7): VF–EF $200–$300 • MS-63 $600–$900 • Only token issuer of this town.

WI, Mayfield • E. Wirth • WI-460-A • *Dry goods, groceries, clothing, and hats* • Dies by Mossin & Marr • Reverse dies: 1174, 1194, 1220 • WI-460-A-2a Rev 1194 (R-6): VF–EF $50–$75 • MS-63 $200–$300 • Only token issuer of this town.

WI, Menasha ("Manash" error) • McCabe Coral Mills • Reverse of WI-480-A • *Mills* • Ascribed to the shop of W.K. Lanphear • This merchant is not listed separately, but is known in connection with a muling used as a *reverse* from John Hunt, Neenah, WI, known as WI-520-A-01a. Location given as MANASH, an error. It should have been Menasha.

WI, Milwaukee • E. Aschermann & Co. • WI-510-A • *Cigars and tobacco* • Dies by Mossin & Marr • Reverse dies: 45950, 45960 • WI-510-A-1a Rev 45960 (R-4): VF–EF $40–$60 • MS-63 $175–$250.

WI, Milwaukee • Ch. Bast, Wisconsin Brewery • WI-510-B • *Brewery* • Dies by Mossin & Marr[121] • Reverse dies: 45980, 45990 • WI-510-B-1a Rev 45980 (R-5): VF–EF $75–110 • MS-63 $300–$450.

WI, Milwaukee • Philip Best, Empire Brewery • WI-510-C • *Lager beer; brewery* • Dies by Mossin & Marr[122] • Reverse die: 46010 • WI-510-C-1a Rev 46010 (R-3): VF–EF $30–$45 • MS-63 $150–$225.

WI, Milwaukee • V. Blatz, City Brewery & Malt House • WI-510-E • *Brewery* • Dies by Mossin & Marr[123] • Reverse dies: 46050, 46060 • WI-510-E-1a Rev 46050 (R-3): VF–EF $60–$90 • MS-63 $200–$300 • The obverse depicts King Gambrinus, fictional Flemish patron of beer.

WI, Milwaukee • M. Bodden • WI-510-F • *Newspaper editor, city treasurer* • Dies by Mossin & Marr[124] • Reverse dies: 1194, 1220 • WI-510-F-1a Rev 1194 (R-5): VF–EF $60–$90 • MS-63 $250–$375.

WI, Milwaukee • A.J. Cooper • WI-510-H • *Lumber yard* • Dies by Mossin & Marr • Reverse dies: 1194, 46080 • WI-510-H-1a Rev 1194 (R-5): VF–EF $30–$45 • MS-63 $100–$150.

WI, Milwaukee • D.J. Doornink • WI-510-I • *Groceries and dry goods* • Dies by Mossin & Marr • Reverse dies: 1194, 46090, 46100 • WI-510-I-1a Rev 46100 (R-5): VF–EF $40–$60 • MS-63 $175–$250.

WI, Milwaukee • A.H. Filner • WI-510-J • *Groceries and bowling* • Dies by Mossin & Marr • Reverse die: 46120 • WI-510-J-1a1 Rev 46120 (R-8): VF–EF $7,500–$11,000 • MS-63 $13,500–$20,000.

WI, Milwaukee • Joseph Fischbein • WI-510-K • *Stoves, hardware, groceries, provisions, etc.* • Dies by Mossin & Marr • Reverse dies: 46130, 46140, 46150, 1461 •

WI-510-K-3a Rev 1461 (R-5): VF–EF $35–$50 • MS-63 $150–$225.

WI, Milwaukee • William Frankfurth • WI-510-L • *Stoves and hardware* • Dies by Mossin & Marr • Reverse dies: 1427F, 46140, 46150 • WI-510-L-1a Rev 46140 (R-3): VF–EF $30–$45 • MS-63 $125–$175.

WI, Milwaukee • Goes & Falk, Wisconsin Malt House & Bavaria Brewery • WI-510-M • *Brewery* • Dies by Mossin & Marr[125] • Reverse die: 46180 • WI-510-M-1a Rev 46180 (R-4): VF–EF $40–$60 • MS-63 $175–$250.

WI, Milwaukee • Goll & Frank's Retail Store, J.H. Hantsch agent • WI-510-N • *Dry goods, fancy goods, Yankee notions, feathers, etc.* • Dies by Mossin & Marr • Reverse die: 46200 • WI-510-N-1a Rev 46200 (R-5): VF–EF $40–$60 • MS-63 $150–$225.

WI, Milwaukee • C.E. Graff • WI-510-O • *Dealer in machinery* • Dies by Mossin & Marr • Reverse dies: 1174, 1194, 1220, 1272 • WI-510-O-2a Rev 1194 (R-6): VF–EF $35–$50 • MS-63 $150–$225.

| WI-510-P • C. Hambach • O-1 used with WI-510-P-1. | WI-510-P • C. Hambach • O-2 used with WI-510-P-2. |

WI, Milwaukee • C. Hambach • WI-510-P • ? • Dies by Mossin & Marr • Reverse die: 1194 • WI-510-P-1a Rev 1194 (R-6), WI-510-P-2a Rev 1194 (R-6): VF–EF $40–$60 • MS-63 $200–$300.

WI, Milwaukee • T.W. Hart, superintendent, M.W.M. Plank Road • WI-510-Q • *Plank road and superintendent*[126] • ? • Reverse die: 46250 • WI-510-Q-1a Rev 46250 (R-7): VF–EF $1,000–$1,500 •

MS-63 $2,500–$3,750 • This is listed as WI-510-Q, of Milwaukee. However, research by Raymond Callan published in *JCWTS*, Fall 1992, "T.W. Hart, Supt. MW.M. Plank Road Co.," revealed that Hart was based in Wauwatosa, not in Milwaukee.

| WI-510-R • Ch. Hermann & Co. • O-1 used with WI-510-R-1 to 4. | WI-510-R • Ch. Hermann & Co. • O-2 used with WI-510-R-5 and 6. |

WI, Milwaukee • Ch. Hermann & Co. • WI-510-R • *Broom and stone ware factory* • Dies by Mossin & Marr • Reverse dies: 1174, 1220, 1272, 46270 • WI-510-R-1a Rev 46270 (R-6): VF–EF $50–$75 • MS-63 $200–$300 • More numismatic strike varieties were made of this issuer than of any other served by Mossin & Marr.

WI, Milwaukee • George Kane • WI-510-S • *Grocer* • Dies by Mossin & Marr • Reverse die: 1194 • WI-510-S-1a Rev 1194 (R-6): VF–EF $60–$90 • MS-63 $200–$300.

| WI-510-T • Kirby Langworthy & Co. • O-1 used with WI-510-T-1. | WI-510-T • Kirby Langworthy & Co. • O-2 used with WI-510-T-2. |

WI, Milwaukee • Kirby Langworthy & Co. Threshing Machine Works • WI-510-T • *Makers of threshing machines, wagons, and other equipment* • Ascribed to the shop of S.D. Childs • Reverse die: 1108 • WI-510-T-1a Rev 1108 (R-7),

WI-510-T-2a Rev 1108 (R-9): VF–EF $250–$375 • MS-63 $750–$1,100.

WI, Milwaukee • A. Kleinsteiber • WI-510-U • *Millinery and fancy goods* • Dies by Mossin & Marr • Reverse dies: 46320, 46330 • WI-510-U-1a Rev 46320 (R-4): VF–EF $150–$225 • MS-63 $400–$600.

WI, Milwaukee • Charles Kleinsteuber • WI-510-V • *Small machinery, models, engraving, stencil cutting, etc.* • Dies by Mossin & Marr • Reverse dies: 46340, 46345, 46355 • WI-510-V-1a Rev 46345 (R-4): VF–EF $50–$75 • MS-63 $200–$300.

WI, Milwaukee • H. Kurt • WI-510-W • *Grocer* • Dies by Mossin & Marr • Reverse die: 1194 • WI-510-W-1a Rev 1194 (R-4): VF–EF $30–$45 • MS-63 $100–$150.

WI, Milwaukee • Louis Kurz • WI-510-X • *Pictorial lithographer* • Dies by Mossin & Marr[127] • Reverse dies: 1194, 1220 • WI-510-X-2a Rev 1220 (R-6): VF–EF $90–$135 • MS-63 $400–$600 • A Kurz & Allison print is illustrated in chapter 3. Kurz relocated to Chicago after the war and was a partner in the firm.

WI-510-Y •
A. Lederer & Co. •
O-1 used with
WI-510-Y-1 and 2.

WI-510-Y •
A. Lederer & Co. •
O-2 used with
WI-510-Y-3 to 5.

WI, Milwaukee • A. Lederer & Co. • WI-510-Y • *Dry goods* • Ascribed to the shop of S.D. Childs • Reverse dies: 1095, 1106, 1108, 1212 • WI-510-Y-1a Rev 1095 (R-6): VF–EF $40–$60 • MS-63 $200–$300.

WI, Milwaukee • Matson & Loomis • WI-510-Ya • *Jewelers, fancy goods* • ? • Custom reverse die • WI-510-Ya-1b.

(R-9): VF–EF $6,000–$9,000 • The firm did business in a three-story building in downtown Milwaukee. Newell Matson and Lucius L. Loomis.

WI, Milwaukee • M.C. Meyer, M.G.B. Pl. Road • WI-510-Z • *Plank road* • Dies by Mossin & Marr • Reverse die: 1194 • WI-510-Z-1a Rev 1194 (R-5): VF–EF $50–$75 • MS-63 $175–$250 • Martin C. Meyer, Milwaukee & Green Bay Plank Road Co.[128]

WI, Milwaukee • A. Miller & Co. • WI-510-AA • *Produce dealer* • Dies by Mossin & Marr • Reverse dies: 1174, 1194, 1220, 1272, 46410 • WI-510-AA-1e Rev 1174 (R-7), WI-510-AA-2a Rev 1194 (R-7): VF–EF $60–$90 • MS-63 $175–$250.

WI, Milwaukee • Friedrich Miller, Plank Road Brewery • WI-510-AB • *Brewery* • Dies by Mossin & Marr • Reverse dies: 0, 46430, 46440, 46460 • WI-510-AB-1a Rev 46430 (R-4): VF–EF $40–$60 • MS-63 $175–$250.

WI, Milwaukee • F. Mitzlaff • WI-510-AC • *Grocery* • Dies by Mossin & Marr • Reverse die: 1194 • WI-510-AC-1a Rev 1194 (R-5): VF–EF $25–$35 • MS-63 $100–$150.

WI, Milwaukee • Mossin & Marr • WI-510-AD • *Diesinkers and engravers* • Dies by Mossin & Marr • Reverse die: 1220 • WI-510-AD-1a Rev 1220 (R-4): VF–EF $60–$90 • MS-63 $250–$375.

WI, Milwaukee • Carl Paeschke • WI-510-AE • *Dry goods, groceries, provisions* • Dies by Mossin & Marr • Reverse dies: 1194, 1220, 46490, 46500 • WI-510-AE-2a Rev 46500 (R-4): VF–EF $30–$45 • MS-63 $125–$175.

WI, Milwaukee • Planer & Kayser's Sewing Machine • WI-510-AF • *Sewing machine sales* • Dies by Mossin & Marr • Reverse die: 1194 • WI-510-AF-1a Rev 1194 (R-6): VF–EF $75–$110 • MS-63 $250–$375 • Milwaukee agent for the Planer & Kayser Patent Sewing Machine Co., 84 Bowery, New York City.

WI, Milwaukee • J. Pritzlaff & Co. • **WI-510-AG** • *Hardware, iron, glass, and stoves* • Dies by Mossin & Marr • Reverse die: 46530 • WI-510-AG-1a1 Rev 46530 (R-4): VF–EF $40–$60 • MS-63 $125–$175.

WI, Milwaukee • J. Scheidhauer • **WI-510-AH** • *Manufacturer of soap and candles* • Dies by Mossin & Marr • Reverse die: 1194 • WI-510-AH-1a Rev 1194 (R-6): VF–EF $100–$150 • MS-63 $350–$500.

WI, Milwaukee • J.B. Schram • **WI-510-AI** • *Wholesale grocer* • Dies by Mossin & Marr • Reverse die: 1194 • WI-510-AI-1a Rev 1194 (R-5): VF–EF $25–$35 • MS-63 $350–$500.

WI, Milwaukee • Severn & Jones • **WI-510-AJ** • *Produce and commission merchants* • Dies by Mossin & Marr • Reverse dies: 1194, 1195, 46560 • WI-510-AJ-1a Rev 1194 (R-5): VF–EF $30–$45 • MS-63 $135–$200 • Thomas Severn and George I. Jones.

WI-510-AK • C.T. Stamm & Co. • O-1 used with WI-510-AK-1.

WI-510-AK • C.T. Stamm & Co. • O-2 used with WI-510-AK-2.

WI, Milwaukee • C.T. Stamm & Son • **WI-510-AK** • *Stoves, tin, and hardware* • AK-1 is ascribed to the shop of S.D. Childs and AK-2 is ascribed to the shop of Mossin & Marr. Stamm & Son ordered tokens from two different merchants. • Reverse dies: 1108, 1194 • WI-510-AK-2a Rev 1194 (R-5): VF–EF $25–$35 • MS-63 $125–$175.

WI, Milwaukee • A.H. Steinmann • **WI-510-AL** • *Groceries, dry goods, and millinery* • Dies by Mossin & Marr • Reverse die: 1194 • WI-510-AL-1a Rev

1194 (R-5): VF–EF $30–$45 • MS-63 $135–$200.

WI, Milwaukee • D. Stoffel • **WI-510-AM** • *Groceries and provisions* • Dies by Mossin & Marr • Reverse die: 1194 • WI-510-AM-1a Rev 1194 (R-5): VF–EF $35–$50 • MS-63 $150–$225.

WI-510-AO • I. Teller • O-1 used with WI-510-AO-1 to 3.

WI-510-AO • I. Teller • O-2 used with WI-510-AO-4.

WI, Milwaukee • I. Teller • **WI-510-AO** • ? • Dies by Mossin & Marr • Reverse dies: 1174, 1194, 46620 • WI-510-AO-2a Rev 1194 (R-4): VF–EF $25–$35 • MS-63 $100–$150 • Listed out of alphabetical order in the Fuld text.

WI, Milwaukee • Friedrich Thiele • **WI-510-AN** • *Meat market* • Dies possibly by Mossin & Marr • Reverse dies: 1194, 1220 • WI-510-AN-1a Rev 1194 (R-6), WI-510-AN-2a Rev 1220 (R-6): VF–EF $30–$45 • MS-63 $135–$200.

WI-510-AP • H. Upmeyer • O-1 used with WI-510-AP-1 and 2, 5.

WI-510-AP I • Upmeyer • O-2 used with WI-510-AP-4.

WI, Milwaukee • H. Upmeyer • **WI-510-AP** • *Jeweler* • Dies by Mossin & Marr • Reverse dies: 1155, 1156, 46640 • WI-510-AP-1a Rev 1155 (R-3): VF–EF $25–$35 • MS-63 $110–$175.

WI, Milwaukee • Hermann Voigt • WI-510-AQ • *Stoves and tinware* • Dies by Mossin & Marr • Reverse die: 46670 • WI-510-AQ-1a Rev 46670 (R-5): VF–EF $40–$60 • MS-63 $150–$225.

WI, Neenah • John Hunt (McCabe reverse) • WI-520-A • *Groceries and provisions* • Ascribed to the shop of W.K. Lanphear • Reverse die: 47010 • WI-520-A-1a Rev 47010 (R-5): VF–EF $75–$110 • MS-63 $300–$450 • See listing under Menasha, Wisconsin, for the McCabe Coral Mills.

WI, Neenah • C.W. Leavens & Co. • WI-520-B • *Groceries* • Dies by Mossin & Marr • Reverse die: 1316 • WI-520-B-1a Rev 1316 (R-6): VF–EF $75–$110 • MS-63 $250–$375.

WI, New Lisbon • J. Ramsey • WI-540-A • *Dry goods, groceries, and general merchandise* • Ascribed to the shop of S.D. Childs • Reverse die: 1205 • WI-540-A-1a Rev 1205 (R-7): VF–EF $150–$225 • MS-63 $500–$750 • Listed out of alphabetical order in the Fuld book.

WI, New Lisbon (and Tomah) • William Runkel • See listing under Tomah, WI-890-B.

WI, New Lisbon • L.C. Wescott • WI-540-B • *Dealer in hardware, stoves, and agricultural implements* • Ascribed to the shop of S.D. Childs • Reverse die: 1107 • WI-540-B-1a Rev 1107 (R-7): VF–EF $150–$225 • MS-63 NA.

WI, Newburg • Franckenburg & Keller • WI-530-A • *Dry goods, groceries, and hardware* • Reverse die: 1194 • WI-530-A-1a Rev 1194 (R-6): VF–EF $135–$200 • MS-63 $500–$750 • Only token issuer of this town.

WI, North Prairie • W.H. Bogardus • WI-550-A • *Dry goods, groceries, and hardware* • Dies by Mossin & Marr[129] • Reverse die: 1194 • WI-550-A-1a Rev 1194 (R-6): VF–EF $175–$250 • MS-63 $600–$900.

WI, North Prairie • J. Remington Sons • WI-550-B • *Dry goods and groceries* • Ascribed to the shop of S.D. Childs • Reverse die: 1106 • WI-550-B-1a Rev 1106 (R-8): VF–EF $600–$900 • MS-63 $1,500–$2,250.

WI, North Prairie • J. Smart Steam Flouring & Planing Mills • WI-550-C • *Mills* • Ascribed to the shop of S.D. Childs • Reverse die: 1205 • WI-550-C-1a Rev 1205 (R-8): VF–EF $500–$750 • MS-63 NA • Mills for processing grain and, separately, wood.

WI, Oconomowoc • Mrs. J. Tate • WI-590-A • *Milliner* • Dies by Mossin & Marr • Reverse die: 1174 • WI-590-A-1a Rev 1174 (R-8): VF–EF $13,500–$20,000 • MS-63 NA • Only token issuer of this town. A classic Wisconsin rarity. Should be Mrs. S.J. Tate.

WI, Oconto County • See Stiles, WI.

WI, Oshkosh • G. Bock, City Hotel • WI-620-A • *Hotel* • Dies by Mossin & Marr • Reverse die: 47120 • WI-620-A-1a Rev 47120 (R-6): VF–EF $125–$175 • MS-63 $350–$500.

WI, Oshkosh • Jos. Boles • WI-620-B • *Merchant tailor and dealer in clothing* • Ascribed to the shop of W.K. Lanphear • Reverse die: 1337 • WI-620-B-1a Rev 1337 (R-6): VF–EF $100–$150 • MS-63 $250–$375.

WI, Oshkosh • Fraker Bro's • WI-620-C • *Dealers in boots, shoes, leather, and hides* • Ascribed to the shop of W.K. Lanphear • Reverse die: 47150 • WI-620-C-1a Rev 47150 (R-5): VF–EF $30–$45 • MS-63 $125–$175.

WI, Oshkosh • Andrew Haben & Co. • WI-620-D • *Dealers in clothing* • Ascribed to the shop of W.K. Lanphear • Reverse dies: 1179, 1181, 1222, 1337 • WI-620-D-3a Rev 1222 (R-6): VF–EF $50–$75 • MS-63 $200–$300.

WI, Oshkosh • Hasbrouck & Fancher • WI-620-E • *Dealers in stoves and tinware* • Reverse die: 1300 • WI-620-E-1a Rev 1300 (R-6): VF–EF $60–$90 • MS-63 $200–$300.

WI, Oshkosh • Hay & Clark • WI-620-F • *Dealers in hardware* • Ascribed to the shop of W.K. Lanphear • Reverse dies: 1179, 1181 • WI-620-F-1a Rev 1179 (R-5): VF–EF $50–$75 • MS-63 $175–$250.

WI, Oshkosh • Jaenicke & Klotzsch • WI-620-G • *Manufacturers of and dealers in leather and hides* • Dies by Mossin & Marr • Reverse die: 1194 • WI-620-G-1a Rev 1194 (R-6): VF–EF $50–$75 • MS-63 $250–$375.

WI, Oshkosh • Kellogg & Hughes • WI-620-H • *Dry goods* • Ascribed to the shop of W.K. Lanphear • Reverse die: 1127 • WI-620-H-1a Rev 1127 (R-6): VF–EF $40–$60 • MS-63 $175–$250.

WI, Oshkosh • Levy & Duncan • WI-620-I • *Dealers in clothing* • Ascribed to the shop of W.K. Lanphear • Reverse dies: 1082, 1125, 1127, 1128, 1171, 1346 • WI-620-I-5a Rev 1171 (R-5): VF–EF $60–$90 • MS-63 $200–$300.

WI, Oshkosh • Lines & Russell • WI-620-J • *Harness makers* • Ascribed to the shop of W.K. Lanphear • Reverse die: 47530 • WI-620-J-1a Rev 47530 (R-6): VF–EF $75–$110 • MS-63 $250–$375.

WI, Oshkosh • A. Neff • WI-620-K • *Hardware and groceries* • Ascribed to the shop of W.K. Lanphear • Reverse die: 1300 • WI-620-K Rev 1300 (R-5): VF–EF $40–$60 • MS-63 $135–$200.

WI, Oshkosh • S.B. & J.A. Paige • WI-620-L • *Grocers* • Ascribed to the shop of W.K. Lanphear • Reverse dies: 1085, 1087, 1179 • WI-620-L-3a Rev 1179 (R-5): VF–EF $50–$75 • MS-63 $200–$300.

WI, Oshkosh • H. Rans • WI-620-M • *Dealer in clothing* • Ascribed to the shop of W.K. Lanphear • Reverse dies: 1082, 1084, 1127, 1128, 1130 • WI-620-M-3a Rev 1127 (R-5): VF–EF $50–$75 • MS-63 $200–$300.

WI, Oshkosh • B.H. Soper • WI-620-N • *Dealer in furniture* • Ascribed to the shop of W.K. Lanphear • Reverse dies: 1082, 1127, 1169 • WI-620-N-1a Rev 1082 (R-6), WI-620-N-3a Rev 1169 (R-6): VF–EF $50–$75 • MS-63 $175–$200.

WI, Oshkosh • Allen Vosburg & Co. • WI-620-O • *Steinway pianos, Smith melodeons, and tremolo harmoniums* • Ascribed to the shop of W.K. Lanphear • Reverse die: 47590 • WI-620-O-1a Rev 47590 (R-6): VF–EF $125–$175 • MS-63 $400–$600.

WI, Oshkosh • William L. Williams • WI-620-P • *Chemist and druggist* • Ascribed to the shop of W.K. Lanphear • Reverse dies: 1123, 1127, 1130 • WI-620-P-2a Rev 1127 (R-6): VF–EF $90–$135 • MS-63 $300–$450.

WI, Port Washington • J. Druecker • WI-680-A • *Dry goods, groceries, clothing, hats, etc.* • Dies by Mossin & Marr • Reverse die: 1194 • WI-680-A-1a Rev 1194 (R-6): VF–EF $75–$110 • MS-63 $300–$450 • Only token issuer of this town. Listed out of order in the Fuld text.

WI, Portage City • T.M. McMillan • WI-660-A • *Groceries and crockery* • Ascribed to the shop of S.D. Childs • Reverse die: 1205 • WI-660-A-1a Rev 1205 (R-7): VF–EF $250–$375 • MS-63 NA • Only token issuer of this town.

WI-700-A •
J.I. Case & Co. •
O-1 used with
WI-700-A-1.

WI-700-A •
J.I. Case & Co. •
O-2 used with
WI-700-A-2 to 5.

WI, Racine • J.I. Case & Co. • WI-700-A • *Thrashing machine manufacturers* • Ascribed to the shop of S.D. Childs • Reverse dies: 1094, 1098, 1105, 1203, 1205 • WI-700-A-2a Rev 1098 (R-5): VF–EF $40–$60 • MS-63 $200–$300.

WI, Racine • J. Clough • WI-700-B • *Fine family groceries, nuts, etc.* • Ascribed to the shop of S.D. Childs • Reverse dies: 1095, 1105, 1108, 1211 • WI-700-B-3a Rev 1108 (R-7): VF–EF $50–$75 • MS-63 $200–$300.

WI, Racine • John Elkins • WI-700-C • *Dealer in watches, jewelry, pianos, etc.* • Ascribed to the shop of S.D. Childs • Reverse dies: 1101, 1105, 1106, 1110, 1205 • WI-700-C-1a Rev 1101 (R-5), WI-700-C-3a Rev 1106 (R-5): VF–EF $35–$50 • MS-63 $150–$225.

| WI-700-D • F. Elmlinger • O-1 used with WI-700-D-1. | WI-700-D • F. Elmlinger • O-2 used with WI-700-D-2. |

WI, Racine • F. Elmlinger • WI-700-D • *Merchant tailor* • Ascribed to the shop of S.D. Childs • Reverse die: 1106 • WI-700-D-1a Rev 1106 (R-4): VF–EF $30–$45 • MS-63 $100–$150.

| WI-700-F • J.W. English • O-1 used with WI-700-F-1 and 2. | WI-700-F • J.W. English • O-2 used with WI-700-F-3. |

WI, Racine • J.W. English • WI-700-E • *Trunk and harness dealer* • Ascribed to the shop of S.D. Childs • Reverse dies: 1105, 1206, 1207 • WI-700-E-3a Rev 1207 (R-6): VF–EF $75–$110 • MS-63 $300–$450.

WI, Racine • Erhardt & Raps • WI-700-F • *Auctioneers* • Dies by Mossin & Marr • Reverse die: 1220 • WI-700-F-1a Rev 1220 (R-4): VF–EF $75–$125 • MS-63 $300–$450.

WI, Racine • Thomas Falvey • WI-700-G • *Manufacturer of reapers and sowers* • Ascribed to the shop of S.D. Childs • Reverse dies: 1101, 1105, 1106, 1110, 1390 • WI-700-G-1a Rev 1101 (R-6), WI-700-G-2a Rev 1105 (R-6), WI-700-G-3a Rev 1106 (R-6), WI-700-G-4a Rev 1110 (R-6): VF–EF $40–$60 • MS-63 $175–$250.

WI, Racine • D.H. Jones • WI-700-H • *Dry goods* • Ascribed to the shop of S.D. Childs • Reverse dies: 1105, 1108, 1110, 1205 • WI-700-H-4a Rev 1205 (R-6): VF–EF $60–$90 • MS-63 $250–$375.

| WI-700-I • J. & H. Miller • O-1 used with WI-700-I-1. | WI-700-I • J. & H. Miller • O-2 used with WI-700-I-2 and 3. |

WI, Racine • J. & H. Miller • WI-700-I • *Dealers in boots and shoes* • Ascribed to the shop of S.D. Childs • Reverse dies: 1105, 1110, 1203 • WI-700-I-1a Rev 1105 (R-7), WI-700-I-2a Rev 1110 (R-7), WI-700-I-3a Rev 1203 (R-7): VF–EF $65–$100 • MS-63 $250–$375.

WI, Racine • Thelen & Deiterich WI-700-J • *Dry goods and groceries* • Ascribed to the shop of S.D. Childs • Reverse dies: 1108, 1357 • WI-700-J-1a Rev 1108 (R-7): VF–EF $200–$300 • MS-63 $500–$750.

WI-720-A •
Greenway & Co. •
O-1 used with
WI-720-A-1 to 5.

WI-720-A •
Greenway & Co. •
O-2 used with
WI-720-A-6 to 8.

WI, Ripon • Greenway & Co. • WI-720-A • *Restaurant, billiard rooms, immense concert hall* • Ascribed to the shop of John Stanton • Reverse dies: 1037, 1042, 1046, 1047, 1069, 47750 • WI-720-A-1a Rev 47750 (R-7): VF–EF $250–$375 • MS-63 $600–$900 • Only token issuer of this town.

WI, Sauk City • C. Nebel • WI-770-A • *Steam mills* • Dies by Mossin & Marr • Reverse dies: 1194, 47760 • WI-770-A-1a Rev 1194 (R-4), WI-770-A-1a1 Rev 1194 (R-4): VF–EF $35–$50 • MS-63 $150–$225 • Only token issuer of this town.

WI, Sheboygan • Trowbridge's Watch, Clock & Jewelry Store • WI-790-A • *Jeweler* • Ascribed to the shop of John Stanton • Reverse dies: 1047, 1319 • WI-790-A-2a1 Rev 1319 (R-8): VF–EF $1,000–$1,500 • MS-63 $2,500–$3,750 • Only token issuer of this town.

WI, Sparta • Hamilton & Co. • WI-830-A • *Grocers* • Ascribed to the shop of S.D. Childs • Reverse die: 1107 • WI-830-A-1a Rev 1107 (R-6): VF–EF $125–$175 • MS-63 $500–$750.

WI, Sparta • W.S. Newton • WI-830-B • *Hardware, stoves* • Ascribed to the shop of S.D. Childs • Reverse die: 1107 • WI-830-B-1a Rev 1107 (R-6): VF–EF $175–$250 • MS-63 $600–$900.

WI, Stiles • Stiles Gang Mills • WI-600-A • *Mills* • Dies by Mossin & Marr • Reverse dies: 1194, 47100 • WI-600-A-1a Rev 1194 (R-5): VF–EF $75–$110 • MS-63 $350–$500 • Only token issuer of this stated location. Address on the token is Oconto County, but the tokens were probably issued in Stiles in that county.

WI, Stoughton • T.P. Camp • WI-860-A • *Watch maker* • Ascribed to the shop of W.K. Lanphear • Reverse dies: 1320, 1427E • WI-860-A-1a Rev 1320 (R-7): VF–EF $200–$300 • MS-63 $600–$900.

WI, Stoughton • Dearbourn & Root • WI-860-B • *Grocers* • Ascribed to the shop of W.K. Lanphear • Reverse die: 1222 • WI-860-B-1a Rev 1222 (R-6): VF–EF $125–$175 • MS-63 $400–$600.

WI, Stoughton • H. Peterson • WI-860-C • *Dry goods, clothing, shoes* • Ascribed to the shop of W.K. Lanphear • Reverse die: 1181 • WI-860-C-1a Rev 1181 (R-5): VF–EF $60–$90 • MS-63 $250–$375.

WI, Tomah • Eaton & Barns • WI-890-A • *Dry goods and groceries* • Dies by Mossin & Marr • Reverse die: 1194 • WI-890-A-1a Rev 1194 (R-6): VF–EF $90–$135 • MS-63 $300–$450.

WI, Tomah (and New Lisbon) • William Runkel • WI-890-B • *Dry goods* • Dies by Mossin & Marr • Reverse die: 1194 • WI-890-B-1a Rev 1194 (R-5): VF–EF $50–$75 • MS-63 $200–$300 • Tomah and New Lisbon are both given as addresses.

WI, Two Rivers • R. Suettinger • WI-900-A • *Manufacturer of and dealer in stoves, tin, and sheet iron ware* • Dies by Mossin & Marr • Reverse die: 1194 • WI-900-A-1a Rev 1194 (R-4): VF–EF $50–$75 • MS-63 $175–$250 • Only token issuer of this town.

WI, Waterloo • Ph. Carpeles & Co. • WI-915-A • *Dry goods, groceries* • Dies by Mossin & Marr • Reverse dies: 1168, 1194 • WI-915-A-2a Rev 1194 (R-5): VF–EF $50–$75 • MS-63 $200–$300 • Only token issuer of this town.

WI, Watertown • H. Bellack • WI-920-A • *Dry goods, groceries, provisions* • Ascribed to the shop of W.K. Lanphear • Reverse die: 1168 • WI-920-A-1a Rev 1168 (R-5): VF–EF $40–$60 • MS-63 $175–$250.

WI, Watertown • Bertram & Co. • WI-920-B • *Boots, shoes* • Ascribed to the shop of W.K. Lanphear • Reverse die: 1317 • WI-920-B-1a Rev 1317 (R-6): VF–EF $75–$110 • MS-63 $300–$450.

WI, Watertown • Cordes & Platz • WI-920-C • *Dry goods, groceries, and liquors* • Ascribed to the shop of W.K. Lanphear • Reverse die: 1085 • WI-920-C-1a Rev 1085 (R-6): VF–EF $35–$50 • MS-63 $135–$200.

WI, Watertown • T. Dervin • WI-920-D • *Dry goods, clothing, groceries* • Dies by Mossin & Marr • Reverse dies: 1174, 1194, 1220, 1272 • WI-920-D-2a Rev 1194 (R-5): VF–EF $40–$60 • MS-63 $135–$200.

WI, Watertown • Patrick Duffy • WI-920-E • *Grocer* • Dies by Mossin & Marr • Reverse die: 1194 • WI-920-E-1a Rev 1194 (R-6): VF–EF $75–$110 • MS-63 $300–$450.

WI-920-F •
Fischer & Rohr •
O-1 used with
WI-920-F-1.

WI-920-F •
Fischer & Rohr •
O-2 used with
WI-920-F-2 and 3.

WI, Watertown • Fischer & Rohr • WI-920-F • *Clothiers* • F-1 is by Mossin & Marr; F-2 and F-3 are by W.K. Lanphear. Fischer & Rohr ordered tokens from two different merchants. • Reverse dies: 0, 1194, 1342 • WI-920-F-1a Rev 1194 (R-5): VF–EF $40–$60 • MS-63 $175–$250.

WI, Watertown • W.C. Fountain • WI-920-G • *Drugs, paint, oils, books, &c.* • Ascribed to the shop of W.K. Lanphear • Reverse dies: 1316, 1323 • WI-920-G-1a Rev 1316 (R-6), WI-920-G-1b Rev 1316 (R-6): VF–EF $50–$75 • MS-63 $150–$225.

WI-920-H •
Charles Goeldner •
O-1 used with
WI-920-H-1 to 3.

WI-920-H •
Charles Goeldner •
O-2 used with
WI-920-H-4.

WI, Watertown • Charles Goeldner • WI-920-H • *Musical instruments, notions, harnesses* • Ascribed to the shop of W.K. Lanphear • Reverse dies: 1091, 1323, 1341 • WI-920-H-4a Rev 1341 (R-5): VF–EF $40–$60 • MS-63 $150–$225.

WI, Watertown • John Heymann • WI-920-I • *Oyster restaurant and beer hall* • Dies by Mossin & Marr • Reverse die: 1194 • WI-920-I-1a Rev 1194 (R-6): VF–EF $100–$150 • MS-63 $300–$450.

WI, Watertown • Daniel Kusel • WI-920-J • *Hardware* • Dies by Mossin & Marr • Reverse die: 1194 • WI-920-J-1a Rev 1194 (R-5): VF–EF $75–$110 • MS-63 $250–$375.

WI, Watertown • J. Moulton • WI-920-K • *Groceries, flour, and feed* • Ascribed to the shop of W.K. Lanphear • Reverse die: 1088 • WI-920-K-1a Rev 1088 (R-6): VF–EF $75–$110 • MS-63 $200–$300.

WI, Watertown • Theodore Racek • WI-920-L • *Restaurant* • Ascribed to the shop of W.K. Lanphear • Reverse die: 1295 • WI-920-L-1a Rev 1295 (R-5): VF–EF $35–$50 • MS-63 $135–$200 • In the third edition of the Fuld text WI-920-L and M will be consolidated under WI-920-L.

WI, Watertown • T. Racek • WI-920-M • *Saloon* • Ascribed to the shop of S.D. Childs • Reverse die: 1356 • WI-920-M-1b Rev 1356 (R-4): VF–EF $40–$60 • MS-63 $125–$175 • "Good for One Glass of Beer." Same merchant as preceding • In the third edition of the

Fuld text WI-920-L and M will be consolidated under WI-920-L.

WI, Waukesha • Charles Cork • WI-930-A • *Groceries, crockery, notions* • Ascribed to the shop of W.K. Lanphear • Reverse die: 1127 • WI-930-A-1a Rev 1127 (R-7): VF–EF $175–$250 • MS-63 $600–$900.

WI, Waukesha • J.A. Dunbar • WI-930-B • *Groceries, provisions, fruit* • Ascribed to the shop of W.K. Lanphear • Reverse die: 1127 • WI-930-B-1a Rev 1127 (R-7): VF–EF $200–$300 • MS-63 $600–$900.

WI, Waukesha • H.W. Sherman • WI-930-C • *Dry goods, hats, groceries* • Ascribed to the shop of W.K. Lanphear • Reverse die: 1317 • WI-930-C-1a Rev 1317 (R-6): VF–EF $150–$225 • MS-63 $500–$750.

WI, Wauwatosa T.W. Hart, superintendent, M.W.M. Plank Road (Madison, Watertown, & Milwaukee Plank Road Co.) • This is listed as WI-510-Q, of Milwaukee. However, research by Raymond Callan published in *JCWTS*, Fall 1992, "T.W. Hart, Supt. MW.M. Plank Road Co.," revealed that Hart was based in Wauwatosa, not in Milwaukee.

WI-960-A •
Gallt & Cole •
O-1 used with
WI-960-A-1 and 2.

WI, Whitewater • Gallt & Cole • WI-960-A • *Dry goods, groceries, shoes* • Ascribed to the shop of S.D. Childs • Reverse dies: 1111, 1115, 1128 • WI-960-A-1a Rev 1111 (R-5): VF–EF $40–$60 • MS-63 $175–$250.

WI, Whitewater • J.S. Lathrop • WI-960-B • *Groceries and provisions* • Ascribed to the shop of W.K. Lanphear • Reverse dies: 1085, 1128 • WI-960-B-1a Rev 1128 (R-6): VF–EF $75–$110 • MS-63 $400–$600.

WI, Whitewater • J.T. Smith • WI-960-C • *Jeweler* • Ascribed to the shop of W.K. Lanphear • Reverse dies: 1320, 1321 • WI-960-C-1a Rev 1320 (R-5), WI-960-C-2a Rev 1321 (R-5): VF–EF $50–$75 • MS-63 $250–$375.

WI, Whitewater • Dr. Van Valkenburgh • WI-960-D • *Druggist, grocer* • Ascribed to the shop of W.K. Lanphear • Reverse dies: 1310, 1316 • WI-960-D-1a Rev 1310 (R-6), WI-960-D-2a Rev 1316 (R-6): VF–EF $50–$75 • MS-63 $175–$250.

WI-960-E •
A. Wahlstedt •
O-1 used with
WI-960-E-1.

WI-960-E •
A. Wahlstedt •
O-2 used with
WI-960-E-2.

WI, Whitewater • A. Wahlstedt • WI-960-E • *Dry goods, groceries, and liquors* • E-1 is ascribed to the shop of W.K. Lanphear, and E-2 is ascribed to the shop of S.D. Childes. Wahlstedt ordered tokens from two different merchants. • Reverse dies: 1085, 1111 • WI-960-E-2a Rev 1111 (R-7): VF–EF $60–$90 • MS-63 $250–$375.

SELECTED CIVIL WAR TOKEN ENGRAVERS AND COINERS

Barkley, C. • New York City, New York • In 1863 he advertised: "Copper Tokens, Checks & Medals forwarded promptly by express to all parts, in any quantity and at the lowest prices. C. Barkley, Die Sinker, No. 70 William St., New York."[1]

Baumgarten, Selig • Baltimore, Maryland.

Bridgens, William H. • New York City, New York • Bridgens, who also dealt in coins, was a highly accomplished engraver. Bridgens had a style all his own, with his hallmarks including the use of triangular dentils on the border and, on some pieces, ornaments in the shape of spearheads. Several of Bridgens's pictorial dies have great appeal, including the French Liberty Head with the misspelled inscription FOR PUBLIC ACCO-MODATION [*sic*], the Washington portrait piece inscribed THE WASHINGTON TOKEN, and the money-laden man exclaiming "go it Buttons" accompanied by the inscription MONEY MAKES THE MARE GO. Others could be cited. He furnished many special pieces to collectors.

"Buffalo engraver," "Buffalo coiner" • Buffalo, New York, or region • Among the more curious issues in the Civil War store card series are several pieces bearing the imprints of Buffalo, New York, merchants. Unique in the series, these have *diagonally reeded* edges. An examination of the die punches suggests that this group of dies stands alone and is not linked with any other grouping. These tokens could just as easily be called "Buffalo primitives," for the reverse dies in particular are very rustic. These issues are known with the following reverses: 1077, 1078, 1079, and 1081. The crudely engraved BUSINESS CARD obverses with eight (instead of the usual nine) feathers, die numbers 1077, 1078, 1079, and 1081, seem to have been made by the same person; these are superficially similar to but have important differences from no. 1080, which is a crude nine-feather BUSINESS CARD die ascribed to A.W. Escherich.

Burr, Montgomery • Philadelphia, Pennsylvania • At one time it was thought that he issued many patriotic tokens and a few store cards.[2] Today facts are scarce.

Charnley, James A. • Providence, Rhode Island • James A. Charnley may be a candidate as the maker of rustic hand-engraved dies used on Rhode Island and related tokens.[3] *See "Rhode Island engraver" below.*

Childs, Shubael D., Jr. • Chicago, Illinois • In the early 1860s the Shubael D. Childs Jr., business was at 117½ Randolph Street, Chicago, Illinois. He made Civil War store cards in quantity beginning in 1861, or a year or two before other prolific issuers. Many featured a woman's head and most used sans-serif letter punches. Childs also produced many sutler tokens. Much about him is in the present narrative text.

Dubois, Frederick N. • Chicago, Illinois • Dubois produced store cards for nearly two dozen merchants in late 1858 or in 1859. Dubois's own store card and most others were combined with a common reverse, known today as Fuld 1368, with a wreath adapted from that used on federal coinage beginning with the gold dollar and $3 in 1854 and continuing with the Flying Eagle cent of 1857. In place of the ONE / CENT on the federal coin of this denomination is BUSINESS / CARD. The obverse or advertising sides of the tokens are quite distinctive. The letters are mostly with serifs and are thick and squat (not tall and narrow). No stars or ornaments appear, nor are there any motifs. Although there are a few exceptions, the lettering fills most of the die, leaving little in the way of large open spaces. Dentils are at the border.[4]

Escherich, A.W. • Chicago, Illinois • In the early 1860s, A.W. Escherich was located at 404 South Clark Street, Chicago. His store card dies are of a rustic or primitive nature lending appeal to numismatists who seek them today.

Glaubrecht, George J. • New York City, New York • George J. Glaubrecht lived in New Jersey during the early 1860s and had a diecutting shop at 95 Fulton Street, New York City. His various Civil War patriotic tokens and store cards are variously signed G.G.; G. G.L. Fuld-NY-630-D-1a (H.L. Bang) is signed GLAUBRECHT.

Gleason, Alexander • Hillsdale, Michigan • Gleason was born in New York State on November 28, 1827. The Gleasons lived in Hillsdale in the 1860s into the 1870s, after which they moved to Jackson, Michigan, and later to Darien, New York, where Alexander died and was buried. This was recorded by the family: "They did stencil work, and I can remember seeing father with a sharp instrument punching out designs."[5] Gleason's dies are of a rustic or primitive nature.[6]

Gminder, Jacob • Baltimore, Maryland • Gminder produced many tokens and store cards in Baltimore, 1859 to 1898.[7] The extent of his Civil War tokens is not known.

Higgins, Henry Darius • Mishawaka, IN • Higgins, a jeweler and manufacturer (of barometers and other devices), cut dies which collectors now refer to as "Indiana primitives." Shubael D. Childs struck some tokens combining Higgins's rustic dies with more finely crafted dies of the Childs shop. Certain of his dies were made by driving a soft steel blank into an actual token made of brass, creating an incuse impression on the blank. This was hardened and later used as a coining die. In the process finer details were lost.[8]

Hörter, Charles D. • New York City, New York • During the Civil War era Hörter maintained a small shop on the second floor of a building at 178 William Street, New York City. Some dies were signed CDH or H.

Hughes, James A. • Cincinnati, Ohio • J.A. Hughes was associated with the shop of William K. Lanphear in Cincinnati during the Civil War–token era. It is not known if he engraved any dies. He also collected tokens and had special strikings made, including in silver. By 1867 he had his own engraving business in addition to commercial printing.

Jacobus, Peter H. • Philadelphia, Pennsylvania • Born in Prussia, Jacobus came to the U.S. at age 16. Set up as an engraver in the late 1830s. In the era 1856–1859 he was a partner with John J. Schell in Jacobus and Shell, diecutters and medalists. The signature of Jacobus is found on dies 1092, 1379, and 1380, and he probably cut others as well. He signed dies as PHJ and JACOBUS. Jacobus continued in business until the early 1870s. • *Directory:* 1861: 135 Dana Street. • 1862: 40 South 3rd Street. Lived at 135 Dana Street. • 1863: 40 South 3rd Street; home at 135 Dana Street. • 1865: 40 South 3rd Street. Home at 313 Crown.

Johnston, H. • Cincinnati, Ohio • A token attributed to Cincinnati, OH-165-CE, bears the name of H. JOHNSTON, 154 Everett Street, but no H. Johnston has been located at this address in the directories. Perhaps this is an error die of William Johnston (of the same address), or perhaps H. Johnston was a relative not listed in the directories.

Johnston, William • Cincinnati, Ohio • William Johnston, of Cincinnati, stated his occupation as a diesinker at 154 Everett Street on tokens classified as OH-165-CF (with reverses 1056, 1247, 1248, 1386, and 1388). His production under his own name was not extensive. One of William Johnston's dies, 1247, is also known in combination with a die bearing the name of M. Lindermann (see listing), whose shop was at the corner of Elm and Henry streets, Cincinnati. In the 1860 *Cincinnati* directory, p. 425, under Covington, Kentucky, William Johnson (*sic*) is listed as an engraver at the northwest corner of 2nd and Greenup streets.

Key, William H. and F.C. Key & Son • Philadelphia, Pennsylvania • During the early 1860s the partnership of F.C. Key & Son, with William H. Key being the son, was located at 329 Arch Street, Philadelphia, Pennsylvania. F.C. Key operated circa 1849–1870. Many tokens and medalets were signed KEY. Born in Brooklyn, New York, circa 1828, William H. Key operated as a diesinker circa 1858–1892. Many of his dies were signed WHK. In 1864 he was appointed an assistant engraver at the United States Mint and remained in service until 1892. He died in 1900.[9] • *Directory listings:* 1861: F.C. Key & Sons was composed of Frederick C. Key, William H. Key, and John C. Odling. Rear of 329 Arch Street. • 1862: F.C. Key & Sons was composed of Frederick C. Key, William H. Key, and John C. Odling. Rear of 329 Arch Street. Frederick C. Key resided on Berkley Street, Camden, New Jersey. William H. Key lived at 827 Market Street, Camden. John C. Odling lived on Henry Street near Royden, Camden. • 1863: F.C. and William H. Key, rear of 329 Arch Street. • 1865 Not listed.

Koehler, Francis X. • Baltimore, Maryland • Koehler was born October 8, 1818, at Swabish, Gmund, Wurttemberg. His mother, a jewelry engraver, was his first teacher of engraving. He served an apprenticeship in Stuttgart and was employed there for a number of years before emigrating to the United States in 1850. Koehler set up business in Baltimore, Maryland, as a die cutter and manufacturer of jewelry circa 1851, but abandoned the manufacture of jewelry in 1863 to devote himself entirely to die cutting. During the Civil War his shop was at 140 West Fayette Street, Baltimore. His death occurred in 1886. During the Civil War he produced sutlers' tokens and some Civil War tokens, the latter resembling sutlers' pieces. Later, circa 1870–1885, he made many tokens with a wreath on the reverse, star at the top, and at the center a number representing the value. He was a member of several German societies in Baltimore. He was also a friend of Anthony C. Paquet, an assistant engraver at the United States Mint.[10] He died in Baltimore on March 22, 1886.[11]

Lang, Charles • Worcester, Massachusetts • Charles Lang issued his own store card during the Civil War, but seems to have done little for others. His only known dies for Civil War tokens were used to strike MA-970-A (in copper and brass), dated 1863, which depicted his portrait on the obverse. His business was taken over by E.A. Timme in Worcester, who later in the 1860s was set up at 251 Main Street, Harrington Corner, Worcester.[12]

Lanphear, William K. • Cincinnati, Ohio, and Chicago, Illinois • Lanphear, located on the second floor of 102 West 4th Street (later 134 West 4th Street), was the second-most prolific issuer of Civil War tokens in Cincinnati, ranking immediately after the shop of John Stanton. His work is remarkable for the variety of motifs used as reverse dies for many store cards and has vastly enriched the repertoire of Civil War issues. He readily accommodated numismatists who desired special strikings and was visited frequently by them. Lanphear seems to have a number of other engravers and artists associated with him, among which are Benjamin C. True, J.A. Hughes, Frederick W. Lutz, William Senour, and Gregory G. Wright, some such as True working off premises. During the Civil War there was a W.K. Lanphear office in Chicago which made stencil plates, stamps, and other products. On October 7, 1864, the American Philosophical Society acknowledged a gift through member Pliny E. Chase "from Mr. Lanphear of Cincinnati consisting of 315 trade tokens."[13] In 1871, Lanphear founded the firm of Lanphear & Ross in Baltimore, which flourished 1871–1873. Subsequently in Baltimore, 1874–1880, he was the owner of the Excelsior Stencil, Stamp & Novelty Co. His output in Baltimore included the stamping of checks and tokens for oyster packers, fruit packers, and fruit pickers.[14]

Lauer, Ludwig Christoph • Nürnberg, Germany • Lauer was a well-known fabricator of brass tokens, medals, and game counters and flourished circa 1848–1873. Apparently, his main business was the making of *spielmarken* (literally, "play money"), some of which bore designs similar to United States coins (such as the Liberty Head by Longacre used on the $20 beginning in 1849). Strasburger & Nuhn (New York City) store cards are ascribed to him.

Leichtweis, Louis • New York City, New York • Leichtweis, an engraver with a shop at 19 Chrystie Street, New York City, made several patriotic dies including 43 which is signed L. LEICHTWEIS below the neck truncation. David D. Gladfelter has ascribed die 18, also known as store card die 2004, to Leichtweis, suggesting it is a transfer copy of a Robert L. Lovett Jr. die.

Lindermann, M. • Cincinnati, Ohio • Lindermann, whose shop was at the corner of Elm and Henry streets, proclaimed his trade as a "check maker" on OH-165-DE. This advertising die was muled with store card dies 1057, 1247, and 1416. These dies are all of a somewhat crude style, at least in comparison with the products of Lanphear and Stanton of the same city. W. Johnston, die cutter at 154 Everett Street, Cincinnati, also issued a token with reverse 1247.

Lovett, George Hampden • New York City, New York • Lovett, a designer, diesinker, and medalist, was born in Philadelphia, February 14, 1824. When he was an infant, Lovett's father moved to New York, and there he spent the greater part of his life. His father, Robert Lovett, and his brothers, John D. and Robert Jr. (all whom he outlived), were all proficient diesinkers. After George received a common-school education, his father took him into his employ, at the age of 17, to learn the art of die sinking and engraving. He spent the rest of his life at that business in New York City. He died in

Brooklyn at age 70 on January 28, 1894. Lovett made certain Washington portrait dies, some pre-war, which have been adopted into the Civil War token series.

Lovett, John D. • New York City, New York • John D. Lovett, a brother of Robert Lovett Jr., and George H. Lovett, was a diecutter at 1 Cortlandt Street, New York City. Little is known concerning the extent of his Civil War token activity, although dies 227 and 228 are ascribed to him.

Lovett, Robert, Jr. • Philadelphia, Pennsylvania • Robert Lovett Jr. was one of three sons of Robert Sr., each of whom became prominent as a diecutter, the others being brothers George Hampden Lovett and John D. Lovett. Robert Jr. was located in Philadelphia, but also had a connection with his New York City brother. His most famous production was the 1861 Confederate States of America cent based on his store card of 1860, in turn copied from the French Liberty Head used on coins of France. The French Liberty Head inspired several engravers to use it on various Civil War tokens, mostly patriotics but with many store cards as well. Lovett made various store card dies with other arrangements such as 1193, 1154, and 1182. 1861–1865: 200 South 5th Street, Philadelphia. Lived at 1109 Wallace Street.

Lutz, Frederick W. • Cincinnati, Ohio • Lutz, residing at 102 West Fourth Street, Cincinnati, produced artistic dies of high quality, some of which were signed LUTZ. It is believed that he worked in the shop of William K. Lanphear at the same address, who struck tokens from Lutz dies. His own store card, OH-165-DG, depicts on the obverse F.W. LUTZ in ornate Old English–style letters, with ARTIST below. This is combined with stock die 1298, illustrating a sewing machine.

Merriam, Joseph H. / Merriam & Co. • Boston, Massachusetts • Merriam, of 18 and 19 Brattle Square, Boston, was very active as a diesinker, seal engraver, and medalist of the era from the 1850s to the 1870s. His work is characterized by a particular boldness, with sharp definition of letters, designs, etc. He seems to have preferred to utilize most of the space on his dies, leaving relatively little open field areas. Certain of his token and medal dies were signed MERRIAM; in the Civil War series these included the famous GOOD FOR A SCENT die with the head of a dog.[15]

H. Miller & Co. • Louisville, Kentucky • H. Miller & Co. made many tokens and medals in the 1850s and 1860s. Ascribed to the Civil War era are those of several merchants whose dies were combined with a standard Miller die depicting a beer mug. These were utilitarian, with no numismatic strikes. Miller's shop was on Third Street, Louisville.

Mossin & Marr • Milwaukee, Wisconsin • The firm of Mossin & Marr, formed by Peter L. Mossin and John Marr, produced many dies for customers in Wisconsin. John Marr seems to have been the principal engraver, and certain of his dies, including the famous "Amazon" depiction, are boldly signed MARR. Most tokens are deeply engraved and well struck.

Müller, Charles • New York City, New York • Müller seems to have been a medalist more than a token issuer. In 1862 he published a circular offering an impressive series of medals he produced relative to Fort Sumter and Fort Pickens, two focal points during the early days of the Civil War.[16] He was the maker of the medalet, NY-630-AV, which advertises John Matthews, maker of soda-water apparatus.

Murdock & Spencer • Cincinnati, Ohio • James Murdock Jr. and William W. Spencer were partners in Murdock & Spencer, engravers at 139 West 5th Street, Cincinnati, Ohio. John Stanton had a share of the business. They bought out Stanton circa 1864, and Murdock is believed to have left in 1868. Murdock & Spencer continued to use Stanton dies. The company made shell cards beginning in 1868.

Murdock, James, Jr. • Cincinnati, Ohio • James Murdock Jr. was born in Belfast, Ireland. From 1855 to 1861 he was employed as a diesinker by John Stanton, Cincinnati diecutter and minter. Later he had his own business within the Stanton shop as part of Murdock & Spencer. The distinction of who struck what is not always clear.

Paquet, Anthony C. • Philadelphia, Pennsylvania • Paquet was born in Hamburg, Germany, in 1814, probably the son of Touissaint François Paquet, a bronze worker in that city. He came to America in 1848, and in the mid-1850s had an engraving shop in New York City. Paquet did contract work for the Mint in early 1857, and on October 20 of that year joined the Mint staff as an assistant engraver. He remained in that post through early 1864, after which he returned to the private sector, but continued to do important commissions for the government, including two designs for Indian Peace medals. His small Washington die for the Great Central Fair, Philadelphia, 1864, was produced at the Mint. At the fair a Mint press was set up to strike the pieces we now know as PA-750-L.

Pilkington, James E. • Steve Tanenbaum: "Pilkington was only at the address on the token (83 Exchange Place) in 1864, thus dating both the Stevens and Krebs tokens. As far as I know, these [Baltimore store cards] are the only tokens with Pilkington-signed reverses."

"Rhode Island engraver(s)," "Rhode Island coiner(s)" • Refers to persons of unknown identity, one of whom created certain dies for Rhode Island and related store cards such as for Charnley, Arcade House, H. Dobson, City Fruit Market, Frank Gay, and others. The style is unique among Civil War token–era dies, inasmuch as the diesinkers seem to have *hand-engraved* the numerals and letters, with no two letters or numerals on the same die being precisely alike. Another hand seems to have done a certain die on which the R's in the inscription H-Y. LEFEVERE. PRO: EMPIRE SALOON are each different in form, as are the E's and other repeated letters. The N's are backward, and punctuation is erratic. No letter or numeral punches were used. It might be said that the makers of these were a die *cutters*, but not die *sinkers*, as few punches were used. *Also see Charnley, James A., above.*

Roloff, Louis • New York City, New York • Roloff conducted an engraving business at 1 New Chambers, New York City, during the Civil War. Certain of his dies are boldly signed DIES BY LOUIS ROLOFF. From time to time there has been speculation that Roloff was a partner with other individuals. Jack R. Detwiler has written that Emil Sigel and Louis Roloff had a working arrangement with each other.[17] On the other hand, David D. Gladfelter, who assumed the daunting task of trying to assign many patriotic token dies to specific issuers, stated that Sigel and Roloff were independent of each other, and also that Charles D. Hörter was not affiliated with Sigel.[18]

Sayre, Joseph J. • Cincinnati, Ohio • 1861 *Williams' Cincinnati Directory:* Joseph Sayre, stamp and brand cutter, 314 West 9th Street, a listing continued later. No Civil War token–era dies specifically ascribed to Sayre have been identified, but likely he made some. A Sayre store card listed in the second edition of *U.S. Civil War Store Cards* as OH-165-FE has since been determined to be non-contemporary.

Scovill Manufacturing Co. • Waterbury, Connecticut • Although the firm was among the better-known strikers of Hard Times tokens (circa 1832–1844) and merchants' tokens of the 1845–1860 era, relatively little is known about its activities with Civil War issues. Many dies have been ascribed to Scovill—particularly the store cards with a brassy appearance (New York state issuers such as Robinson & Ballou, Wing, et al.) and similar patriotics (the 1863 "Flag" issues and others), not much of a factual nature has ever been confirmed. The Waterbury Button Co. may have made some of these or related style dies.[19]

Senour, William • Cincinnati, Ohio • In the 1860s Senour was associated with William K. Lanphear in the production of dies. His address was the same as used by Lanphear and diecutter Frederick W. Lutz: 102 West Forth Street. Certain of his dies have the inscriptions in connected script letters, an unusual style. The obverse die for OH-165-FM, signed in script, *Wm. Senour*, with flourishes above and below, may have been intended as a personal token or business card.

Sigel, Emil • New York City, New York • During the Civil War Sigel was located at 177 William Street, New York City and was that city's most prolific issuer of patriotic tokens and Civil War store cards, including many special issues for the numismatic trade. Sigel was well known in New York City in his time, and after the Civil War worked with the newly reorganized American Numismatic and Archaeological Society in the creation of a medal honoring Abraham Lincoln.

Smith, Frederick B. • New York City, New York • Smith, whose shop was at 122½ Fulton Street during the Civil War, was in the diecutting trade for several decades, including as a partner with Hermann Hartmann in Smith & Hartmann until about 1861, when Hartmann's name disappeared from the directories.

Spencer, William W. • Cincinnati, Ohio • William W. Spencer was born in County Cork in Ireland in 1839. He was a partner with James Murdock Jr. in Murdock & Spencer, engravers who operated in the shop of John Stanton at 139 West 5th Street until about 1868 after which he worked on his own account, including using dies from the former John Stanton and Murdock & Spencer businesses. In the early 1870s he was a partner in Spencer & Stanton.

Stanton, John • Cincinnati, Ohio • John Stanton was a diesinker from about 1852 into the 1870s. In the early years he was a partner with Z. Bisbee (who claimed to be in that trade since 1835, although information is scarce on that point). In *Williams' Directory* for 1861 Stanton is listed as a stamp and brand cutter, 139 West 5th Street. Home at 107 West 5th Street. Benjamin C. True was listed as a diecutter at the same business address. In the advertising section, p. 419, Stanton was not listed under "engravers," but was entered under "stamp cutters," the only other entry being L. Autenreith (southwest corner of 4th and Walnut streets). The *Williams'* directories were notoriously erratic. Stanton hired various engravers and also made an arrangement for Murdock & Spencer to operate in his shop at 139 West 5th Street. This partnership then succeeded to his interests in 1864. Stanton is considered to have been the largest volume producer of Civil War store cards. His products were sold far and wide, except in the Northeast, where most of the trade went to Eastern makers. Stanton was also the most prolific maker of sutlers' tokens, some of which shared store card reverse dies. *As Stanton and Murdock & Spencer used many of the same dies, "Stanton" in the present text also refers to Murdock & Spencer for tokens 1864 and later.*

Waterbury Button Co. • Waterbury, Connecticut • It is thought by some that this manufacturer of buttons, which claimed to have been founded in 1812, was also the maker of many Civil War tokens, but facts are elusive. It was suggested by the late Robert Lindesmith that certain Troy, New York, tokens such as those by Robinson & Ballou and Boutwell, as well as the Dix patriotic tokens, might be the products of this firm.[20] There has been no confirmation of this.

Wilson, J.G. • New York City, New York • The initials JGW, widely spaced, are found below the word CENT on the die of the "Not One Cent" patriotic token known as Fuld 0362. As to whether J.G.W. made store cards is not known, but none have been seen with his initials. The *New York Times*, May 12, 1863, carried this advertisement: "Copper Tokens for Sale. J.G. Wilson, medalist and copper token manufacturer, No. 42 Centre St. (in the rear), New York. Trade supplied at the lowest prices." Little else is known about Wilson, and it is likely that his trade in tokens was ephemeral.[21]

APPENDIX II

LOCATION UNKNOWN CIVIL WAR STORE CARDS

The following Civil War store cards are believed to be contemporary, but the location of the issuer has not been verified. In some instances earlier attributions could not be confirmed. Listed alphabetically by issuer or inscription; LU = Location Unknown.

A. & H. • LU-A • Earlier listed as OH-175-A.

Clark & Co. • LU-D • Earlier listed as PA-985-A. Watch repair check

Consulere Generi Hominum • LU-E • Earlier listed as OH-165-AD. Satirical numismatic token issued by the shop of John Stanton and thus likely deserving of listing as a Stanton CWT of Cincinnati.

Continental Hotel • LU-G • Earlier listed as OH-165-ADb and 165-FM-06. There were multiple hotels with this name, none listed in Cincinnati during the Civil War.

Continental, The • LU-F • Earlier listed as OH-165-ADa. Hotel.

Hill • LU-M • Earlier listed as OH-165-BW 7 to 10. "One Shave." Barber.

Hughes, P. • LU-O • Earlier listed as OH-165-CA. "Good for One 5 Cent Loaf of Bread."

I.X.L. Dairy / Lott Scott • LU-W • Earlier listed as OH-165-K.

K.S. • LU-S • Earlier listed as patriotic 496/497.

Katzenstein, J. • LU-P • Earlier listed as OH-165-CI.

O.G. • LU-K • Earlier listed as OH-165-BE.

Robins Garden • LU-R • New listing.

S. & N. • **LU-T** • Earlier listed as OH-165-FL-3 to 10.

Sam's Inn • LU-V • Earlier listed as AM-115-F. Dies by Merriam; earlier attributed to Boston. No related Boston Civil War directory or other listing has been found.

Scott, Lot / I.X.L. Dairy • LU-W • Earlier listed as OH-165-K. Possibly from Nashville, Tennessee, but not confirmed.

St. Lawrence • LU-U • Earlier listed as OH-165-DZ-2.

Town Branch Store • LU-Z Earlier listed as MI-280-F. May have been in Lexington, Kentucky, but no confirmation has been found.

W.P.E. • LU-H • Earlier listed as patriotic 284A/463

Wilson, S. (S. Wilson's Billiard Saloon) • LU-AB Earlier listed as SNL-4.

Wood & Harrison • LU-AC Earlier listed as OH-165-GQ.

FULD NUMBERS NOW NON-CONTEMPORARY

Fuld numbers assigned to store cards in the second edition of *U.S. Civil War Store Cards*, but which in the third edition will be given NC (Non-Contemporary) designations:

IL-150-AB • NC-IL-A • William Harlev

IL-150-AC • NC-IL-B • Harlev & Johnson

IL-150-BD • NC-IL-D • Peter Stumps

IL-300-A • NC-IL-E • George Van Dorn

IL-692-A (OH-165-EZ earlier) • NC-IL-A • Yankee Robinson. Only postwar issues numbered 14, 17, and 21.

IN-320-A • NC-TX-A • R.S. McKeen & Co.

IN-460-Y • NC-IN-D • J.D. Wilson. Varieties listed as 3 and 4.

IN-730-A • NC-IN-B • J. Holker

IN-890-A • NC-IN-A • Frank Heinig & Bro.

IN-930-A • NC-IN-C • Charles F. Raker

KY-370-A • NC-KY-B • W.S. Johnson & Bro.

MO-880-A • NC-MO-A • John Kenmuir

NY-630-R • NC-NY-A • G.A. Defandorf

OH-005-A • NC-OH-AA • Stoner & Shroyer. Only varieties 5 and 6.

OH-160-C • NC-OH-D • Jas. Driscoll

OH-165-AR • NC-OH-E • Fifth Street Garden

OH-165-AT • NC-OH-F • Fisler & Chance

OH-165-BAa. • NC-OH-H • Galway, Smith & Co.

OH-165-BF • NC-OH-J • R.G.

OH-165-BG • NC-OH-J • Robert Gohs

OH-165-DI • NC-AR-A • R.T. Markham

OH-165-DY • NC-OH-R • James Murdock Jr.

OH-165-U • NC-OH-B • Central Coal Office

OH-165-DZ • NC-OH-S • Murdock & Spencer

OH-165-EI • NC-OH-T • B. Panzer

OH-165-EP • NC-OH-U • H. Ransick

OH-165-EY • NC-OH-V • F.H. Rollins

OH-165-FA • NC-OH-W • Albert Ross

OH-165-FD • NC-OH-X • Sackstedter & Martin

OH-165-FE • NC-OH-Y • Joseph H Sayre

OH-165-FL • NC-OH-Z • Schultz & Negley

OH-170-A • NC-OH-G • French (One French)

OH-170-B • NC-OH-M • James & French

OH-170-C • NC-OH-P • Mauck & Bradbury

OH-345-C • NC-OH-I • S. Goetz

OH-345-D • NC-OH-L • Henking, Allemong & Co.

OH-615-A • NC-OH-A • A.J. Blocksom

PA-750-B • NC-PA-A • M.B. Allebach. Only varieties 2 and 3.

PA-750-J • NC-PA-D • R. Flanagan

PA-750-K • NC-PA-E • J. Henry Gercke

VA-580-A • NC-VA-A • Pfeiffer & Co.

WI-510-D • NC-WI-B • Best & Co.

APPENDIX

NON-CONTEMPORARY STORE CARDS, BY ISSUER

The following store cards were listed as Civil War–era issues earlier but are now classified as having been made before April 1861 or after April 1865. These are classified alphabetically by the name of issuer or inscription plus a letter starting with A for each of the issuers within a given state. Compiled by John Ostendorf for the Civil War Token Society. NC = Non-Contemporary. The next two digits are the state abbreviation. This group is a mixed bag—some tokens that were earlier considered to be of Civil War vintage and others that are obviously not.

There are many pre-1861 store cards that are still listed among regular Civil War store cards, such as those with reverse die 1368. The rationale is that some earlier tokens continued to be *used* during the war. The W. Bell counterstamped cents of 1859 (PA-360-A) are in this category. Such are judgment calls that are inconsistent and can be made as desired.

Allebach, M.B. • NC-PA-A • Earlier listed as PA-750-B. Style is thought to be postwar. Allebach was at the stated address during the war. Combined with reverse dies 1154, 1182, and 1193 (which is dated 1863). Likely, all tokens using these dies are postwar, although others are listed as CWT.[1]

Best & Co. • NC-WI-B • Earlier listed as WI-510-D. Brewer. This name was given to the Empire Brewing Co. in 1869 after it changed hands.[2]

Blocksom, A.J. • NC-OH-A • Earlier listed as OH-615-A. Thought to have been struck after the war, but facts are scarce. A specimen in EF grade sold for $650 in the P.C.A.C. sale of May 30, 1981. Blocksom also issued shell cards in the late 1860s.

Bock, Wm. • NC-PA-B • Earlier listed as NC-4b. Hotel owner. Thought to have been struck circa 1875–1885.

Centennial Advertising Medal Co. • NC-PA-C • Earlier listed as NC-10. Obviously from the 1870s. Made many tokens and medals for the 1876 Centennial Exhibition.

Central Coal Office • NC-OH-B • Earlier listed as OH-165-U. Believed to be postwar. The style is unlike that of the major Cincinnati token shops (Stanton, Spencer, Murdock, and Lanphear).

Central National Home for D.V.S. • NC-OH-C • Earlier listed as PA-750-G and NC-39. Veterans' home in Dayton, Ohio.

Defandorf, G.A. • NC-NY-A • Earlier listed as NY-630-R. Dentist. Began business in 1872.

Dodsworth, Robert • NC-KY-A • Earlier listed as NC-38b. Cold Spring, Kentucky.

Driscoll, Jas. • NC-OH-D • Earlier listed as OH-160-C. CWTS: First listed in Chillicothe in 1876. However: Robert E. Daniel, "Chillicothe, Ohio: C.W. Merchants' Cards," *JCWTS*, Fall 1988: "James Driscoll was proprietor of the Railroad House on Main Street, west of Sugar Street, near the Marietta & Cincinnati Railroad depot. The rate of $1 per day during the Civil War included room and board, the latter indicating that food was served."

Dunlap & Florer Osage Traders • NC-IT-A • Earlier listed as SNL-5 to 7. Post traders in Indian Territory in the 1870s.

Eureka • NC-LU-C • Earlier listed as NC-12; Rulau MV600-615. Dated 1867.

Fifth Street Garden • NC-OH-E • Earlier listed as OH-165-AR. Struck after 1875 as evidenced by the address of minter Murdock on the token.

Fisler & Chance • NC-OH-F • Earlier listed as OH-165-AT. Business commenced on June 19, 1866.

Flanagan, R. • NC-PA-D • Earlier listed as PA-750-J. Listed by Bushnell in 1858. The inscription "Pure Copper Preferable to Paper" is a Civil War sentiment, but here it was used earlier.

Frantz, H. • NC-NY-AB • In the 1870s he counterstamped certain Skidmore Hotel NY-845-A tokens.

French (One French) • NC-OH-G • Earlier listed as OH-170-A. Dated 1873. For years it was thought this was an error for 1863, but it is now known that French was not in business until after the war. Issued by James and French (see listing under J), apparently as one cent (per ONE above the name on the token).

Galway, Smith & Co. • NC-OH-H • Earlier listed as OH-165-BAa. Business started in the 1880s.

Gercke, J. Henry • NC-PA-E • Earlier listed as PA-750-K. Gercke first occupied the address on the token in 1872.

Goetz, S. • NC-OH-I • Earlier listed as OH-345-C. Goetz did not move to Gallipolis until 1872.

Gohs, Robert • NC-OH-K • Earlier listed as OH-165-BG. Struck in 1875 or later as evidenced by the 165 Race Street address of coiner Murdock. Also see R.G. below.

Harlev & Johnson • NC-IL-B • Earlier listed as IL-150-AC. Chicago seller of trunks. In business circa 1873–1875.

Harlev, William • NC-IL-A • Earlier listed as IL-150-AB. Successor to Harlev & Johnson. Chicago seller of trunks.

Heinig, Frank, & Bro. (Frank Heinig & Bro., Union Steam Bakery) • NC-IN-A • Earlier listed as IN-890-A. Business thought to have commenced in 1866.

Henking, Allemong & Co. • NC-OH-L • Earlier listed as OH-345-D. Began business in 1867.

Holker, J. • NC-IN-B • Earlier listed as IN-730-A. Holker is not listed in Oldenburg until 1868.

James & French • NC-OH-M • Earlier listed as OH-170-B. Little information available but thought to be postwar.[3] Same issuer as One French (see listing under F).

Johnson, W.S., & Bro. • NC-KY-B • Earlier listed as KY-370-A. Did not begin business until after the war. Druggists.

Kenmuir, John • NC-MO-A • Earlier listed as MO-880-A. Kenmuir was not in St. Joseph until 1873.

M.B.C. • NC-LU-A • Earlier listed as NC-41a. Dated 1878.

M.S.C. • NC-LU-B • Earlier listed as NC-18a. "Although the reverse die resembles 1194 and 1195 this token was probably struck between 1880 and 1890.[4]

Markham, R.T. • NC-AR-A • Earlier listed as OH-165-DI. Saloon token. Now thought to have been issued in Arkansas in the 1880s.

Martin, S.C. • NC-OH-O • Earlier listed as NC-3b. Thought to have been issued circa 1890–1910.

Mason & Co. • NC-PA-F • Earlier listed as NC-16 despite being dated 1870 and never considered a Civil War token. One of several business styles used by coin dealer Ebenezer Locke Mason Jr.

Mauck & Bradbury • NC-OH-P • Earlier listed as OH-170-C. Business dates from the 1870s.

McKeen, R.S., & Co. • NC-TX-A • Earlier listed as IN-320-A. Thought by Steve Tanenbaum and others to have been issued in Galveston, Indiana. However, the firm is mentioned in Galveston, Texas, soon after the war. Galveston was under blockade and martial law until June 19, 1865.

McLaughlin, Jas. • NC-OH-N • Earlier listed as NC-2. The die style is thought to have dated from no earlier than the 1870s.

Merchants Exchange • NC-OH-Q • Earlier listed as NC-1b. CWTS: Probably struck 1870–1875.

Milwaukee Soldiers Home Fair • NC-WI-C • Earlier listed as NC-17. Event held in June 1865.

Murdock & Spencer • NC-OH-S • Earlier listed as OH-165-DZ. Dates from 1868.

Murdock, James, Jr. • NC-OH-R • Earlier listed as OH-165-DY-1. Address of 165 Race Street dates from 1875.

Needles, C.H. • NC-PA-G • Earlier listed as NC-19. CWTS: Likely struck between 1858 and 1860. Probably *used* during the Civil War.

Panzer, B. • NC-OH-T • Earlier listed as OH-165-EI. Struck circa 1868.

Pfeiffer & Co. • NC-VA-A • Earlier listed as VA-580-A. Struck circa 1870.

Preston, C.W. • NC-IA-A • Earlier listed as NC-5a. General merchant.

R.G. • NC-OH-J • Earlier listed as OH-165-BF. Postwar. Issuer unknown, Robert Gohs (see listing under Gohs) has been suggested. The address of coiner Murdock, 165 Race Street, indicates a date of 1875 or later.

Raker, Charles F. • NC-IN-C • Earlier listed as IN-930-A. Raker was in the Army from June 1861 until March 1865. Unless someone else conducted his business (which sometimes happened during the war) the token was likely postwar.

Rankin & Gibbs Sac & Fox Traders • NC-IT-B • Earlier listed as SNL-5. Post traders in Indian Territory in the 1870s.

Ransick, H. • NC-OH-U • Earlier listed as OH-165-EP. First occupied the location stated on the token in 1872.

Robinson, Yankee • NC-IL-A • Fuld IL-692-A. After the war Yankee Robinson issued more tokens. Earlier Robinson was listed as OH-165-EZ and his several postwar issues were numbered 14, 17, and 21.

Rollins, F.H. • NC-OH-V • Earlier listed as OH-165-EY. Rollins was at the stated address in 1870–1871.

Ross, Albert • NC-OH-W • Earlier listed as OH-165-FA. Slightly pre-war as evidenced by a token appearing at auction in 1860.

Ryan, A.E. • NC-MN-A • Earlier listed as NC-6b. Did not commence business until 1868.

S.B. • NC-WI-A • Earlier listed as NC-37b.

Sackstedter & Martin • NC-OH-X • Earlier listed as OH-165-FD • This partnership was active in 1868 and 1869.

Sage, Augustus B. • NC-NY-C • Earlier listed as NC-21. Dated 1859. Prominent New York City rare-coin dealer 1858–1860, founder of the American Numismatic Society. Faded from the scene in 1861.

Sayre, Joseph H. • NC-OH-Y • Earlier listed as OH-165-FE • At this address beginning in 1868.

Schultz & Negley • NC-OH-Z • Earlier listed as OH-165-FL • This partnership began in 1871.

Small, Robert • NC-MN-B • Earlier listed as NC-7a. 20th-century issue. The listed town was not established until 1905.

Stoner & Shroyer • NC-OH-AA • Earlier listed as OH-005-A-5 and 6 • These particular varieties are postwar; other varieties are listed in chapter 7. It may be that all tokens of this merchant are postwar.

Stumps, Peter • NC-IL-D • Earlier listed as IL-150-BD. Maker of firemen's hats and belts. First listed at the token address in 1870.

Taylor, A.B. • NC-PA-H • This particular token was earlier listed as NC-23. Druggist. For store cards that Taylor *did* issue during the Civil War see his listing in chapter 7.

Van Dorn, George • NC-IL-E • Earlier listed as IL-300-A. Operated as a dry-goods merchant in Fairview after 1866, continuing until about 1873.

Weilacher, John • NC-IN-E • Billiard-hall owner who began business in 1879.

Whitney Glass Works • NC-NJ-A • Earlier listed as NC-29. Issued no earlier than 1869. See postwar listing in Russell Rulau, *Standard Catalog of U.S. Store Cards 1700–1900*.

Wilson, J.D. • NC-IN-D • Earlier listed as IN-460-Y-3 and 4. Believed to have been struck in St. Louis, Missouri, in the late 1850s. Baker.

Wood Co. • NC-WI-D • Earlier listed as NC-30 to 32.

Y. & T. • NC-CT-A • Earlier listed as NC-35a. Possibly Yale & Towne, Stamford, Connecticut, lock manufacturers established in 1868.

APPENDIX
V

ENCASED POSTAGE STAMPS OF 1862

In terms of modern numismatic interest, the most important means of filling the need for small change was the Civil War token. Encased postage stamps, however, also met some of this need. Designed and patented by John Gault, the encasements each consisted of a two-part brass frame. The obverse displayed a current postage stamp visible under a pane of mica; the reverse bore an advertisement. Thirty-one different merchants, products, and services were represented. The stamps, which were legal tender under the Act of July 17, 1862, included the denominations of 1, 3, 5, 10, 12, 24, 30, and 90 cents.

Encasements of most merchants, with stamps of the 1- to 10-cent denominations, come on the market with frequency. Typical grades are Very Fine and Extremely Fine, often with some slight flaking of the mica or with some cracks. Some have traces of silvering on the back. The front frames in a few instances are "ribbed" with closely spaced horizontal ridges.

For values, see *A Guide Book of United States Paper Money.*

Aërated Bread Company (New York City), located on the corner of Lafayette Place and Fourth Street, was founded by Stephen F. Ambler of Brooklyn. Ambler "aerated" his dough by injecting it with carbonated gas, resulting in unusually light bread. His process was at first successful as a novelty item, but ultimately failed for lack of customers.

Ayer's Cathartic Pills (Lowell, Massachusetts) were a product of James C. Ayer and Company, John Gault's biggest single customer, advertising three different patent-medicine products on their encasements. Ayer's Cathartic Pills were advertised as an aid to digestion, with the reverse inscription THE CURRENCY TO PASS (a pun on elimination?). These have Plain Frame and reverses with either Short or Long Arrows. **"Take Ayer's Pills"** was issued in large quantities and are among the most plentiful today. Plain Frame and Ribbed Frame (rare) styles exist. The typeface used on this issue is the largest in the series. **Ayer's Sarsaparilla** exists with AYER'S either small, medium, or large, and with either the Plain or Ribbed Frame style.

Bailey & Company (Philadelphia), a large jewelry firm, was founded in 1832 under the name of Bailey & Kitchen. It moved in 1859 to the address on its encasements: 819 Chestnut (misspelled as "Chesnut") Street. In 1861 an agent for the Confederate government proposed that the company strike cents for the Confederacy. The firm commissioned local diesinker Robert Lovett Jr. to cut the dies. Bailey & Company encasements are fairly scarce; all are of the Plain Frame style.

Joseph L. Bates (Boston) was a purveyor of luxury items for the carriage trade as well as a pioneer in the selling of stereographic viewers and cards. Bates's address, 129 Washington Street, appears on his encasements, which are found with two reverse varieties: FANCY GOODS as two words (normal) and FANCYGOODS.

Brown's Bronchial Troches (Boston) were a product of John I. Brown, who reaped profits from worthless patent medicines, including this one. The encasements are among the more plentiful in the series. All are of the Plain Frame style. The back is one of just two in the series with no beading or dots around the border.

F. Buhl and Company (Detroit, Michigan), dealers in men's and women's hats and furs, were the only Detroit company to commission encasements from Gault. Buhl encasements range from scarce to rare. All are of the Plain Frame style.

H.A. Cook (Evansville, Indiana) was a family business that began as a grocery store and was expanded to carry live poultry, axle grease, brooms, and brushes, along with a line of luxury consumer goods (English ales, Brazilian coffee, French figs, etc.). Cook encasements are among the rarer issues. All are of the Plain Frame style.

Burnett's Cocoaine Kalliston (Boston) was an advertisement for the products of Joseph Burnett, who studied medicine and styled himself "doctor" although he never practiced. Joseph Burnett & Co. marketed perfumes, extracts, and other goods of the sort. Its encasement advertised three personal-care products: Cocoaine (a coconut oil–based hair tonic that had nothing to do with cocaine), Kalliston (a diluted skin cream), and toilet sets. The encasements, issued in large numbers, are plentiful today. All are of the Plain Frame style. **Burnett's Standard Cooking Extracts** was a line of 12 different flavorings for use in cooking. Issued in large numbers, the encasements are plentiful today. All are of the Plain Frame style.

Dougan the Hatter (New York City) was situated on the corner of Nassau and Ann streets in downtown Manhattan. Today part of the financial district, the area was then a warren of narrow, crowded, noisy streets populated by small establishments. In a time and place where men who could afford it seldom went hatless, Dougan's was no doubt popular. The encasements are rare, and are the only issue with an image of the advertised product (in this case, a hat). All are of the Plain Frame style.

Arthur M. Claflin (Hopkinton, Massachusetts) opened a clothing store in his native Massachusetts. He issued a modest quantity of encased postage stamps, and today the Claflin encasement is among the rarest in the series. All are of the Plain Frame style.

Drake's Plantation Bitters (New York City) were a produced by Col. Patrick H. Drake. Made largely of West Indian rum, nearly 100 proof, the drink's flavorings included Angostura bitters, cardamom, and raisins. The backs of the encasements feature the cryptogram S.T.1860.X (S.T. for Saint, 1860 for Croi, and X for itself; together, "St. Croix," the source of the company's rum). This encasement is one of the most plentiful. Most are of the Plain Frame style.

Ellis, McAlpin & Company (Cincinnati) was the wholesale dry-goods business founded by John Washington Ellis and George Washington McAlpin. All encasements of this issuer are scarce, and all are of the Plain Frame style.

G.G. Evans (Philadelphia) was both a highly successful bookstore in 1854 and (as advertised on its encasements) a distributor of wines from California; they were claimed to be "Absolutely Pure" in contrast to the watered-down vintages sometimes shipped to the East. Some specialists believe Evans's encasements were made in violation of Gault's patent: they lack Gault's notice of patent on the back; they are somewhat different in fabric; their backs are concave, with wider, rounded rims; and the pane of mica is usually concave, with a pushed-in appearance, suggesting a thinner cardboard backing than used in Gault products. Evans's encasements are quite scarce. All are of the Plain Frame style.

Gage Brothers & Drake / Tremont House (Chicago) encasements advertise the resplendent Tremont House Hotel.

Opened for business in 1850, the hotel was later purchased by David and George Gage; John B. Drake purchased an interest in the hotel two years afterward. The final S of BROTHERS was inadvertently omitted from the advertisement. Sometimes alphabetized under "Tremont," these encasements are slightly scarce. Nearly all are of the Plain Frame style.

John Gault (Boston and New York City), owner of the encased-postage patent, issued his own encased postage stamps in the summer of 1862, before he became a partner in Kirkpatrick & Gault. Examples are among the most common today, and exist in Plain and Ribbed Frame styles.

L.C. Hopkins & Co. (Cincinnati) was the dry-goods firm of Lewis C. Hopkins. Located at Fifth and Vine streets, the company landed large supply contracts with the Union army during the Civil War. These contracts caused Hopkins to neglect other aspects of his business, which went into decline, ultimately failing in the early 1870s. Hopkins encasements are rare. All are of the Plain Frame style.

Hunt & Nash / Irving House (New York City) is the issue of the fashionable Irving House hotel, at the corner of Broadway and 12th Street. The encasements advertised the hotel's "European Plan": customers were charged a flat rate for their rooms, with all other services at an additional charge. These issues are among the most common, and exist in both Plain and Ribbed Frame styles. The back is one of just two in the series with no beading or dots around the border.

Kirkpatrick & Gault (New York City) was a partnership between Joseph Kirkpatrick and John Gault. Kirkpatrick seems to have been the business manager and general expediter; nothing more is known of his career. Encasements of this issuer are slightly scarcer than the earlier John Gault pieces, and exist in Plain Frame style only. The patent date, but not Gault's name, appears high in the field among the inscriptions.

Lord & Taylor (New York City) began as a small dry-goods business run by English immigrant Samuel Lord, who'd borrowed $1,000 from his wife's uncle, John Taylor. By 1853 Lord & Taylor had become America's first department store. Encasements of Lord & Taylor are slightly scarce, and enjoy a special popularity as the issuer is well known today. All are of the Plain Frame style.

Mendum's Family Wine Emporium (New York City), a wine and foodstuff business, was started by George Mendum in the 1850s. His second store was at the corner of Broadway and Cedar Street, the address found on his encasements. Mendum named his business a "family" emporium to lessen the stigma attached to the sale and consumption of alcohol. These encasements are slightly scarce. Almost all are of the Plain Frame style.

B.F. Miles (Peoria, Illinois), a wholesale and retail drug business, also sold paints, different grades of lubricating oil, and glassware. Owner Benjamin Franklin Miles was a qualified physician but had decided not to go into practice. His shop became a center for the city's social life, and prospered through the Civil War years. The Miles encasement is generally considered the rarest of the issues—the key to a collection. All are of the Plain Frame style.

John W. Norris (Chicago) began in business before 1860, selling books, local newspapers, and magazines, and later expanding to include diaries, song books, and stationery. The business was located at 102 Madison Street; the encasements are among the rarer issues in the series. All are of the Plain Frame style.

North America Life Insurance Company

North America Life Insurance Company (New York City) was founded in 1862 by Nathan Dennison Morgan, and had offices at 63 William Street. The firm prospered during the Civil War by writing insurance policies for Northern soldiers. Due to its involvement in postwar real-estate speculation, the company collapsed following the Panic of 1873. Its encasements' reverses have either INSURANCE straight and with patent information curved along the bottom border, or with INSURANCE in a curve and the patent information in one straight line and one curved line at the bottom. Plain Frame and Ribbed Frame varieties exist of each.

Sands's Ale (Milwaukee, Wisconsin) was founded by Josiah J. Sands, a Chicago brewer who'd developed a lager-making process that gave his products a longer shelf life than those of his competitors. In 1859 Sands sent his brothers to Milwaukee to purchase a brewery already in operation, and during the Civil War years the company enjoyed increased success. By 1867, however, the Milwaukee brewery was sold. Sands's encasements are among the rarest in the series. All are of the Plain Frame style.

Pearce, Tolle, & Holton (Cincinnati), a wholesale dry-goods firm, was formed in Cincinnati in the early 1860s. Partners were William B. Pearce, Alexander M. Holton, Thomas Porter Jr., and W.B. Tolle. Most of the company's products were shipped down the Ohio River to the Mississippi and thence into the interior. The diecutter who punched the message on the back of these encasements incorrectly spelled TOLLE as TOOLE; when the error was noticed, an L was punched over the erroneous O. Encasements of this issuer are rare. All are of the Plain Frame style.

Schapker & Bussing (Evansville, Indiana), seller of dry goods, millinery, and carpets, was the second of Gault's clients in Evansville. Like H.A. Cook, Schapker & Bussing was located on Main Street. Owned by German immigrants Bernard Schapker and John W. Bussing, the firm was hit hard by the Panic of 1873, and eventually dissolved. Encasements of this issuer are fairly plentiful. All are of the Plain Frame style.

John Shillito & Co. (Cincinnati), a dry-goods store, was founded in 1830; its founder, John Shillito, had begun merchandising in 1817, at the age of nine. In 1857 he built the store he later advertised on his encasements. The company remained in Shillito's family until its sale in 1928. Encasements are fairly plentiful. All are of the Plain Frame style.

S. Steinfeld (New York City), located at 70 Nassau Street, began life in 1855 as a confectionery store. Later that year founder Simon Steinfeld secured the agency for French Cognac Bitters (which took advantage of the law that allowed the sale of so-called medicinal alcohol); he then renovated the candy store as a saloon. Steinfeld is one of the rarer issuers; nearly all the examples seen are of the 1¢ denomination. All are of the Plain Frame style.

N.G. Taylor & Co. (Philadelphia) was a metals merchant established around 1810. Its product line grew to include such diverse products as sheet iron and copper, machine tools, tin cans, milk cans, and lead products. N.G. Taylor & Company was one of only four of Gault's clients who also advertised on metal tokens. Taylor encasements are among the rarer issues. All are of the Plain Frame style.

Weir & Larminie (Montreal, Canada), a banking, exchange, and bullion-dealing firm, was Gault's sole foreign client. The company was founded by Scottish immigrant William Weir shortly before the Civil War; G.H. Larminie, of whom little is known, was later a partner. Unfortunately, Weir issued fraudulent statements about the soundness of his operations and made dubious loans. He was indicted, tried for fraud, and convicted. Weir & Larminie encasements are among the rarer issues. All are of the Plain Frame style.

White the Hatter (New York City) was the eponymous hat-making business of George W. White. Located in Greenwich Village, White relocated in 1855 to the ground floor of 216 Broadway, the same building that housed P.T. Barnum's famous American Museum. After two fires on the premises White moved to a new location and expanded his business to include a clothing store, two woolen-goods stores, and a "fancy goods emporium." During 1863 White commissioned a series of Civil War tokens; these are very plentiful in numismatic circles today. White the Hatter issues are rare. All are of the Plain Frame style.

Step Right Up!

What, exactly, were the encased postage stamps of 1862 advertising? Many of the products being hawked were tonics, sarsaparillas, digestive aids, and other marvels of modern medicine—some of them beneficial, others simply "snake oil," at best unproven, possibly fraudulent, and in certain cases addictive or otherwise harmful. The following gallery showcases some of the colorful advertising of the day.

Gentlemen posing with distinctive log-cabin-shaped bottles of Drake's Plantation Bitters— a "digestive aid" that was almost 40% rum. Good for what ails you.

A trade card of Dr. James Cook Ayer of Lowell, Massachusetts, who made a fortune selling patent medicines. Here, Ayer's Cathartic Pills bring a promise of rosy-cheeked good health.

Ayer's Cathartic Pills

are purely vegetable. They contain the active remedial principles, only, of their various ingredients, extracted and highly concentrated, and are scientifically compounded in a manner which insures great certainty and uniformity of medicinal effect. These Pills have won the confidence of physicians, and it is through a knowledge of their composition, and a practical experience of their curative power and safety, that they have become so generally used in practice.

Ayer's Pills, being sugar-coated, will retain their virtues for an indefinite period. They are easy to take; mild, but effective; and may be administered to children with perfect safety.

As an after-dinner Pill, to stimulate digestion in dyspeptic stomachs, Ayer's Pills have no equal. These Pills, used daily in decreasing doses, will restore the stomach, liver, and bowels to natural and heathful action, without causing costiveness. This is a quality in which they are altogether unrivaled.

☞ Not a particle of calomel nor any other deleterious substance enters into the composition of these Pills. They are usually put up in oval wooden boxes; but for hot and damp climates and for export in sealed glass vials.

PREPARED BY

Dr. J. C. AYER & CO., Lowell, Mass., U. S. A.

FOR SALE BY

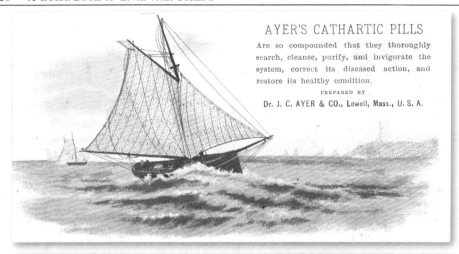

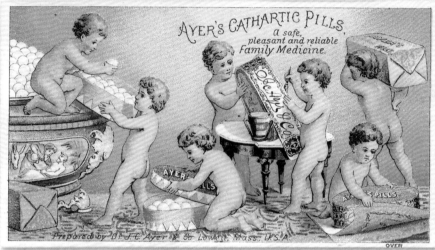

AYER'S PILLS

are the result of years of chemical research and practical experiment. They are compounded from the extracted and concentrated virtues of purely vegetable substances, and combine the choicest cathartic principles in medicine, in proportions accurately adjusted to secure the best curative effects. They are entirely free from croton oil, calomel, or other dangerous substances; they are sugar-coated and pleasant to take, and while sufficiently powerful to act upon the most robust, are the safest physic to employ for children and weakened constitutions, where a gentle yet efficient cathartic is required. They purify, invigorate and enrich the blood, stimulate it to healthy circulation, and, if taken occasionally, keep the system in perfect order. Mild, searching, and effectual, **Ayer's Pills** are specially adapted to the needs of the Stomach, Liver, and Bowels, whose derangements they prevent and cure. They are a sure remedy for Costiveness, Jaundice, Indigestion, Headache, Dizziness, transient attacks of Numbness, Biliousness, and all other diseases resulting from a disordered state of the Digestive Apparatus. As a Dinner Pill they have no equal. Their extensive use by physicians and by the people of all civilized nations, for all the purposes of a family physic, proves their value as a reliable medicine for professional and family use.

Ayer's Pills *are usually put up in oval wooden boxes, as represented on the face of this card; but for hot or damp climates, and for export, in sealed glass vials, as above.*

Prepared by **Dr. J. C. Ayer & Co., Lowell, Mass., U. S. A.**

Sold by all Druggists and Dealers in Medicine.

Ayer's Cathartic Pills were nearly a cure-all, according to their advertising. Headaches, stomachaches, dysentery, heartburn, general crankiness, indigestion, constipation, liver troubles—all would be banished by the sugar-coated pill.

AYER'S PILLS.

ARE you sick, feeble and complaining? Are you out of order, with your system deranged and your feelings uncomfortable? These symptoms are often the prelude to serious illness. Some fit of sickness is creeping upon you, and should be averted by a timely use of the right remedy. Take Ayer's Pills, and cleanse out the disordered humors—purify the blood, and let the fluids move on unobstructed in health again. They stimulate the functions of the body into vigorous activity, purify the system from the obstructions which make disease. A cold settles somewhere in the body and obstructs its natural functions. These, if not relieved, react upon themselves and the surrounding organs, producing general aggravation, suffering and disease. While in this condition, oppressed by the derangements, take Ayer's Pills, and see how directly they restore the natural action of the system, and with it the buoyant feeling of health again. What is true and so apparent in this trivial and common complaint, is also true in many of the deep-seated and dangerous distempers. The same purgative effect expels them. Caused by similar obstructions and derangements of the natural functions of the body, they are rapidly and many of them surely cured by the same means. None who know the virtues of these Pills will neglect to employ them when suffering from the disorders they cure, such as Headache, Foul Stomach, Dysentery, Bilious Complaints, Indigestion, Derangement of the Liver, Costiveness or Constipation. As a Dinner Pill they are both agreeable and effectual.

Price 25 Cents per Box, or Five Boxes for $1.
Prepared by DR. J. C. AYER & CO., Lowell, Mass.

THE FIGHT FOR THE STANDARD.

"'The Fight for the Standard' is over," announced the back side of this trade card, "and it is universally acknowledged that AYER'S PILLS are the only STANDARD cathartic medicine of the age. The disorders which they are designed to cure include Constipation or Costiveness, Indigestion, Dyspepsia, Biliousness, Heartburn, Loss of Appetite, Flatulency, Foul Stomach, Nausea, Dizziness, Headache, Numbness, Jaundice, Diarrhea, Dysentery, and Disorders of the Liver.

Eruptions and Skin Diseases, and Piles, when the result of Indigestion or Constipation, are cured by the use of AYER'S PILLS. These PILLS are often, also, the best remedy for Rheumatism, Gout, Neuralgia, Dropsy, and Kidney Complaints. In Colds they operate beneficially by opening the pores, removing inflammatory secretions, and allaying fever."

Dr. Ayer had graduated from the medical school of the University of Pennsylvania. He never practiced medicine," notes *Appletons' Cyclopædia of American Biography* (1900), "but devoted his principal attention to pharmaceutical chemistry and the compounding of medicines. His success in this line was very great, and soon led him to establish in Lowell a factory for the manufacture of his medicinal preparations, which became one of the largest of its kind in the world, and was magnificently equipped. He accumulated a fortune estimated at $20,000,000. Much of his success was due to his advertising, and he published annually an almanac, 5,000,000 copies of which were gratuitously distributed each year. Editions in English, French, German, Portuguese, and Spanish, were regularly issued."

"Without doubt the Discovery of America is Ayer's SARSAPARILLA," proclaims this advertising card. "This is a COMPOUND CONCENTRATED EXTRACT composed of the Sarsaparilla-root of the tropics, Stillingia, Yellow Dock, Mandrake, and other roots held in high repute for their alterative, diuretic, tonic, and curative properties."

AYER'S SARSAPARILLA

The DEACON: "Land sake Liza, the very sight of that bottle makes me feel like another man."

AYER'S SARSAPARILLA IS A COMPOUND CONCENTRATED EXTRACT-
THE STRONGEST, BEST, CHEAPEST BLOOD MEDICINE.

This advertising card exhorted its reader to "bear in mind that [Ayer's Sarsaparilla] is not a mixture of cheap or dangerous drugs, but a highly concentrated extract of the genuine Honduras Sarsaparilla and other choice medicinal roots, alterative, diuretic, and tonic. . . . If there is a lurking taint of Scrofula about you, AYER'S SARSAPARILLA will expel it from your system."

Customers could send 10¢ in cash or postage stamps to Ayer & Co. and would receive "a fine Chromo-Lithograph (7 x 13 inches, in 'Statuette' style)" of the charming illustration, "The Deacon," along with a set of the firm's elegant album cards.

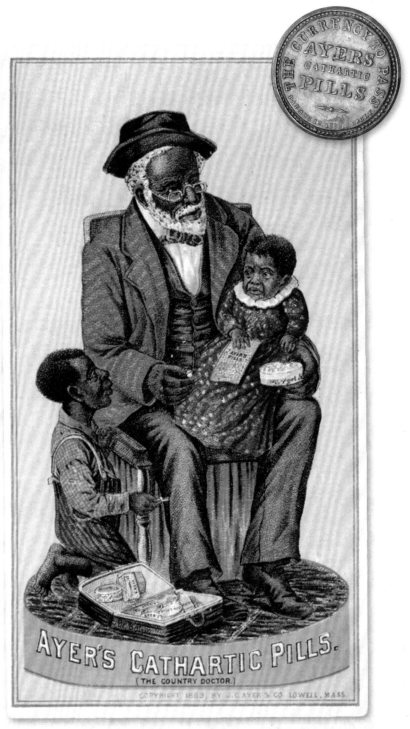

Ayer & Co. would continue to issue colorful and collectible trade cards well after the Civil War. "The Country Doctor" showed a friendly general practitioner ready to ease a troubled baby's ills. Naturally his medical bag is full of Ayer's products.

THIRTY YEARS AGO THE BRONCHIAL TROCHES were introduced, being prepared by combining in a convenient form several medicinal substances held in general esteem among physicians in the treatment of Bronchial Affections and Coughs.

The BRONCHIAL TROCHES contain ingredients acting directly on the organs of the voice. They have an extraordinary effect in all disorders of the Throat and Larynx, restoring a healthy tone when relaxed, either from cold or over-exertion of the voice, and produce a clear and distinct enunciation. To PUBLIC SPEAKERS and SINGERS they will be found invaluable.

Imitations are offered for sale, many of which are injurious. THE GENUINE BRONCHIAL TROCHES ARE SOLD ONLY IN BOXES, with fac-simile of the proprietors on the wrapper.

PRICES, 25 CENTS, 50 CENTS, AND $1 PER BOX.

1850

1880

A COUGH, COLD, or SORE THROAT requires immediate attention. A continuance for any length of time causes irritation of the Lungs, or some chronic Throat Affection. Neglect oftentimes results in some incurable Lung disease. THE TROCHES are not new and untried, but, having been tested by wide and constant use for nearly an entire generation, they have attained well-merited rank among the few staple remedies of the age. BROWN'S BRONCHIAL TROCHES have proved their efficacy by a test of many years, and will almost invariably give immediate relief.

These newspaper ads for John I. Brown & Son of Boston were not as colorful as James Ayer's trade cards, but were just as bombastic in their claims. Every manner of throat and larynx trouble could be cured by Brown's Bronchial Troches. (A *troche* is a medicinal tablet or lozenge.)

BURNETT'S
STANDARD
COOKING
EXTRACTS
OF LEMON VANILLA
ALMOND ROSE &c &c

BURNETT'S

COCOAINE

FOR THE HAIR

IT SOFTENS THE HAIR WHEN HARSH AND DRY. IT SOOTHES THE IRRITATED SCALP. IT AFFORDS THE RICHEST LUSTRE. IT PREVENTS THE HAIR FROM FALLING OFF. IT PROMOTES ITS HEALTHY, VIGOROUS GROWTH. IT IS NOT GREASY NOR STICKY. IT LEAVES NO DISAGREEABLE ODOR. IT KILLS DANDRUFF.

BURNETT'S

KALLISTON

FOR THE SKIN

AS A WASH FOR THE COMPLEXION, IT HAS NO EQUAL. IT IS DISTINGUISHED FOR ITS COOLING AND SOOTHING PROPERTIES, REMOVING TAN, SUNBURN, FRECKLES, REDNESS AND ROUGHNESS OF THE SKIN, ETC.; CURING CHAPPED HANDS, AND ALLAYING THE IRRITATION CAUSED BY THE BITES OF MOSQUITOES AND OTHER ANNOYING INSECTS.

Itching Piles.

BURNETT'S KALLISTON.

A SURE RELIEF
AND A CURE IN MOST CASES.

If your druggist does not keep it, send $1.00 to **JOSEPH BURNETT & CO.,** **27 Central Street, Boston, Mass.** 25 cts. additional will prepay expressage to any part of the United States. Sample by mail on receipt of ten cents.

Burnett's Kalliston,

As a Wash for the Complexion has no Equal. It is distinguished for its soothing and purifying effect, allaying all tendency to inflammation, especially that arising from bites of mosquitoes, stings of insects, &c It is a powerful cleanser of the skin, removing Tan, Freckles, Pimples and all Discolorations. These, with its refreshing and invigorating properties, render it an indispensable requisite for the toilet.

Prepared only by JOSEPH BURNETT & CO., Boston.

For sale By Druggists generally

Price 50 Cents a Bottle. 246-49

Joseph Burnett of Boston had studied pharmacy and medicine but never practiced as a doctor. His products ranged from perfumes to shampoos to extracts and flavorings for cooking. *Cocoaine* in his ads was a reference to the coconut oil used in some tonics, not to cocaine (which was, however, used in various patent medicines of the era).

CINCINNATI : JOHN SHILLITO COMPANY.

INTERIOR VIEW OF JOHN SHILLITO & CO.'S.

The patent-medicine kings weren't the only merchants who issued encased postage stamps. John Shillito opened Cincinnati's first department store, a huge "dry-goods palace" with dining rooms and every manner of retail product a shopper might desire.

APPENDIX

CIVIL WAR
SUTLER TOKENS

Closely related to Civil War tokens are sutler tokens, most of which were made by the same shops that produced Civil War tokens and many of which have Civil War store card dies as reverses. David E. Schenkman wrote the standard reference on this series, *Civil War Sutler Tokens and Cardboard Scrip*, 1983, updated in a second edition (with new reference numbers) by Richard Irons in 2014. In addition to the metal tokens described herein, there are many scrip notes and cardboard tokens that can be found in the Schenkman text. The tokens of H.V. Keep, Schenkman NL-L, bear no mention of a sutler or a military unit and are probably store cards issued years later by Henry Virtner Keep, a New York City manufacturer.

In the era of their use, sutler tokens were usually called "checks." They were issued by licensed contractors who typically operated camp stores in connection with traveling military regiments and companies, although a few had fixed locations such as military posts.

A sutler bringing his goods ashore on the James River, Virginia, summer of 1862. Sketched by Arthur Lumley.

For a soldier in the Union Army, the sutler's tent offered a panorama of delights—comforts and items of pleasure as well as necessities. Products included books, games, stationery, tonics, sweets, shirts, and more. For some regiments ardent spirits were allowed, and for others they were prohibited. Restrictions were easily circumvented by *bitters*—sold for medicinal purposes, but nearly always heavily laced with alcohol.

While most sutlers set up in tents, others did business from wagons and still others occupied stores. In Washington, D.C., in 1865 there were more than 10 sutler shops. Prisons that held captured soldiers were served by sutlers as well.

Most of their tokens were very utilitarian—made of brass and of simple design combining letters and numbers. The most popular denominations were 5, 10, 25, and 50 cents, although a few were 1, 3, 15, and 20 cents in value and some were worth $1.

The leading maker was John Stanton of Cincinnati, Ohio, who operated until 1864, after which the firm was known as Murdock & Spencer. The Cincinnati shop of William Lanphear made many tokens, including the majority with the aforementioned store card reverse dies. Shubael D. Childs of Chicago was a leading maker as well. Francis X. Koehler of Baltimore also made many tokens. Each sutler was registered with the War Department and had to operate under a set of rules. Appointments were made by state governors, military commanders, and government authorities—situations varied. There were no audits of quality for applicants, although successful appointees were supposed to adhere to official rules of conduct. Unofficially and not widely recorded in the annals of the Civil War, now and again Union and Confederate soldiers confronting each other in a combat arena would call a cease-fire for an hour or so, and the soldiers would swap souvenirs and other items, mostly bought from sutlers.

As sutlers enjoyed a monopoly, there were endless complaints about the prices they charged and the freshness of perishable merchandise. In fact, the annals of the Civil

A sutler's tent attached to the 2nd Division, 9th Corps, during the Siege of Petersburg, Virginia (June 1864 to April 1865). Published November 1864.

War, including biographies and recollections, have hardly anything favorable to say about them.

On July 26, 1866, the office of sutler was officially abolished by an act of Congress. Later licensees were generally designated as *post traders*. These issued many tokens similar in certain characteristics to sutler tokens. They are beyond the scope of this book. The term *sutler*, however, continued in popular use for years afterward.

Numismatic interest in sutler tokens began by 1863, at which time they appeared in various public auctions. Some collectors commissioned numismatic strikes in tin (white metal) and copper-nickel, all of which are rarities today.

COLLECTING SUTLER TOKENS

Today sutler tokens are very popular with specialists and, increasingly, with collectors who started out with regular Civil War tokens. While they can be found in many grades, the following cover most in the marketplace:

Fine to Extremely Fine, oxidized: Pieces found by souvenir hunters and detectorists exploring battlefields. Such pieces are usually heavily oxidized. Scattered small nicks or light scratches are normal. Except for rarities, these often sell for significant discounts.

Fine to Extremely Fine, with marks: Pieces with light scratches, nicks, slight bends, or other evidence of handling, but not oxidized. Such examples are often the finest known of certain varieties.

Extremely Fine to About Uncirculated: Pieces that have light wear.

Mint State: Numismatic strikes are usually found in this grade. Regularly issued tokens are usually elusive in such fine preservation.

A newspaper vendor in camp, Meade, Virginia, November 1863. Photographed by Alexander Gardner.

As noted, tokens made for use in the field usually have some marks, light scratches, etc. in catalogs or other sales, mention should be made of them when they are particularly noticeable. Defects such as bending, corrosion, and porosity should be mentioned as well.

Sutler tokens can be collected in several different ways. Seeking one of each issuer is a popular pursuit and is sufficiently challenging that no one has ever obtained all. Collecting one from each state or territory is another way. Issues that have a Civil War token die as the reverse are in great demand.

The Fuld rarity scale for Civil War tokens is used in the present text and can be found in chapter 1. Tokens that were reported years ago, but which have not been verified in recent times, are designated as R-10 (unique). Likely, there are more examples to be discovered. As most sutlers issued tokens of the 5, 10, 25, and 50-cent denominations, if a listing has two or three of these values, probably the other values were issued as well.

Nearly all sutler tokens range from scarce to extremely rare or even unique. Even so, as the series has not been publicized, prices for most are quite affordable in comparison to their rarity. As the auction listings reveal, prices are hardly standard. This is also true for most other tokens and medals in the American series—a departure from most federal coins which are very common in comparison and trade frequently.

Over a long period of time market prices for most sutler tokens have trended upward.

Key to the Listings

Sutler tokens in their as-issued form vary from being struck from expertly prepared dies to pieces on thin metal stamped with single letter and number punches. These classes may aid in their appreciation and affect their value:

"Skedaddler's Hall" at Harrison's Landing, Virginia,
July 1862—a sutler's store. Sketched by Alfred R. Waud.

Class A: Raised lettering on each side, struck from dies that included one side giving the denomination in raised letters. This characterizes most of those made by Childs, Koehler, Lanphear, and Stanton—the leading shops.

Class B: As above, but a stock die was used with the denomination hand-punched.

Class C: Uniface (one-sided) with raised lettering. Denomination may or may not be in raised lettering or punched in.

Class D: Others, including one- or two-sided tokens with incuse lettering and numbers.

The above may be useful in estimating values for rare examples as well as pieces that have not appeared on the market for a long time. Condition being equal, a Class A token is significantly more valuable than a Class D token.

Also affecting value is location. A territorial token, a Virginia (Confederate) token, or á token from a "rare state" will be worth more.

In the following listings, if a token is known to have been issued by a regiment, camp, or post in a given state or territory it is listed under that state or territory. Within the listings the sequence is by regiment number. For a given sutler, denominations are listed in ascending order. Information concerning the design and rarity is given for various issues to the extent that such is known.

Each token is assigned a Whitman number for easy reference. Also included are attribution numbers from David Schenkman's 1983 book, followed by completely new attribution numbers as assigned for the second edition in 2014.

Auction citations: Bleviss = Alan Bleviss Collection, Stack's Bowers Galleries, November 2009; Bunt = Raymond L. Bunt Jr. Collection, Stack's Bowers Galleries, January 2013; Ford XXIII = Stack's Bowers Galleries, August 2013; Hayden = auction by Steve Hayden; PCAC = auction by Presidential Coin & Antique Co., H. Joseph Levine.

Officers and soldiers standing outside a sutler's store during the war.

ARIZONA TERRITORY

Whitman-AZ-100-025b • Samuel Todd, sutler, Fort Mohave • Class C tokens • Incuse lettering: S.T. / SUT-LER / 25.C. Blank reverse. 20 mm. R-8 • Fort Mohave was originally named Camp Colorado when it was established on April 19, 1859, by Lieutenant Colonel William Hoffman during the Mohave War. It was located on the east bank of the Colorado River, at Beale's Crossing, near the head of the Mohave Valley in Mohave County, by the recommendation of Lieutenant Edward Fitzgerald Beale. In November

1864 Todd and his associates were granted the franchise to operate a ferry across the Colorado River • Old and new Schenk-man numbers: NL-X25B / AT-CWG-25B • VF $2,500

W-AZ-100-050b • Brass. 29 mm. Incuse lettering. R-9 • Unlisted / AT-CWG-50B • VF $2,500

W-AZ-100-100b • Brass. 29 mm. Incuse lettering. R-9 • Unlisted / AT-CWG-100B • VF $2,500

CONNECTICUT

Whitman-CT-100-005b • M. Kings-bury, sutler, 18th Regiment Connecticut Volunteer Infantry • Class A tokens • M. KINGSBURY / SUTLER / 18' / CONN. REG / 5 / CTS. IN GOODS. John Stanton backstamp (stamp and brand cutter) on this and the following. 19 mm. R-8 • The 18th Connecticut Volunteer Infantry was organized in Norwich, Connecticut, on August 22, 1862. It was mustered out of service June 27, 1865, at Harpers Ferry, West Virginia. The regiment lost a total of 152 men during service; 4 officers and 67 enlisted men killed or mortally wounded, 1 officer and 80 enlisted men died of disease. • CT-A5B / CT-18-5B. • *Auctions:* Litman (PCAC, December 2003), VF/EF, some encrustation, $1,150.00; Bleviss, EF-45, bent, $420.50; Hayden (September 2010), VF, slightly bent, $950; Ford XXIII, CT A5B, MS-63, $1,762.50

W-CT-100-025b • 22 mm. R-8 • CT-A25B / CT-18-25B • *Auction:* Litman (PCAC, December 2003), VF, $1,351.20

W-CT-120-010b.

W-CT-120-005b • Julius Frank, sutler, 20th Regiment Connecticut Volunteer Infantry • Class A tokens • AT / Liberty head facing left; LIBERTY on headband / FRANK'S. GOOD FOR / 5 / SUTLERS GOODS. 21 mm. • R-10 • Certain tokens of this issuer have triangular marks, probably cancellations. • The 20th Regiment served in the Union Army of the Potomac, which fought in several pivotal battles in the Eastern and Western theaters. It was raised in July 1862. The *Report of Committees for the 43rd Congress 1873–1874* notes that Julius Frank filed a claim to be "compensated for sutler-supplies seized by order of General Thomas in 1864." Further: "Mr. Frank claims that in April, 1864, he was sutler for the Twentieth Regiment of Connecticut volunteers; that at Anderson, Tennessee, some goods were seized by order of the chief quartermaster at Nashville, condemned for a violation of military orders, sold, and the proceeds applied to hospital purposes." • Unlisted / UI-A-5B • *Auction:* Hayden (FPL, August 2014), VF or better detail but slightly porous and cleaned, $1,500

W-CT-120-010b • 21 mm. R-9 • NL-F10B / UI-A-10B • *Auctions:* Litman (PCAC, December 2003), EF, $839.50; Bleviss, Fine-15, heavily porous, $69; Bunt, VF, cleaned $558.13

W-CT-120-025b • 21 mm. R-8 • NL-F25B / UI-A-25B • *Auctions:* PCAC Auc-

tion #67 (June 2000) VF, two reverse triangular counterstamps, $192.50; Bunt, VF-35, cancellation marks, $58.75, VF-35 cancellation marks, $305.50; Ford XXIII, AU, heavy cancellation punches, $164.50

W-CT-120-050b • 21 mm. R-9 • NL-F50B / UI-A-50B • *Auctions:* Litman (PCAC, December 2003), VF, triangular punch marks on reverse, $529; Bleviss, Fine-12, heavily porous, $69

DAKOTA TERRITORY

Whitman-DT-100-010a • **Seth E. Ward, sutler, Fort Laramie.** • **Class B tokens** • S.E. WARD. SUTLER U.S.A. / GOOD FOR / 10c in / SUTLERS GOODS / F. LARAMIE D.T. All are incuse with the reverse being a mirror image of the obverse; made by squeezing on a seal press. 24 mm. R-8 • Tokens of this issuer are typically Mint State. • Ward was appointed sutler to Fort Laramie on April 30, 1857, and held the position until March 1863. He was reappointed in March 1865, near the end of the war. Later he was designated as post trader in the same position. He retired in 1871. The Denver Public Library has a collection of Seth Ward's papers. One of the most important forts in the settlement of the American West, Fort Laramie served many functions throughout its history. • DT-A10C / DT-FL-10C • EF $2,000

W-DT-100-025a • 28 mm. R-8 • DT-A25C / DT-FL-25C • *Auctions:* Hayden (July 2010), AU+, 10% red with small obverse stain, $1,100; Ford XXIII, DT-A25C, AU-58, $646.25, MS-62BN, $646.25, MS-62BN, $646.25; Hayden (FPL, August 2014), MS-63, $2,500

W-DT-100-050a • 33 mm. R-7 • Modern counterfeits exist. • DT-A50C / DT-FL-50C • *Auctions:* Fauver (PCAC July 2006), VF, dug, $345; Hayden (July 2006), EF porous, $496.46; Bleviss, EF-45, $402.50; Bunt, DT A50C, VF-30, $329, EF-40 Schenkman plate token, $587.50; Ford XXIII, DT-A50C, AU-58BN, $705, MS-62, $822.50, MS-63, two planchet clips, $822.50, MS-63BN, small spot, $1,057.50, MS-63BN, $1,410; IL-A25C Hayden (FPL, August 2014), AU+, $1,200

ILLINOIS

W-IL-100-025b.

Whitman-IL-100-005b • **Florian Simmonds, sutler, 12th Regiment Illinois Cavalry** • **Class A tokens** • F. SIMMONDS, SUTLER / 12 / ILLINOIS / CAVALRY. GOOD FOR / 5 / CENTS / KOEHLER (in small letters). The die sinker's name appears retrograde on A5B. 21 mm. R-8 • From 1864 to 1866 Simmonds dealt in sutler goods at 130 West

Lombard Street in Baltimore. This is the only Illinois *cavalry* regiment to issue sutler tokens. The regiment, of volunteers, suffered 38 enlisted men who were killed in action or who died of their wounds and 4 officers and 192 enlisted men who died of disease. • IL-A5B / IL-12a-5B • *Auctions:* Litman (PCAC, December 2003), VF, damaged, $253; Ford XXIII, AU, holed, $282

W-IL-100-010b • 21 mm. R-9 • IL-A10B / IL-12a-10B • EF $1,250

W-IL-100-025a • 21 mm. R-9 • IL-A25C / IL-12a-25C • *Auctions:* Stack's Americana Sale (July 2010), EF, rim nick, $302.50; Hayden (FPL, August 2014), EF, $1,850

W-IL-100-025b • 21 mm. R-9 • IL-A25B / IL-12a-25B • *Auction:* PCAC (December 2005), AU-58, $1,495

W-IL-102-005e • F. SIMMONDS / SUTLER / 5 incuse / 12TH / ILL. CAVALRY. Spread eagle within circle of 13 stars. 18 mm. R-9 • IL-B5WM / IL-12b-5WM • VF $2,500

W-IL-120-005b • **27th Regiment Illinois Volunteer Infantry** • **Class A tokens** • 27 REG. ILL. VOL. / GOOD FOR / 5 / CENTS / IN GOODS. John Stanton backstamp (die sinker). 16 mm. R-8 • This regiment was organized in Camp Butler (near Springfield) in August 1861. In September 1864 those soldiers still in service were transferred to the 9th Illinois Volunteer Infantry Regiment. Most were discharged in June 1865. The regiment suffered a total of 188 fatalities. • IL-C5B / IL-27-5B • EF $1,250

W-IL-120-010b • 19 mm. R-8 • IL-C10B / IL-27-10B • *Auctions:* Hayden (October 2011), Fine+, backstamp worn away, $350; Bunt, EF-45, $528.75; Ford XXIII, MS-63, $1,057.50; Hayden (February 2012), AU+ $900

W-IL-120-025b • 22 mm. R-8 • IL-C25B / IL-27-25B • *Auctions:* Bunt, VF-35, $646.25, AU, scratch, stain, $763.75

W-IL-140-005b • **D.B. Smith, sutler, 28th Regiment Illinois Volunteer Infantry** • **Class C tokens** • D.B. SMITH / 28' / ILL. REG. / 5 / CTS. IN GOODS. Blank reverse. 16 mm. R-9 • The 28th Illinois Infantry was organized in Camp Butler, which had just been opened as a training camp for Illinois soldiers. It was mustered into service on August 15, 1861. Over the course of its service 290 fatalities were recorded. • IL-D5B / IL-28-5B • VF $2,000

W-IL-140-010b • 19 mm. R-9 • *Auction:* Bleviss, EF, holed, $287.50

W-IL-140-010b-x • 25 CETS error. 22 mm. R-9 • IL-D10B / IL-28-10B, IL-D25Ba / IL-28-25Ba • VF $2,000

W-IL-140-025b • John Stanton backstamp (stamp and brand cutter). 22 mm. R-9 • IL-D25Bb / IL-28-25Bb • VF $1,250

W-IL-140-050b • John Stanton backstamp (stamp and brand cutter). 25 mm. R-9 • IL-D50B / IL-28-50B • *Auction:* Slabaugh (PCAC, June 2001), F/VF, $287.50

W-IL-160-005b • **30th Regiment Illinois Volunteer Infantry** • **Class A tokens** • SUTLERS CHECK / FOR / 5 / CENTS IN GOODS. / 30TH REG. ILL. VOL. John Stanton backstamp (die sinker). 16 mm. R-9 • This regiment was organized in Camp Butler and mustered into service on August 28, 1861. It suffered 345 fatalities. • IL-E5B / IL-30-5B • VF $600

W-IL-160-010b • 19 mm. R-9 • IL-E10B / IL-30-10B • VF $1,500

W-IL-160-025b • 22 mm. R-9 • IL-E25B / IL-30-25B • *Auction:* PCAC 7001, Robert Marcus (December 2001), EF, $437

W-IL-180-025b.

W-IL-180-005b • **Inglish & Nantz, sutlers, 32nd Regiment Illinois Volunteer Infantry** • **Class A tokens** • INGLISH & NANTZ / SUTLERS CHECK / 5 / CENTS IN GOODS. / 32 REG. ILL. VOL. John Stanton backstamp (die sinker) on all. 16 mm. R-8 • This regiment was organized in Camp Butler and mustered into service on December 31, 1861. It suffered 268 fatalities during the war. • IL-F5B / IL-32-5B • *Auction:* Litman (PCAC, December 2003), VG, $368

W-IL-180-010b • 22 mm. R-9 • Unlisted / IL-32-10B • VF $1,500

W-IL-180-025b • 19 mm. R-8 • IL-F25B / IL-32-25B • *Auction:* Litman (PCAC, December 2003), AU, $943

W-IL-180-050b • 25 mm. R-9 • IL-F50B / IL-32-50B • EF $1,000

W-IL-200-050a.

W-IL-200-005b • **A. Vance Brown, sutler, 39th Regiment Illinois Volunteer Infantry** • **Class A tokens** • A.

VANCE BROWN / SUTLER, / 39TH / ILL. VET. / KOEHLER (in small letters). GOOD FOR / 5 / CENTS / KOEHLER (in small letters). 21 mm. R-9. Tokens of this issuer are usually seen in circulated grades. • This regiment, nicknamed "Yates' Phalanx," was organized in Chicago and was mustered into service on October 11, 1861, for a three-year term. • IL-G5B / IL-39-5B • *Auction:* Hayden (July 2012), EF, old scratches, obverse die crack as usual, $900

W-IL-200-010b • 21 mm. R-9 • IL-G10B / IL-39-10B • VF $1,500

W-IL-200-025b • 21 mm. R-9 • IL-G25B / IL-39-25B • VF $700

W-IL-200-050a • 21 mm. R-8 • IL-G50C / IL-39-50C • *Auctions:* Litman (PCAC, December 2003), VF/EF, encrustation, $483; Ford XXIII, AU-53BN, $470

W-IL-200-050b • 21 mm. R-9 • IL-G50B / IL-39-50B • VF $1,500

W-IL-220-025a.

W-IL-220-005a • **H.H. Beecher & Co., sutlers, 40th Regiment Illinois Volunteer Infantry** • **Class A tokens** • H.H. BEECHER & CO / 40TH. / ILL. REG. / 5 / CENTS. John Stanton backstamp (stamp and brand cutter). 16 mm. R-8 • A biographical sketch of Beecher was included in a *Portrait & Biographical Album of Sangamon County*, 1891. This regiment was organized in Springfield and mustered into service on August 10, 1861. It suffered 246 fatalities during the war. • IL-H5C / IL-40-5C • EF $550

W-IL-220-010b • 19 mm. R-7 • IL-H10B / IL-40-10B • *Auction:* Bunt, EF, oxidation $499.38, EF, corrosion spot, $305.50

W-IL-220-025a • 22 mm. R-8 • IL-H25C / IL-40-25C • *Auctions:* Litman (PCAC, December 2003); Unc, $747.50; Bleviss, VF, with porosity, $80.50; Bunt, EF, light corrosion, $381.88; Hayden (February 2012), MS-62, $825

W-IL-240-005b.

W-IL-240-005b • Joel C. Benton, sutler, 41st Regiment Illinois Volunteer Infantry • Class A tokens • FORTY FIRST REG'T ILL. V. / Spread eagle; 13 stars above / J.C. BENTON. GOOD FOR FIVE CENTS / IN / GOODS / AT THE / SUTLERS STORE. 20 mm. R-8. Tokens of this issuer are usually seen in circulated grades. • Benton studied medicine in Chicopee Falls, Massachusetts. He moved to Decatur, Illinois. During the war he served as sutler from 1861 to 1865. Later he was a railroad contractor. He died in January 1869 at age 46. The regiment was organized in Decatur and mustered into service on August 5, 1861. It suffered 225 fatalities in the war. • IL-I5B / IL-41-5B • *Auctions:* Litman (PCAC, December 2003), Unc, $846.80; Ford XXIII, AU-55, $587.50

W-IL-240-005h • 20 mm. R-9 • IL-I5L / IL-41-5L • VF $1,000

W-IL-240-010a • 20 mm. R-6 • IL-I10C / IL-41-10C • *Auctions:* PCAC #67 (June 2000), F/VF, $165; Litman (PCAC, December 2003), Ch Red Unc, $592.25; Bunt, VF, cleaned, $235, VF-25, $329, VF-35, clip, $329; Ford XXIII, VF-20, $282; Hayden (July 2014), AU $500

W-IL-240-025g • 20 mm. R-7 • IL-I25L / IL-41-25L • *Auctions:* Litman (PCAC, December 2003), F/VF, $241.15; Bleviss, VF-25, $184; Bunt (January 2013), VF, heavy oxidation, $141; Ford XXIII, EF, damaged. $188

W-IL-260-005b • A.H. Davis, sutler, 45th Regiment Illinois Volunteer Infantry • Class A tokens • AT SUTLERS / STORE / A.H. DAVIS, / W.L.M. / REG. 45. ILL. V. GOOD / FOR 5 CTS / IN GOODS. 16 mm. R-8 • Organized in the mining town of Galena on December 25, 1861, this unit was known as Washburne's Mine Regiment (from Elihu B. Washburne, representative to Congress). It suffered 223 fatalities during the war. • IL-J5B / IL-45-5B • *Auctions:* PCAC Auction #67 (June 2000), EF/AU, $302.50; Litman (PCAC, December 2003), EF/AU, $460

W-IL-260-010b • Reverse: CHILDS MANUFACTURER / (head facing left) / CHICAGO. 22 mm. R-8 • IL-J10B / IL-45-10B • *Auctions:* Litman (PCAC, December 2003), EF/AU, Ch Unc, $825; Hayden (FPL, August 2014), MS-63, $2,250

W-IL-260-025b • Reverse: CHILDS MANUFACTURER / Spread eagle; 13 stars above / CHICAGO. 26 mm. R-8 • IL-J25B / IL-45-25B • *Auctions:* Ford XXIII, VF-35, $470; Hayden (FPL, August 2014), VF, $800

W-IL-280-005b-1390.

W-IL-280-010b.

W-IL-280-005b-1390 • H. Lester, sutler, 51st Regiment Illinois Volunteer Infantry • Class A tokens • GOOD / FOR 5 CTS / IN GOODS AT / SUTLERS / STORE / H. LESTER 51ST R. ILL. V. Reverse: CHILDS MANFR. CHICAGO / Arm holding hammer / 1861. 20 mm. R-8. Tokens of this issuer are usually seen in circulated grades. • Reverse with Civil War store card die 1390. • This regiment was organized in Chicago and mustered into service on December 24, 1861. It suffered 250 fatalities during the war. • IL-K5B / IL-51-5B • *Auctions:* Litman (PCAC, December 2003), VF, encrustation, $287.50; Hayden (FPL, August 2014), VF+, tiny x scratched, $500

W-IL-280-010b • Reverse: CHILDS MANUFACTURER / Head facing left / CHICAGO. 22 mm. R-7 • IL-K10B / IL-51-10B • *Auctions:* Litman (PCAC, December 2003), VF/EF, dents, $184; Bunt, VF-25, $587.50, EF-40, $411.25; Hayden (February 2012), EF, $422.89

WW-IL-280-025b • Reverse: CHILDS MANUFACTURER / Spread eagle; 13 stars above / CHICAGO. 26 mm. R-8 • IL-K25B / IL-51-25B • *Auctions:* PCAC

Auction #67 (June 2000), EF, $247.50; Litman (PCAC, December 2003), EF/AU, slight clip, $431.25; Ford XXIII, EF-45, $381.88; Hayden (FPL, August 2014), MS-63, $1,650

W-IL-300-050a-1390 • S. Patrick, sutler, 54th Regiment Illinois Volunteer Infantry • Class D token • PAYABLE IN GOODS / 50 CTS / S. PATRICK / SUTLER 54TH ILL incuse. R-10 • This regiment was organized in Anna and mustered into service in February 1862. It had 185 fatalities during the war. • Unlisted / IL-54-50C • VF $2,500

W-IL-320-005b • A.A. Lamb, sutler, 70th Regiment Illinois Volunteer Infantry. Camp Butler • Class A tokens • GOOD FOR / 5 / CENTS / IN GOODS AT / A.A. LAMB / SUTLER / 70' ILL. REG. John Stanton backstamp (stamp and brand cutter). 17 mm. R-9 • This regiment was organized in Camp Butler and mustered into service on June 4, 1862. It served on guard duty at Camp Butler, and was not involved in any battles. It lost 23 men who died of disease. • IL-L5B / IL-70-5B • *Auctions:* Slabaugh (PCAC, June 2001), EF, $287.50; Litman (PCAC, December 2003), EF/AU, verdigris, $678.50

W-IL-320-010b • 19 mm. R-9 • IL-L10B / IL-70-10B • VF $700

W-IL-320-025b • 22 mm. R-8 • IL-L25B / IL-70-25B • *Auction:* Litman (PCAC, December 2003), EF/AU, $776.25

W-IL-340-010b • 80th Regiment Illinois Volunteer Infantry • Class A token • 80TH REG'T ILL. VOL SUTLERS CHECK FOR 10 CENTS IN GOODS. John Stanton backstamp (die sinker). 19 mm. R-9. David Schenkman: "I have not seen a specimen of this token, so the description is not exact." • This regiment was composed of ten companies that drew primarily from eight southern Illinois counties. It entered into service on August 25, 1862. Over the course of the war the regiment traveled about 6,000 miles and was involved in more than 20 battles, suffering 218 fatalities. • IL-M10B / IL-80-10B • VF $2,000

W-IL-360-005b • I. August, sutler, 84th Regiment Illinois Volunteer Infantry • Class A tokens • I. AUGUST / 84' REG. / ILL' VOL. / 5 / CENTS IN GOODS. John Stanton backstamp (stamp and brand cutter). 17 mm. R-8. Tokens of this issuer are usually seen in circulated grades. • This regiment suffered 269 fatalities in the war. • IL-N5B / IL-84-5B • *Auctions:* Litman (PCAC, December 2003), AU, a few dark spots, $644; Ford XXIII, AU-55, $587.50

W-IL-360-025b • John Stanton backstamp (stamp and brand cutter). 22 mm. R-9 • IL-N25B / IL-84-25B • EF $900

W-IL-360-050b • John Stanton backstamp (stamp and brand cutter). 25 mm. R-9 • IL-N50B / IL-84-50B • *Auction:* Ford XXIII, MS-62, $1,057.50

W-IL-380-005b • F.A. Packard, sutler, 94th Regiment Illinois Volunteer Infantry • Class A tokens • GOOD FOR / 5 / CENTS / IN GOODS / F.A. PACKARD. / SUTLER / 94' ILL'S REG. John Stanton backstamp (stamp and brand cutter). 16 mm. R-9. Tokens of this issuer are usually seen in circulated grades. • Nicknamed the "McLean Regiment," this unit was organized in McLean County and mustered into service on August 20, 1862. It suffered 175 fatalities in the war. • IL-O5B / IL-94-5B • *Auction:* Ford XXIII, AU-50, $1,645

W-IL-380-010b • 19 mm. R-9 • IL-O10B / IL-94-10B • *Auctions:* Litman (PCAC, December 2003), F/VF, bent, reverse very worn, $632.50; Ford XXIII, MS-61, $1,527.50

W-IL-380-025b • 22 mm. R-9 • IL-O25B / IL-94-25B • *Auctions:* Heritage (June 2007), not graded, $2,151; Ford XXIII, AU-55, $1,645

W-IL-400-005b.

W-IL-402-010a-1009.

W-IL-400-005b • S. Whited & Co., sutlers, 97th Regiment Illinois Volunteer Infantry • Class A tokens • S. WHITED & CO / SUTLERS / 97' ILL. VOL / GOOD FOR / 5 / CTS. IN GOODS. Shield. 17 mm. R-6 • IL-P5B / IL-97-5-B • *Auctions:* PCAC Auction #67 (June 2000), VF, $203.50; Litman (PCAC, December 2003), EF/AU, $208.80; Bleviss, EF-40, $276; Bunt, VF-35, $258.50, VF-30, uneven strike, $223.25, VF-30, $305.50, VF-30, $282, EF-40, $329; Ford XXIII, MS-63, $675.63; Hayden (FPL, August 2014), EF $650

W-IL-402-010a-1009 • 19 mm. R-6 • Reverse with Civil War store card die 1009. • IL-Q10C / IL-97-10Ca • *Auctions:* Litman (PCAC, December 2003),

VF, gouges, $139.20; Heritage (February 2007), EF-40, lightly cleaned, $184; Bleviss, Q10C, VF, cleaned, $178.25; Hayden (March 2010), EF, $375; Bunt, VF, old cleaning, $164.50, VF-25, $223.25, VF-30, $258.50, VF-30, $235, VF-35, $258.50, EF, old cleaning, $270.25, EF-40, $411.25; Hayden (July 2014), VF+, $400; Hayden (FPL, August 2014), EF, $500

W-IL-404-010a-1018 • 19 mm. R-9 • Reverse with Civil War store card die 1018. • IL-R10C / IL-97-10Cb • MS-63 $2,000

W-IL-404-010b-1018 • 19 mm. R-9 • Reverse with Civil War store card die 1018. • IL-R10B / IL-97-10Ba • MS-63 $2,000

W-IL-404-010d-1018 • R-9 • Reverse with Civil War store card die 1018. • IL-R10CN / IL-97-10CN • *Auction:* Ford XXIII, MS-65, $940

W-IL-404-010e • 19 mm. R-9 • IL-R10Z / IL-97-10Za • MS-63 $2,000

W-IL-406-010a-1393 • 19 mm. R-8 • Reverse with Civil War store card die 1393. • IL-S10C / IL-97-10Cc • *Auctions:* Ford XXIII, Unc, Scratches, $329, MS-64BN, $881.25

W-IL-406-010b-1393 • 19 mm. R-9 • Reverse with Civil War store card die 1393. • IL-S10B / IL-97-10Bb • *Auctions:* Litman (PCAC, December 2003), Unc, light staple scratch on reverse, $275; Hayden (FPL, August 2014), MS-62, $1,350

W-IL-406-010e-1393 • 19 mm. R-9 • Reverse with Civil War store card die 1393. • IL-S10Z / IL-97-10Zb • *Auction:* Hayden (FPL, August 2014), MS-63, $2,250

W-IL-440-005b • **H. Rice, sutler, McClernand's Brigade, Illinois Volunteers** • **Class A tokens** • H. RICE /

SUTLER / M'CLERNANDS / BRIGADE / ILLS. VOL. / 5 / CENTS IN GOODS. John Stanton backstamp (die sinker). 17 mm. R-7 • McClernand's Regiment was raised in Illinois by John Alexander McClernand. The unit saw action in many battles. In the papers of Ulysses S. Grant is this letter from General McClernand dated March 1, 1862: "Henry Rice, a man of strict integrity and large fortune, whose appointment as Brigade Sutler at Cairo you approved, and whom you recommended for Post Sutler for the place, wishes your written permission to vend goods in the City of Nashville. I hope it may be within your power and consistent with your views to give him authority to do so." • IL-T5B / IL-MB-5B • *Auctions:* Slabaugh (PCAC, June 2001), EF, $172.50; Litman (PCAC, December 2003), Red Unc, $460; Hayden (June 2005), EF, couple of tiny dents, $385; Hayden (December 2006), $750; Bunt, EF-45, two tiny spots, $528.75, EF, slight oxidation, $646.25, AU-50, $881.25; Ford XXIII, MS-62, $440.63, MS-63, $646.25, MS-64, $763.75, MS-64, $881.25

W-IL-440-010b • 19 mm. R-8 • IL-T10B / IL-MB-10B • *Auctions:* Litman (PCAC, December 2003), EF, $287.50; Bunt, EF, cleaned and retoned, $587.50; Ford XXIII, AU details, bent, $235, MS-62, $881.25; Hayden (FPL, August 2014), EF, slightly wavy planchet, $425

W-IL-440-025b • John Stanton backstamp (die sinker). 22 mm. R-7 • IL-T25B / IL-MB-25B • *Auctions:* Bleviss, EF-45, $373.75; Bunt, EF, cleaned and retoned, $558.13, EF-45, $763.75; Ford XXIII, MS, damaged, $211.50, MS-62, $499.38, MS-62, $558.13

W-IL-440-050b • 25 mm. R-8 • IL-T50B / IL-MB-50B • *Auctions:* Bunt, EF-40, slight oxidation, $646.25; Ford XXIII, MS-62, $646.25

Indiana

Whitman-IN-100-005b • J. Holmes, sutler, 5th Regiment Indiana Volunteer Cavalry • Class A tokens • 5' IND. CAVALRY / GOOD FOR / 5 / CTS IN GOODS / J. HOLMES, SUT. John Stanton backstamp (stamp and brand cutter). 16 mm. R-9 • IN-A5B / IN-5-5B • *Auction:* Hayden (FPL, August 2014), EF, some staining, $1,100

W-IN-100-010b • John Stanton backstamp (stamp and brand cutter). 19 mm. R-9 • IN-A10B / IN-5-10B • VF $1,500

W-IN-100-025a • John Stanton backstamp (stamp and brand cutter). 22 mm. R-8 • IN-A25C / IN-5-25C • *Auctions:* Litman (PCAC, December 2003), VF, $598; Ford XXIII, AU-55BN, $1,057.50

W-IN-100-025b • John Stanton backstamp (stamp and brand cutter). 22 mm. R-10 • IN-A25B / IN-5-25B • VF $1,500

W-IN-120-025b • M. Hughes, sutler, 6th Regiment Indiana Volunteer Infantry • Class A token • M. HUGHES / 6' / REG. IND. VOL. / 25 CENTS / John Stanton backstamp (stamp and brand cutter). 22 mm. R-9 • IN-B25B / IN-6-25B • VF $1,750

W-IN-140-005b • 7th Regiment Indiana Volunteer Infantry • Class A tokens • 7TH IND. REG-T. / 5 / CENTS / IN GOODS. John Stanton backstamp (die sinker). 19 mm. R-9 • IN-C5Ba / IN-7-5Ba • *Auctions:* Bunt, VF, silvered, tiny dent, $528.75; Hayden (FPL, August 2014), MS-64, $2,750

W-IN-140-005b-x • Blank reverse. 19 mm. R-10 • IN-C5Bb / IN-7-5Bb • VF $1,500

W-IN-140-025b • John Stanton backstamp (die sinker). 22 mm. R-7 • IN-C25B / IN-7-25B • *Auctions:* Bunt, VF-35,

$499.38; Ford XXIII, AU, bent, $235; Hayden (FPL, August 2014), Fine+, slightly bent, $575

W-IN-160-005b • 16th Regiment Indiana Volunteer Infantry • Class A tokens • SUTLERS CHECK / 16' IND. VOL / 5 / CTS. IN GOODS. John Stanton backstamp (stamp and brand cutter). 17 mm. R-9 • This infantry unit was organized in Indianapolis in the summer of 1862. It lost nearly 300 soldiers who either were killed outright or died from wounds and disease. • IN-D5Ba / IN-16-5Ba • *Auctions:* Hayden (June 2011), VF, $1,584; Hayden (July 2014), VF, $900; Hayden (FPL, August 2014), AU+ $2,250

W-IN-160-005b-x • Class C tokens • SUTLERS CHECK / 16' IND. VOL / 5 / CTS. IN GOODS. Reverse with obverse inscription incuse and retrograde. 17 mm. R-10 • IN-D5Bb / IN-16-5Bb • VF $2,000

W-IN-160-005b-y • SUTLERS CHECK / 16' IND. VOL. (design over IND.) / 5 / CTS IN GOODS. John Stanton backstamp (stamp and brand cutter). 17 mm. R-10 • IN-D5Bc / IN-16-5Bc • VF $2,000

W-IN-160-005b-z • SUTLERS CHECK / 16' IND. VOL. (design over IND.) / 5 / CTS IN GOODS. 17 mm. R-10. David Schenkman: "I have not seen a specimen of this, so the description may not be exact." • IN-D5Bd / IN-16-5Bd • VF $2,000

W-IN-160-010b • 10 CTS. 19 mm. R-8 • IN-D10B / IN-16-10B • *Auctions:* Hayden (March 2010), VF, $2,090; Bunt, VF, faint scratches, $763.75

W-IN-160-025b • 25 CTS. 22 mm. R-9 • IN-D25B / IN-16-25B • *Auction:* Bunt, VF, faint scratches, $998.75

W-IN-180-005b • 22nd Regiment Indiana Volunteer Infantry • Class A tokens • SUTLERS CHECK / GOOD FOR / 5 / CENTS IN / GOODS / 22 R. IND. VOL. John Stanton backstamp (die sinker). 16 mm. R-8 • IN-E5B / IN-22-5B • EF $750

W-IN-180-010b • 19 mm. R-8 • IN-E10B / IN-22-10B • *Auctions:* Bleviss, EF, rough, $138; Hayden (February 2012), MS-62 or finer, $900

W-IN-180-025b • John Stanton backstamp (die sinker). 22 mm. R-8 • IN-E25B / IN-22-25B • *Auction:* Litman (PCAC, December 2003), AU $690

W-IN-200-005a • J.K. Alexander, sutler, 33rd Regiment Indiana Volunteer Infantry • Class A tokens • J.K. ALEXANDER / SUTLER / 33' / IND. REG. / 5 / CTS. IN GOODS. John Stanton backstamp (stamp and brand cutter). 19 mm. R-7 • IN-F5C / IN-33-5C • *Auctions:* PCAC Auction #67 (June 2000), VF, spots, $330; Litman (PCAC, December 2003), dented and chipped planchet, $402.50; Hayden (July 2007), VF+, $1,062.60; Hayden (March 2010), VF, slightly wavy, $660; Bunt, VF, rough surface, $558.13

W-IN-200-025a • 22 mm. R-9 • IN-F25C / IN-33-25C • VF $2,000

W-IN-220-005b • G. Davidson, sutler, 36th Regiment Indiana Volunteer Infantry • Class A tokens • G. DAVIDSON / 36 IND. VOL. / 5 / CENTS IN GOODS. John Stanton backstamp (die sinker). 16 mm. R-8 • Davidson also issued paper scrip while sutler for the 36th Indiana Volunteers. • IN-G5Ba / IN-36-5Ba • *Auctions:* PCAC Auction #79 (June 2009), AU, $1,138.50; Hayden (December 2012), MS-62, $700; Ford XXIII, MS-63, $822.50

W-IN-220-005b-x • John Stanton backstamp (die sinker). 19 mm (larger diameter for the same denomination). R-8 • IN-G5Bb / IN-36-5Bb • *Auctions:* Hayden (December 2010), MS-63, $1,100; Bunt, VF, retoned, $329; Hayden (FPL, August 2014), MS-63, $1,850

W-IN-220-025b • 22 mm. R-8 • IN-G25Ba / IN-36-25Ba • *Auctions:* eBay (September 2009), AU, $898.88; Hayden (July 2012), MS-63, $750; Bunt, EF-45, light oxidation, $411.25, EF-45, trivial scratches, $470; Hayden (February 2012), MS-62, $600; Hayden (July 2014), MS-63, $600

W-IN-240-005b • John W. Christy, sutler, 37th Regiment Indiana Volunteer Infantry • Class A tokens • JOHN W. CHRISTY / 37 IND. VOL. / 5 / CENTS IN GOODS. John Stanton backstamp (die sinker). 16 mm. R-9 • IN-H5B / IN-37-5B • VF $1,750

W-IN-240-025b • 22 mm. R-9 • IN-H25B / IN-37-25B • VF $1,750

W-IN-260-005b • J.W. Mauzy, sutler, 41st Indiana Volunteer Volunteers / 2d Regiment Indiana Volunteer Cavalry • Class A tokens • 41 REG. IND. VOL / 2ND / CAVALRY / 5 / CENTS / J.W. MAUZY. John Stanton backstamp (die sinker). 16 mm. R-8. Tokens of this issuer are usually seen in circulated grades. • IN-I5B / IN-41-5B • *Auctions:* Bunt, VF, porous, $440.63; Ford XXIII, MS-63, $881.25; Hayden (FPL, August 2014), MS-62, $2,250

W-IN-260-025b • John Stanton backstamp (die sinker). 22 mm. R-8 • IN-I25B / IN-41-25B • *Auctions:* Bunt, VF, clip, light granularity, $381.88, VF, granular, $499.38; Ford XXIII, AU-58, $705, MS-62, $1,057.50

W-IN-280-010b • J.S. Case, sutler, 46th Regiment Indiana Volunteer Infantry • Class A tokens • 46' REG. IND. VOL. / 10 / CENTS IN GOODS. / J.S. CASE. John Stanton backstamp (die sinker). 19 mm. R-9 • IN-J10B / IN-46-10B • VF $2,000

W-IN-280-025b • 22 mm. R-9 • IN-J25B / IN-46-25B • VF $2,000

W-IN-300-025b • Slack & Jones, sutlers, 47th Regiment Indiana Volunteer Infantry • Class C token • 47' IND. REG. / GOOD FOR / 25 / CENTS / SLACK & JONES. Blank reverse. 22 mm. R-9. Tokens of this issuer are usually seen in circulated grades. • IN-K25B / IN-47-25B • *Auction:* Ford XXIII, AU, two holes, $499.38

W-IN-320-005b • J.W. Scott, sutler, 57th Regiment Indiana Volunteer Infantry • Class A tokens • J.W. SCOTT / 57 R. / IND. VOL / 5 / CENTS IN GOODS. John Stanton backstamp (die sinker). 19 mm. R-9. Denomination, 5, is 4 mm high. Tokens of this issuer are usually seen in circulated grades. • IN-L5Ba / IN-57-5Ba • *Auction:* Ford XXIII, MS-62, $822.50

W-IN-320-005b-x • Similar to the preceding, but the denomination, 5, is 3 mm high. 19 mm. R-9 • IN-L5Bb / IN-57-5Bb • *Auction:* Bunt, VF, light oxidation, $587.50

W-IN-320-010b • 22 mm. R-8 • IN-L10B / IN-57-10B • *Auction:* Hayden (FPL, August 2014), EF+, $1,250

W-IN-340-005b • William Show, sutler, 69th Regiment Indiana Volunteer Infantry • Class A tokens • WM. SHOW / SUTLER / 69' IND VOL / 5 / CTS IN GOODS. John Stanton backstamp (stamp and brand cutter). 16 mm. R-9. Tokens of this issuer are usually seen in circulated grades. • IN-M5B / IN-69-5B • VF $1,250

W-IN-340-025b • John Stanton backstamp (stamp and brand cutter). 22 mm. R-9 • IN-M25B / IN-69-25B • *Auctions:* Ford XXIII, MS-63, $1,175; Hayden (FPL, August 2014), AU, $2,500

W-IN-360-005b • W.W. Sibley & Co., sutlers, 71st Regiment Indiana Volunteer Infantry • Class A tokens • W.W. SIBLEY & CO / 71' / REG. IND. VOL / 5 / CENTS. John Stanton backstamp (stamp and brand cutter). 17 mm. R-8 • This regiment started out as an infantry unit in 1862, but which was reorganized as cavalry in early 1863. • IN-N5B / IN-71-5B • *Auctions:* Bleviss, VF, oxidation, verdigris, $414; Hayden (July 2006), EF $1,127.50; Hayden (February 2012), VF with some dents and marks, $600; Bunt, VF, "couple of small dents," $258.50; Hayden (FPL, August 2014), EF, two large dents, $650

W-IN-360-010b • John Stanton backstamp (stamp and brand cutter). 19 mm. R-9 • IN-N10B / IN-71-10B • VF $1,350

W-IN-360-025b • 22 mm. R-9 • IN-N25B / IN-71-25B • VF $1,500

W-IN-380-005b • S.J. Bartlett, sutler, 73rd Regiment Indiana Volunteer Infantry • Class A tokens • S.J. BARTLETT / SUTLER / 73' IND. REG / 5 / CTS. IN GOODS. John Stanton backstamp (stamp and brand cutter). Brass. 16 mm. R-10 • Unlisted / IN-73-5B • VF $3,250

W-IN-380-010b • John Stanton backstamp (stamp and brand cutter). 19 mm. R-10. David Schenkman: "I have not seen this token. The description is as listed in an auction catalog, so it may not be exact." • IN-O10B / IN-73-10B • VF $3,250

W-IN-400-005b • **T.J. Hosford & Co., sutlers, 84th Regiment Indiana Volunteer Infantry** • **Class A tokens** • T.J. HOSFORD & CO / SUTLERS / 84' R. IND. VOL / 5 / CTS. IN GOODS. John Stanton backstamp (stamp and brand cutter). 19 mm. R-9 • Unlisted / IN-84a-5B • VF $2,000

W-IN-400-010b • John Stanton backstamp (stamp and brand cutter). 19 mm. R-9. David Schenkman: "On all specimens examined, the denomination is cut over '5'." • IN-P10B / IN-84a-10B • *Auctions:* Hayden (February 2012), "The first example of this variety we have seen offered, despite its rarity rating [called R-8 at the time]," AU, $1,200; Hayden (FPL, August 2014), MS-63, $3,000

W-IN-400-025b • 22 mm. R-9 • IN-P25B / IN-84a-25B • VF $1,500

W-IN-420-025b.

W-IN-420-005b • **G.S. Maddy & Co., sutlers, 84th Regiment Indiana Volunteer Infantry** • **Class A tokens** • G.S. MADDY & CO. / 84' REG / IND. V. 1. / 5 / CENTS. John Stanton backstamp (stamp and brand cutter). 17 mm. R-9 • IN-Q5B / IN-84b-5B • *Auctions:* Hayden (October 2011), VF, $1,250; Ford XXIII, MS-64, $1,116.25

W-IN-420-010b • 19 mm. R-9 • IN-Q10B / IN-84b-10B • EF $1,100

W-IN-420-025b • 22 mm. R-9 • IN-Q25B / IN-84b-25B • *Auction:* Hayden (February 2012), EF, $750

W-IN-440-005b • **P. Shannon, sutler, 85th Regiment Indiana Volunteer Infantry** • **Class A tokens** • P. SHANNON / SUTLER / 85TH. REG / IND. VOL. / 5 / CTS. IN GOODS. John Stanton backstamp (stamp and brand cutter). 19 mm. R-9 • IN-R5B / IN-85-5B • VF $1,350

W-IN-440-010b • John Stanton backstamp (stamp and brand cutter). 22 mm. R-8 • IN-R10B / IN-85-10B • *Auctions:* Bunt, VF-30, uneven strike, $528.75, EF-40, $528.75

W-IN-460-005a • **[James] Hasson, sutler** • **Class A tokens** • HASSON / 5 / SUTLER. Reverse: Civil War token die 1391. 22 mm. R-9 • Numismatic strikes of this sutler's tokens in copper and in tin (white metal) were in an early Woodward sale. • James Hasson was listed as a post sutler in Indiana in 1863. In 1863 he resided at 127 New Jersey Avenue in Indianapolis, was a sutler, age 34, and was married. In the 1865 *Indianapolis City Directory* he is listed as a sutler in the Soldiers' Home and residing at 299 New Jersey Avenue. • NL-15C / UI-B-5C • MS-63 $1,200

W-IN-460-005b • 22 mm. R-10 • NL-I5Ba / UI-B-5Ba • EF $400

W-IN-460-005bo • Struck over a Lincoln political campaign token for the 1864 presidential contest (DeWitt AL 1864-37). 22 mm. R-10 • NL-I5Bb / UI-B-5Bb

W-IN-460-005e • 22 mm. R-10 • Unlisted / Unlisted

W-IN-460-010a • 22 mm. R-9 • NL-I10C / UI-B-10C • *Auction:* Litman (PCAC, December 2003), Unc RB, $690

W-IN-460-010b • 22 mm. R-8 • NL-I10Ba / UI-B-10Ba • *Auction:* Bleviss, EF-40, holed, $431.25

W-IN-460-010e • 22 mm. R-10 • NL-I10WM / UI-B-10WM • *Auction:* One was in a Woodward sale.

W-IN-460-025a • 22 mm. R-10 • NL-I25C / UI-B-25C • *Auctions:* PCAC Auction #67 (June 2000), VF, small digs and scratch, $187; Litman (PCAC, December 2003), Unc RB, $690

W-IN-460-025b • 22 mm. R-9 • NL-I25Ba / UI-B-25Ba • *Auction:* Hayden (FPL, August 2014), MS-62, over unidentified token, $1,100

W-IN-460-025bo • Struck over an 1864 Lincoln political campaign token (DeWitt AL 1864-37). Reeded edge. 22 mm. Holed at top, as issued. R-10 • NL-I25Bb / UI-B-25Bb • VF $750

W-IN-460-025e • 22 mm. • Unlisted / Unlisted

W-IN-462-005b • **James Hasson, sutler** • **Class A tokens** • JAMES HASSON / SUTLER / 5 / CENTS IN GOODS. John Stanton backstamp (stamp and brand cutter). 17 mm. R-9 • NL-J5B / UI-C-5B • EF $1,500

W-IN-462-010b • John Stanton backstamp (stamp and brand cutter). 19 mm. R-9 • NL-J10B / UI-C-10B • *Auction:* Hayden (FPL, August 2014), EF, small light reverse stain, $1,500

Kentucky

W-KY-100-005a-1391.

Whitman-KY-100-005a-1391 • **James M. Kerr, sutler, Simmonds Battery First Kentucky Volunteer Cavalry** • **Class A tokens** • SIMMONDS / BATTERY / SUTLER / J.M. KERR. Reeded edge. 19 mm. R-9 • Reverse is Civil War token die 1391. • Simmonds Battery was originally known as Company E of the 1st Kentucky Cavalry. It was organized in Pendleton, Ohio, on June 3, 1861, calling volunteers to serve for three years; it was detached from that unit to become Simmonds Battery in July 1862, named for Captain Seth J. Simmonds who was cashiered (removed for violations) on March 13, 1864. It was sometimes referred to as the 1st Kentucky Independent Battery. It was the only unit from Kentucky to serve in the Eastern Theater. James M.

Kerr, sutler, was a first lieutenant of the group. • NL-M5C / KY-1-5C • *Auctions:* Ford XXIII, MS-64BN, $646; Hayden (FPL, August 2014), MS-63, $1,500

W-KY-100-005b-1391 • Reeded edge. 19 mm. R-8 • NL-M5B / KY-1-5B • *Auctions:* Bunt, EF-45, $881.25; Ford XXIII, MS, damaged, $235; Hayden (July 2014), MS-63, $900

W-KY-100-005e-1391 • Reeded edge. 19 mm. R-9 • NL-M5Z / KY-1-5Z • MS-63 $1,750

W-KY-102-010a-1394 • Reeded edge. 19 mm. R-8 • Reverse is Civil War token die 1394. • NL-M10C / KY-1-10C • *Auctions:* Bleviss, VF, bent, gouged, $161; Hayden (October 2011), MS-62, $600; Hayden (December 2012), MS-64, 60% red, $711; Ford XXIII, MS-63RB, $763.75, MS-64BN, $705, MS-66RB, $1,292.50

W-KY-102-010b-1394 • Reeded edge. 19 mm. R-8 • Reverse is Civil War token die 1394. • NL-M10B / KY-1-10B • *Auction:* Hayden (October 2011), MS-62, $600

W-KY-102-010e-1394 • Reeded edge. 19 mm. R-9 • NL-M10Z / KY-1-10Z • MS-63 $1,750

W-KY-104-025a-1399 • Reeded edge. 19 mm. R-7 • Reverse is Civil War token die 1399. • NL-M25C / KY-1-25C • *Auctions:* Bunt, MS-62RB, $1,762.50; Ford XXIII, MS-64RB, $822.50, MS-65BN, $881.25

W-KY-104-025b-1399 • Reeded edge. 19 mm. R-9 • NL-M25B / KY-1-25B • *Auctions:* Hayden (March 2006), VF, marks, $321; Hayden (July 2006), marks, nick, $175; Ford XXIII, MS-62BN, $558

W-KY-104-025e-1399 • Reeded edge. 19 mm. R-9 • NL-M25Z / KY-1-25Z • MS-63 $1,750

W-KY-106-050a-1404 • Reeded edge. 19 mm. R-8 • Reverse is Civil War token die 1404. • NL-M50C / KY-1-50Ca • *Auctions:* Hayden (March 2010), AU, tiny planchet, $406; Ford XXIII, VF-30BN, $258.50

W-KY-106-050b-1404 • Reeded edge. 19 mm. R-9 • NL-M50B / KY-1-50B • *Auction:* Ford XXIII, MS-64, $940

W-KY-106-050e-1404 • Reeded edge. 19 mm. R-9 • NL-M50Z / KY-1-50Z • MS-63 $1,750

W-KY-106-1047d (?) • Reverse Civil War token die 1047. Reeded edge. 19 mm. R-10 • NL-O-CN / KY-1-CNb • MS-63 $2,500

W-KY-108-1069d • Reverse Civil War token die 1069. Reeded edge. 19 mm. R-10 • NL-N-CN / KY-1-Can • MS-63 $3,000

W-KY-108-1069e • Zinc (per David Schenkman). Reeded edge. 19 mm. R-10? Probably white metal, if it exists. Not known to any contributors to this study, nor does the writer know of any 1069 token in zinc or white metal. *Probably an error listing.* • NL-N-Z / KY-1-Z

W-KY-120-005b • **Wilhelm Schulte, sutler, 6th Regiment Kentucky Volunteer Infantry** • **Class D tokens** • The sutler is thought to have been Wilhelm Schulte. Blank reverse. 19 mm. R-9 • Unlisted / KY-6-5B • *Auction:* Hayden (July 2014), VF details, corroded, $1,800; "Steve Tanenbaum had a dark VF of the other known example; quickly sold privately in the $3,000 range."

W-KY-120-020b • Unusual denomination. • 6.K.Y.I. in hallmark punch / 20 incuse. 26 mm. R-10. • Unlisted / KY-6-20B • In July 2014 Steve Hayden noted that he'd had "a nice unique example that quickly sold privately for about $5,000."

W-KY-40-025a-1084.

W-KY-140-005a-1166 • **21st Regiment Kentucky Volunteer Infantry** • **Class A tokens** • GOOD FOR / 5 / CENTS / 21ST. KY. V.I. 19 mm. R-8 • Reverse with Civil War store card die 1166. Tokens made by the shop of William K. Lanphear, Cincinnati. • The regiment was organized in the end of 1861 in Greensburg and remained in service until the early part of December 1865. More than 200 men died in service, more than half succumbing to disease. • KY-A5C / KY-21-5C • *Auctions:* Hayden (June 2011), About Good, cleaned, some detail missing, $110; Hayden (July 2012), VG+, porous, $80; Ford XXIII, MS-64RB, $1,762.50

W-KY-140-010a-1295 • 19 mm. R-9 • Reverse with Civil War store card die 1295. • KY-A10C / KY-21-10C • *Auction:* Bunt, EF, retoned, $646.25

W-KY-40-025a-1084 • 19 mm. R-9 • Reverse with Civil War store card die 1084. • KY-A25C / KY-21-25C • *Auctions:* Hayden (March 2010), EF, heavy punch mark, $400; Ford XXIII, MS-64RB, $1,880

W-KY-160-005b • **R.B. Hall & Co., sutlers. Kentucky Cavalry** • **Class A** tokens • R.B. HALL & CO / KY. / CAVALRY / 5 / CENTS IN GOODS. John Stanton backstamp (die sinker). 16 mm. R-9 • KY-B5B / KY-CV-5B • VF $1,350

W-KY-160-010b • 19 mm. R-8 • KY-B10B / KY-CV-10B • VF $1,350

W-KY-160-025b • 22 mm. R-9 • KY-B25B / KY-CV-25B • VF $1,350

MAINE

Whitman-ME-100-005a • **C.W. Bangs, sutler, 6th Maine Battery (Artillery)** • **Class A tokens** • C.W. BANGS. / 6TH. ME. /BATTERY. GOOD FOR / 5 / CENTS / KOEHLER (in small letters). 21 mm. R-9 • ME-A5C / ME-6-5C • VF $6,000

W-LME-100-010b • 21 mm. R-9 • ME-A10B / ME-6-10B • VF $6,000

W-LME-100-025j • 21 mm. R-9 • ME-A25N / ME-6-25N • *Auction:* Hayden (October 2011), EF, light scratch, $4,375

MARYLAND

Whitman-MD-100-005b • **C. Gilpin, sutler, 2nd Regiment Maryland Volunteer Infantry** • **Class B tokens** • C. GILPIN / SUTLER / CUMBERLAND MARYLAND 2. RT. P.H.B. / 5 / CENTS / IN / GOODS. Denomination, 5, incuse. 19 mm. R-9 • MD-A5B / MD-2-5B • *Auction:* Hayden (FPL, August 2014), Fine/VG, weakness at reverse rims $2,750

W-MD-100-010b • 10 incuse. 19 mm. R-9 • MD-A10B / MD-2-10B • VF $3,250

W-MD-100-015b • 15 incuse. 19 mm. R-8. Unusual denomination. • MD-A15B / MD-2-15B • *Auctions:* PCAC 7707 Auction #77 (June 2007), Fine, $1,552.50; Hayden (September 2010), VF+, $4,290; Hayden (July 2014), VF+ (not the same token as was sold in 2010), $3,400

W-MD-100-025b • 25 incuse. 19 mm. R-9 • MD-A25B / MD-2-25B • VF $3,250

MASSACHUSETTS

Whitman-MA-100-005b • **Edward Pearl, sutler, [19th Regiment Massachusetts Volunteer Infantry]** • **Class D tokens** • Incuse letters on all. Reverse: Blank on all. 27 mm. R-9 • MA-A5B / MA-19-5B

W-MA-100-025b • Incuse letters. 27 mm. R-9 • MA-A25B / MA-19-25B

W-MA-100-050b • Incuse letters. 27 mm. R-9 • MA-A50Ba / MA-19-50Ba

W-MA-100-050b-x • E. PEARL / 50 / SUTLER. 27 mm. R-9 • MA-A50Bb / MA-19-50Bb

W-MA-100-100b • E. PEARL / E. PEARL / ONE / SUTLER. 25 mm. R-8 • MA-A1Ba / Unlisted • *Auction:* Bleviss, VF-20, porous $57.50

W-MA-100-101b-x • E. PEARL / E. PEARL / ONE / SUTLER. C.H. HATCH / C.H. HATCH. Names cross each other in the center of the planchet. 25

mm. R-9. David Schenkman: "The reason for the name on the reverse of the A1Bb is not known. Possibly C.H. Hatch assumed sutlership of the 19th Massachusetts Volunteer Infantry, counterstamped his name on E. Pearl's tokens, and continued to use them." • MA-A1Ba / MA-19-100Ba • *Auction:* Bunt, EF-45, oxidation spot, $940

W-MA-120-005a.

W-MA-120-010a.

W-MA-120-005a • Harvey Lewis, sutler, 23rd 19th Regiment Massachusetts Volunteer Infantry • Class A tokens • HARVEY LEWIS / SUTLER / 23. MASS. / REGIMENT. GOOD / MERRIAM (in tiny letters) / FOR 5 CTS / BOSTON (in tiny letters) / IN GOODS. 19 mm. R-7. This is the scarcest of the four denominations. • The reverse die is the same on all four denominations. The die was modular with a recess at the center

to permit a small die with the denomination to be inserted. This could be changed at will. • MA-B5C / MA-23-5C • *Auctions:* PCAC Auction #67 (June 2000), AU, $357.50; Bleviss, EF-40, corrosion, scratches, $184; Hayden (December 2012), MS-63, $700; Bunt, VF-30, $305.50; Ford XXIII, MS-64BN, $705

W-MA-120-010a • 19 mm. R-6 • MA-B10C / MA-23-10C • *Auctions:* PCAC Auction #67 (June 2000), AU, $214.50; Hayden (December 2010), MS-65, 50% red, $750; Bunt, VF, dig on reverse, $293.75, VF-20, $258.50, VF, $217.38; Hayden (June 2013), VF, $310; Ford XXIII, AU-50BN, $258.50, MS-66RB, $1,292.50

W-MA-120-025a • 19 mm. R-6 • MA-B25C / MA-23-25C • *Auctions:* PCAC Auction #67 (June 2000), Unc, $209 • Hayden (July 2006), AU, $165; Bleviss, EF-45, light corrosion, $356.50; Bunt, VF-30, $164.50, EF, light verdigris, $111.63, EF-45, $381.88, EF-45, $381.88, AU-58, $499.38; Ford XXIII, EF-40, $258.50, AU-50, $305.50, MS-66RB, $1,410; Hayden (July 2014), MS-62, $500

W-MA-120-050a • 19 mm. R-6 • MA-B50C / MA-23-50C • *Auctions:* PCAC Auction #67 (June 2000), EF, cleaned, corrosion, $220; Heritage (February 2008), EF, $529; Heritage (September 2008), EF-40, $546.25; Bleviss, EF-40, $253; Bunt, VF-30, $199.75, VF-30, $211.50, VF-35, $176.25, VF-35, $258.50, EF-40, $199.75, EF-40, $199.75; Ford XXIII, EF-40, $188, EF-40, $258.50, MS-65RB, $822.50, MS-66BN, $822.50; Hayden (FPL, August 2014), MS-64, $1,500

MICHIGAN

Whitman-MI-100-005a • J.A. Leggat, sutler, 3rd 19th Regiment Michigan Volunteer Cavalry • Class A tokens • J.A. LEGGAT / 5 / SUTLER 3D MICH. CAVALRY CHECK / 5 / CENTS /

SUTLER GOODS. 20 mm. R-7. Tokens of this issuer are usually seen in circulated grades. • MI-A5C / MI-3-5C • *Auctions:* PCAC Auction #67 (June 2000), VF/EF, $275; Bleviss, EF-40, corrosion, $115

W-MI-100-010a • 20 mm. R-6 • MI-A10C / MI-3-10C • *Auctions:* Bleviss, VF-20, old cleaning, verdigris, $276; Bunt, VG-10, $199.75, Fine-12, $176.25; Ford XXIII, AU, damaged, $188, AU-55BN, $381.88; Hayden (FPL, August 2014), Fine+, $425

W-MI-100-025a • 20 mm. R-9 • MI-A25C / MI-3-25C • *Auctions:* Litman (PCAC, December 2003), EF/AU, $948.75; Bunt, VF, heavy porosity,

$199.75; Hayden (FPL, August 2014), AU, Schenkman plate token, $1,850

W-MI-100-025b • 20 mm. R-7 • MI-A25B / MI-3-25B • *Auctions:* PCAC Auction #67 (June 2000), VF, $249.70; Bleviss, VF-35, porous, $161; Hayden (March 2010), VF, $488; Hayden (October 2011), EF, porous $450; Hayden (FPL, August 2014), MS-62, $2,250

W-MI-100-025j • 20 mm. R-10 • MI-A25N / MI-3-25N

MISSOURI

Whitman-MO-100-005a • **John W. LaForce, sutler, 1st Regiment Missouri Light Artillery Provisional Battery** • **Class D tokens** • Crudely stamped thin rectangular tags, trimmed corners, usually holed. R-9 • Unlisted / MO-1-5C • VF $4,500

W-MO-100-010a • R-9 • Unlisted / MO-1-10C • VF $4,500

W-MO-100-025a • R-9 • Unlisted / MO-1-25C • VF $4,500

W-MO-100-050a • R-9 • Unlisted / MO-1-50C • VF $4,500

W-MO-120-010b • **A. Schwabacher, sutler, 13th Regiment Missouri Volunteers, U.S. Veteran Reserve Corps** • **Class C token** • 13TH. REGT. / U.S.R.C. / A. SCHWABACHER / 10 CENTS. Blank reverse. 22 mm. R-8 • Thought to have been issued in connection with a Missouri regiment, as the U.S.R.C. abbreviation was widely assigned to military units in that state during the Civil War. • NL-V10B / US-13-10B • *Auctions:* Hayden (July 2007), AU+, 715.77; Bunt, AU-50, $646.25

NEBRASKA TERRITORY

W-NC-100-025a.

Whitman-NT-100-005b • **P. Hoddy & Co., sutlers, 1st Regiment Nebraska Volunteers** • **Class A tokens** • P. HODDY & CO. / FIRST / NEBRASKA / REG. / 5 / CENTS IN GOODS. John Stanton backstamp (stamp and brand cutter). 19 mm.

R-8. Tokens of this issuer are usually seen in circulated grades. • EF $1,000

W-NC-100-025a • John Stanton backstamp (stamp and brand cutter). 22 mm. R-7 • *Auctions:* Hayden (February 2012), EF, with light marks, $500; Bunt, VF-35, $646.25; Ford XXIII, EF-45BN, $705, MS-61BN, $646.25

W-NT-120-005b • **John W. Hugus, sutler, Fort Kearney** • **Class C tokens** • J.W. HUGUS SUTLER U.S.A. / GOOD FOR / 5 CTS / IN SUTLERS / GOODS. / FT KEARNEY Brass. R-10 •

Hugus visited Fort Kearney in mid-August of 1864 on business, but had no business site there at the time. He seems to have acquired his sutler post shortly afterward. By autumn 1865 he was a notary public in that location. Hugus was associated with the First National Bank of Omaha in the late 1860s. He was a post trader at Fort Steele, Wyoming, from 1876 to 1883. • Unlisted / NT-FKa-5B • VF $9,000

W-NT-120-025b • J.W. HUGUS SUTLER U.S.A. / GOOD FOR / 25 CTS / IN SUTLERS / GOODS. / FT KEARNEY N.T. Blank reverse. Brass. R-9 • David Schenkman: "The description of this token was obtained from a photograph. It is assumed to be struck with incuse lettering. The size is not known." • NE-B25B / NT-FKa-25B • VF $12,000

New Hampshire

W-NH-100-005a.

W-NH-100-010b.

Whitman-NH-100-005a • Warren A. Farr, sutler, 24th Regiment New Hampshire Volunteer Infantry • Class A tokens • W.A. FARR / 14 / N.H. VOLS. GOOD FOR / 5 / CENTS / KOEHLER (in small letters). 21 mm. R-9. Tokens of this issuer are usually seen

in low circulated grades, indicating they were used more intensely than the typical sutler's tokens. Farr also issued scrip notes, of which many blank (not filled out) examples exist today. Over a period of time Farr was a retail merchant in Walpole in the Civil War era. Later he was a blacksmith, saw-mill operator, and grist-mill operator in West Chesterfield. • NH-A5C / NH-14-5C • NH-A5C • *Auction:* Hayden (FPL, August 2014), EF, $2,850

W-NH-100-010b • 21 mm. R-9 • NH-A10B / NH-14-10B • *Auction:* Ford XXIII, AU, bent, $329

W-NH-100-025b • 21 mm. R-10 • NH-A25B / NH-14-25B

W-NH-100-025j • 21 mm. R-7 • NH-A25N / NH-14-25N • *Auctions:* Bunt, VF, oxidized, $646.25, EF-40, $1,762.50; Ford XXIII, Fine-12, $352.50, VF, holed, $258.50; Hayden (FPL, August 2014), Fine-12, $600, VF, granular surfaces, $900

New York

W-NY-100-010b.

Whitman-NY-100-005a • John J. Benson, sutler, 1st Mounted Rifles • Class A tokens • J.J. BENSON / GOOD FOR / 5 / CENTS / SUTLER 1ST MTD RIFLES. 5 (within wreath). 19 mm. R-10. Tokens of this issuer are usually seen in circulated grades. • In early 1866 Benson was still sutler for the regiment and bought out the interests of three other traders. • NY-A5C / NY-1-5C

W-NY-100-005g • 19 mm. R-7 • NY-A5L / NY-1-5L • *Auctions:* PCAC Auction #67 (June 2000), EF, dark and granular, $132; Bleviss, VF-25, $184; Hayden (October 2011), EF, $315; Bunt, VF, oxidized, digs, $30.55, VF, oxidized, $152.75; Ford XXIII, EF, damaged, $129.25

W-NY-100-010b • 20 mm. R-6 • NY-A10B / NY-1-10B • *Auctions:* Slabaugh (PCAC, June 2001), VF, $120.75; Heritage (September 2003), EF-45, $184; Heritage (September 2008), EF-45, $322; Bleviss, VF-25, rough and cleaned, $69; Hayden (June 2005), EF, $250; Bunt, VF-30, $176.25, EF-40, $176.25, EF-40, $188, EF-40, $188, EF-45, $182.13, EF-45, $258.50; Ford XXIII, AU-55, $258.50, AU-58, $381.88; Hayden (July 2014), AU, $240; Hayden (FPL, August 2014), VF+, $275, MS-63, $1,000

W-NY-100-010n • 20 mm. Iron (earlier listed as white metal). R-9 • NY-A10WM / NY-1-10I • VF $1,500

W-NY-100-025a • 24 mm. R-6 • NY-A25C / NY-1-25C • *Auctions:* PCAC Auction #67 (June 2000), VF, $165; Slabaugh (PCAC, June 2001), VF, $120.75; Fauver (PCAC July 2006), VF/EF, $166.75; Heritage (September 2008), VF-35, $322; Bleviss, AU-58, $460; Hayden (October 2011), EF, $313.87; Hayden (December 2012), MS-63, 30% red, $750; Bunt, VF, light scratches, $152.75, VF-25, $164.50, VF-30, $211.50, VF-30, $305.50, AU, lightly cleaned, $305.50; Ford XXIII, VF-30BN, $199.75, EF, damaged, $176.25, EF-40, $258.50, EF-40BN, $258.50, EF-45BN, $305.50; Hayden (February 2012), VF+, $269; Hayden (FPL, August 2014), MS-63, $1,500

W-NY-100-025b • 24 mm. R-9 • NY-A25B / NY-1-25B • *Auctions:* eBay (July 2005), EF/AU, $346.69; Bunt, VF-25, rim bump, $188

W-NY-100-050e • 26 mm. R-6 • Listed as NY-A50WM / NY-1-50I • *Auctions:* PCAC Auction #67 (June 2000), Ch AU, $187; Bunt, EF, lightly granular, $188, EF, oxidized, $82.25, EF, oxidized, $99.88, AU, stained, $99.88, AU, stained, $99.88, AU, oxidation, $152.75, AU-50, light oxidation, $282; Hayden (FPL, August 2014), MS-62, $1,000

W-NY-120-005b • **R.S. Parker, sutler, 3rd Regiment New York Volunteer Cavalry** • **Class A tokens** • R.S. PARKER / SUTLER / 3' N.Y. CAV. / 5 / CTS IN GOODS. Reverse: Blank on all. 16 mm. R-9 • NY-B5B / NY-3-5B • VF $1,500

W-NY-120-010b • 19 mm. R-9 • NY-B10B / NY-3-10Ba • *Auctions:* Heritage (March 2010), VF details, damaged, $143.75; Ford XXIII, EF, bent, $470

W-NY-120-025b • 22 mm. R-9 • NY-B25B / NY-3-25B • VF $2,000

W-NY-120-050b • 25 mm. R-10 • NY-B50B / NY-3-50B • VF $2,000

W-NY-120-100b • 100 CENTS. 27 mm. R-9 • NY-B100B / NY-3-100B • EF $2,000

W-NY-140-003g • **G.C. Freedom, sutler, 5th Regiment New York Volunteer Cavalry** • **Class C tokens** • G.C.F. / 3 / SUTLER. Blank reverse. 25 mm. R-9. Unusual denomination. Tokens of this issuer are usually seen in circulated grades. All lettering is incuse. Research by David Schenkman indicates that these tokens were issued by G.C. Freedom, sutler for the 5th New York Volunteers. • NY-C3L / NY-5-3L • VF $1,350

W-NY-140-005g • 25 mm. R-9 • NY-C5L / NY-5-5L • VF $1,350

W-NY-140-010g • 25 mm. R-8 • NY-C10L / NY-5-10L • *Auctions:* Bleviss, EF-40, porous, oxidation, $488.75; Ford

XXIII, EF, damaged, $705, AU-53, $1,057.50, AU-50, $1,292.50

W-NY-140-025g • 25 mm. R-9 • Unlisted / NY-5-25L • VF $1,350

W-NY-140-050g • 25 mm. R-9 • NY-C50L / NY-5-50L • VF $1,350

W-NY-160-010b • **F. Mangold, sutler, 9th Regiment, New York State Militia, Infantry** • **Class B tokens** • NEW YORK ST. M. / 10 / CENTS / IN / GOODS. Denomination, 10, incuse. F. MANGOLD. 19 mm. R-6. Tokens of this issuer are usually seen in circulated grades. • The 9th Regiment New York State Militia was also known as the 83rd Regiment New York Volunteers. • NY-D10B / NY-9-10B • *Auctions:* Slabaugh (PCAC, June 2001), Fine, $166.75; Hayden (December 2008), VF+, $343; Bunt, VF-30, $211.50, VF-30, $258.50, VF-35, $105.75, VF-35, $211.50, D10B VF-35, $329, EF-40, $395.98; Ford XXIII, AU-55, $381.88, AU-58, $411.25, MS-61, $499.38; Hayden (July 2014), AU+, $475; Hayden (FPL, August 2014), EF $375

W-NY-160-020b • 20 incuse. 19 mm. R-7. Unusual denomination. Some are silver plated. • NY-D20B / NY-9-20B • *Auctions:* Ford XXIII, AU-58, $381.88, MS-61, $558.13

W-NY-180-005b • **[G.H. Benedict], sutler, [13th Regiment New York Heavy Artillery]** • **Class A tokens** • G.H. BENEDICT / 5 / CENTS / IN GOODS. 5 (within circle of rays). 18 mm. R-8 • This token, which is included in early listings of sutler tokens, is assumed to have been issued by G.H. Benedict while sutler for the 13th New York Heavy Artillery. • NY-E5B / NY-13-5B • *Auctions:* Hayden (March 2010), VF, $1,000; Ford XXIII, EF, bent, $352.50; Hayden (February 2012), EF+, $950

W-NY-180-025b • 24 mm. R-10 • Unlisted / NY-13-25B • EF $2,500

W-NY-200-005b • **G.C. Platner, sutler, 117th New York Volunteer Infantry Regiment** • **Class D tokens** • G.C PLATNER / 5 / 117 N.Y.V. 23 mm. R-10 • Unlisted / NY-117-5B • VF $2,500

W-NY-200-025b • 23 mm. R-10 • Unlisted / NY-117-25B • VF $2,500

W-NY-220-005b • **E.E. Bedford, sutler, 127th New York Volunteer Infantry Regiment** • **Class A tokens** • E.E. BEDFORD. / 127TH. / N.Y.S.V. / GOOD FOR / 5 / CENTS / KOEHLER (in small letters). 21 mm. R-9. Tokens of this issuer are usually seen in circulated grades. • NY-F5B / NY-127-5B • *Auction:* Ford XXIII, AU, scratches, $188

W-NY-220-010a • 21 mm. R-8 • NY-F10C / NY-127-10C • *Auctions:* Bunt, VF-25, rim bend, $411.25; Ford XXIII, AU-55BN, $998.75, AU-55BN, $822.50; Hayden (July 2014), AU-58, $900; Hayden (FPL, August 2014), VF, fairly large edge dents, $600

W-NY-220-025j • 21 mm. R-8 • NY-F25N / NY-127-25N • *Auctions:* PCAC Auction #67 (June 2000), EF, edge nick, $341; Hayden (June 2011), EF, tiny clip, $1,138.50; Ford XXIII, AU-50, $763

W-NY-240-005b • **F.P. Perkins, sutler, 145th New York Volunteer Infantry Regiment** • **Class A tokens** • F.P.P. / 145 REGT. / N.Y.S.V. 5 / CENTS. 18 mm. R-8 • NY-G5B / NY-145-5B • *Auction:* PCAC Auction #67 (June 2000), VF, $181.50

W-NY-240-010b • 18 mm. R-8 • NY-G10B / NY-145-10B • *Auction:* Hayden (July 2010), VF+, $962.50

W-NY-240-025b • F.P.P. / 145 REGT. / N.Y.S.V. 25 (with six pointed star). 18 mm. R-9 • NY-G25B / NY-145-25B • *Auction:* Bunt, VF, heavy porosity, $381.88

W-NY-240-050b • F.P.P. / 145 REGT. / N.Y.S.V. 50 (within circle of rays). 18 mm. R-9 • NY-G50B / NY-145-50B • VF $1,350

W-NY-260-005b • **William Vanderbeek, sutler, 158th New York Volunteer Infantry Regiment** • **Class C tokens** • WM. VANDERBEEK / SUTLERS CHECK / 5 / CENTS. Blank reverse on all. 22 mm. R-8 • Vanderbeek, recently retired as a sutler, died of yellow fever in New Bern, North Carolina, on September 17, 1864. His tokens were struck by the Scovill Manufacturing Co. of Waterbury, Connecticut. • NL-AD5B / NY-158-5B • *Auctions:* Bunt, MS-62, $528.75; Hayden (FPL, August 2014), MS-63, $1,250

W-NY-260-010a • 20 mm. R-10 • Unlisted / NY-158-10C • MS-63 $1,500

W-NY-260-010b • 20 mm. R-8 • NL-AD10B / NY-158-10B • *Auctions:* Slabaugh (PCAC, June 2001), VF, $184; Bleviss, VF-30, $322; Ford XXIII, MS-62, $558.13

W-NY-260-015b • 22 mm. R-9. Unusual denomination. • NL-AD15B / NY-158-15B • *Auction:* Ford XXIII, MS-63, $1,057.50

W-NY-260-025b • 22 mm. R-9 • NL-AD25B / NY-158-25B • *Auction:* Ford XXIII, MS-62, $587.50

W-NY-260-050a • 28 mm. R-9. American Numismatic Society. • NL-AD50C / NY-158-50C • MS-63 $1,500

W-NY-260-050b • 28 mm. R-6 • NL-AD50B / NY-158-50B • *Auctions:* Bunt, VF, scratches, $141, EF-45, $258.50, AU-50, $129.25, MS-63, Schenkman plate token, $705; Ford XXIII, MS-62, $499.38, MS-62, $558.13, MS-65, $1,028.13; (FPL, August 2014), MS-62, $575

OHIO

Whitman-OH-100-005b • **00 Regiment** • **Class C token** • OH Schenkman A5B • O.V.M. 00' REG'T. / GOOD FOR / 5 CENTS. / IN GOODS. Blank reverse. 22 mm. R-8 • There was no regiment by this name. Likely this was a sample token used to solicit orders. • OH-A5B / OH-00-5B • *Auctions:* Hayden (October 2011), MS-62, 30% bright, $1,775; Bunt, AU-55, Schenkman plate token, $646.25; Ford XXIII, MS-62, $528.75

W-OH-120-005b • **H.D. McKinney, sutler, 1st Regiment Ohio Volunteer Artillery** • **Class A tokens** • H.D. McKINNEY / 1ST. O.V. / ARTILLERY / 5 / CENTS IN GOODS. John Stanton backstamp (die sinker). 16 mm. R-7. Tokens of this issuer are usually seen in circulated grades. • OH-B5B / OH-1-5B • *Auctions:* Bunt, EF-40, $329; Hayden (June 2013), EF, $350; Ford XXIII, MS-61, $528.75

W-OH-140-005b • **2nd Regiment Ohio Volunteer Cavalry** • **Class A tokens** • 2ND. REGIMENT / OHIO / CAVALRY / 5 ? CENTS. John Stanton backstamp (die sinker) on all. 19 mm. R-6 • OH-C5B / OH-2a-5B • *Auctions:* eBay (May 2008), EF, $315.09; Hayden (FPL, August 2014), AU+, $850

W-OH-140-010b • 19 mm. R-10 • OH-C10B / OH-2a-10B • VF $1,500

W-OH-140-025b • 19 mm. R-7 • OH-C25B / OH-2a-25B • *Auction:* Hayden (FPL, August 2014), EF, light marks, $375

W-OH-160-005c • **2nd Regiment Ohio Volunteer Cavalry** • **Class A tokens** • 2ND. REGIMENT / OHIO / CAVALRY / 5 ? CENTS. John Stanton backstamp (stamp and brand cutter) on all. 22 mm. R-9 • OH-D5C / OH-2b-5C • VF $1,500

W-OH-160-010c • 22 mm. R-10 • OH-D10C / OH-2b-10C • VF $2,000

W-OH-160-025c • 22 mm. R-9 • OH-D25C / OH-2b-25C • VF $2,000

W-OH-180-005b • **John I. Metcalf, sutler, 3rd Regiment Ohio Volunteer Cavalry** • **Class A tokens** • JOHN I. METCALF / 3RD REG. / O. CAV. U.S.A. / 10 / CENTS IN GOODS. John Stanton backstamp (die sinker). 16 mm. R-8 • OH-E5B / OH-3-5B • EF $500

W-OH-180-010b • 19 mm. R-8 • OH-E10B / OH-3-10B • *Auctions:* Bleviss, VF-35, porous, $115; Bunt, VF, oxidized, $111.63; Ford XXIII, MS-62, $675.63

W-OH-180-025b • 22 mm. R-6 • OH-E25B / OH-3-25B • *Auctions:* Bleviss, VF-30, holed, $126.50; Hayden (July 2010), EF+, $528; Bunt, VF-30, $129.25, EF, light corrosion, $129.25; Hayden (July 2014), EF+, $466

W-OH-200-005b • **E.W. Hamlin, sutler, 4th Regiment Ohio Volunteer Cavalry** • **Class A tokens** • 4TH REG. O.V.C. / GOOD FOR / 5 / CENTS IN / GOODS / E.W. HAMLIN SUT. John Stanton backstamp (die sinker). 16 mm. R-7. Tokens of this issuer are usually seen in circulated grades. • OH-F5B / OH-4a-5B • *Auctions:* PCAC Auction #67 (June 2000), EF with scattered spots

throughout, $154; Bunt, VF, oxidized, $35.25, EF-40, $176.25

W-OH-200-010b • 4TH. REG. O.V.C. / GOOD FOR / 10 / CENTS IN / GOODS / E.W. HAMLIN, SUT. Reverse: John Stanton backstamp (die sinker). Brass. 19 mm. R-8 • OH-F10B / OH-4a-10B • *Auctions:* Bunt, EF-40, $282, AU, lightly cleaned, $211.50; Hayden (June 2013), AU+, $450; Ford XXIII, MS-62, $646.25

W-OH-200-025b • 22 mm. R-7 • OH-F25B / OH-4a-25B • *Auctions:* Hayden (October 2011), EF, $350; Bunt, VF-25, $188

W-OH-220-005b • **Charles Stevens, sutler, 4th Regiment Ohio Volunteer Infantry** • **Class A tokens** • CHAS. STEVENS / 5 / CENTS / IN GOODS. Reverse: PILKINGTON / MAKER / 83 / EXCHANGE PLACE / BALTIMORE. 18 mm. R-9. From David Schenkman: "According to F.G. Duffield's 1907 *Numismatist* listing of Baltimore tokens, 'Charles Stevens appears in the directories of 1864 and 1865 as a sutler, at 287 Hollins Street and 675 Lexington Street, respectively.'" Stevens was also sutler of the 4th Regiment of the Ohio Volunteer Infantry, as listed here. J.E. Pilkington, the die sinker whose advertisement is on the reverse of the token, was at 83 Exchange Place only during 1864. • MD-B5B / OH-4b-5B • VF $2,500

W-OH-220-025b • The reverse is an incuse impression of the obverse. 18 mm. R-9 • Unlisted / OH-4b-25B • VF $2,500

W-OH-240-005b • **5th Regiment Ohio Volunteer Cavalry** • **Class C tokens** • IN GOODS / 5 / CENTS / 5TH REG'T O.V. Reverse is an incuse mirror image of the obverse. 22 mm. R-7. Tokens of this issuer are usually seen in circulated grades.

• J.A. Hunt and F.E. Arnold both served as sutlers for the 5th Ohio Volunteers but are not mentioned on the token. • OH-G5B / OH-5-5B • *Auctions:* Hayden (March 2010), EF, hairlines, $385; Bunt (January 2013), VF-25, $199.75, VF-30, $329, AU-50, $152.75; Ford XXIII, AU, bent, $199.75, MS-62, $646.25; Hayden (February 2012), AU, $300; Hayden (FPL, August 2014), VF, $325, MS-62, $1,250

W-OH-240-005g • IN GOODS / 5 / CENTS / 5TH REG'T O.V. Reverse is an incuse mirror image of the obverse. 22 mm. R-10 • OH-G5L / OH-5-5L

W-OH-260-005b • **S. Hatch, sutler, 7th Regiment Ohio Volunteer Cavalry** • **Class C tokens** • S. HATCH. / 7TH REG / O.V.M. / 5 / CENTS. Reverse: Blank on all. 22 mm. R-8 • OH-H5B / OH-7-5B • *Auctions:* Bunt, VF, retoned, $223.25, EF-45, $329; Hayden (FPL, August 2014), MS-63, $1,100

W-OH-260-025b • S. HATCH / 7TH REG / O.V.M. / 25 / CENTS. Reverse: 25 mm. R-8 • OH-H25Ba / OH-7-25Ba • *Auctions:* Bunt, AU, cleaned, $329, AU-50, small spot, $352.50; Ford XXIII, MS-62, $470, MS-62, $558.13

W-OH-260-025b-x • S. HATCH / 7TH REG / O.V.M. / 25 / CENTS. John Stanton backstamp (stamp and brand cutter). 25 mm. R-10 • OH-H25Bb / OH-7-25Bb • VF $1,500

W-OH-280-005b • **Phineas P. Merwin, sutler, 8th Regiment Ohio Volunteer Cavalry** • **Class A tokens** • P. MERWIN, / 5 / CENTS / 8TH. REG. O.V.M. John Stanton backstamp (die sinker). 17 mm. R-8. An obverse brockage of I5B exists. • OH-I5B / OH-8-5B • *Auctions:* Bunt, VF-35, $381.88, EF, cleaned, $223.25; Ford XXIII, MS-62, $587.50

W-OH-280-025b • John Stanton backstamp (die sinker). 22 mm. R-7 • OH-I25B / OH-8-25B • *Auctions:* Bunt, VF, small dent, $188, VF-25, $235, AU-50, $411.25; Ford XXIII, MS-61, $587.50

W-OH-300-005b • **T.E Burke, sutler, 10th Regiment Ohio Volunteer Infantry** • **Class A tokens** • T.E. BURKE / 10 / REG. O.V.I. / 5 / CENTS. John Stanton backstamp (stamp and brand cutter). 17 mm. R-9 • OH-J5B / OH-10a-5B • VF $1,750

W-OH-300-010b • John Stanton backstamp (stamp and brand cutter). 19 mm. R-10 • OH-J10Ba / OH-10a-10Ba • VF $1,750

W-OH-300-010b-x • Denomination, 10, cut over 25. 19 mm. R-9 • OH-J10Bb / OH-10a-10Bb • EF $2,250

W-OH-300-025b • 22 mm. R-9 • OH-J25B / OH-10a-25B • EF $2,250

W-OH-320-025b • **Ferguson, sutler, 10th Regiment Ohio Volunteer Infantry** • **Class A tokens** • 10TH REG. O.V. / FERGUSON. / 25 CENTS IN GOODS. John Stanton backstamp (die sinker). Brass. 19 mm. R-9 • OH-K25B / OH-10b-25B • EF $3,000

W-OH-320-050b • John Stanton backstamp (die sinker). 22 mm. R-9 • OH-K50B / OH-10b-50B • AU $3,000

W-OH-340-005b • **12th Regiment Ohio Volunteer Cavalry** • **Class A tokens** • SUTLERS CHECK / 12' / O.V.C. / 5 / CTS. IN GOODS. John Stanton backstamp (stamp and brand cutter). 17 mm. R-9 • OH-L5B / OH-12-5B • VF $2,000

W-OH-340-025b • 22 mm. R-10 • Unlisted / OH-12-25B • VF $2,250

W-OH-360-005h • 21st Regiment Ohio Volunteer Infantry • 21ST O.V.I. / 5 / 1863. GOOD FOR / 5 / IN GOODS. Black hard rubber, 32 mm. R-9. Denominations are incuse and painted white. An example exists with no incuse denominations. • OH-M5R / OH-21-5R • VF $3,500

W-OH-360-010h • Black hard rubber, oval, 25 x 35 mm. R-9. Denominations are incuse and painted white. An example exists with no incuse denominations. • OH-M10R / OH-21-10R • VF $3,500

W-OH-360-025h • Black hard rubber, oval, 35 x 45 mm. R-9. Denominations are incuse and painted white. • OH-M25R / OH-21-25R • VF $3,500

W-OH-380-025a-1082.

W-OH-380-005a-1168 • **G.W. Forbes, sutler, 23rd Regiment Ohio Volunteer Infantry** • **Class A tokens** • G.W. FORBES / SUTLER / 5 / CENTS / 23D O. U.S.A. 19 mm. R-7 • Reverse with Civil War store card die 1168. Some were made for the numismatic trade. Edward Cogan's auction of September 1863 had a set of all three varieties. Forbes was Jewish and provided the soldiers of that religion with matzos and prayer books suitable for the celebration of the 1863 Passover Seder. • OH-N5C / OH-23-5C • *Auctions:* Bunt, Fine-12, $129.25, VF-20, $528.75; Hayden (July 2014), MS-64RB, $2,100. "This is only the second Uncirculated example we have seen offered."

W-OH-380-010a-1295 • 19 mm. R-8 • Reverse with Civil War store card die 1295. • OH-N10C / OH-23-510 • *Auc-*

tions: Hayden (October 2011), MS-64, 40% red, $1,475; Ford XXIII, AU-55BN, $440.63, MS-65RB, $1,292.50

W-OH-380-025a-1082 • 19 mm. R-8 • Reverse with Civil War store card die 1082. • OH-N25C / OH-23-25C • *Auction:* Bunt, AU-58, $3,525

W-OH-400-005a • **Piatt's Zouaves, 34th Regiment Ohio Volunteer Infantry** • **Class A tokens** • 5 CTS. IN GOODS / ZOUAVE / 34TH. REG. O.V.M. John Stanton backstamp (die sinker). 22 mm. R-6. Tokens of this issuer are usually seen in circulated grades. • In his diary entry for June 3, 1862, future president Rutherford B. Hayes noted: "All our regiments have behaved reasonably well except [the] Thirty-fourth, Piatt's Zouaves, and Paxton's Cavalry. Don't abuse them, but they were pretty shabby. The Zouaves were scattered seventy miles, reporting us all cut to pieces, etc., etc." Other observers felt the unit to be comical with its red pants and zouave attire and to be poorly organized. Units that called themselves zouaves often were outfitted in colorful uniforms, sometimes with Oriental or other ornate headwear. • OH-O5C / OH-34-5C • *Auctions:* Hayden (June 2011), MS-63, 10% red, $2,035; Hayden (December 2012), AU, $775; Bunt, VF, light scratches, $211.50, EF-45, $440.63, EF-45, $587.50, AU-55, tiny scratch, $998.75; Ford XXIII, EF-45BN, $499.38, EF-45BN, $528.75; Hayden (FPL, August 2014), EF+, $750

W-OH-400-005b • John Stanton backstamp (die sinker). 22 mm. R-9 • OH-O5B / OH-34-5B • *Auction:* Bleviss, VF-20, porous, $80.50

W-OH-420-005b • **41st Regiment Ohio Volunteer Infantry** • **Class C tokens** • SUTLERS CHECK / 41 REG. O.V.M. / 5 / CENTS. Blank reverse. 19

mm. R-5. Tokens of this issuer are usually seen in circulated grades. • OH-P5B / OH-41-5B • *Auctions:* Bunt, VF, oxidation, split planchet, $88.13, VF, light oxidation, $105.75, VF, oxidation, cracked planchet, clip, $99.88, EF, light oxidation, $176.25; Hayden (FPL, August 2014), EF, porous, $250

W-OH-420-025b • 22 mm. R-7 • OH-P25Ba / OH-41-25Ba • *Auctions:* Bleviss, Fine-15, split, porous, $57.50; Hayden (March 2006), Fine, dark and corroded, $50; Bunt, VF, granular, $94, AU-50, $646.25; Ford XXIII, MS-63, $763.75

W-OH-420-025b-x • John Stanton backstamp (die sinker). 22 mm. R-8 • OH-P25Bb / OH-41-25Bb • EF $550

W-OH-440-005b • **McBeth & Aull, sutlers, 45th Regiment Ohio Volunteer Infantry** • **Class A tokens** • McBETH & AULL / O.V.I. 45' REG. / 5 / CTS. IN GOODS. John Stanton backstamp (stamp and brand cutter). 19 mm. R-8. Tokens of this issuer are usually seen in circulated grades. • OH-Q5B / OH-45-5B • *Auctions:* Bleviss, VF-35, oxidation, $299; Bunt, VF-20, $199.75, VF-30, $199.75; Ford XXIII, AU-58, $558.13

W-OH-440-010b • 22 mm. R-8 • OH-Q10B / OH-45-10B • EF $600

W-OH-460-005b • **B. Howell, sutler, 46th Regiment Ohio Volunteer Infantry** • **Class A tokens** • B. HOWELL / 5 / CENTS / IN GOODS. / 46 REG. O.V. U.S.A. John Stanton backstamp (stamp and brand cutter). 17 mm. R-8. Tokens of this issuer are usually seen in circulated grades. • OH-R5B / OH-46-5B • *Auctions:* Ford XXIII, EF, damaged, $176.25

W-OH-460-010b • B. HOWELL / 10 / CENTS IN GOODS. / 46 REG. O.V. U.S.A. John Stanton backstamp (stamp and brand cutter). 19 mm. R-9 • OH-R10B / OH-46-10B • *Auction:* Ford XXIII, AU-58, $528.75

W-OH-460-025b • John Stanton backstamp (stamp and brand cutter). 22 mm. R-9 • OH-R25B / OH-46-25B • *Auction:* Bunt, VF, retoned, $176.25

W-OH-480-005b • **A. Hirsch, sutler, 47th Regiment Ohio Volunteer Infantry** • **Class C token** • O.V.M. 47' REG'T. / A. HIRSCH / GOOD FOR / 5 / CENTS. / IN GOODS. Blank reverse. 22 mm. R-7. Most tokens of this issuer are in circulated grades. • OH-S5B / OH-47-5B • *Auctions:* eBay (September 2009), VF, corrosion, $791; Bunt, VF-30, light bend, $188, EF-45, $499.38; Ford XXIII, MS-62, $528.75, MS-63, $646.25

W-OH-500-005b • **M.H. Sullivan & Co., sutlers, 50th Regiment Ohio Volunteer Infantry** • **Class A tokens** • M.H. SULLIVAN & CO. / SUTLERS / 5 / CENTS IN GOODS / 50TH. REG. O. VOL. John Stanton backstamp (die sinker). 19 mm. R-7. Tokens of this issuer are usually seen in high circulated grades. • OH-T5B / OH-50-5B • *Auctions:* Hayden (July 2007), EF+, $500.50; Bunt, AU, retoned, spot, $211.50, VF-35, $440.63, AU-50, $558.13; Ford XXIII, AU, damaged, $199.75

W-OH-500-025b • Blank reverse. 25 mm. R-9 • OH-T25B / OH-50-25B • *Auction:* Ford XXIII, AU-55, $411.25

W-OH-520-005b • **S. Brown, sutler, 51st Regiment Ohio Volunteer Infantry** • **Class A tokens** • S. BROWN / 51' O. REG / 5 / CENTS IN GOODS. John Stanton backstamp (die sinker). 16 mm. R-9. Tokens of this issuer are usually seen in circulated grades. • OH-U5B / OH-51-5B • EF $750

W-OH-520-010b • John Stanton backstamp (die sinker). 19 mm. R-9 • OH-U10B / OH-51-10B • EF $750

W-OH-520-025b • John Stanton backstamp (die sinker). 22 mm. R-9 • Unlisted / OH-51-25B • EF $750

W-OH-540-005d-1346.

W-OH-540-050d-1122.

W-OH-540-005a-1346 • **James B. Spitzer, sutler, 55th Regiment Ohio Volunteer Infantry • Class A tokens** • J.B. SPITZER / SUTLER. / 5 / CENTS / 55 O.V.I. 19 mm. R-8 • Reverse with Civil War store card die 1346. All tokens were made by the shop of William K. Lanphear, Cincinnati. • OH-V5C / OH-55a-5C • *Auctions:* Hayden (December 2008), MS-63, $825; Bunt, VF-25, $223.25

W-OH-540-005d-1346 • 19 mm. R-10 • OH-V5CN / OH-55a-5CN • MS-63 $2,000

W-OH-540-010a-1226 • 19 mm. R-8 • Reverse with Civil War store card die 1226. • OH-V10C / OH-55a-10C • *Auctions:* Hayden (July 2010), MS-63, 20% red, $875; Hayden (July 2014), MS-63, 20% red, $959

W-OH-540-010b-1226 • 19 mm. R-10 • Reverse with Civil War store card die 1226. • Unlisted / OH-55a-10B • VF $1,500

W-OH-540-010d-1226 • 19 mm. R-10 • OH-V10CN / OH-55a-10CN • MS-63 $2,000

W-OH-540-025a-1168 • 19 mm. R-7 • Reverse with Civil War store card die 1168. • OH-V25C / OH-55a-25C • *Auctions:* Bleviss, VF-25, light porosity, $299; eBay (January 2011), Unc RB, $1,200; Bunt, VF-30, $329, AU-55, $1,292.50, AU-58, $822.50; Ford XXIII, MS-64BN, $1,997.50

W-OH-540-025d-1168 • 19 mm. R-10 • OH-V25CN / OH-55a-25CN • MS-63 $2,000

W-OH-540-050a-1122 • 19 mm. R-8 • Reverse with Civil War store card die 1122. • OH-V50C / OH-55a-50C • *Auctions:* Hayden (December 2006), VF, retoned, clip, $257.13; Bleviss, Fine-12, rough, cleaned, $138; Hayden (July 2012), MS-63, 30% red, $1,075; Ford XXIII, MS-63BN, $3,055; Heritage (January 2014, Internet), AU-55, $246.75

W-OH-540-050d-1122 • 19 mm. R-10 • OH-V50CN / OH-55a-50CN • MS-63 $2,000

W-OH-560-005b • **M. Sullivan, sutler, 55th Regiment Ohio Volunteer Infantry • Class A tokens** • M. SULLIVAN / SUTLER / 5 / CENTS IN GOODS. / 55 REG. O.V.M.U.S. John Stanton backstamp (die sinker). 16 mm. R-8. Tokens of this issuer are usually seen in circulated grades. • M. Sullivan evidently served as sutler for the 57th Ohio Volunteer Regiment Volunteer Militia before becoming sutler of the 55th Regiment. The same dies were utilized to strike tokens for both regiments, the 7 of 57 being re-engraved into a 5. • OH-W5B / OH-55b-5b • EF $400

W-OH-560-010b • John Stanton backstamp (die sinker). 19 mm. R-7 • OH-W10B / OH-55b-10B • *Auctions:* Bleviss, EF-40, porous, $172.50; Bunt, VF, light bends, $111.63, EF-40, $117.50

W-OH-560-025b • 22 mm. R-8 • OH-W25B / OH-55b-25B • *Auction:* Bunt, EF, cleaned $88.13

W-OH-560-050b • 25 mm. R-10 • OH-W50Ba / OH-55b-50Ba • *Auctions:* Bunt, VF-25, $176.25, EF, reverse scratches, $129.25, EF-40, $223.25, EF-45, tiny spot, $117.50

W-OH-560-050b-x • **Class C token (exception)** • Blank reverse. 25 mm. R-7 • OH-W50Bb / OH-55b-50Bb • *Auctions:* Hayden (March 2010), VF, marks, clip, $286; eBay (February 2011), Unc, uneven toning, $295; Ford XXIII, AU, damaged, $199.75

W-OH-580-005b • **M. Sullivan, sutler, 57th Regiment Ohio Volunteer Infantry** • **Class C tokens** • M. SULLIVAN / SUTLER / 5 / CENTS IN GOODS. / 57 REG. O.V.M.U.S. Blank reverse. 16 mm. R-10. Tokens of this issuer are usually seen in circulated grades. • OH-X5Ba / OH-57-5Ba • EF $1,500

W-OH-580-005b-x • John Stanton backstamp (die sinker). 16 mm. R-10 • OH-X5Bb / OH-57-5Bb • EF $1,500

W-OH-580-010b • John Stanton backstamp (die sinker). 19 mm. R-9 • OH-X10B / OH-57-10B • *Auction:* Hayden (FPL, August 2014), EF+, $1,000

W-OH-580-025b • 22 mm. R-9 • David Schenkman has not seen an example of this token. • OH-X25B / OH-57-25B • EF $1,500

W-OH-580-050b • Blank reverse. 25 mm. R-9 • OH-X50B / OH-57-50B • *Auction:* Ford XXIII, AU-50, $1,116.25

W-OH-600-005b • **59th Regiment Ohio Volunteer Infantry** • **Class A tokens** • SUTLERS CHECK / 59 REG. O.V.M. / 5 / CENTS IN GOODS. John Stanton backstamp (die sinker). 16 mm. R-8. Tokens of this issuer are usually seen in circulated grades. • J.B. Goodwin was a sutler for the 59th Ohio Volunteer Regiment Volunteers, organized in Ripley in September 1861. • OH-Y5Ba / OH-59-5Ba • *Auctions:* Bunt, VF-30, $282, EF, small spot, $176.25, EF-45, $411.25, EF-45, Schenkman plate token, $499.38

W-OH-600-005b-x • SUTLERS CHECK / 59. REG. O.V.M. / 5 / CENTS IN GOODS. John Stanton backstamp (die sinker). 16 mm. R-9. Y5Bb is struck from a different die than the preceding. In addition to the period after 59 there is a period (or die chip) above the denomination, 5. CENTS IN GOODS is farther away from the other lettering than on Y5Ba. • OH-Y5Bb / OH-59-5Bb • AU $1,100

W-OH-600-025b • John Stanton backstamp (die sinker). R-8 • OH-Y25B / OH-59-25B • *Auctions:* Bleviss, EF-40, $322; Bunt, VF-30, light scratches, $188; Ford XXIII, AU-50, $352.50; Hayden (FPL, August 2014), MS-63, $1,250

W-OH-620-005b • **61st Regiment Ohio Volunteer Infantry** • **Class A tokens** • O.V.U.S.A. / 61ST REGT / 5 / CENTS. John Stanton backstamp (die sinker). 16 mm. R-7. Tokens of this issuer are usually seen in circulated grades. This regiment was organized in Columbus in April 1862 and was consolidated into the 82nd Ohio Infantry in March 1865. • OH-Z5B / OH-61-5B • *Auctions:* Bunt, EF-40, $352.50, EF-40 $470, AU, lightly cleaned, $411.25, AU-50, Schenkman plate token, $587.50; Ford XXIII, Unc, damaged, $329, MS-62, $528.75, MS-63, $587.50

W-OH-620-010b • John Stanton backstamp (die sinker). 19 mm. R-8 • OH-Z10B / OH-61-10B • *Auctions:* Bunt, EF-45, $352.50; Ford XXIII, MS-61, $499

W-OH-620-025b • 22 mm. R-7 • OH-Z25B / OH-61-25B • *Auctions:* Bunt, VF, small digs, $188, VF-25, $305.50, AU-50, $998.75

W-OH-640-005b • Hosmer & Crowther, sutlers, 62nd Regiment Ohio Volunteer Infantry • Class A tokens • HOSMER & CROWTHER / SUTLERS CHECK / 5 / CENTS / 62 REG. O.V.M. John Stanton backstamp (die sinker). 16 mm. R-8. Tokens of this issuer are usually seen in circulated grades. • OH-AA5B / OH-62-5B • *Auctions:* Slabaugh (PCAC, June 2001), EF, $247.25; Bunt, EF-45, $366.60; Ford XXIII, AU-58, $616.88

W-OH-640-010b • 19 mm. R-8 • OH-AA10B / OH-62-10B • *Auctions:* Bleviss, 87 OH-AA10B, Fine-15, porous, $69; Bunt, AU-50, $440.63

W-OH-640-025b • 22 mm. R-8 • OH-AA25B / OH-62-25B • *Auctions:* Bleviss, EF-45, cleaned, holed, $149.50; Bunt, EF-45, $381.88; Ford XXIII, AU, damaged, $176.25; Hayden (FPL, August 2014), AU+ $700

W-OH-640-100b • ONE / DOLLAR. 25 mm. R-8 • OH-AA100B / OH-62-100B • *Auction:* Bunt, EF, cleaned, $282

W-OH-640-100b silver plated • 25 mm. R-9 • OH-AA100PB / OH-62-100PB • *Auctions:* Bunt (SBG, January 2013) EF, cleaned, $282

W-OH-660-005b • R.C. Hine, sutler, 63rd Regiment Ohio Volunteer Infantry • Class C tokens • R.C. HINE / 63D / REG. O.V. / 5 / CENTS. Blank reverse. 18 mm. R-9 • OH-AB5B / OH-63-5B • *Auctions:* Bunt, VF, holed, $188

W-OH-660-010b • 22 mm. R-8 • OH-AB10B / OH-63-10B • *Auction:* Bunt, VF, heavy porosity, $176.25

W-OH-660-025b • 24 mm. R-9. David Schenkman has not seen an example; size is approximate. • OH-AB25B / OH-63-25B • VF $1,350

W-OH-680-005b • William W. Drennan, sutler, 64th Regiment Ohio Volunteer Infantry • Class A tokens • WM W. DRENNAN / 64 REG. O.V. / 5 / CENTS IN GOODS. John Stanton backstamp (die sinker). 16 mm. R-8 • Prior to the Civil War Drennan was a shopkeeper. • OH-AC5B / OH-64-5B • *Auctions:* Bunt, EF-40, $305.50; Hayden (February 2012), AU+, $1,200; Hayden (FPL, August 2014), EF+, $1,500

W-OH-680-010b • John Stanton backstamp (die sinker). 19 mm. R-9 • OH-AC10B / OH-64-10B • VF $1,200

W-OH-680-025b • 22 mm. R-8 • OH-AC25B / OH-64-25B • *Auction:* Hayden (March 2010), EF, $1,584

W-OH-700-005a • J.T. Strong, sutler, 66th Regiment Ohio Volunteer Infantry • Class A tokens • J.T. STRONG. / 66 / O.V.I. GOOD FOR / 5 / CENTS / KOEHLER (in small letters). 21 mm. R-8. Tokens of this issuer are usually seen in circulated grades. • OH-AD5C / OH-66-5C • *Auctions:* Bunt, Fine to VF, holed and corroded, $54.05; Ford XXIII, AU-50BN, spot, $881.25

W-OH-700-010b • 21 mm. R-9 • OH-AD10B / OH-66-10B • VF $1,500

W-OH-700-025b • 21 mm. R-10 • Unlisted / OH-66-25B • VF $2,000

W-OH-700-025j • 21 mm. R-10 • Unlisted / OH-66-25N • VF $2,000

W-OH-720-005b • Launderer's check, 71st Regiment Ohio Volunteer Infantry • Class A token • LAUNDERER'S / CHECK / 71 REG O.V.M. 5 CENTS IN WASHING. John Stanton backstamp (die sinker). Brass. R-10 • Elmstedt, who served as sutler for three and a half years, is not mentioned on the token and may or may not have been involved with the laundry service. • Unlisted / OH-71-5B • EF $3,500

W-OH-740-005a • A. Sampson, sutler, 78th Regiment Ohio Volunteer Infantry • Class C tokens • O.V.U.S.A. / 78 / A. SAMPSON / 5 / CENTS IN GOODS. Blank reverse. 16 mm. R-9 • OH-AE5B / OH-78-5C • VF $900

W-OH-740-005b • Blank reverse. 16 mm. R-9 • OH-AE5C / OH-78-5B • *Auction:* Bunt, EF, minor verdigris, $305.50

W-OH-740-025a • 22 mm. R-10 • OH-AE25C / OH-78-25C

W-OH-740-025b • 22 mm. R-9 • OH-AE25B / OH-78-25B • *Auction:* Bleviss, 89 OH-AE25B, EF-45, handling marks, reverse dents, $488.75

W-OH-760-005d-1290.

W-OH-760-010d-1295.

W-OH-760-025d-1176.

W-OH-760-005a-1290 • J.W. Cruikshank, sutler, 81st Regiment Ohio Volunteer Infantry • Class A tokens • J.W.

CRUIKSHANK. / 5 / CENTS / 81ST / REG. O.V.I. 19 mm. R-7 • Reverse with Civil War store card die 1290. All tokens were made by the shop of William K. Lanphear, Cincinnati. Five different Cruikshank tokens sold in Edward Cogan's sale of September 1863. • OH-AF5C / OH-81a-5C • *Auctions:* Bleviss, VF-25, rough, $103.50; Bunt, AU-55, $528.75

W-OH-760-005b-1290 • 19 mm. R-10 • OH-AF5B / OH-81a-5B

W-OH-760-005d-1290 • 19 mm. R-10 • OH-AF5CN / OH-81a-5CN • MS-63 $2,000

W-OH-760-010a-1295 • 19 mm. R-8 • Reverse with Civil War store card die 1295. • OH-AF10C / OH-81a-10C • *Auctions:* Heritage (February 2013), AU-53, $440.63; Hayden (FPL, August 2014), EF, short scratch, edge marks, and cut, $450

W-OH-760-010b-1295 • 19 mm. R-10 • OH-AF10B / OH-81a-10B • MS-63 $1,750

W-OH-760-010d-1295 • 19 mm. R-10 • OH-AF10CN / OH-81a-10CN • MS-63 $2,000

W-OH-760-025a-1176 • 19 mm. R-7 • Reverse with Civil War store card die 1176. • OH-AF25C / OH-81a-25C • *Auctions:* Bleviss, AU-58, $488.75; Bunt, VF-20, $152.75, EF, etched, $199.75, AU-58, $881.25; Hayden (FPL, August 2014), VF, $400

W-OH-760-025b-1176 • 19 mm. R-9 • OH-AF25B / OH-81a-25B • MS-63 $1,750

W-OH-760-025d-1176 • 19 mm. R-10 • OH-AF25CN / OH-81a-5CN • MS-63 $2,000

W-OH-762-025a-1127.

Close-up of altered inscription.

W-OH-762-005a-1295 • J.W. Cruikshank, sutler, 81st Regiment [altered inscription], Infantry • Class A tokens • J.W. CRUIKSHANK. / 5 / CENTS / 81ST obliterated by cutting a design over it in the die / REG. O.V.I. 19 mm. R-7 • Reverse with Civil War store card die 1295. • OH-AG5C / OH-81b-5C • *Auctions:* Bleviss, VF-20, $345; Bunt, VF, minor corrosion, $152.75

W-OH-762-010a-1346 • J.W. CRUIKSHANK / 10 / CENTS. / 81 obliterated by cutting a design over it in the die / REG. O.V.I., 19 mm. R-8 • Reverse with Civil War store card die 1346. • OH-AG10C / OH-81b-10C • *Auctions:* Bleviss, EF-45, light corrosion, $230; Hayden (June 2011), VF, light stain, $331.10

W-OH-762-025a-1127 • J.W. CRUIKSHANK / 25 / CENTS / 81 obliterated by cutting a design over it in the die / REG. O.V.I. 19 mm. R-8 • Reverse with Civil War store card die 1127. • OH-AG25C / OH-81b-25C • *Auctions:* Bleviss, EF-40, verdigris, $402.50; Bunt, VF, damaged, $117.50, VF-30, $381.88; Hayden (June 2013), VF, planchet flaw, Schenkman plate token, $260

W-OH-780-005b • Hofer & Jones, sutlers, 86th Regiment Ohio Volunteer Infantry • Class A tokens • HOFER & JONES / 5 / CENTS / 86' / REG. O.V.I. John Stanton backstamp (stamp and brand cutter). 17 mm. R-8 • OH-AH5B / OH-86-5B • *Auction:* Bunt, VF-35, $352.50

W-OH-780-010b • John Stanton backstamp (stamp and brand cutter). 19 mm. R-9 • OH-AH10B / OH-86-10B • VF $750

W-OH-780-025b • 22 mm. R-9 • OH-AH25B / OH-86-25B • VF $750

W-OH-800-005b • 101st Regiment Ohio Volunteer Infantry • Class C tokens • 101ST. REG. O.V.I. / 5 / CENTS / IN GOODS. Blank reverse. 19 mm. R-9 • This regiment was organized in Monroeville in August 1862 and completed service in June 1865. • OH-AI5Ba / OH-101-5Ba • *Auction:* Hayden (October 2011), EF, slightly bent, $600

W-OH-800-005b-x • John Stanton backstamp (stamp and brand cutter). 19 mm. R-10 • OH-AI5Bb / OH-101-5Bb

WW-OH-800-010a • 22 mm. R-9 • OH-AI10C / OH-101-10C • *Auction:* Bunt (SBG, January 2013) EF, reverse scratches, $646.25

W-OH-800-010b • 22 mm. R-10 • OH-AI10B / OH-101-10B

W-OH-800-028b • 25 mm. R-9 • OH-AI25B / OH-101-25B • VF $1,500

W-OH-820-010b • 102nd Regiment Ohio Volunteer Infantry • Class A tokens • A. SLOCUM / 102' / REG. O.V.I. / 10 / CTS. IN GOODS. John Stanton backstamp (stamp and brand cutter). 19 mm. R-8 • OH-AJ10B / OH-102-10B • EF $500

W-OH-820-025b • 22 mm. R-9 • OH-AJ25B / OH-102-25B • EF $650

W-OH-840-005a • **D.J. Church, sutler, 105th Regiment Ohio Volunteer Infantry** • **Class A tokens** • GOOD FOR / 5 / CENTS / IN GOODS AT / D.J. CHURCH'S / SUTLER / 105' REG. O.V.I. John Stanton backstamp (stamp and brand cutter). 17 mm. R-9 • OH-AK5C / OH-105-5C • EF $700

W-OH-840-005b • John Stanton backstamp (stamp and brand cutter). 17 mm. R-8 • OH-AK5B / OH-105-5B • EF $700

W-OH-840-010b • 19 mm. R-9 • OH-AK10B / OH-105-10B • EF $700

W-OH-840-025b • 22 mm. R-8 • OH-AK25B / OH-105-25B • *Auction:* PCAC Auction #67 (June 2000), VF, $264

W-OH-860-005b • **C.B. Jones, sutler, 116th Regiment Ohio Volunteer Infantry** • **Class B tokens** • C.B. JONES / 5 / 116. O.V.I. Denomination, 5, incuse. Spread eagle within a circle of 13 stars. 18 mm. R-9 • OH-AL5B / OH-116-5B • *Auction:* Ford XXIII, Fine-15, $1,997.50

W-OH-860-050b • 50 incuse. 18 mm. R-9 • OH-AL50B / OH-116-50B • VF $2,000

W-OH-880-005b • **W.M. Burke, sutler, 117th Regiment Ohio Volunteer Infantry** • **Class A tokens** • O.V.I. 117' REG'T / W.M. BURKE / GOOD FOR / 5 / CTS. IN GOODS. John Stanton backstamp (stamp and brand cutter). 16 mm. R-9 • OH-AM5B / OH-117-5B • VF $1,500

W-OH-880-010b • John Stanton backstamp (stamp and brand cutter). 19 mm. R-9 • OH-AM10B / OH-117-10B • *Auction:* Hayden (FPL, August 2014), EF+, reverse a bit weak, $2,500

W-OH-880-025b • 22 mm. R-9 • OH-AM25B / OH-117-25B • VF $1,500

W-OH-900-010a • **S. Oldham and D.H. Smith, sutlers, 122nd Regiment Ohio Volunteer Infantry** • **Class C tokens** • SUTLER / 10 / 122 RGT. O.V. 20 mm. Blank reverse. R-9 • Unlisted / OH-122-10C • EF $2,250

W-OH-900-050a • 20 mm. Blank reverse. R-10 • Unlisted / OH-122-50C • EF $2,250

W-OH-920-025b • **G.W. Story, sutler, 187th Regiment Ohio Volunteer Infantry** • **Class A tokens** • OH Schenkman AN25B • G.W. STORY / SUTLER / 187' REG. O.V.I. / 25 / CENTS IN GOODS. MURDOCK & SPENCER / 139 / 5' ST / CIN'O. 22 mm. R-9 • OH-AN25B / OH-187-25B • VF $1,500

W-OH-940-005b • **William Jamison, sutler, Camp Chase** • **Class A tokens** • WM. JAMISON / CAMP / CHASE / 5 / CENTS. John Stanton backstamp (die sinker). 16 mm. R-9. Jamison was post sutler at Camp Chase beginning in August of 1861. His license was revoked on January 4, 1862, but he evidently regained it and continued in business until August, 1864. • OH-AO5B / OH-CC-5B • VF $1,500

W-OH-940-010b • 19 mm. R-9 • OH-AO10B / OH-CC-10B • VF $1,500

W-OH-940-025b • John Stanton backstamp (die sinker). 22 mm. R-9 • OH-AO25B / OH-CC-25B • *Auction:* Bunt, Fine-15, $646.25

W-OH-960-005h black • **Isa A. Hutchinson. Story, sutler, Camp Dennison** • I.A. HUTCHINSON / POST / SUTLER, / CAMP / DENNISON.

GOOD FOR / 5 / CENTS / IN GOODS. Black hard rubber. 32 mm. R-9 • Hutchinson is said to have been associated in some way with the 16th Ohio Volunteer Regiment. • OH-AP5Ra / OH-CD-5Ra • *Auction:* Ford XXIII, AU-55, $2,173.75

W-OH-960-005h brown • Brown hard rubber. 32 mm. R-9 • OH-AP5Rb / OH-CD-5Rb • AU $1,850

W-OH-960-005h maroon • Maroon hard rubber. 32 mm. R-8 • OH-AP5Rc / OH-CD-5Rc • *Auction:* Bunt, EF-45, $1,586.25

PENNSYLVANIA

Whitman-PA-100-005g • **T.J. Doyle, sutler, Battery A, Pennsylvania Artillery** • **Class D token** • SUTLER / BATTERY A / 1ST P. ART. T.J. DOYLE / 10. 18 mm. R-9. All lettering is incuse. • PA-A10L / PA-1-10L • VF $3,000

W-PA-120-025a • **William Wood, sutler, 2nd Regiment, Pennsylvania Artillery** • **Class A token** • WM. W. WOOD / (two cannons crossed) / SUTLER / 2ND PA. ARTY. GOOD FOR / 25 / CENT/ IN TRADE. 21 mm. R-6. Tokens of this issuer are usually seen in circulated grades. • With more than 5,000 officers and enlisted men at one time, this was the largest regiment to serve in the Union Army. • PA-B25C / PA-2-25C • *Auctions:* PCAC Auction #67 (June 2000), VF, $192.50, EF $231; Marcus PCAC (December 2001), VF/EF, $218.50; Litman (PCAC, December 2003), F/VF, digs, $161; Bleviss, VF-35, $373.25; Hayden (July 2006), Fine+, $190; Bunt, VF-25, $188, VF-35, $235, VF-35, $258.50, EF, porous, $141, EF-45, rim bruise, $258.50; Ford XXIII, EF, damaged, $188, EF-40BN, $223.25, AU-50BN, $440.63, AU-53BN, $528.75, AU-53BN, $440.63; Hayden (July 2014), EF+, $425

W-PA-140-005b • **George McAlpin, sutler, 11th Regiment Pennsylvania Volunteer Cavalry** • **Class B tokens** • G. McALPIN / SUTLER / 11. / PENN. CAVALRY. 5 within wreath. Denomination incuse, 6 mm high. 20 mm. R-8. Tokens of this issuer are usually seen in circulated grades. • Tokens made by Francis X. Koehler, Baltimore. • PA-D5Ba / PA-11b-5Ba • *Auctions:* PCAC Auction #67 (June 2000), VF, corrosion spots, $192.50; Hayden (July 2010), VF+, $435

W-PA-140-005b-x • Same as preceding, but denomination incuse; 6 mm high. 20 mm. R-9 • PA-D5Bb / PA-11b-5Bb • AU $900

W-PA-140-010b • 10 incuse; 5 mm high. 20 mm. R-8 • PA-D10Ba / PA-11b-10Ba • *Auctions:* Bleviss, VF-25, lightly porous, $253; Bunt, VF-25, $329; Hayden (June 2013), VF, $300

W-PA-140-010b-x • 10 incuse; 4 mm high. 20 mm. R-8 • PA-D10Bb / PA-11b-10Bb • *Auctions:* Bunt, VF-30, $305.50; Ford XXIII, AU-50BN, $646.25; Hayden (February 2012), EF, $477

W-PA-140-025a • "McAlpen" error • GEO. McALPEN / (two swords crossed) / SUTLER / JACOBUS PHILA (in tiny letters) / 11TH PA. CAV. GOOD FOR / 25 CENT. 21 mm. R-6. Dies by P.J. Jacobus, Philadelphia. • Surname misspelled. • PA-C25C / PA-11a-25Ca • *Auctions:* Heritage (February 2007), EF-40, corroded, $230; Bleviss, EF-40, holed, $126.50; Hayden (December 2005), AU, light scratches, $467.50; Bunt, VF-30, $440.63; Ford XXIII, EF-40, $258.50, AU, damaged, $176.25, AU, damaged, $188, AU-50BN, $329

W-PA-140-025b • 25 incuse. 20 mm. R-9 • PA-D25Ba / PA-11b-25Ba • *Auction:* Hayden (December 2005), EF, with light marks, $710

W-PA-140-025b-x • 25 incuse on reverse. 20 mm. R-9 • PA-D25Bb / PA-11b-25Bb • AU $1,500

W-PA-140-025b-y • 25 incuse on reverse. 20 mm. R-8 • PA-D25Bc / PA-11b-25Bc • EF $550

W-PA-140-050b • 50 incuse. 20 mm. R-9 • PA-D50Ba / PA-11b-50Ba • *Auction:* Bunt, VF, porous, $282

W-PA-140-050b-x • 50 incuse on reverse. 20 mm. R-9 • PA-D50Bb / PA-11b-50Bb • EF $1,000

W-PA-160-005b • **11th Regiment Pennsylvania Volunteer Infantry** • **Class C tokens** • SUTLER / 5 / 11. REG. / P.V. Blank reverse. 17 mm. R-8. Tokens of this issuer are usually seen in circulated grades. • W.B. Hellings, John H. Shyrock, and E.C. Wells all were sutlers for the 11th Regiment Pennsylvania Volunteer Infantry. • PA-E5B / PA-11c-5B • EF $750

W-PA-160-010b • 19 mm. R-9 • PA-E10B / PA-11c-10B • EF $1,250

W-PA-160-025b • 24 mm. R-9 • *Auctions:* Ford XXIII, AU-50, $558.13

W-PA-160-025g • 24 mm. R-10 • PA-E25L / PA-11c-25L • VF $1,500

W-PA-180-005b • **L. Lang, sutler, 12th Regiment Pennsylvania Volunteer Cavalry** • **Class C tokens** • GOOD / 5 / 12. PA. CAV. REG. / L. LANG, sutler. Reverse: Blank on all. 17 mm. R-9. Tokens of this issuer are usually seen in circulated grades. • PA-F5B / PA-12-5B • *Auction:* Ford XXIII, MS-62, $1,762.50

W-PA-180-010b • 19 mm. R-9 • PA-F10B / PA-12-10B • *Auctions:* Bunt, VF, rim damage, $940; Hayden (February 2012), VF, with some digs, $1,000

W-PA-180-025b • 24 mm. R-9 • PA-F25B / PA-12-25B • VF $1,500

W-PA-200-005b • **23rd Regiment Pennsylvania Volunteer Infantry** • **Class C tokens** • SUTLER / 5 / 23. REG. / P.V. Blank reverse. 17 mm. R-9. Tokens of this issuer are usually seen in circulated grades. • George Gates and F.C. Crowley were sutlers for this regiment. Crowley was also sutler for the 7th U.S. Infantry. • PA-G5B / PA-23-5B • PA Schenkman G5B • VF $900

W-PA-200-010b • 21 mm. R-8 • PA-G10B / PA-23-10B • *Auctions:* Ford XXIII, MS-62, $1,116.25, MS-64, $1,997.50

W-PA-200-025b • 24 mm. R-9 • PA-G25B / PA-23-25B • *Auction:* Hayden (June 2011), EF, dark, $962.50

W-PA-220-005b.

W-PA-220-005b • **C. & S., sutlers, 28th Regiment Pennsylvania Volunteer Infantry** • **Class C tokens** • SUTLER / 5 / 28. REG. / P.V. / C. & S. Reverse: Blank on all. 19 mm. R-8. Tokens of this issuer are usually seen in circulated grades. • Josiah M. Christy was a partner. • PA-H5B / PA-28-5B • PA Schenkman H5B • *Auctions:* Hayden (July 2007), EF, $996.60; Bunt, EF-40, $329, $822.50

W-PA-220-010b • 19 mm. R-8 • PA-H10B / PA-28-10B • PA-H25B / PA-28-25B • *Auction:* Bunt, $646.25

W-PA-220-025b • 24 mm. R-8 • *Auction:* Bunt, Fine-15, $282

W-PA-240-003b.

W-PA-240-003b • J.A. Garman, sutler, 54th Regiment Pennsylvania Volunteer Infantry • Class B tokens • J.A. GARMAN / SUTLER / 3 / 54 / PA. VOLS. Denomination, 3, incuse. Spread eagle within circle of 13 stars. 18 mm. R-5. Unusual denomination. Tokens of this issuer are usually seen in circulated grades. Ford had a token of this issuer, without denomination (MS-61, $1,525.50). • PA-I3B / PA-54-3B • *Auctions:* PCAC Auction #67 (June 2000), AU, $198; Hayden (July 2006), MS-62, 40% bright, $411; Heritage (February 2008), Ch AU, $276; Heritage (September 2008), EF, $299; eBay (September 2009), Unc, $220.68; Bleviss (November 2009), AU-50, $253; Hayden (October 2011), MS-62, 40% bright, $395; Bunt, AU-58, $235, AU-55, minor oxidation, $223.25

W-PA-240-005b • 5 incuse. 18 mm. R-6 • PA-I5Ba / PA-54-5Ba • *Auctions:* Slabaugh (PCAC, June 2001), VF, $161; Heritage (February 2008), Ch AU, $373.75; Heritage (June 2010), MS-62, $253, MS-62, $373.75, MS-64, $402.50; Hayden (FPL, August 2014), MS-62, $650

W-PA-240-005b-x • Denomination 5X, 5X incuse. 18 mm. R-8 • David Schenkman: "The incuse 'X' after the denomination of this and a following token were added to prevent enterprising soldiers from raising the value of the 5¢ and 10¢ tokens by adding a zero." • PA-I5Bb / PA-54-5Bb • *Auctions:* Bleviss, VF-35, $184; Bunt, EF-45, minor spots, $164.50; Ford XXIII, AU, damaged, $305.50

W-PA-240-010b • 10 incuse. 18 mm. R-6 • PA-I10Ba / PA-54-10Ba • *Auctions:* PCAC Auction #67 (June 2000), EF, $192.50; Heritage (September 2007), Ch AU, $402.50 • Heritage (February 2008), Ch AU, $345; Heritage (June 2010), EF-45, $207; Hayden (July 2010), MS-63, 60% bright, $440; Hayden (December 2012), MS-62, $450; Bunt, EF, harshly cleaned, $94, EF-45, $235

W-PA-240-010b-x • 10X incuse. 18 mm. R-7 • PA-I10Bb / PA-54-10Bb • *Auctions:* Heritage (February 2008), Ch AU, $402.50; Heritage (September 2008), Ch AU, $345; Heritage (March 2010), EF details, scratches, $184

W-PA-240-025b • 25 incuse. 18 mm. R-5 • PA-I25B / PA-54-25B • *Auctions:* Hayden (March 2006), VF, $254.10; Heritage (February 2008), Ch AU, $299; Heritage (September 2008), AU-55, $345; Bleviss, EF-45, $276; Heritage (February 2010), EF-45, $149.50, AU-50, $184, AU-53, $253, MS-63, $287.50, MS-64, $299; Heritage (June 2010), MS-63, $402.50; Hayden (December 2010), MS-62, 30% bright, $550; Bunt, EF, harshly cleaned, $129.25, EF-45, minor toning spots, $164.50, AU, oxidation spot, $164.50, AU-58, $188; Hayden (June 2013), AU, $375; Ford XXIII, VF-35, $223.25; Hayden (FPL, August 2014), AU, $350

W-PA-240-050b • 50 incuse. 18 mm. R-7 • PA-I50B / PA-54-50B • *Auctions:* Heritage (February 2008), EF, $322; Heritage (September 2008), AU-50, $345; Heritage (June 2010), AU-58, $402.50, MS-61, $299; eBay (February 2011), EF, uneven toning, $168.50; Bunt, VF-25, $164.50, EF-40, $199.75, AU-50, $258.50

W-PA-240-100b • 100 incuse. R-8. David Schenkman: "A variety exists with no incuse denomination. There is also a variety with an incuse denomination '2.' Both of these are no doubt errors, the former missing the incusing process completely, and the latter missing the '5' punch." • PA-I100Ba / PA-54-100Ba • *Auctions:* Heritage (February 2008), Ch AU, $299; Heritage (September 2008), EF-45, $345; Heritage (February 2010), MS-63, $345; Heritage (June 2010), MS-63, $373.75, MS-64, $431.25; Ford XXIII, VF-25, $188

W-PA-260-003g • **William H. McCutcheon, sutler, 67th Regiment Pennsylvania Volunteer Infantry** • **Class D tokens** • W.H.M. / SUTLER / 67. P.V. 5 / IN GOODS. 15 mm. R-9. Tokens of this issuer are usually seen in circulated grades. All lettering is incuse. David Schenkman has not seen a specimen; the size is approximate. • PA-J5L / PA-67-5L • VF $1,750

W-PA-260-010g • 18 mm. R-9 • PA-J10L / PA-67-10L • VF $1,750

W-PA-260-025g • 25 mm. R-9 • PA-J25L / PA-67-25L • VF $1,750

W-PA-260-050g • 29 mm. R-9 • PA-J50L / PA-67-50L • *Auction:* Hayden (October 2011), EF, heavily corroded, $475

W-PA-280-005b • **A.W.H, sutler, Baxter's Philadelphia Fire Zouaves, 72nd Infantry** • **Class C tokens** • BAXTER'S FIRE ZOUAVES. / SUTLER'S / 5 / TICKET. / A.W.H. Blank reverse. 17 mm. R-8 • Baxter's Fire Zouaves was organized by DeWitt Clinton Baxter in 1861. Many of the soldiers had served as firemen, hence the regiment's name. Losses due to combat and disease amounted to more than 250 officers and enlisted men. • NL-H5B / PA-72-5B • *Auctions:* Litman (PCAC, December 2003), H10B, AU, $414; PCAC (December 2005),

EF-40, $552; Hayden (December 2005), AU, $1,050; Bunt, VF-30, $329; Ford XXIII, MS-62, $587.50; Hayden (FPL, August 2014), AU, $1,650

W-PA-280-010b • 21 mm. R-8 • NL-H10B / PA-72-10B • *Auctions:* Ford XXIII, AU-58, $822.50, AU-58, $998.75; Hayden (July 2014), AU-58, $900

W-PA-280-025b • 24 mm. R-8 • NL-H25B / PA-72-25B • *Auctions:* Bunt, VF-30, $763.75

W-PA-300-005b • **A. Krebs, sutler, 103rd Regiment Pennsylvania Volunteer Infantry** • **Class A token** • A. KREBS / 5 CENTS / IN GOODS. Reverse: PILKINGTON / MAKER / 83 EXCHANGE PLACE / BALTIMORE. 16 mm. R-10 • Unlisted / PA-103-5B

W-PA-300-010b • **Class A token** • As above but 10 denomination. 18 mm. R-9 • Unlisted / PA-103-10B • EF $2,500

W-PA-300-025b • **Class D token** • A. KREBS / 25 / CENTS / IN GOODS. Blank; obverse inscription shows incuse and retrograde. 25 mm. R-9 • Counterstamped TAYLOR on one or both sides. • PA-K25Ba / PA-103-25Ba • *Auctions:* Hayden (FPL, August 2014), VF, but much loss of detail due to TAYLOR counterstamped on obverse, $1,250

W-PA-320-010h • **Samuel Pollock, sutler, 155th Regiment Pennsylvania Volunteer Infantry** • SAMUEL POLLOCK / 155TH / PENNA VOLS / SUTLER. FIRST UNITED STATES ZUAVE BRIGADE. / 10 / 1864. Brown hard rubber. 32 mm. R-10. Denomination is incuse and painted white. Zouave is misspelled. • Unlisted / PA-155-5R • VF $4,000

W-PA-320-010h • Black hard rubber. 32 mm. R-9 • PA-L10R / PA-155-10R • VF $4,000

W-PA-320-025h • Black hard rubber. 32 mm. R-9. Denomination is incuse and painted white. • PA-L25R / PA-155-25R • *Auction:* Hayden (June 2013), EF, $6,450

W-PA-340-005e • **John H. Gotschall, sutler, 172nd Regiment Pennsylvania Volunteer Infantry** • **Class B tokens** • JOHN H. GOTSHALL / SUTLER / 5 / 172 / PENN. REG. S.M. Denomination 5 incuse. Spread eagle within circle of 13 stars. 19 mm. R-9 • PA-M5WM / PA-172-5WM • *Auction:* Ford XXIII, VF, damaged, $3,055

W-PA-340-010e • 10, 10 incuse. 19 mm. R-9. The only specimen David Schenkman has seen is on an oval (19 x 23 mm) planchet. This was probably caused by the token being struck without a collar. • PA-M10WM / PA-172-10WM • VF $4,000

Virginia

Whitman-VA-100-005b • **L. Goldheim, sutler, 1st Virginia Cavalry Regiment** • **Class B tokens** • L. GOLDHEIM / 5 / 1ST CAVALRY. Denomination, 5, incuse. Spread eagle within circle of 13 stars. 18 mm. R-8. Tokens of this issuer are usually seen in circulated grades. • Also see W-NL-180-025b for another Goldheim token. • VA-A5B / VA-1a-5B • *Auctions:* Ford XXIII, VF-30, $558.13, EF-45, $1,410

W-VA-100-010b • 10 incuse. Spread eagle within circle of 13 stars. 18 mm. R-9 • VA-A10B / VA-1a-10B • *Auction:* Ford XXIII, VF-20, $1,292

W-VA-100-025b • 25 incuse. 18 mm. R-8 • VA-A25B / VA-1a-25B • *Auctions:* Hayden (July 2012), EF+, $2,850; Bunt, Fine-12, $1,645; Ford XXIII, Fine-12, $1,057

W-VA-120-005b • **A. Kohn, sutler, 1st Virginia Regiment** • **Class A token** • A. KOHN / SUTLER / FIRST / VIRGINIA / REG'T / 5 / CTS. IN GOODS. John

W-PA-360-005a • **Christian Inhoff, sutler, Carlisle Barracks** • **Class A tokens** • C. INHOFF, / SUTLER / CARLISLE / BARRACKS. GOOD FOR / 5 / IN TRADE. 20 mm. R-9 • Christian Inhoff became the sutler at Carlisle Barracks in 1854. • PA-N5C / PA-CB-5C • VF $700

W-PA-360-010a • 20 mm. R-8 • PA-N10C / PA-CB-10C • VF $500

W-PA-360-025a • 20 mm. R-9 • PA-N25C / PA-CB-25C • *Auction:* Ford XXIII, MS-66RB, $2,115

W-PA-360-050a • 20 mm. R-7 • PA-N50C / PA-CB-50C • *Auctions:* Bunt, VF-35, $822.50, MS-62RB, $1,410; Ford XXIII, AU, cleaned, $329

Stanton backstamp (stamp and brand cutter). 19 mm. R-9 • Also see W-VA-220-005b. • VA-B5B / VA-1b-5B • EF $3,000

W-VA-140-005a.

W-VA-140-005a • **J.L. O'Neal, sutler, 2nd Regiment Virginia Cavalry** • **Class A tokens** • J.L. O'NEAL / 2'D VA. / CAVALRY / 5 / CENTS. John Stanton backstamp (stamp and brand cutter). 16 mm. R-8 • VA Schenkman C5C • VA-C5C / VA-2a-5C • *Auction:* Bleviss, F-12, porous, $80.50

W-VA-140-005b • John Stanton backstamp (stamp and brand cutter). 16 mm. R-10 • VA-C5B / VA-2a-5B

W-VA-140-025b • 22 mm. R-8 • VA-C25B / VA-2a-25B • *Auctions:* Heritage (September 2007), not graded, $862.50; Bunt, VF, minor dents, $258.50, VF-25, $705

W-VA-160-005b • **2nd Regiment Virginia Cavalry** • **Class A tokens** • 2ND. REGIMENT / VIRGINIA / CAVALRY / 5 / CENTS. John Stanton backstamp (die sinker). 16 mm. R-8 • VA-D5B / VA-2b-5B • *Auctions:* Bunt, VF-35, $528.75, EF-45, minor flecks, clip, $705; Hayden (July 2014), MS-63, $1,305

W-VA-160-025b • 22 mm. R-9 • VA-D25B / VA-2b-25B • AU $2,000

W-VA-180-005b • **M. Ezekiel, sutler, 3rd Virginia Regiment** • **Class C tokens** • M. EZEKIEL / 3RD. VIR. REGT. / GOOD FOR / 5 / CENTS IN GOODS. Blank reverse. 22 mm. R-7 • VA-E5B / VA-3-5B • *Auctions:* Litman (PCAC, December 2003), EF/AU, $1,127; Bunt, EF-40, $1,645; Ford XXIII, MS-62, $998.75

W-VA-180-005b-x • Blank reverse. 22 mm. R-9 • VA-E5PB / VA-3-5PB • AU $1,500

W-VA-180-005e • 22 mm. R-10 • Unlisted / VA-3-5Z • VF $1,500

W-VA-200-005b • **4th Virginia Regiment** • **Class A tokens** • VA 4TH VIRGINIA REG T. / 5 / CENTS / IN GOODS. John Stanton backstamp (stamp and brand cutter). 16 mm. R-9 • VA-F5B / VA-4-5B • VF $1,250

W-VA-200-025b • 22 mm. R-9 • VA-F25B / VA-4-25B • EF $1,750

W-VA-220-005b • **A. Kohn, sutler, 5th Virginia Regiment** • **Class A tokens** • A. KOHN / SUTLER / FIFTH / VIRGINIA / REG'T / 5 / CTS. IN GOODS.

John Stanton backstamp (stamp and brand cutter). 19 mm. R-7 • These tokens were struck from the same obverse die used to strike W-VA-120-005b; the die was altered by cutting FTH over RST of FIRST. Evidently A. Kohn was the sutler for the 1st Virginia Regiment prior to becoming sutler for the 5th Regiment. Three specimens of W-VA-220-B have been seen by David Schenkman. • VA-G5Ba / VA-5-5Ba • *Auctions:* Bunt, VF, minor dents, $381.88, VF, heavy porosity, $470

W-VA-220-005bo • Same as preceding but struck over a token of A. Kohn, 1st Virginia Regiment. 19 mm. R-9 • VA-G5Bb / VA-5-5Bb • *Auctions:* Litman (PCAC, December 2003), EF/AU, spot, $1,840; Bunt, Fine-15, granular, $381.88

W-VA-240-005b • **G.G. Sawtell, sutler, 8th Virginia Regiment** • **Class A tokens** • G.G. SAWTELL / 8TH VIR. REG. / 5 / CENTS IN GOODS. John Stanton backstamp (stamp and brand cutter). 22 mm. R-9 • Also see tokens of Sawtell under W-VA-320. • VA-H5B / VA-8-5B • *Auctions:* Heritage (March 2013), VF-35, $3,525

W-VA-240-025b • John Stanton backstamp (stamp and brand cutter). 25 mm. R-9 • VA-H25B / VA-8-25B • VF $1,250

W-VA-260-005b • **H. Asher, sutler, 9th Virginia Regiment** • **Class A tokens** • H. ASHER / SUTLER / 9' VIR. REG. / 5 / CENTS. John Stanton backstamp (stamp and brand cutter). 17 mm. R-8 • VA-I5B / VA-9a-5B • VA Schenkman I5B • EF $1,000

W-VA-260-005g • 17 mm. R-10 • VA-J5L / VA-9b-5L • *Auction:* Litman (December 2003), EF, $2,064.25

W-VA-260-025b • Stanton backstamp (stamp and brand cutter). 22 mm. R-9 • VA-I25B / VA-9a-25B • EF $1,000

W-VA-280-005g.

W-VA-280-005g • A & K, sutlers, 10th Virginia Regiment • Class D tokens • 10TH VA. / 5 / A & K. Blank reverse. 15 mm. R-8. All lettering incuse on this and the following. • VA-K5L / VA-10-5L • *Auction:* Ford XXIII, AU-55, $2,585

W-VA-280-010g • 25 mm. R-10 • VA-K10L / VA-10-10L • VF $2,000

W-VA-280-025g • 25 mm. R-9 • VA-K25L / VA-10-25L • VF $2,000

W-VA-300-005b • W.W. Sherwood, sutler, 13th Virginia Regiment • Class A tokens • VA W.W. SHERWOOD / 13' / VIRGINIA / REG / 5 / CTS. IN GOODS. John Stanton backstamp (stamp and brand cutter). 16 mm. R-9 • VA-L5Ba / VA-13-5Ba • AU $2,850

W-VA-300-005b-x • W.W. SHER-WOOD / 13' / VIRGINIA / REG. / 5 /

West Virginia

Whitman-WV-100-005b • Bare & Rauch, sutlers, 11th Regiment West Virginia Volunteer Infantry • Class A tokens • BARE & RAUCH / SUTLERS / 11' W. VA. REG. / 5 / CTS. IN GOODS. John Stanton backstamp (stamp and brand cutter). 19 mm. R-9 • WV-A5Ba / WV-11-5Ba • VF $8,500

W-WV-100-005b-x • Blank reverse. 19 mm. R-10 • David Schenkman has not

Wisconsin

Whitman-WI-100-005e • T.W. Eddy, sutler, 6th Regiment Wisconsin Volunteer Infantry • Class B tokens • T.W. EDDY / SUTLER / 5 / WIS. VOLS. 5

CTS. IN GOODS. John Stanton backstamp (stamp and brand cutter). 16 mm. R-9 • This and the preceding were struck from the same obverse die. The period after REG. was added to create W-VA-300-005b-x. • VA-L5Bb / VA-13-5Bb • EF $2,000

W-VA-300-025b • 22 mm. R-9 • VA-L25B / VA-13-25B • VF $1,250

W-VA-320-005b • G.G. Sawtell, sutler, 15th Virginia Regiment • Class A tokens • G.G. SAWTELL / 15 VIR. REG / 5 / CENTS IN GOODS. 15 incuse over 8TH. John Stanton backstamp (stamp and brand cutter). 22 mm. R-9 • David Schenkman: "Apparently G.G. Sawtell was first sutler for the 8th Virginia Regiment, later becoming sutler for the 15th Regiment. These tokens were made by simply stamping the number 15 over 8TH on his tokens of the 8th Regiment; also see W-VA-240." • VA-M5B / VA-15-5B • EF $3,500

W-VA-320-025b • 15 incuse over 8TH. John Stanton backstamp (stamp and brand cutter). 25 mm. R-9 • VA-M25B / VA-15-25B • VF $3,000

seen this token. • WV-A5Bb / WV-11-5Bb • VF $8,500

W-WV-100-010b • 22 mm. R-10 • David Schenkman has not seen this token. • WV-A10B / WV-11-10B • VF $8,500

W-WV-100-025b • 25 mm. R-9 • WV-A25B / WV-11-25B • *Auction:* Litman (PCAC, December 2003), F/VF, wavy planchet, $5,405

incuse. Spread eagle within circle of 13 stars. 18 mm. R-10 • Unlisted / WI-6-5WM • VF $4,500

W-WI-100-010e • 10 incuse. 18 mm. R-9 • WI-A10WM / WI-6-10WM • VF $4,500

W-WI-100-025e • 25 incuse. 18 mm. R-9 • WI-A25WM / WI-6-25WM • VF $4,500

W-WI-120-010b.

W-WI-120-025b.

W-WI-120-005b • Sid. Wright, sutler, 11th Regiment Wisconsin Volunteer Infantry • Class A tokens • AT SUT-LERS / STORE / SID. WRIGHT. / 11. R. WIS. V. GOOD / FOR 5 CTS / IN GOODS. 15 mm. R-8 • WI-B5B / WI-11-5B • *Auctions:* Hayden (December 2005), EF, light hairlines, $1,100; Heritage (March 2013), VF-35, $3,525; Ford XXIII, AU-55, $1,762.50; Hayden (July 2014), EF, $1,350

W-WI-120-010b • Reverse: CHILDS MANUFACTURER / Head facing left / CHICAGO. 22 mm. R-7 • No period after MANUFACTURER on reverse die. • WI-B10Ba / WI-11-10Ba • *Auctions:* Litman (PCAC, December 2003), Brilliant Mint State, $1,265; Hayden (March 2010), VF, with obverse scratches, $770; Bunt, Fine, granular, $258.50, VF, light granularity, $282, EF-40, $440.63; Hayden (FPL, August 2014), MS-63, $3,500

W-WI-120-010b • CHILDS MANU-FACTURER. / Head facing left / CHI-CAGO. 22 mm. R-9 • Period after MANUFACTURER on reverse die. • WI-B10Bb / WI-11-10Bb • *Auction:* PCAC Auction #67 (June 2000), EF, $385

W-WI-120-025b • Reverse: CHILDS MANUFACTURER / Spread eagle; 13 stars above / CHICAGO. 25 mm. R-9 • WI-B25B / WI-11-25B • *Auctions:* Hayden (June 2005), VF, $1,023; Heritage (September 2007), Ch AU, $2,070

COLORED INFANTRY

Although troops for various so-called colored infantry units, also called colored troops, were raised in different states, they are usually attributed to the federal government in Washington, D.C.

Whitman-CI-100-005b • 27th U.S. Colored Infantry • Class A tokens • 27' U.S.C.I. / GOOD FOR / 5 / CTS IN GOODS. MURDOCK & SPENCER / 139 / 5' ST / CIN' O. 19 mm. R-8 • At one time Gilbert S. Blackman was sutler. • NL-Z5B / US-27-5B • *Auctions:* Litman (PCAC, December 2003), VF/EF, $1,224.75; Bleviss, Fine-15, porous, $92; Ford XXIII, AU-53, $1,645

W-CI-100-025b • 25 mm. R-8 • NL-Z25B / US-27-25B • *Auction:*Hayden (December 2010), EF, scratches $2,500

W-CI-120-010b • 48th Regiment U.S. Colored Infantry • Class A tokens • Reverse in small letters: SCHULZE BRO'RS / ST. LOUIS. 23 mm. R-10 • The 48th U.S. Colored Infantry was organized in Milliken's Bend, Louisiana, on May 23, 1863, as the 11th Regiment Infantry (African Descent). The name was changed to 48th U.S. Colored Troops on March 11, 1864. • The shop of Schulze Brothers, stencil makers and engravers, was at 212 Vine Street. • Unlisted / US-48-10B • EF $7,500

W-CI-120-025b • 48th U.S. Colored Infantry • 48' U.S.C.I. GOOD FOR 25 CENTS. 22 mm. R-9. David Schenkman has not seen this token; the description is not complete, and is as listed by Curto. • NL-AA25B / US-48-25B • VF $5,000

W-CI-140-005b • C.H. Smith, sutler, 117th U.S. Colored Troops • Class C tokens • C.H. SMITH SUTLER / 5 / 117. U.S. COL. TR. Denomination, 5, incuse. Blank reverse. 23 mm. R-9 • NL-W5B / US-117-5B • VF $3,000

W-CI-140-010b • 10 incuse. 23 mm. R-9 • NL-W10B / US-117-10B • EF $3,500

W-CI-140-025b • 25 incuse. 23 mm. R-10 • Unlisted / US-117-25B • VF $3,000

W-CI-140-050b • 50 incuse. 23 mm. R-9 • NL-W50B / US-117-50B • VF $3,000

W-CI-160-005a-1047.

W-CI-160-005a-1047 • J.M. Longwell, sutler, 119th U.S. Colored Infantry • Class A tokens • J.M. LONGWELL / SUTLER / 119 / U.S.C.I. Reeded edge. 19 mm. R-9 • Reverse with Civil War store card die 1047, die state II. A numismatic strike. • This unit was organized in Camp Nelson, Kentucky, in January 1865 and mustered out of duty in April 1866. • NL-R-C / US-119-C • *Auction:* Hayden (February 2012), MS-62, $2,300

W-CI-160-005d-1047 • 19 mm. R-10 • Reverse with Civil War store card die 1047, die state II. A numismatic strike. • Unlisted / US-119-CN • *Auction:* Ford XXIII, MS-64, $4,259.38

W-CI-160-010a • J.M. LONGWELL / SUTLER / 119 / U.S.C.I. GOOD FOR / 10 / CENTS / IN GOODS ONLY. Reeded edge. 19 mm. R-9 • NL-S10C / US-119-10C • MS-63 $2,750

W-CI-160-010e • 19 mm. R-8 • NL-S10WM / US-119-10WM) • *Auction:* PCAC Auction #67 (June 2000), VF/EF, $742.50

W-CI-160-025e • R-9 • NL-S25WM / US-119-25WM) • *Auctions:* Hayden (June 2005), EF, $3,036; Heritage (September 2006), EF-40, $2,415; Hayden (FPL, August 2014), MS-62, $3,000

W-CI-160-050e • 30 mm. R-8 • NL-S50WM / US-119-50WM • *Auction:* Bunt, AU-50, $1,292.50

NON-LOCAL

Whitman-NL-100-005b • **Victor Beaudry, sutler, 1st Regiment, U.S. Cavalry • Class B tokens** • V. BEAUDRY, SUTLER / 5 / 1ST. REG. / U.S. CAVALRY. Denomination, 5, incuse. Reverse: Ornamental design. 23 mm. Made by Koehler. R-9 • Beaudry, a French Cana-

dian, came to California in 1849 during the Gold Rush. In 1855 he moved to Los Angeles. In 1861 he was appointed sutler of the 1st Regiment, U.S. Cavalry, and saw service in the war. He was also a sutler for the 4th Regiment, U.S. Cavalry. His tokens were issued in that connection in the East. As such they are only peripherally related to California. Later he was sutler at Fort Independence in the Owens Valley (not related to the 1st Regiment, U.S. Cavalry). After the war he operated a store and a highly successful lead and silver mine in nearby Cerro Gordo (today a ghost town). He was the brother of Prudent Beaudry, mayor of Los Angeles from 1874 to 1876. Victor Beaudry died in the city of his birth, Montreal, in 1888. • Certain examples sold as *California* sutler tokens have brought higher prices than might have been the case otherwise. • NL-B5B / US-1a-5B • *Auction:* Hayden (July 2012), VF, $700

W-NL-100-010b • 23 mm. R-9 • NL-B10B / US-1a-10B • EF $800

W-NL-100-025b • V, BEAUDRY / SUTLER / 25 / 1ST REG. / U.S. CAVALRY. Denomination 25 incuse. 21 mm. R-10 • Unlisted / US-1a-25B • VF $1,500

W-NL-100-050b • 21 mm. R-9 • NL-B50B / US-1a-50B • *Auctions:* Bleviss, Fine-12, $431.25; Hayden (FPL, August 2014), EF, with some light reverse digs, $1,250

W-NL-101-005b • Class A tokens with Koehler imprint • V. BEAUDRY / 1ST REG. / U.S. CAVALRY. GOOD FOR / 5 / CENTS / KOEHLER (in small letters) / DOLLAR. 21 mm. R-9 • NL-C5B / US-1b-5B • VF $550

W-NL-101-010b • Reverse: GOOD FOR / 10 / CENTS . KOEHLER. 21 mm. R-9 • NL-B10B / US-1b-10B • EF $750

W-NL-101-025b • 21 mm. R-10 • Unlisted / US-1b-25B • VF $1,500

W-NL-101-050b • 21 mm. R-9 • NL-C-50B / US-1b-50B • VF $550

W-NL-101-100b • V. BEAUDRY / 1ST REG. / U.S. CAVALRY. ONE / 100 / KOEHLER (in small letters) / DOLLAR. 21 mm. R-8 • NL-C100B / US-1b-100B • *Auctions:* PCAC Auction #67 (June 2000), VF, many small obverse digs,

$203.50; Litman (PCAC, December 2003), EF/AU, $805

W-NL-120-005c • W.C.C, sutler, 39th Regiment U.S. Infantry • Class D token • Incuse lettering. Blank reverse. R-10 • Unlisted / US-39b-5C • VF $2,500

W-NL-140-005b • C. & R., sutlers, 39th Regiment U.S. Infantry • Class C tokens • 39TH U.S.I. / 10c / C. & R. Reverse: Blank on all. 22 mm. R-10. All lettering is incuse. • NL-D5B / US-39a-5B

W-NL-140-010b • R-9 • Unlisted / US-39a-10B • VF $2,250

W-NL-140-025b • R-10 Unlisted / US-39a-25B

W-NL-140-050b • R-10 • Unlisted / US-39a-50B • VF $2,250

W-NL-180-010b.

W-NL-180-025b.

W-NL-180-005b • J.W. Donohoe, sutler, 5th Regiment U.S. Cavalry • Class B tokens • J.W. DONOHOE, / SUTLER / 5 / 5. REG. / U.S. CAVALRY. 5 incuse. Reverse: Arabesque design. 23 mm. R-9 • NL-E5B / US-5b-5B • *Auction:* Bleviss, VF-25, porous, $253

W-NL-180-010b • 10 incuse. 23 mm. R-9 • NL-E10B / US-5b-10B • *Auction:* Hayden (FPL, August 2014), Fine+, $1,000

W-NL-180-025b • 25 incuse. 23 mm. R-9 • NL-E25B / US-5b-25B • *Auction:* Litman (PCAC, December 2003), F/VF, $609.50

W-NL-180-050b • 50 incuse. 23 mm. R-10 • NL-E50B / US-5b-50B • VF $1,500

W-NL-200-005b • **L. Goldheim, sutler, 8th U.S. Infantry** • **Class B tokens** • 23 mm. R-8. Tokens of this issuer are usually seen in circulated grades. • Also see W-VA-100, other Goldheim tokens. • Unlisted / US-8-5B • VF $2,000

W-NL-200-010b • R-9 • Unlisted / US-8-10B • VF $2,000

W-NL-200-160-025b • L. GOLD-HEIM / 25 / 8TH U.S. INFTY. Denomination, 25, incuse. Ornamental design. 23 mm. R-9 • NL-G25B / US-8-25B • VF $1,250

W-NL-200-160-050b • Similar to preceding, but 50 incuse. R-8 • Unlisted / US-8-50B • VF $1,750

W-NL-220-005b-x-1391.

W-NL-220-005b-1391 • **William H. Jones, sutler** • **Class A tokens** • SUTLER CHECK / REDEEMED / IN / GOODS TO / SOLDIERS / ONLY / BY / WM. H. JONES. 5 / CENTS (11 stars around). Reeded edge. 20 mm. R-7 • Reverse is Civil War token die 1391. •

According to the 1869 *Newport, Kentucky Directory* the United States Sutler Store was operated by William H. Jones at 45 Cabot Street. Jones was the post sutler at Fort Bradford, Ohio, years later, from 1880 to 1891. • NL-K5Ba / UI-D-5Ba • *Auctions:* Bleviss, VF-30, dark and porous, $92; eBay (February 2011), Unc, obverse spots, $280; Bunt, VF-30, tiny clip, $164.50, VF, $141, VF-30, $199.75

W-NL-220-005b-x-1391 • Denomination, 5, is 6 mm high. 19 mm. R-8 • NL-K5Bb / UI-D-5Bb • *Auctions:* Bleviss, EF-40, cleaned, $195.50; Bunt, VF, cleaned, $176.25, VF-20, $152.75

W-NL-220-005b-y • Denomination, 5, is 5 mm high. 19 mm. R-9 • NL-K5Bc / UI-D-5Bc • VF $400

W-NL-220-010b-1396 • SUTLER CHECK / REDEEMED / IN / GOODS TO / SOLDIERS / ONLY / BY / WM. H. JONES. Reverse is Civil War token die 1396. Reeded edge. 20 mm. R-8 • NL-K10Ba / UI-D-10Ba • *Auctions:* Litman (PCAC, December 2003), EF/AU, $402.50; Bunt (January 2013), VF-25, $199.75

W-NL-220-010b-x-1396 • Obverse as preceding. Reverse is Civil War token die 1396. 19 mm. R-9 • NL-K10Bb / UI-D-10Bb • *Auction:* PCAC Auction #67 (June 2000), VF, $302.50

W-NL-220-025b-1399 • Obverse as preceding. Reverse is Civil War token die 1399. Reeded edge. 19 mm. R-9 • Reverse is Civil War token die 1399. • Fuld NL-14b. NL-K25Ba / UI-D-25Ba • *Auction:* Hayden (FPL, August 2014), VF, $650

W-NL-220-025b-x • Similar to the preceding but from a different reverse die. 19 mm. R-9. David Schenkman has not seen a specimen of this token. • NL-K25Bb / UI-D-25Bb • VF $450

W-NL-220-050b-1404 • Obverse as preceding. Reverse is Civil War token die

1404 (CENTS without period). Reeded edge. 19 mm. R-8 • NL-K50Ba / UI-D-50Ba • *Auctions:* Hayden (June 2005), Fine, $446.60; Hayden (July 2007), F+, some marks, $330; Heritage (September 2007), not graded, $299; Bleviss, VF-25, heavily porous, $92; Bunt, VF, $141

W-NL-220-050b-x • Obverse as preceding. • Reverse is similar to Civil War token die 1404, but with CENTS in taller letters and with a period. 19 mm. R-9 • NL-K50Bb / UI-D-50Bb • *Auction:* Bunt, VF-30, $199.75

W-NL-240-005B • **L. & Co. Sutlers** • **Class C tokens** • R-10 • Unlisted / UI-E-5B • EF $2,000

W-NL-240-010n • L. & Co. / 10 / SUTLERS. Blank reverse. Iron. 21 mm. R-9. All lettering is incuse. David Schenkman: "The metallic composition of this token is assumed to be iron; it is strongly attracted to a magnet. At the present time only one specimen is known." • NL-P10I / UI-E-10I • EF $2,000

W-NL-260-005a • **R.R. 2nd Volunteer Regiment** • **Class A tokens** • Obverse: * / R.R. / * * / 2V / KOEHLER. Dentilated border. Reverse: GOOD FOR / 5 / CENTS / -------- / KOEHLER. Dentilated border. 22 mm. R-9 • Some have attributed this to Robinson's Regiment (also known as the 2nd Regiment Volunteers of Tennessee), which fought on the Confederate side, but this seems to be questionable. • Unlisted / UI-G-5B • *Auction:* Hayden (July 2014), EF, $900

W-NL-260-010a • 22 mm. R-9 • Unlisted / UI-G-10Ba • *Auction:* Ford (August 2013), EF, $2,829

W-NL-260-025b • 21 mm. Identical to the reverse of W-NH-100-025b. R-9 • Unlisted / UI-G-25Ba • *Auction:* Bunt, VF, light porosity, $1,645

W-NL-280-005b • **R.R. Landon, sutler, First Regiment, U.S.M.F.** • **Class A tokens** • AT SUTLERS / STORE / R.R. LANDON / 1ST R. / U.S.M.F. GOOD / FOR 5 CTS / IN GOODS. 16 mm. R-9 • NL-Q5B / US-1c-5B • *Auction:* Litman (PCAC, December 2003), EF/AU, $759

W-NL-280-010b • Reverse: CHILDS MANUFACTURER / Head facing left / CHICAGO. 22 mm. R-8 • NL-Q10B / US-1c-10B • *Auctions:* Bleviss, EF-40, cleaned, holed, $172.50; Hayden (December 2005), VF, $550; Hayden (March 2010), EF, $550; Bunt, Fine-15, $88.13, VF, granular, $88.13; Hayden (FPL, August 2014), MS-62, $1,250

W-NL-280-025b • Reverse: CHILDS MANUFACTURER / CHICAGO (spread eagle; 13 stars above) / CHICAGO. 26 mm. R-9 • NL-Q25B / US-1c-25B • EF $600

W-NL-300-010g • **16th Regiment, Mounted Volunteers** • 16TH REG. M.V. 10. 29 mm. R-10. Lettering is incuse. David Schenkman has not seen this token; the description is not complete, and is as described by Curto. • NL-T10L / UI-K-10L

W-NL-320-005b • **Sutlers, 25th Regiment** • **Class C token** • SUTLERS / 5 / 25 R.E.G. / T V. Blank reverse. 19 mm. R-10 • David Schenkman: "This token is listed as number 1693 in Benjamin P. Wright's *American Business Tokens*." • NL-Y5B / UI-L-5B

W-NL-340-005b • **William W. Updegraff, sutler, 5th U.S. Heavy Artillery** • **Class C tokens** • WM. W. UPDEGRAFF / SUTLER / 5TH U.S.H.A. / GOOD FOR / 5 / CTS IN GOODS. Reverse: Blank on all. 19 mm. R-10. David Schenkman has not seen an example of this token. • NL-AC5B / US-5a-5B

W-NL-340-010b • 22 mm. R-9 • NL-AC10B / US-5a-10B • MS-63 $2,750

WW-NL-340-025b • 25 mm. R-10 • NL-AC25B / US-5a-25B

W-NL-360-005b • **Charles P. West-cott, sutler, 16th Regiment, U.S. Infan-try • Class A tokens** • G.P. WESTCOTT. / 16 I. U.S.A. / 5 / cutter). 16 mm. R-9 • G in G.P., instead of correct C. • Charles P. Westcott was sutler for the 16th Infan-try from August 1861 to August 1864. • NL-AE5Ba / US-16-5Ba • VF $450

W-NL-360-005b-x • John Stanton back-stamp (die sinker). 16 mm. R-9 • G in G.P., instead of correct C. • NL-AE5Bb / US-16-5Bb • VF $700

W-NL-360-010b • John Stanton back-stamp (stamp and brand cutter). 19 mm. R-8 • NL-AE10Ba / US-16-10Ba • *Auc-tions:* Bunt, AU-50, $235; Hayden (FPL, August 2014), MS-62, $750

W-NL-360-010b-x • John Stanton back-stamp (die sinker). 19 mm. R-9 • NL-AE10Bb / US-16-10Bb • VF $600

W-NL-360-020b • John Stanton back-stamp (stamp and brand cutter). 22 mm.

R-7. Unusual denomination. • NL-AE20Ba / US-16-20Ba • *Auctions:* Bunt, VF-20, $176.25, EF-45, $258.50, AU-50, $235, AU-50, $646.25; Hayden (FPL, August 2014), MS-60, $650

W-NL-360-020b-x • John Stanton back-stamp (die sinker). 22 mm. R-9 • NL-AE20Bb / US-16-20Bb • VF $450

W-NL-360-025b • 22 mm. R-10 • NL-AE25B / US-16-25B

W-NL-380h • **D.A. Wray, sutler, 6th Regiment, U.S. Infantry** • 6TH U.S. CAVALRY, D.A. WRAY SUTLER. Hard rubber. R-10. Description is not complete. The only mention David Schenkman has found of this token is in George and Mel-vin Fuld's 1954 *Numismatist* listing of hard rubber tokens (number 477). NL AF-R / US-6-50R • VF $4,500

W-NL-400-050j • **NLA, sutler, • Class A token** • Obverse: NLA in script. Reverse: GOOD FOR / 50 CENTS / KOEHLER. 22 mm. R-9 • Unlisted • *Auction:* Ford (August 2013), EF, $129.25

Non-Contemporary

These are tokens issued by sutlers after the Civil War ended.

Whitman-NC-100-005b • **S.W. Beall, sutler, Fort Kearney** • **Class A tokens** • S.W. BEALL. / 5. CTS / SUTLER. GOOD / FOR 5 CTS / IN GOODS. 16 mm. R-8. Tokens of this issuer are usually seen in worn grades. • Unlike certain other Western forts, Kearney had no stockades or guard houses. It consisted of a number of two-story buildings arranged around a parade ground. • NE-A5B / NT-FKb-5B • EF $550

W-NC-100-010b • GOOD FOR / 10 / CENTS IN / SUTLERS / GOODS / S.W. BEALL. SUTLER 10 (within circle of 13 stars). 20 mm. R-7 • NL-A10B / NT-FKb-10B • *Auctions:* Bleviss, EF-40, verdigris, $402.50; Ford XXIII, damaged, $199.75, AU-55, $646.25

W-NC-100-025b • GOOD FOR / 25. / CENTS IN / SUTLERS / GOODS. / S.W. BEALL, sutler, Spread eagle and 13 stars around / 1866. 22 mm. R-6 • NL-A25B / NT-FKb-25B • *Auctions:* Bleviss, EF-40, light corrosion, $316.25; Bunt, VF, heavy porosity, $223.25; Ford XXIII, VF-20, $235, EF, tooled, $188, EF-40, $329, MS-62, $646.25

W-NC-100-050a • GOOD FOR / 50. / CENTS IN / SUTLERS / GOODS. / S.W. BEALL, sutler, Liberty head facing left similar to a $5 half eagle; 13 stars around / 1866. 26 mm. R-10 • Unlisted / NT-FKb-50C • AU $1,000

W-NC-100-050b • GOOD FOR / 50. / CENTS IN / SUTLERS / GOODS. / S.W. BEALL, sutler, Liberty head facing left similar to a $5 half eagle; 13 stars around / 1866. 26 mm. R-7 • NL-A50B / NT-FKb-50B • *Auctions:* Hayden (October 2011), VF, $450; Ford XXIII, VF, damaged, $188, VF-35, $293.75, EF, damaged, $199.75, EF-45, $411.25; Hayden (FPL, August 2014), MS-62, $1,650

W-NC-120-005a-1391 • **Rice & Byers (Frank R. Rice & Joseph K. Byers), sutlers** • SUTLER CHECK / REDEEMED / IN / GOODS TO / SOLDIERS / ONLY / BY / RICE & BYERS. 5 / CENTS. Reeded edge. 20 mm. R-10 • Reverse is Civil War token die 1391. • The firm of Rice & Byers, dealers in cigars and tobacco, was formed in St. Louis, Missouri, in 1871. These tokens are not sutler issues in the traditional sense of the term. In that decade they also operated a trading post at Fort Sill in Indian Territory. • Unlisted / IT-FS-5C • VF $1,000

W-NC-120-005b-1391 • 20 mm. • R-8 • Reverse is Civil War token die 1391. • NL-U5B / IT-FS-5Ba • EF $500

W-NC-120-010b-1394 • Reeded edge. 20 mm. R-9 • Reverse is Civil War token die 1394. • NL-U10Ba / IT-FS-10Ba • VF $375

W-NC-120-010b-x • SUTLER CHECK / REDEEMED / IN / GOODS TO / SOLDIERS / ONLY / BY / RICE & BYERS. Reeded edge. 20 mm. R-9 • David Schenkman: "The 0 of the denomination is incuse over a struck 5. There are two possible explanations for this token. One is that it was struck as a 15-cent denomination on purpose, and the denomination later changed to 10 cents by stamping a 0 over the 5. Alternatively, the wrong reverse die could have been used, and the incusing done by the manufacturer to correct his error." • NL-U10Bb / IT-FS-10Bb • VF $375

W-NC-120-015b • Reeded edge. Reverse with 15 / CENTS with 11 stars around. 19 mm. R-10 • Unlisted / IT-FS-15B • VF $1,000

W-NC-120-025b-1399 • Reeded edge. 19 mm. R-9 • Reverse is Civil War token die 1399. • NL-U25B / IT-FS-25B • *Auctions:* Slabaugh (PCAC, June 2001), EF, $299; Bleviss, VF-35, $920

W-NC-120-050b-1404A • Reeded edge. 19 mm. R-9 • Reverse is Civil War token die 1404A • NL-U50B / IT-FS-50B • MS-63 $1,500

W-NC-120-100b • SUTLER CHECK / REDEEMED / IN / GOODS TO / SOLDIERS / ONLY / BY / RICE & BYERS. ONE / DOLLAR (within circle of 16 stars). 26 mm. R-9 • NL-U100B / IT-FS-100B • *Auction:* Bleviss, VF-25, porous, lightly bent, $161

NOTES

Chapter 2

1. Donald Erlenkotter, "Frederick Nelson Dubois (IL-150-P): Father of the Civil War Token?" *Civil War Token Journal*, Winter 2011. Credit was given to D. Albert Soeffing, "Some Store Card History," *TAMS Journal*, June 1992, for Dubois's own account.
2. Copy provided by Charles McSorley.
3. This is the price for *three* candidates' medals. Just as Lincoln was not on the local ballot, his election medal was not included in the sample offering.

Chapter 3

1. Citation furnished by Don Erlenkotter.
2. Citation furnished by Don Erlenkotter.
3. Excerpted from *Harper's New Monthly Magazine's* issue of June 1861. This account covered events from April 7 to May 6, 1861. From the outset it was noted in Northern newspapers and other accounts that Fort Sumter had been *evacuated*, not *surrendered*. A description of the bombardment of Fort Sumter published in *Harper's Weekly*, April 27, 1861, differs in some details, notes that the Confederate forces suffered loss of men, that two Union defenders were killed during the gun salute, etc. Anderson went to New York City aboard the steamer *Baltic*, having been transferred to that ship from the remains of Fort Sumter by the *Isabel*.
4. Hugh McCulloch, *Men and Measures of Half a Century*, 160–161.
5. *Annual Report of the Secretary of the Treasury*, 1861, 7. The precise nature of the estimate arose from Chase adding together estimates received from various departments and not rounding them off.
6. *John Sherman's Recollections*, 1895, 278–283, includes this and many other comments about paper money.
7. Also see William Luitje, "IN-260-A Moves to Michigan," *The Civil War Token Journal*, Summer 2009. Brooks had a larger facility in Battle Creek than in Elkhart, so instead of listing alphabetically by state as usual practice, it was opted to move the token to Michigan.
8. From the *Worcester* (Massachusetts) *Palladium*, May 28, 1862, courtesy of Don Munro.
9. However, in 1864 the legislation was dusted off and threats were made against several token issuers.
10. Neil Carothers, *Fractional Money*, 177–178.
11. No documentation this has been found, but the Scovill archives include a collection of encased postage stamps; see narrative text.
12. Citation courtesy of Richard Winslow III.
13. Weir, *Sixty Years in Canada*, 137, 138, 159, 167.
14. Langley's *San Francisco Directory* (1864–1865), 12 (chronicle of events).
15. *Ibid.*, 17 (chronicle of events).
16. Hubert Howe Bancroft, *History of Oregon*, vol. II. (1848–1888), 641, citing the *Portland Oregonian*, August 30, 1864.
17. *Ibid.*, 642. Discussion of California and Oregon finances.
18. In *Numisgraphics*, 1876.
19. Chester Robinson, "A. Gleason," *Journal of the Civil War Token Society*, Spring 1971, 26.

20. In November 1860 Bangs, Merwin & Co., the New York City auction house, issued a *Catalogue of Coins, Medals, Medalets, Etc., from the Collection of W.C. Prime and B. Haines.*

21. Fred Reed and Don Erlenkotter both furnished citations and information regarding Gault's token advertisements.

Chapter 4

1. *New York Daily Reformer* (Watertown, NY), September 10, 1863.

2. *New York Herald*, May 16, 1863.

3. Reprinted in the *American Stamp Mercury and Numismatist*, January 1870. The date of publication in the *New York Mercury* was not given. Citation furnished by Remy Bourne.

4. Clipping furnished by Bob Chandler, curator of the Wells Fargo History Museum, San Francisco.

5. For many years Franklin Peale had been chief coiner at the Philadelphia Mint, but he was fired in the mid-1850s for alleged misconduct.

6. Usually cited as "if any one attempts . . . ," occasionally as "if any man attempts . . ."

7. For extensive information see "Pliny Chase," Fred L. Reed, *Journal of the Civil War Token Society*, Summer 1975. Chase was born in Worcester, Massachusetts, August 18, 1820, was brought up as a Quaker, and completed his education with a college degree in 1839, after which he taught in public schools in Leicester and Worcester, Masschusetts, and Providence, Rhode Island. He left that profession in 1848 and went to work for a stove and foundry company. Before the Civil War he moved to Philadelphia and resumed teaching. He later became prominent in science and published many important papers. Chase died in Haverford, Pennsylvania, on December 17, 1886.

8. During his collecting career George Fuld was only able to acquire four different reverses. These were sold to Harry W. Bass Jr. in 1972. Stephen L. Tanenbaum owned only one, OH-165-AK-7b. OH-165-AK-2 is unique and in the collection of the American Numismatic Society.

9. Howard L. Adelson, *The American Numismatic Society 1858–1958*, 77.

10. Alvin Robert Kantor and Marjorie Sered Kantor, *Sanitary Fairs: A Philatelic and Historical Study of Civil War Benevolences* (Glencoe, IL: Amos Philatelics, SF Publishing), 1992. Contains various information concerning the Cincinnati event, especially pp. 174–175.

11. A notice proclaimed: "Donations will be brought free by Express and by Railroad, to be sold for U.S. Sanitary Commission. Exhibition for two weeks commencing on 21st December. Money or anything salable accepted. Excursion Trains daily at half rate."

12. For the "Arms of the State" and "Sporting Scenes" tokens struck to his order see chapter 6, dies 489 to 493.

13. Also see David E. Schenkman, "Mr. Levick's Auction," *Journal of the Civil War Token Society*, Spring 1976.

14. In 1888, Dr. George F. Heath, of Monroe, Michigan, started a publication called *The American Numismatist*, apparently unaware of Leal's priority. After the first issue Heath changed the name to *The Numismatist*, a title which is still used today.

15. From Hetrich, "Civil War Tokens and Store Cards," *The Numismatist*, June 1922.

16. Every generation builds on the shoulders of those before, and today there are more than 15,000 patriotic tokens and store cards described. Some earlier thought to

have been qualifying tokens have been delisted, including the two Barnet tokens noted for Virginia, and many others have been added.

17. *The Numismatist*, June 1937.

18. George Fuld conversation with the author, September 17, 2012. Also see the reminiscences by Fuld in the fore part of the present text.

Chapter 5

1. Certain items under "The Marketplace" have been adopted from books Dave Bowers has written for Whitman Publishing, LLC, and are copyrighted by them.

2. This is a curious aspect. Among federal issues, specialists in, say, early copper cents highly prize scarce issues in lower grades such as Good to Fine, whereas specialists in gold coins do not want them in low grades except in rare instances in which there are no higher grades available.

3. Charlotte Gale and David M. Gale, "Philadelphia Merchant Tokens: Directory Study of Store Cards," *Journal of the Civil War Token Society*, Spring 1985, 9.

4. *Rare Coin Review* No. 3, 1875; David D. Gladfelter, "The Gies Token Hoard, An Update," *Journal of the Civil War Token Society*, Winter 1975, 120–121, who noted that today the family pronounces its name like *geese* (with this in mind the heading on this section does not rhyme); Jesse Patrick, "Facts on the Gies Hoard of Civil War Tokens," *Journal of the Civil War Token Society*, Winter 1976. A hoard of 1,064 Gies tokens was sold by the family and was later auctioned by Bowers & Ruddy Galleries. Some tokens with the correct spelling were also counterstamped as were some issued by other merchants, specifically MI-225-B-2a, MI-225-G-1a, MI-225-CS-1a, MI-615-A-1a, and NY-105-Q-3a (information from William Luitje, August 5, 2012).

5. The illustrations for the reverses of MI-225-AF-1a and ME-225-AE-3a are from different specimens than the illustrations for the obverses (which are from the obverse-only Civil War Token Society files).

6. Recollection published in the Baraboo *Republic*, May 14, 1884.

7. John and Alice Durant, *Pictorial History of the American Circus* (Cranbury, NJ: A.S. Barnes & Co., 1957), 319.

8. Also see Bill Massey, "Yankee Robinson, Portrait of a Showman," *Journal of the Civil War Token Society*, Fall 1975.

Chapter 6

1. See the Sheldon Collection Sale, Lot 2607, Bowers and Merena Galleries, April 1983.

2. Attributions are to David Gladfelter, "Patriotic CWT Dies and Ascriptions," *Patriotic Civil War Tokens*.

3. Certain information regarding 9A and 9B is courtesy of David Gladfelter, Ken Bauer, and Wayne Stafford.

4. See *Journal of the Civil War Token Society*, vol. 12, no. 1, 18, and vol. 17, no. 4, 25.

5. Revised by Mark Glazer from the second edition of *U.S. Civil War Store Cards*.

6. Elemental analysis showed a "copper" token to be 56 percent copper and 44 percent silver, a strange alloy.

Chapter 7

1. "What is a Civil War Token?" *Journal of the Civil War Token Society*, Winter 1989, 2–5.

2. Also see Waldo C. Moore, "The Washington House Token," *The Numismatist*, February 1931. Moore was not aware that the token was issued after the war.

3. Excerpted from "Rhode Island Tokens," *Token and Medal Society Journal*, July–September 1964.

4. Also see Donald Erlenkotter and William Luitje, "Relocating the 'City of New York' (NY-630-Q) to Norwich, Connecticut," Fall 2011.

5. Abstracted from directory search for years 1858–1866 (Gary L. Lyon, "Chicago's Merchants and Their Store Cards," *Journal of the Civil War Token Society*, Winter 1982, 6–9).

6. Abstracted from directory search for years 1858–1866 (Gary L. Lyon, "Chicago's Merchants and Their Store Cards," *Journal of the Civil War Token Society*, Winter 1982, 6–9).

7. Also see Donald Erlenkotter, "Jacob Ulrich Mingers (IL-150-AO)," Spring 2012.

8. Abstracted from *The Civil War Token Journal*. From directory search for years 1858–1866 (Gary Lr Store Cards," *Journal of the Civil War Token Society*, Winter 1982, pp. 6–9).

9. Also see "I.L. Elwood," by Milton J. Gordon, "prepared by the Archivist, Northern Illinois University," in *Journal of the Civil War Token Society*, Winter 1973.

10. Also see James Higby, "Edward Weibezahn and His Rare Store Cards," *Civil War Token Journal*, Spring 2009.

11. Also see Leland Stickle, "A. Alschuler, Men's Clothier, Ottawa, Illinois," *Journal of the Civil War Token Society*, Winter 1971.

12. O-2 was discovered by the author on May 24, 2000.

13. Also see "M.B. Castle of Sandwich, Ill.," by Gary R. Peterson, *Journal of the Civil War Token Society*, Winter 1980.

14. This study was the main source for historical information given in the present listing of Indiana store cards.

15. Also see Constantina Lyla Spath, "Calvin Crooks & Co.: Issuer of the IN-355-A Tokens," *Civil War Token Journal*, Spring 2010.

16. *Sic transit gloria:* In 1977, Richard E. Brown, of Fostoria, Ohio, who had served as president of the Civil War Token Society 1975–1976, stated his most prized token is OH-175-B-01d as it was the last Cleveland merchant token he needed. *Journal of the Civil War Token Society*, Fall 1977. Little did he know it was a misattribution at the time.

17. In "Bill Lanphear's Big Goofs," *Journal of the Civil War Token Society*, Fall 1975, David D. Gladfelter illustrated and discussed the two Lanphear dies with the wrong *state*, IN-550-G (shows Ligonier, MICH. instead of the correct IND.) and WI-320-A (shows Juneau, MICH. instead of the correct WIS.).

18. Also see Scott A. Blickensderfer, "Bartholomew & McClelland, Valparaiso, Indiana," *Civil War Token Journal*, Spring 2008.

19. Also see Scott A. Blickensderfer, "Wheeling, Indiana, Single Merchant 'Franchise' Town," Summer 2009.

20. "Store Card Names," Michael J. Sullivan, *Journal of the Civil War Token Society*, Winter 1986.

21. Also see Spencer I. Radnich Jr., "Leavenworth, Kansas and the Cohen Token," *Journal of the Civil War Token Society*, Winter 1977. Adolph Cohen arrived in Leavenworth in the 1850s, possibly in late 1858.

22. David Gladfelter, correspondence with the author, July 12, 2012.

23. Also see Jud Petrie, "The Maine Tokens of R.S. Torrey," *Journal of the Civil War Token Society*, Spring 1992.

24. General reference for attribution changes from Chicago, Illinois, to Baltimore is George Fuld and David D. Gladfelter, "The Long Lost Baltimore Twelve," *Journal of the Civil War Token Society*, Spring 1978, 5–8.

25. Also see Jane Sears, "Ahern & Broadbent Civil War Token," *Civil War Token Journal*, Winter 2008.

26. Also see Russ Sears, "George Bauernschmidt: Baltimore Brewer," *Journal of the Civil War Token Society*, Spring 1987.

27. "The Maryland Civil War Tokens," by Russ Sears, *Journal of the Civil War Token Society*, Summer 1993, 11–12.

28. The Eastman National Business College, Poughkeepsie, New York, token, NY-760-A, was of similar intent.

29. Also see Donald Erlenkotter, "The Pulmonales Story (MA-115-Ea)," *The Civil War Token Journal*, Spring 2012.

30. Also see Alan Chetson Jr., and Don Erlenkotter, "Dunn & Co.'s Oyster House," *Civil War Token Journal*, Spring 2010.

31. Also see Alvin Robert Kantor and Marjorie Sered Kantor, *Sanitary Fairs: A Philatelic and Historical Study of Civil War Benevolences;* and Bill Jones, "The Sanitary Fair Tokens," *Journal of the Civil War Token Society*, Summer 1994.

32. Steve Tanenbaum, letter to the author, January 14, 1998.

33. Citation located by Clifton A. Temple.

34. Information from "The Popular Innkeeper," by Chet Robinson, *Journal of the Civil War Token Society*, Summer 1974, 61. The name of the novel is not given.

35. Also see Al Rayburn, "Wm. S. Wilcox of Adrian, Michigan," *Civil War Token Journal*, Winter 2010.

36. Also see William Luitje, "IN-260-A Moves to Michigan," Summer 2009. Brooks had a larger facility in Battle Creek than in Elkhart, so instead of listing alphabetically by state as usual practice, it was opted to move the token to Michigan.

37. Also see William Luitje, "MI-060-A and V.P. Collier," *Civil War Token Journal*, Summer 2008.

38. Also see Otis Titus, "Congdon Brothers' Store to be Restored," *Journal of the Civil War Token Society*, Spring 1978.

39. Also see Cathryn Sutherland, "George Washington Goodell, Druggist, Corunna, Michigan (MI-200-B)," Spring 2012.

40. Also see information from Clifton A. Temple, *Journal of the Civil War Token Society*, Fall 1975, adapting a 19th-century account about Armstrong.

41. Also see W. David Perkins, "Alexander Copland's Steam Bakery," *Civil War Token Journal*, Summer 2006.

42. Also see Clifton A. Temple, "Token Small Talk," *Journal of the Civil War Token Society*, Winter 1972, history of the hotel, formerly a part of the old National Hotel.

43. Dennis P. Wierzba, "Collector Strikes and the Cataloging Errors They Caused," *Journal of the Civil War Token Society*, Summer, 1990, 12–13.

44. Also see W. David Perkins, "C.B. Goodrich 'Opposite the Perkins Hotel,'" *Civil War Token Journal*, Winter 2005.

45. Also see Edwin Graf, "The Merchant Unionists of Detroit, *Journal of the Civil War Token Society*, Spring 1972.

46. Also see Bart Woloson, "David B. Herrinton (MI-225-A) and His Double Thread $15 Sewing Machine," *Civil War Token Journal*, Winter 2011.

47. Also see Clifton Temple, "Die Proofs," *Journal of the Civil War Token Society*, Fall 1975.

48. Also see W. David Perkins, "Putting Up at the Perkins Hotel in Detroit," *Civil War Token Journal*, Fall 2006.

49. Also see W. David Perkins, "The Day William Perkins Met C.C. Randall in Detroit," *Civil War Token Journal*, Summer 2007.

50. Dennis P. Wierzba, "Collector Strikes and the Cataloging Errors They Caused," *Journal of the Civil War Token Society*, Summer, 1990, 12–13.

51. Citation furnished by Clifton Temple, *Journal of the Civil War Token Society*, Fall 1971, 26. Also see Temple, "Small Talk," *Journal of the Civil War Token Society*, Spring 1973.

52. Also see Clifton A. Temple, "The International Token of W.E. Tunis," *Journal of the Civil War Token Society*, Winter 1972.

53. Also see Thomas P. Gardner, "Captain Eber Ward and the Soo Locks," *Journal of the Civil War Token Society*, Summer 1996 and "Eber Ward's Steamer PLANET: Further Reflections on OH-175-Q," *Journal of the Civil War Token Society*, Summer 1987; Donald Erlenkotter and William Luitje, "Eber Ward's Steamer *PLANET* Revisited," *Civil War Token Journal*, Summer 2012.

54. Also see William Luitje, "W.W. Whitlark and the Grover & Baker Company," *Civil War Token Journal*, Spring 2009.

55. Also see Richard Maki, "John McKay of East Saginaw, Michigan," *Civil War Token Journal*, Spring 2007.

56. Also see Patrick Flannery, "Dr. James W. Phelps, Mason, Michigan," *Civil War Token Journal*, Spring 2009.

57. Also see Roswell Burrows, "The Mussey Token," *Journal of the Civil War Token Society*, Winter 1971, using information supplied by Robert R. Hailey.

58. Also see Paul Cunningham, "Fisher & Hendryx," *Journal of the Civil War Token Society*, Fall 1976.

59. Also see Paul Cunningham, "Dr. Hause's Card," *Journal of the Civil War Token Society*, Winter 1996.

60. Also see Paul Cunningham, "George Ketcham," *Journal of the Civil War Token Society*, Winter 1977; Cunningham, "CWT Issuer Ketcham Lived Here," *Civil War Token Journal*, Fall 2006.

61. Also see Paul Cunningham, "Patterson, Druggist," *Journal of the Civil War Token Society*, Spring 1978.

62. Information from David D. Gladfelter, September 13, 2012.

63. Also see Jack R. Detwiler, "Blood Treats Gout in St. Louis," *Journal of the Civil War Token Society*, Spring 1986.

64. Also see Grovenor C. Nudd, "A.W. Gale's Store Card," *Journal of the Civil War Token Society*, Summer 1976, and narrative in chapter 3 of the present work.

65. Also see David D. Gladfelter, "New Jersey Civil War Tokens," *Journal of the Civil War Token Society*, Fall 1971, which covers other New Jersey issuers as well.

66. Also see Howard H. Kurth, "Civil War Tokens of D.L. Wing & Co." *Numismatic Scrapbook*, March 1941.

67. Also see Don Prybyzerski, "Hussey's Special Message Post," *Journal of the Civil War Token Society*, Spring 1985.

68. Also see Werner G. Mayer, "N.Y.C. Brewery Tokens," *Journal of the Civil War Token Society*, Spring 1978, for this and other breweries of the city.

69. Also see Benj. G. Lowenstam, "A Civil War Oddity," *The Numismatist*, September 1930.

70. Also see Donald Prybyzerski, *Journal of the Civil War Token Society*, Fall 1981.

71. Also see Donald Erlenkotter, "Gustavus Lindenmueller: The Myth, the Man, the Mystery," *Civil War Token Journal*, Fall 2010.

72. Also see Jack R. Detwiler, "A $2.00 View of New York City," *Journal of the Civil War Token Society*, Summer 1983.

73. Also see Bill Jones, "John Matthews: The Father of the American Soft Drink Industry," *Journal of the Civil War Token Society*, Fall 1994.

74. Also see Warren G. Mayer, "The Bohemians," *Journal of the Civil War Token Society*, Summer 1978. Extensive information is available on the Internet as well.

75. Also see Glenn Firestone, "The New York Metropolitan Fair," *Journal of the Civil War Token Society*, Summer 1974.

76. Also see Werner G. Mayer, "Jones Wood and Hotel," *Journal of the Civil War Token Society*, Summer 1982.

77. Many sources including *Historical Magazine*, March 1874, 180; *American Antiquarian*, April 1889, 472–473.

78. Bill Anderson, "All's Weller That Ends Weller," *Journal of the Civil War Token Society*, Fall 1995. Discovery made by Steven L. Tanenbaum.

79. Also see A.R. Frey, "Morgan L. Marshall," *The Numismatist*, March 1904; Donald Erlenkotter, "Morgan L. Marshall, 1862," *Civil War Token Journal*, Spring 2012.

80. Also see A.R. Frey, biography of Marshall, *The Numismatist*, March 1904.

81. Also see Donald Prybyzerski, "Eastman National Business College of New York," *Journal of the Civil War Token Society*, Fall 1982.

82. Melvin and George Fuld, "The Tokens of the Boutwells of Troy, New York," *The Numismatist*, April 1952.

83. Also see Ed Quagliana, "The Memorial Day Story," *TAMS Journal*, June 1971. In 1865 Welles made the suggestion that led to this holiday.

84. In *Journal of the Civil War Token Society*, Winter 1979, in "Private Scrip—Blood Brothers to Civil War Tokens," Sterling A. Rachootin illustrated an 1862 10-cent scrip note issued by Hall, noting he was a "chemist, druggist, bookseller & stationer." Also see Donald Erlenkotter, "Henry C. Welles, 1861," *The Civil War Token Journal*, Winter 2011.

85. Also see Waldo C. Moore, "The Stoner and Shroyer Tokens," *The Numismatist*, January 1943; Max M. Schwartz, "A New View of the Stoner and Shroyer Tokens," *The Numismatist*, May 1943.

86. Also see Thomas P. Gardner, "The Grindstone Store Cards," *Journal of the Civil War Token Society*, Fall 1989.

87. Also see Robert E. Daniel, "Chillicothe, Ohio: C.W. Merchants' Cards," *Journal of the Civil War Token Society*, Fall 1988. Information is also given on other Chillicothe merchants listed here.

88. Also see Frederick S. Ball and Donald Erlenkotter, "John Kirchenschlager (now OH-160-Da): Reassigned from Cincinnati to Chillicothe, Ohio," *Civil War Token Journal*, Summer 2011.

89. For extensive information on Cincinnati merchants see John Ostendorf, *Civil War Store Cards of Cincinnati*, Civil War Token Society (2007).

90. Also see Waldo C. Moore, "The Boman Copperheads," *The Numismatist*, September 1917.

91. Also see John Ostendorf, "City Hosiery Store (OH-165-X)," Summer 2005.

92. Also see John Ostendorf, "Elizabeth Heinzmann: Female CWT Store Card Issuer," *Civil War Token Journal*, Spring 2006.

93. Russell Rulau, *Standard Catalogue of United States Tokens, 1700–1900*, 2nd ed., 1997.

94. Also see Waldo C. Moore, "B. Kittredge & Co.," *The Numismatist*, December 1917.

95. Also see Waldo C. Moore, "The Ratterman Copperheads," *The Numismatist*, April 1916.

96. *Journal of the Civil War Token Society*, Summer 1976, included "The D.B.S. Civil War Token," written decades earlier by Henry Clay Ezekiel of Cincinnati.

97. Also see Thomas P. Gardner, "The Grindstone Store Cards," *Journal of the Civil War Token Society*, Fall 1989.

98. Also see Terry Stahurski, "The End of an Era—Geo. Worthington & Co.," *Journal of the Civil War Token Society*, Summer 1992.

99. Also see Alan S. DeShazo, "W.B. Eager of Elyria, Ohio," *Civil War Token Journal*, Winter 2009.

100. Also see Sterling A. Rachootin, "H.H. Robinson Civil War Token Issuer," *Journal of the Civil War Token Society*, Spring 1982.

101. For information on the two Sharonvilles see Frederick S. Ball and John Ostendorf, "Sharonville, Ohio: A Civil War 'Tale of Two Cities'," *Civil War Token Journal*, Spring 2011.

102. Also see Dana Zaiser, "W.G. Brain—Druggist-Springfield, Ohio, "*Civil War Token Journal*, Spring 2006.

103. Also see Dana Zaiser, "Ludlow and Bushnell—Druggists," *Civil War Token Journal*, Summer 2006.

104. "New Jersey Civil War Tokens," *Journal of the Civil War Token Society*, Fall 1971, 16–23.

105. Also see Rich Bottles Jr., "Pittsburgh Wood Planing," *Journal of the Civil War Token Society*, Summer 1992.

106. Also see William Groom, "The Erie Storecard," *Journal of the Civil War Token Society*, Fall 1983.

107. Also see Russ Daisley, "The Meadville Civil War Token," *Journal of the Civil War Token Society*, December 1999.

108. Also see Donald Erlenkotter, "Michael Francis Beirn: Civil War Token Issuer Prosecuted!" *Civil War Token Journal*, Summer 2008.

109. Also see Melvin and George Fuld, "The Tokens of the Great Central Fair of Philadelphia," *The Numismatist*, September 1952; Bill Jones, "The Sanitary Fair Tokens," *Journal of the Civil War Token Society*, Summer 1994.

110. David D. Gladfelter, "The Largest Civil War Token," *Journal of the Civil War Token Society*, Summer 1974, 48–49.

111. Also see Melvin Fuld, "Pittock's Pittsburgh Civil War Tokens," *The Numismatist*, February 1970.

112. "Store Card Names," Michael J. Sullivan, *Journal of the Civil War Token Society*, Winter 1986.

113. Also see *Civil War Token Society Journal* articles by Mrs. Elizabeth Steinle, David Schenkman, Jim Hall, Steve Gorman, and David D. Gladfelter. The last contributed an article, "Make that Snow Hill, West Virginia," to the *Journal of the Civil War Token Society*, Winter 1977.

114. Also see Jim Hartman, "Christopher Elias Stifel," *Journal of the Civil War Token Society*, Winter 1980.

115. Also see John Stock, "The Civil War Tokens of Baraboo, Wisconsin," Summer 2005.

116. Also see A.T. Glaze, "An 1848 Tin Shop," *Incidents and Anecdotes of Early Days and History of Business in the City and County of Fond du Lac from Early Times to the Present* (1905), 257 (citation from P W. David Perkins, September 5, 2003).

117. For his biography see *The History of Fond du Lac County, Wisconsin*, Western Historical Company, Chicago, [19th century], 44 (citation from P.W. David Perkins, September 5, 2003).

118. Also see David D. Gladfelter, "Emigranten," *Journal of the Civil War Token Society*, Summer 1972.

119. Also see Robert C. Kraft, "R.K. Findlay, Druggist and Grocer?" *Journal of the Civil War Token Society*, Summer 1997.

120. Also see Werner G. Mayer, "Additional Brewery Tokens," *Journal of the Civil War Token Society*, Spring 1977.

121. Several citations could be mentioned, especially Ray Callan, "Best & Co.'s Beer Hall on Market Street," *Journal of the Civil War Token Society*, Spring 1996.

122. Also see Werner G. Mayer, "The Best Brewers in Milwaukee," *Civil War Token Journal*, Fall 2006.

123. Also see Werner G. Mayer, "More Beer," *Journal of the Civil War Token Society*, Winter 1976.

124. Also see Raymond Callan, "M. Bodden," *Journal of the Civil War Token Society*, Winter 1993.

125. Also see Werner G. Mayer, "More Beer," *Journal of the Civil War Token Society*, Winter 1976.

126. Also see Raymond Callan, "M.W.M. Plank Road Co.," *Journal of the Civil War Token Society*, Winter 1993.

127. Also see Glenn H. Firestone, "Louis Kurz, Pictorial Photographer," *Journal of the Civil War Token Society*.

128. Also see Raymond Callan, "M.C. Meyer," *Journal of the Civil War Token Society*, Winter 1993.

129. For general information see Roger A. Lalich, "North Prairie, WI CWT Issuers: Three Merchants and Three Die Errors," *Civil War Token Journal*, Fall 2010.

Appendix I

1. *New York Daily Reformer* (Watertown, NY), December 16, 1863.

2. *Journal of the Civil War Token Society*, Winter 1980, 96, but later (2012) David D. Gladfelter stated that based on new information the Burr attributions were uncertain (and hence not used in the present text).

3. His case has been advanced by several contributors to *Journal of the Civil War Token Society*, beginning with Michael Saks, "The Charnleys of Providence, Part 2," *Journal of the Civil War Token Society*, Fall 1981. However, a contemporary biography of Charnley indicates he was a highly competent professional, not an amateur. Positive attribution awaits the future.

4. Also see Don Erlenkotter, "Frederick Nelson Dubois (IL-150-P): Father of the Civil War Token," *Civil War Token Journal*, Winter 2011.

5. "A. Gleason," by Chester Robinson, *Journal of the Civil War Token Society*, Spring 1971, p. 26.

6. *Journal of the Civil War Token Society*, Spring 1983, includes "In Search of Alexander Gleason," by Dennis P. Wierzba.

7. "Wartime Baltimore," Melvin Fuld, *Journal of the Civil War Token Society*, Fall 1972.

8. Wayne Stafford, "H.D. Higgins and His Indiana Frontier Mint," *Civil War Token Journal*, Summer 2003 is a prime source for information on Higgins. David D. Gladfelter has also contributed articles about Higgins and his tokens.

9. W. Elliot Woodward's Sixty-Ninth Sale, October 13–18, 1884, contained many Key medals and tokens.

10. "Wartime Baltimore," Melvin Fuld, *Journal of the Civil War Token Society*, Fall 1972.

11. Also see Frank G. Duffield, "Francis X. Koehler, Die Cutter, of Baltimore," *The Numismatist*, September 1916.

12. *New England Business Directory*, 1868; also *The Worcester Directory for 1870* (Henry J. Howland, Worcester, 1870).

13. *Proceedings of the American Philosophical Society*, vol. 9, 425.

14. Melvin Fuld, "Wartime Baltimore," *Journal of the Civil War Token Society*, Fall 1972.

15. David E. Schenkman, "Joseph H. Merriam, Die Sinker," *The Numismatist*, April 1980, is the definitive study.

16. Attinelli, *Numisgraphics*, 1876, 88.

17. *Journal of the Civil War Token Society*, Spring 1984, 19.

18. *Journal of the Civil War Token Society*, Winter 1978, 134.

19. Also see Lyman H. Low, "Hard Times Tokens," *American Journal of Numismatics*, July 1899; "J.M.L. & W.H. Scovill," Edgar H. Adams, *The Numismatist*, July 1912; and *Brass Roots*, published by the company in 1952.

20. David D. Gladfelter, crediting Robert J. Lindesmith, *Journal of the Civil War Token Society*, Winter 1980, 102.

21. Donald Erlenkotter, "The Outing of JGW: A Civil War Token Manufacturer Revealed," *Journal of the Civil War Token Society*, Winter 2005. An earlier article by Jack Detwiler, "Fuld 363—Who is JGW," in *The Copperhead Courier*, Spring 1984, was found to be irrelevant.

Appendix IV

1. Also see Benj Fauver, "The Scope of Civil War Tokens," *Journal of the Civil War Token Society*, Spring 1988.

2. Werner G. Mayer, "The Best Brewers in Milwaukee," *Journal of the Civil War Token Society*, Fall 1976.

3. George Hetrich, "Civil War Tokens and Tradesmen's Tokens," *The Numismatist*, June 1922.

4. John Ostendorf database.

Selected Bibliography and Resources

Books and Society Journals

These books and scholarly journals either focus exclusively on Civil War tokens or include articles or commentary on the subject.

American Journal of Numismatics. American Numismatic and Archaeological Society; American Numismatic Society, 1866 to the 21st century.

Civil War Token Journal (and title variations). Civil War Token Society, 1960s to date.

Coffee, John M. Jr., and Harold V. Ford. *The Atwood-Coffee Catalogue of United States and Canadian Transportation Tokens,* fifth edition, American Vecturist Association, Boston, MA, 1996.

Fuld, George and Melvin Fuld. *U.S. Civil War Store Cards,* second edition. Quarterman Publications, Inc., Lawrence, MA, 1975.

———, *Patriotic Civil War Tokens,* fifth edition. Krause Publications, Iola, WI, 2005.

Hamm, William E. *Indiana Merchant Issuers of Civil War Tokens.* Civil War Token Society, Garnerville, NY, 1993.

Hartzog, Rich. *Wisconsin Civil War Tokens—The Robert C. Kraft* Collection. World Exonumia Press, Rockford, IL, 1991.

Hetrich, George, and Julius Guttag. *Civil War Tokens and Tradesmens' Store Cards.* Birdsboro, PA, 1924.

Miller, Donald M. *A Catalog of U.S. Store Cards or Merchant Tokens.* Indiana, Pennsylvania, 1962.

Musante, Neil E. *The Medallic Work of John Adams Bolen.* Published by the author, Springfield, MA, 2002.

The Numismatist. George F. Heath, American Numismatic Association, 1888 to date.

Ostendorf, John. *Civil War Store Cards of Cincinnati.* Civil War Token Society, 2007.

Rulau, Russell, *Standard Catalog of United States Tokens,* fourth edition. Krause Publications, Iola, WI, 2004.

Schenkman, David E. *Merchant Tokens of Washington, D.C.* Jade House Publications, Bryans Road, Maryland, 1982.

———, *Civil War Sutler Tokens and Cardboard Scrip.* Jade House Publications, Bryans Road, Maryland, 1983.

———, *Maryland Merchant Tokens.* Maryland Token and Medal Society, Baltimore, MD, 1986.

———, *Merchant Tokens of Hard Rubber and Similar Compositions.* Jade House Publications, Bryans Road, Maryland, 1991.

Token and Medal Society Journal. Token and Medal Society, 1960s to date.

Selected Web Sites

These Web sites cater to the numismatist—the general coin collector, the collector of tokens and medals, or the specialist in Civil War tokens and/or sutler tokens.

American Numismatic Association. www.money.org

American Numismatic Society. www.numismatics.org

"Civil War Token Collecting by Type." www.cwtoken.com

Civil War Sutler Tokens. www.sutlertoken.com

Civil War Token Society. www.cwtsociety.com

Token and Medal Society. www.tokenandmedal.org

Selected Bibliography Specific to Sutler Tokens

Curto, James J. "Sutlers and Their Tokens: 1861–1866," published serially in *The Numismatist* beginning in July 1946.

Curto, James J. "Sutler Issues of the Civil War," published serially in *The Numismatist* beginning in June 1959, with additions to his 1946 series.

Delo, David M. *Peddlers and Post Traders: The Army Sutler on the Frontier.* University of Utah Press, Salt Lake City, 1992.

Lord, Francis A. *Civil War Sutlers and Their Wares.* Thomas Yoseloff, Cranbury, NJ, 1969.

Frossard, E. "Sutlers' Checks." *Numisma*, published serially in 1880.

Schenkman, David E. *Civil War Sutler Tokens and Cardboard Scrip.* Jade House Publications, Bryans Road, MD, 1983.

Schenkman, David E., and Richard W. Irons (editor). *Civil War Sutler Tokens and Cardboard Scrip*, second edition. Yurchak Printing, Lansdale, PA: 2014.

Trowbridge, C.O., and Howland Wood. "Sutlers' Checks Used in the Federal Army During the Civil War." *American Journal of Numismatics*, published serially in 1903 and 1904.

Wright, Benjamin P. "The American Store or Business Cards," published serially in *The Numismatist* beginning in January 1898.

ABOUT THE AUTHOR

Q. David Bowers has been a professional numismatist since he was a teenager in the early 1950s. He has served as president of the American Numismatic Association (1983–1985) and as president of the Professional Numismatists Guild (1977–1979); is a recipient of the ANA's Farran Zerbe Award; was the first ANA member to be named Numismatist of the Year (1995); in 2005 was given the ANA Lifetime Achievement Award; and has been inducted into the ANA Numismatic Hall of Fame. Bowers was awarded the highest honor given by the Professional Numismatists Guild (the Founder's Award) and has received more "Book of the Year" awards and "Best Columnist" honors from the Numismatic Literary

Guild than has any other writer. He is the author of more than 50 books, hundreds of auction and other catalogs, and several thousand numismatic articles. He has graded and cataloged many of the finest coin collections ever brought to the market. He is numismatic director of Whitman Publishing, LLC, chairman emeritus of Stack's Bowers Galleries, and research editor of *A Guide Book of United States Coins* (popularly known as the "Red Book").

CREDITS AND ACKNOWLEDGMENTS

The author expresses appreciation to the Civil War Token Society, which has generously provided many images and much information. The *Patriotic Civil War Tokens* and *Civil War Store Cards* books, both by George and Melvin Fuld tance from many contributors, have been   ournal, currently titled the *Civil Wa*   al Society as well and the *TAMS Jou*

    Thanks to the following: **American Antiquarian Society** for printed source material • **American Numismatic Association Dwight N. Manley Library** for loaning requested catalogs and books • **American Numismatic Society** for providing images from its remarkable collection based on and expanded from the Edward Groh cabinet donated in the early 20th century • The late **Herman Aqua** for research information and sharing information regarding the tokens in his extensive collection • **Ken Bauer** for many images from his extensive photographic files and for valuable suggestions • **Alan Chetson** furnished an illustration • **Alan Bleviss** whose extensive collection was studied • The late **Dale Cade** for correspondence and encouragement over the years • The late **Jack Detwiler** for information on patriotic token dies • **Larry Dziubek** for correspondence and research over many years and for providing images • **Donald Erlenkotter** for extensive correspondence regarding store cards and sharing of research findings and for editing suggestions • **Benj Fauver** for discussions about designs and motifs • **Roberta French** for research assistance and many transcriptions • The late **George J. Fuld** for a lifetime of sharing information since the late 1950s and for providing reminiscences for this book • The late **Melvin Fuld** for research and historical information • **David Gladfelter** for technical advice, historical information, insights, and more, dating back many years • **Mark Glazer** for sharing information and also images from his collection of patriotic tokens • **Robert L. Hailey** for correspondence • **Richard Hartzog** for information on store cards and rare varieties • **Steve Hayden** as an associate in handling the Tanenbaum estate tokens, for sharing images, for rarity information, for pricing information, and many more things; he was one of the most important contributors to this book • **Jon Harris** for information on rare varieties • **Robert Hoge,** then curator of the American Numismatic Society Collection, facilitated an arrangement between the author and also the Civil War Token Society for the photographing of certain rare and even unique tokens • **Scott Hopkins** for providing historical information regarding sutler tokens • The late **Bryon Kanzinger** for discussions concerning the token market • **Christine Karstedt** for assistance in many areas • **Paul Koppenhaver** as a source for rare varieties in the late 20th century • **H. Joseph Levine / Presidential Coin & Antique Co.** for providing many auction citations for sutler tokens • The late **Walter Korzick** for sharing information on rare varieties • **Ernie Latter** for providing images • The late **Robert J. Lindesmith** for research information • **William Luitje** for information regarding store card dies • **H. Joseph Levine** for sharing information over a long period of time • **Massachusetts Historical Society** for printed source material • The late **Charles McSorley** for historical information and ephemera • The late **Donald M. Miller** for sharing information • **Evelyn Mishkin** helped with copyediting, suggestions, and in other ways • **John Ostendorf,** editor of the forthcoming third edition of *U.S. Civil War Store Cards*, for countless communications, questions answered, and other help regarding store cards during the preparation of the manuscript; our correspondence file would occupy many hundreds of pages; was one of the most important contributors to this book • **Jud Petrie** for help on research inquiries and publications • **Sterling Rachootin** for comments and correspondence over the years • **Fred L. Reed,** longtime scholar in the field of Civil War history and numismatics, for suggestions, citations, and writing the foreword to the first edition • **Richard Rossa** for help in many ways dating back to the 1980s • **Russell Rulau** for extensive discussions over a long period of years • **David Schenkman** for historical and technical information over a long period of time • **Rick Snow** for assistance in several areas • The late **Henry G. Spangenberger** for information and ephemera • **Stack's Bowers Galleries** for providing images and information regarding the Alan Bleviss, Raymound Blunt, and John J. Ford Jr. sutler token collections and other offerings • **Wayne Stafford** for providing information on Henry D. Higgins and his "Indiana primitive" tokens and helping clarify errors from the first edition • The late **Kenneth N. Trobaugh** for information on rare store cards • The late **Stephen L. Tanenbaum** for being a constant correspondent, advisor, mentor, and research associate from the early 1970s onward • **Susan Trask** for providing introductions and sources for information, for sharing images, and for much excellent advice • The late **Larkin Wilson** for discussions and correspondence regarding metals, striking, and technical aspects.

INDEX